INTERNATIONAL POLITICAL ECONOMY

PERSPECTIVES ON GLOBAL POWER AND WEALTH

THIRD EDITION

Jeffry A. Frieden
University of California, Los Angeles

David A. Lake
University of California, San Diego

London and New York

First published 1995 by
St. Martin's Press
175 Fifth Avenue, New York, NY 10010

Executive editor: Don Reisman
Managing editor: Patricia Mansfield Phelan
Project editor: Amy Horowitz
Production supervisor: Joe Ford
Art director: Sheree Goodman
Cover design: Jeannette Jacobs

Reprinted 1997 by Routledge

Simultaneously published and distributed outside North America by
Routledge
11 New Fetter Lane, London, EC4P 4EE
and representatives throughout the world.

Printed in Great Britain by T. J. Press Ltd., Padstow, Cornwall

British Library Cataloguing in Publication Data

A catalogue record for this book is available from the British Library.

ISBN: 0–415–12047–0

*Acknowledgments and copyrights can be found on the title page of each chapter and
constitute an extension of the copyright page.*

PREFACE

The readings in *International Political Economy: Perspectives on Global Power and Wealth* are primarily intended to introduce the study of international political economy to those with little or no prior knowledge of it. The book is designed for use in courses in international political economy, international relations, and international economics. The selections present both clear and identifiable theoretical arguments and important substantive material. Twenty-two of the thirty-three articles are new to this third edition of our book, and the theoretical approach has been revised substantially to reflect both changes in the real world and intellectual progress in the field of international political economy.

Although the selections can be used in any order, they are grouped in seven parts that reflect some of the more common organizing principles used in international political economy courses. Each part begins with an introduction by the editors that provides background information and highlights issues raised in the readings. Each reading is preceded by an abstract summarizing its specific arguments and contributions. The readings were edited to eliminate extraneous or dated information, and most footnotes were removed.

The introduction defines the study of international political economy, summarizes major analytic frameworks in the field, and identifies several current debates. In past editions, the introduction and readings were largely structured around three analytic perspectives: Realism, Marxism, and Liberalism. This framework is retained in this edition, but substantially downplayed. The field of international political economy has made significant progress over the past decade, and this division—while useful as a pedagogic device—has become increasingly obsolete. To capture the most important work and current debates in international political economy, we now highlight the analytic tensions between international and domestic explanations, on the one hand, and state- and society-centered explanations, on the other. These two dimensions create four distinct views, which we refer to as the international political, international economic, domestic statist, and domestic societal approaches. Part I presents examples of these different perspectives in international political economy. The readings in this part are intended to suggest the underlying logic and types of arguments used by proponents of each approach. Although they are representative of their respective schools, they do not necessarily capture the wide range of opinion within each approach.

Part II, which reviews the history of the international economy since the nineteenth century, provides the background and perspective necessary to understand the contemporary international political economy. The selections describe the major developments in the history of the modern international economy from a variety of different theoretical viewpoints.

The remainder of the book is devoted to the post-1945 international political economy. Separate sections on production, money and finance, and trade look at the principal broad issue areas associated with the politics of international economic relations. Part VI, wholly new to this edition, focuses on the particular political and economic problems of developing and formerly centrally planned economies. Finally, Part VII examines current problems in the politics of international economics.

The selections in this volume have been used successfully in our courses on international political economy at the University of California, Los Angeles, and the University of California, San Diego. In our own research, we approach the study of international political economy from very different perspectives. Yet, we find that this set of readings accommodates our individual approaches to the subject matter while simultaneously covering the major questions of the field.

David Dollar made helpful suggestions on the editors' introductions, as did Ronald A. Francisco, and the following reviewers for St. Martin's Press: Stephen Anderson, University of Wisconsin at Madison; Thomas J. Bellows, University of Texas at San Antonio; Richard Ganzel, University of Nevada; Lowell Gustafson, Villanova University; Anne R. Hornsby, Spelman College; Charles K. Kennedy, Wake Forest University; Robert McIntire, Millikin University; Elizabeth Norville, Lewis and Clark College; Frances H. O'Neal, University of Alabama; John G. Speer, University of Houston; and Scot A. Stradley, University of North Dakota. For this edition, Don Reisman and Mary Hugh Lester of St. Martin's Press helped us shepherd the project through the publication process; Risa Brooks, Barbara Butterton, Bart Fischer, and Roland Stephen provided research and editorial assistance. Finally, we want to thank our respective spouses, Anabela Costa and Wendy K. Lake, for their encouragement.

Jeffry A. Frieden
David A. Lake

CONTENTS

INTERNATIONAL POLITICAL ECONOMY

PERSPECTIVES ON

GLOBAL POWER

AND WEALTH

THIRD EDITION

Introduction

INTERNATIONAL POLITICS AND INTERNATIONAL ECONOMICS

Over the past twenty-five years, the study of international political economy has undergone a remarkable resurgence. Virtually nonexistent before 1970 as a field of study, international political economy is now a popular area of specialization for both undergraduates and graduate students, as well as the source of much innovative and influential work by modern social scientists. The revival of international political economy after nearly forty years of dormancy has enriched both social science and public debate, and promises to continue to do both.

International political economy is the study of the interplay of economics and politics in the world arena. In the most general sense, the economy can be defined as the system of producing, distributing, and using wealth; politics is the set of institutions and rules by which social and economic interactions are governed. *Political economy* has a variety of meanings. For some, it refers primarily to the study of the political basis of economic actions, the ways in which government policies affect market operations. For others, the principal preoccupation is the economic basis of political action, the ways in which economic forces mold government policies. The two focuses are in a sense complementary, for politics and markets are in a constant state of mutual interaction.

It should come as no surprise to inhabitants of capitalist societies that markets exist and are governed by certain fundamental laws that operate more or less independently of the will of firms and individuals. Any shopkeeper knows that an attempt to raise the price of a readily available and standardized product—a pencil, for example—above that charged by nearby and competing shopkeepers will very rapidly cause customers to stop buying pencils at the higher price. Unless the shopkeeper wants to be left with piles of unsold pencils, he or she will have to bring the price back into line with "what the market will bear." The shopkeeper

1

will have learned a microcosmic lesson in what economists call the market-clearing equilibrium point, the price at which the number of goods supplied equals the number demanded, or the point at which supply and demand curves intersect.

At the base of all modern economics is the general assertion that, within certain carefully specified parameters, markets operate in and of themselves to maintain balance between supply and demand. Other things being equal, if the supply of a good increases far beyond the demand for it, the good's price will be driven down until demand rises to meet supply, supply falls to meet demand, and the market-clearing equilibrium is restored. By the same token, if demand exceeds supply, the good's price will rise, thus causing demand to decline and supply to increase until the two are in balance.

If the international and domestic economies functioned like perfectly competitive markets, they would be relatively easy to describe and comprehend. Fortunately or unfortunately, however, the freely functioning market is only a highly stylized or abstract picture that is rarely reproduced in the real world. A variety of factors influence the workings of domestic and international markets in ways that a focus on purely economic forces does not fully capture. Consumer tastes can change—how large is the American market for spats or sarsaparilla today?—as can the technology needed to make products more cheaply, or even to make entirely new goods that displace others (stick shifts for horsewhips, calculators for slide rules). Producers, sellers, or buyers of goods can band together to try to raise or lower prices unilaterally, as the Organization of Petroleum Exporting Countries (OPEC) did with petroleum in 1974 and 1979. And governments can act, consciously or inadvertently, to alter patterns of consumption, supply, demand, prices, and virtually all other economic variables.

It is this last fact, political "interference" with economic trends, that is the most visible, and probably the most important, reason to go beyond market-based, purely economic explanations of social behavior. Indeed, many market-oriented economists are continually surprised by the ability of governments, or of powerful groups pressuring governments, to contravene economic tendencies. When OPEC first raised oil prices in December 1973, some market-minded pundits, and even a few naive economists, predicted that such naked manipulation of the forces of supply and demand could last only a matter of months. What has emerged from the past twenty years' experience with oil prices is that they are a function of both market forces and the ability of OPEC's member states to organize concerted intervention in the oil market.

Somewhat less dramatic are the everyday operations of local and national governments that affect prices, production, profits, wages, and almost all other aspects of the economy. Wage, price, and rent controls; taxation; incentives and subsidies; tariffs; and government spending all serve to mold modern economies and the functioning of markets themselves. Who could understand the suburbanization of the United States after World War II without taking into account government tax incentives to home mortgage-holders, government-financed highway construction, and politically driven patterns of local educational expenditures? How many

American (or Japanese or European) farmers would be left if agricultural subsidies were eliminated? How many Americans would have college educations were it not for public universities and government scholarships? Who could explain the proliferation of nonprofit groups in the United States without knowing the tax incentives given to charitable donations?

In these instances, and many more, political pressure groups, politicians, and government bureaucrats have at least as much effect on economic outcomes as do the fundamental laws of the marketplace. Social scientists, especially political scientists, have spent decades trying to understand how these political pressures interact to produce government policy. Many of the results provide as elegant and stylized a view of politics as the economics profession has developed of markets. As in economics, however, social science models of political behavior are little more than didactic devices whose accuracy depends on a wide variety of unpredictable factors, including underlying economic trends. If an economist would be foolish to dismiss the possibilities of intergovernmental producers' cartels (such as OPEC) out of hand, a political scientist would be foolish not to realize that the economic realities of modern international commodity markets ensure that successful producers' cartels will be few and far between.

It is thus no surprise that political economy is far from new. Indeed, until a century ago, virtually all thinkers concerned with understanding human society wrote about political economy. For individuals as diverse as Adam Smith, John Stuart Mill, and Karl Marx, the economy was eminently political and politics was obviously tied to economic phenomena. Few scholars before 1900 would have taken seriously any attempt to describe and analyze politics and economics separately.

Around the turn of the century, however, professional studies of economics and politics became more and more divorced from one another. Economic investigation began to focus on understanding more fully the operation of specific markets and their interaction; the development of new mathematical techniques permitted the formalization of, for example, laws of supply and demand. By the time of World War I, an economics profession per se was in existence, and its attention was focused on understanding the operation of economic activities in and of themselves. At the same time, other scholars were looking increasingly at the political realm in isolation from the economy. The rise of modern representative political institutions, mass political parties, more politically informed populations, and modern bureaucracies all seemed to justify the study of politics as an activity that had a logic of its own.

With the exception of a few isolated individuals and an upsurge of interest during the politically and economically troubled years of the Great Depression, the twentieth century saw an increasing separation of the study of economics and politics. Economists developed ever more elaborate and sophisticated models of how economies work. Similarly, other social scientists spun out ever more complex theories of political development and activity.

The resurgence of political economy since 1970 has had two interrelated sources. The first was dissatisfaction among academics with the gap between abstract models of political and economic behavior, on the one hand, and the actual behavior of polities and economies, on the other. Theory became more ethereal and seemed less realistic. Many scholars began to question the intellectual justifications for a strict analytic division between politics and economics. Second, as the stability and prosperity of the first twenty-five postwar years started to disintegrate in the early 1970s, economic issues became politicized, and political systems became increasingly preoccupied with economic affairs. In August 1971, Richard Nixon ended the gold–dollar standard that had formed the basis for postwar monetary relations; two and a half years later, OPEC, a previously little-known group, succeeded in substantially raising the price of oil. In 1974 and 1975, the industrial nations of Western Europe, North America, and Japan fell into the first worldwide economic recession since the 1930s; unemployment and inflation were soon widespread realities and explosive political issues. In the world arena, the underdeveloped countries—most of them recently independent—burst onto center stage as the Third World, demanding a fairer division of global wealth and power. If in the 1950s and 1960s economic growth was taken for granted and politics occupied itself with other matters, in the 1970s and 1980s economic stagnation fed political strife while political conflict exacerbated economic uncertainty.

For both intellectual and practical reasons, then, social scientists began seeking, once more, to understand how politics and economics interact in modern society. As interest in political economy grew, a series of fundamental questions were posed, and a broad variety of contending approaches arose.

To be sure, today's political economists have not simply reproduced the studies of earlier (and perhaps neglected) generations of political economists. The professionalization of both economics and political science has led to major advances in both fields, and scholars now understand both economic and political phenomena far better than they did a generation ago. It is on this improved basis that the new political economy is being constructed, albeit with some long-standing issues in mind.

Just as in the real world, where politicians must pay close attention to economic trends and economic actors must keep track of political tendencies, those who would understand the political process must take the economy into account and vice versa. A much richer picture of social processes emerges from an integrated understanding of both political and economic affairs than from the isolated study of politics and economics as separate realms. This much is by now hardly controversial; it is in application that disagreements arise. Government actions may color economic trends, but these actions themselves may simply reflect the pressures of economic interest groups. Economic interest groups may be central in determining government policy, yet the political system—democratic or totalitarian, two-party or multiparty, parliamentary or presidential—may crucially color the outlooks and influence of economic interests. In the attempt to arrive at an integrated view of how politics and economics interact, we must disentangle economic and political causes and effects. In this effort, different scholars have different approaches, with different implications for the resulting view of the world.

CONTENDING PERSPECTIVES ON
INTERNATIONAL POLITICAL ECONOMY

All analysts of the international political economy are faced with the daunting task of understanding the interaction of many disparate forces. It is possible to simplify many such factors so that they can be arrayed on two dimensions. These two dimensions also capture many of the theoretical disagreements that characterize scholarship on the politics of international economic relations. One set of disagreements has to do with the relationship between the international and domestic political economies; another set concerns the relationship between the state and social forces.

The first dimension of interest concerns the degree to which the causes of international political and economic trends are to be found at the domestic or international level. All observers agree that in a complex world, both global and national forces are important. But different analysts place different emphases on the importance of one or the other. Some focus on how international forces tend to overpower domestic interests; others emphasize the degree to which national concerns override global considerations.

It should surprise no one that American tariff policy, Japanese international financial goals, and South Korean development strategies are important in the world's political economy. Disagreements arise, however, over how best to explain the sources of the foreign economic policies of individual nations, or of nation-states in general. At one end of the spectrum, some scholars believe that national foreign economic policies are essentially determined by the global environment. The actual room for national maneuver of even the most powerful of states, these scholars believe, is limited by characteristics inherent in the international system. At the other end of the spectrum are scholars who see foreign economic policies primarily as the outgrowth of national, domestic-level political and economic processes. For them, the international system exists only as a jumble of independent nation-states, each with its own political and economic peculiarities.

The international-domestic division is at the base of many debates within international political economy, as in the world at large. While some argue, for example, that the cause of Third World poverty is in the unequal global economic order, others blame domestic politics and economics in developing nations. Many see multinational corporations as powerful independent forces in the world—whether for good or for evil—while others see international firms as extensions of their home countries. For some, global geopolitical relations among nations dominate the impulses that arise from their domestic social orders.

The distinction between the two approaches can be seen quite clearly, for example, in explanations of trade policy. To take a specific instance, starting in the early 1980s the United States and many European governments imposed restrictions on the import of Japanese automobiles. The form of the controls varied widely: the United States and Japanese governments negotiated "voluntary" export restraints that Japanese producers agreed to abide by, while in some European countries quantitative quotas were imposed unilaterally. Concerned about stiff

Japanese competition that was reducing profits and employment, European and North American automakers and the trade unions that represent their employees provided key support for these policies.

From this example, one clear analytic conclusion would be that domestic political and economic pressures—the electoral importance of the regions where auto industries are concentrated; the economic centrality of the sector to the European and North American economies; government concern about the broad national ramifications of the auto industry; and the political clout of the autoworkers' unions—led to important foreign economic measures: the restriction of Japanese automobile imports. Indeed, many scholars saw the restrictions as confirmation of the primacy of domestic concerns in the making of foreign economic policy.

Yet, analysts who search for the causes of national foreign economic policies in the international, rather than the domestic, arena, could also find support in the auto import restrictions. After all, the policies responded to the rise of Japan as a major manufacturer and exporter of automobiles, a fact that had little to do with the domestic scene in the United States and Europe. Many North American and European industries have lost competitive ground to rapidly growing overseas manufacturers, a process that is complex in origin but clearly one of worldwide proportions. Some have argued that trade policies are a function of realities inherent in the international system, such as the existence of a leading, hegemonic power and the eventual decline of that state (see Krasner, Reading 1). In this view, the decline of American power set the stage for a proliferation of barriers to trade.

The internationally minded scholar might also argue that it is important to understand why the European and American measures took the relatively mild form they did, simply limiting the Japanese to established (and often very appreciable) shares of the markets. If the measures had been adopted solely to respond to the distress of local auto industries, the logical step would have been to exclude foreign cars from the markets in question. Yet, the position of Europe and the United States in the global economic and political system—including everything from world finance to international military alliances—dictated that European and North American policymakers not pursue overly hostile policies toward the Japanese.

More generally, scholars have explained long-term changes in trade policy in very different ways. During the period between World Wars I and II, and especially in the 1930s, almost all European nations and the United States were highly protectionist. Since World War II, on the other hand, the North American and Western European markets have been opened gradually to one another and to the rest of the world.

Scholars whose theoretical bent is international point out that domestic politics in Europe and the United States have not changed enough during this period to explain such a radical shift. But the role of the United States and Western Europe in the international political and economic system has indeed been different from what it was during the 1930s: after 1945, North American and Western European countries were united in an American-led military and economic alliance against the Soviet Union. Some internationally oriented analysts argue that the causes of postwar foreign economic policies in North America and Western Europe can be found in the international geopolitical positions of these regions—the increase in American power, the decline of Europe, the Soviet challenge, and the rise of the Atlantic Alliance. Others point to broad technological and economic developments, such as dramatic improvements in telecommunications and transportation, that have altered governments' incentives to protect or open their economies.

Scholars who support domestic-level explanations take the opposite tack. For them, the postwar system was itself largely a creation of the United States and the major Western European powers. To cite the modern international political economy as a source of American or British foreign economic policy, these scholars argue, is to put the cart before the horse, since it was the United States and its allies that created the institutions—the Marshall Plan, the Bretton Woods agreement, the European Community—of today's international political economy. We must therefore search for the true roots of the shift in trade policy in North America and Western Europe within these nations.

The example of trade policy demonstrates that serious scholars can arrive at strikingly different analytic conclusions on the basis of the same information. For some, domestic political and economic pressures caused the adoption of auto import restrictions. For others, geopolitical, economic, or technological trends in the international environment explain the same action.

The second dimension along which analysts differ in their interpretation of trends in the international political economy has to do with the relative importance of politicians and political institutions, on the one hand, and private social actors, on the other. The interaction between state and society—between national governments and the social forces they represent, rule, or ignore—is indeed another dividing line within the field of international political economy. In the study of the politics of the world economy, questions continually arise about the relative importance of independent government action and institutions versus a variety of societal pressures on the policy-making process.

The role of the state is at the center of all political science; international political economy is no exception. Foreign economic policy is made, of course, by foreign economic policymakers; this much is trivial. But just as scholars debate the relative importance of overseas and domestic determinants of foreign economic policies, so too do they disagree over whether policymakers represent a logic of their own, or reflect domestic lobbies and interest groups. According to one view, the state is relatively insulated or autonomous from the multitude of social, political, and economic pressures that emanate from society. The most that pluralistic interest groups can produce is a confused cacophony of complaints and demands, but coherent national policy comes from the conscious actions of national leaders and those who occupy positions of political power and from the institutions in which they operate. The state, in this view, molds society, and foreign economic policy is one part of this larger mold.

The opposing school of thought asserts that policymakers are little more than the transmitters of underlying societal demands. At best, the political system can organize and regularize these demands, but the state is essentially a tool in the hands of socioeconomic and political interests. Foreign economic policy, like other state actions, evolves in response to social demands; it is society that molds the state, and not the other way around.

We can illustrate the difference in focus with the previously discussed example of trade policy in North America and Western Europe before and since World War II. Many of those who look first and foremost at state actors would emphasize the dramatic change in the overall foreign policy of these governments after World War II, starting with the Atlantic Alliance to meet the demands of European reconstruction and the Cold War, which required that the American market be opened to foreign goods in order to stimulate the economies of the country's allies. Eventually the European Community (the Common Market) arose as a further effort to cement the Atlantic Alliance against the Soviet Union.

According to this view, trade liberalization arose out of national security concerns, understood and articulated by a very small number of individuals in the American and Western European governments, who then went about "selling" the policies to their publics. Alternatively, it might be argued that the traumas of the Great Depression taught the managers of states that a descent into protectionism could lead to intolerable social tensions. In this context, political leaders may have developed a strong belief in the desirability of trade relations that are generally open. In this view of the world, what takes explanatory precedence is the opinions, beliefs, and desires of national political leaders—the state.

Other scholars, for whom society is determinant, emphasize the major socioeconomic and political changes that had been gaining force within the industrial capitalist nations after World War I. Corporations became more international, and came to fear overseas competition less. For important groups, trade protection was counterproductive because it limited access to the rest of the world economy; freer trade and investment opened broad and profitable new horizons for major economic actors in North America and Western Europe.

By the same token, socioeconomic trends at a global level were also pushing toward international trade liberalization. The rise of internationally integrated financial markets and global corporations, for example, have created private interests that oppose interference with the free movement of goods and capital across national borders. This new group of social forces has, in the opinion of some (see for example, Strange, Reading 4), fundamentally transformed the very nature of economic policy making in all nations.

These two dimensions combined give rise to four different perspectives in international political economy. An *international political* view emphasizes the constraints imposed on states by the global geostrategic and diplomatic environment within which they operate. It focuses on the inherent conflict among states in a hostile world, within which cooperation, although often desirable and feasible, can be difficult to achieve.

The *international economic* perspective similarly emphasizes the importance of constraints external to individual nations, but highlights global socioeconomic factors rather than political ones. For them, international developments in technology, telecommunications, finance, and production fundamentally affect the setting within which national governments make policy. Indeed, these can matter to the point of making some choices practically impossible to implement, and making others so attractive as to be impossible to resist.

Domestic approaches look inside nation-states for explanations of the international political economy. The *domestic statist* view turns its attention to states, as does the international political perspective, but it emphasizes the role and institutions of the state in a domestic setting rather than in the global system. This view, which at times is called simply *statism,* tends to downplay the impact of constraints emanating both from the international system and from domestic societies. National policymakers are thus seen as the predominant actors in determining national priorities and implementing policies to carry out these goals.

The *domestic societal* perspective shares this emphasis on developments within national borders, but looks first and foremost at economic and sociopolitical actors rather than political leaders. This view, at times known simply as *societal,* tends to minimize international constraints and to emphasize socioeconomic pressures that originate at home. Here what determines national policy are the demands made by individuals, firms, and groups rather than independent action by policymakers.

The contending perspectives can once again be illustrated by recalling their approaches to the example of trade policy tendencies. International political interpretations would rely on geopolitical trends among states at the global level to explain changing patterns of trade relations. An international economic view would emphasize trends in market forces, technologies, and the like, which alter the environment in which governments make trade policy. The domestic statist approach focuses on the goals and actions of the government within the national political system, for which foreign trade can represent ways to help them stay in power. And a domestic societal perspective looks primarily at the pressures brought to bear on policy by socioeconomic groups, some desirous of trade liberalization and others interested in protection from imports.

It should be noted that these simplistic categories hardly describe the nuance and complexity of actual theoretical approaches; all scholars recognize that the foreign economic policies of all countries are constrained by both international and domestic, and both political and economic, factors. It may indeed be the case that one set of forces matters more or less in some issue areas than in others, in some times than in others, in some countries than in others. International geopolitical concerns presumably have more impact on a small, weak country surrounded by enemies than on a large, powerful nation far away from any threat. Domestic concerns, whether statist or societal, may matter more to policy in times of great social and political conflict than in less turbulent times.

Nonetheless, analysts of the international political economy do differ in their interpretations. Rather than being absolute, the disagreements are over relative weights to be assigned to each set of causes. Some scholars assign primacy to social forces, others to autonomous state action; some to global factors, others to domestic.

These perspectives can lead to widely different explanations of specific events and general processes within the international political economy. Their differences have generated numerous debates in the field, many of which are contained in the readings discussed below.

THREE ALTERNATIVE VIEWS OF
INTERNATIONAL POLITICAL ECONOMY

In addition to the above perspectives, some scholars attempt to classify interpretations of global political and economic developments in a somewhat different manner. Many theories of international political economy can also be categorized into one of three perspectives: Liberalism, Marxism, and Realism.

In the field of international political economy, advocates of free trade and free markets are still referred to as Liberals. In twentieth-century American domestic politics, on the other hand, the term has come to mean something different. In the United States today, "Conservatives" generally support free markets and less government intervention, while "Liberals" advocate greater governmental intervention in the market to stimulate growth and mitigate inequalities. These contradictory usages of the term *Liberal* may seem confusing, but the context usually makes the author's meaning clear.

The Liberal argument emphasizes how both the market and politics are environments in which all can be made better off by entering into voluntary exchanges with others. If there are no impediments to trade among individuals, Liberals reason, everyone can be made as well-off as possible given existing stocks of goods and services. All participants in the market, in other words, will be at their highest possible level of utility. Neoclassical economists, who are generally Liberals, believe firmly in the superiority of the market as the allocator of scarce resources.

Liberals therefore reason that the economic role of government should be quite limited. Many forms of government intervention in the economy, they argue, intentionally or unintentionally restrict the market and thereby prevent potentially rewarding trades from occurring.

Liberals do generally support the provision by government of certain "public goods," goods and services that make society better off but that would not be provided by private markets.[1] The government, for example, plays an important role in supplying the conditions necessary for the maintenance of a free and competitive market. Governments must provide for the defense of the country, protect property rights, and prevent unfair collusion or concentration of power within the market. The government should also, according to most Liberals, educate its citizens, build infrastructure, and provide and regulate a common currency. The proper role of government, in other words, is to provide the necessary foundation for the market.

At the level of the international economy, Liberals assert that a fundamental harmony of interests exists between as well as within countries. They argue that all countries are best off when goods and services move freely across national borders in mutually rewarding exchanges. If universal free trade were to exist, all countries would enjoy the highest level of utility and there would be no economic basis for international conflict and war.

Liberals also believe that governments should manage the international economy in much the same way as they manage their domestic economies. They should establish rules and regulations, often referred to as "international regimes," to govern exchanges between different national currencies and to ensure that no country or domestic group is damaged by "unfair" international competition.

Marxism originated with the writings of Karl Marx, a nineteenth-century political economist and perhaps the severest critic of capitalism and its Liberal supporters. Marx saw capitalism and the market creating extremes of wealth for capitalists and poverty for workers. While everyone may have been better off than before, the capitalists were clearly expanding their wealth more rapidly than all others. Marx rejected the assertion that exchange between individuals necessarily maximizes the welfare of the whole society. Accordingly, Marx perceived capitalism as an inherently conflictual system that both should and would be inevitably overthrown and replaced by socialism.

Marxists believe that classes are the dominant actors in the political economy. Specifically, Marxists identify two economically determined aggregations of individuals, or classes, as central: capital, or the owners of the means of production, and labor, or the workers. Marxists assume that classes act in their economic interests, that is, to maximize the economic well-being of the class as a whole. The basis of the capitalist economy, according to Marxists, is the exploitation of labor by capital: capitalism by its very nature denies labor the full return for its efforts.

Marxists see the political economy as necessarily conflictual, since the relationship between capitalists and workers is essentially antagonistic. Because the means of production are controlled by a minority within society, the capitalists, labor does not receive its full return; conflict between the classes is inevitable because of this exploitation. Marxists also believe that capitalism is inherently prone to periodic economic crises. Such crises will, they believe, ultimately lead to the overthrow of capitalism by labor and the erection of a socialist society in which the means of production will be owned jointly by all members of society and exploitation will cease.

Lenin extended Marx's ideas to the international political economy to explain imperialism and war (see Lenin, Reading 7). Imperialism, Lenin argued, was endemic to modern capitalism. As capitalism decayed in the most developed nations, capitalists would attempt to solve their problems by exporting capital abroad. As this capital required protection from both local and foreign challengers, governments would colonize regions to safeguard the interests of their foreign investors. Eventually, capitalist countries would compete for control over these areas and intracapitalist wars would follow.

Today, Marxists who study the international political economy are primarily concerned with two issues. The first is the fate of labor in a world of increasingly internationalized capital. The growth of multinational corporations and the rise of globally integrated financial markets appear to have weakened the economic and political power of labor. If workers in a particular country demand higher wages or improved health and safety measures, for example, the multinational capitalist can simply shift production to another country where labor is more compliant. As a result, many Marxists fear that labor's ability to negotiate with capital for a more equitable division of wealth has been significantly undermined.

Second, Marxists are concerned with the poverty and continued underdevelopment of the Third World. Some Marxists argue that development is blocked by domestic ruling classes who pursue their own narrow interests at the expense of national economic progress. Others, known as "dependency" theorists, extend class analysis to the level of the international economy. According to these Marxists, the global system is stratified into a wealthy area, the "core" or First World, and a region of oppression and poverty, the "periphery" or Third World. International capitalism, in this view, exploits the periphery and benefits the core, just as capitalists exploit workers within a single country. The principal questions here focus on the mechanisms of exploitation—whether they be multinational corporations, international financial markets and organizations, or trade—and the appropriate strategies for stimulating autonomous growth and development in the periphery.

Realism traces its intellectual roots back to Thucydides' writings in 400 B.C., as well as those of Niccoló Machiavelli, Thomas Hobbes, and the mercantilists Jean-Baptiste Colbert and Friedrich List. Realists believe that nation-states pursue power and shape the economy to this end. They assume that nation-states are the dominant actors within the international political economy. According to Realists, the international system is anarchical, a condition under which nation-states are sovereign, the sole judge of their own behaviors, and subject to no higher authority. If no authority is higher than the nation-state, Realists believe, then all actors are subordinate to the nation-state. While private citizens can interact with their counterparts in other countries, Realists assert that the basis for this interaction is legislated by the nation-state. Thus, where Liberals focus on individuals and Marxists on classes, Realists concentrate on nation-states.

Realists also argue that nation-states are fundamentally concerned about international power relations. Because the international system is based upon anarchy, the use of force or coercion by other nation-states is always a possibility and no higher authority is obligated to come to the aid of a nation-state under attack. Nation-states are thus ultimately dependent upon their own resources for protection. For Realists, then, each nation-state must always be prepared to defend itself to the best of its ability. For them, politics is largely a zero-sum game and by necessity conflictual. If one nation-state wins, another must lose.

Realists believe, additionally, that nation-states can be thought of as rational actors in the same sense that others assume individuals are rational. Nation-states are assumed to perform cost-benefit analyses and choose the option that yields the greatest value, especially as regards the nation's international geopolitical and power positions.

It is the emphasis on power that gives Realism its distinctive approach to the study of international political economy. While economic considerations may often complement power concerns, the former are, in the Realist view, subordinate to the latter. Realists allow for circumstances in which nation-states sacrifice economic gain to weaken their opponents or strengthen themselves in military or diplomatic terms. Thus, trade protection, which might reduce a country's overall income by restricting the market, may be adopted for reasons of national political power.

Realist political economy is primarily concerned with how changes in the distribution of international power affect the form and type of international economy. The best known Realist approach to this question is the "Theory of Hegemonic Stability," which holds that an open international economy—that is, one characterized by the free exchange of goods, capital, and services—is most likely to exist when a single dominant or hegemonic power is present to stabilize the system and construct a strong regime (see Krasner, Reading 1, and Lake, Reading 8). For Realists, then, the pursuit of power by nation-states shapes the international economy.

Each of these three perspectives features different assumptions and assertions. Liberals assume that individuals are the proper unit of analysis, while Marxists and Realists make similar assumptions for classes and nation-states, respectively. The three perspectives also differ on the inevitability of conflict within the political economy. Liberals believe economics and politics are largely autonomous spheres; Marxists maintain that economics determines politics; and Realists argue that politics determines economics.

This tripartite division of international political economy is useful in many ways, especially as it highlights differing evaluations of the importance of economic efficiency, class conflict, and geostrategic considerations. However, the lines between the three views are easily blurred. Some Marxists agree with the Realist focus on interstate conflict, while others agree with the Liberal emphasis on economic interests. There are many Liberals who use neoclassical tools to analyze interstate strategic interaction in much the same way Realists do, or to investigate the clash of classes as do Marxists. Such substantial overlap, in our view, makes the two-dimensional categorization outlined above somewhat clearer. We also believe that these two dimensions, international–domestic and state–society, more accurately characterize analytic differences among scholars and observers of the international political economy.

THE CONTEMPORARY INTERNATIONAL POLITICAL ECONOMY: AN OVERVIEW

After initial sections on theoretical perspectives and historical background, the remainder of this book of readings is about the politics of international economic relations since World War II. Developments since 1945 have, indeed, raised a wide variety of theoretical, practical, and policy issues.

The contemporary international political economy is characterized by unprecedented levels of multinational production, cross-border financial flows, and international trade. It is also plagued by increasing political conflict as individuals, groups, classes, and countries clash over the meaning and implications of these economic transactions. The contradiction between increasing economic integration and the wealth that it produces, on the one hand, and the desire for political control and national autonomy, on the other, define much of what happens in the global political economy.

For over thirty years, the general pattern of relations among non-Communist nations was set by American leadership, and this pattern continues to influence the international political economy today. In the political arena, formal and informal alliances tied virtually every major non-Communist nation into an American-led network of mutual support and defense. In the economic arena, a wide-ranging set of international economic organizations—including the International Monetary Fund (IMF), the General Agreement on Tariffs and Trade (GATT), and the International Bank for Reconstruction and Development (World Bank)—grew up under a protective American umbrella, and often as direct American initiatives. The world economy itself was heavily influenced by the rise of modern multinational corporations and banks, whose contemporary form is largely of United States origin.

American plans for a reordered world economy go back to the mid-1930s. After World War I, the United States retreated into relative economic insularity, for reasons explored in Part II, "Historical Perspectives." When the Great Depression hit, American political leaders virtually ignored the possibility of international economic cooperation in their attempts to stabilize the domestic economy. Yet, even as the Roosevelt administration looked inward for recovery, by 1934 new American initiatives were signaling a shift in America's traditional isolationism. Roosevelt's secretary of state, Cordell Hull, was a militant free trader, and in 1934 he convinced Congress to pass the Reciprocal Trade Agreements Act, which allowed the executive to negotiate tariff reductions with foreign nations. This important step toward trade liberalization and international economic cooperation was deepened as war loomed in Europe and the United States drew closer to Great Britain and France.

The seeds of the new international order, planted in the 1930s, began to grow even as World War II came to an end. The Bretton Woods agreement, reached among the Allied powers in 1944, established a new series of international economic organizations that became the foundation for the postwar American-led system. As the wartime American–Soviet alliance began to shatter, a new economic order emerged in the non-Communist world. At its center were the three pillars of the Bretton Woods system: international monetary cooperation under the auspices of the IMF, international trade liberalization negotiated within the GATT, and investment in the developing countries stimulated by the World Bank. All three pillars were essentially designed by the United States and dependent on American support.

As it developed, the postwar capitalist world reflected American foreign policy in many of its details. One principal concern of the United States was to build a bulwark of anti-Soviet allies; this was done with a massive inflow of American aid under the Marshall Plan, and the encouragement of Western European cooperation within a new Common Market. At the same time, the United States dramatically lowered its barriers to foreign goods, and American corporations began to invest heavily in foreign nations. Of course, the United States was not only acting altruistically: European recovery, trade liberalization, and booming international investment helped ensure great prosperity within the United States as well.

American policies, whatever their motivation, had an undeniable impact on the international political economy. Trade liberalization opened the huge American market to foreign producers. American overseas investment provided capital, technology, and expertise for both Europe and the developing world. American government economic aid, whether direct or channeled through such institutions as the World Bank, helped finance economic growth abroad. In addition, the American military "umbrella" allowed anti-Soviet governments in Europe, Japan, and the developing world to rely on the United States for security and to turn their attentions to encouraging economic growth.

All in all, the non-Communist world's unprecedented access to American markets and American capital provided a major stimulus to world economic growth, not to mention to the profits of American businesses and to general prosperity within the United States. For over twenty-five years after World War II, the capitalist world experienced impressive levels of economic growth and development, all within a general context of international cooperation under American political, economic, and military tutelage.

This period is often referred to as the Pax Americana because of its broad similarity to the British-led international economic system that reigned from about 1820 until World War I, known as the Pax Britannica. In both instances, general political and economic peace prevailed under the leadership of an overwhelming world power—the United Kingdom in one case, the United States in the other. There were, nonetheless, major differences between the two eras (see Lake, Reading 8).

Just as the Pax Britannica eventually ended, however, the Pax Americana gradually eroded. By the early 1970s, strains were developing in the postwar system. Between 1971 and 1975, the postwar international monetary system, which had been based on a gold-backed United States dollar, fell apart and was replaced by a new, improvised pattern of floating exchange rates in which the dollar's role was still strong but no longer quite so central. At the same time, pressures for trade protection from uncompetitive industries in North America and Western Europe began to mount; and, although tariff levels remained low, a variety of nontariff barriers to world trade, such as import quotas, soon proliferated. In the political arena, détente between the United States and the Soviet Union seemed to make the American security umbrella less relevant for the Japanese and Western Europeans; in the less developed countries, North–South conflict appeared more important than East–West strife. In short, as American economic strength declined, the Bretton Woods institutions weakened, the Cold War thawed during the 1970s, and the Pax Americana drew to a close.

The quickening pace of change in the Soviet Union and its allies eventually culminated in the collapse of the former Soviet bloc in the late 1980s and early 1990s, and ultimately in the disintegration of the former Soviet Union. The end of the Cold War did not, of course, mean an end to international conflict, but it did put an end to the East–West divide that had dominated global politics for so long. To some extent, most of the former centrally planned economies joined the ranks of the developing world, struggling to overcome poverty and privation. But Russia is no typical Third World nation, and its problems, and the problems it raises for the rest of the world, are unprecedented in both type and scope.

Within a rapidly changing environment, the United States remains the most important country in the contemporary international political economy, but it is no longer dominant. The era of American hegemony has been replaced by a new multilateral order based on the joint leadership of Western Europe, Japan, and the United States. Together, these countries have successfully managed—or, some would say, muddled through—the "oil shocks" of the 1970s, the debt crisis of the early 1980s, and the exchange rate, trade, and financial gyrations of the Reagan–Bush era. Despite greater success than many thought possible, multilateral leadership and the liberal international order remain fragile. Conflicts of interest and economic tensions remain muted, but they could erupt at any time.

As might be expected, the rise and decline of the Pax Americana and the emergence of the new multilateral order, along with the end of the Cold War, have led to great scholarly controversy. For some analysts, America's global dominance and the East–West divide were the principal determinants of Western interests and policies and, in turn, of the liberal international economy. The decline of the United States in a post–Cold War world, in this view, presages the eventual collapse of international openness. For others, the policies of the United States, and other countries, were affected in more important ways by domestic economic and political pressures; from this perspective, the decline of American hegemony is expected to have little effect on international openness. For still others, the consequences of the liberal order have fundamentally altered the interests of the United States and other countries; the internationalization of production and finance and the rise of economic interdependence have created vested interests in favor of the free flow of goods, services, and capital across national borders.

The remainder of this book is devoted to understanding the contemporary international political economy and its likely future. Throughout this text, a variety of thematic issues are addressed; in each cluster of issues, alternative theoretical and analytic perspectives compete. The selections in this reader serve both to provide information on broad trends in the politics of international economic relations, and to give an overview of the contending approaches to be found within the discipline.

NOTE

1. More specifically, a public good is one that, in its purest form, is *nonrival in consumption* and *nonexcludable*. The first characteristic means that consumption of the good by one person does not reduce the opportunities for others to consume the good; for example, clean air can be breathed by one person without reducing its availability to others. The second characteristic means that nobody can be prevented from consuming the good: those who do not contribute to pollution control are still able to breathe clean air. These two conditions are fully met only rarely, but goods that come close to them are generally considered public goods.

I

CONTENDING PERSPECTIVES ON INTERNATIONAL POLITICAL ECONOMY

As outlined in the introduction, there are two principal theoretical dimensions that can be used to organize debates within international political economy. The first addresses the relative importance of international- and domestic-level variables in accounting for trends in the international political economy, the second, the significance of statist and societal factors. Part I contains four selections, one representing each approach as applied to a specific issue. In a classic example of an international political approach, Stephen D. Krasner examines patterns of trade openness within the international economy over the nineteenth and twentieth centuries. Barry Eichengreen uses a domestic society-centered theory to account for the Smoot–Hawley Tariff, which contained some of the highest duties in history. Adopting a domestic statist approach, Stephan Haggard and Chung-in Moon provide an explanation for South Korea's export-oriented development program. Finally, Susan Strange explores how international economic factors have altered both the relationship between states and firms and the nature of diplomacy between countries. Exemplars of their respective approaches, these essays are intended only to illustrate basic themes and arguments; all four approaches contain a rich diversity of styles and conclusions, and the essays selected here are only a sample. Nonetheless, they serve to highlight key analytic debates and provide a useful empirical introduction to critical trends and cases in international political economy.

1

State Power and the Structure
of International Trade

STEPHEN D. KRASNER

In this essay, Stephen D. Krasner addresses the relationship between the interests and power of major states and the trade openness of the international economy. In this international political analysis, he identifies four principal goals of state action: political power, aggregate national income, economic growth, and social stability. He then combines the goals with different national abilities to pursue them, relating the international distribution of potential economic power to alternative trade regimes. Krasner maintains, most significantly, that the hegemony of a leading power is necessary for the creation and continuance of free trade. He applies his model to six periods. Krasner's analysis in this 1976 article is a well-known attempt to use international political theory, and Realism more generally, to explain international economic affairs. The theory he propounds, which has been dubbed the "theory of hegemonic stability," has influenced many subsequent analyses.

INTRODUCTION

In recent years, students of international relations have multinationalized, transnationalized, bureaucratized, and transgovernmentalized the state until it has virtually ceased to exist as an analytic construct. Nowhere is that trend more apparent than in the study of the politics of international economic relations. The basic conventional assumptions have been undermined by assertions that the state is trapped by a transnational society created not by sovereigns, but by nonstate actors. Interdependence is not seen as a reflection of state policies and state choices (the perspective of balance-of-power theory), but as the result of elements beyond the control of any state or a system created by states.

Stephen D. Krasner. "State Power and the Structure of International Trade." From *World Politics*, 28, 3 (April 1976). Reprinted by permission of The Johns Hopkins University Press.

This perspective is at best profoundly misleading. It may explain developments within a particular international economic structure, but it cannot explain the structure itself. That structure has many institutional and behavioral manifestations. The central continuum along which it can be described is openness. International economic structures may range from complete autarky (if all states prevent movements across their borders), to complete openness (if no restrictions exist). In this paper I will present an analysis of one aspect of the international economy—the structure of international trade; that is, the degree of openness for the movement of goods as opposed to capital, labor, technology, or other factors of production. Since the beginning of the nineteenth century, this structure has gone through several changes. These can be explained, albeit imperfectly, by a state-power theory: an approach that begins with the assumption that the structure of international trade is determined by the interests and power of states acting to maximize national goals. The first step in this argument is to relate four basic state interests—aggregate national income, social stability, political power, and economic growth—to the degree of openness for the movement of goods. The relationship between these interests and openness depends upon the potential economic power of any given state. Potential economic power is operationalized in terms of the relative size and level of economic development of the state. The second step in the argument is to relate different distributions of potential power, such as multipolar and hegemonic, to different international trading structures. The most important conclusion of this theoretical analysis is that a hegemonic distribution of potential economic power is likely to result in an open trading structure. That argument is largely, although not completely, substantiated by empirical data. For a fully adequate analysis it is necessary to amend a state-power argument to take account of the impact of past state decisions on domestic social structures as well as on international economic ones. The two major organizers of the structure of trade since the beginning of the nineteenth century, Great Britain and the United States, have both been prevented from making policy amendments in line with state interests by particular societal groups whose power had been enhanced by earlier state policies.

THE CAUSAL ARGUMENT: STATE INTERESTS, STATE POWER, AND INTERNATIONAL TRADING STRUCTURES

Neoclassical trade theory is based upon the assumption that states act to maximize their aggregate economic utility. This leads to the conclusion that maximum global welfare and Pareto optimality are achieved under free trade. While particular countries might better their situations through protectionism, economic theory has generally looked askance at such policies. . . . Neoclassical theory recognizes that trade regulations can . . . be used to correct domestic distortions and to promote infant industries, but these are exceptions or temporary departures from policy conclusions that lead logically to the support of free trade.

State Preferences

Historical experience suggests that policy makers are dense, or that the assumptions of the conventional argument are wrong. Free trade has hardly been the norm. Stupidity is not a very interesting analytic category. An alternative approach to explaining international trading structures is to assume that states seek a broad range of goals. At least four major state interests affected by the structure of international trade can be identified. They are: political power, aggregate national income, economic growth, and social stability. The way in which each of these goals is affected by the degree of openness depends upon the potential economic power of the state as defined by its relative size and level of development.

Let us begin with aggregate national income because it is most straightforward. Given the exception noted above, conventional neoclassical theory demonstrates that the greater the degree of openness in the international trading system, the greater the level of aggregate economic income. This conclusion applies to all states regardless of their size or relative level of development. The static economic benefits of openness are, however, generally inversely related to size. Trade gives small states relatively more welfare benefits than it gives large ones. Empirically, small states have higher ratios of trade to national product. They do not have the generous factor endowments or potential for national economies of scale that are enjoyed by larger—particularly continental—states.

The impact of openness on social stability runs in the opposite direction. Greater openness exposes the domestic economy to the exigencies of the world market. That implies a higher level of factor movements than in a closed economy, because domestic production patterns must adjust to changes in international prices. Social instability is thereby increased, since there is friction in moving factors, particularly labor, from one sector to another. The impact will be stronger in small states than in large, and in relatively less developed than in more developed ones. Large states are less involved in the international economy: a smaller percentage of their total factor endowment is affected by the international market at any given level of openness. More developed states are better able to adjust factors: skilled workers can more easily be moved from one kind of production to another than can unskilled laborers or peasants. Hence social stability is, *ceteris paribus,* inversely related to openness, but the deleterious consequences of exposure to the international trading system are mitigated by larger size and greater economic development.

The relationship between political power and the international trading structure can be analyzed in terms of the relative opportunity costs of closure for trading partners. The higher the relative cost of closure, the weaker the political position of the state. Hirschman has argued that this cost can be measured in terms of direct income losses and the adjustment costs of reallocating factors. These will be smaller for large states and for relatively more developed states. Other things being equal, utility costs will be less for large states because they generally have a smaller proportion of their economy engaged in the international economic system. Reallocation costs will be less for more advanced states because their factors are more mobile. Hence a state that is relatively large and more developed will find its political power enhanced by an open system because its opportunity costs of closure are less. The large state can use the threat to alter the system to secure economic or noneconomic objectives. Historically, there is one important exception to this generalization—the oil-exporting states. The level of reserves for some of the states, particularly Saudi Arabia, has reduced the economic opportunity costs of closure to a very low level despite their lack of development.

The relationship between international economic structure and economic growth is elusive. For small states, economic growth has generally been empirically associated with openness. Exposure to the international system makes possible a much more efficient allocation of resources. Openness also probably furthers the rate of growth of large countries with relatively advanced technologies because they do not need to protect infant industries and can take advantage of expanded world markets. In the long term, however, openness for capital and technology, as well as goods, may hamper the growth of large, developed countries by diverting resources from the domestic economy, and by providing potential competitors with the knowledge needed to develop their own industries. Only by maintaining its technological lead and continually developing new industries can even a very large state escape the undesired consequences of an entirely open economic system. For medium-size states, the relationship between international trading structure and growth is impossible to specify definitively, either theoretically or empirically. On the one hand, writers from the mercantilists through the American protectionists and the German historical school, and more recently analysts of *dependencia,* have argued that an entirely open system can undermine a state's effort to develop, and even lead to underdevelopment. On the other hand, adherents of more conventional neoclassical positions have maintained that exposure to international competition spurs economic transformation. The evidence is not yet in. All that can confidently be said is that openness furthers the economic growth of small states and of large ones so long as they maintain their technological edge.

From State Preferences to International Trading Structures

The next step in this argument is to relate particular distributions of potential economic power, defined by the size and level of development of individual states, to the structure of the international trading system, defined in terms of openness.

Let us consider a system composed of a large number of small, highly developed states. Such a system is likely to lead to an open international trading structure. The aggregate income and economic growth of each state are increased by an open system. The social instability produced by exposure to international competition is mitigated by the factor mobility made possible by higher levels of development. There is no loss of political power from openness because the costs of closure are symmetrical for all members of the system.

Now let us consider a system composed of a few very large, but unequally developed states. Such a distribution of potential economic power is likely to lead to a closed structure. Each state could increase its income through a more open system, but the gains would be modest. Openness would create more social instability in the less developed countries. The rate of growth for more backward areas might be frustrated, while that of the more advanced ones would be enhanced. A more open structure would leave the less developed states in a politically more vulnerable position, because their greater factor rigidity would mean a higher relative cost of closure. Because of these disadvantages, large but relatively less developed states are unlikely to accept an open trading structure. More advanced states cannot, unless they are militarily more powerful, force large backward countries to accept openness.

Finally, let us consider a hegemonic system—one in which there is a single state that is much larger and relatively more advanced than its trading partners. The costs and benefits of openness are not symmetrical for all members of the system. The hegemonic state will have a preference for an open structure. Such a structure increases its aggregate national income. It also increases its rate of growth during its ascendancy—that is, when its relative size and technological lead are increasing. Further, an open structure increases its political power, since the opportunity costs of closure are least for a large and developed state. The social instability resulting from exposure to the international system is mitigated by the hegemonic power's relatively low level of involvement in the international economy, and the mobility of its factors.

What of the other members of a hegemonic system? Small states are likely to opt for openness because the advantages in terms of aggregate income and growth are so great, and their political power is bound to be restricted regardless of what they do. The reaction of medium-size states is hard to predict; it depends at least in part on the way in which the hegemonic power utilizes its resources. The potentially dominant state has symbolic, economic, and military capabilities that can be used to entice or compel others to accept an open trading structure.

At the symbolic level, the hegemonic state stands as an example of how economic development can be achieved. Its policies may be emulated, even if they are inappropriate for other states. Where there are very dramatic asymmetries, military power can be used to coerce weaker states into an open structure. Force is not, however, a very efficient means for changing economic policies and it is unlikely to be employed against medium-size states.

Most importantly, the hegemonic state can use its economic resources to create an open structure. In terms of positive incentives, it can offer access to its large domestic market and to its relatively cheap exports. In terms of negative ones, it can withhold foreign grants and engage in competition, potentially ruinous for the weaker state, in third-country markets. The size and economic robustness of the hegemonic state also enable it to provide the confidence necessary for a stable international monetary system, and its currency can offer the liquidity needed for an increasingly open system.

In sum, openness is most likely to occur during periods when a hegemonic state is in its ascendancy. Such a state has the interest and the resources to create a structure characterized by lower tariffs, rising trade proportions, and less regionalism. There are other distributions of potential power where openness is likely, such as a system composed of many small, highly developed states. But even here, that potential might not be realized because of the problems of creating confidence in a monetary system where adequate liquidity would have to be provided by a negotiated international reserve asset or a group of national currencies. Finally, it is unlikely that very large states, particularly at unequal levels of development, would accept open trading relations.

These arguments, and the implications of other ideal typical configurations of potential economic power for the openness of trading structures, are summarized in [Chart 1].

THE DEPENDENT VARIABLE: DESCRIBING THE STRUCTURE OF THE INTERNATIONAL TRADING SYSTEM

The structure of international trade has both behavioral and institutional attributes. The degree of openness can be described both by the flow of goods and by the *policies* that are followed by states with respect to trade barriers and international payments. The two are not unrelated, but they do not coincide perfectly.

In common usage, the focus of attention has been upon institutions. Openness is associated with those historical periods in which tariffs were substantially lowered: the third quarter of the nineteenth century and the period since the Second World War.

Tariffs alone, however, are not an adequate indicator of structure. They are hard to operationalize quantitatively. Tariffs do not have to be high to be effective. If cost functions are nearly identical, even low tariffs can prevent trade. Effective tariff rates may be much higher than nominal ones. Nontariff barriers to trade, which are not easily compared across states, can substitute for duties. An undervalued exchange rate can protect domestic markets from foreign competition. Tariff levels alone cannot describe the structure of international trade.

A second indicator, and one which is behavioral rather than institutional, is

CHART 1. Probability of an Open Trading Structure with Different Distributions of Potential Economic Power

LEVEL OF DEVELOPMENT OF STATES	SIZE OF STATES		
	Relatively Equal		Very Unequal
	Small	Large	
Equal	Moderate-High	Low-Moderate	High
Unequal	Moderate	Low	Moderate-High

trade proportions—the ratios of trade to national income for different states. Like tariff levels, these involve describing the system in terms of an agglomeration of national tendencies. A period in which these ratios are increasing across time for most states can be described as one of increasing openness.

A third indicator is the concentration of trade within regions composed of states at different levels of development. The degree of such regional encapsulation is determined not so much by comparative advantage (because relative factor endowments would allow almost any backward area to trade with almost any developed one), but by political choices or dictates. Large states, attempting to protect themselves from the vagaries of a global system, seek to maximize their interests by creating regional blocs. Openness in the global economic system has in effect meant greater trade among the leading industrial states. Periods of closure are associated with the encapsulation of certain advanced states within regional systems shared with certain less developed areas.

A description of the international trading system involves, then, an exercise that is comparative rather than absolute. A period when tariffs are falling, trade proportions are rising, and regional trading patterns are becoming less extreme will be defined as one in which the structure is becoming more open.

Tariff Levels

The period from the 1820's to 1879 was basically one of decreasing tariff levels in Europe. The trend began in Great Britain in the 1820's, with reductions of duties and other barriers to trade. In 1846 the abolition of the Corn Laws ended agricultural protectionism. France reduced duties on some intermediate goods in the 1830's, and on coal, iron, and steel in 1852. The *Zollverein* established fairly low tariffs in 1834. Belgium, Portugal, Spain, Piedmont, Norway, Switzerland, and Sweden lowered imposts in the 1850's. The golden age of free trade began in 1860, when Britain and France signed the Cobden-Chevalier Treaty, which virtually eliminated trade barriers. This was followed by a series of bilateral trade agreements between virtually all European states. It is important to note, however, that the United States took little part in the general movement toward lower trade barriers.

The movement toward greater liberality was reversed in the late 1870's. Austria-Hungary increased duties in 1876 and 1878, and Italy also in 1878; but the main breach came in Germany in 1879. France increased tariffs modestly in 1881, sharply in 1892, and raised them still further in 1910. Other countries followed a similar pattern. Only Great Britain, Belgium, the Netherlands, and Switzerland continued to follow free-trade policies through the 1880's. Although Britain did not herself impose duties, she began establishing a system of preferential markets in her overseas Empire in 1898. The United States was basically protectionist throughout the nineteenth century. The high tariffs imposed during the Civil War continued with the exception of a brief period in the 1890's. There were no major duty reductions before 1914.

During the 1920's tariff levels increased further. Western European states protected their agrarian sectors against imports from the Danube region, Australia, Canada, and the United States, where the war had stimulated increased output. Great Britain adopted some colonial preferences in 1919, imposed a small number of tariffs in 1921, and extended some wartime duties. The successor states of the Austro-Hungarian Empire imposed duties to achieve some national self-sufficiency. The British dominions and Latin America protected industries nurtured by wartime demands. In the United States the Fordney-McCumber Tariff Act of 1922 increased protectionism. The October Revolution removed Russia from the Western trading system.

Dramatic closure in terms of tariff levels began with the passage of the Smoot-Hawley Tariff Act in the United States in 1930. Britain raised tariffs in 1931 and definitively abandoned free trade at the Ottawa Conference of 1932, which introduced extensive imperial preferences. Germany and Japan established trading blocs within their own spheres of influence. All other major countries followed protectionist policies.

Significant reductions in protection began after the Second World War; the United States had foreshadowed the movement toward greater liberality with the passage of the Reciprocal Trade Agreements Act in 1934. Since 1945 there have been seven rounds of multilateral tariff reductions. The first, held in 1947 at Geneva, and the Kennedy Round, held during the 1960's, have been the most significant. They have substantially reduced the level of protection.

The present situation is ambiguous. There have recently been some new trade controls. In the United States these include a voluntary import agreement for steel, the imposition of a 10 per cent import surcharge during four months of 1971, and export controls on agricultural products in 1973 and 1974. Italy imposed a deposit requirement on imports during parts of 1974 and 1975. Britain and Japan have engaged in export subsidization. Nontariff barriers have become more important. On balance, there has been movement toward greater protectionism since the end of the Kennedy Round, but it is not decisive. The outcome of the multilateral negotiations that began in 1975 remains to be seen.

In sum, after 1820 there was a general trend toward lower tariffs (with the notable exception of the United States), which culminated between 1860 and 1879; higher tariffs from 1879 through the interwar years, with dramatic increases in the 1930's; and less protectionism from 1945 through the conclusion of the Kennedy Round in 1967.

Trade Proportions

With the exception of one period, ratios of trade to aggregate economic activity followed the same general pattern as tariff levels. Trade proportions increased from the early part of the nineteenth century to about 1880. Between 1880 and 1900 there was a decrease, sharper if measured in current prices than constant ones, but apparent in both statistical series for most countries. Between 1900 and

1913—and here is the exception from the tariff pattern—there was a marked increase in the ratio of trade to aggregate economic activity. This trend brought trade proportions to levels that have generally not been reattained. During the 1920's and 1930's the importance of trade in national economic activity declined. After the Second World War it increased.

. . . There are considerable differences in the movement of trade proportions among states. They hold more or less constant for the United States; Japan, Denmark, and Norway . . . are unaffected by the general decrease in the ratio of trade to aggregate economic activity that takes place after 1880. The pattern described in the previous paragraph does, however, hold for Great Britain, France, Sweden, Germany, and Italy.

. . . Because of the boom in commodity prices that occurred in the early 1950's, the ratio of trade to gross domestic product was relatively high for larger states during these years, at least in current prices. It then faltered or remained constant until about 1960. From the early 1960's through 1972, trade proportions rose for all major states except Japan. Data for 1973 and 1974 show further increases. For smaller countries the trend was more erratic, with Belgium showing a more or less steady increase, Norway vacillating between 82 and 90 per cent, and Denmark and the Netherlands showing higher figures for the late 1950's than for more recent years. There is then, in current prices, a generally upward trend in trade proportions since 1960, particularly for larger states. The movement is more pronounced if constant prices are used.

Regional Trading Patterns

The final indicator of the degree of openness of the global trading system is regional bloc concentration. There is a natural affinity for some states to trade with others because of geographical propinquity or comparative advantage. In general, however, a system in which there are fewer manifestations of trading within given blocs, particularly among specific groups of more and less developed states, is a more open one. Over time there have been extensive changes in trading patterns between particular areas of the world whose relative factor endowments have remained largely the same.

Richard Chadwick and Karl Deutsch have collected extensive information on international trading patterns since 1890. Their basic datum is the relative acceptance indicator (RA), which measures deviations from a null hypothesis in which trade between a pair of states, or a state and a region, is precisely what would be predicted on the basis of their total share of international trade. When the null hypothesis holds, the RA indicator is equal to zero. Values less than zero indicate less trade than expected, greater than zero more trade than expected. For our purposes the critical issue is whether, over time, trade tends to become more concentrated as shown by movements away from zero, or less as shown by movements toward zero. . . .

There is a general pattern. In three of the four cases, the RA value closest to zero—that is the least regional encapsulation—occurred in 1890, 1913, or 1928; in the fourth case (France and French West Africa), the 1928 value was not bettered until 1964. In every case there was an increase in the RA indicator between 1928 and 1938, reflecting the breakdown of international commerce that is associated with the Depression. Surprisingly, the RA indicator was higher for each of the four pairs in 1954 and in 1938, an indication that regional patterns persisted and even became more intense in the postwar period. With the exception of the Soviet Union and Eastern Europe, there was a general trend toward decreasing RA's for the period after 1954. They still, however, show fairly high values even in the late 1960's.

If we put all three indicators—tariff levels, trade proportions, and trade patterns—together, they suggest the following periodization.

Period I (1820–1879): Increasing openness—tariffs are generally lowered; trade proportions increase. Data are not available for trade patterns. However, it is important to note that this is not a universal pattern. The United States is largely unaffected; its tariff levels remain high (and are in fact increased during the early 1860's) and American trade proportions remain almost constant.

Period II (1879–1900): Modest closure—tariffs are increased; trade proportions decline modestly for most states. Data are not available for trade patterns.

Period III (1900–1913): Greater openness—tariff levels remain generally unchanged; trade proportions increase for all major trading states except the United States. Trading patterns become less regional in three out of the four cases for which data are available.

Period IV (1918–1939): Closure—tariff levels are increased in the 1920's and again in the 1930's; trade proportions decline. Trade becomes more regionally encapsulated.

Period V (1945–c. 1970): Great openness—tariffs are lowered; trade proportions increase, particularly after 1960. Regional concentration decreases after 1960. However, these developments are limited to non-Communist areas of the world.

THE INDEPENDENT VARIABLE: DESCRIBING THE DISTRIBUTION OF POTENTIAL ECONOMIC POWER AMONG STATES

Analysts of international relations have an almost pro forma set of variables designed to show the distribution of potential power in the international *political* system. It includes such factors as gross national product, per capita income, geographical position, and size of armed forces. A similar set of indicators can be presented for the international economic system.

Statistics are available over a long time period for per capita income, aggregate size, share of world trade, and share of world investment. They demonstrate that, since the beginning of the nineteenth century, there have been two first-rank economic powers in the world economy—Britain and the United States. The United States passed Britain in aggregate size sometime in the middle of the nineteenth century and, in the 1880's, became the largest producer of manufactures. America's lead was particularly marked in technologically advanced industries turning out sewing machines, harvesters, cash registers, locomotives, steam pumps, telephones, and petroleum. Until the First World War, however, Great Britain had a higher per capita income, a greater share of world trade, and a greater share of world investment than any other state. The peak of British ascendance occurred around 1880, when Britain's relative per capita income, share of world trade, and share of investment flows reached their highest levels. Britain's potential dominance in 1880 and 1900 was particularly striking in the international economic system, where her share of trade and foreign investment was about twice as large as that of any other state.

It was only after the First World War that the United States became relatively larger and more developed in terms of all four indicators. This potential dominance reached new and dramatic heights between 1945 and 1960. Since then, the relative position of the United States has declined, bringing it quite close to West Germany, its nearest rival, in terms of per capita income and share of world trade. The devaluations of the dollar that have taken place since 1972 are reflected in a continuation of this downward trend for income and aggregate size.

The relative potential economic power of Britain and the United States is shown in [Tables I and II].

In sum, Britain was the world's most important trading state from the period after the Napoleonic Wars until 1913. Her relative position rose until about 1880 and fell thereafter. The United States became the largest and most advanced state

TABLE I. Indicators of British Potential Power
          (Ratio of British value to next highest)

	Per Capita Income	Aggregate Size	Share of World Trade	Share of World Investment*
1860	.91(US)	.74(US)	2.01(FR)	n.a.
1880	1.30(US)	.79(1874–83 US)	2.22(FR)	1.93(FR)
1900	1.05(1899 US)	.58(1899 US)	2.17(1890 GERM)	2.08(FR)
1913	.92(US)	.43(US)	1.20(US)	2.18(1914 FR)
1928	.66(US)	.25(1929 US)	.79(US)	.64(1921–29 US)
1937	.79(US)	.29(US)	.88(US)	.18(1930–38 US)
1950	.56(US)	.19(US)	.69(US)	.13(1951–55 US)
1960	.49(US)	.14(US)	.46(1958 US)	.15(1956–61 US)
1972	.46(US)	.13(US)	.47(1973 US)	n.a.

*Stock 1870–1913; Flow 1928–1950

Years are in parentheses when different from those in first column.

Countries in parentheses are those with the largest values for the particular indicator other than Great Britain.

TABLE II. Indicators of U.S. Potential Power (Ratio of U.S. value to next highest)

	Per Capita Income	Aggregate Size	Share of World Trade	Share of World Investment Flows
1860	1.10(GB)	1.41(GB)	.36(GB)	Net debtor
1880	.77(GB)	1.23(1883 GB)	.37(GB)	Net debtor
1900	.95(1899 GB)	1.73(1899 GB)	.43(1890 GB)	n.a.
1913	1.09(GB)	2.15(RUS)	.83(GB)	Net debtor
1928	1.51(GB)	3.22(USSR)	1.26(GB)	1.55(1921–29 UK)
1937	1.26(GB)	2.67(USSR)	1.13(GB)	5.53(1930–38 UK)
1950	1.78(GB)	3.15(USSR)	1.44(GB)	7.42(1951–55 UK)
1960	2.05(GB)	2.81(USSR)	2.15(1958 GB)	6.60(1956–61 UK)
1972	1.31(GERM)	n.a.	1.18(1973GERM)	n.a.

Years are in parentheses when different from those in first column.

Countries in parentheses are those with the largest values for the particular indicator other than the United States.

in economic terms after the First World War, but did not equal the relative share of world trade and investment achieved by Britain in the 1880's until after the Second World War.

TESTING THE ARGUMENT

The contention that hegemony leads to a more open trading structure is fairly well, but not perfectly, confirmed by the empirical evidence presented in the preceding sections. The argument explains the periods 1820 to 1879, 1880 to 1900, and 1945 to 1960. It does not fully explain those from 1900 to 1913, 1919 to 1939, or 1960 to the present.

1820–1879. The period from 1820 to 1879 was one of increasing openness in the structure of international trade. It was also one of rising hegemony. Great Britain was the instigator and supporter of the new structure. She began lowering her trade barriers in the 1820's, before any other state. The signing of the Cobden-Chevalier Tariff Treaty with France in 1860 initiated a series of bilateral tariff reductions. It is, however, important to note that the United States was hardly involved in these developments, and that America's ratio of trade to aggregate economic activity did not increase during the nineteenth century.

Britain put to use her internal flexibility and external power in securing a more open structure. At the domestic level, openness was favored by the rising industrialists. The opposition of the agrarian sector was mitigated by its capacity for adjustment: the rate of capital investment and technological innovation was high enough to prevent British agricultural incomes from falling until some thirty years after the abolition of the Corn Laws. Symbolically, the Manchester School led by

Cobden and Bright provided the ideological justification for free trade. Its influence was felt throughout Europe where Britain stood as an example to at least some members of the elite.

Britain used her military strength to open many backward areas: British interventions were frequent in Latin America during the nineteenth century, and formal and informal colonial expansion opened the interior of Africa. Most importantly, Britain forced India into the international economic system. British military power was also a factor in concluding the Cobden-Chevalier Treaty, for Louis Napoleon was more concerned with cementing his relations with Britain than he was in the economic consequences of greater openness. Once this pact was signed, however, it became a catalyst for the many other treaties that followed.

Britain also put economic instruments to good use in creating an open system. The abolition of the Corn Laws offered continental grain producers the incentive of continued access to the growing British market. Britain was at the heart of the nineteenth-century international monetary system which functioned exceptionally well, at least for the core of the more developed states and the areas closely associated with them. Exchange rates were stable, and countries did not have to impose trade barriers to rectify cyclical payments difficulties. Both confidence and liquidity were, to a critical degree, provided by Britain. The use of sterling balances as opposed to specie became increasingly widespread, alleviating the liquidity problems presented by the erratic production of gold and silver. Foreign private and central banks increasingly placed their cash reserves in London, and accounts were cleared through changing bank balances rather than gold flows. Great Britain's extremely sophisticated financial institutions, centered in the City of London, provided the short-term financing necessary to facilitate the international flow of goods. Her early and somewhat fortuitous adherence to the gold—as opposed to the silver or bimetallic—standard proved to be an important source of confidence as all countries adopted at least a *de facto* gold standard after 1870 because of the declining relative value of silver. In times of monetary emergency, the confidence placed in the pound because of the strength of the British economy allowed the Bank of England to be a lender of last resort.

Hence, for the first three-quarters of the nineteenth century, British policy favored an open international trading structure, and British power helped to create it. But this was not a global regime. British resources were not sufficient to entice or compel the United States (a country whose economy was larger than Britain's by 1860 and whose technology was developing very rapidly) to abandon its protectionist commercial policy. As a state-power argument suggests, openness was only established within the geographical area where the rising economic hegemony was able to exercise its influence.

1880–1900. The last two decades of the nineteenth century were a period of modest closure which corresponds to a relative decline in British per capita income, size, and share of world trade. The event that precipitated higher tariff levels was the availability of inexpensive grain from the American Midwest, made possible by the construction of continental railways. National responses varied.

Britain let her agricultural sector decline, a not unexpected development given her still dominant economic position. Denmark, a small and relatively well-developed state, also refrained from imposing tariffs and transformed its farming sector from agriculture to animal husbandry. Several other small states also followed open policies. Germany, France, Russia, and Italy imposed higher tariffs, however. Britain did not have the military or economic power to forestall these policies. Still, the institutional structure of the international monetary system, with the City of London at its center, did not crumble. The decline in trade proportions was modest despite higher tariffs.

1945–1960.   The third period that is neatly explained by the argument that hegemony leads to an open trading structure is the decade and a half after the Second World War, characterized by the ascendancy of the United States. During these years the structure of the international trading system became increasingly open. Tariffs were lowered; trade proportions were restored well above interwar levels. Asymmetrical regional trading patterns did begin to decline, although not until the late 1950's. America's bilateral rival, the Soviet Union, remained—as the theory would predict—encapsulated within its own regional sphere of influence.

Unlike Britain in the nineteenth century, the United States after World War II operated in a bipolar political structure. Free trade was preferred, but departures such as the Common Market and Japanese import restrictions were accepted to make sure that these areas remained within the general American sphere of influence. Domestically the Reciprocal Trade Agreements Act, first passed in 1934, was extended several times after the war. Internationally the United States supported the framework for tariff reductions provided by the General Agreement on Tariffs and Trade. American policy makers used their economic leverage over Great Britain to force an end to the imperial preference system. The monetary system established at Bretton Woods was basically an American creation. In practice, liquidity was provided by the American deficit; confidence by the size of the American economy. Behind the economic veil stood American military protection for other industrialized market economies—an overwhelming incentive for them to accept an open system, particularly one which was in fact relatively beneficial.

The argument about the relationship between hegemony and openness is not as satisfactory for the years 1900 to 1913, 1919 to 1939, and 1960 to the present.

1900–1913.   During the years immediately preceding the First World War, the structure of international trade became more open in terms of trade proportions and regional patterns. Britain remained the largest international economic entity, but her relative position continued a decline that had begun two decades earlier. Still, Britain maintained her commitment to free trade and to the financial institutions of the City of London. A state-power argument would suggest some reconsideration of these policies.

Perhaps the simplest explanation for the increase in trade proportions was the burst of loans that flowed out of Europe in the years before the First World War, loans that financed the increasing sale of goods. Germany and France as well as

Britain participated in this development. Despite the higher tariff levels imposed after 1879, institutional structures—particularly the monetary system—allowed these capital flows to generate increasing trade flows. Had Britain reconsidered her policies, this might not have been the case.

1919–1939. The United States emerged from the First World War as the world's most powerful economic state. Whether America was large enough to have put an open system in place is a moot question. As Table II indicates, America's share of world trade and investment was only 26 and 55 per cent greater than that of any other state, while comparable figures for Great Britain during the last part of the nineteenth century are 100 per cent. What is apparent, though, is that American policy makers made little effort to open the structure of international trade. The call for an open door was a shibboleth, not a policy. It was really the British who attempted to continue a hegemonic role.

In the area of trade, the U.S. Fordney-McCumber Tariff of 1922 increased protection. That tendency was greatly reinforced by the Smoot-Hawley Tariff of 1930 which touched off a wave of protective legislation. Instead of leading the way to openness, the United States led the way to closure.

In the monetary area, the American government made little effort to alter a situation that was confused and often chaotic. During the first half of the 1920's, exchange rates fluctuated widely among major currencies as countries were forced, by the inflationary pressures of the war, to abandon the gold standard. Convertibility was restored in the mid-twenties at values incompatible with long-term equilibrium. The British pound was overvalued, and the French franc undervalued. Britain was forced off the gold standard in September 1931, accelerating a trend that had begun with Uruguay in April 1929. The United States went off gold in 1933. France's decision to end convertibility in 1936 completed the pattern. During the 1930's the monetary system collapsed.

Constructing a stable monetary order would have been no easy task in the political environment of the 1920's and 1930's. The United States made no effort. It refused to recognize a connection between war debts and reparations, although much of the postwar flow of funds took the form of American loans to Germany, German reparations payments to France and Britain, and French and British war-debt payments to the United States. The Great Depression was in no small measure touched off by the contraction of American credit in the late 1920's. In the deflationary collapse that followed, the British were too weak to act as a lender of last resort, and the Americans actually undercut efforts to reconstruct the Western economy when, before the London Monetary Conference of 1933, President Roosevelt changed the basic assumptions of the meeting by taking the United States off gold. American concern was wholly with restoring the domestic economy.

That is not to say that American behavior was entirely obstreperous; but cooperation was erratic and often private. The Federal Reserve Bank of New York did try, during the late 1920's, to maintain New York interest rates below those in London to protect the value of the pound. Two Americans, Dawes and Young, lent their names to the renegotiations of German reparations payments, but most of the actual work was carried out by British experts. At the official level, the first manifestation of American leadership was President Hoover's call for a moratorium on war debts and reparations in June 1931; but in 1932 the United States refused to participate in the Lausanne Conference that in effect ended reparations.

It was not until the mid-thirties that the United States asserted any real leadership. The Reciprocal Trade Agreements Act of 1934 led to bilateral treaties with twenty-seven countries before 1945. American concessions covered 64 per cent of dutiable items, and reduced rates by an average of 44 per cent. However, tariffs were so high to begin with that the actual impact of these agreements was limited. There were also some modest steps toward tariff liberalization in Britain and France. In the monetary field, the United States, Britain, and France pledged to maintain exchange-rate stability in the Tripartite Declaration of September 1936. These actions were not adequate to create an open international economic structure. American policy during the interwar period, and particularly before the mid-thirties, fails to accord with the predictions made by a state-power explanation of the behavior of a rising hegemonic power.

1960–Present.   The final period not adequately dealt with by a state-power explanation is the last decade or so. In recent years, the relative size and level of development of the U.S. economy has fallen. This decline has not, however, been accompanied by a clear turn toward protectionism. The Trade Expansion Act of 1962 was extremely liberal and led to the very successful Kennedy Round of multilateral tariff cuts during the mid-sixties. The protectionist Burke-Hartke Bill did not pass. The 1974 Trade Act does include new protectionist aspects, particularly in its requirements for review of the removal of nontariff barriers by Congress and for stiffer requirements for the imposition of countervailing duties, but it still maintains the mechanism of presidential discretion on tariff cuts that has been the keystone of postwar reductions. While the Voluntary Steel Agreement, the August 1971 economic policy, and restrictions on agricultural exports all show a tendency toward protectionism, there is as yet no evidence of a basic turn away from a commitment to openness.

In terms of behavior in the international trading system, the decade of the 1960's was clearly one of greater openness. Trade proportions increased, and traditional regional trade patterns became weaker. A state-power argument would predict a downturn or at least a faltering in these indicators as American power declined.

In sum, although the general pattern of the structure of international trade conforms with the predictions of a state-power argument—two periods of openness separated by one of closure—corresponding to periods of rising British and American hegemony and an interregnum, the whole pattern is out of phase. British commitment to openness continued long after Britain's position had declined. American commitment to openness did not begin until well after the United States had become the world's leading economic power and has continued during a period of relative American decline. The state-power argument needs to be amended to take these delayed reactions into account.

AMENDING THE ARGUMENT

The structure of the international trading system does not move in lockstep with changes in the distribution of potential power among states. Systems are initiated and ended, not as a state-power theory would predict, by close assessments of the interests of the state at every given moment, but by external events—usually cataclysmic ones. The closure that began in 1879 coincided with the Great Depression of the last part of the nineteenth century. The final dismantling of the nineteenth-century international economic system was not precipitated by a change in British trade or monetary policy, but by the First World War and the Depression. The potato famine of the 1840's prompted abolition of the Corn Laws; and the United States did not assume the mantle of world leadership until the world had been laid bare by six years of total war. Some catalytic external event seems necessary to move states to dramatic policy initiatives in line with state interests.

Once policies have been adopted, they are pursued until a new crisis demonstrates that they are no longer feasible. States become locked in by the impact of prior choices on their domestic political structures. The British decision to opt for openness in 1846 corresponded with state interests. It also strengthened the position of industrial and financial groups over time, because they had the opportunity to operate in an international system that furthered their objectives. That system eventually undermined the position of British farmers, a group that would have supported protectionism, if it had survived. Once entrenched, Britain's export industries, and more importantly the City of London, resisted policies of closure. In the interwar years, the British rentier class insisted on restoring the prewar parity of the pound—a decision that placed enormous deflationary pressures on the domestic economy—because they wanted to protect the value of their investments.

Institutions created during periods of rising ascendancy remained in operation when they were no longer appropriate. For instance, the organization of British banking in the nineteenth century separated domestic and foreign operations. The Court of Directors of the Bank of England was dominated by international banking houses. Their decisions about British monetary policy were geared toward the international economy. Under a different institutional arrangement more attention might have been given after 1900 to the need to revitalize the domestic economy. The British state was unable to free itself from the domestic structures that its earlier policy decisions had created, and continued to follow policies appropriate for a rising hegemony long after Britain's star had begun to fall.

Similarly, earlier policies in the United States begat social structures and institutional arrangements that trammeled state policy. After protecting import-competing industries for a century, the United States was unable in the 1920's to opt for more open policies, even though state interests would have been furthered thereby. Institutionally, decisions about tariff reductions were taken primarily in congressional committees, giving virtually any group seeking protection easy access to the decision-making process. When there were conflicts among groups, they were resolved by raising the levels of protection for everyone. It was only after the cataclysm of the depression that the decision-making processes for trade policy were changed. The presidency, far more insulated from the entreaties of particular societal groups than congressional committees, was then given more power. Furthermore, the American commercial banking system was unable to assume the burden of regulating the international economy during the 1920's. American institutions were geared toward the domestic economy. Only after the Second World War, and in fact not until the late 1950's, did American banks fully develop the complex institutional structures commensurate with the dollar's role in the international monetary system.

Having taken the critical decisions that created an open system after 1945, the American government is unlikely to change its policy until it confronts some external event that it cannot control, such as a worldwide deflation, drought in the great plains, or the malicious use of petrodollars. In America perhaps more than in any other country "new policies," as E. E. Schattschneider wrote in his brilliant study of the Smoot-Hawley Tariff in 1935, "create new politics,"[1] for in America the state is weak and the society strong. State decisions taken because of state interests reinforce private societal groups that the state is unable to resist in later periods. Multinational corporations have grown and prospered since 1950. International economic policy making has passed from the Congress to the Executive. Groups favoring closure, such as organized labor, are unlikely to carry the day until some external event demonstrates that existing policies can no longer be implemented.

The structure of international trade changes in fits and starts; it does not flow smoothly with the redistribution of potential state power. Nevertheless, it is the power and the policies of states that create order where there would otherwise be chaos or at best a Lockian state of nature. The existence of various transnational, multinational, transgovernmental, and other nonstate actors that have riveted scholarly attention in recent years can only be understood within the context of a broader structure that ultimately rests upon the power and interests of states, shackled through they may be by the societal consequences of their own past decisions.

NOTE

1. E. E. Schattschneider, *Politics, Pressures and the Tariff: A Study of Free Enterprise in Pressure Politics as Shown in the 1929–1930 Revision of the Tariff* (New York: Prentice-Hall, 1935), p. 288.

2

The Political Economy
of the Smoot-Hawley Tariff

BARRY EICHENGREEN

Barry Eichengreen presents a domestic societal explanation of the passage of the Smoot-Hawley Tariff Act of 1930. Eichengreen argues that economic interest groups were the key actors underlying the passage of the act. Specifically, he asserts that certain sectors of agriculture and industry supported each other's desire for protection and together pressured the government to pass the highly restrictive Smoot-Hawley Tariff. He shows both how the actions of self-interested groups in national societies affect the making of foreign economic policy and how international political and market forces can influence the interests of societal actors.

The intimate connection between the Great Depression and the Smoot-Hawley Tariff of 1930 was recognized by contemporaries and continues to be emphasized by historical scholars. But just as contemporaries, while agreeing on its importance, nonetheless viewed the tariff in a variety of different ways, historians of the era have achieved no consensus on the tariff's origins and effects. The definitive study of the Smoot-Hawley's origins, by Schattschneider [1935], portrays the tariff as a classic example of pork-barrel politics, with each member of Congress after his particular piece of pork. Revisionist treatments characterize it instead as a classic instance of party politics; protectionism being the household remedy of the Republican Party, the tariff's adoption is ascribed to the outcome of the 1928 election. Yet proponents of neither interpretation provide an adequate analysis of the relationship of Smoot-Hawley to the Depression. . . .

POLITICS, PRESSURES AND THE TARIFF

The debate surrounding the passage of the Tariff Act of 1930 remains a classic study in the political economy of protection. A number of theories have been de-

Barry Eichengreen. "The Political Economy of the Smoot-Hawley Tariff." From *Research in Economic History,* Vol. 12 (1989), pp. 1–43. Reprinted by permission of JAI Press Inc.

veloped to explain Smoot-Hawley's adoption, starting with that advanced in Schattschneider's [1935] classic monograph whose title this section bears.

Schattschneider's influential study "set the tone for a whole generation of political writing on pressure groups. . . ." and "cut the lens through which Americans have since visualized the making of U.S. foreign trade policy. . . ."[1] Schattschneider focused on the influence of special interest groups. In his account, the actions of lobbyists and special interests were responsible for both the tariff's adoption and its form.

Schattschneider dubbed the principle around which the tariff coalition organized "reciprocal noninterference." The coalition was assembled by offering limited protection to everyone involved. Since only moderate protection was provided and no single import-competing sector reaped extraordinary benefits at the expense of others, they could combine in support of tariff legislation. In addition, under provisions of the original House and Senate bills, credits (or "debentures") were to be made available to exporters, extending the coalition beyond the import-competing to the export-producing sector. Not just the number of duties raised but the very process by which the bill was passed is invoked in support of the log-rolling interpretation. Passage required 14 months from when Hoover called a special session of Congress to when the final bill was signed. The record of public hearings in which the bill was discussed ran to 20,000 pages, while the final bill provided tariff schedules for more than 20,000 items. Since insurgency was easier under Senate than House rules, log-rolling was more conspicuous there: the Senate amended the House bill over 1,200 times, most of them on the Senate floor. Still other changes were engineered in conference committee.

If the distinguishing feature of the Tariff Act of 1930 was the dominance of special interests, one must ask why they had grown so much more powerful. Schattschneider provides no explicit answer, although he indicts Hoover for failing to guide the legislation through Congress. But the systematic explanation implicit in his analysis is the rise of the "new lobby." Although fraternal, religious, social, and economic groups had always been part of the American scene, they had never been so well organized or visible in the Capitol as in the 1920s. . . .

A number of influences prompted the rise of the new lobby. First, the activities of the "muckrakers" in the first decade of the twentieth century had intensified public scrutiny of political affairs. Second, whereas businessmen had traditionally dealt with government in "a spasmodic and haphazard fashion," the panic of 1907 spurred them to cultivate more systematic representation. Simultaneously, the U.S. Chamber of Commerce took a more prominent role in representing the interests of business. . . . Finally, much as the Chamber of Commerce represented business's general interests, trade associations filled this role for more specialized groups. A Department of Commerce publication listed some 1,500 organizations classified as trade associations, nearly double the number known to exist in 1914. Some were organized by products produced, others by materials used, still others by markets in which sales took place. Like the other three influences, the growth of trade associations was a distinctively twentieth-century development, but in contrast to other trends, which had been underway in the early years of the century, the sudden rise to prominence of trade associations was attributable to World War I. The war effort required closer ties between government and industry, but upon attempting to establish them the authorities found it difficult to deal with individual enterprises and requested that associations be formed. If the war occasioned the formation and growth of trade associations, the armistice by no means signalled their demise. Once formed into an association the process of marshalling a constituency was no longer so difficult. Improvements in communication, notably the telephone, reinforced these advantages, and associations quickly learned to use pamphlets and other media to publicize their case. The adoption of new Congressional rules made it more difficult for powerful individuals to dictate policy, opening the legislative process to competing interests.

The same forces tending to promote effective representation of industrial interests in Washington encouraged the formation of effective organizations representing farmers and labor. The American farm movement had long been distinguished by its inability to organize effectively and represent its interests before Congress. The ad hoc methods of agricultural organizations, such as sending a representative to Washington in response to specific developments, had proven ineffectual. For agriculture as for industry, World War I and the impetus it provided for the formation of the War Trade Board and the Food Administration permitted farmers' organizations to assume new importance. In 1918 the National Grange opened a permanent legislative office in Washington, and the militant American Farm Bureau Federation, founded in 1919, lobbied actively for farm legislation. In 1921 a bipartisan Farm Bloc of senators and congressmen from the South and West was formed, and it acquired a pivotal position in the balance of power in the 66th and 67th Congresses. Although it had at best mixed success in passing farm legislation before falling into disarray, the prominence of the Farm Bloc did much to alert agricultural interests to the advantages of effective congressional representation.

By encouraging the development of direct government-labor relations, the war had a similar impact on the American Federation of Labor. While maintaining its distance from party politics, by the 1920s the AFL was commonly acknowledged as the most formidable group in the United States other than the political parties. Thus, in the 1920s the three principal American interest groups—business, agriculture, and labor—were for the first time ably represented in Washington.

The rise of the new lobby is consistent with Schattschneider's characterization of Smoot-Hawley as an instance of pork-barrel politics. But his theory of reciprocal noninterference—that the Smoot-Hawley bill by offering something for everyone garnered widespread support—fails to confront the question of why the vote on the final bill so closely followed party lines, with only 5 Democratic Senators voting in favor and 11 Republicans against. Neither does it explain why tariff-rate increases differed so widely by schedule.

An alternative explanation, recently advanced by Pastor [1980], is that Smoot-Hawley is simply an instance of party politics. Protection in general and for industry in particular was regularly advocated by the Republican Party. With the White House occupied by a Republican President and the Senate in Republican hands, there were few obstacles to revising upward existing tariff schedules. It is curious that this straightforward explanation has attracted so little attention. It may be that partisan aspects of the debate were disguised by the absence of a change in party in 1928 like that following the 1920 election which preceded the 1922 Fordney-McCumber Tariff Act. Moreover, the issue of protection had not been hotly disputed in the 1928 campaign. Although the Democrats had traditionally campaigned on the basis of staunch opposition to protectionist measures, in 1928 they moderated their position and joined the Republicans in endorsing protection, albeit in vague and reserved terms. . . . Given the extent of consensus, there was little debate in the subsequent Congress over principles of free trade and protection. Hence even Free Traders among the Democrats were ill positioned to mount effective opposition to tariff increases.

The problem with this partisan interpretation is that it provides no explanation for Smoot-Hawley's timing or its form. It is suggested that Congress was simply accustomed to engaging in tariff revision every seven years (the average life of a tariff law between the Acts of 1883 and 1930), and that by 1929 Congress and the public had recovered from the exhausting Fordney-McCumber deliberations of 1920–22. But this mechanical explanation neither recognizes links between protectionist pressure and economic events nor provides an explanation for the observed variation in import duty levels.

The explanation coming closest to satisfying these requirements is the view of Smoot-Hawley as a response to the problems of American agriculture. The explanation runs as follows. While the 1920s were boom years for the country as a whole, prosperity was unevenly distributed. After benefiting from high prices from 1917 to 1920, American agriculture failed to recover from the recession of 1920–21. For much of the decade, farm gate prices declined relative to the prices of nonagricultural goods. . . . In 1926, a relatively favorable year for farmers when average wholesale prices were 51 percent above their 1913 levels, the prices of farm products were only 42 percent above those levels. The explanation for lagging prices was that World War I had prompted the expansion of agricultural production outside Europe. While European sugar production, for example, fell by 50 percent during the war, the shortfall was offset by expanding output in Cuba, Java, and South America. Once European production recovered, often under cover of import duties or production subsidies, world prices were depressed. Similarly, wartime disruptions of the global wheat market greatly stimulated production in Argentina, Australia, Canada, and the United States. The consequent decline in prices was magnified in the second half of the 1920s by the imposition of import duties on wheat by Germany, Italy, and France.

Agrarian distress in the United States took various forms, notably farm foreclosures which, after averaging 3.2 per thousand farms between 1913 and 1920, rose to 10.7 per thousand in 1921–25 and 17.0 per thousand in 1926–29. Foreclosure reflected not just the declining relative price of agricultural products but overall price level trends; since much agricultural land had turned over between 1917 and

1920 when prices were high, the subsequent deflation greatly augmented the burden of mortgage debt. The value of total farm mortgage debt rose by 45 percent between 1917 and 1920 and by a further 28 percent between 1920 and 1923 despite the deflation that set in after the beginning of the decade. The foreclosures of the second half of the 1920s were most heavily concentrated in Idaho, Montana, North and South Dakota, Colorado, and Arizona, the sources of strongest pressure for agrarian relief.

In the 1928 presidential campaign Hoover laid stress on tariff protection for agriculture. Previously, agriculture had been the recipient of only modest tariffs, in part because duties on farm imports would have been ineffective given U.S. status as a net exporter of most agricultural goods (sugar, wool and hides being the principal exceptions). In 1922, for reasons detailed above, the U.S. balance of trade in farm products turned negative, where it remained except in 1925 for the duration of the decade. Hence an expanding segment of American agriculture grew to appreciate the relevance of tariff protection.

By this interpretation, Smoot-Hawley was predominantly a form of agricultural relief. . . . Farm interests were well positioned to press their case. Although the United States had grown increasingly urbanized over preceding decades, Congress had not been reapportioned following the 1920 Census. Consequently, farm interests were overrepresented in the House, just as, on the two senator per state rule, they were overrepresented in the Senate.

This characterization of Smoot-Hawley as an agricultural measure won by the West over the opposition of the East is consistent not only with the partisan interpretation, given the regional concentration of Democratic and Republican voters, but it explains a number of defections from party ranks. To the extent that agricultural distress intensified with the onset of the Depression, it links the tariff to macroeconomic conditions. Where it falls short is in explaining why tariffs on manufactured imports were raised as part of an agrarian relief measure, or why the tariff was supported not only by representatives of agricultural districts but by those of industrial regions as well. Many accounts emphasize the extent of discord between agriculture and industry. . . . What explains the pattern of voting and the tariff schedule that emerged from Congressional debate?

A MODEL OF THE TARIFF-MAKING PROCESS

The framework I use to analyze the adoption of Smoot-Hawley is a variant of Gerschenkron's [1943] model of the political economy of protection. This is a member of the class of "interest-group models" of tariff formation. . . . I first review Gerschenkron's application of his model to Bismarckian Germany before adapting it to analysis of the Smoot-Hawley Tariff.

In Gerschenkron's model, a tariff is adopted when narrow yet well-placed interest groups combine in its support. Gerschenkron divides German society not merely along sectorial lines but into heavy industry (producers of basic products such as coal, iron and steel), light industry (manufacturers of consumer goods, along with whom might be included artisans and shopkeepers), large agriculture (the Junkers, or estate owners of the east), and small agriculture (commercial producers located primarily west of the Elbe). He explains the Bismarckian tariff as a coalition of iron and rye, allying large agriculture and heavy industry.

In the 1870s as in the 1920s, the impetus for agrarian protection was the fall in grain prices. The position of traditional German agriculture, which specialized in grain, was seriously undermined. The alternative to continued grain production behind tariff walls was to shift into the production of high quality foodstuffs such as dairy products and meat for rapidly expanding urban markets. Cheap imported grain could serve as an input into such production. But, crucially, large and small agriculture differed in their capacity to adjust. Variations in soil quality and proximity to urban markets provided greater scope for the production of dairy products and meat west of the Elbe. In addition, dairy products, meats and vegetables were most efficiently produced on small owner-managed farms. Hence costs of adjustment were lowest where long-term leaseholders and small owner-managed farms predominated—west of the Elbe—and highest where landless laborers worked large estates. The model predicts that small agriculture should have opposed agricultural protection due to its impact on costs, while large agriculture should have favored it.

Neither light nor heavy industry, with the possible exception of yarn spinning, desperately required protection from import competition. Under competitive conditions, Germany probably would have imported grain and exported both light manufactures and the products of the basic industries. While it is not clear that import duties on industrial goods would have succeeded in raising the prices of domestically-produced goods, given competition at home but the net export position of German manufacturers, heavy industry in fact supported the imposition of a tariff on manufactured goods. One interpretation is that, with high levels of fixed capital, heavy industry was exceptionally susceptible to cyclical fluctuations. Tariffs may have reduced the risk of falling prices, thereby encouraging the fixed investments which permitted scale economies to be reaped. A more compelling interpretation is that barriers to cheap imports were a necessary condition for firms producing basic goods to combine and extract monopoly profits from domestic users. Consistent with this interpretation, producers of final goods like stoves, pots and pans, shovels and rakes opposed tariffs on the products of basic industries because of their impact on production costs.

What is relevant for our purposes is that no group favored the final outcome: high tariffs on both agricultural and industrial goods. But because of the dispersion of interests, action required compromise. The two likely outcomes were a coalition of large industrialists and landowners obtaining general protection, and a coalition of small manufacturers and farmers successfully defending free trade. Gerschenkron ascribes the victory of the protectionist coalition to institutional factors. The Junkers, as members of the squirearchy, occupied a privileged position in the political system. Not only did they staff the bureaucracy and judiciary but, like the wealthy industrialists, they benefitted from the structure of the electoral system. Heavy industry, aided by smaller numbers, organized more effectively than small manufacturing. Managers of large enterprises formed new associations and worked to convert existing ones to protectionism. Their cause was not hurt by the fact that the Chancellor found protection a useful tool for achieving his political goals and played an active role in forging the alliance of iron and rye.

Gerschenkron's model can be applied to the case of the Smoot-Hawley Tariff by again distinguishing industry by size and agriculture by region. Naturally, the interests of the groups and the coalitions are entirely different from those observed in Bismarckian Germany. So is the role of national leadership. Nonetheless, distinctions of region and scale shed considerable light on the American case.

In the case of Smoot-Hawley, it is useful to distinguish sheltered from unsheltered agriculture and, as in Germany, light from heavy industry, where it is light industry and unsheltered agriculture that combined to support protection. As noted previously, critics of the Smoot-Hawley Tariff argued that duties on agricultural products would not be "effective" in raising prices because the United States was a net exporter of these goods. . . . The problem with this contention is that net trade may not be the appropriate indicator of the effectiveness of a tariff. It may mislead either if there existed segmented regional markets or if products were heterogeneous. For goods such as wheat with a high ratio of value to volume, there existed not merely a national but an international market. But wheat was not a homogenous product, and the United States both imported and exported different grades of what was often regarded in policy debate as a single commodity. Since, for example, little if any exportable surplus of high grade milling wheat was produced in the United States, it was argued that a tariff would therefore be effective in raising the Minneapolis price relative to that prevailing in Winnipeg. Even if the product was homogenous, for perishable products the United States was sufficiently large geographically that transport costs might impede the equalization of prices across regions. . . . Northern states like Minnesota and Eastern seaboard states like Massachusetts might find their markets flooded by cheap Canadian potatoes, milk, cream, butter and eggs. Since these goods could not penetrate further into the interior because of their high ratio of volume to value or due to the danger of spoilage, inland producers remained insulated from imports. Moreover, Southern farmers who engaged in the production of cotton (other than the long staple variety, which was imported and received a generous increase in tariff protection under the 1930 Act) were oriented toward the export market. Northern farmers close to the Canadian border had reason to favor protection to a much greater extent than their counterparts in the interior or the South.

There existed equally sharp divisions within manufacturing. The pressure for protection was greatest in light industry concentrating in the batch production of goods tailored to market. Heavy industry and manufacturers of standardized products had mechanized their operations and largely held their own against foreign competition. But labor-intensive industries dominated by small-scale firms experienced growing competition from abroad. In the bottle-making industry, producers of "fancy ware" such as perfume and toilet water bottles suffered from an increasing volume of French imports. Manufacturers of watches faced Swiss competition and producers of jewelry complained of German imports. Eastern glove manufacturers experienced difficulty in matching the prices of foreign goods. The New England shoe industry experienced competition from Czechoslovak producers. Some producers were sheltered by relatively generous Fordney-McCumber duties. But, for most, foreign trends such as the desperate attempts of English mills to hold onto market share exacerbated their woes. Still, only a minority of American industries were seriously injured by competition from foreign goods.

In opposition stood heavy industries producing standardized products, particularly segments which relied on the assembly line, mass production, the latest technology and the multi-divisional form. By the turn of the century, the United States had gained a competitive advantage in many of the industries of the Second Industrial Revolution, automobiles being a prime example. In 1929 motor cars and parts comprised 10 percent of total U.S. merchandise exports, while imports were negligible due only partially to a modicum of tariff protection. Given the importance of export sales and the anticipated impact of a tariff on production costs, the automobile producers, led by Henry Ford, made clear their opposition to the tariff bill. The same was true of producers of farm machinery, iron and steel bars, sheet, rails and metal manufactures.

The banking community had traditionally supported the protectionist system. Bankers doing business in industrial regions where firms depended on the tariff favored the maintenance of protection. But in the 1920s their support was tempered by events. World War I had transformed the United States from a debtor to a creditor nation and reoriented America's banking business abroad. Already in 1923 spokesmen for the financial community acknowledged that Europe's continued ability to service its dollar debt hinged upon foreign industries' access to American markets.

The opposite shift was evident in the attitudes of organized labor. Traditionally, labor had opposed protection for its impact on the cost of living. Those groups of workers injured by import competition were incapable of changing this policy. For half a century the AFL's position on the tariff had been one of carefully cultivated neutrality. Although individual unions might lobby for protection against imported goods or for lower duties on raw materials, the Federation's policy was to take no position on the issue. In 1930 it went only so far as to accede to individual unions' requests for legislative assistance. However, at the November 1928 AFL convention the first official caucus of pro-tariff unions was formed. This "Wage Earners Protective Conference" represented 8 or 9 percent of the Federation's membership, the leading participants including the photo-engravers, wall paper craftsmen, glass-bottle blowers and potters. Clearly, labor's traditional opposition to protection was attenuated by the success of pro-tariff unions in organizing to lobby for a change in policy.

In sum, the situation in 1930 appeared as follows. Farmers along the Canadian border and Eastern seaboard desired higher protection but, comprising only a minority of American agriculture, found it difficult to obtain alone. Light industries producing goods tailored to market also desired protection but similarly comprised only a portion of American manufacturing. In principle, neither group favored protection for the other, but each was willing to support the claims of its counterpart in return for participation in the coalition. While agriculture received generous protection under the final Smoot-Hawley bill, so did light industry producing goods tailored to market. . . .

This interpretation has advantages over the view of Smoot-Hawley that divides the American economy into monolithic agricultural and industrial blocs. It explains why sections of the industrial Midwest and East should have complained about the height of agricultural tariffs, and why certain agrarian interests, notably in the South, should have complained of industrial protection. It is consistent also with the observed alliance of industrial and agricultural protectionists and explains why the Smoot-Hawley Tariff, originally conceived as agricultural relief, evolved into a bill extending protection to portions of both industry and agriculture. It is consistent with Schattschneider's emphasis on log-rolling aspects of the legislative process, but rather than characterizing log-rolling as entirely general suggests that "reciprocal noninterference" should have favored border agriculture and light industry. It is consistent with the notion that Hoover lost control of the legislative process by permitting the debate to extend beyond the question of agricultural relief and with the inference that Hoover failed to take forceful action on the grounds that he saw the small businesses which dominated light industry as his constituency, but not necessarily with the opinion of Senator Borah that a narrowly agricultural tariff could have passed in 1929 had Hoover taken the bit in his teeth. National leadership, while important in both Gerschenkron's and this paper's application of the model, plays opposite roles in the two instances, since Bismarck favored widespread protection and played a prominent role in obtaining it, while Hoover personally opposed blanket protection but failed to effectively guide the legislative process. Finally, by invoking the rise of the trade association, the model can be used to explain how diverse agricultural and industrial interests succeeded in influencing the legislative process.

The model can be elaborated in various directions. One extension would introduce the long history of protectionism in the United States and the country's habit of neglecting the impact of its economic policies on the rest of the world. Another would build on the tendency of the Depression to undermine confidence in the self-equilibrating nature of the market. In many countries, the depth of the Depression provided a rationale for the extension of economic planning. In Britain, for example, Keynes went so far for a time as to argue for central planning along Soviet lines. In the United States this desire for intervention and control was most clearly manifest in the New Deal, but the same tendencies contributed to the pressure for tariff protection in 1930. . . .

At the same time the Depression worked to promote Smoot-Hawley by undermining confidence in the stability of the market, it altered the costs and benefits of protection as perceived by interest groups. By further lowering already depressed agricultural prices, it increased the pressure agricultural interests brought to bear on elected officials. By further undermining the already tenuous position of light industries engaged in the production of specialty products, it reinforced their efforts to acquire insulation from foreign competition. . . .

CONCLUSION

. . . Economic histories view the Great Depression and the Smoot-Hawley Tariff as inextricably bound up with one another. They assign a central role to the Depression in explaining the passage of the 1930 Tariff Act and at the same time emphasize the role of the tariff in the singular depth and long duration of the slump. This paper has reexamined the historical evidence on both points. It is not hard to identify relationships linking the tariff to the Depression and vice versa. But the evidence examined here suggests that previous accounts have conveyed what is at best an incomplete and at worst a misleading impression of the mechanisms at work. It is clear that the severity of the initial business cycle downturn lent additional impetus to the campaign for protection. But it is equally clear that the impact of the downturn on the movement for protection worked through different channels than typically posited. Rather than simply strengthening the hand of a Republican Executive predisposed toward protection, or increasing the burden borne by a depressed agricultural sector which had long been agitating for tariff protection, the uneven impact of the Depression occasioned the birth of a protectionist coalition comprising producers particularly hard hit by import competition: border agriculture and small-scale industry engaged in the production of specialty goods. That coalition was able to obtain for its members substantial increases in levels of tariff protection because of an unusual conjuncture of distinct if related developments including reforms of Congressional procedure, the rise of trade associations and the growth of interventionist sentiment. The experience of Smoot-Hawley documents how macroeconomic distress accompanied by import penetration gives rise to protectionist pressure, but does so only once the analysis transcends the model of monolithic agricultural and industrial blocs. . . .

NOTE

1. The first quote is from Bauer et al. [1972: 25], the second from Pastor [1980: 70].

REFERENCES

Bauer, de Sola Pool, and Dexter [1972]. Raymond Bauer, Ithiel de Sola Pool, and L. A. Dexter. *American Business and Public Policy*. Chicago: Aldine-Atherton, 1972.

Gerschenkron [1943]. Alexander Gerschenkron. *Bread and Democracy in Germany*. University of California Press, 1943.

Pastor [1980]. Robert A. Pastor. *Congress and the Politics of U.S. Foreign Economic Policy, 1929–1976*. University of California Press, 1980.

Schattschneider [1935]. E. E. Schattschneider. *Politics, Pressures and the Tariff*. Prentice-Hall, 1935.

3

The South Korean State in the International Economy: Liberal, Dependent, or Mercantile?

STEPHAN HAGGARD
AND CHUNG-IN MOON

Stephan Haggard and Chung-in Moon present a domestic statist interpretation of South Korea's economic development. They argue that the government's ability to insulate itself from domestic interest groups permitted it to pursue its own export-oriented development program. Also important was the ability of the state to extract resources from society and distribute them selectively in accordance with its development strategy. The authors point to the existence of a reformist political leadership interested in the general welfare of the country as key to South Korea's development success. In contrast with societal and international political or economic approaches, the central assertion of this reading is that the state was the primary actor directing South Korea's development.

To many economists, South Korea represents the paradigmatic case of a developing country realizing high levels of growth through specialization and close integration into the international division of labor. Unlike the majority of LDCs [less developed countries] which have continued to pursue inward-looking import-substituting growth strategies, South Korea "took off" following a liberalization of tariffs and the exchange rate regime and increased incentives toward foreign direct investment and borrowing. Realizing an initial comparative advantage in low-wage labor, the South Korean economy has continued to undergo structural

Stephan Haggard and Chung-in Moon. "The South Korean State in the International Economy: Liberal, Dependent, or Mercantile?" From John Gerard Ruggie, ed., *The Antinomies of Interdependence: National Welfare and the International Division of Labor*, pp. 131–189. Copyright © by Columbia University Press, New York. Reprinted with permission of the publisher.

transformation which would seem to vindicate theories of the product cycle and international comparative advantage. With growth initially led by exports of light manufactures such as textiles, the diffusion of technology through multinationals and learning by Korean firms has resulted in a gradual upgrading of South Korea's exports. The dimensions of the "miracle" have been widely documented: average annual growth of GNP [gross national product] over the seventies of 9.7 percent, manufacturing growth averaging 18 percent and annual export growth over 20 percent. . . .

The purpose of this paper is to explore the political economy of export-led industrialization in South Korea as a way of clarifying a number of interrelated debates on strategies of association and dissociation in the international political economy. These include the domestic political prerequisites of export-led growth and the range of international maneuverability open to small trading states. Finally, we seek to address some of the theoretical problems raised by both liberal and dependency analyses of peripheral industrialization. The following arguments will be made.

The turning point in South Korean growth came with a series of liberalizing policy reforms taken between 1963 and 1965. An analysis of these reforms suggests that liberalization has important domestic political prerequisites ignored by liberal economists. First, the state must be strong enough to impose stabilization and resist pressures from domestic business and other groups favored by closure. This proves not to be a once-and-for-all task. Despite the purported benefits of export-led growth, the South Korean government has been faced with continuing political opposition to its economic policies. Second, the state must possess adequate resources and the ability to channel them selectively to ease the reorientation of the economy in an outward direction. "Liberalization" does not correspond with domestic laissez-faire. Indeed, state control of business through credit allocation policies is one hallmark of the Korean model. Finally, the shift would never have occurred without the ascendence of a new reformist leadership which saw economic reform in its long-term *political* interest. In South Korea, this leadership was provided by the military following the coup of 1961.

South Korea has faced a series of external constraints including protectionism, competitive pressures, and the transmission of various international economic disturbances, which also tend to be ignored by advocates of export-led growth. These international pressures have generated countervailing strategies which demonstrate the precarious range of maneuver open to small trading-states.

South Korea's strategy toward existing regimes such as the GATT, and to international reform efforts such as NIEO [New International Economic Order], differs somewhat from those of the large, more inward-oriented NICs [newly industrialized countries]. With their large external sectors, the small trading NICs are particularly vulnerable to political pressure to participate in the trade regime as equal partners. As major beneficiaries of the liberal trading order, their long-term interest is in sustaining the openness of the trading system and in strengthening those regime mechanisms which will protect them from the arbitrary actions of their larger trading partners. This remains a long-term goal, however. Pursuing effective bilateral bargaining strategies has gained in importance as increasing amounts of NIC trade are managed under "exceptionalist" trade arrangements.

Geographic diversification of external economic ties, a classic risk-reduction strategy, has become a key component of South Korea's foreign economic policy. Diversification has not only occurred as a firm-level response to market opportunities, but has been facilitated, prompted, and controlled by the state. The interest of the NICs in market diversification suggests that they are likely to be in the forefront of the construction of new South-South ties.

Export product diversification has been one of the major challenges to the export-oriented NICs over the course of the seventies. As labor costs have risen, comparative advantage in light manufactures has eroded. South Korea's aggressive effort to break its previous pattern of international specialization proved politically and economically disastrous at least in the short run. The crisis provoked a rethinking of strategy and has raised important questions on the limits of industrial deepening in small, open economies.

A final, more theoretical, theme of this paper stems from the observation that export-led growth has been accompanied by a somewhat different pattern of social and political control and external dependency than the pattern in the large Latin American NICs. This suggests that modifications are required if models of bureaucratic authoritarianism and dependency developed in the Latin American context are to be extended to East Asia. These models stress the determinancy of underlying economic forces, both domestic and international, on state policy. We argue, however, that Korean development is best understood in terms of a statist model, in which the state is conceived as having relative autonomy in its ability to define developmental goals and the power to build the social coalitions to support them. Such an approach appears suited to South Korean development which has been led by a state that is relatively strong vis-à-vis social actors. If we look at some of the other NICs however—particularly Brazil, Mexico, Taiwan, and Singapore—they seem to differ from other developing countries precisely in the existence of relatively strong states. Indeed, much of their economic success appears attributable to such state strength.

As a trading nation, South Korea's economic "dependency" is as much a function of external market relations, international macroeconomic conditions, and changes in international comparative advantage as it is of the penetration of foreign firms. Foreign investment has played a different role in industrialization and trade in Korea than in the Latin American NICs. This is in part due to the trade-oriented strategy itself, in part because the South Korean leadership has self-consciously fostered an internationally oriented and competitive domestic bourgeoisie. In general, it appears that dependency theorists have overestimated the effects of multinational corporations on national development, while paying inadequate attention to the constraints transmitted through external market relations. Dependency is often treated as a rigid, determinate international structure, rather than as a set of shifting constraints within which states seek to maneuver. A country's position in the international division of labor is not pre-given, but is in part determined by state industrialization and development strategies. While significantly constrained by both external market and corporate pressures, the South Korean state has sought to use both for the purpose of expanding its power and flexibility both domestically and internationally. In this sense, South Korea's foreign economic policy and industrial strategy are best understood as mercantile rather than either liberal or dependent.

THE POLITICAL PREREQUISITES OF EXPORT-LED GROWTH

The consensus on the value of manufactured exports to LDC industrialization is surprisingly wide. From the Brandt Commission to the IMF, from UNCTAD [the United Nations Conference on Trade and Development] to the World Bank, a group of otherwise querulous economists seem to agree that export promotion pays off in efficiency, employment, and growth. The domestic political bases of the policy shift toward export-led growth remain largely unexamined, however. The South Korean case suggests several likely prerequisites for such policy reform that are not likely to be found widely in the developing world.

Strong State

The first prerequisite for liberalization is a strong state. The relative strength of the state can be measured along two dimensions, what may be called "autonomy" and "capacity." First, the state may be considered strong to the extent that decision-making elites are capable of organizationally insulating themselves from societal pressures by controlling channels of interest representation and autonomously defining "national" tasks. Second, state strength can be measured by the capacity to extract resources and to implement policies which change the behavior of private actors and that ultimately may lead to changes in the social structure itself.

Korea achieved independence with a strong state apparatus already in place. The Japanese had developed the colonial bureaucracy to realize their interests in the country. Rather than reforming it, the American occupation forces strengthened the state still further as a bulwark against the Left. Syngman Rhee's autocratic course continued the centralizing tradition, though his lack of interest in economic development resulted in an incoherent strategy.

One result of the military coup of 1961 was the further centralization of political power. All existing political organizations were disbanded, as was the National Assembly. The labor union structure, already weakened by its close ties to Rhee's Liberal party, was reorganized, with the government having a hand in selecting the new leadership. The National Agricultural Cooperatives Federation was tightly integrated into the central bureaucracy. New business organizations such as traders' and manufacturers' associations were formed under government auspices. Perhaps the most powerful instrument of social and political control was the Korean Central Intelligence Agency, created in 1961. Responsible only to the executive, the KCIA's significance in all matters—ranging from intelligence gathering and secret police functions to the implementation of economic policy and interbureaucratic coordination—cannot be overestimated.

At the same time the military restructured and strengthened the economic policymaking machinery into an Economic Planning Board having wide responsibilities including control of the budget. Even more important was the organization of the Presidential Secretariat within the presidential mansion or Blue House. This extremely insulated policymaking unit concentrated decision-making authority closely around Park Chung-hee. These organizational reforms were to survive the transition to civilian rule in 1964. The National Assembly's power vis-à-vis the executive was to remain small, while interest groups were to have few channels of access not controlled directly by the government. Even Park's own party was only a weak source of policy initiative. This political insulation and institutional centralization was to prove important in initiating and sustaining the outward-looking course.

First, export promotion demanded financial stabilization. After an initially inflationary course, the military imposed stabilizing measures which compressed real wages, restricted credit to domestic firms, and raised the prices of inputs to domestic farmers. One needs only to look to the two previous South Korean governments for contrasts: stabilization efforts, undertaken at the insistence of the Americans, contributed to the downfall of both the Rhee and Chang Myon governments.

Equally important was the need to resist pressure from domestic entrepreneurs privileged under the old, import-substituting regime. . . .

Under Rhee, close links had developed between the U.S. aid program, the governing Liberal party, and the state and domestic entrepreneurs. The bureaucracy, which controlled import licenses and foreign exchange allocation, could funnel money and goods to supporters of the regime in return for kickbacks or simply to retain a base of political support. Domestic business could either process these goods, realizing high rates of return due to the level of protection, or simply profit through pure arbitrage. This system was attacked by the military's campaign against "illicitly accumulated wealth." Many of these entrepreneurs were not heavily penalized and were finally co-opted into the planning efforts of the new regime. Corrupt relations between government and business continued to be a political issue over the 1960s and 1970s. Nonetheless, the entrepreneurial context was dictated by a new policy orientation which severely restricted the potential for zero-sum arbitrage.

The strong state has continued to be of importance in maintaining an outward orientation even after the initial policy reforms. Over the course of the 1960s, Park pursued a high-growth, inflationary course, heavily biased in favor of industrialization. This strategy had disruptive consequences for a number of social groups, providing the political base for the opposition. Agriculture was ignored, leading to a relative decline in rural incomes. Despite growing urban employment, rapid internal migrations produced a large class of urban marginals and squatters. Labor continued to be tightly controlled. At the same time, a visibly wealthy business class with close relations with the state had emerged, providing a target for critics of the regime. The tight centralization of political power around Park and the atrophy of democratic institutions served as the rallying point for the opposition. While its economic program remained inchoate, the imbalanced export-led growth strategy was held accountable for many of the country's problems. Ineffective in the 1967 election, which came at the height of the economic successes of the sixties, the opposition New Democratic party (NDP) launched a vigorous campaign in 1971, losing the presidential election narrowly amid charges of election fraud.

Park's declaration of emergency in December 1971 and the institution of the authoritarian Yushin Constitution in the following year further consolidated executive authority. In the name of national security—the state interest par excellence—Park placed new controls on labor, student, and dissident activity. The "New Village Movement," launched in 1970, sought to tie the countryside closer to the regime, while reversing the perception of rural neglect. The state's role in settling labor disputes was enhanced. Direct repression became an increasingly important tool of government control.

This consolidation of state power in the name of national security had the consequence of destroying the political bases for the articulation of alternative development strategies. It is far from clear that the opposition could have abandoned export-led growth. Nonetheless, there has been a continuity in opposition programs since the sixties, emphasizing balanced growth, redistributive and welfare policies, expansion of the domestic market, and a reduction of the degree of reliance on exports and foreign capital. Since the late seventies, some opposition analysis has become increasingly leftist, emphasizing the connections between export-led capitalist industrialization, external dependency, exploitation of workers and peasants and authoritarianism.

The position of the state vis-à-vis labor deserves further comment. . . .

. . . Korean labor had traditionally been weak. The American occupation had weakened the militant elements of Korean labor in the forties. Rhee built quasi-corporatist ties between his Liberal party and the unions in the fifties which facilitated top-down control. Import substitution was not carried out under the auspices of a populist coalition linking a mobilized working class and domestic business against rural elites. The labor unions grew in membership *after* the policy reforms of 1964 and 1965 as labor was pulled out of the countryside into the cities.

The shift to export-led growth was premised on an international comparative advantage in low-wage labor. The government could not prevent wages from rising beginning in the late sixties in response to labor scarcity and inflation. The government *could,* however, control and actively repress efforts on the part of labor to increase its political voice and organizational strength, thus maintaining a relatively free market in labor. There has been, for example, no effective minimum-wage legislation in Korea. By the end of the seventies, membership in Korean unions was only 24.4 percent of the total organizable work force. The close relationship between export-led growth and control of labor was seen most clearly in the special labor law enacted in January 1970. Following lengthy labor disputes with two export-oriented American firms, this law placed special restrictions on labor organization and collective action in foreign invested firms. Following the declaration of the state of emergency these provisions were extended to workers in all enterprises. There has clearly been an "elective affinity" between state controls on labor and export-led growth.

The strong state proved important for the pursuit of outward-oriented growth for several reasons. Previous regimes had proved politically incapable of imposing domestic stabilization. In addition, policy reform demanded a reorientation and internationalization of domestic firms and control of labor, even if these changes did not motivate the coup and subsequent consolidation of state power. Finally, the closure of the political realm and control of the opposition limited the political base from which a more inward-looking strategy could be articulated. Accomplishing all of these goals was facilitated by state control over finance and the generation of new resources, both domestic and foreign.

State Control over Economic Resources

Undoubtedly, the growth of Korean manufactured exports can be partly explained in neoclassical terms. A realistic exchange rate signaled firms about their international comparative advantage. Exporters were exempted from numerous import restrictions and enjoyed access to inputs at world market prices. The government also provided certain public goods, such as market information and infrastructure, which enhanced profitability.

But the government also promoted exports by indirect subsidies channeled through the financial system in the form of highly differential interest rates. Subsidized credit helped finance exports, imported inputs, and new investment in export-related industries. The military had seized the outstanding private shares of the commercial banking system as part of its campaign against illegally accumulated wealth. Even more important, the military drafted new legislation to govern the Bank of Korea, giving the executive wide discretionary power over any decisions taken by its governing board. Initially, export incentives were granted with little attention given to sectoral composition or domestic value-added. The state "followed the market" allowing firm-level initiative to determine the allocation of resources and supporting those industries demonstrating success. As early as 1964, however, the Bank of Korea was granted the authority to designate sectors to receive special attention. Financial institutions were required to concentrate their portfolios in those sectors. State control over credit thus came to play three mutually supportive functions. First, it provided a powerful tool of microeconomic control. Second, it subsidized the initial entry of firms into foreign markets. Finally, it built the political support of domestic business, cementing a close business-state alliance, though one in which the government held powerful levers of control. . . .

Reformist Leadership

The third prerequisite for liberalization is a reformist leadership. Within the policymaking apparatus, there must be planners, indigenous or foreign, who can articulate a liberal course in such a way that it corresponds with the interests of political elites. Economic ideologies and political interests matter: one only needs to look at the influence of Prebisch's ECLA [Economic Commission on Latin America] on the inward-looking industrialization strategies chosen by so many Latin American states in the fifties. In Korea, a significant influence was exercised by the U.S. Agency for International Development [AID], a fact which would appear to underline Korea's external dependence. An examination of the political forces behind liberalization demonstrates, however, that it was motivated by the quest for increased *autonomy* from the United States on the one hand, and domestic political consolidation on the other.

Initially, the military showed little interest in pursuing economic stabilization. The expansion of manufactured exports was not seen as the primary vehicle for promoting growth, but rather as a measure for increasing self-reliance by generating new sources of foreign exchange. The military's exchange rate policy even increased the gap between the official and effective rate. The ambitious First Five-Year Plan, unveiled hastily in 1961, stressed the building of a heavy industrial base under a form of "guided capitalism," with little attention to the inflationary consequences. Primary exports were to be expanded to finance imports, implying a very different position in the international division of labor than that which developed.

This economic strategy put the military government at cross-purposes with its American donors, who protested the mismanagement of the economy and the tendency to inflation throughout the fifties. Park tried to get around AID objections and maintain the elements of the plan by obtaining private credits, but lack of experience in international borrowing quickly led to overextension. A number of factors pushed toward reconciliation with the Americans and the emergence of a reformist consensus within the state.

The first was the political consolidation within the military of senior officers favoring a more "managerial" as opposed to "revolutionary" approach to economic policy. These "managerial" forces came to be centered in the executive and the cabinet, forming a tacit alliance with the younger technocrats given wider recognition following a purge of the bureaucracy. The more radical junior officers, favoring a more nationalist economic posture, had developed their base of support in the military-created Democratic Republican party, which never fulfilled the vanguard role some of the colonels had envisioned.

Second was the condition of the economy itself, particularly the inflation which had resulted from government spending, rapid increases in the money supply, and an abortive currency reform in 1962. A major justification for the coup had been the need to foster rapid economic development. The military was reformist from the beginning. The question was: what kind of reforms would work? As Park was forced to admit publicly, the military's expansionist course had not. Scandals in certain industries and the stock market had tarnished the military's image. In addition, the Americans had taken advantage of the rice crisis of 1963 to push both economic and political reforms, in particular, a return to democracy. Park, who was to run as a civilian, was thus open to ideas which would provide legitimation by improving economic performance. After his election, Park turned increasingly to civilian technocrats for economic advice, giving them the full political backing required to implement reforms.

While the role of the United States in pushing reforms is undeniable, it must be recognized that from Park's perspective, policy reform held out the promise of sustained growth and foreign exchange to replace declining aid commitments, both conducive to his broader national security and developmental aims. As with the liberalized posture toward foreign capital, the liberalization efforts became a way of *strengthening* the government's position, both domestically and internationally, a point overlooked by theorists of dependency and imperialism who tend to see the penetration of corporate and market forces as *weakening* the state.

South Korea thus seemed to possess important domestic political preconditions for external liberalization, particularly a strong state with flexible control of finance and a reformist leadership. The reforms of 1964, which unified the exchange rate and dismantled numerous trade controls, should not be equated with either domestic or external laissez-faire, however. As noted, the state wielded a powerful discretionary instrument through control of credit allocation. An analysis of South Korea's strategy for managing external interdependencies shows that the state's use of "liberal" policy-instruments has been highly selective. It also demonstrates that the state has recognized interdependence as a liability and has aggressively sought to reduce the costs associated with it.

INTERNATIONAL CONSTRAINTS AND STATE RESPONSES

As a small trading nation, South Korea has been exposed to a number of pressures emanating from the international system. While some of these may be attributed to size and resource endowment, or lack of it, many are a function of the particular development strategy South Korea has pursued. States pursuing ISI [Import Substituting Industrialization] have faced different external constraints than those pursuing export-led growth. This point is routinely overlooked by theorists of dependency. The precise character of a country's external economic relations is not reducible to backwardness or "structural position" in the international system alone. The relationship between the "international system" and the domestic political economy is established by state policies concerning tariff levels, exchange rate, foreign investment, borrowing, and industrialization. Similarly, economists advocating openness tend to downplay both the political and economic dilemmas of interdependence, stressing the gains in efficiency and output to be had through specialization. The concepts of dependence, sensitivity, and reliance allow us to avoid the rigid determinism of structuralist models of dependency while illustrating some of the political and adjustment costs of market integration overlooked by economists.

The first constraint South Korea has faced is dyadic dependence. The classic formulation of the political power generated through such inequality remains Albert Hirschman's *National Power and the Structure of International Trade*. Focusing on the economic concept of "gains from trade," Hirschman argued that a trade, financial, or investment relation which is more important for a small country than for a large one gives the larger partner a basis for influence by creating bilateral dependencies. By 1970 this had become a clearly recognized problem for the political leadership. In that year, 46 percent of South Korea's exports were going to the United States with another 28 percent going to Japan. On the import side, dependence on Japan was extremely large, creating trade imbalances which have become a standing political issue between the two countries. While Hirschman was concerned with the overt manipulation of bilateral ties, a possibility which obviously worried the Koreans during the Carter administration, this has not been the only concern. Bilateral dependence also tied South Korea to the economic performance of the United States and Japan.

This increased economic sensitivity, a second international constraint. Sensitivity is the extent to which domestic economic performance is determined by the performance of and trends in the international economy. There are of course numerous channels through which international disturbances may be transmitted to the domestic economy, including capital markets, the prices and quantities of traded goods, and so on. One rough indicator of South Korea's sensitivity and the openness of the economy may be seen in the ratio of exports plus imports to GDP [gross domestic product]. While in 1960, two-way trade was 16 percent of GDP, it had risen to 24 percent by 1965, 38 percent by 1970 and 64 percent by 1975. During times of turbulence, small open economies experience shocks more dramatically, and, of course, the seventies was just such a period. In rapid succession, the 1970s saw the breakdown of the Bretton Woods regime, which immediately upset the *won*-dollar exchange rate, the rise in raw material prices, the oil crises, the deep recession and weak recovery, and massive increases in worldwide inflation. These external shocks demanded major macroeconomic adjustments.

Equally troubling was the long-run trend in South Korea's international competitive position. South Korean export growth had been built around a fairly narrow range of products. In 1970 almost 60 percent of exports were accounted for by textiles, apparel, plywood, and wigs. This mix was vulnerable for a number of reasons. Real wages in the other Asian NICs had risen much more slowly than those in South Korea over the late 1960s. New low-wage entrants were seeking to replicate East Asia's success in the export of light manufactures. In 1971 the United States and South Korea initialed their first bilateral trade-restraint agreement in textiles, ushering in the era of protection. Export-led growth not only produced a general vulnerability to macroeconomic disturbances, but had placed pressure at the microeconomic, sectoral level as well.

A third constraint associated with outward-looking growth may be called reliance. Reliance refers to the need for external inputs—capital, technology, raw materials, energy—to pursue a given development strategy. While all developing countries rely on external inputs and savings, South Korea's export-led growth has proved import and debt intensive. External reliance not only establishes the balance of payments as a constraint on growth, but poses what may be called an economic security dilemma by making the success of a given development strategy contingent on resources held by foreign actors: it is in part this contingency which has given rise to the Third World's call for increased self-reliance. While the costs of economic autarchy are high in terms of efficiency, the costs of interdependence are high in terms of security, vulnerability, and political autonomy. The political problems of external reliance are highly visible in those conflicts between host governments and multinational firms that have been detailed by writers in the dependency tradition. But the need for capital and technology from MNCs [multinational corporations] is not the only form of external reliance. Korean policymakers have become increasingly concerned by "resource nationalism," the increasing politicization of, and competition over, access to raw materials and energy, inflation in the cost of various intermediate inputs, and soaring interest rates.

In a highly militarized, national-security state, such as Korea, external reliance is closely related to the traditional security dilemma as well. An examination of Park's writings and speeches reveals the close links he drew between economic development, national security, and anti-Communism. Park's calls for an independent and self-sufficient economy seem ludicrous in light of Korea's openness and specialization. The reassessment of America's position in the Pacific under Nixon, the troop withdrawal that followed, the debacle of Vietnam, and the apparent moves toward further disengagement under Carter, all posed the question of vulnerability in stark form and motivated the quest for increased self-reliance, particularly in defense-related industries.

Some of these international constraints are endemic to export-led growth. Sensitivity and external reliance are probably unavoidable for small countries, regardless of their level of development. Our interest here, however, is not the effect of these external relations on various domestic economic outcomes, such as rates of growth and inequality. This has been the purview of traditional economic writing and has become the focus of a growing body of literature purporting to test dependency theories. Our interest is rather on the strategies that states pursue to manage these constraints. . . . It has been found that South Korea's foreign economic and industrial policy over the seventies was dictated by two overriding concerns: the need for markets and the need to remain internationally competitive. In responding to both of these external constraints, the state played a decisive role. . . .

CONCLUSION

Despite its intellectual and prescriptive appeal, the strategy of radical dissociation from the international system is not an option for most developing countries. Even China and Tanzania, much heralded cases of self-reliance, have hardly pursued autarchic courses. The questions then become, what kind of association? Under what conditions? And with what effects?

We have argued that association is a function of the broader strategies of development and industrialization, and that these, in turn, are rooted in domestic political processes and structures. We must ask not only what policies are good, but under what conditions certain policies are likely to emerge and prove feasible. One particularly close form of association—export-led growth—appears to have been facilitated in South Korea by a set of important political prerequisites, which may not be easily transferrable to other cases: a strong reformist state wielding highly discretionary financial instruments and pressure from a powerful ally.

We have attempted to show some of the limitations on either liberal or dependency interpretations of Korean development. Korean growth has been, above all, state-led. The Korean state, and the state in other NICs as well, has substantial power in designing and implementing development policy and in controlling the economy. More importantly, however, the state appears to have substantial power in insulating itself from social and political pressures, and in controlling the classes and interests—including domestic and foreign business as well as labor—which serve as the bases for export-led growth.

We have also attempted to show that *association* has a number of discreet dimensions and must be disaggregated. External vulnerabilities are not reducible to the relationship with foreign capital or a dominant military partner. They also include a set of market vulnerabilities which have dictated and constrained South Korea's foreign economic and industrial policies. The Korean state has sought to neutralize the costs of association, though not always with complete success. Though under growing pressure to "graduate," South Korea, to date, has been selective in its liberalism, controlling direct investment and using trade and financial instruments to develop a domestic business class. South Korea has sought with some success to diversify its external trade relations and has bargained successfully to increase market access under conditions of growing protection. Finally, the state has acted to force industrial development. Although proving a short-term disaster, this policy may be seen in the future as having produced important gains.

The advocacy of close association via export-led growth may involve a fallacy of composition which has not been adequately recognized, however. The East Asian NICs entered the export game at an historically auspicious moment. Rapid world growth facilitated Korea's entry into the world trading system. By the time protectionist pressures and slowed macroeconomic conditions manifested themselves, Korea had developed a flexible state policy apparatus and a set of domestic firms seasoned to international competition. New entrants face a different set of prospects. The smooth absorption of LDCs into the international division of labor is now hindered by slowed world growth and the political and economic rigidities in the advanced industrial states which prohibit rapid industrial adjustment. Successful "association" is partly a function of timing.

Finally, we must ask what effect export-led growth has had on welfare and equity. A major contention of dependency analysis has been that close association and integration are associated with political exclusion and social marginalization and polarization. Indeed, explaining these social-structural distortions has been a major aim of dependency thinking. Korea, however, has often been cited as an example of the benefits to be gained by close integration into the international economy and the possibilities for redistribution with growth. Several caveats are in order on both sides.

First, Korea's rapid growth has been accompanied by rising incomes, expanded employment and the virtual elimination of the levels of poverty of the forties and fifties. These rising incomes have largely been generated in the urban industrial sector: agriculture has been "pulled" by industrial expansion, rather than leading it.

Second, by any standards, Korea has a relatively egalitarian distribution of income. This is partly attributable to export-led growth, based on labor-intensive manufactures, and expanding employment, which is beneficial to distribution. By keeping wages low, disparities between rural and urban incomes and within the urban working class were narrowed. Most seem to agree, however, that land reforms and the Korean War itself were the critical factors in redistributing assets. These events have little to do with export-led growth; indeed, they preceded it. As we have argued, the reforms may have been a critical political precondition for any rapid industrialization.

The relative neglect of agriculture over the 1950s and 1960s resulted in some reconcentration of holdings and a deterioration of the rural-urban terms of trade as rates of productivity in the two sectors diverged. Critics of the Korean model have argued that neglect of the rural sector was a conscious state policy aimed at creating a large pool of low-wage labor. As Taiwan shows, however, rural neglect is not intrinsic to export-led growth itself. Moreover, rural decline elsewhere has been identified with ISI strategies as well. Rather, political choices about the countryside appear as important as industrialization strategies per se. The ratio of rural to urban household incomes had sunk to 63 percent in 1968. To reverse the perception of rural decline, Park instituted several policies aimed at maintaining rural political support, including a change in rice pricing policy and the launching of the New Village movement. By 1975, rural and urban income levels had reached rough parity.

As the Fifth plan itself admits, there has been a significant erosion of income equality over the seventies. Recent work has also demonstrated that the earlier picture of overall levels of equality has probably been distorted by the failure to adequately include the very wealthy in income statistics used in distribution studies. A number of indicators, such as automobile ownership and tax data, suggest that incomes among the upper class have been increasing rapidly. At the same time, rapid growth resulted in large internal migrations and the creation of a significant squatter and marginal class in the cities. However, over the seventies, Korean growth has also produced a new urban middle class so that erosion in the overall level of income equality should not be interpreted as implying a general polarization of society.

As anyone familiar with Korea is aware, growth has been accompanied by authoritarian controls and the sometimes violent repression of political opposition. Making causal links between political structure and development strategy is not as easy as it might appear. Authoritarian controls predate the turn to export-led growth and have a history not only in the American and Japanese occupations, but in the traditional structure of Korean politics and society. Developing states pursuing different development strategies, including dissociationist ones, also have authoritarian regimes.

Given these caveats, we have argued that there have been some affinities between Korea's associationist strategy and authoritarianism. The first concerns labor. While not always successful in controlling wages directly, the state has acted to strictly control labor organization and political activity. The second affinity is a broader one, and concerns the leadership's capacity to autonomously define and implement a particular development orientation. Whatever its *motivation,* the government's political strategy has had the effect of fragmenting the opposition and limiting the channels through which popular demands could be articulated. It was in part this autonomy which permitted the government to pursue a strategy based on the rapid accumulation of capital and close integration into the international economy.

4

States, Firms and Diplomacy

SUSAN STRANGE

Susan Strange argues that changes in the international economy have altered the relationship between states and multinational corporations and have given rise to new forms of diplomacy in the international arena. Highlighting the crucial importance of international economic factors, Strange points out how such worldwide trends as technological development, the growing mobility of capital, and the decreasing costs of communication and transportation have led more firms to plan their activities on a global basis. This has increased competition among states as they encourage firms to locate within their territories. The international economic environment within which all states operate has been fundamentally transformed, and governments are being forced to adapt to this new reality.

. . . Three propositions will be advanced here. First, that many seemingly unrelated developments in world politics and world business have common roots and are the result in large part of the same structural changes in the world economy and society. Second, that partly in consequence of these same structural changes, there has been a fundamental change in the nature of diplomacy. Governments must now bargain not only with other governments, but also with firms or enterprises, while firms now bargain both with governments and with one another. As a corollary of this, the nature of the competition between states has changed, so that macroeconomic management and industrial policies may often be as or even more important for governments than conventional foreign policies as conventionally conceived. The third proposition follows from the second, and concerns the significance of firms as actors influencing the future course of transnational relations—not least for the study of international relations and political economy.

Susan Strange. "States, Firms, and Diplomacy." This is an edited text of an article which first appeared in *International Affairs*, London, Vol. 68, no. 1 January 1992, pp. 1–15, and is reproduced with permission.

STRUCTURAL CHANGE

Most commentators on international affairs have in our opinion paid far too little attention to structural change, particularly to change in the structure of production in the world economy. Our recent work argues that most of the recent changes in world politics, however unrelated they may seem on the surface, can be traced back in large part to certain common roots in the global political economy. We see common driving forces of structural change behind the liberation of Central Europe, the disintegration of the former Soviet Union, the intractable payments deficit of the United States, the Japanese surpluses, the rapid rise of the East Asian newly industrialized countries, and the U-turns of many developing country governments from military or authoritarian government to democracy, and from protection and import substitution towards open borders and export promotion.

These common driving forces of change, in brief, are the accelerating rate and cost of technological change, which has speeded up in its turn the internationalization of production and the dispersion of manufacturing industry to newly industrialized countries; increased capital mobility, which has made this dispersion of industry easier and speedier; and those changes in the structure of knowledge that have made transnational communications cheap and fast and have raised people's awareness of the potential for material betterment in a market economy. These common roots have resulted, at the same time and in many countries, in the demand for democratic government and for the economic flexibility that is impossible in a command economy. . . .

Technological Change, Mobile Capital, Transborder Communications

Most obvious of the structural changes acting as the driving force on firms and governments alike were those in the technology of industrial and agricultural production; related to them were changes in the international financial structure. The accelerating pace of technological change has enhanced the capacity of successful producers to supply the market with new products, and/or to make them with new materials or new processes. At the same time, product and process lifetimes have shortened, sometimes dramatically. Meanwhile, the costs to the firm of investment in R & D, research and development—and therefore of innovation—have risen. The result is that all sorts of firms that were until recently comfortably ensconced in their home markets have been forced, whether they like it or not, to seek additional markets abroad in order to gain the profits necessary to amortize their investments in time to stay up with the competition when the next technological advance comes along. It used to be thought that internationalism was the preserve of the large, privately owned Western "multinational" or transnational corporations. Today, thanks to the imperatives of structural change, these have been joined by many smaller firms, and also by state-owned enterprises and firms based in developing countries. Thus it is not the phenomenon of the transnational corporation that is new, but the changed balance between firms working only for a local or domestic market, and those working for a global market and in part producing in countries other than their original home base.

Besides the accelerating rate of technological change, two other critical developments contributed to the rapid internationalization of production. One was the liberalization of international finance, beginning perhaps with the innovation of Eurocurrency dealing and lending in the 1960s, and continuing unchecked with the measures of financial deregulation initiated by the United States in the mid-1970s and early 1980s. As barriers went down, the mobility of capital went up. The old difficulties of raising money for investment in offshore operations and moving it across the exchanges vanished. It was either unnecessary for the transnational corporations to find new funds, or they could do so locally.

The third contributing factor to internationalization has often been overlooked—the steady and cumulative lowering of the real costs of transborder transport and communication. Without them, central strategic planning of far-flung affiliates would have been riskier and more difficult, and out-sourcing of components as in car manufacture would have been hampered.

Broader Perspectives

These structural changes have permeated beyond finance and production to affect global politics at a deep level. They have, for instance, significantly affected North–South relations. The so-called Third World no longer exists as a coalition of developing countries ranged, as in UNCTAD (the UN Conference on Trade and Development), in opposition to the rich countries. Developing countries are now acutely aware that they are competing against each other, the laggards desperately trying to catch up with the successful newly industrialized countries. The transnational corporations' search for new markets was often a major factor leading them to set up production within those markets. Sometimes this was done for cost reasons. Other times it was done simply because the host government made it a condition of entry. The internationalization of production by the multinationals has surely been a major factor in the accelerated industrialization of developing countries since the 1950s. For it is not only the Asian newly industrialized countries whose manufacturing capacity has expanded enormously in the last two or three decades, but also countries like India, Brazil, Turkey and Thailand.

At the same time, the internationalization of production has also played a major part in the U-turn taken in economic policies by political leaders in countries as diverse and far apart as Turkey and Burma, Thailand and Argentina, India and Australia. Structural change, exploited more readily by some than others, has altered the perception of policy-makers in poor countries both about the nature of the system and the opportunities it opens to them for the present and the future. In the space of a decade, there has been a striking shift away from policies of import-substitution and protection towards export promotion, liberalization and privatization.

It is no accident that the "dependency school" writers of the 1970s have lost so much of their audience. Not only in Latin America (where most of this writing was focused), we see politicians and professors who were almost unanimous in the 1970s in castigating the multinationals as agents of American imperialism who now acknowledge them as potential allies in earning the foreign exchange badly needed for further development.

Nor, we would argue, is the end of the Cold War, the detente in East–West relations and the liberation of Central Europe from Soviet rule and military occupation to be explained by politics or personalities alone. Here too there are ways in which structural change has acted, both at the level of government and the bureaucracy, and at the popular level of consumers and workers.

In the production structure, even in the centrally planned economies, industrialization has raised living standards from the levels of the 1930s and 1940s, at least for the privileged classes of society. Material progress has not been as fast as in the market economy, but in the socialist countries as in Latin America or Asia, the ranks have multiplied of a middle class of managers, professional doctors, lawyers, engineers and bureaucrats, many of whom are significantly better educated than their parents. With this *embourgeoisement* has come greater awareness of what is going on in other countries, and of the widening gap between living standards in the affluent West and their own.

In the world market economy, competition among producers has lowered costs to consumers and widened their choice of goods, while raising their real incomes. Under the pressures of shortening product life cycles, heavier capital costs and new advances in technologies, rivalry among producers has unquestionably contributed to material wealth for the state as well as for consumers. Witness the spread down through income groups of cars, colour TV, washing machines, freezers, video recorders, telephones, personal computers. In any Western home, a high proportion of these consumer goods carry the brand names of foreign firms.

By contrast, the Soviet consumer has suffered the deprivation consequent on the economy's insulation from the fast-changing global financial and production structures. But the information about what others enjoyed in the West could not altogether be kept from people even in the Soviet Union, let alone in Central Europe. The revolution in communications, and thus in the whole global knowledge structure, helped to reveal the widening gap between standards of living for similar social groups under global capitalism and under socialism.

At the same time, the new bourgeoisie, aware of the inefficiencies of the command economy, saw that economic change was being blocked by the entrenched apparatus of centralized government and could only be achieved through political change and wider participation. While the burden of defence spending certainly played a part in both East and West in furthering detente and making possible the liberation of Central Europe, political change was accelerated within the socialist countries by the rise of a new middle class and their perception of the gap in living standards and of the apparent inability of centrally planned systems to respond to the structural change in technologies of production.

We would argue that similar structural forces also lie behind the worldwide trend to democratic government and the rejection of military and authoritarian rule. In short, people have become better off and better educated and are making their material dissatisfaction and their political aspirations strongly felt. We would argue that this wave of political change has the same universal roots, whether in Greece, Portugal or Spain, in Turkey, or in Burma, Brazil or Argentina. . . .

TWO NEW SIDES TO DIPLOMACY

State–Firm Diplomacy

The net result of these structural changes is that there now is greatly intensified competition among states for world market shares. That competition is forcing states to bargain with foreign firms to locate their operations within the territory of the state, and with national firms not to leave home, at least not entirely. . . .

. . . The transnational firm has command of an arsenal of economic weapons that are badly needed by any state wishing to win world market shares. The firm has, first, command of technology; second, ready access to global sources of capital; third, ready access to major markets in America, Europe and, often, Japan. If wealth for the state, as for the firm, can be gained only by selling on world markets—for the same reason that national markets are too small a source of profit for survival—then foreign policy should now begin to take second place to industrial policy; or perhaps, more broadly, to the successful management of society and the efficient administration of the economy in such a way as to outbid other states as the preferred home to the transnational firms most likely to win and hold world market shares.

While the bargaining assets of the firm are specific to the enterprise, the bargaining assets of the state are specific to the territory it rules over. The enterprise can operate in that territory—even if it just sells goods or services to people living there—only by permission and on the terms laid down by the government. Yet it is the firm that is adding value to the labour, materials and know-how going into the product. States are therefore competing with other states to get the value-added done in their territory and not elsewhere. That is the basis of the bargain.

Firm–Firm Diplomacy

A third dimension, equally the product of the structural changes noted earlier, is the bargaining that goes on between firms. This too may lead to partnerships or alliances in which, while they may be temporary or permanent, each side contributes something that the other needs, so that both may enhance their chances of success in the competition for world market shares. Firms involved in this third dimension of diplomacy may be operating in the same sector (as in aircraft design, development and manufacturing) or in different sectors (where, for instance, one party may be contributing its expertise in computer electronics, the other in satellite communications).

For scholars of international relations, both new dimensions are important. The significance of the state–firm dimension is that states are now competing more for the means to create wealth within their territory than for power over more territory. Power, especially military capability, used to be a means to wealth. Now it is more the other way around. Wealth is the means to power—not just military power, but the popular or electoral support that will keep present ruling groups in their jobs. Without this kind of support, even the largest nuclear arsenals may be of little avail. Nowadays, except perhaps for oilfields and water resources, there is little material gain to be found in the control of more territory. As Singapore and Hong Kong have shown, world market shares—and the resulting wealth—can be won with the very minimum of territory. Even where, as in Yugoslavia or the Soviet Union, there is a recurrence of conflict over territory, the forces behind it are not solely ethnic nationalism of the old kind. Many Slovenes, Croats, Russians or Georgians want to wrest control over their territory from the central power because they believe they would be able to compete better in the world economy on their own than under the control of their old federal bosses. Autonomy is seen as a necessary condition for economic transformation and progress.

Successfully Managing Society and Economy

Having got control over territory, government policy-makers may understand well enough what is needed to bargain successfully with foreign firms to locate with them. But they may not always be able to deliver. For though the forces of structural change affect everyone, even the old centrally planned economies, the capacity of governments to respond are extremely diverse. . . .

. . . The diversity of government responses to structural change usually reflects the policy dilemmas peculiar to the government of that society. But precisely because of increased integration in the world market economy, it is more and more difficult for governments to "ring-fence" a particular policy so that implementing it does not directly conflict with, perhaps negate, some other policy. . . .

Contemplation of the diversity of host-country policies in monetary management, trade and competition policy very soon brings home the fact that there are no shortcuts and no magic tricks in wooing foreign firms. However, some general advice is still possible. One piece of advice is obviously to pinpoint the policy dilemmas where objectives clash. Another is to cut out the administrative delays and inefficiencies that bedevil the work of local managers. . . . Another good piece of advice, already stressed in the growing literature on the management of international business, is to break up monopolies and enforce competition among producers. . . .

. . . The diversity of government responses . . . is surely due not only to mulish stupidity or ignorance of the keys to success. Governments are, after all, political systems for the reconciliation of conflicting economic and social, and sometimes ethnic, interests. Moreover, the global structural changes that affect them all do so very differently, sometimes putting snakes, sometimes ladders in their path. Some small boats caught by a freak low tide in an estuary may escape grounding on the mud by alert and skilful management; others may be saved by luck. Our research suggests that the crucial difference between states these days is not, as the political scientists used to think, that between "strong" states and "weak" ones, but between the sleepy and the shrewd. States today have to be alert, adaptable to external change, quick to note what other states are up to. The name of the game, for governments just as for firms, is competition.

FIRMS AS DIPLOMATS

Our third general point—the importance of firms as major actors in the world system—will be obvious enough to leaders of finance and industry. They will not need reminding that markets may be moved, governments blown off course and balances of power upset by the big oil firms, by the handful of grain dealers, by major chemical or pharmaceutical makers. It will come as no surprise to them that the game of diplomacy these days has two extra new dimensions as well as the conventional one between governments.

But while I have scratched the surface of one of these—the bargaining between firms and governments—I have not said much about the third, bargaining between firms. This deserves to be the subject of a whole new research programme. Examples have recently multiplied of firms which were and may remain competitors but which under the pressures of structural change have decided to make strategic or even just tactical alliances with other firms in their own or a related sector of business. In the study of international relations it is accepted as normal that states should ally themselves with others while remaining competitors, so that the bargaining that takes place between allies is extremely tough about who takes key decisions, how risks are managed and how benefits are shared.

The implications for international relations analysis of the three-sided nature of diplomacy are far-reaching. The assertion that firms are major actors is at odds with the conventions of international relations as presently taught in most British universities and polytechnics. The standard texts in the subject subscribe to the dominant "realist" school of thought, which holds that the central issue in international society is war between territorial states, and the prime problematic therefore is the maintenance of order in the relations between these states. This traditional view of international relations also holds that the object of study is the behaviour of states towards other states, and the outcome of such behaviour *for states:* whether they are better or worse off, less or more powerful or secure. Transnational corporations may be mentioned in passing, but they are seen as adjuncts to or instruments of state policy.

Our contention is that transnational corporations should now be put centre stage; that their corporate strategies in choosing host countries as partners are already having great influence on the development of the global political economy, and will continue increasingly to do so. In common with many contemporary political economists, our interest is not confined to the behaviour of states or the outcomes for states. Who-gets-what questions must also now be asked—about social groups, generations, genders, and not least, about firms and the sectors in which they operate. Ten years from now we anticipate that the conventions and limitations of what has sometimes been called the British school of international relations will be regarded as impossibly dated, its perceptions as démodé as 1950s fashions. This is not to say, of course, that there are no lessons to be learned by economic ministries and corporate executives from the diplomatic history of interstate relations. Only that the study of international relations must move with the times, or be marginalized as a narrow specialism. . . .

To sum up. Much more analytical work is needed on firm–firm bargaining as well as on state–firm bargaining in all its multivariant forms. It needs recognizing that both types of bargaining are interdependent with developments in state–state bargaining (the stock in trade of international relations), and that this in turn is interdependent with the other two forms of transnational diplomacy. In the discipline of management studies, corporate diplomacy is becoming at least as important a subject as analysis of individual firms and their corporate strategies for finance, production and marketing. In the study of international relations, an interest in bargaining is already beginning to supplant the still-fashionable analysis of international regimes.

A focus on bargaining, and the interdependence of the three sides of diplomacy that together constitute transnational bargaining, will necessarily prove more flexible and better able to keep up with change in global structures. No bargain is for ever, and this is generally well understood by anyone with hands-on experience of negotiation. The political art for corporate executives, as for government diplomats, is to devise bargains that will hold as long as possible, bargains that will not easily be upset by changes in other bargaining relationships. This is true for political coalitions between parties, or between governments and social groups, such as labour; and it is equally true for bargains between governments and foreign firms, and between firms and other firms. The multiplicity of variables in the pattern of any one player's interlocking series of bargains is self-evident.

A final point about the interlocking outcomes of transnational bargaining relates to theories of international relations and political economy. Social scientists like to think that the accumulation of more and more data, the perfecting of analytical tools and their rigorous application according to scientific principles will some day, somehow, produce a general theory to explain political and economic behaviour. They are a bit like peasants who still believe there is a pot of gold buried at the end of the rainbow despite their repeated failures to track it down. Today, the complexity of the factors involved in each of the three forms of transnational bargaining, and the multiplicity of variables at play, incline us to deep scepticism about general theories. Not only are economics—*pace* the economists—inseparable from the real world of power and politics, but outcomes in the global political economy, the product of this complex interplay of bargains, are subject to the great divergences that we have observed.

II

HISTORICAL PERSPECTIVES

A truly international economy first emerged during the "long sixteenth century," the period from approximately 1480 to 1650. In its earliest form, the modern international economy was organized on the basis of mercantilism, a doctrine that asserted that power and wealth were closely interrelated and legitimate goals of national policy. Thus, wealth was necessary for power, and power could be used to obtain wealth. Because power is a relative concept, as one country can gain it only at the expense of another, mercantilist nations perceived themselves to be locked into a zero-sum conflict in the international economy.

During this period countries pursued a variety of policies intended to expand production and wealth at home while denying similar capabilities to others. Six policies were of nearly universal importance. First, countries sought to prevent gold and silver, a common mercantilist measure of wealth, from being exported. At the beginning of the sixteenth century Spain declared the export of gold or silver punishable by death. France declared the export of coined gold and silver illegal in 1506, 1540, 1548, and 1574, thereby demonstrating the difficulty of enforcing such regulations. Second, regulations (typically, high tariffs) were adopted to limit imports to necessary raw materials. Importing raw materials was desirable because it lowered prices at home and thereby reduced costs for manufacturers. By limiting imports of manufactured and luxury items, on the other hand, countries sought to stimulate production at home while reducing it abroad. Third, exports of manufactured goods were encouraged for similar reasons. Fourth, just as they sought to encourage imports of raw materials, countries sought to limit the export of these goods so as to both lower prices at home and limit the ability of others to develop a manufacturing capability of their own. Fifth, exports of technology—including both machinery and skilled artisans—were restricted in order to inhibit potential foreign competitors. Finally, many countries adopted navigation laws mandating that a certain percentage of their foreign trade had to be carried in native ships. This last trade regulation was intended to stimulate the domestic shipping and shipbuilding industries—both necessary resources for successful war making.

By the early nineteenth century, mercantilist trade restrictions were coming under widespread attack, particularly in Great Britain. Drawing upon the Liberal writings of Adam Smith and David Ricardo, Richard Cobden and other Manchester industrialists led the fight for free trade, which culminated in 1846 in the abolition of the Corn Laws (restrictions on grain imports), the last major mercantilist impediment to free trade in Britain. Other countries soon followed the British example. Under Britain's hegemonic leadership, Europe entered a period of free trade that lasted from 1860 to 1879 (see Kindleberger, Reading 5). This trend toward freer trade was reversed in the last quarter of the nineteenth century. The purported causes of this reversal are many, including the decline of British hegemony, the onset of the first Great Depression of 1873–1896, and the new wave of industrialization on the Continent, which led to protection for domestic manufacturers from British competition (see Gourevitch, Reading 6). For whatever reason—and the debate continues even today—by 1890, nearly all countries except Great Britain had once again imposed significant restrictions on imports.

Coupled with this trend toward increased protection was a new wave of formal colonialism. For reasons discussed by V. I. Lenin (Reading 7), Britain had already begun to expand its holdings of foreign territory during the period of free trade. After 1880, it was joined by Germany and France. In 1860, Great Britain possessed 2.5 million square miles of colonial territory and France, only 0.2 million; Germany had not yet entered the colonial race. By 1899, Britain's holdings had expanded to 9.3 million square miles, France's to 3.7 million, and Germany's to 1.0 million. This expansion occurred primarily in Africa and the Pacific. In 1876, slightly less than 11 percent of Africa and nearly 57 percent of Polynesia were colonized. By 1900, over 90 percent of Africa and almost 99 percent of Polynesia were controlled by European colonial powers and the United States.

World War I, which many analysts believe to have been fueled by the race for colonies and in particular by Germany's aggressive attempt to catch up with Great Britain, destroyed the remaining elements of the Pax Britannica. The mantle of leadership, which had previously been borne by Britain, was now divided between Britain and the United States. Yet, neither country could—or desired to—play the leadership role previously performed by Britain.

World War I was indeed a watershed in American international involvement. The terrible devastation caused by the war in Europe served to weaken the traditional world powers, while it brought the United States a period of unexpected prosperity. The Allies, short of food and weapons, bought furiously from American suppliers. To finance their purchases, they borrowed heavily from American banks and, once the United States entered the war, from the American government. As a result, American factories and farms hummed as the war dragged on; industrial production nearly doubled during the war years. And because the war forced the European powers to neglect many of their overseas economic activities, American exporters and investors were also able to move into areas they had never before influenced. When the war began, the United States was a net debtor of the major European nations; by the time it ended, the United States was the world's principal lender, and all of the Allies were deeply in debt to American banks and the American government.

Despite the position of political and economic leadership the United States shared with Great Britain after World War I, the country rapidly retreated into its traditional inward orientation. To be sure, many American banks and corporations continued to expand abroad very rapidly in the 1920s, and the United States remained an important world power, but the United States refused to join the League of Nations or any of the other international organizations created in this period. American tariff levels, reduced on the eve of World War I, were once again raised. The reasons for the country's post–World War I isolationism, as it is often called, are many and controversial. Chief among them were the continued insularity of major segments of the American public, traditionally inward looking in political and economic matters; the resistance to American power of such European nations as Great Britain and France; and widespread revulsion at the apparently futile deaths that had resulted from involvement in the internecine strife of the Old World.

Whatever the reasons for the isolationism of the 1920s, these tendencies were heightened as the world spiraled downward into depression after 1929. In the Smoot–Hawley Act of 1930, the United States dramatically increased its tariffs, and by 1933 the world was engulfed in a bitter trade and currency conflict. In 1933, desperate to encourage domestic economic recovery, Franklin Roosevelt significantly devalued the dollar, sounding the death knell of what remained of the nineteenth-century international economic order.

During the nearly four centuries summarized here, the international economy underwent several dramatic transformations. From a closed and highly regulated mercantilist system, the international economy evolved toward free trade in the middle of the nineteenth century. After a relatively brief period of openness, the international economy reversed direction and, starting with the resurgence of formal imperialism and accelerating after World War I, once again drifted toward closure. This historical survey highlights the uniqueness of the contemporary international political economy, which is the focus of the rest of this reader; David A. Lake (Reading 8) compares the central characteristics of the international economy in the nineteenth and twentieth centuries. This survey also raises a host of analytic questions, many of which appear elsewhere in the book as well. Particularly important here is the question of what drives change in the international economy. In the readings that follow, Charles Kindleberger, in a domestic societal approach, focuses on interest groups and ideology; Peter Gourevitch examines interest groups and state structures; Lenin finds the locus of change in the stages of capitalism; and Lake emphasizes changes in the international political and economic systems.

5

The Rise of Free Trade
in Western Europe
CHARLES P. KINDLEBERGER

Charles P. Kindleberger, a leading economic historian, examines the process by which mercantilist trade restrictions were dismantled and evaluates several of the best-known theses concerning the ascendance of free trade in Western Europe. Presenting a domestic society-centered argument, Kindleberger contends that free trade in many instances arose as individual entrepreneurs pressured their governments to lift restrictions on international trade and finance so that they could pursue overseas business opportunities. Yet, Kindleberger points out that political activity by entrepreneurs cannot explain the rapid expansion of free trade in Europe after 1850. He suggests that this "second wave" of free trade may have been motivated by ideology rather than by economic or political interests. This important article offers a persuasive explanation of how and why the market principle gained dominance within the international economy during the nineteenth century.

I

. . . The beginnings of free trade internationally go back to the eighteenth century. French Physiocratic theory enunciated the slogan *laisser faire, laisser passer* to reduce export prohibitions on agricultural products. Pride of place in practice, however, goes to Tuscany, which permitted free export of the corn of Sienese Maremma in 1737, after the Grand Duke Francis had read Sallustio Bandini's *Economical Discourse*. Beset by famine in 1764, Tuscany gradually opened its market to imported grain well before the Vergennes Treaty of 1786 between France and Britain put French Physiocratic doctrine into practice. Grain exports in Tuscany had been restricted under the "policy of supply," or "provisioning," or

Charles P. Kindleberger. "The Rise of Free Trade in Western Europe." From *The Journal of Economic History*, 35, 1 (1975). Copyright © 1975 by the Economic History Association. Reprinted with the permission of Cambridge University Press.

"abundance," under which the city-states of Italy limited exports from the surrounding countryside in order to assure food to the urban populace. Bandini and Pompeo Neri pointed out the ill effects this had on investment and productivity in agriculture.

The policy of supply was not limited to food. In the eighteenth and early nineteenth century exports were restricted in, among others, wool and coal (Britain), ashes, rags, sand for glass and firewood (Germany), ship timbers (Austria), rose madder (the Netherlands), and silk cocoons (Italy). The restrictions on exports of ashes and timber from Germany had conservation overtones. The industrial revolution in Britain led further to prohibitions on export of machinery and on emigration of artisans, partly to increase the supply for local use, but also to prevent the diffusion of technology on the Continent. We return to this below.

What was left in the policy of supply after the Napoleonic Wars quickly ran down. Prohibition of export of raw silk was withdrawn in Piedmont, Lombardy and Venetia in the 1830's, freedom to export coal from Britain enacted in the 1840's. Details of the relaxation of restrictions are recorded for Baden as part of the movement to occupational freedom. The guild system gradually collapsed under the weight of increasing complexity of regulations by firms seeking exceptions for themselves and objecting to exceptions for others. A number of prohibitions and export taxes lasted to the 1850's—as industrial consumers held out against producers, or in some cases, like rags, the collectors of waste products. Reduction of the export tax on rags in Piedmont in 1851 produced a long drawn-out struggle between Cavour and the industry which had to close up thirteen plants when the tax was reduced. To Cavour salvation of the industry lay in machinery and the substitution of other materials, not in restricting export through Leghorn and Messina to Britain and North America.

Elimination of export taxes and prohibitions in nineteenth-century Europe raises doubt about the universal validity of the theory of the tariff as a collective good, imposed by a concentrated interest at the expense of the diffuse. The interest of groups producing inputs for other industries are normally more deeply affected than those of the consuming industries, but it is hardly possible that the consuming is always less concentrated than the producing industry.

II

The question of export duties sought by domestic manufacturers on their raw materials, and of import duties on outputs demanded by producers for the domestic market, was settled in the Netherlands in the eighteenth century in favor of mercantile interests. These were divided into the First Hand, merchants, shipowners and bankers; the Second Hand, which carried on the work of sorting and packing in staple markets, and wholesaling on the Continent; and the Third Hand, concerned with distribution in the hinterland. Dutch staple trade was based partly on mercantile skills and partly on the pivotal location of Amsterdam, Rotterdam, and other staple towns dedicated to trade in particular commodities, largely perishable, nonstandardized and best suited to short voyages. The First Hand dominated Dutch social and political life and opposed all tariffs on export or import goods, above a minimum for revenue, in order to maximize trade and minimize formalities. From 1815 to 1830 when Holland and Belgium were united as the Low Countries, the clash between the Dutch First Hand and Belgian producers in search of import protection from British manufactures was continuous and heated.

The First Hand objected to taxes for revenue on coffee, tea, tobacco, rice, sugar, and so on, and urged their replacement by excises on flour, meat, horses and servants. Tariffs for revenue must be held down to prevent smuggling and to sustain turnover. The safe maximum was given variously as three percent, five percent, and on transit even as one-half percent. Transit in bond, and transit with duty-cum-drawback were thought too cumbersome. The Dutch made a mistake in failing to emulate London which in 1803 adopted a convenient entrepôt dock with bonding. Loss of colonies and of overseas connections in the Napoleonic Wars made it impossible from early in the period to compete with Britain in trade. Equally threatening was Hamburg which supplied British and colonial goods to Central Europe in transit for one-half percent revenue duty maximum, many products free, and all so after 1839. More serious, however, was the rise of direct selling as transport efficiency increased. Early signs of direct selling can be detected at the end of the seventeenth century when Venice and Genoa lost their role as intermediary in traffic between Italy and the West. By the first half of the nineteenth century, they were abundant. "By the improved intercourse of our time (1840), the seller is brought more immediately into contact with the producer." Twenty years earlier, the Belgian members of a Dutch Belgian fiscal commission argued that "there was no hope of restoring Holland's general trade. Owing to the spread of civilization, all European countries could now provide for themselves in directly trading."[1]

It is a mistake to think of merchants as all alike. As indicated, First, Second and Third Hands of the Netherlands had different functions, status and power. In Germany, republican merchants of Hamburg differed sharply from those of the Imperial city, Frankfurt, and held out fifty years longer against the Zollverein. Within Frankfurt there were two groups, the English-goods party associated with the bankers, and the majority, which triumphed in 1836, interested in transit, forwarding, retail and domestic trade within the Zollverein. In Britain a brilliant picture had been drawn of a pragmatic free trader, John Gladstone, father of William, opposed to timber preferences for Canada, enemy of the East India Company monopoly on trade with China and India, but supportive of imperial preference in cotton and sugar, and approving of the Corn Laws on the ground of support for the aristocracy he hoped his children could enter via politics. The doctrinaire free traders of Britain were the cotton manufacturers like Gladstone's friend, Kirman Finlay, who regarded shipowners and corn growers as the two great monopolists.

The doctrinaire free trade of the Dutch merchants led to economic sclerosis, or economic sickness. Hamburg stayed in trade and finance and did not move into industry. In Britain, merchants were ignorant of industry, but were saved by the coming of the railroad and limited liability which provided an outlet for their surplus as direct trading squeezed profits from stapling. The economic point is simple: free trade may stimulate, but again it may lead to fossilization.

III

The movement toward freer trade in Britain began gross in the eighteenth century, net only after the Napoleonic Wars. In the initial stages, there was little problem for a man like Wedgewood advocating free trade for exports of manufactures under the Treaty of Vergennes with France, but prohibitions on the export of machinery and emigrations of artisans. Even in the 1820's and 1830's, a number of the political economists—Torrens, Baring, Peel, Nassau Senior—favored repeal of the Corn Laws but opposed export of machinery. The nineteenth century is seen by Brebner not as a steady march to *laisser-faire* but as a counterpoint between Smithian *laisser-faire* in trade matters and, after the Reform Bill, Benthamic intervention of 1832 which produced the Factory, Mines, Ten Hours and similar acts from 1833 to 1847.

First came the revenue aspect, which was critical to the movement to freer trade under Huskisson in the 1820's, Peel in the 1840's, and Gladstone in the 1850's. Huskisson and Gladstone used the argument that the bulk of revenue was produced by taxes on a few items—largely colonial products such as tea, coffee, sugar, tobacco, and wine and spirits—and that others produced too little revenue to be worth the trouble. Many were redundant (for example, import duties on products which Britain exported). Others were so high as to be prohibitory or encouraged smuggling and reduced revenue. When Peel was converted to free trade, it was necessary to reintroduce the income tax before he could proceed with repeal of 605 duties between 1841 and 1846, and reductions in 1035 others. The title of Sir Henry Parnell's treatise on freer trade (1830) was *Financial Reform.*

But Huskisson was a free trader, if a cautious one. He spoke of benefits to be derived from the removal of "vexatious restraints and meddling interference in the concerns of internal industry and foreign commerce."[2] Especially he thought that imports stimulated efficiency in import-competing industry. In 1824 the prohibition on silk imports had been converted to a duty of thirty percent regarded as the upper limit of discouragement to smuggling. In a speech on March 24, 1826, said by Canning to be the finest he had heard in the House of Commons, Huskisson observed that Macclesfield and Spitalfield had reorganized the industry under the spur of enlarged imports, and expanded the scale of output. Both Michel Chevalier and Count Cavour referred to this positive and dynamic response to increased imports in England.

Restrictions on export of machinery and emigration of artisans went back, as indicated, to the industrial revolution. Prohibition of export of stocking frames was enacted as early as 1696. Beginning in 1774 there was a succession of restrictions on tools and utensils for the cotton and linen trades and on the emigration of skilled artisans. The basis was partly the policy of supply, partly naked maintenance of monopoly. Freedom had been granted to the emigration of workmen in

1824. After the depression of the late 1830's, pressure for removal of the prohibition came from all machinery manufacturers. Following further investigation by a Select Committee of Parliament, the export prohibition was withdrawn.

The main arguments against prohibition of the export of machinery and emigration of artisans were three: they were ineffective, unnecessary, and harmful. Ineffectuality was attested to by much detail in the Select Committee reports on the efficiency of smuggling. Machinery for which licenses could not be obtained could be dispatched illegally in one of a number of ways—by another port, hidden in cotton bales, in baggage or mixed with permitted machinery and in a matter of hours. Guaranteed and insured shipments could be arranged in London or Paris for premia up to thirty percent.

That prohibition was unnecessary was justified first by the inability of foreigners, even with English machinery and English workmen, to rival English manufacturers. Britain had minerals, railways, canals, rivers, better division of labor, "trained workmen habituated to all industrious employments."[3] "Even when the Belgians employed English machines and skilled workers, they failed to import the English spirit of enterprise, and secured only disappointing results."[4] In 1825, the Select Committee concluded it was safe to export machinery, since seven-year-old machinery in Manchester was already obsolete.

In the third place it was dangerous. Restriction on emigration of artisans failed to prevent their departure, but did inhibit their return. Restriction of machinery, moreover, raised the price abroad through the cost of smuggling, and stimulated production on the Continent. Improvement in the terms of trade through restriction of exports (but failure to cut them off altogether) was deleterious for its protective effect abroad.

Greater coherence of the Manchester cotton spinners over the machinery makers spread over Manchester, Birmingham and London may account for the delay from 1825 to 1841 in freeing up machinery, and support Pincus' theory on the need of concentrated interests. But the argument of consistency was telling. In 1800 the Manchester manufacturers of cloth had demanded a law forbidding export of yarn, but did not obtain it. The 1841 Second Report concluded that machinery making should be put on the same footing as other departments of British industry. It is noted that Nottingham manufacturers approved free trade but claim an exception in regard to machinery used in their own manufacture. Babbage observed that machinery makers are more intelligent than their users, to whose imagined benefits their interests are sacrificed, and referred to the "impolicy of interfering between two classes."[5] In the end, the Manchester Chamber of Commerce became troubled by the inconsistency and divided; the issue of prohibition of machinery was subsumed into the general attack on the Corn Laws. In the 1840's moreover, the sentiment spread that Britain should become the Workshop of the World, which implied the production of heavy goods as well as cotton cloth and yarn.

Rivers of ink have been spilled on the repeal of the Corn Laws, and the present paper can do little but summarize the issues and indicate a position. The questions relate to the Stolper-Samuelson distribution argument, combined with the Reform

Bill of 1832 and the shift of political power from the landed aristocracy to the bourgeois; incidence of the Corn Laws and of their repeal, within both farming and manufacturing sectors; the potential for a dynamic response of farming to lower prices from competition; and the relation of repeal to economic development on the Continent, and especially whether industrialization could be halted by expanded and assured outlets for agricultural produce, a point of view characterized by Gallagher and Robinson as "free-trade imperialism." A number of lesser issues may be touched upon incidentally: interaction between the Corn Laws and the Zollverein, and its tariff changes in the 1840's; the question of whether repeal of the Corn Laws and of the Navigation Acts would have been very long delayed had it not been for the potato famine in Ireland and on the Continent; and the question of whether the term "free-trade imperialism" is better reserved for Joseph Chamberlain's Empire preference of fifty years later.

In the normal view, the Reform Bill of 1832 shifted power from the land and country to the factory and city, from the aristocratic class to the bourgeois, and inexorably led to changes in the trade policies which had favored farming and hurt manufacturing. One can argue that repeal of the Corn Laws represented something less than that and that the Reform Bill was not critical. The movement to free trade had begun earlier in the Huskisson reforms; speeches in Parliament were broadly the same in 1825 when it was dominated by landed aristocrats as in the 1830's and 1840's. Numbers had changed with continued manufacturing expansion, but nothing much more. Or one can reject the class explanation, as Polanyi does, and see something much more ideological. "Not until the 1830's did economic liberalism burst forth as a crusading passion." The liberal creed involved faith in man's secular salvation through a self-regulating market, held with fanaticism and evangelical fervor. French Physiocrats were trying to correct only one inequity, to break out of the policy of supply and permit export of grain. British political economists of the 1830's and 1840's, who won over Tories like Sir Robert Peel and Lord Russell, and ended up in 1846 with many landlords agreeable to repeal of the Corn Laws, represented an ideology. "Mere class interests cannot offer a satisfactory explanation for any long-run social process."[6]

Under a two-sector model, free trade comes when the abundant factor acquires political power and moves to eliminate restrictions imposed in the interest of the scarce factor which has lost power. In reality factors of production are not monolithic. Some confusion in the debate attached to the incidence of the tax on imported corn within both farming and manufacturing. The Anti-Corn Law League of Cobden and Bright regarded it as a tax on food, taking as much as twenty percent of the earnings of a hand-loom weaver. Cobden denied the "fallacy" that wages rose and fell with the price of bread. Benefits, moreover, went to the landlord and not to the farmer or farm-laborer, as rents on the short leases in practice rose with the price of corn. There are passages in Cobden which suggest that hurt of the Corn Laws fell upon the manufacturing and commercial classes rather than labor but the speeches run mainly in terms of a higher standard of living for the laborer who would spend his "surplus of earnings on meat, vegetables, butter, milk and cheese," rather than on wheaten loaves. The Chartists were interested not in repeal, but in other amenities for the workers. Peel's conversion waited on his conclusion that wages did not vary with the price of provision, and that repeal would benefit the wage earner rather than line the pockets of the manufacturer.

In any event, with Gladstone's reductions in duties on meat, eggs and dairy products, with High Farming, and an end to the movement off the farm and out of handwork into the factory real wages did rise in the 1850's, but so did profits on manufacturing. As so often in economic debates between two alternatives, history provides the answer which economists abhor, both. Nor did repeal bring a reduction in incomes to landlords—at least not for thirty years—as the farm response to repeal, and to high prices of food produced by the potato famine, was more High Farming.

Cobden may have only been scoring debating points rather than speaking from conviction when on a number of occasions he argued that the repeal would stimulate landlords "to employ their capital and their intelligence as other classes are forced to do in other pursuits" rather than "in sluggish indolence," and to double the quantity of grain, or butter, or cheese, which the land is capable of providing, with "longer leases, draining, extending the length of fields, knocking down hedgerows, clearing away trees which now shield the corn" and to provide more agricultural employment by activity to "grub up hedges, grub up thorns, drain, ditch." Sir James Caird insisted that High Farming was the answer to the repeal of the Corn Laws and many shared his view. The fact is, moreover, that the 1850's were the Golden Age of British farming, with rapid technical progress through the decade though it slowed thereafter. Repeal of the Corn Laws may not have stimulated increased efficiency in agriculture, but it did not set it back immediately, and only after the 1870's did increases in productivity run down.

The political economists in the Board of Trade—Bowring, Jacob, MacGregor—sought free trade as a means of slowing down the development of manufacturing on the Continent. They regarded the Zollverein as a reply to the imposition of the Corn Laws, and thought that with its repeal Europe, but especially the Zollverein under the leadership of Prussia, could be diverted to invest more heavily in agriculture and to retard the march to manufacturing. There were inconsistencies between this position and other facts they adduced: Bowring recognized that Germany had advantages over Great Britain for the development of manufacturing, and that Swiss spinning had made progress without protection. The 1818 Prussian tariff which formed the basis for that of the Zollverein was the lowest in Europe when it was enacted—though the levying of tariffs on cloth and yarn by weight gave high effective rates of protection despite low nominal duties to the cheaper constructions and counts. Jacob noted that the export supply elasticity of Prussian grain must be low, given poor transport. "To export machinery, we must import corn,"[7] but imports of corn were intended to prevent the development of manufacturers abroad, whereas the export of machinery assisted it. The rise and progress of German manufacturing was attributed to restrictions on the admission of German agricultural products and wood, imposed by France and England, but also to "the natural advantages of the several states for manufacturing industry, the genius and laborious character and the necessities of the German people, and . . .

especially the unexampled duration of peace, and internal tranquility which all Germany enjoyed."[8]

The clearest statements are those of John Bowring. In a letter of August 28, 1839, to Lord Palmerston he asserted that the manufacturing interest in the Zollverein "is greatly strengthened and will become stronger from year to year unless counteracted by a system of concessions, conditional upon the gradual lowering of tariffs. The present state of things will not be tenable. The tariffs will be elevated under the growing demands and increasing power of the manufacturing states, or they will be lowered by calling into action, and bringing over to an alliance, the agricultural and commercial interests."[9] In his testimony before the Select Committee on Import Duties in 1840 he went further: "I believe we have created an unnecessary rivalry by our vicious legislation; that many of these countries never would have dreamed of being manufacturers."

On this showing, the repeal of the Corn Laws was motivated by "free-trade imperialism," the desire to gain a monopoly of trade with the world in manufactured goods. Zollverein in the 1830's merely indicated the need for haste. Torrens and James Deacon Hume, among others, had been pushing for importing corn to expand exports in the 1820's, before Zollverein was a threat.

Reciprocity had been a part of British commercial policy in the Treaty of Vergennes in 1786, in treaties reducing the impact of the Navigation Laws in the 1820's and 1830's. The French were suspicious, fearing that they had been outtraded in 1786. They evaded Huskisson's negotiations in 1828. But reciprocity was unnecessary, given David Hume's law. Unilateral reduction of import duties increased exports. Restored into the British diplomatic armory in 1860, reciprocity later became heresy in the eyes of political economists, and of the manufacturing interest as well.

The view that ascribes repeal of the Corn Laws to free-trade imperialism, however, fails adequately to take account of the ideology of the political economists, who believed in buying in the cheapest market and selling in the dearest, or of the short-run nature of the interests of the Manchester merchants themselves. It was evident after the 1840's that industrialization on the Continent could not be stopped, and likely that it could not be slowed down. The Navigation Acts were too complex; they had best be eliminated. The Corn Laws were doomed, even before the Irish potato famine, though that hastened the end of both Corn Laws and Navigation Acts, along with its demonstration of the limitation of market solutions under some circumstances.

"A good cause seldom triumphs unless someone's interest is bound up with it."[10] Free trade is the hypocrisy of the export interest, the clever device of the climber who kicks the ladder away when he has attained the summit of greatness. But in the English case it was more a view of the world at peace, with cosmopolitan interests served as well as national.

It is difficult in this to find clear-cut support for any of the theories of tariff formation set forth earlier. Free trade as an export-interest collective good, sought in a representative democracy by concentrated interests to escape the free rider, would seem to require a simple and direct connection between the removal of the tariff and the increase in rents. In the repeal of the Corn Laws, and the earlier tariff reductions of Huskisson and Peel, the connection was roundabout—through Hume's law, which meant that increased imports would lead to increased prices or quantities (or both) exported on the one hand, and/or through reduced wages, or higher real incomes from lower food prices on the other. Each chain of reasoning had several links.

Johnson's view that free trade is adopted by countries with improving competitiveness is contradictory to the free-trade-imperialism explanation, that free trade is adopted in an effort to undermine foreign gains in manufacturing when competitiveness has begun to decline. The former might better account in timing for Adam Smith's advocacy of free trade seventy years earlier—though that had large elements of French Physiocratic thought—or apply to the 1820's when British productivity was still improving, before the Continent had started to catch up. In turn, free-trade imperialism is a better explanation for the 1830's than for the end of the 1840's, since by 1846 it was already too late to slow, much less to halt, the advance of manufacturing on the Continent.

Vested interests competing for rents in a representative democracy, thrusting manufacturers seeking to expand markets, or faltering innovators, trying as a last resort to force exports on shrinking markets—rather like the stage of foreign direct investment in Vernon's product cycle when diffusion of technology has been accomplished—none of these explanations seems free of difficulties as compared with an ideological explanation based on the intellectual triumph of the political economists, their doctrines modified to incorporate consistency. The argument took many forms: static, dynamic, with implicit reliance on one incidence or another, direct or indirect in its use of Hume's law. But the Manchester School, based on the political economists, represented a rapidly rising ideology of freedom for industry to buy in the cheapest and sell in the dearest market. It overwhelmed the Tories when it did not convert them. Britain in the nineteenth century, and only to a slightly lesser extent the Continent, were characterized by a "strong, widely-shared conviction that the teachings of contemporary orthodox economists, including Free Traders, were scientifically exact, universally applicable, and demanded assent."[11] In the implicit debate between Thurman Arnold who regarded economic theorists (and lawyers) as high priests who rationalize and sprinkle holy water on contemporary practice, and Keynes who thought of practical men as responding unconsciously to the preaching of dead theorists, the British movement to free trade is a vote, aided by the potato famine, for the view of Keynes.

IV

France after 1815 was a high-tariff country which conformed to the Pincus model for a representative democracy with tariffs, for various interests, except that (a) there were tariffs for all, and (b) it was not a democracy. The Physiocratic doctrine of *laisser-faire* for agricultural exports had been discredited in its reciprocal form by the disaster wreaked by imports up to 1789 under the Treaty of Vergennes. The

Continental system, moreover, provided strong protection to hothouse industries which was continued in the tariff of 1816, and elaborated in 1820 and 1822. To the principles of Turgot, that there should be freedom of grain trade inside France but no imports except in periods of drought, were added two more: protection of the consumer by regulating the right of export of wheat—a step back from Physiocratic doctrine—and protecting the rights of producers by import tariffs. In introducing the tariff of 1822 for manufactures, Saint-Cricq defended prohibitions, attacked the view that an industry which could not survive with a duty of twenty percent should perish, saying that the government intended to protect all branches together: "agriculture, industry, internal commerce, colonial production, navigation, foreign commerce finally, both of land and of sea."[12]

It was not long, however, before pressures for lower duties manifested themselves. Industries complained of the burden of the tariff on their purchases of inputs, and especially of the excess protection accorded to iron. It was calculated that protection against English iron cost industrial consumers fifty million francs a year and had increased the price of wood—used for charcoal, and owned by the many noble *maîtres de forges*—by thirty percent on the average and in some places fifty percent. Commissions of inquiry in 1828 and 1834 recommended modifications in duties, especially to enlarge supplies which local industry was not in a position to provide, and to convert prohibitions into tariffs. A tumult of conflict broke out in the Chamber among the export interests of the ports, the textile interests of Alsace and Normandy, the *maîtres de forges* and the consumers of iron, with no regard, says the protectionist Gouraud, for the national interest. The Chambers were then dissolved by the cabinet, and tariffs adjusted downward, in coal, iron, copper, nitrates, machinery, horses. Reductions of the 1830's were followed in the peaks of business by similar pressure for reductions in prosperous phases of the cycle of the 1840's and 1850's.

A troubling question that involved conflicting interests in this period was presented by sugar, for which it was impossible to find a solution agreeable at the same time to colonial planters, shipowners, port refiners, consumers and the treasury. Colonial supply was high cost and a 55 francs per 100 kilograms duty on foreign supplies was needed to keep the sugar ports content. This, however, made it economical to expand beet-sugar production, begun during the Continental blockade, and the sugar ports turned to taxing this domestic production, less heavily at first, but with full equality in 1843. By this time it was too late, and with the freeing of the slaves in 1848, French colonial sugar production no longer counted.

The free-trade movement in France had its support in Bordeaux, the wine-exporting region; Lyon, interested in silk; and Paris, producer of so-called Paris articles for sale abroad (cabinet ware, perfumes, imitation jewelry, toys, and so on). Later Norman agricultural interests in the export of butter and eggs to London teamed up with Bordeaux in wine to resist the attempts by textile interests to enlist agriculture in favor of higher tariffs.

Intellectual support to free trade led by Bastiat from Bordeaux, and with Michel Chevalier as its most prestigious member, is dismissed by Lévy-Leboyer as unimportant. Nonetheless, Chevalier had an important part in the negotiation of the treaty, and in persuading Napoleon III to impose it on France in the face of the united opposition of the Chamber of Deputies. Some attention to his thought is required.

The prime interest of the *Société d'Economie Politique* and of Chevalier was growth. His two-year visit to the United States in 1833–1835 impressed him with the contribution of transport to economic growth and contributed to his 1838 major work on *The Material Interests of France in Roads, Canals and Railroads.* American protectionist doctrine of Henry Carey seems not to have affected him. Polytechnician, graduate of the *Ecole des Mines,* Chevalier's first interest in freer trade came from a project to establish woolen production in the Midi, and to obtain cheaper wool. Much of his later reasoning was in terms of the penalty to industry from expensive materials: Charging 35 francs for a quintal of iron worth 20 imposes on industry "the labor of Sisyphus and the work of Penelope."[13] His major argument, at the *Collège de France,* and in his *Examen du Système Commercial,* cited the success of Spitalfield and Macclesfield when Huskisson permitted competition of imports; and the experience of the manufacturers of cotton and woolen textiles in Saxony who were worried by the enactment of Zollverein but sufficiently stimulated by import competition so that in two or three years their industry was flourishing. The letter of Napoleon III to Fould talks in specifics of the need to abolish all duties on raw materials essential to industry to encourage production, and to reduce by stages the duties on goods which are consumed on a large scale. In the more general introduction it states that "lack of competition causes industry to stagnate," echoing the Chevalier view. Chevalier himself was one of the judges of the Universal Exposition of 1855 in Paris and noted that France received so many prizes that no one dared confess to being a protectionist.

There were economic purposes behind the Anglo-French treaty, as evidenced by the proposal in France in 1851 for tariffs of twenty percent, ten percent and a duty-free on wholly manufactured goods, semi-finished manufactures and raw materials; by actual reductions in duties on coal, iron and steel in 1852 as the railroad boom picked up; and by the legislative proposal designed by Napoleon III in 1855, but not put forward until after the Crimean War, to admit 241 items duty free, reduce tariffs on 19 others, remove all prohibitions and set a top limit of thirty percent. This last was turned down by the Chamber and Napoleon promised not to submit a new tariff proposal before 1861.

Economic interests were involved, and the theories of great men like Cobden and Chevalier. However, there was more: Napoleon III was starting to engage in foreign adventure. He wanted to rid Italy of Austrian rule by use of arms. The British opposed his military measures, despite their recent use of force in Crimea. The treaty was used to hold British neutrality, as much as or more than to stimulate growth in France. Moreover, it did not need to be submitted to the Chamber. Under the Constitution of 1851, the Emperor had the sole power to make treaties, and such treaties encompassed those dealing with trade.

The move was successful both politically and economically. With the help of the French armies, Italy was unified under the leadership of Piedmont, and French growth never faltered under the impetus of increased imports. French industries met competition successfully and checked the growth of imports after two years. While its effects are intermingled with those of the spread of the French railroad network, it "helped to bring about the full development of the industrial revolution in France."

Further, it added impetus to the free-trade movement in Europe. This was under way in the early 1850's, following repeal of the Corn Laws. The Swiss constitution of 1848 had called for a tariff for revenue only and protective duties were reduced progressively from 1851 to 1855. The Netherlands removed a tariff on ship imports and a prohibition against nationalization of foreign ships. Belgium plugged gap after gap in its protective system in the early 1850's, only to turn around at the end of the decade and adopt free trade down the line. Piedmont, as we shall see, and Spain, Portugal, Norway and Sweden (after 1857) undertook to dismantle their protective and prohibitive restrictions. With the Anglo-French treaty the trickle became a flood. France, Germany, Italy and Britain engaged in negotiating reciprocal trade treaties with the most-favored nation clause.

Following French defeat at Sedan in 1870 and the abdication of Louis Napoleon, the Third Republic brought in the protectionist Thiers. The Cobden treaty was denounced in 1872. Reversal of policy waited upon the repeal of the Le Chapelier law of 1791, taken in the heat of the French revolution against associations, which forbade economic interests from organizing. Dunham claims that a country with leadership would have accepted a moderate tariff in 1875, but that the free traders had neither organization nor conviction, that is, too many free riders.

The French movement to free trade was taken against the weight of the separate interests, in the absence of strong export interests, with an admixture of economic theory of a dynamic kind, and imposed from above. The motivation of that imposition was partly economic, partly, perhaps even mainly, political. Moreover, it had a bandwagon effect in spreading freer trade.

In the French case, the leadership overwhelmed the concentrated economic interests. That leadership earned its surplus, to use Frohlich, Oppenheimer and Young's expression, in a coin different than economic, that is, in freedom to maneuver in foreign policy. It may be possible to subsume increases in leadership surplus in this form into an "economic theory of national decision-making" with costs to vested interests accepted in exchange for political benefits to a national leader, ruling by an imposed constitution, the legitimacy of which is not questioned. The effort seems tortured.

V

As mentioned earlier, the Prussian tariff of 1818 was regarded when it was enacted as the lowest in Europe. But the duties on coarse yarns and textiles were effectively high, since the tariff was levied by weight. Jacob in 1819 noted that the "system of the Prussian government has always been of manufacturing at home everything consumed within the Kingdom; of buying from others, nothing that can be dispensed with," adding "As scarcely any competition exists, but with their

own countrymen, there is little inducement to adopt the inventions of other countries, or to exercise their facilities in perfecting their fabrics; none of these have
kept pace. . . ."[14] Baden, on joining the Zollverein which adopted the Prussian
tariff for the totality, believed itself to be raising its tariff level when it joined.
What Baden did, however, was to acquire enforcement: its long border had previously been effectively open.

The Prussian tariff dominated that of the Zollverein, organized in the years
from 1828 to 1833, primarily because Prussia took a very liberal view of tariff
revenues. Most goods by sea entered the German states via Prussia, directly or by
way of the Netherlands, but the text of the Zollverein treaty of 1833 provided that
the revenues from the duties after deduction of expenses would be divided among
the contracting states according to population. Prussia thus received 55 percent,
Bavaria 17 percent, Saxony 6.36 percent, Wurtemberg 5.5 percent, and so on, and
[Prussia] was said in 1848 to have sacrificed about two million talers a year, exclusive
of the fiscal loss sustained by smuggling along the Rhine and Lake Constance. This
can be regarded as a side-payment made by the beneficiary of income-distribution
under Pareto-optimal conditions to gain its policy, or as the disproportionate share
of overhead costs of the collective good saddled on the party that most wanted it.

Despite adjustments made in Prussian customs duties between 1819 and 1833,
the tariff remained low by British standards. Junker grain growers were hopeful of
importing British manufactures in order to sell Britain more grain. Junker bureaucrats, brought up on Adam Smith and free trade by instinct, were fearful that
highly protective rates would reduce the revenue yield.

Outside of Prussia plus Hamburg and Frankfurt and the other grain-growing
states of Mecklenburg, Pomerania, and so on, there was interest in higher tariffs,
but apart from the Rhineland, little in the way of organized interests. Von
Delbrück comments that Prussia and Pomerania had free trade interests and shipping interests, but that outside the Rhineland, which had organized Chambers of
Commerce under the French occupation, there were few bureaucrats, or organs
with views on questions of trade and industry. Nor did the Prussian government
see a need to develop them.

Saxony was sufficiently protected by its interior location so as not to feel
threatened by low tariffs, which, as mentioned, were not really low on coarse
cloths. On joining the Zollverein, Baden was concerned over raising its tariff, and
worried lest it be cut off from its traditional trading areas of Switzerland and Alsace. It fought with the Zollverein authorities over exemptions for imported capital equipment, but gradually evolved into a source of pressure, with Bavaria and
Wurtemberg, for higher tariffs on cotton yarns and iron. Fischer points out the
request for lifting the duty on cotton yarns from two talers per centner to five was
resisted by the weavers of Prussia (the Rhineland) and Silesia.

Cotton yarns and iron were the critical items. Shortly after the formation of the
Zollverein, a trend toward protection was seen to be under way. The Leipsig consul reported a new duty on iron to the Board of Trade in February 1837 and observed that the switch from imports of cotton cloth to imports of yarn pointed in
the direction of ultimate exclusion of both. Bowring's letter of August 1839 noted

that the manufacturing interest was growing stronger, that the existing position was untenable, and that tariffs would be raised under the growing demands and increasing power of the manufacturing states, or would be lowered by an alliance between the agricultural and commercial interests.

Open agitation for protection began two and one-half years after the formation of the Zollverein when the South pushed for duties on cotton yarns. Linen yarns and cloth went on the agenda in 1839 and iron, protection for which was sought by Silesian and west German ironwork owners, beginning in 1842. But these groups lacked decisive power. The Prussian landed nobility covered their position by citing the interests of the consumers, and Prince Smith, the expatriate leader of the doctrinaire free traders, in turn tried to identify free trade and low tariffs with the international free-trade movement rather than with the export interests of the Junkers. The tariff on iron was raised in 1844, those on cotton yarns and linen yarns in 1846. Von Delbrück presents in detail the background of the latter increases, starting with the bureaucratic investigations into linen, cotton, wool, and soda, with their negative recommendations, continuing through the negotiations, in which Prussia was ranged against any increase and all the others in favor, and concluding that the Prussian plenipotentiary to the Zollverein conference was right in not vetoing the increases, as he could have done, operating on the theory that a compromise was more important than the rationally correct measure of this or that tariff. The head of the Prussian Handelsamt was not satisfied with the outcome of the conference but had to accept it.

From 1846 on, the direction of Zollverein tariffs was downward, aided first by the repeal of the Corn Laws and secondly by the Cobden-Chevalier treaty. With the increases of the 1840's and English reductions, the Zollverein tariff from one of the lowest in Europe had become relatively high. Von Delbrück was one of the doctrinaire free traders in the Prussian civil service and notes that in 1863 he had been trying for a reduction on the tariff in pig iron for seven years, since the tariff reform of 1856, which reordered but did not lower duty schedules. He also wanted a reduction in the tariff on cotton cloth; duties on woolens were no longer needed. The opportunity came with the announcement of the Anglo-French treaty. He noted that Austria had gone from prohibitions to tariffs, that the Netherlands had reformed its tariffs with a five percent maximum on industrial production, and that the levels of Italian duties were lower than those in Germany. "Could we stay away from this movement? We could not."[15]

Bismarck was no barrier to the Junker bureaucracy. His view about tariff negotiations was expressed in 1879 in the question: "Who got the better of the bargain?" Trade treaties, he believed, were nothing in themselves but an expression of friendship. His economic conscience at this time, he said later, was in the hands of others. Moreover, he had two political ends which a trade treaty with France might serve: to gain her friendship in the Danish question, and to isolate Austria which was bidding for a role in the German Confederation. Austrian tariffs were high. The lower the levels of the Zollverein the more difficulty she would have in joining it and bidding against Prussia for influence. The Zollverein followed the 1863 treaty with France with a series of others.

Exports of grain from Prussia, Pomerania, and Mecklenberg to London as a percentage of total English imports hit a peak in 1862 at the time of the Civil War and proceeded down thereafter as American supplies took over. The free-trade movement nonetheless continued. Only hesitation prevented a move to complete free trade at the peak of the boom in 1873. There is debate whether the crash later in the year triggered off the return to protection in 1879 or not. Victory in 1871 had enlarged competition in iron and cotton textiles by including Alsace and Lorraine in the new German Empire. Radical free traders and large farmers achieved the reduction in duties on raw iron in 1873 and passed legislative provision for their complete removal in 1877. But Lambi notes that *Gewerbefreiheit* (freedom of occupation) had caused dissatisfaction and in some versions subsumed free trade. By 1875 the iron interests are organizing to resist the scheduled elimination of iron duties in 1877.

The difference between the 1873 depression which led to tariffs, and the 1857 crisis which did not, lay in (a) the fact that the interests were not cohesive in the earlier period and (b) that Britain did not keep on lowering duties in the later period as it had in the first. On the first score the Verein Deutscher Eisen- und Stahl-Industrielle was formed in 1873 after vertical integration of steel back to iron mining had removed the opposition between the producers and consumers of iron. This much supports the view of the effectiveness of concentrated interests achieving their tariff goals when scattered interests will not—though again it has nothing to do with representative democracy. On the other hand, the free traders also organized; in 1868 the Kongress Nord-Deutscher Landwirte was organized, and in 1871 it was broadened to cover all Germany. In 1872, a Deutsche Landwirtschaftsrat was formed. Many of these organizations and the once free-trade Congress of German Economists were subverted and converted to protection after 1875, but a new Union for the Promotion of Free Trade was formed in September 1876. German economic interests as a whole became organized, and the struggle was among interests concentrated on both sides.

Abandonment of the opposition of the landed interests is perhaps critical. Consumers of iron in machinery, they opposed tariffs on iron up to 1875, but with the decline in the price of grain and the threat of imports, their opposition collapsed. It might have been possible to support tariffs for grain and free trade for iron, but inconsistency is open to attack. After von Delbrück's resignation or discharge in April 1876, Bismarck forged the alliance of bread and iron. As widely recounted, he had strong domestic political motives for higher tariffs on this occasion, as contrasted with his international political gains from lower tariffs up to 1875.

In general, however, the German case conforms to the Stolper-Samuelson explanation: the abundant factor wants free trade; when it becomes relatively scarce, through a gain in manufacturing at home and an expansion of agriculture abroad, it shifts to wanting tariffs. Doctrine was largely on the side of free trade. List's advocacy of national economy had little or no political force. His ultimate goal was always free trade, and his early proposal of ten percent duties on colonial goods, fifteen percent on Continental and fifty percent on British was more anti-British than national. In the 1840's he was regarded in Germany, or at least by the

Prussians, as a polemicist whose views were offered for sale. Bismarck is often regarded as the arch-villain of the 1879 reversal of Zollverein low tariffs, but it is hard to see that his role was a major one. . . .

VI

My first conclusion reached from this survey was that free trade in Europe in the period from 1820 to 1875 had many different causes. Whereas after 1879, various countries reacted quite differently to the single stimulus of the fall in the price of wheat—England liquidating its agriculture, France and Germany imposing tariffs, though for different political and sociological reasons, Italy emigrating (in violation of the assumptions of classical economics), and Denmark transforming from producing grain for export to importing it as an input in the production of dairy products, bacon and eggs—before that the countries of Europe all responded to different stimuli in the same way. Free trade was part of a general response to the breakdown of the manor and guild system. This was especially true of the removal of restrictions on exports and export taxes, which limited freedom of producers. As more and conflicting interests came into contention, the task of sorting them out became too complex for government (as shown in *Gewerbeförderung* in Baden, and the refinement of the Navigation Laws in England), and it became desirable to sweep them all away.

Part of the stimulus came from the direct self-interest of particular dominant groups, illustrated particularly by the First Hand in the Netherlands. In Britain, free trade emerged as a doctrine from the political economists, with a variety of rationalizations to sustain it in particular applications: anti-monopoly, increases to real wages, higher profits, increased allocative efficiency, increased productivity through innovation required by import competition. In France, the lead in the direction of free trade came less from the export interests than from industrial interests using imported materials and equipment as inputs, though the drive to free trade after 1846 required the overcoming of the weight of the vested interests by strong governmental leadership, motivated by political gain in international politics. The German case was more straightforward: free trade was in the interest of the exporting grain- and timber-producing classes, who were politically dominant in Prussia and who partly bought off and partly overwhelmed the rest of the country. The Italian case seems to be one in which doctrines developed abroad which were dominant in England and in a minority position in France, were imported by strong political leadership and imposed on a relatively disorganized political body.

Second thoughts raise questions. The movement to free trade in the 1850's in the Netherlands, Belgium, Spain, Portugal, Denmark, Norway and Sweden, along with the countries discussed in detail, suggests the possibility that Europe as a whole was motivated by ideological considerations rather than economic interests. That Louis Napoleon and Bismarck would use trade treaties to gain ends in foreign policy suggests that free trade was valued for itself, and that moves toward it would earn approval. Viewed in one perspective, the countries of Europe in this period should not be considered as independent economies whose reactions to various phenomena can properly be compared, but rather as a single entity which moved to free trade for ideological or perhaps better doctrinal reasons. Manchester and the English political economists persuaded Britain which persuaded Europe, by precept and example. Economic theories of representative democracy, or constitutional monarchy, or even absolute monarchy may explain some cases of tariff changes. They are little help in Western Europe between the Napoleonic Wars and the Great Depression.

NOTES

1. H. R. C. Wright, *Free Trade and Protection in the Netherlands, 1816–1830: A Study of the First Benelux* (Cambridge: Cambridge University Press, 1955) p. 124.

2. *William Huskisson, (The Speeches of the Right Honorable)* (London: John Murray, 1832), 11, p. 328.

3. Report of the Select Committee on the Laws Relating to the Export of Tools and Machinery, 30 June 1825, in *Parliamentary Papers, Reports of Committee,* (1825), Vol. V, p. 12.

4. H. R. C. Wright, *Free Trade and Protection,* p. 130.

5. Charles Babbage, *The Economy of Machinery and Manufactures* (London: Charles Knight, 4th ed., 1835), p. 364.

6. Karl Polanyi, *The Great Transformation* (New York: Farrar & Rinehart, 1944), p. 152–53.

7. Testimony of Thomas Ashton, in *First Report of the Select Committee,* para. 235.

8. John McGregor, *Germany, Her Resources, Government, Union of Customs and Power under Frederick William IV* (London: Whittaker and Co., 1948), p. 68.

9. John Bowring, "Report on the Prussian Commercial Union 1840," *Parliamentary Papers,* 1840, Volume XXI, p. 287.

10. Mill, cited by Bernard Semmel, *The Rise of Free Trade Imperialism: Classical Political Economy, The Empire of Free Trade and Imperialism, 1750–1850* (Cambridge: Cambridge University Press, 1970), p. 207.

11. Kenneth Fielden, "The Rise and Fall of Free Trade," in C. J. Bartlett, ed., *Britain Pre-eminent: Studies in British World Influence in the Nineteenth Century* (London: Macmillan, 1969), p. 78.

12. Charles Gouraud, *Histoire de la politique commerciale de la France et son influence sur le progrès de la richesse publique depuis le moyen age jusqu'à nos jours,* 1, 11 (Paris: Auguste Durand, 1854), p. 208.

13. Michel Chevalier, *Cours d'economie politique, Fait au Collège de France,* 1, 11, 111 (2nd ed., Paris: No publisher stated, 1855), p. 538.

14. William Jacob, *A View of the Agriculture, Manufactures, Statistics and Society in the State of Germany and Parts of Holland and France* (London: John Murray, 1820), pp. 201–12.

15. Rudolph von Delbrück, *Lebenserinnerungen, I* (Leipsig: Duncker u. Humblot, 1905), p. 200.

6

International Trade, Domestic Coalitions, and Liberty: Comparative Responses to the Crisis of 1873–1896

PETER ALEXIS GOUREVITCH

Peter Alexis Gourevitch examines the impact upon the trade policies and political coalitions of four countries of the Great Depression of 1873–1896, during which Germany and France adopted high tariffs on both agricultural and industrial products, Great Britain maintained its historic policy of free trade, and the United States protected industry but not agriculture. In attempting to explain this pattern of response, Gourevitch compares four alternative hypotheses: economic explanations, emphasizing domestic societal interests; political system explanations, focusing on domestic statist variables; international system explanations, combining international political and economic factors; and economic ideology explanations. Domestic societal interests supplemented by a concern with state structures, he concludes, provide the most persuasive account of these four cases. Gourevitch not only gives a detailed and informative history of the trade policies of the four great economic powers of the late nineteenth century, but he also provides a useful test of several of the main approaches in international political economy.

For social scientists who enjoy comparisons, happiness is finding a force or event which affects a number of societies at the same time. Like test-tube solutions that respond differently to the same reagent, these societies reveal their characters in

Peter Alexis Gourevitch. "International Trade, Domestic Coalitions, and Liberty: Comparative Responses to the Crisis of 1873–1896." Reprinted from *The Journal of Interdisciplinary History*, VIII (1977), 281–313, with the permission of the editors of *The Journal of Interdisciplinary History* and the MIT Press, Cambridge, Massachusetts. © 1977 by The Massachusetts Institute of Technology and the editors of *The Journal of Interdisciplinary History*.

divergent responses to the same stimulus. One such phenomenon is the present worldwide inflation/depression. An earlier one was the Great Depression of 1873–1896. Technological breakthroughs in agriculture (the reaper, sower, fertilizers, drainage tiles, and new forms of wheat) and in transportation (continental rail networks, refrigeration, and motorized shipping) transformed international markets for food, causing world prices to fall. Since conditions favored extensive grain growing, the plains nations of the world (the United States, Canada, Australia, Argentina, and Russia) became the low-cost producers. The agricultural populations of Western and Central Europe found themselves abruptly uncompetitive.

In industry as well, 1873 marks a break. At first the sharp slump of that year looked like an ordinary business-cycle downturn, like the one in 1857. Instead, prices continued to drop for over two decades, while output continued to rise. New industries—steel, chemicals, electrical equipment, and shipbuilding—sprang up, but the return on capital declined. As in agriculture, international competition became intense. Businessmen everywhere felt the crisis, and most of them wanted remedies.

The clamour for action was universal. The responses differed: vertical integration, cartels, government contracts, and economic protection. The most visible response was tariffs. . . .

Although the economic stimuli were uniform, the political systems forced to cope with them differed considerably. Some systems were new or relatively precarious: Republican France, Imperial Germany, Monarchical Italy, Reconstruction America, Newly-Formed Canada, Recently Autonomous Australia. Only Britain could be called stable. Thirty years later when most of these political systems had grown stronger, most of the countries had high tariffs. The importance of the relation between the nature of the political system and protection has been most forcefully argued by Gershenkron in *Bread and Democracy in Germany*. The coalition of iron and rye built around high tariffs contributed to a belligerent foreign policy and helped to shore up the authoritarian Imperial Constitution of 1871. High tariffs, then, contributed to both world wars and to fascism, not a minor consequence. It was once a commonly held notion that free trade and democracy, protection and authoritarianism, went together. . . .

These basic facts about tariff levels and political forms have been discussed by many authors. What is less clear, and not thoroughly explored in the literature, is the best way to understand these outcomes. As with most complex problems, there is no shortage of possible explanations: interest groups, class conflict, institutions, foreign policy, ideology. Are these explanations all necessary though, or equally important? This essay seeks to probe these alternative explanations. It is speculative; it does not offer new information or definitive answers to old questions. Rather, it takes a type of debate about which social scientists are increasingly conscious (the comparison of different explanations of a given phenomenon) and extends it to an old problem that has significant bearing on current issues in political economy—the interaction of international trade and domestic politics. The paper examines closely the formation of tariff policy in late nineteenth-century Germany, France, Britain, and the United States, and then considers the impact of the tariff policy quarrel on the character of each political system.

EXPLAINING TARIFF LEVELS

Explanations for late nineteenth-century tariff levels may be classified under four headings, according to the type of variable to which primacy is given.

1. Economic Explanations Tariff levels derive from the interests of economic groups able to translate calculations of economic benefit into public policy. Types of economic explanations differ in their conceptualization of groups (classes vs. sectors vs. companies) and of the strategies groups pursue (maximizing income, satisfying, stability, and class hegemony).

2. Political System Explanations The "statement of the groups" does not state everything. The ability of economic actors to realize policy goals is affected by political structures and the individuals who staff them. Groups differ in their access to power, the costs they must bear in influencing decisions, prestige, and other elements of political power.

3. International System Explanations Tariff levels derive from a country's position in the international state system. Considerations of military security, independence, stability, or glory shape trade policy. Agriculture may be protected, for example, in order to guarantee supplies of food and soldiers, rather than to provide profit to farmers (as explanation 1 would suggest).

4. Economic Ideology Explanations Tariff levels derive from intellectual orientations about proper economic and trade policies. National traditions may favor autarchy or market principles; faddishness or emulation may induce policy makers to follow the lead given by successful countries. Such intellectual orientations may have originated in calculations of self-interest (explanation 1), or in broader political concerns (explanation 2) or in understandings of international politics (explanation 3), but they may outlive the conditions that spawned them.

These explanations are by no means mutually exclusive. The German case could be construed as compatible with all four: Junkers and heavy industry fought falling prices, competition, and political reformism; Bismarck helped organize the iron and rye coalition; foreign policy concerns over supply sources and hostile great powers helped to create it; and the nationalist school of German economic thought provided fertile ground for protectionist arguments. But were all four factors really essential to produce high tariffs in Germany? Given the principle that a simple explanation is better than a complex one, we may legitimately try to determine at what point we have said enough to explain the result. Other points may be interesting, perhaps crucial for other outcomes, but redundant for this one. It would also be useful to find explanations that fit the largest possible number of cases.

Economic explanation offers us a good port of entry. It requires that we investigate the impact of high and low tariffs, both for agricultural and industrial products, on the economic situation of each major group in each country. We can then turn to the types of evidence—structures, interstate relations, and ideas—required by the other modes of reasoning. Having worked these out for each country, it will then be possible to attempt an evaluation of all four arguments.

GERMANY

Economic Explanations What attitude toward industrial and agricultural tariffs would we predict for each of the major economic groups in German society, if each acted according to its economic interests? A simple model of German society contains the following groups: small peasants; Junkers (or estate owners); manufacturers in heavy, basic industries (iron, coal, steel); manufacturers of finished goods; workers in each type of industry; shopkeepers and artisans; shippers; bankers; and professionals (lawyers, doctors). What were the interests of each in relation to the new market conditions after 1873?

Agriculture, notes Gerschenkron, could respond to the sharp drop in grain prices in two ways: modernization or protection. Modernization meant applying the logic of comparative advantage to agriculture. Domestic grain production would be abandoned. Cheap foreign grain would become an input for the domestic production of higher quality foodstuffs such as dairy products and meat. With rising incomes, the urban and industrial sectors would provide the market for this type of produce. Protection, conversely, meant maintaining domestic grain production. This would retard modernization, maintain a large agricultural population, and prolong national self-sufficiency in food.

Each policy implied a different organization for farming. Under late nineteenth-century conditions, dairy products, meats, and vegetables were best produced by high-quality labor, working in small units, managed by owners, or long-term leaseholders. They were produced least well on estates by landless laborers working for a squirearchy. Thus, modernization would be easier where small units of production already predominated, as in Denmark, which is Gerschenkron's model of a modernizing response to the crisis of 1873. The Danish state helped by organizing cooperatives, providing technology, and loaning capital.

In Germany, however, landholding patterns varied considerably. In the region of vast estates east of the Elbe, modernization would have required drastic restructuring of the Junkers' control of the land. It would have eroded their hold over the laborers, their dominance of local life, and their position in German society. The poor quality of Prussian soil hindered modernization of any kind; in any case it would have cost money. Conversely, western and southern Germany contained primarily small- and medium-sized farms more suited to modernization.

Gerschenkron thinks that the Danish solution would have been best for everyone, but especially for these smaller farmers. Following his reasoning, we can impute divergent interests to these two groups. For the Junkers, protection of agriculture was a dire necessity. For the small farmers, modernization optimized their welfare in the long run, but in the short run protection would keep them going; their interests, therefore, can be construed as ambivalent.

What were the interests of agriculture concerning industrial tariffs? Presumably the agricultural population sought to pay the lowest possible prices for the industrial goods that it consumed, and would be opposed to high industrial tariffs. Farmers selling high-quality produce to the industrial sector prospered, however, when that sector prospered, since additional income was spent disproportionately on meat and eggs. Modernizing producers might therefore be receptive to tariff and other economic policies which helped industry. For grain, conversely, demand was less elastic. Whatever the state of the industrial economy, the Junkers would be able to sell their output provided that foreign sources were prevented from undercutting them. Thus, we would expect the Junkers to be the most resolutely against high industrial tariffs, while the smaller farmers would again have a less clear-cut interest.

Neither were the interests of the industrial sector homogenous. Makers of basic materials such as iron and steel wanted the producers of manufactured products such as stoves, pots and pans, shovels, rakes, to buy supplies at home rather than from cheaper sources abroad. Conversely the finished goods manufacturers wanted cheap materials; their ideal policy would have been low tariffs on all goods except the ones that they made.

In theory, both types of industries were already well past the "infant industry" stage and would have benefited from low tariffs and international specialization. Indeed, German industry competed very effectively against British and American products during this period, penetrating Latin America, Africa, Asia, and even the United States and United Kingdom home markets. Low tariffs might not have meant lower incomes for industry, but rather a shift among companies and a change in the mix of items produced.

Nevertheless tariffs still offered certain advantages even to the strong. They reduced risk in industries requiring massive investments like steel; they assured economies of scale, which supported price wars or dumping in foreign markets; and to the extent that cartels and mergers suppressed domestic production, they allowed monopoly profits. Finally, iron and steel manufacturers everywhere faced softening demand due to the declining rate of railroad building, not wholly offset by shipbuilding. As we shall see, steelmen were in the vanguard of protectionist movements everywhere including Britain (their only failure).

All industrialists (except those who sold farm equipment) had an interest in low agricultural tariffs. Cheap food helped to keep wages down and to conserve purchasing power for manufactured goods.

The interests of the industrial workforce were pulled in conflicting directions by the divergent claims of consumer preoccupations and producer concerns. As consumers, workers found any duties onerous, especially those on food. But as producers, they shared an interest with their employers in having their particular products protected, or in advancing the interests of the industrial sector as a whole.

Shippers and their employees had an interest in high levels of imports and exports and hence in low tariffs of all kinds. Bankers and those employed in finance had varied interests according to the ties each had with particular sectors of the economy. As consumers, professionals and shopkeepers, along with labor, had a general interest in keeping costs down, although special links (counsel to a steel company or greengrocer in a steel town) might align them to a high-tariff industry.

This pattern of group interests may be represented diagrammatically. Table 1 shows each group's position in relation to four policy combinations, pairing high and low tariffs for industry and agriculture. The group's intensity of interest can be conveyed by its placement in relation to the axis: closeness to the origin suggests ambiguity in the group's interest; distance from the intersection suggests clarity and intensity of interest.

Notice that no group wanted the actual policy outcome in Germany—high tariffs in both sectors. To become policy, the law of 1879 and its successors required trade-offs among members of different sectors. This is not really surprising. Log-rolling is expected of interest groups. Explanation 1 would therefore find the coalition of iron and rye quite normal.

Nevertheless, a different outcome—low tariffs on both types of goods—also would have been compatible with an economic interest group explanation. Log-rolling could also have linked up those parts of industry and agriculture that had a plausible interest in low tariffs: finished goods manufacturers, shippers and dockworkers, labor, professionals, shopkeepers, consumers, and farmers of the West and South. This coalition may even have been a majority of the electorate, and at certain moments managed to impose its policy preferences. Under Chancellor Georg von Caprivi (1890–1894), reciprocal trade treaties were negotiated and tariffs lowered. Why did this coalition lose over the long run? Clearly because it was weaker, but of what did this weakness consist?

Political Explanations   One answer looks to aspects of the political system which favored protectionist forces at the expense of free traders: institutions (weighted voting, bureaucracy); personalities who intervened on one side or another; the press of other issues (socialism, taxation, constitutional reform, democratization); and interest group organization.

TABLE 1. Interests of Different Groups in Relation to Industrial and Agricultural Tariffs (Germany)

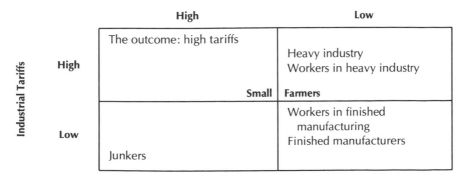

In all these domains, the protectionists had real advantages. The Junkers especially enjoyed a privileged position in the German system. They staffed or influenced the army, the bureaucracy, the judiciary, the educational system, and the Court. The three-class voting system in Prussia, and the allocation of seats, helped overrepresent them and propertied interests in general.

In the late 1870s, Bismarck and the emperor switched to the protectionists' side. Their motives were primarily political. They sought to strengthen the basic foundations of the conservative system (autonomy of the military and the executive from parliamentary pressure; a conservative foreign policy; dominance of conservative social forces at home; and preservation of the Junkers). For a long time, industry and bourgeois elements had fought over many of these issues. Unification had helped to reconcile the army and the middle classes, but many among the latter still demanded a more liberal constitution and economic reforms opposed by the Junkers. In the 1870s Bismarck used the Kulturkampf to prevent a revisionist alliance of Liberals, Catholics, and Federalists. In the long run, this was an unsatisfactory arrangement because it made the government dependent on unreliable political liberals and alienated the essentially conservative Catholics.

Tariffs offered a way to overcome these contradictions and forge a new, conservative alliance. Industrialists gave up their antagonism toward the Junkers, and any lingering constitutionalist demands, in exchange for tariffs, anti-Socialist laws, and incorporation into the governing majority. Catholics gave way on constitutional revision in exchange for tariffs and the end of the Kulturkampf (expendable because protection would now carry out its political function). The Junkers accepted industry and paid higher prices for industrial goods, but maintained a variety of privileges, and their estates. Peasants obtained a solution to their immediate distress, less desirable over the long run than modernization credits, but effective nonetheless. Tariff revenues eased conflicts over tax reform. The military obtained armaments for which the iron and steel manufacturers received the contracts. The coalition excluded everyone who challenged the economic order and/or the constitutional settlement of 1871. The passage of the first broad protectionist measure in 1879 has aptly been called the "second founding" of the Empire.

Control of the Executive allowed Bismarck to orchestrate these complex trade-offs. Each of the coalition partners had to be persuaded to pay the price, especially that of high tariffs on the goods of the other sector. Control of foreign policy offered instruments for maintaining the bargain once it had been struck. . . . The Chancellor used imperialism, nationalism, and overseas crises to obscure internal divisions, and particularly, to blunt middle-class criticism. Nationalism and the vision of Germany surrounded by enemies, or at least harsh competitors, reinforced arguments on behalf of the need for self-sufficiency in food and industrial production and for a powerful military machine. . . .

The protectionists also appear to have organized more effectively than the free traders. In the aftermath of 1848, industry had been a junior partner, concerned with the elimination of obstacles to a domestic German free market (such as guild regulations and internal tariffs). Its demands for protection against British imports were ignored. . . . The boom of the 1860s greatly increased the relative importance of the industrialists. After 1873, managers of heavy industry, mines and some of the banks formed new associations and worked to convert old ones: in 1874 the Association of German Steel Producers was founded; in 1876, the majority of the Chambers of Commerce swung away from free trade, and other associations began to fall apart over the issue. These protectionist producers' groups were clear in purpose, small in number, and intense in interest. Such groups generally have an easier time working out means of common action than do more general and diffuse ones. Banks and the state provided coordination among firms and access to other powerful groups in German society.

The most significant of these powerful groups—the Junkers—became available as coalition allies after the sharp drop in wheat prices which began in 1875. Traditionally staunch defenders of free trade, the Junkers switched very quickly to protection. They organized rapidly, adapting with remarkable ease, as Gerschenkron notes, to the *ère des foules*. Associations such as the Union of Agriculturalists and the Conservative Party sought to define and represent the collective interest of the whole agricultural sector, large and small, east and west. Exploiting their great prestige and superior resources, the Junkers imposed their definition of that interest—protection as a means of preserving the status quo on the land. To legitimate this program, the Junker-led movements developed many of the themes later contained in Nazi propaganda: moral superiority of agriculture; organic unity of those who work the land; anti-Semitism; and distrust of cities, factories, workers, and capitalists. . . .

The alternative (Low/Low) coalition operated under several political handicaps. It comprised heterogeneous components, hence a diffuse range of interests. In economic terms, the coalition embraced producers and consumers, manufacturers and shippers, owners and workers, and city dwellers and peasants. Little in day to day life brought these elements together, or otherwise facilitated the awareness and pursuit of common goals; much kept them apart—property rights, working conditions, credit, and taxation. The low tariff groups also differed on other issues such as religion, federalism, democratization of the Constitution, and constitutional control of the army and Executive. Unlike the High/High alliance, the low-tariff coalition had to overcome its diversity without help from the Executive. Only during the four years of Caprivi was the chancellor's office sympathetic to low-tariff politics, and Caprivi was very isolated from the court, the kaiser, the army, and the bureaucracy.

Despite these weaknesses, the low-tariff alliance was not without its successes. It did well in the first elections after the "refounding" (1881), a defeat for Bismarck which . . . drove him further toward social imperialism. From 1890, Caprivi directed a series of reciprocal trade negotiations leading to tariff reductions. Caprivi's ministry suggests the character of the programmatic glue needed to keep a low-tariff coalition together: at home, a little more egalitarianism and constitutionalism (the end of the antisocialist laws); in foreign policy, a little more internationalism—no lack of interest in empire or prestige, but a greater willingness to insert Germany into an international division of labor.

International System Explanations   A third type of explanation for tariff levels looks at each country's position in the international system. Tariff policy has consequences not only for profit and loss for the economy as a whole or for particular industries, but for other national concerns, such as security, independence, and glory. International specialization means interdependence. Food supplies, raw materials, manufactured products, markets become vulnerable. Britain, according to this argument, could rely on imports because of her navy. If Germany did the same, would she not expose her lifeline to that navy? If the German agricultural sector shrank, would she not lose a supply of soldiers with which to protect herself from foreign threats? On the other hand, were there such threats? Was the danger of the Franco-British-Russian alliance an immutable constituent fact of the international order, or a response to German aggressiveness? This brings us back to the Kehr-Wehler emphasis on the importance of domestic interests in shaping foreign policy. There were different ways to interpret the implications of the international system for German interests: one view, seeing the world as hostile, justified protection; the other, seeing the world as benevolent, led to free trade. To the extent that the international system was ambiguous, we cannot explain the choice between these competing foreign policies by reference to the international system alone.

A variant of international system explanations focuses on the structure of bargaining among many actors in the network of reciprocal trade negotiations. Maintenance of low tariffs by one country required a similar willingness by others. One could argue that Germany was driven to high tariffs by the protectionist behavior of other countries. A careful study of the timing of reciprocal trade treaties in this period is required to demonstrate this point, a type of study I have been unable to find. The evidence suggests that at least in Germany, the shift from Caprivi's low tariff policy to Bernhard Bulow's solidarity bloc (protection, naval-building, nationalism, antisocialism) did not come about because of changes in the behavior of foreign governments. Rather, the old Bismarckian coalition of heavy industry, army, Junkers, nationalists, and conservatives mobilized itself to prevent further erosion of its domestic position.

Economic Ideology   A fourth explanation for the success of the protectionist alliance looks to economic ideology. The German nationalist school, associated with Friedrich List, favored state intervention in economic matters to promote national power and welfare. Free trade and laissez-faire doctrines were less entrenched than they were in Britain. According to this explanation, when faced with sharp competition from other countries, German interests found it easier to switch positions toward protection than did their British counterparts. This interpretation is plausible. The free trade policies of the 1850s and 1860s were doubtless more shallowly rooted in Germany and the tradition of state interventionism was stronger.

All four explanations, indeed, are compatible with the German experience: economic circumstances provided powerful inducements for major groups to support high tariffs; political structures and key politicians favored the protectionist

coalition; international forces seemed to make its success a matter of national security; and German economic traditions helped justify it. Are all these factors really necessary to explain the protectionist victory, or is this causal overkill? I shall
reserve judgement until we have looked at more examples.

FRANCE

The French case offers us a very different political system producing a very similar policy result. As with Germany, the causes may explain more than necessary.
The High/High outcome (Table 1) is certainly what we would expect to find looking at the interests of key economic actors. French industry, despite striking gains
under the Second Empire and the Cobden-Chevalier Treaty, was certainly less
efficient than that of other "late starters" (Germany and the United States). Hence
manufacturers in heavy industry, in highly capitalized ones, or in particularly vulnerable ones like textiles had an intense interest in protection. Shippers and successful exporters opposed it.

Agriculture, as in Germany, had diverse interests. France had no precise equivalent to the Junkers; even on the biggest farms the soil was better, the labor force
freer, and the owners less likely to be exclusively dependent on the land for income. Nonetheless, whether large or small, all producing units heavily involved
in the market were hard hit by the drop in prices. The large proportion of quasi-
subsistence farmers, hardly in the market economy, were less affected. The
prevalence of small holdings made modernization easier than in Prussia, but still
costly. For most of the agriculture sector, the path of least resistance was to maintain past practice behind high tariff walls.

As we would expect, most French producer groups became increasingly protectionist as prices dropped. In the early 1870s Adolphe Thiers tried to raise tariffs
largely for revenue purposes but failed. New associations demanded tariff revision. In 1881, the National Assembly passed the first general tariff measure, which
protected industry more than agriculture. In the same year American meat products were barred as unhealthy. Sugar received help in 1884, grains and meats in
the tariffs of 1885 and 1887. Finally, broad coverage was given to both agriculture
and industry in the famous Méline Tariff of 1892. Thereafter, tariffs drifted up-
wards, culminating in the very high tariff of 1910.

This policy response fits the logic of the political system explanation as well.
Universal suffrage in a society of small property owners favored the protection of
units of production rather than consumer interests. Conflict over nontariff issues,
although severe, did not prevent protectionists from finding each other. Republican, Royalist, Clerical, and anti-Clerical protectionists broke away from their free
trade homologues to vote the Méline Tariff. Méline and others even hoped to reform the party system by using economic and social questions to drive out the
religious and constitutional ones. This effort failed but cross-party majorities continued to coalesce every time the question of protection arose and high tariffs
helped reconcile many conservatives to the Republic.

In France, protection is the result we would expect from the international system explanation: international political rivalries imposed concern for a domestic food supply and a rural reservoir of soldiers. As for the economic ideology explanation, ideological traditions abound with arguments in favor of state intervention. The Cobden-Chevalier Treaty had been negotiated at the top. The process of approving it generated no mass commitment to free trade as had the lengthy public battle over the repeal of the Corn Laws in Britain. The tariffs of the 1880s restored the *status quo ante*.

Two things stand out in the comparison of France with Germany. First, France had no equivalent to Bismarck, or to the state mechanism which supported him. The compromise between industry and agriculture was organized without any help from the top. Interest groups and politicians operating through elections and the party system came together and worked things out. Neither the party system, nor the constitution, nor outstanding personalities can be shown to have favored one coalition over another.

Second, it is mildly surprising that this alliance took so long to come about— perhaps the consequence of having no Bismarck. It appears that industry took the lead in fighting for protection, and scored the first success. Why was agriculture left out of the Tariff of 1881 (while in Germany it was an integral part of the Tariff of 1879), when it represented such a large number of people? Why did it take another eleven years to get a general bill? Part of the answer may lie in the proportion of people outside the market economy; the rest may lie in the absence of leaders with a commanding structural position working to effect a particular policy. In any case, the Republic eventually secured a general bill, at about the same time that the United States was also raising tariffs.

GREAT BRITAIN

Britain is the only highly industrialized country which failed to raise tariffs on either industrial or agricultural products in this period. Explanation 1 appears to deal with this result quite easily. British industry, having developed first, enjoyed a great competitive advantage over its rivals and did not need tariffs. International specialization worked to Britain's advantage. The world provided her with cheap food, she supplied industrial products in exchange and made additional money financing and organizing the exchange. Farmers could make a living by modernizing and integrating their units into this industrial order. Such had been the logic behind the repeal of the Corn Laws in 1846.

Upon closer inspection, British policy during the Great Depression seems less sensible from a materialist viewpoint. Conditions had changed since 1846. After 1873, industry started to suffer at the hands of its new competitors, especially American and German ones. Other countries began to substitute their own products for British goods, compete with Britain in overseas markets, penetrate the British domestic market, and erect tariff barriers against British goods. Britain was beginning that languorous industrial decline which has continued uninterrupted to the present day.

In other countries, industrial producers, especially in heavy industry, led agitation for protection in response to the dilemma of the price slump. Although some British counterparts did organize a Fair Trade league which sought protection within the context of the Empire (the policy adopted after World War I), most industrialists stayed with free trade.

If this outcome is to be consistent with explanation 1, it is necessary to look for forces which blunted the apparent thrust of international market forces. British producers' acceptance of low tariffs was not irrational if other ways of sustaining income existed. In industry, there were several. Despite Canadian and Australian tariff barriers, the rest of the Empire sustained a stable demand for British goods; so did British overseas investment, commercial ties, and prestige. International banking and shipping provided important sources of revenue which helped to conceal the decline in sales. Bankers and shippers also constituted a massive lobby in favor of an open international economy. To some degree, then, British industry was shielded from perceiving the full extent of the deterioration of her competitive position.

In agriculture, the demand for protection was also weak. This cannot be explained simply by reference to 1846. Initially the repeal of the Corn Laws affected farming rather little. Although repeal helped prevent sharp price increases following bad harvests, there was simply not enough grain produced in the world (nor enough shipping capacity to bring it to Europe) to provoke a major agricultural crisis. The real turning point came in the 1870s, when falling prices were compounded by bad weather. Why, at this moment, did the English landowning aristocracy fail to join its Junker or French counterpart in demanding protection? The aristocrats, after all, held a privileged position in the political system; they remained significantly overrepresented in the composition of the political class, especially in the leadership of Parliament; they had wealth and great prestige.

As with industry, certain characteristics of British agriculture served to shield landowners from the full impact of low grain prices. First, the advanced state of British industrial development had already altered the structure of incentives in agriculture. Many landowners had made the change from growing grain to selling high quality foodstuffs. These farmers, especially dairymen and meat producers, identified their interests with the health of the industrial sector, and were unresponsive to grain growers' efforts to organize agriculture for protection.

Second, since British landowners derived their income from a much wider range of sources than did the Junkers the decline of farming did not imply as profound a social or economic disaster for them. They had invested in mining, manufacturing, and trading and had intermarried with the rising industrial bourgeoisie. Interpenetration of wealth provided the material basis for their identification with industry. This might explain some Tories' willingness to abandon protection in 1846, and accept that verdict even in the 1870s.

If repeal of the Corn Laws did not immediately affect the British economy it did profoundly influence politics and British economic thought in ways, following the logic of explanations 2 and 4, that are relevant for explaining policy in the 1870s. The attack on the Corn Laws mobilized the Anti-Corn Law League (which received some help from another mass movement, the Chartists). Over a twenty year period, the League linked the demand for cheap food to a broader critique of landed interest and privilege. Its victory, and the defection of Peel and the Tory leadership, had great symbolic meaning. Repeal affirmed that the British future would be an industrial one, in which the two forms of wealth would fuse on terms laid down for agriculture by industry. By the mid-1850s even the backwoods Tory rump led by Disraeli had accepted this; a decade later he made it the basis for the Conservative revival. To most of the ever larger electorate, free trade, cheap food, and the reformed political system were inextricably linked. Protection implied an attack on all the gains realized since 1832. Free trade meant freedom and prosperity. These identifications inhibited the realization that British economic health might no longer be served by keeping her economy open to international economic forces.

Finally, British policy fits what one would expect from analysis of the international system (explanation 3). Empire and navy certainly made it easier to contemplate dependence on overseas sources of food. It is significant that protection could be legitimated in the long run only as part of empire. People would do for imperialism what they would not do to help one industry or another. Chamberlain's passage from free trade to protection via empire foreshadows the entire country's actions after World War I.

UNITED STATES

Of the four countries examined here, only the United States combined low-cost agriculture and dynamic industry within the same political system. The policy outcome of high industrial tariffs and low agricultural ones fits the logic of explanation 1. Endowed with efficient agriculture, the United States had no need to protect it; given the long shadow of the British giant, industry did need protection. But despite its efficiency (or rather because of it) American agriculture did have severe problems in this period. On a number of points, it came into intense conflict with industry. By and large industry had its way.

Monetary Policy   The increasing value of money appreciated the value of debt owed to Eastern bankers. Expanding farm production constantly drove prices downward, so that a larger amount of produce was needed to pay off an ever increasing debt. Cheap money schemes were repeatedly defeated.

Transportation   Where no competition among alternative modes of transport or companies existed, farmers were highly vulnerable to rate manipulation. Regulation eventually was introduced, but whether because of the farmers' efforts or the desire of railroad men and other industrialists to prevent ruinous competition—as part of their "search for order"— is not clear. Insurance and fees also helped redistribute income from one sector to the other.

Tariffs   The protection of industrial goods required farmers to sell in a free world market and buy in a protected one.

Taxation   Before income and corporate taxes, the revenue burden was most severe for the landowner. Industry blocked an income tax until 1913.

Market Instability   Highly variable crop yields contributed to erratic prices, which could have been controlled by storage facilities, government price stabilization boards, and price supports. This did not happen until after World War I.

Monopoly Pricing Practices   Differential pricing (such as Pittsburgh Plus, whereby goods were priced according to the location of the head office rather than the factory) worked like an internal tariff, pumping money from the country into the Northeast. The antitrust acts addressed some of these problems, but left many untouched.

Patronage and Pork-Barrel   Some agrarian areas, especially the South, fared badly in the distribution of Federal largesse.

In the process of political and industrial development, defeat of the agricultural sector appears inevitable. Whatever the indicator (share of GNP, percentage of the workforce, control of the land) farmers decline; whether peasants, landless laborers, family farmers, kulaks, or estate owners, they fuel industrialization by providing foreign exchange, food, and manpower. In the end they disappear.

This can happen, however, at varying rates: very slowly, as appears to be the case in China today, slowly as in France, quickly as in Britain. In the United States, I would argue, the defeat of agriculture as a *sector* was swift and thorough. This may sound strange in light of the stupendous agricultural output today. Some landowners were successful. They shifted from broad attacks on the system to interest group lobbying for certain types of members. The mass of the agricultural population, however, lost most of its policy battles and left the land.

One might have expected America to develop not like Germany, . . . but like France: with controlled, slower industrial growth, speed sacrificed to balance, and the preservation of a large rural population. For it to have happened the mass of small farmers would have to have found allies willing to battle the Eastern banking and industrial combine which dominated American policy-making. To understand their failure it is useful to analyze the structure of incentives among potential alliance partners as was done for the European countries. If we take farmers' grievances on the policy issues noted above (such as money and rates) as the functional equivalent of tariffs, the politics of coalition formation in the United States become comparable to the equivalent process in Europe.

Again two alliances were competing for the allegiance of the same groups. The protectionist core consisted of heavy industry, banks, and textiles. These employers persuaded workers that their interests derived from their roles as producers in the industrial sector, not as consumers. To farmers selling in urban markets, the protectionists made the familiar case for keeping industry strong.

The alternative coalition, constructed around hostility toward heavy industry and banks, appealed to workers and farmers as consumers, to farmers as debtors and victims of industrial manipulation, to the immigrant poor and factory hands against the tribulations of the industrial system, . . . and to shippers and manufacturers of finished products on behalf of lower costs. Broadly this was a Jackson-type coalition confronting the Whig interest—the little man versus the man of property. Lower tariffs and more industrial regulation (of hours, rates, and working conditions) were its policies.

The progressive, low-tariff alliance was not weak. Agriculture employed by far the largest percentage of the workforce. Federalism should have given it considerable leverage: the whole South, the Midwest, and the trans-Mississippi West. True, parts of the Midwest were industrializing, but then much of the Northeast remained agricultural. Nonetheless the alliance failed: the explanation turns on an understanding of the critical realignment election of 1896. The defeat of Populism marked the end of two decades of intense party competition, the beginning of forty years of Republican hegemony and the turning point for agriculture as a sector. It will be heuristically useful to work backwards from the conjuncture of 1896 to the broader forces which produced that contest.

The battle of 1896 was shaped by the character and strategy of William Jennings Bryan, the standard bearer of the low-tariff alliance. Bryan has had a bad historical press because his Populism had overtones of bigotry, anti-intellectualism, archaism, and religious fundamentalism. Politically these attributes were flaws because they made it harder to attract badly needed allies to the farmers' cause. Bryan's style, symbols, and program were meaningful to the trans-Mississippi and Southern farmers who fueled Populism, but incomprehensible to city dwellers, immigrants, and Catholics, to say nothing of free-trade oriented businessmen. In the drive for the Democratic nomination and during the subsequent campaign, Bryan put silver in the forefront. Yet free coinage was but a piece of the Populist economic analysis and not the part with the strongest appeal for nonfarmers (nor even the most important element to farmers themselves). The city dweller's grievances against the industrial economy were more complex. Deflation actually improved his real wages, while cheap money threatened to raise prices. In the search for allies other criticisms of the industrial order could have been developed but Bryan failed to prevent silver from overwhelming them.

Even within the agrarian sector, the concentration on silver and the fervid quality of the campaign worried the more prosperous farmers. By the 1890s, American agriculture was considerably differentiated. In the trans-Mississippi region, conditions were primitive; farmers were vulnerable, marginal producers: they grew a single crop for the market, had little capital, and no reserves. For different reasons, Southern agriculture was also marginal. In the Northeast and the Midwest farming had become much more diversified; it was less dependent on grain, more highly capitalized, and benefited from greater competition among railroads, alternative shipping routes, and direct access to urban markets. These farmers related to the industrial sector, rather like the dairymen in Britain, or the Danes. Bryan frightened these farmers as he frightened workers and immigrants. The qualities which made him attractive to one group antagonized others. Like Sen. Barry Goldwater and Sen. George McGovern, he was able to win the nomination, but in a manner which guaranteed defeat. Bryan's campaign caused potential allies to define their interests in ways which seemed incompatible with those of the agricultural sector. It drove farmers away rather than attracting them. Workers saw Bryan not as an ally against their bosses but as a threat to the industrial sector of the economy of which they were a part. To immigrants, he was a nativist xenophobe. Well-to-do Midwestern farmers, Southern Whigs, and Northeast shippers all saw him as a threat to property.

The Republicans, on the other hand, were very shrewd. Not only did they have large campaign funds, but, as Williams argues, James G. Blaine, Benjamin Harrison, and William McKinley understood that industrial interests required allies the support of which they must actively recruit. Like Bismarck, these Republican leaders worked to make minimal concessions in order to split the opposition. In the German coalition the terms of trade were social security for the workers, tariffs for the farmers and the manufacturers, guns and boats for the military. In America, McKinley, et al., outmaneuvred President Grover Cleveland and the Gold Democrats on the money issue; when Cleveland repealed the Silver Purchase Act, some of the Republicans helped pass the Sherman Silver Purchase Act. The Republican leaders then went after the farmers. Minimizing the importance of monetary issues, they proposed an alternative solution in the form of overseas markets: selling surpluses to the Chinese or the Latin Americans, negotiating the lowering of tariff levels, and policing the meat industry to meet the health regulations Europeans had imposed in order to keep out American imports. To the working class, the Republicans argued that Bryan and the agrarians would cost them jobs and boost prices. Social security was never mentioned—McKinley paid less than Bismarck.

In 1896, the Republican candidate was tactically shrewd and the Democratic one was not. It might have been the other way around. Imagine a charismatic Democrat from Ohio, with a Catholic mother, traditionally friendly to workers, known for his understanding of farmers' problems, the historical equivalent of Senator Robert Kennedy in the latter's ability to appeal simultaneously to urban ethnics, machine politicians, blacks, and suburban liberals. Unlikely but not impossible: had he existed, such a candidate would still have labored under severe handicaps. The difference between Bryan and McKinley was more than a matter of personality or accident. The forces which made Bryan the standard bearer were built into the structure of American politics. First, McKinley's success in constructing a coalition derives from features inherent in industrial society. As in Germany, producers' groups had a structural advantage. Bringing the farmers, workers, and consumers together was difficult everywhere in the industrial world during that period. In America, ethnic, geographic, and religious differences made it even harder.

Second, the industrialists controlled both political parties. Whatever happened at the local level, the national Democratic party lay in the firm grip of Southern conservatives and Northern businessmen. Prior to 1896, they wrote their ideas into the party platforms and nominated their man at every convention. The Gold Democrats were not a choice but an echo. . . . A Bryan-type crusade was structurally necessary. Action out of the ordinary was required to wrest the electoral machine away from the Gold Democrats. But the requirements of that success also sowed seeds for the failure of November, 1896.

Why, in turn, did the industrialists control the parties? The Civil War is crucial. At its inception, the Republican party was an amalgam of entrepreneurs, farmers, lawyers, and professionals who believed in opportunity, hard work, and self-help; these were people from medium-sized towns, medium-sized enterprises, medium-sized farms. These people disliked the South not because they wished to help the black race or even eliminate slavery, but because the South and slavery symbolized the very opposite of "Free Soil, Free Labor, Free Men." By accelerating the pace of industrialization, the Civil War altered the internal balance of the Party, tipping control to the industrialists. By mobilizing national emotions against the South, the Civil War fused North and West together, locking the voter into the Republican Party. Men who had been antibusiness and Jacksonian prior to 1860 were now members of a coalition dominated by business.

In the South, the Old Whigs, in desperate need of capital, fearful of social change, and contemptuous of the old Jacksonians looked to the Northern industrialists for help in rebuilding their lands and restoring conservative rule. What would have been more natural than to have joined their Northern allies in the Republican party? In the end, the hostility of the Radical Republicans made this impossible, and instead the Old Whigs went into the Democratic Party where they eventually helped sustain the Gold Democrats and battled with the Populists for control of the Democratic organization in the South.

There were, then, in the American system certain structural obstacles to a low-tariff coalition. What of economic ideology (explanation 4) and the international system (explanation 3)? Free trade in the United States never had the ideological force it had in the United Kingdom. Infant industries and competition with the major industrial power provided the base for a protectionist tradition, as farming and distrust of the state provided a base for free trade. Tariffs had always been an important source of revenue for the Federal government. It is interesting that the "Free Soil, Labor and Men" coalition did not add Free Trade to its program.

Trade bore some relation to foreign policy. . . . Nonetheless, it is hard to see that the international political system determined tariff policy. The United States had no need to worry about foreign control of resources or food supply. In any case the foreign policy of the low-tariff coalition was not very different from the foreign policy of the high-tariff coalition.

In conclusion, four countries have been subjected to a set of questions in an attempt to find evidence relevant to differing explanations of tariff levels in the late nineteenth century. In each country, we find a large bloc of economic interest groups gaining significant economic advantages from the policy decision adopted concerning tariffs. Hence, the economic explanation has both simplicity and power. But is it enough? It does have two weaknesses. First, it presupposes a certain obviousness about the direction of economic pressures upon groups. Yet, as the argumentation above has sought to show, other economic calculations would also have been rational for those groups. Had farmers supported protection in Britain or opposed it in Germany and France, we could also offer a plausible economic interpretation for their behavior. The same is true for industrialists: had they accepted the opposite policy, we could find ways in which they benefited from doing so. We require an explanation, therefore, for the choice between two economic logics. One possibility is to look at the urgency of economic need. For protectionists the incentive for high tariffs was intense and obvious. For free traders, the advantages of their policy preference, and the costs of their opponents' victory, were more ambiguous. Those who wanted their goals the most, won.

Second, the economic explanation fails to flesh out the political steps involved in translating a potential alliance of interest into policy. Logrolling does take some organization, especially in arranging side payments among the partners. The iron-rye bargain seems so natural that we forget the depth of animosity between the partners in the period preceding it. To get their way, economic groups had to translate their economic power into political currency.

The political structures explanation appears to take care of this problem. Certain institutions and particular individuals helped to organize the winning coalition and facilitate its victory. Looking at each victory separately, these structures and personalities bulk large in the story. Yet viewed comparatively, their importance washes out. Bismarck, the Junkers, the authoritarian constitution, the character of the German civil service, the special connections among the state, banking, and industry—these conspicuous features of the German case have no equivalents elsewhere. Méline was no Bismarck and the system gave him no particular leverage. Mobilization against socialism did not occur in the United States, or even in Britain and France. Yet the pattern of policy outcomes in these countries was the same, suggesting that those aspects of the political system which were *idiosyncratic* to each country (such as Bismarck and regime type) are not crucial in explaining the result. In this sense the political explanation does not add to the economic one.

Nonetheless, some aspects of the relation between economic groups and the political system are *uniform* among the countries examined here and do help explain the outcome. There is a striking similarity in the identity of victors and losers from country to country: producers over consumers, heavy industrialists over finished manufacturers, big farmers over small, and property owners over laborers. In each case, a coalition of producers' interests defined by large-scale basic industry and substantial landowners defeated its opponent. It is probable, therefore, that different types of groups from country to country are systematically not equal in political resources. Rather, heavy industrialists and landowners are stronger than peasants, workers, shopkeepers, and consumers. They have superior resources, access to power, and compactness. They would have had these advantages even if the regimes had differed considerably from their historical profiles. Thus a republicanized or democratized Germany would doubtless have had high tariffs (although it might have taken longer for this to come about, as it did in France). A monarchist France (Bourbon, Orleanist, or Bonapartist) would certainly have had the same high tariffs as Republican France. An authoritarian Britain could only have come about through repression of the industrialists by landowners, so it is possible a shift in regime might have meant higher tariffs; more likely, the industrialists would have broken through as they did in Germany. Certainly Republican Britain would have had the same tariff policy. In the United States, it is possible (although doubtful) that without the critical election of 1896, or with a different party system altogether, the alternation between protectionist Republicans and low-tariff Democrats might have continued.

Two coalitions faced each other. Each contained a variety of groups. Compared to the losers, the winners comprised: (1) groups for which the benefits of their policy goal were intense and urgent, rather than diffuse; (2) groups occupying strategic positions in the economy; and (3) groups with structurally superior positions in each political system. The uniformity of the winners' economic characteristics, regardless of regime type, suggests that to the extent that the political advantages derive from economic ones, the political explanation is not needed. The translation of economic advantage into policy does require action, organization, and politics; to that extent, and to varying degrees, the economic explanation by itself is insufficient. It is strongest in Germany, where the rapidity of the switch from free trade to protection is breathtaking, and in France where economic slowness made the nation especially vulnerable to competition. It works least well for Britain where the policy's advantages to the industrialists seem the least clear, and for the United States, where the weakness of agriculture is not explicable without the Civil War. Note that nowhere do industrialists fail to obtain their preferences.

In this discussion, we have called the actors groups, not classes, for two reasons. First, the language of class often makes it difficult to clarify the conflicts of interest (e.g., heavy industry vs. manufacture) which exist within classes, and to explain which conception of class interest prevails. Second, class analysis is complex. Since interest group reasoning claims less, and works, there is no point in going further.

The international system and economic ideology explanations appear the least useful. Each is certainly compatible with the various outcomes, but has drawbacks. First, adding them violates the principle of parsimony. If one accepts the power of the particular economic-political explanation stated above, the other two explanations become redundant. Second, even if one is not attracted by parsimony, reference to the international system does not escape the difficulty inherent in any "unitary actor" mode of reasoning: why does a particular conception of the national interest predominate? In the German case, the low-tariff coalition did not share Bismarck's and Bulow's conception of how Germany should relate to the world. Thus the international system explanation must revert to some investigation of domestic politics.

Finally, the economic ideology explanation seems the weakest. Whatever its strength in accounting for the free trade movement of the 1850s and 1860s, this explanation cannot deal with the rapid switch to protection in the 1870s. A national culture argument cannot really explain why two different policies are followed within a very short span of time. The flight away from free trade by Junkers, manufacturers, farmers, and so on was clearly provoked by the price drop. For the United Kingdom, conversely, the continuity of policy makes the cultural argument more appropriate. Belief in free trade may have blunted the receptivity of British interest groups toward a protectionist solution of their problems. The need for the economic ideology explanation here depends on one's evaluation of the structure of economic incentives facing industry: to whatever extent empire, and other advantages of having been first, eased the full impact of the depression, ideology was superfluous. To whatever extent industry suffered but avoided protection, ideology was significant.

7

Selections from *Imperialism: The Highest Stage of Capitalism*

V. I. LENIN

In this 1916 pamphlet, V. I. Lenin offers both an analysis of the world's predicament at the time and a call for future action. He outlines the development of "monopoly capitalism" and the domination of the world's leading countries by finance capital. In order to escape declining rates of profit at home, according to Lenin, capitalists invest abroad with the support of their governments. As more and more land is seized by imperial powers, economic and military competition between the capitalist nation-states escalates. Lenin compares his view of this new phase of capitalism to other explanations. He goes on to describe the characteristics of monopoly capitalism and the process of imperialism intrinsic to it. In this domestic society-centered and Marxist interpretation, Lenin provides an important account of imperialism in the late nineteenth century.

THE EXPORT OF CAPITAL

Under the old type of capitalism, when free competition prevailed, the export of *goods* was the most typical feature. Under modern capitalism, when monopolies prevail, the export of *capital* has become the typical feature.

Capitalism is commodity production at the highest stage of development, when labour power itself becomes a commodity. The growth of internal exchange, and particularly of international exchange, is a special feature of capitalism. The uneven and spasmodic character of the development of individual enterprises, of individual branches of industry and individual countries, is inevitable under the capitalist system. England became a capitalist country before any other, and in the middle of the nineteenth century, having adopted free trade, claimed to be the "workshop of the world," the great purveyor of manufactured goods to all other countries, which in exchange were to keep her supplied with raw materials. In the last quarter of the nineteenth century, *this* monopoly was already undermined. Other countries, protecting themselves by tariff walls, had developed into independent capitalist countries. On the threshold of the twentieth century, we see a new type of monopoly coming into existence. First, there are monopolist capitalist combines in all advanced capitalist countries; secondly, a few rich countries, in which the accumulation of capital reaches gigantic proportions, occupy a monopolist position. An enormous "superfluity of capital" has accumulated in the advanced countries.

It goes without saying that if capitalism could develop agriculture, which today lags far behind industry everywhere, if it could raise the standard of living of the masses, who are everywhere still poverty stricken and underfed, in spite of the amazing advance in technical knowledge, there could be no talk of a superfluity of capital. This "argument" the petty-bourgeois critics of capitalism advance on every occasion. (But if capitalism did these things it would not be capitalism; for uneven development and wretched conditions of the masses are the fundamental and inevitable conditions and premises of this mode of production.) As long as capitalism remains what it is, surplus capital will never be utilized for the purpose of raising the standard of living of the masses in a given country, for this would mean a decline in profits for the capitalists; it will be used for the purpose of increasing those profits by exporting capital abroad to the backward countries. In these backward countries, profits usually are high, for capital is scarce, the price of land is relatively low, wages are low, raw materials are cheap. The possibility of exporting capital is created by the entry of numerous backward countries into international capitalist intercourse; main railways have either been built or are being built there; the elementary conditions for industrial development have been created, etc. The necessity of exporting capital arises from the fact that in a few countries capitalism has become "over-ripe" and (owing to the backward state of agriculture and the impoverished state of the masses) capital cannot find "profitable" investment.

Here are approximate figures showing the amount of capital invested abroad by the three principal countries:

Capital Invested Abroad (In billions of francs)

Year	Great Britain	France	Germany
1862	3.6	–	–
1872	15.0	10 (1869)	–
1882	22.0	15 (1880)	?
1893	42.0	20 (1890)	?
1902	62.0	27–37	12.5
1914	75–100	60	44.0

This table shows that the export of capital reached formidable dimensions only in the beginning of the twentieth century. Before the war the capital invested abroad by the three principal countries amounted to between 175 and 200 billion francs. At the modest rate of 5 per cent, this sum brought in from 8 to 10 billion a year. This provided a solid basis for imperialist oppression and the exploitation of most of the countries and nations of the world; a solid basis for the capitalist parasitism of a handful of wealthy states!

How is this capital invested abroad distributed among the various countries? *Where* does it go? Only an approximate answer can be given to this question, but sufficient to throw light on certain general relations and ties of modern imperialism.

Approximate Distribution of Foreign Capital (about 1910) (In billions of marks)

Continent	Great Britain	France	Germany	Total
Europe	4	23	18	45
America	37	4	10	51
Asia, Africa, Australia	29	8	7	44
Total	70	35	35	140

The principal spheres of investment of British capital are the British colonies, which are very large also in America (for example, Canada), as well as in Asia, etc. In this case, enormous exports of capital are bound up with the possession of enormous colonies, of the importance of which for imperialism we shall speak later. In regard to France, the situation is quite different. French capital exports are invested mainly in Europe, particularly in Russia (at least ten billion francs). This is mainly *loan* capital, in the form of government loans and not investments in industrial undertakings. Unlike British colonial imperialism, French imperialism might be termed usury imperialism. In regard to Germany, we have a third type; the German colonies are inconsiderable, and German capital invested abroad is divided fairly evenly between Europe and America.

The export of capital greatly affects and accelerates the development of capitalism in those countries to which it is exported. While, therefore, the export of capital may tend to a certain extent to arrest development in the countries exporting capital, it can only do so by expanding and deepening the further development of capitalism throughout the world. The countries which export capital are nearly always able to obtain "advantages," the character of which throws light on the peculiarities of the epoch of finance capital and monopoly. The following passage, for instance, occurred in the Berlin review, *Die Bank,* for October 1913:

> "A comedy worthy of the pen of Aristophanes is being played just now on the international money market. Numerous foreign countries from Spain to the Balkan states, from Russia to the Argentine, Brazil and China, are openly or secretly approaching the big money markets demanding loans, some of which are very urgent. The money market is not at the moment very bright and the political outlook is not yet promising. But not a single money market dares to refuse a loan for fear that its neighbor might grant it and so secure some small reciprocal service. In these international transactions the creditor nearly always manages to get some special advantages: an advan-

tage of a commercial-political nature, a coaling station, a contract to construct a harbour, a fat concession, or an order for guns."

Finance capital has created the epoch of monopolies, and monopolies introduce
everywhere monopolist methods: the utilization of "connections" for profitable
transactions takes the place of competition on the open market. The most usual
thing is to stipulate that part of the loan that is granted shall be spent on purchases
in the country of issue, particularly on orders for war materials, or for ships, etc. In
the course of the last two decades (1890–1910), France often resorted to this
method. The export of capital abroad thus becomes a means for encouraging the
export of commodities. In these circumstances transactions between particularly
big firms assume a form "bordering on corruption," as Schilder "delicately" puts
it. Krupp in Germany, Schneider in France, Armstrong in England, are instances
of firms having close connections with powerful banks and governments whose
"share" must not be forgotten when arranging a loan.

France granted loans to Russia in 1905 and by the commercial treaty of September 16, 1905, she "squeezed" concessions out of her to run till 1917. She did
the same thing when the Franco-Japanese commercial treaty was concluded on
August 19, 1911. The tariff war between Austria and Serbia, which lasted with a
seven months' interval, from 1906 to 1911, was partly caused by competition between Austria and France for supplying Serbia with war material. In January
1912, Paul Deschanel stated in the Chamber of Deputies that from 1908 to 1911
French firms had supplied war material to Serbia to the value of 45,000,000
francs.

A report from the Austro-Hungarian Consul at Sao-Paulo (Brazil) states:

"The construction of the Brazilian railways is being carried out chiefly by
French, Belgian, British and German capital. In the financial operations
connected with the construction of these railways the countries involved
also stipulate for orders for the necessary railway material."

Thus, finance capital, almost literally, one might say, spreads its net over all
countries of the world. Banks founded in the colonies, or their branches, play an
important part in these operations. German imperialists look with envy on the
"old" colonizing nations which in this respect are "well established." In 1904,
Great Britain had 50 colonial banks with 2,279 branches (in 1910 there were 72
banks with 5,449 branches); France had 20 with 136 branches; Holland, 16 with
68 branches; and Germany had a "mere" 13 with 70 branches.

The American capitalists, in their turn, are jealous of the English and German:
"In South America," they complained in 1915, "five German banks had forty
branches and five English banks had seventy. . . . During the last twenty-five
years, Great Britain and Germany have invested in the Argentine, Brazil and Uruguay about four billion dollars, which places under their control 46 per cent of the
total trade of these three countries."

The capital exporting countries have divided the world among themselves in
the figurative sense of the term. But finance capital has also led to the *actual* division of the world.

IMPERIALISM AS A SPECIAL STAGE OF CAPITALISM

We must now try to sum up and put together what has been said above on the subject of imperialism. Imperialism emerged as the development and direct continuation of the fundamental attributes of capitalism in general. But capitalism only became capitalist imperialism at a definite and very high stage of its development, when certain of its fundamental attributes began to be transformed into their opposites, when the features of the period of transition from capitalism to a higher social and economic system began to take shape and reveal themselves all along the line. The fundamental economic factor in this process is the substitution of capitalist monopolies for capitalist free competition. Free competition is the fundamental attribute of capitalism and of commodity production generally. Monopoly is exactly the opposite of free competition; but we have seen the latter being transformed into monopoly before our very eyes, creating large-scale industry and eliminating small industry, replacing large-scale industry by still larger-scale industry, finally leading to such a concentration of production and capital that monopoly has been and is the result: cartels, syndicates and trusts, and merging with them, the capital of a dozen or so banks manipulating thousands of millions. At the same time monopoly, which has grown out of free competition, does not abolish the latter, but exists alongside it and hovers over it, as it were, and, as a result, gives rise to a number of very acute antagonisms, friction and conflicts. Monopoly is the transition from capitalism to a higher system.

If it were necessary to give the briefest possible definition of imperialism we should have to say that imperialism is the monopoly stage of capitalism. Such a definition would include what is most important, for, on the one hand, finance capital is the bank capital of the few big monopolist banks, merged with the capital of the monopolist combines of manufacturers; and, on the other hand, the division of the world is the transition from a colonial policy which has extended without hindrance to territories unoccupied by any capitalist power, to a colonial policy of the monopolistic possession of the territories of the world which have been completely divided up.

But very brief definitions, although convenient, for they sum up the main points, are nevertheless inadequate, because very important features of the phenomenon that has to be defined have to be especially deduced. And so, without forgetting the conditional and relative value of all definitions, which can never include all the concatenations of a phenomenon in its complete development, we must give a definition of imperialism that will embrace the following five essential features:

1. The concentration of production and capital developed to such a stage that it creates monopolies which play a decisive role in economic life.
2. The merging of bank capital with industrial capital, and the creation, on the basis of "finance capital," of a financial oligarchy.
3. The export of capital, which has become extremely important, as distinguished from the export of commodities.

4. The formation of international capitalist monopolies which share the world among themselves.
5. The territorial division of the whole world among the greatest capitalist powers is completed.

Imperialism is capitalism in that stage of development in which the domination of monopolies and finance capital has established itself; in which the export of capital has acquired pronounced importance; in which the division of the world among the international trusts has begun; in which the partition of all the territories of the globe among the great capitalist powers has been completed.

We shall see later that imperialism can and must be defined differently if consideration is to be given, not only to the basic, purely economic factors—to which the above definition is limited—but also to the historical place of this stage of capitalism in relation to capitalism in general, or to the relations between imperialism and the two main tendencies in the working class movement. The point to be noted just now is that imperialism, as interpreted above, undoubtedly represents a special stage in the development of capitalism. In order to enable the reader to obtain as well grounded an idea of imperialism as possible, we deliberately quoted largely from *bourgeois* economists who are obliged to admit the particularly indisputable facts regarding modern capitalist economy. With the same object in view, we have produced detailed statistics which reveal the extent to which bank capital, etc., has developed, showing how the transformation of quantity into quality, of developed capitalism into imperialism, has expressed itself. Needless to say, all the boundaries in nature and in society are conditional and changeable, and, consequently, it would be absurd to discuss the exact year or the decade in which imperialism "definitely" became established. . . .

We notice three areas of highly developed capitalism, that is, with a high development of means of transport, of trade and of industry. These are the Central European, the British and the American areas. Among these are three states which dominate the world: Germany, Great Britain, the United States. Imperialist rivalry and the struggle between these countries have become very keen because Germany has only a restricted area and few colonies (the creation of "central Europe" is still a matter for the future; it is being born in the midst of desperate struggles). For the moment the distinctive feature of Europe is political disintegration. In the British and American areas, on the other hand, political concentration is very highly developed, but there is a tremendous disparity between the immense colonies of the one and the insignificant colonies of the other. In the colonies, capitalism is only beginning to develop. The struggle for South America is becoming more and more acute.

There are two areas where capitalism is not strongly developed: Russia and Eastern Asia. In the former the density of population is very small, in the latter it is very high; in the former political concentration is very high; in the latter it does not exist. The partition of China is only beginning, and the struggle between Japan, U.S.A., etc., in connection therewith is steadily gaining in intensity. . . .

Finance capital and the trusts are aggravating instead of diminishing the differences in the rate of development of the various parts of world economy. When the relation of forces is changed, how else, *under capitalism,* can the solution for contradictions be found, except by resorting to *violence?*

Railway statistics provide remarkably exact data on the different rates of development of capitalism and finance capital in the world economy. . . .

. . . The development of railways has been more rapid in the colonies and in the independent or semi-independent states of Asia and America. Here, as we know, the finance capital of the four or five biggest capitalist states reigns undisputed. Two hundred thousand kilometres of new railways in the colonies and in the other countries of Asia and America represent more than 40,000,000,000 marks in capital, newly invested under particularly advantageous conditions, with special guarantees of a good return and with profitable orders for steel works, etc., etc.

Capitalism is growing with the greatest rapidity in the colonies and in transoceanic countries. Among the latter, *new* imperialist powers are emerging (*e.g., Japan*). The struggle of world imperialism is becoming aggravated. The tribute levied by finance capital on the most profitable colonial and trans-oceanic enterprises is increasing. In sharing out this booty, an exceptionally large part goes to countries which, as far as the development of productive forces is concerned, do not always stand at the top of the list. . . .

About 80 percent of the total existing railways are concentrated in the hands of the five great powers. But the concentration of the *ownership* of these railways, that of finance capital, is much greater still: French and English millionaires, for example, own an enormous amount of stocks and bonds in American, Russian and other railways.

Thanks to her colonies, Great Britain has increased "her" length of railways by 100,000 kilometres, four times as much as Germany. And yet it is well known that the development of productive forces in Germany, and especially the development of the coal and iron industries, has been much more rapid during this period than in England—not to mention France and Russia. In 1892, Germany produced 4,900,000 tons of pig iron, and Great Britain produced 6,800,000 tons; in 1912, Germany produced 17,600,000 tons and Great Britain, 9,000,000 tons. Germany, therefore, had an overwhelming superiority over England in this respect!

We ask, is there *under capitalism* any means of remedying the disparity between the development of productive forces and the accumulation of capital on the one side, and the division of colonies and "spheres of influence" by finance capital on the other side—other than by resorting to war?

THE PLACE OF IMPERIALISM IN HISTORY

We have seen that the economic quintessence of imperialism is monopoly capitalism. This very fact determines its place in history, for monopoly that grew up on the basis of free competition, and out of free competition, is the transition from the capitalist system to a higher social economic order. We must take special note of the four principal forms of monopoly, or the four principal manifestations of monopoly capitalism, which are characteristic of the period under review.

1. Monopoly arose out of the concentration of production at a very advanced stage of development. This refers to the monopolist capitalist combines: cartels, syndicates and trusts. We have seen the important role these play in modern economic life. At the beginning of the twentieth century, monopolies acquired complete supremacy in the advanced countries. And although the first steps towards the formation of the combines were first taken by countries enjoying the protection of high tariffs (Germany, America), England, with her system of free trade, was not far behind in revealing the same phenomenon, namely, the birth of monopoly out of the concentration of production.

2. Monopolies have accelerated the capture of the most important sources of raw materials, especially for the coal and iron industry, which is the basic and most highly trustified industry in capitalist society. The monopoly of the most important sources of raw materials has enormously increased the power of big capital, and has sharpened the antagonism between trustified and non-trustified industry.

3. Monopoly has sprung from the banks. The banks have developed from modest intermediary enterprises into the monopolists of finance capital. Some three or five of the biggest banks in each of the foremost capitalist countries have achieved the "personal union" of industrial and bank capital, and have concentrated in their hands the power to dispose of thousands upon thousands of millions which form the greater part of the capital and revenue of entire countries. A financial oligarchy, which throws a close net of relations of dependence over all the economic and political institutions of contemporary bourgeois society without exception—such is the most striking manifestation of this monopoly.

4. Monopoly has grown out of colonial policy. To the numerous "old" motives of colonial policy, finance capital has added the struggle for the sources of raw materials, for the export of capital, for "spheres of influence," *i.e.,* for spheres of good business, concessions, monopolist profits, and so on; in fine, for economic territory in general. When the colonies of the European powers in Africa comprised only one-tenth of that territory (as was the case in 1876), colonial policy was able to develop by methods other than those of monopoly—by the "free grabbing" of territories, so to speak. But when nine-tenths of Africa had been seized (approximately in 1900), when the whole world had been shared out, there was inevitably ushered in a period of colonial monopoly and, consequently, a period of intense struggle for the partition and the repartition of the world.

The extent to which monopolist capital has intensified all the contradictions of capitalism is generally known. It is sufficient to mention the high cost of living and the power of the trusts. This intensification of contradictions constitutes the most powerful driving force of the transitional period of history, which began at the time of the definite victory of world finance capital.

Monopolies, oligarchy, the striving for domination instead of the striving for liberty, the exploitation of an increasing number of small or weak nations by an extremely small group of the richest or most powerful nations—all these have given birth to those distinctive features of imperialism which compel us to define it as parasitic or decaying capitalism. More and more there emerges, as one of the tendencies of imperialism, the creation of the "bondholding" (*rentier*) state, the usurer state, in which the bourgeoisie lives on the proceeds of capital exports and by "clipping coupons." It would be a mistake to believe that this tendency to decay precludes the possibility of the rapid growth of capitalism. It does not. In the epoch of imperialism, certain branches of industry, certain strata of the bourgeoisie and certain countries betray, to a greater or less degree, one or other of these tendencies. On the whole capitalism is growing far more rapidly than before, but it is not only that this growth is becoming more and more uneven; this unevenness manifests itself also, in particular, in the decay of the countries which are richest in capital (such as England).

In regard to the rapidity of Germany's economic development, Riesser, the author of the book on the great German banks, states:

"The progress of the preceding period (1848–70), which had not been exactly slow, stood in about the same ratio to the rapidity with which the whole of Germany's national economy and with it German banking progressed during this period (1870–1905), as the mail coach of the Holy Roman Empire of the German nation stood to the speed of the present-day automobile . . . which in whizzing past, it must be said, often endangers not only innocent pedestrians in its path, but also the occupants of the car."

In its turn, this finance capital which has grown so rapidly is not unwilling (precisely because it has grown so quickly) to pass on to a more "tranquil" possession of colonies which have to be captured—and not only by peaceful methods—from richer nations. In the United States, economic development in the last decades has been even more rapid than in Germany, and *for this very reason* the parasitic character of modern American capitalism has stood out with particular prominence. On the other hand, a comparison of, say, the republican American bourgeoisie with the monarchist Japanese or German bourgeoisie shows that the most pronounced political differences become insignificant during the imperialist period—not because they are unimportant in general, but because throughout it is a case of a bourgeoisie with definite traits of parasitism.

The receipt of high monopoly profits by the capitalists in one of the numerous branches of industry, in one of numerous countries, etc., makes it economically possible for them to corrupt individual sections of the working class and sometimes a fairly considerable minority, and win them to the side of the capitalists of a given industry or nation against all the others. The intensification of antagonism between imperialist nations for the partition of the world increases this striving. And so there is created that bond between imperialism and opportunism, which revealed itself first and most clearly in England, owing to the fact that certain features of imperialist development were observable there much sooner than in other countries. . . .

From all that has been said in this book on the economic nature of imperialism, it follows that we must define it as capitalism in transition, or, more precisely, as moribund capitalism. It is very instructive in this respect to note that the bourgeois economists, in describing modern capitalism, frequently employ terms like "interlocking," "absence of isolation," etc.; "in accordance with their functions and course of development," banks are "not purely private business enterprises; they are more and more outgrowing the sphere of purely private business regulations." And this very Riesser, who uttered the words just quoted, declares with all seriousness that the "prophecy" of the Marxists concerning "socialization" has not been realized!

What then does this word "interlocking" express? It merely expresses the most striking feature of the process going on before our eyes. It shows that the observer counts the separate trees without seeing the wood. It slavishly copies the superficial, the fortuitous, the chaotic. It reveals the observer as one overwhelmed by the mass of raw material and utterly incapable of appreciating its meaning and importance. Ownership of shares and relations between owners of private property "interlock in a haphazard way." But the underlying factor of this interlocking, its very base, is the changing social relations of production. When a big enterprise assumes gigantic proportions, and, on the basis of exact computation of mass data, organizes according to plan the supply of primary raw materials to the extent of two-thirds, or three-fourths of all that is necessary for tens of millions of people; when these raw materials are transported to the most suitable place of production, sometimes hundreds or thousands of miles away, in a systematic and organized manner; when a single centre directs all the successive stages of work right up to the manufacture of numerous varieties of finished articles; when these products are distributed according to a single plan among tens of hundreds of millions of consumers (as in the case of the distribution of oil in America and Germany by the American "Standard Oil")—then it becomes evident that we have socialization of production, and not mere "interlocking"; that private economic relations and private property relations constitute a shell which is no longer suitable for its contents, a shell which must of necessity begin to decay if its destruction be postponed by artificial means; a shell which may continue in a state of decay for a fairly long period (particularly if the cure of the opportunist abscess is protracted), but which must inevitably be removed. . . .

8

British and American Hegemony Compared: Lessons for the Current Era of Decline

DAVID A. LAKE

Analysts often look to the precedent of British decline, which is said to have contributed to international political and economic unrest, in attempting to understand the impact of America's relative decline. In this essay, David A. Lake points out that the analogy is deeply flawed. International political and economic structures were fundamentally different in the two hegemonic eras, as were the specific processes associated with the relative decline of Britain and the United States. Lake summarizes the salient characteristics of the two periods, and on this basis projects a continuation of past international economic openness even as American hegemony wanes.

America's decline has gained new prominence in the current political debate. There is little doubt that the country's economic competitiveness has, in fact, waned since its hegemonic zenith in the 1950s. The immediate post–Second World War era was anomalous; with Europe and Japan devastated by the war, the United States enjoyed a period of unchallenged economic supremacy. As other countries rebuilt their economies, this lead had to diminish. Yet, even in the 1970s and 1980s, long after the period of "catch up" had ended, America's economy continued to weaken relative to its principal trading partners.

Popular attention has focused on the appropriate policy response to this self-evident decline. One critical issue, which cuts across the traditional liberal–conservative spectrum, is America's relations with its allies. Should the United States maintain a policy of free trade premised on broad reciprocity as in the General Agreement on Tariffs and Trade (GATT), or must it "get tough" with its trading partners, demand equal access industry-by-industry to foreign markets, balance trade between specific countries, and retaliate if others fail to abide by America's understanding of the international trade regime? This is a question which all present and future American governments will have to address—and the answer is by no means ideologically predetermined or, for that matter, clear.

The issue of American decline is not new, despite the recent attention devoted to it. It has been a topic of lively academic debate for almost twenty years—a debate which, while not directly focused on such issues, can shed considerable light on the question of America's relations with its trading partners. The so-called theory of hegemonic stability was developed in the early 1970s to explain the rise and fall of the *Pax Britannica* and *Pax Americana,* periods of relative international economic openness in the mid-nineteenth and mid-twentieth centuries respectively. In its early form, the theory posited that hegemony, or the existence of a single dominant economic power, was both a necessary and sufficient condition for the construction and maintenance of a liberal international economy. It followed that once the hegemon began to decline, the international economy would move toward greater conflict and closure. The theory has since been refined and extended, with nearly all revisions concluding that a greater potential exists for non-hegemonic international economic cooperation than was allowed for in the original formulation. All variants of the theory of hegemonic stability suggest, nonetheless, that Britain's relative decline after 1870 is the closest historical analogy to the present era and a fruitful source of lessons for American policy. Many have drawn pessimistic predictions about the future of the liberal international economy on the basis of this comparison, with the implication that a more nationalist foreign economic policy is necessary to halt the breakdown of the open international economy into a series of regional trading blocs. To understand and judge this, one must recognize and begin with the parallels between the *Pax Americana* and the *Pax Britannica* and their subsequent periods of decline. Yet, one must also recognize that the differences between these two cycles of hegemony are just as important as the similarities. The two periods of declining hegemony are similar, but not identical—and the differences have tremendous import for the future of the liberal international economic order and the nature of American policy.

THE HISTORICAL ANALOGY

From the sixteenth to the eighteenth centuries, the international economy was dominated by mercantilism—a pervasive set of state regulations governing the import and export of goods, services, capital, and people. Britain was no exception to this general trend and, in fact, was one of its leading proponents. While restrictions on trade may have been adopted largely as a result of rent-seeking by domestic groups, they also stimulated home production and innovation and allowed Britain to build an industrial base from which to challenge Dutch hegemony.

With the industrial revolution, and the resulting economic take-off, Britain slowly began dismantling its mercantilist system. Various restraints were removed, and by the 1830s few industrial tariffs and trade restrictions remained. Agricultural protection persisted, however, until industry finally triumphed over landed interests in the repeal of the Corn Laws in 1846. Britain's shift to free trade ushered in a period of international economic liberalization. For reasons discussed below, the repeal of the Corn Laws facilitated the rise of free trade coalitions in both the emerging Germany and the United States. Moreover, Britain finally induced France to join in the emerging free trade order in 1860, trading its acquiescence in France's military excursions into Northern Italy for lower tariffs in a bargain which underlay the important Cobden–Chevalier Treaty. Interlocking trade treaties premised on the unconditional most-favored-nation principle then served to spread these reductions throughout Europe.

British hegemony peaked in approximately 1870, after which its national product, trade and labor productivity—while continuing to grow in absolute terms—began to shrink relative to its principal economic rivals. With Britain's decline, the free trade order began to unravel. The United States returned to a policy of high protection after the Civil War. Germany adopted high tariffs in its coalition of Iron and Rye in 1879. France followed suit in the Méline Tariff of 1892.

Just as Britain had used mercantilism as a weapon against Dutch hegemony, the United States and Germany used protection to build up their infant industries, which were then able to challenge and defeat British industry in global competition. Despite a large measure of protectionist rent-seeking by various uncompetitive groups in both countries, this strategy of industrial stimulation was successful. By the late 1890s, the United States surpassed Britain in relative labor productivity and other key indicators of industrial production. Germany also emerged as a major threat to British economic supremacy, particularly in the race for colonies in the developing world.

Despite these threats, Britain continued to dominate and manage the international economy until the outbreak of the First World War. With its industrial base slipping, Britain moved into services—relying on shipping, insurance and international finance to offset its increasing trade deficits. The British pound remained the international currency and the City of London the core of the international financial system.

British weakness, however, was revealed and exacerbated by the First World War. Britain sold off many of its overseas assets to pay for the necessary wartime supplies. As a result, repatriated profits were no longer sufficient to offset its trade deficit. Moreover, the war generated several deep and insidious sources of international economic instability—war debts, German reparations, America's new status as a net creditor nation, and, at least partly through Britain's own mistakes, an overvalued pound.

Eventually, the international economy collapsed under the weight of its own contradictions, despite futile efforts at joint Anglo–American international economic leadership in the 1920s. American capital, previously channeled to Germany, which in turn used its international borrowings to pay reparations to Britain and France, was diverted to the stock market after 1927, feeding the speculative fever and precipitating a wave of bank closures in Austria and Germany. As the banking panic spread across Europe and eventually across the Atlantic, the stock market became its own victim. While the crash of 1929 did not cause the Great Depression, it certainly exacerbated the underlying instabilities in international commodity markets. As the depression worsened, each country turned inward upon itself, adopting beggar-thy-neighbor policies in a vain attempt to export the pain to other states.

The roots of American hegemony lie in the period following the Civil War. With the defeat of the South, government policy shifted in favor of the North and industrialization. By the First World War, the United States had emerged as Britain's equal. The two competed for international economic leadership (and occasionally for the abdication of leadership) throughout the inter-war period.

The United States began the process of liberalization in 1913 with the passage of the Underwood Tariff Act. While pressure for freer trade had been building for over a decade, this was the first concrete manifestation of reform. This nascent liberalism, however, was aborted by the war and the international economic instability it engendered; tariffs were raised in 1922 and again in 1930. The United States returned to international liberalism in the Reciprocal Trade Agreements Act of 1934. While free trade remained politically tenuous throughout the 1930s and early 1940s, it was locked securely in place as the centerpiece of American foreign economic policy by the end of the Second World War.

Like Britain, the United States was the principal impetus behind international economic liberalization. It led the international economy to greater economic openness through the GATT, the International Monetary Fund (IMF), the World Bank, and a host of United Nations–related organizations. The United States also made disproportionately large reductions in its tariffs and encouraged discrimination against its exports as a means of facilitating economic reconstruction. Real trade liberalization was delayed until the 1960s, when the Kennedy Round of the GATT substantially reduced tariffs in all industrialized countries. This success was soon followed by the equally important Tokyo Round, which further reduced tariffs and rendered them essentially unimportant impediments to trade.

Despite these successes, and in part because of them, challenges to international liberalism began to emerge in the late 1960s. As America's economic supremacy receded, the exercise of international power became more overt and coercive. This was especially true in the international monetary arena, where the series of stopgap measures adopted during the 1960s to cope with the dollar overhang were abandoned in favor of a more unilateral approach in the appropriately named "Nixon Shocks" of August 1971. More importantly, as tariffs were reduced and previously sheltered industries were exposed to international competition, new pressures were placed on governments for trade restrictions. These pressures have been satisfied, at least in part, by the proliferation of non-tariff barriers to trade, the most important of which take the form of "voluntary" export restraints by foreign producers. While the net effect of reduced tariffs and increased non-tariff barriers to trade is difficult to discern, it is clear that domestic political support for free trade in the United States and other advanced industrialized countries has eroded.

In summary, during their hegemonic ascendancies, both Britain and the United States played leading roles in opening the international economy. And in both cases, brief successes were soon followed by increasing challenges to global liberalism. The parallels are clear. The historical analogy suggests a period of increasing economic conflict, a slide down the "slippery slope of protection," and a return to the beggar-thy-neighbor policies of the inter-war period.

THE HISTORICAL REALITY

Despite the plausibility and attractiveness of this historical analogy, it is deeply flawed. The similarities between the *Pax Britannica* and *Pax Americana* have overshadowed the differences, but those differences may in the end prove to be more important. The points of contrast between the two periods of hegemony can be grouped into four categories.

I. International Political Structures

In the nineteenth century, and throughout the period of British hegemony, the United Kingdom, France, and then Germany all pursued empire as a partial substitute for trade within an open international economy. No country relied entirely on intra-empire trade, but as the international economy became more competitive in the late nineteenth century all three countries turned toward their colonies. This stimulated a general breakdown of the international economy into regional trading blocs and substituted government legislation and regulations for international market forces.

At the height of its hegemony, for instance, Britain pursued an open door policy within its colonies. Parliament repealed the mercantilist Navigation Laws in 1828 and soon thereafter opened the trade of the colonies to all countries on equal terms. Despite the absence of formal trade restrictions in the colonies, however, Britain continued to dominate their trade through informal means, counting on the ties between colonial administrators and the home state to channel trade in the appropriate directions.

Beginning in the late 1890s, however, Britain began to accept and, later, actively to promote preferential trade measures within the empire. While the earliest preferences took the form of unilateral reductions in colonial tariffs on British exports, by the First World War, Britain, under pressure from the colonies, began to reciprocate. The McKenna Duties, passed in 1915, and the Safeguarding of Industry Duties, enacted after the war, all discriminated against non-empire trade. In 1932, Britain returned to protection and adopted a complete system of Imperial Preference. In short, as its economic strength deteriorated in the late nineteenth century, even Britain, the paragon of international liberalism, turned inward to its empire.

Since 1945, on the other hand, formal imperialism has all but disappeared. Instead of a system of geographically dispersed empires, there now exists a system of sovereign states. As the American-dominated "Dollar bloc" of the 1930s attests, a formal empire is not necessary for the creation of a regional trade bloc. Yet the present international system is less likely to break down into regional economic blocs for two reasons.

As Hobson, Lenin and other theorists of late nineteenth-century imperialism correctly pointed out, imperialism is a finite process, the end point of which is determined by the quantity of available land. Once the hinterland is exhausted, countries can expand only through the redistribution of existing colonies. Thus, the quest for imperial trading blocs transforms exchange, at least in part, from a positive into a zero-sum game and increases the level of economic conflict endemic in the international system. Despite the decline of American hegemony, the gains from trade today are both more visible and less exclusive, helping to make the liberal international economy more durable than in the past.

In addition, colonies are not fully sovereign and have, at best, abridged decision-making powers. As a result, intra-imperial trade and trade agreements are not subject to the same possibilities for opportunism as are trade arrangements between independent states. Today, even if two countries undertake a bilateral trade treaty, as in the case of the United States and Canada, each remains fully sovereign and capable of cheating and exploiting the other. Indeed, as regional specialization expands, the quasi-rents potentially appropriable by either party will also increase, thereby raising the gains from opportunism. The higher the gains and, therefore, the risk of opportunism, the less likely it is that two countries will enter into binding bilateral relationships. As a result, trade blocs between sovereign states will always be more fragile, less beneficial and, it follows, less prevalent than those based upon imperial preference.

II. International Economic Structures

A. The Bases of British and American Hegemony   While both Britain and the United States enjoyed a position of international economic dominance, the bases of their economic hegemony differed in important ways. Britain's share of world *trade* was substantially larger than that obtained by the United States, while America's share of world *product* was far larger than Britain's.

In 1870, Britain controlled approximately 24 per cent of world trade, declining to less than 15 per cent by the outbreak of the First World War. The United States, however, accounted for only 18.4 per cent of world trade in 1950, and its share fell to less than 15 per cent by the mid 1960s. Collective goods theory suggests that Britain had a stronger interest in acting as a benevolent hegemon and, specifically, in regulating and maintaining an open international economy. This interest in providing the international economic infrastructure, furthermore, was reinforced by Britain's higher dependence on trade, which reached 49 per cent of national product in 1877–85 and 52 per cent in 1909–13. For the United States, trade accounted for only 17 per cent of national product in the 1960s, although this ratio has risen in recent years. These figures indicate that Britain also faced considerably higher opportunity costs of international economic closure.

While British hegemony was based upon control of international trade, the United States—still the largest trader of its era—relied on the relatively greater size of its domestic economy. Throughout its hegemonic rise and decline, the British economy (measured in terms of national product) was relatively small compared to its trading rivals, and to that of the United States at a similar stage in its hegemonic cycle. In 1860, Britain's economy was only three-quarters the size of America's. Conversely, in 1950, the domestic economy of the United States was over three times larger than the Soviet Union's, its next largest rival. This difference between British and American hegemony, while highlighting variations in the opportunity costs of closure, also has important implications for the international political processes discussed below.

B. The Trajectories of Decline   Not only were the economic bases of British and American hegemony different, but their respective declines have also followed alternative trajectories. In the late nineteenth century, Britain was confronted by two dynamic, vibrant and rapidly growing rivals: the United States and Germany. Perhaps because of its latecomer status or its geographical position in Europe, Germany was singled out as Britain's principal challenger for hegemony. With the eventual assistance of the United States, Britain defeated Germany in war, and Germany was eliminated as an important economic actor.

The waning of British hegemony thus found the United States and the United Kingdom in roughly equal international economic positions. In the years immediately before the First World War, an economic *modus vivendi,* grounded in substantial tariff reductions in the United States, appeared possible between these two powers. Yet, Anglo–American cooperation and the potential for joint leadership of the international economy were cut short by the war and its aftermath. The breakdown of the international economy during the war created difficult problems of reconstruction and generated high international economic instability, which shortened time horizons in both the United States and Britain and rendered postwar cooperation substantially more difficult. In the absence of such cooperation, the conflicts over reconstruction were insoluble, and the international economy eventually collapsed in the Great Depression.

The decline of American hegemony has occurred primarily through a general levelling of international economic capabilities among the Western powers. Today, the international economy is dominated by the United States, the Federal Republic of Germany, France, and Japan, all substantial traders with a strong interest in free trade, even if they desire some protection for their own industries. The greatest structural threat to continued cooperation is not the absence of partners capable of joint management, but too many partners and the corresponding potential for free riding that this creates.

Despite the instability generated by the oil shocks of the 1970s, moreover, these four economic powers have successfully managed the international economy—or at least muddled through. They have coped with a major change in the international monetary regime, the rise of the Euromarkets, and the Third World debt crisis. The most immediate threats to continued cooperation are the large and, apparently, endless budget and trade deficits of the United States. Barring any further increase in international economic instability, however, even these problems may be manageable.

III. International Political Processes

A. The Three Faces of Hegemony   Elsewhere, Scott James and I have distinguished three "faces" or strategies of hegemonic leadership.[1] The first face of hegemony, as we define it, is characterized by the use of positive and negative sanctions aimed directly at foreign governments in an attempt to influence their choice of policies. Through inducements or threats, the hegemon seeks to alter the international costs and benefits of particular state actions. Economic sanctions, foreign aid and military support (or lack thereof) exemplify the strategic use of direct and overt international power central to this first face.

In the second face, the hegemon uses its international market power, or the ability to influence the price of specific goods, to alter the incentives and political influence of societal actors in foreign countries. These individuals, firms, sectors, or regions then exert pressure upon their governments for alternative policies, which—if the hegemon has used its market power correctly—will be more consistent with the interests of the dominant international power. This is a "Trojan Horse" strategy in which the hegemon changes the constellation of interests and political power within other countries in ways more favorable to its own interests.

The third face focuses on the hegemon's use of ideas and ideology to structure public opinion and the political agenda in other countries so as to determine what are legitimate and illegitimate policies and forms of political behavior. In other words, the hegemon uses propaganda, in the broadest sense of the word, to influence the climate of opinion in foreign countries.

In the mid-nineteenth century, Britain used its dominance of world trade to pursue an essentially second face strategy of hegemonic leadership. By repealing its Corn Laws, and allowing unfettered access to its markets, Britain effectively restructured the economic incentives facing producers of raw materials and foodstuffs. Over the long term, by altering factor and sector profit rates, and hence investment patterns, Britain augmented and mobilized the political influence of the interests within non-hegemonic countries most amenable to an international division of labor. All this was premised on complementary production and the free exchange of primary goods for British manufactures. Thus, in the United States, repeal of the Corn Laws facilitated the rise of a free trade coalition between Southern cotton growers, the traditional force for international economic openness in the American politics, and Western grain producers who had previously allied themselves with the more protectionist Northeastern industrialists. This South–West coalition was reflected in almost two decades of freer trade in the United States, begun with the passage of the Walker Tariff in 1846. A similar process can be identified in Prussia, where the repeal of the Corn Laws reinforced the political power and free trade tendencies of the Junkers. This is not to argue, of course, that Britain relied exclusively on the second face of hegemony, only that it was an important theme in British trade policy and international leadership.

The United States, as noted above, has never dominated international trade to the same extent as Britain, but instead bases its leadership and influence upon its large domestic market. American strategy follows from this difference. Where Britain used its trade dominance to pursue a second face strategy, the United States relies to a larger extent on a first face strategy, trading access to its own market for reciprocal tariff reductions abroad. Accordingly, the United States did not unilaterally reduce tariffs, except for the period immediately after the Second World War, but instead linked reductions in, at first, bilateral treaties under the Reciprocal Trade Agreements Act and, later, in the GATT.

The explicitly reciprocal nature of American trade policy facilitates greater multilateral openness. British liberalization was spread throughout Europe by the unconditional most-favored-nation principle, but free trade remained fragile. As soon as alternative political coalitions obtained power, as in the United States in the aftermath of the Civil War and in Germany in the coalition of Iron and Rye, liberal trade policies were quickly jettisoned in favor of protection. Committed to free trade, Britain made clear its reluctance to retaliate against new protectionism by its trading partners. As a result, it allowed countries like the United States and Germany to free ride on its leadership—specifically, to protect their domestic industries while continuing to take advantage of British openness. The reciprocal trade policy adopted by the United States has brought more countries into the fold, so to speak, by linking access to American markets to participation in the GATT system. This system of generalized reciprocity, as well as the increasing willingness of the United States to retaliate against unfair foreign trade practices, acts to restrain protectionism in foreign countries. Paradoxically, a trade strategy based upon the first face of hegemony, despite its more overt use of international power, may prove more resilient.

B. International Regimes   A second and related difference in the international political processes of British and American hegemony is the latter's greater reliance upon international institutions and international economic regimes. Britain led the international economy in the nineteenth century without recourse to any formal international institutions and with few international rules governing exchange relations between countries. The nineteenth century, in other words, was a period of weak or, at best, implicit international economic regimes.

In the present period, on the other hand, international economic regimes are highly prevalent, even pervasive. The GATT, the IMF, the World Bank, and many United Nations organizations all give concrete—and lasting—substance to America's global economic leadership. As a result, international liberalism has been institutionalized in international relations.

As Robert Keohane has persuasively argued, international regimes are instruments of statecraft and are created to facilitate cooperation, specifically, by (a) providing a legal liability framework, (b) reducing transactions costs, and (c) reducing uncertainty by providing information and constraining moral hazard and irresponsibility. States comply with their dictates, Keohane continues, because of reputational considerations, because regimes provide a service which is of value, and because they are easier to maintain than to create. For these same reasons, Keohane suggests, international regimes are likely to persist even though the interests which brought them into being change. International regimes are thus important because they create more consistent, routinized and enduring international behavior.[2]

To the extent that this argument is correct, the greater reliance of American hegemony on international regimes can be expected to preserve the liberal international economic order for some unspecifiable period, not only in the United States but throughout the international economy as well. America's hegemonic "afterglow" may well be longer than Britain's.

C. Issue Linkage   The "low" politics of trade have always been linked with the "high" politics of national security—the views of certain liberal economists notwithstanding. Military issues have been linked with trade treaties, as in the Cobden–Chevalier treaty between Britain and France in 1860. Trade policy also impinges upon economic growth and the basis for long-term military strength.

The free trade order constructed under British leadership bridged the political divide by including both allies and antagonists, friends and foes. In this system, not only was British influence over its military competitors limited, but the free trade order benefited all participants, often stimulating growth in antagonists and undermining the long-term strength of the United Kingdom. As Robert Gilpin noted, perhaps the most important contradiction of a free trade order, and international capitalism more generally, is that it develops rather than exploits potential competitors for international leadership.[3]

The liberal international economic regimes of American hegemony, on the other hand, have been built exclusively on one side of a bipolar political divide. All of America's important trading partners are also its allies. This provides great potential leverage for the United States in trade issues. America's contributions to the public good of common defense can be diplomatically and tactically linked to liberal trade policies. In addition, the greater benefits derived from specialization and the international division of labor are confined to allies of the United States. All economic benefits, in other words, reinforce America's security needs. As a result, challengers to American hegemony are less likely to emerge. And the United States, in turn, may be willing to make greater economic sacrifices to maintain the long-term strength and stability of the Western alliance.

IV. International Economic Processes

A. The Pattern of Specialization   The nineteenth-century international economy was built upon a pattern of complementary trade. Britain, and later a handful of other industrialized countries, exported manufactured goods and imported raw materials and foodstuffs. To the extent that complementary products were not available within any particular economy, or available only at a substantially higher cost, this system of North–South trade created conditions of mutual dependence between core and peripheral states and, in turn, high opportunity costs of closure. As the Great Depression of the early 1930s clearly demonstrated, the economic costs of international closure were considerable.

The largest and most rapidly growing area of international trade after 1945, on the other hand, has been intra-industry trade—or the exchange of similar commodities between similarly endowed countries. Accordingly, the United States is both a major importer and exporter of chemicals, machine tools and numerous other products. Similar patterns can be found in Europe and, to a lesser extent, for Japan.

This pattern of intra-industry trade creates two important but offsetting pressures, the net impact of which is unclear. First, intra-industry trade has a lower opportunity cost of closure than does complementary trade. The welfare loss of trade restraints on automobiles in the United States, for instance, is considerably less than it would be in the absence of a significant domestic car industry. In short, countries can more easily do without intra-industry trade. Second, the primary stimulus for intra-industry trade is economies of scale in production. To the extent that these economies are larger than the domestic market, and can be satisfied only by exporting to foreign countries, they create important domestic political interest in favor of free trade and international openness. This restraint on protection, of course, will vary across countries, weighing more heavily in, say, Switzerland, than in the United States.

B. International Capital Flows   In both the mid-nineteenth and mid-twentieth centuries, Britain and the United States, respectively, were the centers of the international financial system and the primary source of foreign investment. Both hegemons invested considerable sums abroad, perhaps at the expense of their own domestic economies. Nonetheless, an important difference exists between the two cases. Britain engaged almost exclusively in portfolio investment; the United States relied to a greater extent upon foreign direct investment.

During the period of British decline, a deep conflict emerged between the City of London, the primary source of international capital, and British manufacturers. As the latter found themselves less competitive within the international economy, they began to demand and lobby for a return to protection. The protectionists, or so-called tariff reformers, had grown strong enough to split the Conservative Party by 1903, costing it the parliamentary election of January 1906. By 1912, the tariff reformers dominated the party and, before the trade issue was displaced on the political agenda by Irish home rule, appeared likely to win the next legislative battle. The City, on the other hand, remained solidly liberal. Increasingly, financial profits depended upon new capital outflows and prompt repayment of loans made to developing countries. With an international horizon stretched before it, the City would bear the costs of protection in the form of higher domestic prices and, more importantly, in the reduced ability of exporting countries to repay their loans, but would receive few if any benefits. Where the manufacturers desired to return to an industrially based economy and a trade surplus, the City was content with the reliance on services and recognized the need for Britain to run a trade deficit for the foreseeable future. This conflict lasted throughout the inter-war period, with the City emerging triumphant with the return of pre-war parity in 1925, only to be defeated on the question of protection in 1932.

Until the 1970s, on the other hand, the United States engaged primarily in foreign direct investment. The export of both capital and ownership alters the nature of America's political cleavages, creating intra-industry and capital–labor conflicts rather than an industry–finance division. The overseas manufacturing assets, globally integrated production facilities, and enhanced trade dependence of multinational corporations reduce the demands for protection by firms engaged in foreign investment, but not by labor employed in those sectors. In this sense, the trade interests of multinational corporations are more similar to those of the international financial community than they are to domestic or non-internationalized firms. While nationally oriented firms and labor may still seek rents through domestic protection, the presence of a large multinational sector creates offsetting trade policy pressures within manufacturing and, indeed, often within the same sector, thereby strengthening the free trade lobby in the United States.

WHITHER THE *PAX AMERICANA?*

The differences between British and American hegemony are considerable, and serve to call into question the appropriateness of the historical analogy. The decline of the *Pax Americana* will not follow the same path blazed by the decline of the *Pax Britannica.* Simplistic historical analogies fully deserve the scepticism with which they are greeted. What then is the likely future of the international economic order? Will openness endure, or is closure imminent?

The international constraints discussed above point in different directions. The absence of formal imperialism, the emerging structure of the post-hegemonic international economy, the moderate (so far) level of international economic instability, greater American reliance on a first face strategy of explicit reciprocity, the institutionalization of liberal international economic regimes, the overlap between the security and economic issue areas, and the importance of foreign direct investment, all suggest that international liberalism is robust and likely to endure. The potential for free riding among the great economic powers, the pattern of economic specialization, and the growing importance of intra-industry trade, are the most important challenges to the liberal international economy—and are a source of caution about the future.

While certainly more fragile than in, say, the 1960s, the open international economy has several underlying sources of resiliency. Even though America's economic competitiveness has declined, relatively free and unrestricted commerce is likely to remain the international norm. The international economy is not being held open simply through inertia; there are real interests supporting international liberalism.

This relatively optimistic view of the future of the international trading order supports continued commitment by the United States to free trade and generalized reciprocity as found in the GATT. Japan- or Korea-bashing is unnecessary; other countries share America's interest in maintaining free trade within the international economy. The United States does not carry the burden of maintaining international openness alone.

Narrow policies of reciprocity, which seek equal access industry-by-industry or balanced trade between specific countries, may prove counterproductive, encouraging a decline into bilateralism that will redound to everyone's disadvantage and create the result which pessimists fear. As recent work on iterated prisoners' dilemma shows, cooperation can be sustained best by reciprocating cooperation. To the extent that the United States is perceived as defecting from the open international economy, it encourages similar behavior in others. Economic instability enhanced this problem in the 1920s, but it is inherent in the current system as well.

On the other hand, the United States cannot benefit by being the "sucker" in international trade. It must make clear that the continued openness of the American market is contingent upon similar degrees of openness in other countries. A broad or generalized policy of reciprocity is sufficient for this task, and promises to calm rather than exacerbate international economic tensions.

CONCLUSION

Statesmen and stateswomen undoubtedly base their decisions on theories of international politics, even if such theories are so implicit and amorphous as to resemble nothing more than "world views." No policy is made in a theoretical vacuum. Rather, beginning from selected assumptions or principles of human action, all policy-makers rely upon means–ends relationships and estimates of costs and benefits either derived from or validated by historical experience. These theories can be quite wrong or poorly understood, in which case the policy is likely to fail. Good theories, well employed, lead to more positive outcomes—or at least one hopes they do.

Scholars are an important source of the theories upon which decision-makers base their policies. This is especially true of the theory of hegemonic stability. Developed just as the first signs of American decline were becoming apparent and long before the pattern and its implications were recognized in diplomatic circles, the theory of hegemonic stability has slowly crept out of the ivory tower and into the public consciousness. It has helped spark a debate on the limits of American power in the late twentieth century. It has also led to demands for more aggressive trade policies under the generally accepted but nonetheless dangerous standard of "specific reciprocity."

No theory is widely accepted unless it has some empirical support and intuitive plausibility. The danger is, however, that even theories that meet these criteria may be underdeveloped and inadequately specified by their scholarly progenitors or oversimplified by those who translate academic jargon and subtlety into the language of public debate. The theory of hegemonic stability has been poorly served on both counts, leading to overly pessimistic predictions on the future of the international economy and to far too aggressive trade policies which threaten to bring about the results they are supposedly designed to prevent.

NOTES

1. Scott C. James and David A. Lake, "The Second Face of Hegemony: Britain's Repeal of the Corn Laws and the American Walker Tariff of 1846," *International Organization* 43, 1 (1989): 1–29.

2. Robert O. Keohane, *After Hegemony: Cooperation and Discord in the World Political Economy* (Princeton: Princeton University Press, 1984).

3. Robert Gilpin, *U.S. Power and the Multinational Corporation: The Political Economy of Foreign Direct Investment* (New York: Basic Books, 1975).

III

PRODUCTION

Productive activity is at the center of any economy. Agriculture, mining, and manufacturing are the bases upon which domestic and international commerce, finance, and other services rest. No society can survive without producing. Production is crucial to both domestic and international political economies.

In the international arena, production abroad by large corporations has gained enormously in importance since World War I. The establishment of productive facilities in foreign lands is nothing new, however. The planters who settled the southern portion of the thirteen colonies under contract to, and financed by, British merchant companies were engaging in foreign direct investment in plantation agriculture. Before the twentieth century, indeed, foreign investment in primary production—mining and agriculture—was quite common. European and North American investors financed copper mines in Chile and Mexico, tea and rubber plantations in India and Indochina, and gold mines in South Africa and Australia.

Around the turn of the century, and especially after World War I, a relatively novel form of foreign direct investment arose: the establishment of overseas branch factories of manufacturing corporations. In its origin, the phenomenon was largely North American, and remained so until the 1960s, when European and then Japanese manufacturers also began investing in productive facilities abroad. These internationalized industrial firms were called multinational or transnational corporations, or enterprises (MNCs, TNCs, MNEs, or TNEs), usually defined as firms with productive facilities in three or more countries. Such corporations have been extraordinarily controversial for both scholars and politicians.

There are about 16,000 MNCs in the world. Most are relatively small, but the top several hundred are so huge, and so globe straddling, as to dominate major portions of the world economy. It has in fact been estimated that the 350 largest MNCs in the world, with over 25,000 affiliates, account for 28 percent of the world's output. The largest MNCs have annual sales larger than the gross national product of all but a few of the world's nations.[1]

One major analytic task is to explain the very existence of multinational manufacturing corporations. It is, of course, simple to understand why English investors would finance tea plantations in Ceylon—they could hardly have grown tea in

Manchester. Yet, in the abstract, there is little logic in Bayer producing aspirin in the United States. If the German aspirin industry is more efficient than the American, Bayer could simply produce the pills in its factories at home and export them to the United States. Why, then, does Ford make cars in England and Volkswagen make cars in the United States, and why do both companies make cars in Mexico, instead of simply shipping them, respectively, across the Atlantic or the Rio Grande?

For the answer, students of the MNC have examined both economic and political factors. The political spurs to overseas direct investment are straightforward. Many countries maintain trade barriers in order to encourage local industrialization; this makes exporting to these nations difficult, and MNCs choose to "jump trade barriers" and produce inside protected markets. Similar considerations apply where the local government uses such policies as "Buy American" regulations, which favor domestic products in government purchases, or where, as in the case of Japanese auto investment in the United States, overseas producers fear the onset of protectionist measures.

Economic factors in the spread of MNCs are many and complex. The simplest explanation is that foreign direct investment moves capital from more-developed regions where capital is abundant and cheap to less developed nations where capital is scarce and expensive. This captures some of the story, but leaves much unexplained. Why, for example, does this transfer of capital not take the form of foreign lending rather than the much more complex form of foreign direct investment? And why is most foreign direct investment among developed countries with similar endowments of capital rather than between developed and developing nations?

Economists have often explained foreign direct investment by pointing to certain size-related characteristics of multinational corporations. Because MNCs are very large in comparison to local firms in most countries, they can mobilize large amounts of capital more easily than local enterprises can. Foreign corporations may then, simply by virtue of their vast wealth, buy up local firms in order to eliminate competitors. In some lines of business, such as large-scale appliances or automobiles, the initial investment necessary to begin production may be prohibitive for local firms, giving MNCs a decisive advantage. Similarly, MNC access to many different currencies from the many markets in which they operate may give them a competitive advantage over firms doing business in only one nation and currency. And the widespread popularity of consumption patterns formed in North America and Western Europe and then transplanted to other nations—a process that often leads to charges of "cultural imperialism"—may lead local consumers to prefer foreign brand names to local ones: much of the Third World brushes with Colgate and drinks Coke, brands popularized by American literature, cinema, television, and advertising. However, though these points may be accurate, they do not amount to a systematic explanation of foreign direct investment.

The first step in the search for a more rigorous explanation of foreign direct investment was the "product cycle theory" developed by Raymond Vernon.[2] Vernon pointed out that products manufactured by MNCs typically follow similar patterns or cycles. A firm begins by introducing a new product that they manufacture and sell at home; over time, they expand exports to foreign markets; as the product becomes more widely known, they eventually engage in foreign investment; finally, as production of the good is standardized, they begin exporting back to the home market. This jibes with observations that MNCs tend to operate in oligopolistic markets (those dominated by a few firms); that their products often are produced with new technologies; and that MNCs tend to have important previous exporting experience.

The product cycle theory did not answer all the economic questions, however. For most neoclassical economists there was still no explanation of why firms would invest abroad instead of simply exporting from their presumably more congenial home base, or licensing the production technology, trademark, or other distinguishing market advantage to local producers. In the past twenty years most economists have come to regard the multinational corporation as a special case of the vertically or horizontally integrated corporation. In this view, large companies conduct certain activities inside the firm rather than through the marketplace, because some transactions are difficult to carry out by normal market means—especially where prices are hard to calculate or contracts hard to enforce. Applied to MNCs, this approach suggests that foreign direct investment takes place because these firms have access to unique technologies, managerial skills, or marketing expertise that is more profitable when maintained within the corporate network than sold on the open market. In Reading 9, neoclassical economist Richard Caves surveys the modern economic theories of MNCs.

If the origins of MNCs are analytically controversial, their effects are debated with even more ferocity. In the 1950s and 1960s, as American-based corporations expanded rapidly into Western Europe, protests about foreigners buying up the European economies were common. Most Americans regarded these protests as signs of retrograde nationalism, for Americans have traditionally taken MNCs for granted—few Americans even realize that such firms as Shell, Bayer, Saks Fifth Avenue, Nestlé, CBS Records, and Firestone Tires are foreign owned.

As investment in the United States by firms from the rest of the world has grown, however, a significant body of thought has arisen to argue that this development represents a threat to American control over the United States. Readings 12 and 13, by Cletus Coughlin and Thomas Omestad respectively, present two contending views on the issue: Coughlin sees little or no risk in allowing foreign firms free access to American assets and markets, while Omestad believes that doing so does indeed pose a threat to American sovereignty.

While foreign direct investment is controversial in the developed countries, it is far more contentious in the Third World. Developed nations, after all, have technically advanced regulatory agencies and relatively large economies, while most less developed countries (LDCs) have economies smaller than the largest MNCs, and the regulatory bureaucracies of many LDC governments are no match for MNC executives. In many LDCs, then, the very presence of MNCs is viewed with suspicion. MNCs have been known to interfere in local politics, and local businesspeople often resent the competition created by huge foreign enterprises.

Over the years many LDCs have imposed stringent regulations on foreign direct investors, although most of them continue to believe that on balance MNCs have a beneficial impact on national economic and political development. In the section that follows, the articles by Shah Tarzi (Reading 10) and David Fieldhouse (Reading 11) evaluate the arguments in favor of and opposed to multinational corporations in the Third World.

NOTES

1. United Nations Centre on Transnational Corporations, *Transnational Corporations in World Development: Third Survey* (New York: United Nations, 1983), 46.
2. Raymond Vernon, "International Investment and International Trade in the Product Cycle," *Quarterly Journal of Economics* 80, 2 (1966): 190–207.

9

The Multinational Enterprise
as an Economic Organization
RICHARD E. CAVES

Richard E. Caves, a neoclassical economist, provides a survey of economic explanations of the multinational enterprise (MNE). He focuses on how certain circumstances can make it difficult to carry out transactions in the marketplace. For example, it is hard to measure or establish a "fair" price for assets such as new technologies or managerial expertise. In these cases, firms, including MNEs, can overcome the problems of market transactions involving such hard-to-price assets by carrying out transactions internally, within the corporation. This reading presents the predominant economic explanation for the rise and existence of MNEs.

The multinational enterprise (MNE) is defined here as an enterprise that controls and manages production establishments—plants—located in at least two countries. It is simply one subspecies of multiplant firm. We use the term "enterprise" rather than "company" to direct attention to the top level of coordination in the hierarchy of business decisions; a company, itself multinational, may be the controlled subsidiary of another firm. The minimum overseas "plant" needed to make an enterprise multinational is, as we shall see, judgmental. The transition from an overseas sales subsidiary or a technology licensee to a producing subsidiary is not always clear cut, for good economic reasons. What constitutes "control" over a foreign establishment is another judgmental issue. Not infrequently an MNE will hold a minor fraction of the equity of a foreign affiliate, and we shall see that what fraction of equity a parent holds in its foreign subsidiary is itself an economic decision. Countries differ in regard to the minimum percentage of equity ownership that they count as a "direct investment" abroad, as distinguished from a "portfolio investment," in their international-payments statistics.

The purpose of this study is not to sort the MNEs from the national firms in the world's enterprises. However, the definition does have the valuable function of identifying the MNE as essentially a multiplant firm. We are back to Coase's classic question of why the boundary between the administrative allocation of resources within the firm and the market allocation of resources between firms falls where it does. In the environment of a market economy, entrepreneurs are free to try their hand at displacing market transactions by increasing the scope of transactions handled administratively within their firms. In the Darwinian tradition we expect that the most profitable pattern of enterprise organization will ultimately prevail: Where more profit results from placing plants under a common administrative control, multiplant enterprises will predominate, and single-plant firms will merge or go out of business. In order to explain the existence and prevalence of MNEs, we require models that predict where the multiplant firm enjoys "transactional" advantages from displacing the arm's-length market and where it does not. In fact, the prevalence of multiplant (multinational) enterprises varies greatly from sector to sector and from country to country, affording a ready opportunity to test any models of the MNE that we develop.

The models of the multiplant firm potentially relevant to explaining the presence of MNEs are quite numerous and rather disparate in their concerns. It proves convenient to divide them into three groups: (1) One type of multiplant firm turns out essentially the same line of goods from its plants in each geographic market. Such firms are common in U.S. domestic industries such as metal containers, bakeries, and brewing. Similarly, many MNEs establish plants in different countries to make the same or similar goods. We refer to these firms as horizontally integrated. (2) Another type of multiplant enterprise produces outputs in some of its plants that serve as inputs to other of its plants. We then describe the firm as vertically integrated. Vertically integrated firms, MNE or domestic, may make physical transfers of intermediate products from one of their plants to another, but that practice is not required by our definition; they need only be producing at adjacent stages of a vertically related set of production processes. (3) The third type of multiplant firm is the diversified company whose plants' outputs are neither vertically nor horizontally related to one another. As an international firm, we refer to it as a diversified MNE.

HORIZONTAL MULTIPLANT ENTERPRISES AND THE MNE

We start by equating the horizontal MNE to a multiplant firm with plants in different countries. Its existence requires, first, that *locational forces* justify spreading the world's production around so that plants are found in different national markets. Given this dispersion of production, there must be some *transactional advantage* to placing the plants (some plants, at least) under common administrative control. This is the abstract, static approach that provides the most general and most satisfying avenue to explaining the multinational company. . . . We assume at first that plant A was located in southeast England because that was the lowest-cost way to serve the market it in fact serves. We also assume that this locational choice was not essentially influenced by whether the plant was built by an MNE, bought by an MNE, or not owned by an MNE at all. The static approach also puts aside the vital question of why a company grows into MNE status—something we can explain much better once the static model is in hand.

The transactional approach asserts, quite simply, that horizontal MNEs will exist only if the plants they control and operate attain lower costs or higher revenue productivity than if the plants function under separate managements. Why should this net-revenue advantage arise? Some of the reasons have to do with minimizing costs of production and closely associated logistical activities of the firm. The more analytically interesting reasons—and, we shall see, surely the more important ones empirically—concern the complementary nonproduction activities of the firm.

Intangible Assets

The concept that has proved most fruitful for explaining the nonproduction bases for the MNE is that of intangible assets belonging to the firm. Successful firms in most industries possess one or more types of intangible assets. An asset may represent technology—knowledge about how to produce a cheaper or better product at given input prices, or how to produce a given product at a lower cost than competing firms. This intangible asset might take the specific form of a patented process or design, or it might simply rest on know-how shared among employees of the firm. Or the intangible might take the form of a marketing asset. The firm may possess special skills in styling or promoting its product that make it such that the buyer can distinguish it from those of competitors. Such an asset has a revenue productivity for the firm because it signifies the willingness of some buyers to pay more for that firm's product than for an otherwise comparable variety of the same good that lacks this particular touch. Assets of this type are closely akin to product differentiation, a market condition in which the distinctive features of various sellers' outputs cause each competing firm to face its own downward-sloping demand curve. Once again, the intangible asset may take the form of a specific property—a registered trademark or brand—or it may rest in marketing and selling skills shared among the firm's employees. Finally, the distinctiveness of the firm's marketing-oriented assets may rest with the firm's ability to come up with frequent innovations; its intangible asset then may be a patented novelty, or simply some new combination of attributes that its rivals cannot quickly or effectively imitate.

An intangible asset yields a rent to the time and makes the firm appear successful. But why should that cause it to be multiplant and multinational? The answer lies in the problems of market failure associated with arm's-length transactions in intangible assets. These failures deter a successful one-plant firm from selling or renting its intangible assets to other single-plant firms and thereby foster the existence of multiplant (and multinational) firms. Intangible assets are subject to a daunting list of infirmities for being put to efficient use by conventional markets:

1. They are, at least to some degree, *public goods.* Once a piece of knowledge has been developed and applied at a certain location, it can be put to work elsewhere at little extra cost and without reducing the "amount" of the idea available at the original site. From society's point of view, the marginal conditions for efficient allocation of resources then require that the price of the intangible asset be equal to its marginal cost, zero or approximately zero. But no one gets rich selling his bright ideas for zero. Therefore, intangible assets tend to be underprovided or to be priced inefficiently (at a net price exceeding their marginal cost) or both.
2. Transactions in intangibles suffer from *impactedness* combined with *opportunism.* This problem is best explained by examples: I have a piece of knowledge that I know will be valuable to you. I try to convince you of this value by describing its general nature and character. But I do not reveal the details, because then the cat would be out of the bag, and you would be free to use the knowledge without paying for it. But you therefore decline to pay me as much as the knowledge would in fact be worth to you, because you suspect that I am opportunistic and overstate my claims. With these conditions present, I cannot collect in an arm's-length transaction the full net-revenue productivity of my knowledge. I will underinvest in the knowledge, or I may try to earn the most I can from what knowledge I do acquire by putting it to work myself.
3. An element amplifying the problem of impactedness is *uncertainty.* If the knowledge were the recipe for a truly superb chocolate cake, I could bring about an efficient arm's-length transaction by letting you taste the cake and guaranteeing that (once you have bought the recipe and executed it properly) yours will taste just as good. Conversely, if neither of us can predict accurately how well the knowledge will perform when you use it, and if we are both risk averse, too small a volume of transactions will take place in the intangible knowledge.

Consider what these propositions imply for the MNE: There are seven soap factories in seven countries—each an independent firm. One discovers a way to make its product especially attractive to buyers at little added cost, and its rivals, by assumption, cannot imitate the innovation simply by copying it. The innovator could license its discovery to the other six firms, but would (for reasons set forth earlier) probably be able to collect less than the full net-revenue productivity. It could expand its output and export to the other six markets, but that would incur excessive transportation costs if the plants were all efficiently located at the start (as we assume). The most profitable solution for the seven plants (firms) jointly is to band together into one MNE in order to share the intangible asset. This analysis generates the empirical prediction that we should find a greater incidence of

MNEs in industries where intangible assets are important. Tests of the proposition will be reviewed later. . . .

Scale Economies and Cost Minimization

The theory of multiplant operation has also indicated a number of economies more directly relating to the firm's production activities, and these could apply to the MNE if they do not stop at the national boundary. There may be transactional economies in the procurement of raw materials that go beyond the input needs of the single plant. Economies may arise in the transportation network for outbound shipments of finished goods that extend beyond the single plant's output. Localized demand fluctuations may call for pooling plants' capacities so that several plants' outputs can be flexibly shipped wherever the peak demand is occurring. If the industry's output consists of a line of goods, it may be efficient for each plant to specialize in some items rather than for each to turn out the whole array. It is an empirical question how fully these economies are available to a multiplant firm operating across national boundaries, because they depend on the free movement of goods (inputs and outputs) among plants or the common use of managerial resources. But the hypothesis is there to be tested.

Empirical Evidence

These hypotheses about horizontal MNEs have received rather extensive statistical testing. The usual strategy of research involves correlating the prevalence of MNEs in an industry with structural traits of that industry: If attribute x promotes the formation of MNEs, and successful firms in industry A have a lot of x, then MNEs should be prevalent in industry A. One can analyze the shares of sales held by foreign subsidiaries in a national market such as Canada or the United Kingdom to determine whether or not high shares occur in industries marked by the traits that should give rise to MNEs. One can perform the same exercise by examining interindustry differences in the relative sizes of foreign assets held by companies based in the various manufacturing industries of the United States or Sweden. One can compare the activities of national companies to those of MNEs. Let us summarize the conclusions that have emerged from these studies.

The presence of intangible assets as an encouragement to foreign investment has been affirmed in many studies. Although intangible assets by their nature resist any direct measurement, their prevalence is revealed by the outlays that companies make for the purpose of producing them. As indicators of these assets, economists have seized on the outlays for advertising and research and development (R&D) undertaken by firms classified to an industry. That the share of the foreign-subsidiary assets in the total assets of U.S. corporations increases significantly with the importance of advertising and R&D outlays in the industry has been confirmed statistically in many studies. . . . [T]he influence of advertising appears most strongly in the food and chemicals sectors (the latter includes phar-maceuticals, soaps and detergents, and some other consumer goods), whereas the influence of the industry's research intensity appears strongest in the machinery sectors. This pattern closely matches one's sense of the apparent importance of different sorts of intangible assets in those industries. . . .

Other statistical investigations have dealt with inflows of foreign investment to countries such as Canada and the United Kingdom. Once again, R&D and adver-tising levels, especially when measured in the United States—the principal source country for the foreign investors—are significantly related to the shares of the local market held by the subsidiaries. . . .

Although horizontal manufacturing investments have held the attention of re-searchers, horizontal MNEs have expanded vigorously in banking and other ser-vices as well. The descriptive literature indicates that the intangible-assets hypoth-esis again makes a good showing—especially when expanded to take in an ongoing selling contractual relationship between the service enterprise and the nonfinancial MNE with which it does business. A bank, advertising agency, or accounting firm acquires a good deal of specific knowledge about its client's busi-ness, and the two firms may sustain an ongoing relation based on trust that lowers the cost of contracting and the risks of opportunistic behavior. If the service firm has such a quasi-contractual relation with a parent MNE, it enjoys a transactional advantage for supplying the same service to the MNE's foreign subsidiaries. But the service must be supplied locally, and so the service firm goes multinational to follow its customers.

Much casual evidence reveals this intangible asset of a quasi-contractual custo-mer relation behind service industries' foreign investments. The banking sector's case is particularly well documented. Grubel affirmed the transactional model but also pointed to two other factors. Some banks may acquire particular product-differentiating skills analogous to those found in some goods-producing indus-tries; although these cut little ice in most banking markets, they may explain banks' foreign investments in less-developed countries. Also, national banking markets often appear somewhat noncompetitive because of cartelization or regu-lation or both, and foreign banks are well-equipped potential entrants. The Euro-currency markets can be largely explained on this basis. The traits of foreign banks' operations in the United States affirm these propositions. Their assets in-clude proportionally more commercial and industrial loans than those of their do-mestic competitors, reflecting the primacy of business with their foreign-MNE customers. As they age, they develop other business from this base—drumming up other loan and deposit customers, undertaking large interbank transactions to balance their foreign parents' dollar positions.

Dynamics of the MNE

The transactional approach to the MNE has the advantage that it can explain the dynamic course of development of the firm over time, as well as the prevalence of

MNEs at a given time—the approach we have explored thus far. If the MNE can sometimes seize an advantage to displace a market and reduce transactions costs, the firm itself faces costs of securing information and arranging transactions that shape its behavior. Here we shall set forth some propositions that arise from this fact. . . .

The dynamic transactional approach first makes an elementary point about why MNEs are not ubiquitous. Each person is normally a citizen of some particular country and brings to his business a general knowledge of the legal and social system, the "ways of doing things," peculiar to that nation. The business firm, unless already a mature MNE, has a clear-cut national base and identity, with its internal planning and decision making carried out in the context of that nation's legal and cultural framework. When the entrepreneurial unit extends itself to found or acquire subsidiaries in foreign lands, it must incur a fixed transactions cost of learning how things are done abroad. If it sends home-office personnel to run and develop the subsidiary, they will (for a time, at least) be less effective than at home for this reason. Foreign nationals can be hired to run the shop, but then a similar fixed cost must be incurred to teach them the firm's way of doing things. Either choice leaves the potential MNE facing a virtual disadvantage in the foreign market with respect to its local competitors, who are steeped in their social and cultural milieu and need incur no such fixed transactions cost. The transactional advantages of the MNE are necessary to get it over this intrinsic transactional disadvantage.

The transactional approach also implies that intangible assets are developed by firms in some national market. These assets influence a series of investment decisions taken over time by successful firms, including decisions to begin and expand foreign investments. The approach helps to predict how these decisions will be made. First, the firm that comes to possess some rent-yielding skill or intangible asset cannot overnight undertake all the profitable projects it can find utilizing that asset. Various constraints limit the firm's growth, because there is a limit to how rapidly it can expand its management cadre and its equity-capital base. The firm ponders various strategies for using its distinctive assets so as to maximize the expected present value of its future profits. Suppose that its decisive advantage over (at least some of) its rivals becomes clear when it is a single-nation firm holding 10 percent of its national market. For its next big investment, does it expand into foreign markets, or does it go for another 10 percent of the domestic market? The answer could go either way, but information costs do create a bias toward continuing domestic expansion. This is "more of the same" and does not require the firm to incur new information and search costs associated with going abroad.

If fortune continues to smile on the firm and its share of the domestic market grows, the marginal returns to additional expansion there eventually decline. Given the elasticity of the market demand curve, the higher our expanding firm's market share, the lower the demand elasticity that it perceives. Also, its increasing market share comes at the cost of dislodging stronger and stronger competitors. Expanding to serve overseas markets becomes more and more attractive.

Once investments abroad rise to the top of the list of profitable investments for the firm, the choice of destination should be affected by information costs as they vary among foreign destinations. The first overseas investment is likely to be made in the national market where the entrepreneur faces the least disadvantage of language and culture.

The empirical evidence on patterns of expansion by multinational firms strongly supports these propositions. Horst compared firms within industries to see what traits discriminate between those that go abroad and those not yet holding MNE status. The only significant difference he found was in the size (market share) they had already attained in the domestic market. This result supports the hypothesis that the successful firm runs out its successes in the domestic market before incurring the transactions costs of going abroad. Another strong pattern of evidence bears on the countries that firms pick for their first ventures abroad. For example, U.S. firms tend strongly to make Canada the first stop. Evidence . . . shows that each source country's MNEs pick their debut foreign markets so as to minimize the information and transactions costs associated with foreign investment. The new MNE can easily accommodate to the familiar environment while it is learning the ropes—acquiring knowledge that reduces the cost (or risk) of future expansions into more alien terrain. And its intangible assets provide it with some offsetting advantages at the earliest stages. It can work its plant at designed capacity sooner than a comparable independent firm, and a product innovation borrowed from its parent involves fewer shakedown difficulties for the subsidiary.

VERTICALLY INTEGRATED MNES

It is now an easy step to identify the vertically integrated MNE as simply a species of vertically integrated firm whose production units lie in different nations. Our quest for models to explain the vertically integrated multinational immediately turns to the economic analysis of vertically integrated firms. Again, we suppose that production units are placed around the world according to conventional locational pressures—the bauxite mine where the bauxite is, the smelter that converts alumina into aluminum near a source of low-cost electric power. The question is, why do they come under common administrative control?

Until recent years the economic theory of vertical integration contained only a small and unsatisfying inventory of models. Some dealt with the physical integration of production processes: If you make structural shapes out of the metal ingot before it cools, you need not incur the cost of reheating it. Such gains from physical integration explain why sequential processes are grouped in a single plant, but they hardly explain the common ownership of far-flung plants. The other group of traditional models proposed that vertical integration might be preferable to a stalemate between a monopolistic seller and a monopsonistic buyer. The deduction is reasonable enough, but it hardly explains vertical integration in the many markets that do not represent bilateral monopoly (even if they are less than purely competitive).

Transactional Explanations of Vertical Integration

The great source of enrichment to the theory of vertical integration has been a transactional approach of the same genus we employed to explain horizontal MNEs. Vertical integration occurs, the argument goes, because the parties prefer it to the contracting costs and uncertainties that would mar the alternative state of arm's-length transactions. The vertically integrated firm internalizes a market for an intermediate product, just as the horizontal MNE internalizes markets for intangible assets. Suppose that there were universal pure competition in each intermediate-product market, with large numbers of buyers and sellers, the product homogeneous (or its qualities readily evaluated by the parties), information about prices and availability in easy access to all parties in the market. Neither seller nor buyer would then have any reason (other than personal esteem) to maintain a long-term relation with any particular transactor on the other side of the market. When these assumptions no longer hold, however, both buyers and sellers acquire a variety of motives to make long-term alliances. To retain our emphasis on transactions costs, suppose that parties in the market incur a substantial fixed cost if they shift from one transactions partner to another. Each seller's product may be somewhat different, and the buyer incurs significant costs of testing or adapting to new varieties, or merely learning the requirements and organizational routines of new partners. The buyer and seller have an incentive to enter into some kind of long-term arrangement.

If buyers and sellers are still numerous, however, why should these switching costs impair the operation of a competitive market? The disappointed transactions partner can always switch in the long run. Why does that consideration not keep everyone honest? The answer is that under plausible assumptions it can pay to be opportunistic and try to improve one's deal with an ongoing transactions partner. If everyone knows this, there is an incentive to enter into long-term contracts with terms fully specified in advance so as to avoid any uncertainty and entrapment.

But that effort bumps into another problem with arm's-length vertical relations. Suppose the parties sit down to work out a contract that specifies how each will behave under all possible contingencies and provides policing and enforcement mechanisms that avert the problem of opportunism. Well and good, but the bargaining sessions may be prolonged indeed. The alternative to the uncertainty about how one will fare in an ongoing bargain is the high cost of negotiating in advance a contract that will anticipate every uncertainty and close every loophole. Careful definition of the agreement in advance bargaining saves on the costs of monitoring the agreement and haggling over unexpected developments after it is signed, of course, but only at the expense of greater negotiation costs. There is, as usual, no free lunch.

Internalizing the market through vertical integration at that point becomes an attractive option. Although internal coordination of a vertically related MNE is not without its costs and strains on managerial capacity, it does allow adapting to the flow of events without concern for who benefits more.

To summarize this somewhat complex argument, intermediate-product markets can be organized in a spectrum of ways stretching from anonymous spot market transactions through a variety of long-term contractual arrangements at arm's-length to vertical integration. Switching costs and durable, specific assets discourage spot transactions and favor one of the other modes. If, in addition, the costs of negotiating and monitoring arm's-length contracts are high, the choice falls on vertical integration. These are the empirical predictions of the "transactions" approach to vertical integration.

One other aspect of the theory of vertical integration holds promise for explaining MNEs of this type. Vertical integration can occur because of failings in markets for information, as analyzed earlier in the context of intangible assets. A processing firm must plan its capacity on some assumption about the future price and availability of its key raw material. The producers of that raw material have the cheapest access (and perhaps exclusive access) to that information. But they may have an incentive not to reveal it accurately to the prospective customer; the more capacity those customers can be induced to build, the higher the price they are likely to bid in the future for any given quantity of the raw material. Therefore, vertical integration may occur in order to get around impacted information coupled with opportunism.

Empirical Evidence

The available literature testing these hypotheses has included far fewer statistical studies than has the literature concerned with horizontal MNEs. . . .

A great deal of information exists on individual extractive industries in which MNEs operate on a worldwide basis, and this case-study evidence merits a glance in lieu of more systematic findings. For example, Stuckey found the international aluminum industry to contain not only MNEs integrated from the mining of bauxite through the fabrication of aluminum products but also a network of long-term contracts and joint ventures. All of these indicate a general unwillingness of market participants to settle for spot transactions in bauxite (the raw ore) and alumina (output of the first processing stage). Stuckey likewise did not assign much importance to the small number of market participants worldwide. Rather, the problem is that switching costs are extremely high. That is, alumina refining facilities need to be located physically close to bauxite mines (to minimize transportation costs), and they are constructed to deal with the properties of specific ores. Likewise, for technical and transportation-cost reasons, aluminum smelters are somewhat tied to particular sources of alumina. Therefore, arm's-length markets tend to be poisoned by the problems of small numbers and switching costs. And the very large specific and durable investments in facilities also invoke the problems of long-term contracts that were identified earlier. . . .

A good deal of evidence on vertical integration also appears in the vast and contentious literature on the oil industry. The more ambitious investigations of vertical integration have addressed the U.S. segment of the industry, but there appears to be no central difference between the forces traditionally affecting vertical integration in national and international oil companies. These studies give considerable emphasis to the risks faced by any nonintegrated firm in petroleum extraction or refining. Refineries normally operate at capacity and require a constant flow of crude-oil input. Storing large inventories of input is quite costly, and so backward integration that reduces uncertainty about crude supplies can save the refiner a large investment in storage capacity. It also reduces risks in times of "shortages" and "rationing," when constraints somewhere in the integrated system (crude-oil supplies are only the most familiar constraint) can leave the unintegrated firm out in the cold. . . .

Finally, country-based studies of the foreign-investment process have also underlined vertical MNEs as the outcome of failed arm's-length market transactions. Japanese companies have tended to become involved with extractive foreign investments only after the experience of having arm's-length suppliers renege on long-term contracts, and they have also experimented with low-interest loans to independent foreign suppliers as a way to establish commitment.

Vertical Integration: Other Manifestations

The identification of vertically integrated foreign investment with extractive activities is traditional and no doubt faithful to the pattern accounting for the bulk of MNE assets. However, it gives too narrow an impression of the role of vertically subdivided transactions in MNEs.

First of all, it neglects a form of backward integration that depends not on natural resources but on subdividing production processes and placing abroad those that are both labor-intensive and footloose. For example, semiconductors may be produced by capital-intensive processes and assembled into electronic equipment by similarly mechanized processes both undertaken in the United States. But, in between, wires must be soldered to the semiconductors by means of a labor-intensive technology. Because shipping costs for the devices are low relative to their value, it pays to carry out the labor-intensive stage in a low-wage country. The relationship of the enterprises performing these functions in the United States and abroad must obviously be a close one, involving either detailed contractual arrangements or common ownership. This subdivision of production processes should occur through foreign investment to an extent that depends again on the transactional bases for vertical integration. Some theoretical models have suggested that this type of vertical dis-integration proceeds as an industry enlarges, permitting real gains from an expanded division of labor as more and more separable processes are carried out by firms specializing in them. The model probably is applicable to the type of foreign investment just described. The gains from an expanded division of labor . . . may depend on the geographical dispersion of production processes to specialized establishments and may have little to do with the form of transactions between the specialized establishments (spot, contract, or vertical MNE relationships).

Writers on the rapid expansion of offshore procurement and the associated international trade always refer to the role of foreign investment in transplanting the necessary know-how and managerial coordination. Jarrett has explored statistically both the structural determinants of this type of trade and the role of MNEs in carrying it out. His data pertain to imports under a provision of the U.S. tariff whereby components exported from the United States for additional fabrication abroad can be reimported with duty paid only on the value added abroad; his statistical analysis addresses both the total value of imports of such articles and the value added abroad. Furthermore, the analysis explains how these activities vary both among U.S. industries and among countries taking part in this trade. His results confirm the expected properties of the industries that make use of vertically dis-integrated production: Their outputs have high value per unit of weight, possess reasonably mature technology (so are out of the experimental stage), are produced in the United States under conditions giving rise to high labor costs, and are easily subject to decentralized production. Among overseas countries, U.S. offshore procurement favors those not too far distant (transportation costs) and with low wages and favorable working conditions. With these factors controlled, there is a positive relation of the component flows to the extent of U.S. foreign investment, both among industries and among foreign countries.

A considerable amount of vertical integration is also involved in the "horizontal" foreign investments described earlier in this chapter, and we shall see that the behavior of horizontal MNEs cannot be fully understood without recognizing the complementary vertical aspects of their domestic and foreign operations. Often the foreign subsidiary does not just produce the parent's good for the local market; it processes semifinished units of that good, or it packages or assembles them according to local specifications. Pharmaceuticals, for example, are prepared in the locally desired formulations using basic preparations imported from the parent. The subsidiary organizes a distribution system in the host-country market, distributing partly its own production, but with its line of goods filled out with imports from its parent or other affiliates. Or the subsidiary integrates forward to provide local servicing facilities of information and customer service. These activities are bound up with the development and maintenance of the enterprise's goodwill asset, as described earlier, through a commitment of resources to the local market. The firm can thereby assure local customers, who are likely to incur fixed investments of their own in shifting their purchases to the MNE, that the company's presence is not transitory; because the MNE has sunk some costs locally, it will continue even in the face of some adverse disturbances. This consideration helps explain foreign investment in some producer-goods industries for which the intangible-assets hypothesis otherwise seems rather dubious. All of these activities represent types of forward integration by the MNE, whether into final-stage processing of its goods or into ancillary services.

The evidence of this confluence of vertical and horizontal foreign investments mainly takes the form of casual descriptions rather than systematic data. . . . It is implied by the available data on the extent of intracorporate trade among MNE affiliates—flows that would be incompatible with purely horizontal forms of intracorporate relationships. We can, for example, turn to data on imports of finished goods by Dutch subsidiaries from their U.S. parents. These were high as percentages of the affiliates' total sales in just those sectors where imports might complement local production for filling out a sales line—chemicals (24.9 percent), electrical equipment (35.4 percent), and transportation equipment (65.5 percent). The prevalence of intracorporate trade in engineering industries also suggests the importance of components shipments.

Recently, some statistical evidence has appeared on U.S. exports and imports passing between corporate affiliates that sheds light on this mixture of vertical and horizontal foreign investment. Lall analyzed the factors determining the extent of U.S. MNEs' exports to their affiliates (normalized either by their total exports or by their affiliates' total production). He could not discriminate between two hypotheses, although he concluded that they jointly have significant force: (1) that trade is internalized where highly innovative and specialized goods are involved and (2) that trade is internalized where the ultimate sales to final buyers must be attended by extensive customer engineering and after-sales services. Jarrett confirmed these hypotheses with respect to the importance in U.S. imports of the interaffiliate component, which in his data includes exports by foreign MNEs to their manufacturing and marketing subsidiaries in the United States as well as imports by U.S. MNEs from their overseas affiliates. Jarrett also found evidence that interaffiliate trade in manufactures reflects several conventional forms of vertical integration: More of it occurs in industries populated (in the United States) by large plants and companies, capable of meeting the scale-economy problems that arise in the international dis-integration of production, and in industries that carry out extensive multiplant operations in the United States. . . .

PORTFOLIO DIVERSIFICATION AND THE DIVERSIFIED MNE

The formal purpose of this section is to complete the roster of international multiplant firms by accounting for those whose international plants have neither a horizontal nor a vertical relationship. An obvious explanation of this type of MNE (though not the only one, it turns out) lies in the goal of spreading business risks. Going multinational in any form brings some diversification gains to the enterprise, and these reach their maximum when the firm diversifies across "product space" as well as geographical space.

The hypothesis that companies act to avoid risks may seem obvious, but it requires some explanation. The risk-averse investor generally must choose between investments involving greater risks and higher expected returns and those involving lesser risks and lower expected returns (somebody else has already seized any high-return low-risk options). Because foreign investment itself usually is supposed to be a risky activity, the risk-averse business would be expected to avoid it. However, that conjecture neglects the process of diversification. Pool the cash-flow streams from two risky projects, and the uncertainty of the combined stream is almost always less than the uncertainty of either stream separately. The reduction demands only that the expected returns of the two projects be imperfectly correlated: Among various possible states of nature, A and B do not always have their ups and downs at the same time. A has the greatest diversification value for B if A's ups coincide with B's downs and vice versa, but some diversification is achieved whenever they are not perfectly correlated. As an explanation of MNEs, this analysis suggests quite simply that the risk-averse corporation may find that plants operated in different countries offer good prospects for diversification. . . .

Now we can assess diversification as a motive for the MNE. Within national economies, many shocks affect all firms rather similarly—recessions, major changes in government policy. Between countries, such disturbances are more nearly un-correlated, creating opportunities for international diversification. Also, changes in exchange rates and terms of trade tend to favor business profits in one country while worsening them elsewhere. Statistical evidence confirms that MNEs enjoy diversification gains: The larger the share of foreign operations in total sales, the lower the variability of the firm's rate of return on equity capital. . . .

None of this evidence, it should be stressed, directly affirms the hypothesis that diversified foreign investment has a premium value for risk spreading. However, risk spreading is not inconsistent with any of the positive influences on diversified foreign investment that have been uncovered. And those influences account for only a small proportion of the observed diversified foreign investment, leaving plenty of room for risk spreading, and other influences yet unidentified.

SUMMARY

The existence of the MNE is best explained by identifying it as a multiplant firm that sprawls across national boundaries, then applying the transactional approach to explain why decentralized plants should fall under common ownership and con-trol rather than simply trade with each other (and with other agents) on the open market. This approach is readily applied to the horizontal MNE (its national branches produce largely the same products), because the economies of multiplant operation can be identified with use of the firm's intangible assets, which suffer many infirmities for trade at arm's length. This hypothesis receives strong support in statistical studies, which also identify an influence of other "excess capacities" in the firm, such as managerial skills.

A second major type of MNE is the vertically integrated firm, and several eco-nomic models of vertical integration stand ready to explain its existence. Once again, the transactional approach holds a good deal of power, because vertical MNEs in the natural-resources sector seem to respond to the difficulties of work-ing out arm's-length contracts in small-numbers situations where each party has a durable and specific investment at stake. Evading problems of impacted informa-tion also seems to explain some vertical foreign investment. The approach also works well to explain the rapid growth of offshore procurement by firms in indus-trial countries, which involves carrying out labor-intensive stages of production at low-wage foreign locations. Although some procurement occurs through arm's-length contracts rather than foreign investment, the foreign-investment proportion is clearly large. Finally, numerous vertical transactions flow between the members of apparently horizontal MNEs as the foreign subsidiary undertakes final fabrication, fills out its line with imports from its corporate affiliates, or provides ancillary services that complement these imports.

Diversified foreign investments, which have grown rapidly in recent decades, suggest the use of foreign investment as a means of spreading risks to the firm. Foreign investment, whether diversified from the parent's domestic product line or not, does apparently offer some diversification value. Diversified foreign investments can be explained in part by the parent's efforts to utilize its diverse R&D discoveries, and certain other influences as well. But the evidence at hand does not specifically tie diversified foreign investment to the corporate motive of spreading risks through diversification among both products and national markets.

10

Third World Governments and Multinational Corporations: Dynamics of Host's Bargaining Power

SHAH M. TARZI

Shah M. Tarzi examines the bargaining relationship between Third World host governments and multinational firms. While host governments seek to encourage firms to locate within their countries on the best terms possible, MNCs want to minimize the conditions and restrictions the host government is able to impose on their operations. Tarzi identifies several factors that affect the bargaining power of the host government. He distinguishes between factors that influence the potential power of the state, such as its managerial skills, and those that affect the ability of the state to exercise its bargaining power. Actual power, as he terms it, is determined by societal pressures the host government faces, the strategy of the MNC, and the international pressures from the MNC's home government.

INTRODUCTION

In their economic relationships with multinational corporations, Third World countries would seem to have the critical advantage, inasmuch as they control access to their own territory. That access includes internal markets, the local labour supplies, investment opportunities, sources of raw materials, and other resources that multinational firms need or desire. In practical terms, however, this apparent bargaining advantage on the part of the host nation, in most instances, is greatly surpassed by the superior advantages of the multinationals. Multinational

Shah M. Tarzi. "Third World Governments and Multinational Corporations: Dynamics of Host's Bargaining Power." This first appeared as an article in *International Relations,* vol. X, no. 3, May 1991, pp. 237–49. Reprinted by permission of The David Davies Memorial Institute of International Studies.

corporations possess the required capital, technology, managerial skills, access to world markets, and other resources that governments in the Third World need or wish to obtain for purposes of economic development.

In addition to firm-specific assets—technology, managerial skills, capital and access to markets—the economic power of the multinationals grows out of a combination of additional factors. First, foreign investment accounts for large percentages of the total stock of local investment, local production and sales. Secondly, multinationals tend to dominate key sectors of the economy that are critical to the host states' economic development. Thirdly, multinationals usually prevail in the highly concentrated industries in the Third World—petroleum, aluminum, chemicals, transportation, food products and machinery. This economic concentration in single industries gives the multinational firms oligopoly power, allowing them to monopolize and control supply and price in a way that does not occur in more competitive industries.

In the first decade and a half after World War II, the multinational corporations were so powerful that they could essentially prevent any challenges to their dominance from host governments. The unique position they held as the sole source of capital, technology and managerial expertise for the Third World states gave them special negotiating advantages. Third World governments in their developing state could not easily duplicate the skills of the corporations, and when they did attempt to bypass the assistance of the multinationals, the cost to them in reduced efficiency was extremely high. Furthermore, the exposure of individual corporations was low, except for corporations in natural resources, plantations and utilities. In Latin America and the Middle East, where most of direct foreign investment in raw materials was concentrated, long-term concession contracts protected companies from immediate risk exposure. Host countries could neither remove nor replace them without sustaining enormous costs to their economies. Thus, the multinationals were usually able to exercise de facto sovereign power over the pricing and marketing of output.

Nevertheless, despite the colossal power of the multinational corporations, the historic trend has been one of increasing ascendance of Third World host states. By the 1960s the multinationals were facing pressure from the host states to make substantial contributions to the long-term goals of economic development. Regarding foreign investment in natural resources, for example, ownership and control over raw material production was transferred to OPEC members. In the process, the Seven Sisters (the major oil companies) were relegated from their positions of independence and dominance to the role of junior partners of host governments in the Middle East. Similarly, in manufacturing there is a visible trend toward a sharing of ownership and control in foreign manufacturing ventures.

Several factors help to explain the relative ascendancy or improved position of some Third World host states with respect to their relationships with multinationals. A number of changes have increased the bargaining power of the Third World countries. And in addition to favourable changes in their bargaining power, other constraining factors in both domestic and international environments of the host countries have been eased, improving the ability of the hosts to exact better terms from the multinational corporations.

THIRD WORLD GOVERNMENTS: DYNAMICS OF POTENTIAL BARGAINING POWER

In order to examine the extent to which host states in the Third World can influence the behaviour of multinational corporations, we call attention to the distinction between potential power and actual power (the power to exercise or implement).

Potential power connotes the relative bargaining power of the host state which is dependent upon: (1) the level of the host government's expertise, (2) the degree of competition among multinationals, (3) the type of direct foreign investment, and (4) the degree or extent of prevailing economic uncertainty.

Actual power, on the other hand, may be defined as the ability and willingness of host governments to exercise their bargaining power in order to extract more favourable terms from foreign firms. Domestic factors, including host country politics, along with international factors, such as foreign political and economic coercion, constrain Third World host states in their efforts to translate potential bargaining power into power that engenders favourable outcomes with foreign investors. These domestic and international factors act as a wedge between potential and actual power. The dynamics of potential bargaining power for the Third World governments is examined below.

Level of Host's Expertise

Most host states have antiquated government structures and inadequate laws for collecting taxes and controlling foreign business. These institutional weaknesses impair the ability of host states in their negotiations with multinational corporations. Shortages of competent, trained and independent administrators exacerbate these institutional problems and make it difficult for host states to manage multinationals and monitor their behaviour. . . .

The trend, however, has been toward tougher laws in the host countries. Frequently, the host countries become dependent upon the revenue generated by foreign investors in order to finance government services and meet domestic requirements for employment. In turn, the desire for economic growth produces certain incentives within host states to strengthen their administrative expertise in international tax law, corporate accounting and industrial analysis. Thus, the development of economic and financial skills in host states is facilitated by the need to monitor multinational corporations and negotiate with them more effectively. Over time, therefore, host countries have developed or acquired many of the managerial skills which had long been employed by the multinationals as bargaining tools. By improving their expertise and capacity to monitor the corporations more closely, some host states were able to renegotiate terms when conditions permitted. The development of producer cartels also created a strong impetus for improving expertise within host countries to manage multinationals better. . . . Multinational corporations can be expected to regain their bargaining advantage vis-à-vis a Third World government, however, when certain conditions arise: (1) the rate of change in technological complexity of the foreign investment regime grows faster relative to the host country's capabilities and rate of innovations; and/or (2) if the optimum scale of the investment regime expands so as to make it extremely difficult for the host government to manage it, in spite of initial strides in managerial expertise.

Both technological and managerial complexity for developing products or extracting resources correlate positively with bargaining power for the multinational corporations. Nevertheless, during the last two decades, the cumulative effect of improvement in the host countries' expertise has resulted in a relative tightening of terms with respect to direct foreign investment. This phenomenon has resulted in a relative improvement in Third World governments' bargaining positions.

Level of Competition for Investment Opportunities

Competition among multinational corporations for investment opportunities in a Third World country also affects the bargaining power of host countries. Essentially, a lack of competition among multinationals predicts a weak bargaining position for the host country. Conversely, increased competition is likely to improve the bargaining power of the host government. Competition among multinationals is likely to be greater where a host country provides a cheap source of needed labour and also functions as an "export platform" when the purpose of the investment project is to serve external markets. Competition for investment projects is likely to be limited, however, when projects are both capital intensive and designed to serve only local markets.

During the 1950s and 1960s, the absence of competition for investment opportunities served to diminish the bargaining power of host states in the Third World. The availability of alternative sources of raw materials and the existence of cheap labour elsewhere also work together to weaken the bargaining power of any individual country. In the last two decades, the spread of multinational corporations of diverse national origins (American, Japanese, European) has provided host countries with alternatives. In the international oil industry, for example, host countries have successfully used competition among multinationals to increase revenues from oil production. As a case in point, J. Paul Getty's Pacific Western Oil Company upset the stability of other corporations' agreements when it acquired an oil concession in Saudi Arabia by offering larger tax payments than the established oil companies were then willing to pay.

The option of choice from several willing foreign investors is extremely important to a host country. The ability to choose allows a host state to avoid the concentration of investment from one traditionally dominant Western country. Thus, for instance, Japanese multinationals have emerged as an alternative to US firms in Latin America, and American firms have, in turn, emerged as an alternative to French firms in Africa.

If competition were to intensify among the multinational corporations for the resources of Third World countries and host governments' ability to manage and monitor multinationals were to improve, it is likely that host nations would pay less than before for services provided by the corporations.

Economic Uncertainty and the Obsolescing Bargain

Uncertainty about the success of a particular foreign investment project, its final cost, and the desire of a host country to attract investment create a marked asymmetry of power favouring the multinational corporations. During this initial phase, the host country must pursue permissive investment policies with the corporations. But as uncertainty decreases and the investment projects become successful, the multinational's initial bargaining advantage begins to erode. Invested fixed capital becomes "sunk," a hostage to and a source of the host country's bargaining strength as it acquires jurisdiction over valuable foreign assets. The foreign firm's financial commitment to assets located in host nations weakens the bargaining advantage it enjoyed at the beginning of the investment cycle. Consequently, when the bargaining advantage begins to shift to the host state, the initial agreements that favoured the multinationals are renegotiated.

In manufacturing, high technology, and services ventures, the probability of obsolescence is extremely low. Multinational corporations in natural resources, on the other hand, are most vulnerable. . . .

This paradigm interprets the interaction between multinational corporations and host countries as a dynamic process. Furthermore, given the level of economic uncertainty for both parties, the interests of host countries and foreign investors are likely to diverge. The two parties then become antagonists. Gradually, a change in the bargaining advantages on the side of the multinational shift to that of the host country. The developments that follow may result in the renegotiation by the government of the initial concession agreement.

Characteristics of the Foreign Investment Project

As noted earlier, the probability of obsolescence is, to a large extent, a function of the foreign investment assets. Thus, the bargaining power or negotiating ability of a host country substantially depends on the type of direct foreign investment that is involved. Characteristics of the foreign investment project affecting the outcome of the bargaining process are: (1) absolute size of fixed investment; (2) ratio of fixed to variable costs; (3) the level of technological complexity of the foreign investment regime; and (4) the degree of marketing complexity.

Those foreign investment projects which do not require high fixed investments have a low fixed-to-relative cost ratio. Based on changeable technology and marketing complexity, they are less vulnerable to the dynamics of obsolescing bargaining than are foreign investment projects having high fixed costs, slowly changing technology and undifferentiated project lines. Investment projects in natural resources, plantation agriculture and utilities fall into this group. Once the investment is sunk and the project becomes profitable, foreign firms may be exposed to the threat of nationalization or, more likely, the renegotiation of the original terms of investment.

Knowing these economic and political risks, multinational corporations would not commit large sums of money unless they were likely to get extremely generous terms. These "over-generous" terms to which the host country initially agrees often become a major source of national discontent and resentment against the foreign firm.

In manufacturing, where marketing skills are complex and products differentiated, foreign corporations have considerable flexibility in their response to the host country's demands. In order to counter the demands of the host government, these firms can diversify product lines, move to a new activity such as export, incorporate additional technology, or threaten to withdraw their operation altogether.

Corporations in the vanguard of scientific and technological development such as computers or electronics have only recently begun to penetrate Third World economies. This group is especially immune to the obsolescing bargain. The pace and complexity of research and development (R & D) in computers and electronics is, for the most part, beyond the capability and geographic reach of any of the host governments in the Third World.

Constraints on the Exercise of Power: Implementation

The literature on bargaining provides a prevailing conceptual framework of bilateral monopoly to describe Third World–multinational corporation interaction. According to this model, the distribution of benefits between multinationals and Third World countries is a function of relative power. It is assumed that power is a function of the demand of each party for resources that the other possesses. This model is essentially static, however, because it does not deal with political and economic constraints on the exercise of power arising from the international environment. Similarly, it fails to account for constraints that are posed by the multinational's economic power. More importantly, it ignores the constraints posed by the host country's domestic politics. Specifically, the bilateral monopoly model does not distinguish between potential bargaining power and its implementation. Domestic politics within a host country, as well as international political and economic pressures from multinationals (or their home governments), may hinder host countries in their efforts to exploit the bargaining advantage once gained from the relative demand for its resources.

In order to fill this theoretical gap in the literature, we identify and analyse various constraining factors in both the domestic and international environments. The objective is to illuminate the extent to which a host government is able or willing to translate its bargaining advantage into actual power, to exercise this power in order to extract favourable terms from foreign investors. These relationships are presented below.

Domestic Constraints on the Exercise of Power

Key determinants in translating potential power into actual power are the attitudes and beliefs of the ruling elite regarding foreign investment, and their willingness and ability to discount international economic and political pressure in their confrontation with multinational corporations. During the 1950s and 1960s, Third World governments provided stability to foreign investments by working to preserve the status quo, despite changes that improved their bargaining power. At least two reasons can be given for the leadership of these countries to favour the status quo. One possibility is that their ideological predisposition was such that they saw multinationals as a benevolent force for economic development. Another possibility is that they may have feared that the international political and economic costs of seeking change would outweigh the benefits. There were also, of course, those instances where individual leaders in host countries were known to accept private payments in exchange for their efforts to preserve the status quo. In other instances, changes in the host country's leadership led to classic confrontations. The new elite, having divergent ideological and policy priorities, attempted to persuade the foreign investment regimes to become more responsive to domestic economic priorities. When Mossadeq became the prime minister of Iran in the early 1950s, for example, in efforts to finance Iran's First Development Plan he attempted to nationalize the British-owned Anglo-Iranian Oil company. Similarly, the Kinshasa government's struggle to use earnings from the copper mines of Katanga to pay for post-independence development of the Congo led to a major confrontation. The ultimate result was the nationalization of foreign assets.

Since the mid-1960s there has been a change in attitude among most Third World leaders with respect to foreign investment. Exposés of political intervention by multinational corporations in the domestic politics of host states, the IT & T scandal in Chile in particular, contributed to this change. Unlike IT & T's interference in Chilean politics, most multinationals do not pursue such ruthless politics of intervention. Nevertheless, the degree to which multinationals can influence, by legal or illegal means, the domestic political process can reduce the host country's ability to change corporate behaviour and to make it cater to domestic needs.

A major force for change has been the emergence of new diverse groups which have become involved in the host country's political processes. Students, labour, business, intelligentsia, middle echelon government technocrats and even farmers' associations have greater political clout than ever before. Mobilized by the processes of industrialization and urbanization, and facilitated by global technology, these groups came to place intense pressure on their governments for improving the domestic economy, providing welfare, housing, transportation, and creating jobs. The extractive sector in particular, dominated by foreign firms, became a focus for nationalistic demands of an intensity that could not be ignored by the leadership of Third World states. Among the above groups, business and labour are especially noteworthy. The lack of a strong labour movement, however, remains a major source of institutional weakness in underdeveloped countries. . . .

In a similar vein, the lack of competition from local businesses creates another source of institutional weakness. Too often local businesses, for whom multinational corporations might mean intense competition, are unable to compete with the giant corporations because the latter have access to cheaper sources of capital, better terms from suppliers, and marketing and distribution advantages. The absence of countervailing power via a competitive indigenous business sector helps to explain why the global corporations are able to continue to exert dominant power in underdeveloped countries. A similar and more prevalent situation is one wherein local business owners find that by cooperating with global firms, they too can benefit.

There often exists a strong alliance between the foreign corporation and various powerful home state groups such as landowners, or other pro-business conservative groups. All these groups tend to share the multinationals' distaste for radical social change. This alliance serves as a major constraint on the ability of host countries to translate their bargaining power into favourable outcomes. The effect is the perpetuation of the status quo.

International Constraints: Non-State Actors

We can distinguish between two types of constraints in the international environment. First, there are constraints posed by non-state actors. Second, constraints often emerge as a result of home governmental actions on behalf of the multinational corporations. Constraints posed by non-state actors include the level of global integration of multinationals, local political risk and transnational risk management strategies.

Global integration includes the flow of raw materials, components and final products as well as flows of technology, capital and managerial expertise between the units and subsidiaries of a global corporation. In essence, it is a complex system of a globally integrated production network, at the disposal of the corporation. This complex transnational system is augmented by global logistical and information networks, global advertising and sometimes global product differentiation. The host government's desire to acquire access to this global network and the dependence of host states on the foreign firms who created it produce a constraint on the former's bargaining power.

Global integration, therefore, is an important determinant of multinational strategy. Increasingly, multinational corporations have developed globally based systems of integrated production, marketing and distribution networks in order to reduce costs and enhance their global outreach. A host country that engages in joint ventures with highly integrated and sophisticated foreign firms invariably becomes dependent on the multinationals' controlled globally integrated networks.

Global integration is usually found in companies having very complex technology. There is little that the host country can do to influence integration, and consequently the host country may be severely constrained in its bargaining position. The majority of research and development is undertaken by highly integrated firms and is located in the industrialized home countries. As a result technological developments are beyond the reach or control of developing host countries. Royalties charged by highly integrated firms on the use of their technologies further increase the relative vulnerability of host states. International Business Machines, for instance, continues to maintain an unconditional 10 per cent royalty for the use of its technology despite the efforts of host countries to reduce it.

Another constraint on a host government's ability to exercise power arises from the use of political risk management strategies by multinational corporations. In order to diminish or control better their political risks, multinationals often establish transnational alliances that dramatically increase the cost to the host state of changing the foreign investment regime in their favour. The experience of Third World governments with the pharmaceutical and automobile industries demonstrates how a web of alliances built by the global corporations can seriously impair their exercise of governmental power.

One tactic used by the multinationals is to spread the equity in the foreign investment project over a number of companies from other developed countries. This strategy increases the legal, political and economic obstacles to unilateral alterations in contracts with host states. Another tactic is to raise debt capital for the foreign investment project from banks of different countries (United States, Japan, Germany). Multinationals structure the financing in such a way that banks are paid only if the project is profitable. Host governments' retaliatory actions against the corporations could, therefore, alienate these powerful global banks which have bankrolled the investment project. In view of the significant role of some of the largest global banks involved in the Third World debt problem, this particular risk management strategy may act as a powerful constraint on the host state's ability to turn its potential bargaining power into actual power. Another tactic that multinationals use for protection is to involve the World Bank, IMF and Inter-American Development Banks. The formidable power and prestige of these institutions and their ability to deny financing to host governments' development projects can also deter the host governments from taking actions against multinational corporations.

These and other transnational risk management strategies tend to support the general proposition that multinationals can structure the international economic system and respond to their own financial needs to the detriment of host states in the Third World.

International Constraint: Home Government of Multinational Corporations

The extent to which multinational corporations can mobilize the support of their home government, and the ability (or inability) of the Third World government to withstand retaliation from the powerful governments of the United States and Western Europe on behalf of multinationals, can also affect the bargaining equation. For example, between 1945 and 1960 the bargaining power of the multinationals was strengthened by the actions of the United States, which was home to most of the corporations. The American government prevented the emergence of multilateral lending institutions that might have provided alternative capital sources to multinationals. It promoted instead direct foreign investment in the Third World as a major aspect of its foreign assistance program. It also provided diplomatic support to protect the assets of American multinationals. In a few instances, the American government used covert operations and force to protect economic and strategic interests and, in the process, promoted corporate interests.

The home government may support multinational corporations for a variety of national security reasons, to maintain access to cheap sources of foreign raw materials, to improve its balance of payments position or to use the corporations to transfer aid to pro-Western governments in the Third World. In addition, global corporations are powerful domestic political actors in their own right. They can (and do) take advantage of the fragmentation and decentralization of the democratic political process in Western countries in order to influence government policy. Since business groups are likely to be the best organized and best financed groups, with a persistent interest in the outcome of US policy, they could bias the "pluralism" of the political process in the Western countries. For example, in the United States, the Hickenlooper Amendment and the Gonzalez Amendment were the result of corporate lobbying, and both tied American foreign economic interests to the preservation of corporate interests in the Third World.

To be sure, there is no systematic relationship between the home government's interests and corporate interests that might automatically trigger home government support for multinational corporations vis-à-vis Third World governments. In the first place, if there is a conflict between the strategic interests of the nation and narrow corporate interests, the former is likely to prevail. An example of this is American support for Israel in the Arab-Israeli conflict. Secondly, there often exist sharp divisions among multinationals so that they cannot articulate a unified view of their interests. Finally, the result of American extraterritorial diplomatic support on behalf of established corporations—Alcoa, Reynolds, Anaconda, Exxon—in Latin America did not result in favourable outcomes for the corporations. As a result, corporations are becoming more reluctant to seek the support of their home government.

In spite of the above reasons, the potential for conflict with the US government weighs heavily in Third World governments' decisions to confront foreign firms. Since investment in the Third World tends to be highly concentrated according to the interests of the multinationals' home country (often raw materials are key to national security), and because multinationals are highly influential political actors in the politics of their home country, Third World governments' fears of the US superpower are well-founded. Thus, the host government's willingness (or lack of it) to discount the corporation's home government's potential retaliation (in the form of economic, political or military pressure) may crucially alter both decision-making processes and potential bargaining advantages.

SUMMARY AND CONCLUSION

. . . [T]he model presented in this paper predicts that multinational corporation/Third World country interaction will tend to be unstable over time and that the interests of the two actors are likely to diverge increasingly as the relative bargaining position of the host country improves.

In order to model the bargaining power of Third World countries with respect to multinational corporations, we have made a distinction between potential and actual power. The former is the capability, as yet unrealized, of a host Third World country to alter or influence the behaviour of multinationals. The latter connotes the ability or willingness of the host government to exercise this power in order to extract favourable terms from foreign firms. Potential power is a function of four variables: (1) the level of the host country's expertise, (2) the degree of competition among multinationals, (3) economic uncertainty, and (4) the type of direct foreign investment.

This discussion leads to policy implications for host governments. Obviously, they need to build national capabilities that would help them to regulate better the multinationals. More importantly, in order for them to be effective, national policies need to be revised to conform more closely to the stage of foreign investment cycle. This article's principal thesis is that, despite their apparent bargaining advantage, the dependence of Third World countries which are host to multinational corporations on the international economic system severely limits the ability of host countries to exercise their potential power.

11

"A New Imperial System"?
The Role of the Multinational
Corporations Reconsidered
DAVID FIELDHOUSE

David Fieldhouse discusses the impact of MNCs on the development experiences of Third World states. He starts with the "dependency" school's view that MNCs reinforce the underdevelopment of the Third World, then reviews the potential costs and benefits to developing countries of multinational production. He concludes that the impact of the MNC depends on the host government's ability to manage its relations with the firm. Many factors might affect the state's position in regard to foreign firms, especially advantages a host state has in the bargaining relationship. Fieldhouse concludes that without looking at specific cases it is impossible to know in general whether an MNC will benefit or harm a host country.

A multinational company (alias multinational corporation, transnational enterprise and many other synonyms, but hereafter referred to as MNC) can be defined as a firm which owns or controls income-generating assets in more than one country. The substance has existed for more than a century, but it was only twenty-five years ago that it was given a special name within the framework of foreign direct investment (FDI) and so became a defined concept. . . .

. . . [O]nce it was christened, the MNC assumed an autonomous existence as a special category of capitalist organization and was seized on by intellectuals and publicists of many types as a convenient pole on which to raise their particular flags. In this, of course, the MNC resembled "imperialism," once the word came into vogue in the later nineteenth century, though with this difference. It might be possible to house all books of any significance written on the theory of imperial-

David Fieldhouse. "A New Imperial System? The Role of the Multinational Corporations Reconsidered." From Wolfgang Mommsen and Jurgen Osterhammel, eds. *Imperialism and After*, Allen & Unwin, 1986, pp. 225–40. © The German Historical Institute. Reprinted by permission.

ism since, say, 1900 on one short shelf. The literature on MNCs is now so large that books are published as guides to the bibliography. An historian of European overseas expansion can hope only to know a selection of those works that he can understand (that is, not in the shorthand of the mathematical economists) and which bear on the questions the historian thinks important.

There are many such questions, but this chapter concentrates on one only: is the MNC an affront to the sovereignty of the Third World, a form of imperialism after empire and a cause of "underdevelopment"? I do not claim to answer it, merely to summarize the issues and to suggest a broad line of approach.

THE MULTINATIONAL AS "A NEW IMPERIAL SYSTEM" IN THE THIRD WORLD

The most important question concerning the modern MNC is why its character and activities should be regarded as a special problem. At one level, of course, the MNC is liable to the same criticism as any capitalist enterprise: that it exists to extract surplus value and thus exploit the proletariat. Its two special features are that, in common with all forms of FDI, it operates across national frontiers and that control is retained by one global centre. It might, therefore, have been expected that the first and main attack on MNCs would have come from Marxists; yet this was one dog that did not bark until there was a chorus into which it could join. It is always difficult to explain why something did not happen. The probable explanation is that . . . Lenin and later Marxist–Leninists chose not to distinguish between different forms of capitalist enterprise that collectively constituted what they called "imperialism." Thus it was not until 1968 that those two stalwart New England Marxists, Baran and Sweezy, included in their book *Monopoly Capital,* a direct Marxist appreciation of MNCs. Ironically, this stemmed from their reading an article in the Wall Street journal, *Business Week,* for 20 April 1963. Following *Business Week* . . . they took Standard Oil (NJ) as their model of an MNC, noting with surprise that it really was a world-wide enterprise and that, far from exporting capital in the way finance capital was supposed to do, its post-1945 expansion had been financed almost entirely by its overseas earnings. Moreover, they realized that since 1945 sales and profits of American overseas subsidiaries had been rising faster than those in the United States. Clearly, the MNC needed special analysis; but this led Baran and Sweezy only to the somewhat naïve conclusion that the main reason why the United States opposed the growth of socialism in the Third World was that this would restrict further opportunities for expanding FDI, despite the fact that socialist states, being industrialized, were the best trading partners.

Baran and Sweezy did not, then, pursue the matter further. They were, in fact, merely getting on to a bandwagon that had been set in motion the previous year by J.-J. Servan-Schreiber, a Frenchman whose *American Challenge* is conventionally taken to have been the first widely noticed rationalization of the impact of American industrial investment on post-1945 Europe. His central argument was that American corporations had seen the opportunity presented first by postwar reconstruction and the shortage of dollars which inhibited normal imports, then by the integration of the market following the Treaty of Rome in 1958. They had moved into Europe on a very large scale, concentrating mainly in the more technologically advanced industries, in which they now had a commanding lead, using the products of their research and development facilities (R&D) at home to make money abroad. Paradoxically, 90 per cent of this "investment" had been raised by loans and government grants within Europe. But the most important fact was that Europe stood in danger of becoming dependent on the United States not only for its most sophisticated industries but, more serious, for the technology that made them possible. Europe would thus be condemned to remain in perpetuity on the second rung of a five-rung ladder, as an "advanced industrial" economy below the . . . "post-industrial" states—the United States, Canada, Japan and Sweden. The solution was not to exclude American investment but for Europe to compete more effectively through a genuine federation, including Britain, state support for R&D, specialization by major European corporations in advanced products and improved technical education.

Servan-Schreiber's book aroused much interest and may have helped to trigger off widespread investigation into the character of MNCs (a term, incidentally, which he did not use). Probably his most influential concept was that of an emerging "hierarchy" of countries in different stages of technological development which might, because of the unprecedented advantage then possessed by American companies, become ossified. This challenged the then conventional assumption that all economies were on the same escalator which would bear them from poverty to affluence. It is uncertain whether this idea was his own creation; but there is no doubt that within a year or two this became the key element in two quite different strands of radical thinking on MNCs and Third World development. On the one hand, some of the Latin American dependency theorists who, as a group, had hitherto shown no great interest in MNCs, now quickly built them into their existing concept of "underdevelopment." This was frankly derivative and is not worth discussing here. Much more important and influential was the work of S. H. Hymer whose seminal ideas, published between 1970 and 1972, are central to the modern debate over the role of the MNC in less developed countries.

Hymer accurately reflects the way in which assessments of the MNC became increasingly hostile after about 1960. His PhD dissertation, completed at MIT in 1960 but not published until 1976, was widely read in typescript and seems to have been the origin of the argument that the primary function of FDI was to exploit control of overseas investment to obtain a monopoly rent. Yet in 1960 Hymer was not an unqualified critic of MNCs; his position was that of a conventional North American liberal (he was a Canadian) who believed in an anti-trust approach to large enterprises of all types in order to counter monopoly and promote competition within a competitive economy. By the later 1960s, however, he had become a Marxist; and it was from this standpoint that he developed a more radical critique of the MNC in a series of articles which were subsequently collected and published after his accidental death (1974) in 1979.

Hymer's central message was that, although MNCs might increase the world's wealth through their efficient use of resources, the benefits would go mainly to the countries in which the MNCs were based, while the rest of the world paid the price of their monopoly profits. The result would be an hierarchical world order as corporations developed a complex division of labour within individual firms and throughout the international economy. . . .

These ideas form the starting point of most recent assessments of the impact of the MNC on host countries in which it has subsidiaries under its effective control. The essence of Hymer's concept of an international hierarchy was that the interests of its lower echelons must be subordinated to those of the highest level: that is, subsidiaries exist only to serve the shareholders in the parent company at the top of the pyramid; so that, when a conflict of interest arises, the interests of the base will necessarily be sacrificed to those of the apex. Without this assumption the debate over the role of the MNC would be merely technical, concerned with its motivation, organization and profitability. By contrast, most of the literature since about 1970 has turned on two different issues. First, whether there is a necessary conflict of interest between MNCs and host countries. Secondly, whether the specific methods adopted by MNCs in particular countries are to the disadvantage of their hosts, even if the MNC performed a generally useful role; and if so, what measures the host should adopt to minimize or reduce these disadvantages.

It is important to recognize that these issues are not necessarily related. That is, we could take the view that FDI may, in principle, be in the best interests of host countries, while accepting that particular corporations, types of enterprise, or the way in which they operate may be disadvantageous to the host. I propose very briefly to outline the standard arguments on both these issues. To simplify, I shall concentrate on two of the four generally accepted types of MNC: those that manufacture in host countries for international markets ("off-shore" enterprises) and those that manufacture for the host market. That is not to ignore the importance of enterprises which specialize in the extraction of minerals and petroleum or in production of agricultural commodities. These are central to the debate over the MNC and will be considered in the conclusion. But most of the modern literature tends to assume, rightly, that these are now historic phenomena, rapidly losing their importance as host countries nationalize oil supplies, mines and plantations. The central issue in the debate over the MNC turns on its industrial investments, now the largest single element in FDI and its dynamic sector. Let us consider first the general theoretical arguments for and against direct investment in manufacturing from the standpoint of host countries, then some evidence of their actual effects.

It is conventional to discuss the effects of MNCs under two heads: the "direct" economic effect on the host country and "externalities" or side effects. The direct economic effect of establishing a manufacturing subsidiary of an MNC should consist of an increase in the real income of the host country resulting from the import of capital, skills and technology which would otherwise not be available. Provided the total increase of the income of the host government (through taxes) and of the society (through higher incomes or cheaper goods) exceeds the amount accruing to the owners of the MNC as profits, we would expect the direct economic effect to be favourable. Only if the profits made by the MNC are, in effect, provided by the host government in the form of subsidies (direct, by remission of taxes or through public investment in the infrastructure made solely to attract or facilitate the MNC's operations); or, alternatively, if the level of effective protection is so high that the subsidiary adds no value (because the goods it makes could be bought more cheaply on world markets) should there fail to be a net direct benefit to the host economy.

The list of actual or potential indirect benefits is much longer and can, in fact, be cut to taste. Let us take the relatively simple example of FDI in a developed economy. In his pioneering survey of American direct investment in Britain, published in 1958, J. H. Dunning singled out the following indirect benefits. The general effect on British industrial development was good because of the diffusion of imported skills and the creation of close links with the more dynamic American economy. The impact of this imported efficiency was both vertical (affecting British suppliers of American firms "upstream" and consumers of American products "downstream" of the subsidiary), and horizontal, affecting many other parts of the British economy. American firms set higher standards of pay and conditions, which had a valuable demonstration effect on British labour and employers. Some American factories were set up in development areas. Although these caused some strain on the supply of skilled labour, this was not a general or serious problem. Finally, American firms had a directly measurable effect on the British balance of payments. Partly because they were geared to exporting to established markets for their products, American firms had an excellent export record and, in 1954, accounted for 12 per cent of total British manufacturing exports. In that year the net balance of payments effect was plus £231 million. In addition, Britain was saved an unmeasurable quantity of dollars through the import-substituting effect of American industries in Britain.

Dunning therefore sums up the direct and indirect benefits of American FDI to Britain before 1958 in terms of the law of comparative costs. Just as, under Ricardo's law of comparative advantage, and in a free trade world, any two countries could trade to their mutual advantage provided each concentrated on those products in which it had a relative (though not necessarily absolute) advantage, so in the modern age of protection and economic management, American FDI in Britain enabled each country to use its respective assets more effectively than either could have done in isolation. . . .

There could be no clearer statement of both the theoretical and actual benefits of FDI in a developed country: Servan-Schreiber's clarion call nine years later was a false alarm, since the Continent had benefited as much as Britain, and in much the same ways, from the activities of American MNCs. Moreover, the United States had long since lost the monopoly of advanced technology it had briefly held in the 1940s and was no longer the only large-scale foreign investor: by 1978 Western Europe's accumulated stock of FDI had almost caught up with that of the United States. Clearly, what had been sauce for the goose was now sauce for the gander. Europe had nothing to fear from the United States because it could play the same game.

The question that is central to the study of the multinational in the Third World is whether the same holds true there as in developed countries. On any principle of comparative costs or comparative advantage it ought, of course, to do so. The main reason for wondering whether it does is that for less developed countries (LDCs) FDI is a one-way, not a two-way process: they are almost entirely recipients of foreign investment, not investors. Defined as "underdeveloped" countries, they do not, for the most part, possess the technology, capital, or know-how which might enable them to reverse roles. Their governments may not have the sophistication (or, perhaps, as dependency theorists commonly argue, the patriotism and concern for public welfare) which is expected of Western governments and which might enable them to judge whether the cost of providing conditions attractive to MNCs will outweigh the "direct" economic benefits their countries might obtain. Above all, the indirect effects may be very different because the host country may not be able to respond to the stimulus of foreign enterprise in the way expected in developed countries. Thus, even if Dunning's law of comparative costs holds good at a purely economic level, there may be other non-economic considerations specific to LDCs which outweigh the direct benefits provided by MNCs.

This, indeed, is the basic assertion made by a large number of critics of MNCs who do not seriously question their utility in the developed world but argue, from very diverse standpoints, that they are of dubious benefit to LDCs. To adopt Sanjay Lall's typology, there are three common ways of looking at the deficiencies of the MNC in poor countries: that of the "nationalists," who accept the potential benefits of FDI but have reservations about certain aspects of it; the *dependencia* approach, which (according to Lall) cannot be incorporated into any formal economic analysis; and that of some Marxists, who deny all possibility that an MNC can convey any benefits on host countries. All three are interesting; but, since most criticism of MNCs falls under the first head, let us consider the reservations made by Lall himself and Paul Streeten from a "nationalist" standpoint.

Their starting-point is the dual proposition that the proper criterion for assessing the role of MNCs in LDCs must be social welfare in the broadest sense; but also that there is no possibility of making a final objective judgement on their welfare implications. The reasons are limited information on many aspects of MNC activities, unmeasurable "externalities," different economic theories of development, differing value judgements on "welfare" and wide contrasts in defining "alternative situations." Nevertheless, conventional assessments of the costs and benefits of MNCs which use these difficulties as a ground for mere agnosticism are vulnerable to the accusation of circularity. Thus, if we accept the neo-classical Paretian welfare paradigm, which assumes a basic harmony of interests in society, the ability of individuals to know and pursue their own interests and the neutrality of the state, which pursues a "national" interest, then MNCs are bound to be in the best interests of a host country because they satisfy individual preferences in the market and provide technology, marketing, management skills and other externalities. Adverse effects can simply be blamed on the policies of the host government: transfer prices within MNCs alone lie to some extent beyond state control. Thus, to obtain any grip on the subject, we must look for limitations in this basic welfare critique.

Lall and Streeten point to four possible defects in welfare theory as it relates to MNCs. It makes no distinction between "wants" on ethical or social grounds: that is, consumer preference may not be the ultimate criterion of welfare. Wants may not be genuine but learnt. Income distribution is excluded. The state may not be neutral, rather reflecting class or group control of state power in its own interests. . . .

This means that we have to go beyond the actual activities of MNCs into a normative assessment of "desirable" forms of social and economic development in LDCs. Or, to put it bluntly, the standard of assessment must be what conduces most to the sort of society the critic would like to see. For Lall and Streeten, as for most "nationalist" critics of MNCs, this would seem to be one in which the needs of the poor majority take precedence over the wants of the relatively affluent minority, so that the character and distribution of the benefits provided by MNCs are more important as a measure of their contribution to "growth" than undifferentiated figures of per capita or national income, which conceal the distribution of advantages.

Once this is conceded, it is possible to construct a quite different critique of the desirability of MNCs, in which the test is whether some alternative source of a desired good would make a greater contribution to social welfare, as defined above. Lall and Streeten therefore survey the various benefits conventionally ascribed to MNCs under three main heads, in each case emphasizing concomitant costs and alternative policies.

(1) Capital

MNCs have preferential access to the capital market and their investment may stimulate further aid from foreign governments. But, in fact, MNCs bring in very little capital, which might benefit the host's foreign-exchange position, instead reinvesting local profits and raising funds in the host country. This is desirable in so far as the MNC raises equity capital, since it reduces the "rent" and the foreign-exchange costs of servicing the investment; but less good if it uses local loan capital, since this diverts local savings from other activities. Thus the main capital import consists of machinery, know-how, patents, and so on; and here the danger is that these things, coming as part of a "package," may be overpriced. Thus the role of MNCs as a source of capital is far from simple. Each case must stand alone and there may be better ways for an LDC to acquire these capital assets than through an MNC.

(2) Organization and Management

In this field the superiority of an MNC is undoubted, both as an efficient user of resources and as a demonstrator of sound business methods in countries where corporate "management" is a novelty. Yet, once again, there may be hidden costs, seen from a "nationalist" or "welfare" position.

First, as Hymer argued, the price of accepting an MNC may be subordination as a "branch-plant" in an hierarchical world system, which means dependence.

Secondly, there is transfer-pricing within MNCs, which Lall and Streeten define as follows.

> The problem arises from the fact that transfer prices, being under the control of the firm concerned, can be put at levels which differ from prices which would obtain in "arms-length" transactions, and so can be manipulated to shift profits clandestinely from one area of operations to another. If the different units of a MNC behaved like independent firms, clearly the problem would not arise. However, given the growing extent of intra-firm trade, it is the *centralization of authority* and the growth of a *global business strategy* that creates fears on the part of governments (both host and home) that they are losing legitimate tax revenue.[1]

Obviously the host government can and should attempt to monitor such transactions so as to ensure that profits declared reflect actual profits made. But there are technical difficulties in doing so, particularly for LDCs with comparatively weak bureaucracies; and transfer-pricing remains one of the most suspect aspects of MNCs.

Thirdly, the very efficiency of an MNC may have an adverse effect on domestic entrepreneurship in the host country. If all the dynamic and technically advanced sectors of the LDC's economy pass into the hands of foreign firms, this may check economic development by reducing the rate of capital accumulation. But this, in fact, is very unlikely. It would happen only in any of three hypothetical cases: first, if the MNC made no higher profits than local men and repatriated a proportion of these profits, by contrast with local capitalists, if these are assumed to reinvest all their retained profits at home; secondly, if subsidiaries were made to pay more for technology than local entrepreneurs could have paid for the same thing on an open market; and, thirdly, if the MNCs created an oligopolistic market structure, as contrasted with an assumed competitive market if local capitalists had it entirely to themselves.

These are potentially disadvantageous economic consequences of the organizational superiority of the MNC. But other, non-economic, costs may also have weight in a nationalistic welare balance sheet. National ownership of the means of production may be intrinsically desirable. MNCs may adversely affect social, cultural and political values. Patterns of development may be distorted, local élites reinforced and the road to "socialist" change blocked. The inclusion of such criteria in almost any "nationalist" or "radical" critique of the MNC is significant. However valid, they are necessarily subjective and incompatible with economic assessment of the value of MNCs to developing countries.

(3) Technology

. . . Technology, rather than capital, is now usually taken to be the main contribution made by MNCs to LDCs and . . . two questions have to be asked in each case.

First, could the same benefits have been obtained by the LDC except through the medium of a multinational so that some of the associated costs could have been avoided: for example, by licensing indigenous producers? Secondly, and characteristic of the "radical" critique, are the technologies imported by MNCs "appropriate" to the circumstances of LDCs? For example, are they excessively capital-intensive and do they serve the desires of an élite rather than the "basic needs" of the masses? Such questions, of course, reflect normative assumptions: there are "optimal" patterns of production which are "appropriate" to the special circumstances of LDCs and should therefore be preferred on welfare criteria. The same applies to another MNC specialty, marketing skills. However valuable these may be in stimulating an internal market and domestic production, MNC advertising may create "unsuitable" tastes, inducing the starving to spend their money on Coca Cola rather than on milk.

To sum up, the common denominator of such reservations is that the apparent economic benefits of the types of industrial activity normally associated with MNCs may be outweighed for LDCs either by the economic costs included in the "package" in which they are imported or, alternatively, by the fact that they are "inappropriate" by other, non-economic criteria. In either case, the standard answer is that it is up to the host government to decide and to control. But on this also most radical critics of MNCs tend to question whether the state in most LDCs can match up to its assigned role. If not, if it is too weak or class-dominated, if its officials are too ignorant or corrupt to promote "suitable" policies, then sovereignty becomes no defence against the MNC. So, ultimately, our assessment of the probable and potential impact of MNCs on host countries must turn on how effectively the host state performs its role as maker of policy and defender of the "national interest." Let us, therefore, finally consider the capacity of the nation-state to use and control the potential of the MNC and whether the multinational constitutes a form of economic imperialism after the end of formal empire.

STATE SOVEREIGNTY AND THE MULTINATIONAL

It is only when one poses these questions that the fundamental difficulty of studying MNCs becomes fully evident. Unless one is an unqualified believer in dependency theory, or a neo-Marxist of the sort denounced by Warren and Emmanuel—both of whom reject the possibility that a nonsocialist state could wish, let alone be competent, to subordinate class or sectoral interests to those of the society as a whole—there is no possibility of providing a definite answer. This is not to be evasive: there are two sound reasons for agnosticism.

First, there is very little hard information on the operations of MNCs. Their operations can be studied at two levels: the general and the specific. Most published information is general, based on surveys of a very large number of firms and their activities in host countries. So far as it goes, such information is valuable as the basis for making general statements concerning both the source and distribution of FDI by country of origin and investment and as between the several hundred largest MNCs. It also throws light on methods of entry into host countries, the extent of local equity holding, output, profitability according to published accounts, receipts from royalties and fees, expenditure on R&D and on the contribution to export earnings. Such information makes possible broad statements indicating the importance of the economic role of the MNC in the modern world economy; but it has two obvious limitations. It gives no insight into the motivation and internal operations of individual corporations or the attitudes and policies of host governments; and, consequently, it cannot provide the evidence by which we might assess the "welfare" implications of FDI as we have defined it. The first need can only be met by detailed research on particular corporations with deliberate emphasis on the issues raised by theorists.

But even if the flow of specific information increases greatly (and both large corporations and host governments are commonly very reluctant to allow their inner secrets to be revealed) there is a second reason why no comprehensive answer could be given on the compatibility of the MNC and the welfare of host countries. Each corporation and each country is a special case. Individual examples can neither prove nor disprove general propositions. Thus no general theory of the MNC and its relationship with the sovereign state can be drawn up. At most I can suggest some broad propositions that seem to be reasonably consistent with the facts of the case in the 1980s. Let me, therefore, attempt a broad answer to the main question posed in this chapter: what is the role of the MNC in the world economy? Is it a key weapon in the armoury of a new informal imperialism?

The fundamental point is that while the public image of the MNC in the Third World has remained virtually static for over two decades, the reality has changed and is changing very fast. In the 1950s, when the alarm bells started to ring, the common assumption was that most MNCs were American-owned, expressing the United States' postwar economic and political hegemony throughout the world; and that most of these enterprises extracted oil or minerals, or ran plantations. Neither assumption was valid then, and they have become almost entirely untrue three decades later. Western Europe has now achieved rough parity with the United States as the source of FDI; and in the Third World the focus of MNC activity has shifted decisively from "exploitation" of "irreplaceable" reserves of oil and minerals or growing tropical crops to investment in manufacturing for re-export or for local consumption. This structural change is reflected in the critical literature: where once Standard Oil and United Fruit were the villains, now it is the multitude of industrial companies who are accused of debauching indigenous tastes and extracting Baran's "surplus" through excessive profits and the abuse of transfer prices, royalty payments, and so on. My argument is that the change in the functions of the multinational has significantly affected its relationship with the sovereign state in which it operates; and that, even if accusations of "imperialism" might have been to some extent justified in a Third World context in the past, they are much less relevant in the present.

The most legitimate criticism of MNCs has always been that their very function was to make competition imperfect, distorting the economic process and obtaining a "monopoly rent" by internalizing the market. This makes them agents of a new mercantilism, which has historically tended towards some form of imperialism. Is this, indeed, their common aim and, if so, why can private firms frustrate market forces in this way?

First, the question of intention. There are a number of alternative theoretical explanations of why large business firms should wish to establish overseas subsidiaries, and all assume that they do so to obtain a higher overall profit by "internalizing" their total operations than they might do by using some alternative strategy. Their reasons, however, vary according to the nature of their activities and the environment in which they operate; and the main contrast is between the extractive and utility companies, on the one hand, and those which manufacture in host countries on the other.

The salient fact about the utility, oil, mineral and agricultural corporations is that, by and large, they grew in a more or less free-trade environment: that is, the things they dealt in were seldom subject to protective duties, quantity controls (except in wartime), or tariffs. These firms engaged in production and trade in commodities for many reasons, but most did so either to achieve vertical integration within a single firm, or to sell to third parties on the international market. In both cases, however, and also in that of public utilities, one of their primary aims was to erect some form of monopoly as a defence against the risks of a competitive free-trade market. Oil companies, primarily concerned with refining and marketing, nevertheless bought leases of oil deposits so that they could control the price of their raw material and balance supplies from low- and high-cost areas within their global operations. Mineral firms and agricultural producers were both notorious for using monopoly, monopsony, cartels, rings, and so on, to force down the price paid to host governments, peasant producers, and so on, and conversely to force up the price they could charge to consumers.

Thus MNCs of this type attempted to create some form of monopoly in a free-trade environment as their best means of maximizing profits. As an important by-product, they tended also to be "imperialistic." Because their activities commonly depended on concessions (for oil, mines, plantations) or, if they were engaged in trade, on satisfactory access to the producers of their commodity, relations with host governments were of crucial importance. And because much of their business was done with the relatively weak states of Latin America and the Middle East and with the early post-colonial states of Africa and Asia, they commonly achieved a position approaching dominance over their hosts: hence the concept of United Fruit's "banana republics" and the near-sovereignty of Standard Oil or Anglo-Iranian in some parts of the Middle East. In this sense it was characteristic of MNCs engaged in the commodity trade, and some in public utilities (ITT, for example) that they established "informal empires" as a response to the need to establish monopoly as the basis of profitability in a competitive environment.

Exactly the opposite is generally true of the modern manufacturing multinationals. They are, by their nature, interested in freedom of trade outside their protected home base. They do not need physical control over their markets. Above all, they normally engage in manufacture in other countries as a direct response to some form of obstruction in the market, which either threatens an established export trade or offers opportunities for higher profit through some form and degree of monopoly in a previously competitive market. The chronology of FDI in manufacturing shows this to be universally true. The timing of the great spate of direct industrial investment, which started in the 1920s in Britain after the McKenna duties of the First World War, and from the 1950s in most LDCs as they adopted severe protectionism along with their new independence constitutions, shows that (with probably the sole exception of post-1950 American "off-shore" industries in South-East Asia) the manufacturing multinational was conjured up by protectionist governments. The effect was a double distortion of the market. "Effective protection" raised domestic prices above international prices, so creating for the first time a market that might be profitable for modern industry, despite the restricted demand and high production costs of the Third World countries. For their part, the multinationals, compelled or tempted by protectionism to jump the tariff wall, further distorted the market by exploiting the opportunities provided by their monopoly of technology and know-how. Thus, as Hymer argued as early as 1960, it was indeed imperfections in the market that attracted MNCs to undertake overseas manufacturing; but in the Third World these imperfections were created by the protectionist state.

If, then, the power held by the MNCs in the Third World is in any sense "a New Imperial System" (or perhaps a "third colonial occupation") then it must be said that the gates were opened from the inside. But we must not beg this question. Empire means the imposition of external authority, the transfer of the power to make final decisions to a central metropolis. Hymer's concept of a world hierarchy assumed that senior corporate executives in Manhattan could determine what happened in Manchester, Bombay, or Nairobi; that the power of the great corporations was greater than that of small or even middling states. Is this really so, or is his New Imperial System merely a fable?

Paradoxically, there was more substance in Hymer's vision in the past than when he saw it and there is still less in the 1980s. His prototypes were the big utility and extractive corporations. These, as we have seen, were a special case. They needed power to achieve their objectives and were able to hold it because of the weakness of many of the states (including some colonies) in which they operated. They were, indeed, states within states, largely autonomous, latter-day feudal barons, able to bargain, even dictate, because of the importance of their activities to the host states. It was precisely because they were so powerful that the new sovereign states found it essential, whenever they had the power, to destroy them: in many countries effective decolonization consisted in the nationalization of telecommunications, oil wells and copper mines.

It is entirely different with the modern, manufacturing multinational. Its very presence in the host country reflects local policy decisions: it is a genie summoned to serve protectionism. It depends for its profit on the continuance of that policy. It has little power because, in most cases, the only sanction it could impose on a hostile state would be to stop production; and, since this is seldom for export, the economic consequences for the host would be negligible. Physically, moreover, a factory bears no resemblance to a large mine or plantation. It is in no sense autonomous or remote, not a city-state. It is easy to starve out by simply refusing li-

censes for essential inputs. Indeed, virtually the only threat the modern manufacturing multinational can make to its host government is that unreasonable treatment may inhibit further foreign investment or technological transfer. The threat
is real but seldom compelling. A determined state will normally act as it wishes
and risk the consequences.

My conclusion, therefore, is that in so far as there is a latent tension between
the power of the MNC and that of the sovereign host state, it is the state that now
holds most of the cards and can determine the rules of the game. At the macroeconomic level it can adjust its policies in such a way that it is no longer possible
for MNCs to make "excessive" profits or attractive for them to import factors of
production. At the administrative level, it is always possible to use anti-trust laws
against excessive concentration, to impose quotas, limit prices, above all to insist
on a minimal level of local participation in the equity and of nationals in employment. Nationalization is a rare last resort simply because experience shows that
very large foreign corporations will normally accept the bid from the very small
states.

Yet we must end on a note of caution. I have argued that the modern multinational chief executive in Hymer's allegorical skyscraper is not the ruler of an informal overseas empire. The humblest LDC is in no danger from the power of a
multinational which is engaged in manufacturing and technology transfer. But
there are other, more subtle dangers. The main danger of the modern MNC to the
LDC lies not in its power but in two much less dramatic qualities: its superior
cunning and its apparent harmlessness. The cunning of an MNC is one aspect of
its managerial efficiency and its ability to take a global view of its interests. Without it an MNC could not operate successfully in Third World states with their
jungle of regulations. The problem is to draw the line between cunning and dis-
honesty as, for example, represented by abuse of transfer-pricing; and much of the
substance in criticisms made by "nationalist" and "radical" critics of MNC
behaviour amounts to the accusation that this line has been crossed. Lall's study of
the pharmaceutical industry supports the general prejudice that this is commonly
the most guilty type of multinational. Yet, while such practices may cause loss to
LDCs, they are unlikely to cause disaster. The real danger lies rather in the seduc-
tiveness of the industrial MNC. The benefits a foreign corporation can offer to a
poor, non-industrial state are extremely attractive: an instant, advanced factory at
little or no immediate cost with payments due only when, and if, the subsidiary
flourishes. It is not surprising that during the optimistic "development" decades
before the mid-1970s so many LDCs welcomed manufacturing corporations with
open arms and failed to see the long-term risks they were running.

The analogy with much of the borrowing in which many Latin American and
Islamic states in the Mediterranean indulged during the nineteenth century is obvious and the dangers equally great: on the economic side a growing and ultimately intolerable strain on foreign-exchange earnings to pay for imported inputs
and to meet the cost of repatriated profits, and so on; more generally, a host of
social and political problems at home as the alien presence makes itself felt. In the
later twentieth century the result will not be the formal imperialism of a Dual Con-

trol or a protectorate; but a number of LDCs have now learnt that excessive foreign investment, if coupled with inappropriate economic and social management, may lead to virtual bankruptcy, dictation by the World Bank or the IMF and possibly domestic revolution. Sovereignty, in fact, may be proof against the multinational, but it carries no guarantee against lack of wisdom; and the essential message of the "national" or "radical" critic of the MNC to developing countries should be *caveat emptor. . . .*

NOTE

1. S. Lall and P. Streeten, *Foreign Investment, Transnationals, and Developing Countries* (London, 1977), 59; italics in original.

12

Foreign-Owned Companies in the United States: Malign or Benign?
CLETUS C. COUGHLIN

Cletus C. Coughlin examines the nature of foreign investment in the United States and discusses its possible causes and effects. Foreign investment in the United States has increased dramatically since the 1970s. Coughlin attributes the growth in inward foreign direct investment (that coming *into* the United States) primarily to increases in other industrialized countries' exports of technology and growing incentives to locate production in foreign areas. He concludes that foreign investment benefits the American economy by promoting trade, allowing for transfers of technology, and improving America's trade balance by making United States firms more competitive and productive.

Foreign direct investment in the United States increased more than elevenfold between 1977 and 1990. The rapid increase in U.S. businesses acquired or established by foreign firms has generated much controversy. Some observers worry that foreign-owned firms are more likely than U.S. firms to take actions that would reduce employment, worsen the U.S. trade deficit, inhibit technological progress or threaten national security. Defenders of foreign direct investment stress the increased economic activity stemming from new jobs and the transfer to the United States of improved management, marketing and production techniques.

This paper examines three aspects of foreign direct investment in the United States (FDIUS) to assess whether foreign-owned companies are more likely to have malign or benign effects on the U.S. economy. First, the paper highlights the basic facts about FDIUS—its amount, the home countries of the foreign-owned companies, its distribution across industries and the relative share of the U.S. economy controlled by foreign companies. Second, it summarizes research on what causes FDIUS. Third, it scrutinizes the economic effects of this investment.

Cletus C. Coughlin. "Foreign-Owned Companies in the United States: Malign or Benign?" *Federal Reserve Bank of St. Louis Review*, May/June 1992.

THE WHO, WHERE, HOW AND HOW MUCH OF FDIUS

Foreign direct investment (FDI) is the purchase of ownership in, or the flow of lending to, an enterprise located in a foreign country that is largely owned by residents of the investing country. FDIUS results in a foreign enterprise operating in the United States under the control of a firm (or individuals) of a country other than the United States. Thus, FDI is ownership with actual control of the enterprise, which is what distinguishes FDI from portfolio investment. . . .

How Much FDIUS

The most common measure of FDIUS uses the cumulative stock of prior FDI. This measure is the sum of foreign owners' equity (including retained earnings) for all foreign affiliates, plus net lending to these affiliates from their parents. This investment is measured at its historical cost, that is, the value of the investment when it actually occurred. . . . [T]he book value of FDIUS rose from $13.3 billion in 1970 to $403.7 billion in 1990, an annual growth rate of 18.6 percent. This rapid growth has made the United States the leading host country in the world for FDI.

Unfortunately, the use of historical cost ignores the effects of both real and nominal changes in the value of the investment. For example, changes in the earnings prospects of a foreign-owned firm in the United States can change the value of a specific investment, and changes in the overall price level can affect the value of FDI generally. These drawbacks prompted the development of two other measures of FDI. The first, called current cost, re-values investment using estimates of the current value of the net stock of direct investment capital, land and inventories. A second, more general measure is the market value of a firm's net worth. This measure implicitly values both tangible and intangible assets, such as patents and trademarks, because a firm's net worth is the difference between its assets and liabilities.

The current cost and market value measures . . . reveal two facts. First, like the book value measure, both have grown rapidly in recent years and, second, both differ from the book value of FDIUS. Between 1982 and 1990, the current cost value of FDIUS increased from $173.2 billion to $465.9 billion, an annual growth rate of 13.2 percent, while the market value measure increased from $133.0 billion to $530.4 billion, an annual growth rate of 18.9 percent. These different growth rates have resulted in a book value of FDIUS for 1990 that is 87 percent of the current cost value and 76 percent of the market value.

By themselves, these levels of FDIUS are not especially revealing. One way to provide perspective is to examine the counterpart of FDIUS, the levels of FDI held by U.S. firms. Not only is the United States the leading host country in the world for FDI, it is also the leading source country. Despite the rapid growth of FDIUS, FDI held by U.S. firms as of 1990 exceeds FDIUS, irrespective of the method of measurement. For example, FDI held by U.S. firms in 1990 was $421.5 billion using the book value, $598.1 billion using current cost value and $714.1 billion using the market value. Thus, FDI held by U.S. firms exceeded FDIUS by $17.8 billion, $132.2 billion or $183.7 billion, respectively.

A second way to provide perspective is to calculate the ratio of FDIUS to the total net worth of U.S. non-financial corporations (using the book value of each). Between 1977 and 1990, according to Graham and Krugman (1991), this ratio increased from 2.1 percent to 10.5 percent. This suggests "foreign control" of about 10 percent of the U.S. economy.

Another way to assess the extent of foreign control is to examine the share of U.S. workers employed by foreign-owned firms. Between 1977 and 1988, employment at non-bank foreign-affiliated firms rose from 1.7 percent to 4.3 percent of all U.S. non-bank employment. When one focuses only on the manufacturing sector, the share rises from 3.5 percent to 8.9 percent.

No matter which measure is used, foreign ownership and control have increased substantially in recent years. The level of foreign control, however, is not as high as it is in most other developed countries. For example . . . the share of foreign-owned firms' manufacturing employment in 1986 was 7 percent in the United States, 21 percent in France, 13 percent in Germany, 14 percent in the United Kingdom and 1 percent in Japan. Except for Japan, the rapid increase in FDIUS has made the level of foreign control in the United States closer to that of other developed countries.

The How of FDIUS

FDIUS occurs in either of two ways. One way, termed "greenfield" investment, involves the construction of new production facilities in the United States—either brand-new subsidiaries or expansions of existing subsidiaries. The other method of FDIUS is the acquisition of existing U.S. firms. Despite some greenfield investments that have generated much publicity, such as the opening of Japanese-owned automobile plants, FDIUS has occurred primarily by way of acquisitions. . . . For example, the $56.8 billion outlay in 1990 by foreign firms to acquire existing firms was more than seven times larger than the $7.7 billion outlay to establish new subsidiaries.

The Who and Where of FDIUS

FDIUS occurs in various industries and involves numerous, primarily developed, foreign countries. . . . [T]he United Kingdom, whose share of FDIUS was 26.8 percent in 1990, is the leading source country. The other leading investors and their shares in 1990 are: Japan—20.7 percent; the Netherlands—15.9 percent; Germany—6.9 percent; and Canada—6.9 percent. Despite having a smaller share than the British, Japanese FDIUS has generated much more publicity than British

FDIUS. Part of the reason for this attention is due to the industries in which the Japanese are involved, of which more is said later, and part is due to the rapid rise of Japanese FDIUS in the 1980s. Between 1980 and 1990, Japanese FDIUS increased at an annual rate of 33.3 percent, boosting the Japanese share from 5.7 percent to 20.7 percent. . . .

. . . [T]he largest share of FDIUS remains in manufacturing. Between 1980 and 1990, investment in this sector increased nearly fivefold. Since total FDIUS increased similarly, the manufacturing share of FDIUS was slightly less than 40 percent in both 1980 and 1990. The United Kingdom is the leading foreign investor in manufacturing by a wide margin. In 1990, its share was 33.1 percent, more than double the Netherlands' 15.3 percent. The other leading investors are: Germany—9.5 percent; Japan—9.5 percent; and Canada—5.8 percent. The largest portion (26 percent) of manufacturing FDIUS in 1990 was in chemicals, followed by machinery (18.5 percent), food processing (14.3 percent) and primary and fabricated metals (11 percent).

The wholesale and retail trade sector has the second-largest share of FDIUS. Its share was 15.4 percent in 1990, down from 18.3 percent in 1980. These shares, however, are likely overstated because of the method used to allocate industry statistics: wholesale trade in automobiles includes some manufacturing of automobiles. As automobile production by Japanese-owned affiliates increases, sales of automobiles manufactured in the United States will rise relative to the sales of automobiles imported from Japan for resale. As this occurs, more affiliates will be reclassified from wholesale trade into manufacturing, causing reported FDIUS in transportation equipment manufacturing to rise and FDIUS in wholesale trade to fall.

Finance and insurance accounted for 9.7 percent of FDIUS in 1990, up from 8.9 percent in 1980. Countries with major financial markets—Japan, the Netherlands, Switzerland, Canada and the United Kingdom—account for the majority of this investment.

The share of FDIUS in petroleum, the fourth-leading industry, declined from 14.7 percent in 1980 to 9.4 percent in 1990. . . . In fact, both foreign and domestic investment in the petroleum industry grew relatively slowly during the 1980s.

The remaining industries, real estate and banking, are probably the most controversial. The share of FDIUS in real estate increased from 7.3 percent in 1980 to 8.6 percent in 1990. The $34.6 billion of real estate FDIUS reflects the investment of foreign parents in U.S. affiliates whose major activity is real estate. Large amounts of U.S. real estate are also held by affiliates classified in other industries. Thus, the actual level of real estate FDIUS exceeds $34.6 billion. In addition, the value of assets actually controlled by foreign owners is likely much greater because of the high debt leverage in this industry (foreign investors are able to control real estate valued far greater than their own equity by borrowing from unrelated parties).

Some of the controversy surrounding this investment is because foreign ownership of real estate tends to be concentrated in a few locations, such as Hawaii, downtown Los Angeles and Houston and a few other urban areas. . . . A final cause of controversy is the large share of Japanese ownership.

The Japanese also play a prominent role in the FDIUS that has occurred in banking. Between 1980 and 1990, the share of FDIUS in banking declined from 5.5 percent to 4.7 percent; however, foreign ownership in the U.S. banking industry is large and has been increasing. In 1980, 11.9 percent of the total assets of all U.S. banks were held by financial affiliates of foreign banks and holding companies. By 1990, this figure had risen to 21.2 percent, more than half of which is held by Japanese-owned banks.

THE WHY OF FDIUS

Much research has been devoted to developing theoretical explanations of FDI. The importance of specific factors that might explain FDIUS has also been examined thoroughly. Rather than provide an in-depth review of this voluminous literature, let's examine the primary explanation of FDI, which is based on the "industrial-organization" approach, and the commonly identified determinants of FDI. It is important to stress that this explanation is most useful in discussing FDI in manufacturing.

FDI Theory: The Industrial-Organization Approach

Standard FDI theories rely on "firm-specific advantages" to explain why it occurs. The foreign investor must have some advantage over local firms to compensate for the fact that the multinational corporation (MNC) incurs additional costs because of (1) cultural, legal, institutional and linguistic differences; (2) a lack of knowledge about local market conditions; and (3) lengthier lines of communication and, therefore, an increase in communication failures.

A foreign investor's advantages can take many forms. Technology is the primary advantage; access to large amounts of capital, superior management and products differentiated by successful advertising are also important.

A foreign company's advantages are exploited by FDI only if, given its information and expectations about prices, costs and legal environment, it can earn higher profits. Any technological advantage, defined broadly as economically valuable knowledge, can be exploited by exports to a country instead of foreign production and sales in that same country. Thus, the firm selects FDI over exporting only if the former is more profitable. FDI and exporting, however, are not the only alternatives. A firm with a technological advantage may license a firm in another country to produce a good using its technology. Once again, the firm with the technological advantage will choose the route with the highest anticipated profits. . . .

Empirical Evidence on FDIUS

The rapid rise of FDIUS since the late 1970s has prompted much research that attempts to isolate specific factors that explain it. Since FDI theory stresses the importance of technological differences, the role of technology in the rapid growth of FDIUS is examined first. The effects of exchange rate changes, taxation, protectionist pressures and the business cycle on FDIUS are then explored.

Technology and FDIUS   The preceding views of FDI stress the importance of the transfer of technology from a parent to its foreign affiliate. MNCs, however, can also transfer technology from the affiliate to the parent. Rapid increases in foreign direct investment in the United States during the 1980s have worried some observers that foreign firms are investing primarily to acquire U.S. technology, which could harm the competitive position of U.S. firms.

One way to assess international transfers of technology involving U.S. affiliates of foreign-based MNCs is to compare receipts of royalties and license fees *from* their foreign parents with payments of such fees *to* their foreign parents. Receipts measure the value of technology transferred from foreign-owned companies in the United States to their parents, while payments measure purchases of technology from their parents. . . . [B]oth measures have increased at annual rates of more than 20 percent since 1982. Payments by U.S. affiliates, however, far exceed receipts in each year and were nearly six times the value of receipts in 1990. Thus, technology transfers are occurring to a far greater extent from foreign-based MNCs to their American affiliates than the reverse.

While the preceding evidence is consistent with FDI theory, it still does not explain why FDIUS has risen faster than FDI by U.S. firms. Once again, the role of technology in FDI theory provides insights. One explanation revolves around the shrinking and, in some cases, reversal of U.S. technological superiority. Generally speaking, from the end of World War II until 1970, U.S.-based firms had substantial advantages over foreign-based firms in technology and management skills. These advantages caused FDI abroad by U.S.-based firms to exceed FDIUS. Over the last 20 years, however, foreign-based firms have developed such advantages of their own to a far greater extent than they had previously; these advantages have provided a stimulus to FDIUS. Thus, the increasing role of foreign firms in U.S. production can be related to changing patterns of the development of new technology and management innovations throughout the world.

Exchange Rate Changes and FDIUS   While a pre-eminent role in explaining FDIUS can be ascribed to technology, other factors can affect FDIUS. One common argument is that a "weak" foreign exchange value of the dollar encourages FDIUS. In many discussions, a weak dollar is not defined formally, but is used informally as a value lower than its value at some previous point. The lower value of the dollar has two effects that could stimulate FDIUS. First, it deters exports to the United States as U.S. consumers are faced with higher prices. Therefore, foreign firms might find it more attractive to locate production in the United States rather than export a smaller quantity. Second, the lower value of the dollar makes U.S. productive assets cheaper for foreign firms than they were previously.

While a weak dollar makes production in the United States more attractive, all other things the same, it is crucial to emphasize that FDIUS depends on whether the U.S. productive assets are worth more to a foreign-based firm than to a U.S.-based firm. A declining dollar raises the expected returns to both a U.S. owner and a foreign owner. How might the expected returns rise more for the latter than the former?

One argument focuses on the changing composition of production in the United States. As the dollar declines, U.S. competitiveness shifts from non-traded sectors, such as services and retail trade, to traded sectors, such as manufacturing. Since FDI is more substantial in traded than non-traded sectors, production in the United States shifts from areas in which foreign-owned companies have little involvement to areas in which they have much more involvement.

It is unclear exactly what impact changes in the foreign exchange value of the dollar have on FDIUS. What is clear is that the long-run upward trend in FDIUS beginning in the late 1970s took place during a strengthening as well as a weakening of the dollar. Thus, the evidence suggests that changes in the value of the dollar are, at most, a factor that has had slight effects.

Tax Rate Changes and FDIUS   Changes in tax policy have also been viewed as a potential determinant of FDIUS. Two major changes in U.S. tax policy in 1981 and 1986 may have contributed to the timing of changes in the rate of FDIUS. To assess the impact of U.S. tax changes on FDIUS, such changes must be viewed in conjunction with the tax systems of the source countries.

Generally speaking, two types of tax systems can be identified in the leading source countries for FDIUS. Countries with "territorial" corporate taxation, like the Netherlands and Canada, do not attempt to tax the income earned by the subsidiaries of firms based in their countries. Countries with "worldwide" systems, like the United Kingdom and Japan, tax the earnings of subsidiaries while granting a tax credit for taxes paid to host-country governments. For example, under a worldwide system, subsidiaries of foreign firms pay corporate profit taxes similar to those paid by domestic firms. When they repatriate income to their parent, the income is subject to taxation at the home-country rate, with a credit for taxes paid to the U.S. government.

The differing tax systems provide different investment incentives for given U.S. tax changes. In the early 1980s, U.S. corporate taxes were reduced by accelerated depreciation allowances. By allowing firms to reduce their taxable incomes, these cuts were valuable to U.S.-owned corporations. The cuts should also have been valuable to foreign firms, though they were more valuable to those subject to territorial rather than worldwide taxation. Firms subject to worldwide taxation faced the offsetting effects of reduced tax credits.

Overall, the tax cuts provided relatively more benefits to U.S.-owned firms than foreign-owned firms and, thus, were biased against FDIUS. In addition, the bias against firms from the United Kingdom and Japan, countries with worldwide systems, was greater than against firms from the Netherlands and Canada, countries with territorial systems. These incentives were reduced in 1986 when tax legislation eliminated the special investment incentives.

Generally speaking, little empirical evidence suggests that tax rate changes have played a major role in FDIUS. The share of FDIUS from the Netherlands and Canada relative to Japan and the United Kingdom did not rise from 1981 to 1986 and fall thereafter. . . .

There is, however, some empirical evidence that changes in taxes matter. The preceding argument suggested that U.S. tax cuts deterred FDIUS, while tax increases encouraged FDIUS. . . . Overall, the empirical evidence points, at most, to a very small role for tax policy in affecting FDIUS.

Trade Barriers and FDIUS   Another factor identified as a potential determinant of FDIUS is actual or potential protectionist measures. The basic idea is that a trade barrier, or the threat of imposing one, will induce FDIUS because the profitability of production in the United States by the foreign-owned firm would rise relative to exporting to the United States. Underlying such behavior, of course, is some advantage possessed by the foreign-owned firm.

The fact that trade barriers are frequently thought of as protecting U.S.-owned firms is ironic. In fact, such protection tends to increase foreign control in the U.S. economy. A domestic industry demanding protection is likely to be one in which foreign firms have special advantages. Trade barriers erected in that industry simply attract FDIUS, stimulating additional foreign-owned production.

Protectionism has played a role in FDIUS. The production of automobiles and color television sets are two examples. Nonetheless, protectionism is not likely to have become so large a factor that it can explain the rapid increase in FDIUS.

The Business Cycle and FDIUS   A final factor affecting FDIUS is the business cycle. The business cycle characterizes the extent to which the level of economic activity in the United States and abroad changes over time. . . . [A] study of inflows into France, Germany, Japan, the United Kingdom and the United States found that FDI rose faster than output during economic recoveries and fell faster during recessions. Changes in economic activity, however, are not likely to affect the relative shares of foreign- vs. U.S.-controlled production substantially because the business cycle affects the profit expectations of foreign and domestic investors similarly.

THE EFFECTS OF FDIUS

The major controversies about the effects of FDIUS encompass economic as well as political issues. In addition, there are national security issues that involve economic and political considerations. This paper, however, examines the issues that are primarily economic.

Technology Transfer and Research and Development Effects

FDI facilitates the movement across national borders of goods, services and, most important, technology by reducing some transaction costs that inhibit trade. For example, reaching an agreement to transfer technology within a MNC is much easier (that is, less costly) than it is with two separate companies.

The benefits of the trade stimulated by the expansion of MNCs come from three sources. The first source is known as comparative advantage. Countries have different combinations of productive resources, and goods are produced with different combinations of these resources. Trade allows countries to benefit by producing goods that, relative to other countries, they can produce and sell cheaply and exchanging them for goods that can be produced and sold more cheaply abroad. The second source of gains from trade requires increasing returns to scale. With trade, countries can produce a narrower range and larger quantities of goods than they could otherwise. Longer production runs may allow firms to achieve lower per unit production costs. Finally, trade reduces the power of firms to set prices (that is, increases competition) and allows consumers to enjoy larger quantities and lower prices.

Looking specifically at trade in technology, FDI allows a firm to appropriate (or capture) the benefits of its own research and development. When the foreign investor produces goods and services using its own technology, it is as if there were trade in the results of research and development. From the firm's point of view, its appropriation of benefits provides the incentive to engage in research and development in the first place. . . .

Proponents of FDI frequently stress the generation of what are termed "external benefits." Foreign firms may not be able to appropriate all of the gains from the technology they transfer. Instead, domestic firms can learn and imitate the transferred technology and management methods, and workers may take their acquired skills and use them in other jobs. Unfortunately, these external benefits are difficult to measure.

On the other hand, critics argue that FDIUS tends to reduce the spillover of external benefits, particularly those associated with engaging in research and development. Research and development involves many complex intellectual activities undertaken by highly skilled employees. Critics suggest that these activities tend to be located near the headquarters of the parent firm. Since the headquarters of foreign-owned firms are located outside the United States, some are concerned that research and development activities might be shifted out of the United States. For example, as more of the U.S. chemical industry is controlled by foreign-owned firms, critics charge that larger shares of research and development in this industry will be shifted abroad.

One way to assess the importance of this "headquarters" effect is to compare research and development expenditures in the United States by all U.S. firms with those by U.S. affiliates of foreign firms. . . . [R]esearch and development expenditures per worker for all industries were nearly twice as large for affiliates of foreign firms ($2,040) as for all U.S. firms ($1,070). If one limits research and development expenditures to those that are company-funded, the difference becomes even larger.

These differences partially reflect the industrial composition of FDIUS, because most research and development occurs in manufacturing. U.S. manufacturing firms spend larger amounts per employee on research and development ($4,640) than U.S. affiliates of foreign firms ($3,780), a pattern that is reversed when only company-funded expenditures ($3,110) are counted. All in all, there is little evidence that a headquarters effect exists.

Employment and Wage Effects

Without question, the most controversy about FDIUS concerns employment. Advocates of FDIUS suggest that the rising number of U.S. employees in foreign-owned firms represents the creation of new jobs. Critics stress that FDIUS is a dynamic process, which may or may not create jobs. While critics concede that new plants and expansions of existing plants lead to the creation of new jobs, they reject the general presumption that acquisitions create new jobs. For acquisitions to create jobs, one would have to argue that, without the foreign purchase, the jobs in the acquired firm would have been eliminated and no other U.S. firm would have expanded following the closing of an acquired firm. Such an argument strains credibility. A more realistic view is that acquisitions have little effect on jobs and primarily reflect the transfer of jobs from U.S. to foreign owners.

. . . [T]he focus on job creation reflects a fundamental misunderstanding of how the U.S. macroeconomy functions. The supply of labor is the key determinant of employment in the long run. Aggregate demand for goods and services and, thus, the demand for labor, can vary in the short run, causing employment to change; however, in the long run, the economy will move toward its so-called natural rate of unemployment. This rate is unaffected by the degree of foreign ownership of firms in the United States. Thus, the net impact of FDIUS on U.S. employment is negligible.

More important than the number of jobs associated with FDIUS is the types of jobs. This issue is frequently described as "good" jobs being replaced by "bad" jobs. One argument is that foreign-based firms prefer to engage in high-wage activities at home, while engaging in low-wage activities in the United States. Some contrary evidence has already been presented. For example, there is no evidence that foreign-based firms perform research and development in the United States, a high-wage activity, to a lesser degree than U.S. firms do.

Another way to examine job quality is to compare the wages of workers employed by foreign owners with those of U.S. owners. . . . [C]ompensation per worker in U.S. affiliates of foreign firms is comparable to that in U.S. firms. For all industries, pay by U.S. affiliates of foreign firms was $29,800 in 1987, substantially more than the $24,200 paid by U.S. firms. This difference, however, is primarily because the distribution of FDIUS tends to be more pronounced in higher-paying industries than U.S. investment generally.

Looking at specific industries, there is little difference in compensation per worker between the two sets of firms, except in petroleum and finance, insurance and real estate. For example, workers employed by U.S. affiliates of foreign firms in the primary and fabricated metals manufacturing sector averaged $3,000 more in compensation than all U.S. workers in this sector. Meanwhile, in the chemicals and allied products manufacturing sector, the former averaged $2,900 less than the latter. Thus, there is no evidence that FDIUS is causing good (high-paying) jobs to be replaced by bad (low-paying) jobs.

Trade Balance Effects

Another source of controversy concerns the export and import activity of foreign-owned firms in the United States. Critics charge that foreign-owned firms are major contributors to U.S. trade deficits. . . .

Comparing parent companies of U.S.-based MNCs in manufacturing with U.S. affiliates of foreign firms in manufacturing, one finds that U.S. affiliates of foreign firms export less per worker ($13,780 vs. $15,070) and import more per worker ($17,920 vs. $7,060) than parent companies of U.S.-based MNCs. Caution is required in interpreting these numbers, however. First, to infer that, on average, when a foreign firm acquires a firm in the United States, imports per worker will more than double, is inappropriate. There is no reason to expect the newly acquired firm to change its trading pattern substantially simply because of a change in owners.

Second, especially with greenfield investments, FDI in manufacturing frequently begins with assembly operations that require many imported inputs; however, over time, local sourcing grows. Japanese auto manufacturing in the United States provides an example of how local content has increased over time. For example . . . the U.S. content of output by Japanese-owned U.S. automobile affiliates increased from 38 percent in 1988 to 50 percent in 1989.

Closely related is the fact that FDIUS might be displacing imports. In other words, the production associated with FDIUS could reduce imports. For example, prior to Japanese automobile production in the United States, purchases of Japanese automobiles were entirely imports. Now, even though the typical Japanese automobile produced in the United States might have less U.S. content than the typical U.S. automobile produced in the United States, the fact that some portion of the Japanese automobile is produced in the United States means less imports than previously.

Finally, it is important to note that the trading behavior of foreign-owned firms, like trading behavior in general, is beneficial. The technology being transferred from foreign firms to their U.S. affiliates, which the affiliate is importing, makes the affiliate more productive and, thus, more competitive. Similar statements can be made about other imported inputs. To the extent that trade allows the U.S. affiliate to make better use of its resources, the U.S. economy gains.

CONCLUSION

No matter how it is measured, foreign direct investment in the United States has increased substantially since the late 1970s, primarily via acquisitions. The current level of foreign ownership, however, is not high relative to that in most other developed countries. In addition, the foreign direct investment of U.S. firms still exceeds FDIUS.

Overall, the rise in FDIUS can be viewed as the result of technological developments abroad that are being transferred to the United States. Other factors have also affected FDIUS. There is general agreement, for example, that the business cycle affects FDIUS and that, in some industries, the threat of protectionism or protectionism itself has influenced the investment decisions of foreign firms. Foreign exchange and tax rate changes have had, at most, slight effects.

The transfers of technology are a positive development in that they reflect the expectation that production in the United States will be profitable. For the United States as a whole, this transfer of technology allows resources to be more productive, not only in the industry directly affected by the FDI, but also possibly in other industries because of external benefits.

Critics have raised numerous concerns about whether foreign-owned firms in the United States behave differently than U.S. firms and whether this behavior might be detrimental to U.S. interests. These concerns do not stand up to empirical scrutiny. For instance, more technology is being transferred into the United States than out of the United States. The research and development activity of foreign-owned firms is similar to that of U.S. firms. Compensation in foreign-owned firms is similar to U.S. firms, suggesting that foreign ownership is not replacing good jobs with bad ones. Finally, while foreign-owned firms tend to import more than they export, it is far from certain that this is detrimental to U.S. interests.

Overall, foreign-owned companies are a positive factor in making the U.S. economy more competitive and productive. Advocates of public policies to deter foreign ownership should be viewed with skepticism.

13

Selling Off America

THOMAS OMESTAD

Thomas Omestad argues forcefully that the current laissez-faire policy of the United States toward foreign direct investment within its borders threatens to weaken America's international economic strength and political power. Since the early 1980s, Omestad finds, the United States has experienced a rapidly rising influx of foreign investment. Because the United States is more open to foreign investment than other countries, he argues, this influx unfairly and inappropriately increases America's economic and political dependence on others. Moreover, he maintains, foreign investment has not created a significant number of new jobs in the United States. In its concern for America's international power and position, this article contrasts sharply with the views of Coughlin (Reading 12).

Foreigners with fistfuls of devalued dollars now comb America for banks, businesses, factories, land, and securities. This shopping spree began in the 1970s, but its growing strength is a principal legacy of Reaganomics. As long as America consumes more than it produces, the imbalance must be made up with foreign money that purchases IOUs and equity. In the 1980s America began trading ownership of assets (and the future incomes they provide) for the privilege of living beyond its means. The result is a continuing erosion of control over decision making and technologies that are crucial to the creation of national wealth and power.

How long Americans will sustain this grand financial experiment is an open question. Anxieties that foreigners, particularly Japanese, are buying up America have coalesced into an emotional political issue, as seen in the 1988 presidential campaign. The anti-investment appeal reflects a serious weakening of public support for traditional U.S. policy toward foreign funds. A 1988 opinion survey taken for *The International Economy* revealed that 74 per cent of Americans believe foreign investment has lessened U.S. economic independence, 78 per cent favor a law restricting foreign ownership of businesses and real estate, and 89 per cent want foreign investors to register with the government. The gulf between current

Thomas Omestad. "Selling Off America." Reprinted with permission from *Foreign Policy* 76 (Fall 1989) by the Carnegie Endowment for International Peace.

policy and public attitudes means that the Bush administration will come under intensifying pressure to consider controls on foreign ownership, particularly as foreign takeovers continue or even accelerate in the 1990s.

The debate on foreign investment may not bring out the best in the American people. Politicizing foreign investment appeals to the insular, nativist streak in U.S. politics. Foreign purchases offer highly visible signs of America's declining position in the world economy and of the increasing penetration of its economic and political system by foreign interests. When the British purchase Pillsbury, the Japanese buy CBS Records, the West Germans take control of A&P, and the Canadians amass Manhattan skyscrapers, public resentment stirs.

For Canadians and West Europeans, this growing public concern seems premature. Their own unease did not develop until American penetration had reached far greater levels. In the late 1960s and 1970s, distress over extensive American control of key Canadian industries prompted more than 200,000 people to join Independent Canada Associations. But by that time foreign ownership of Canada's manufacturing and energy industries had climbed above 50 per cent. The Canadian government's response was to create a screening agency for foreign acquisitions. In Western Europe, after U.S. investment reached high levels in a number of major industries, the best-selling 1967 book *The American Challenge* galvanized public concern about American economic power. French author Jean-Jacques Servan-Schreiber warned darkly that "fifteen years from now the world's third greatest industrial power, just after the United States and Russia, may not be Europe, but American industry in Europe."

Today, it is America's turn to exploit the opportunities and meet the challenges of foreign economic power. The public dialogue on foreign investment is all too easily dominated by those with isolationist instincts on one side and those with vested interests on the other. Needed is a dispassionate debate, but a debate nonetheless. The issues themselves are too important to be dismissed as xenophobic or narrowly nationalistic, as the Reagan and Bush administrations have sought to do.

While the overall degree of foreign ownership in the American economy does not seem excessive at this point, its rate of growth is cause for concern. America's new vulnerability stems above all from the self-inflicted wounds of U.S. macroeconomic policies. Yet it also follows decades of allowing other countries asymmetrically broad access to U.S. companies, especially to high-technology concerns. The foreign investment wave therefore calls for a reassessment of policy in order to ensure that U.S. interests are being preserved, that acquisitions in industries critical to national defense and civilian high-technology are scrutinized, and that the country proceeds along a path of economic interdependence rather than mere dependence.

TRADITIONAL POLICY

Throughout its history the United States has taken an essentially laissez-faire approach to foreign investment on the premise that free capital flows maximize economic efficiency. "A world with strong foreign investment flows is the opposite of a zero-sum game," President Ronald Reagan stated in September 1983. "We believe there are only winners, no losers, and all participants gain from it." U.S. international investment policy rests on the principle of national treatment: With few exceptions, the same laws govern investment from foreign and domestic sources. Foreign acquisitions are not routinely screened. The policy reflects both a free-market philosophy and the significant profits American companies have reaped by establishing operations abroad, particularly after World War II in capital-hungry Europe, Japan, and Latin America. Through the 1950s and 1960s foreign investment was largely one-way; for every dollar foreigners invested in the United States, Americans plunked down four or five overseas.

By the early 1970s production by the overseas units of U.S. companies had surpassed total exports from the United States itself. Some American multinational corporations deployed more than half of their total assets abroad and drew more than half of their earnings from those holdings. This outward investment sacrificed manufacturing jobs at home, but it allowed American companies as a whole to hold onto a nearly constant share of world exports from the late 1960s on.

For U.S. policymakers the principle of free capital movement served larger geopolitical purposes. As economist Robert Gilpin pointed out in *The Political Economy of International Relations* (1987), "Foreign direct investment has been considered a major instrument through which the United States could maintain its relative position in world markets, and the overseas expansion of multinational corporations has been regarded as a means to maintain America's dominant world economic position in other expanding economies." Open investment was part of the broader U.S.-led effort to liberalize and expand international economic activity through the creation of the General Agreement on Tariffs and Trade (GATT), the International Monetary Fund, and the Organization for Economic Cooperation and Development (OECD). U.S. overseas investments and trade relationships were credited with fostering the economic recovery of Western Europe and Japan and strengthening the anticommunist military alliances.

Since the early 1970s, however, the pattern of foreign investment among industrial countries has shifted significantly. The growth of U.S. overseas investment has slowed, and, with economic recovery achieved, investors in Japan and Western Europe have looked to America and elsewhere for commercial opportunities. Financial deregulation and vastly improved communications technologies have allowed investors to move decisively into foreign securities markets. Meanwhile, multinational corporations have come to view overseas investment as part of a larger strategy. Gaining market shares abroad has become synonymous with staying competitive globally, maximizing long-run returns, and hedging against protectionism. That has been especially true of the world's biggest consumer market, the United States.

By investing in America, foreigners advance a number of goals: They place their capital in a political and legal safe haven, exploit economies of scale, secure distribution networks and improve product-related services, gain access to a skilled workforce and research and development efforts, and circumvent protectionist barriers. The final reason grew especially important during the Reagan years as the value of U.S. imports subject to protectionist restraint doubled to 24 per cent.

Constraining Japanese imports has had the paradoxical effect of creating new competitors at home. Restraints on imported cars, semiconductors, and televisions, for example, have spurred the establishment of Japanese assembly plants in the United States.

During the Reagan years foreign investment was also driven by an improvident macroeconomic policy. Reagan entered office with the dual ideological mission of building up U.S. military power and cutting tax rates. Borrowing to cover the new military expenditures drained some three-quarters of America's chronically meager savings. Interest rates rose as government and private sources competed for funds. Foreign investors, attracted to higher rates of return than were available elsewhere, flocked to America, initially plowing their funds into securities, especially government debt. As foreigners bought up dollars with which to invest in America, the dollar's value increased. But the price of U.S. exports also rose, crippling some U.S. industries and pushing more production abroad. America's international investment fortunes were soon reversed; by 1985 the United States had become a net debtor for the first time since World War I. The mounting imbalance led to monetary coordination among the top industrial countries that since 1985 has sharply devalued the dollar and improved U.S. trade performance. However, the currency's drop undercut the value of dollar-denominated securities at the same time it made hard assets exceedingly cheap for foreign concerns. Thus began a grand debt-for-equity swap that has been dubbed the "fire sale" of America.

Though growing rapidly, foreign investment in the United States is often overstated. Today, foreigners own 4–5 per cent of total U.S. assets. Foreign interests employ around 3 million Americans—3.5 per cent of the labor force. At the end of 1988, according to Commerce Department data, foreigners had $1.79 trillion invested in the United States, while Americans held $1.25 trillion in investments abroad. Thus the United States was a net debtor of $533 billion. (This figure is actually overstated because investments are tabulated according to their book value—the price paid when the asset was acquired. U.S. overseas investments tend to be older than foreign investments here, so their book value falls below current market value to a greater degree than do foreign holdings in America.) Of foreigners' total investment in America in 1988, $329 billion, or just 18 percent, was direct investment, which the Commerce Department defines as the book value of enterprises in which a foreigner owns at least 10 per cent of the voting securities. All other holdings—such as U.S. Treasury and private bonds and smaller equity stakes—are considered portfolio investments. Portfolio holdings are passive in that they do not confer actual control as foreign direct investment (FDI) usually does. Portfolio investment, however, is more volatile because of its high liquidity and sensitivity to interest rate differences.

FDI in the United States has been advancing briskly since the early 1970s. In 1971 it stood at $14 billion, in 1980 $83 billion, and by the end of 1988 $329 billion, a 23-fold jump since 1971 and almost a quadrupling under Reagan. In

1988 FDI grew 21 per cent. Meanwhile, American direct investment abroad has grown more slowly. U.S. FDI rose from $83 billion in 1971 to $215 billion in 1980 and to $327 billion in 1988. In 1988 it grew only 6 per cent. America's worsening financial position suggests that foreign investment here will be outpacing U.S. investment abroad for some time to come.

The top direct investors are first the British and then the Japanese, the latter group advancing quickly during 1988 to displace the Netherlands as the second largest. Canada and West Germany trail in fourth and fifth place.

Much of the public concern over foreign investment stems from its concentration in particular sectors and localities. About 20 per cent of total banking assets in America are held by foreign banks; foreigners control 12 per cent of the U.S. manufacturing base, though slightly less than 1 per cent of its agricultural land. Foreign interests own 25–30 per cent of chemical industry assets and about half of the consumer electronics and cement industries. They are making strong inroads in insurance, publishing, machine tools, semiconductors, and wholesale trade.

Foreigners are also buying heavily into America's major cities: In Los Angeles, they own an estimated 46 per cent of the prime commercial real estate, in Houston 39 per cent, and in the nation's capital 33 per cent. The state of Hawaii received more than one quarter of all Japanese real estate investment in the United States from 1985 to 1987, and home prices in Honolulu soared.

AUTONOMY FOREGONE

The most pervasive concern about foreign investment is that it will reduce America's economic and political autonomy. Foreign held debt and foreign ownership imply dependence and vulnerability. With ownership goes control over economic decisions and influence over political ones. Senator Frank Murkowski (R-Alaska) summed up this view bluntly in the December 30, 1985, *New York Times:* "Once they own your assets, they own you."

While foreigners through their investments gain a direct stake in the health of the U.S. economy, they also can pose a unique problem: Their ultimate political loyalties and interests lie elsewhere. For this reason, all countries at least partially shelter their political systems from foreign influence, even when the system is as grounded in the values of openness and pluralism as is America's.

From a historical standpoint, Washington has good reason for concern about the leverage foreigners have on it. This is particularly apparent when the investors are government-controlled, such as the central banks in Europe and Japan that have amassed huge holdings of U.S. government securities in recent years. Economic pressure is a prime tool of foreign-policy influence, which is exerted even against close allies if necessary. In 1956 the United States demonstrated its alarm at the British-French invasion of Egypt's Suez Canal by withholding badly needed oil supplies from Britain and France and by refusing to help halt a damaging run on the pound. After the 1973 oil embargo Saudi Arabian holdings of U.S. dollars and government securities emerged as a potential "money weapon" against U.S.

foreign policy. The Treasury Department refused to reveal the amount of Saudi holdings to Congress for fear that the Saudis would sell them off and trigger a plunge of the dollar.

America's heavy reliance on foreign capital in the 1980s has greatly accelerated the decline of its global economic power. By 1986 nearly two-thirds of America's net investment in plant, equipment, and housing was being supplied by foreigners. Indeed, without foreign capital, interest rates during 1983–84 might have been five percentage points higher than they were. Foreigners in recent years have financed more than half of the federal budget deficit, and they now hold about 10 per cent of the national debt.

In May 1987 foreign investors showed their clout by balking for two days at the purchase of 30-year Treasury securities; the Treasury quickly cut the price to draw them back into the market. The dumping of Treasury securities by Japanese fund managers, who panicked at the announcement of a poor U.S. trade performance, helped set off the October 1987 stock market crash. And rumors during the 1988 presidential campaign held that Bush was benefiting from an implicit agreement with Bonn and Tokyo to prop up the dollar through election day. Whether or not such an understanding existed, the rumors were a sign of the potential for foreign influence over U.S. economic policy and electoral outcomes.

Dependence on foreign money forced the Reagan administration to replace the previously neutral posture toward foreign investment with an unrestrained welcome. Although couched in terms of free-market economics, the public welcome masked administration fears that foreign funds might flow elsewhere, triggering a hard landing for the economy, the Reagan revolution, and Republican presidential hopes. Thus in 1984 the administration pushed through Congress the repeal of the 30 per cent withholding tax on earnings from foreign-held government and corporate securities. The following year the Treasury allowed publicity-shy foreigners to buy U.S. government bonds anonymously. And Reagan threatened to veto the 1988 trade bill until a proposal for more public disclosure of foreign holdings was removed.

To protect and enhance the value of their investments, foreign interests have stepped up their lobbying and campaign-related activities. Lobbyists and lawyers representing foreign interests are now frequent visitors to Capitol Hill, federal agencies, state legislatures, and city halls. Foreign interests have banded together to form several new lobbying groups, the most influential being the Washington-based Association for Foreign Investment in America led by the prominent former cabinet officer Elliot Richardson.

Foreign interests pressured Florida, California, and other states to repeal their unitary taxes, which are assessed on a company's worldwide sales of goods produced in a state rather than only on the sales made within the state. Sony of America executives threatened to scrap plans to build factories in both California and Florida if their unitary taxes were not lifted. Florida agreed after the governor called a special legislative session during Christmas week 1984. In California foreign interests funneled contributions into the campaign coffers of state legislators. They stressed the state's investment potential and threatened to transfer operations to nonunitary tax states. British Prime Minister Margaret Thatcher asked Reagan to wade back into California politics on the side of repeal; Reagan later announced his support of federal legislation to outlaw the unitary tax nationwide. The legislature in Sacramento eventually scrapped the tax, losing an estimated $300 million in revenue in 1986 alone.

Congress has also faced skillful foreign lobbying efforts. In 1987–88 Toshiba Corporation and its U.S. subsidiary, Toshiba America, orchestrated a grassroots campaign in excess of $9 million that succeeded in easing sanctions intended to punish Toshiba for its sale of high-technology military equipment to the Soviet Union. Toshiba's message to lawmakers was simple: A ban on sales would cost the jobs of thousands of constituents. Toshiba America's lobbyists coordinated protests by companies using its components or selling Toshiba products under their own labels. Ironically, because Toshiba America is considered a U.S. corporation, its lobbyists were not required to register as foreign agents. Another fierce lobbying drive took place in 1988 when foreign investors weighed in against the so-called Bryant amendment, named for Texas Democratic Representative John Bryant, which would have required disclosure of large foreign holdings. Many foreign investors said that they would take their money elsewhere if the amendment were adopted.

The Japanese have been the most active politically. According to Pat Choate, an economist studying foreign political influence in America, 152 Japanese companies and government agencies hired 113 firms for representation in Washington in 1988, three times as many as the British. For this the Japanese paid more than $100 million—"more than the combined budgets of the U.S. Chamber of Commerce, the National Association of Manufacturers, the Business Roundtable, the Committee for Economic Development and the American Business Conference—the five most influential business organizations in Washington," Choate reported in the June 19, 1988, *Washington Post*. Washington lobbying was only part of the elaborate Japanese public relations activities. Japanese corporate philanthropy in America came to $140 million in 1988, while research contracts with universities reached $30 million. Other support goes to museums, think tanks, and public television stations. Clearly, the Japanese have excelled at the American art of winning friends and influencing people.

Foreign investors have also used a major legal loophole to directly influence federal and state campaigns. The Federal Election Campaign Act of 1974 specifically forbids foreign nationals from making contributions to political campaigns. But the Federal Election Commission, in a series of divided opinions, has interpreted the law to permit U.S. subsidiaries owned by foreign firms to donate campaign funds through political action committees (PACs). This interpretation has defeated the congressional intent of barring foreigners from U.S. elections. Foreign-company PACs reportedly contributed more than $1.1 million toward the 1986 election and at least $2 million toward the 1988 election. About 100 foreign-company PACs are now in operation.

Foreign acquisitions raise concerns of another kind when they take place in the defense industry. Thus in 1976 President Gerald Ford set up the Committee on

Foreign Investment in the United States (CFIUS), a Treasury-led interagency body that meets on an ad hoc basis to review such investments for their national security implications. Until new legislation was passed recently, the president would have had to declare a national emergency to block such an acquisition. There seemed to be little need, however, because no president has ever found the need formally to bar a sale through CFIUS.

Growing foreign ownership in the U.S. defense industry is one facet of a broader erosion of the defense industrial base. According to a tally of sales reported in the journal *Mergers and Acquisitions,* 11 companies in military-related industries were sold to foreigners in 1983, while 37 such takeovers, some hostile, occurred in just the first half of 1988.

Defense Department officials have felt that certain purchases could increase the chances of espionage or other transfers of military technology to adversaries. Thus the Pentagon has sought to safeguard defense activities by obtaining private assurances that research and development and production remain in the United States. The government can demand that foreigners divest themselves of units involved in especially sensitive operations or order the U.S. units to operate as blind trusts, allowing foreign owners to collect the profits but keeping them out of management. It can also continue to limit foreign acquisitions of defense contractors to allied countries. Finally, the Pentagon can deny contracts and security clearances to a foreign-owned firm it considers a risk. Still, Pentagon monitors of foreign investment are handicapped by a troubling lack of timely information about takeovers. The Defense Department often discovers the sale of a defense firm only after the fact, and it does not systematically track ownership trends among its contractors and subcontractors. Consequently, no one really knows the true extent of foreign ownership of defense-related firms.

Anxieties about relying on foreign-owned defense firms came to a head in 1987 when the Japanese electronics giant Fujitsu made a $200–$225 million bid for Fairchild Semiconductor Corporation. Ironically, Fairchild was already owned by a French firm, Schlumberger Ltd., and was supplying $100 million in advanced circuitry annually for U.S. defense efforts. Well-publicized Pentagon criticisms of the sale led Fujitsu to withdraw its bid before CFIUS could issue a recommendation. Fairchild, the financial loser, was later sold for $120 million to a U.S. firm, National Semiconductor Corp.

Driven by such security concerns, Congress inserted in the 1988 trade bill a provision authored by Senator James Exon (D-Nebraska) and Representative James Florio (D-New Jersey) that allows the president to block foreign acquisitions if they appear to endanger national security. Reagan called the provision unnecessary but did not veto it. The first test of the Exon-Florio amendment came in February 1989 when President George Bush decided against blocking the sale of the Monsanto Company's semiconductor subsidiary to a West German chemical group. The Monsanto firm was the last major U.S. manufacturer of silicon wafers, a vital component of advanced semiconductors. Although CFIUS deliberated on the deal's implications for the defense industry, it proved difficult to justify blocking the sale to a close ally, particularly after the purchaser, Huels A. G., privately committed to keep Monsanto's research and development in the United States.

RESTRICTIONS ABROAD

Political support for foreign investment has been shaken by the long-time imposition of tougher limits on foreign ownership by other countries. The United States places fewer restrictions on foreign investment than any other industrial power. While the Reagan administration publicly prodded trading partners to lower their trade barriers, it exerted little pressure in the investment field. The Bush administration will find itself pressed by Congress to seek treatment for American overseas investment roughly equivalent to treatment of investment here.

Foreign acquisitions in America are blocked in only a few areas related to national security as specified by OECD guidelines. Foreigners may not invest in nuclear energy, control oil pipelines, own U.S.-flag vessels, buy more than 25 per cent of a U.S. airline, or hold a broadcasting license. Thirty states limit foreign purchases of land, particularly farmland. Foreign investors need to register with the federal government only for purchases of farmland. Abroad, a trend toward liberalization of investment regulations is underway, but most countries continue to put up stiffer barriers than the United States. . . .

The Reagan administration quietly sought to lower . . . barriers to U.S. investment by placing foreign investment into an expanded GATT. But progress has been slow. Several Third World countries have opposed the idea out of fear that it would diminish sovereign control of their economies.

Reagan administration officials maintained that a more assertive approach aimed at achieving reciprocity would invite retaliation abroad. They also argued that it would violate the principle of national treatment and undercut efforts to get other countries to liberalize investment regulations. Still, the political pressure for a level playing field in investment led the Reagan and now Bush administrations to consider reciprocity, if only rhetorically, as a policy goal. This pressure will intensify with the approach of Western Europe's internally free market in 1992. The EC is likely to add another (supranational) layer of review for large foreign acquisitions in Europe. And it is gravitating toward a strategy of capturing the value-added production of high-technology companies that want to do business in the EC. Tough new local content rules on the import of integrated circuits for semiconductors, for example, will probably force U.S. computer chip makers to shift advanced production from America to Europe.

JOBS AND TECHNOLOGY

Proponents routinely contend that foreign investment will help spark the reindustrialization of the American economy. Foreign investors are said to be creating millions of jobs. Lured by this prospect, states and cities entice them with hundreds of millions of dollars annually in incentive packages—tax write-offs, financing, and new infrastructure—that often lead to expensive bidding wars. But the common wisdom that foreign investment is an important source of new jobs may simply be wrong, according to a surprising new analysis of employment data. Economists Norman Glickman and Douglas Woodward, in their 1989 book *The New Competitors: How Foreign Investors Are Changing the U.S. Economy,* analyzed the employment effects of foreign direct investment from new plants and expansions on one hand and cutbacks on the other. They concluded that foreign investment in the United States actually reduced total employment between 1982 and 1986 by 55,900 jobs. If the recession years of 1982 and 1983 are excluded, foreigners created only a net 55,500 jobs, barely 1 per cent of all employment growth over the 1984–86 period. Thus foreign investment is hardly the engine of job growth that is claimed. From a national standpoint, states and cities may be wasting money and unfairly favoring new foreign-owned manufacturers with subsidies.

How is this conclusion possible given the rapid growth of foreign investment? The vast share of FDI represents purchases of existing assets; in 1986, for example, 81 per cent of the value of FDI and 97 per cent of all employment added to foreign payrolls came through mergers and acquisitions. These transactions transfer control of assets and do not necessarily create jobs. Indeed, mergers and acquisitions often lead to corporate restructuring that results in job losses as the new owners move to ease the burden of takeover debt. After the takeovers of Allied Giant and Federated Department Stores by Canadian corporate raider Robert Campeau, for example, more than 10,000 workers were laid off and a number of retail chains were sold. On the other hand, new foreign owners can rescue failing companies, saving jobs that might otherwise be lost. The number of foreign acquisitions that fall into this category is unknown, but one was Japanese Bridgestone's purchase of Firestone Tire and Rubber. Bridgestone appears to have arrested Firestone's downward slide by introducing quality and cost-saving measures and by soothing union-management tensions.

Even more important, foreign investors, chiefly the Japanese, are strategically picking off American competitors. In 1987 the Japanese bought an incredible 20 times as many U.S. high-tech firms as Americans bought in Japan. Japanese multinational corporations have concentrated their U.S. investments in basic industries and in the high-tech and service sectors, and they often bring along their suppliers. Japanese firms, more than European and Canadian ones, have been prone to keep top management, high value-added production, and research and development operations at home, often preferring to build "screwdriver" assembly plants that pay lower wages. "Time after time, the Japanese reserve for themselves the part of the value-added chain that pays the highest wages and offers the greatest opportunity for controlling the next generation of production and product technology," economists Robert Reich and Eric Mankin wrote in the March–April 1986 *Harvard Business Review.*

Most Japanese multinationals have not transferred technology or allowed local control to the degree that American and West European corporations have for decades. Japanese firms have launched many joint ventures in computers, biotechnology, and other high-tech areas with the apparent aim of transporting advanced research to Japan. As a result, American companies lose development and manufacturing experience and are drained of their research findings. As it stands now, some become mere marketers and distributors for Japanese-made products, exacerbating America's deindustrialization. A survey of companies operating in the U.S. automobile, computer and semiconductor industries—where Japanese firms dominate among foreign competitors—taken by Glickman and other researchers found that the proportion of American workers involved in research and development for foreign firms is less than half (3.1 per cent) of that for domestically owned firms (6.6 per cent). In short, some foreign acquisitions weaken the economy's capacity to generate wealth and translate new technologies into commercial applications.

Particularly worrisome is the growing reliance of American high-tech start-up companies on foreign partners for cash and manufacturing expertise. The quid pro quo is usually a transfer of new technologies to the foreign investors, creating future industrial competitors. One case is that of Japan's Kubota, a tractor company that is now making mini-supercomputers after investing in five Silicon Valley firms. The design, chips, and software all came from cash-hungry American firms in which Kubota staked money in exchange for minority shares and the transfer of technology. For a $75 million investment, Kubota is gaining the expertise to make a computer entirely on its own in a few years. Another example is the cash investment by Taiwan's Microtek International in Mouse Systems Corporation, a troubled U.S. maker of optical scanning equipment. Microtek used the deal to secure a source of technology and rights to buy all of Mouse. These cases illustrate a dangerous trend: U.S. companies, acting on short-term needs, are selling off the very technologies that have given them (and the economy) long-term competitive advantages.

In lower-tech areas, American manufacturers are benefiting from joint ventures through an infusion of Japanese management and manufacturing techniques, though others are facing painful competition on their home turf. U.S. automobile and auto parts manufacturers, for example, are being squeezed by Japanese competitors. The United Auto Workers estimated that 200,000 jobs might be lost by 1990 because U.S.-based Japanese manufacturers use labor more efficiently than American firms and import more parts.

However, the competition also motivates American producers to improve efficiency, quality control, and coordination between parts suppliers and assemblers; some U.S. firms are adopting the more demanding Japanese methods, such as just-in-time inventory purchases. At a General Motors–Toyota joint venture in Fremont, California, Japanese manufacturing know-how and management has turned around a failed operation. General Motors says the cars produced there are its best and most efficient. Similar improvements have been reported through joint ventures in the steel industry. From a national policy standpoint, however, the key test will be whether General Motors and other U.S. joint-venture participants can transfer new technology and production expertise to their other operations.

The surge in foreign investment warrants a fresh look at U.S. policy. But the aim of that reassessment must not be a general constriction of the influx of money. Given America's overreliance on foreign funds, that could prompt a recession or provoke even greater restrictions abroad. Yet the emerging public reaction to foreign ownership cannot be assuaged merely by touting the principle of open investment, which most countries thwart in practice, or by preaching the benefits of foreign investment, which are usually overstated. Policymakers need to reassure the public that long-term U.S. interests are being protected amid growing overseas ownership.

The underlying tenet of America's international investment policy must be to end its macroeconomic addiction to foreign money. Accepting the benefits of integration into the world economy does not mean endorsing a fiscal policy that unnecessarily increases U.S. dependence on foreign investors. This policy is unsustainable economically and politically; it also raises the cost of capital and diverts foreign and domestic savings to consumption rather than to the investment that will raise future living standards. It is, in short, no way for an economic superpower to run its affairs. . . .

Refining U.S. investment policy should not degenerate into an attempt to wall off the world economy. Rather, the goal should be to advance American interests within the framework of increasing interdependence. The point is not to blame foreign firms for assertively pursuing their own interests but to recognize that fact and adapt U.S. policy accordingly. The laissez-faire attitude that continues to guide policy needs to be shelved in favor of a more pragmatic orientation—one that recognizes the problems, as well as the benefits, of foreign investment.

IV

MONEY AND FINANCE

The international economy, like domestic economies, requires a common monetary standard to function smoothly. For individuals and firms to buy and sell and to save and invest, they need some generally acceptable and predictable unit of account against which other goods can be measured, a medium of exchange with which transactions can be carried out, and a store of value in which wealth can be held. National currencies serve this purpose within countries: Americans buy, sell, save, and invest in dollars. In international trade and payments, a variety of possible common measures can be imagined; in practice, the two purest cases are a commodity standard and an international currency standard. Economic actors could use a widely traded commodity, such as gold or pork bellies, against which to measure other goods; or they might arrive at some fictitious unit in which goods could be priced. The former approximates the classical gold standard, the latter, present-day special drawing rights, which are a sort of "paper gold" issued by the International Monetary Fund and equal to a mix of national currencies. Because agreement on a fictitious international currency is difficult, such national currencies as the dollar or the pound sterling have often been used as the basis for international payments.

If the international monetary system provides the measures needed to conduct world trade and payments, the international financial system provides the means to carry out trade and payments. For many hundreds of years, financial institutions—especially banks—have financed trade among clients in different nations, sold and bought foreign currencies, transferred money from one country to another, and lent capital for overseas investment. If, as is often averred, the international monetary system is the Great Wheel that allows goods to move in international trade, the international financial system is the grease that allows the wheel itself to turn.

In the modern era, since 1820 or so, there have been essentially four well-functioning international monetary systems in the non-Communist world; each has had corresponding international financial characteristics. From about 1820 until World War I, the world was on or near the classical gold standard, in which many major national currencies were tied to gold at a legally fixed rate. In principle, as Benjamin J. Cohen explains in Reading 14, the gold standard was self-regulating; should any national currency (and economy) get out of balance, it would be forced back into equilibrium by the very operation of the system. In practice, the pre–World War I system was actually a gold–sterling standard; the British pound sterling, backed by a strong government and the world's leading financial center, was "as good as gold," and most international trade and payments were carried out in sterling.

The world financial system in the century before World War I was indeed dominated by British banks, which financed much of world trade and channeled enormous amounts of investment capital to such rapidly developing countries as the United States, Australia, Argentina, and South Africa. As time wore on, the financial institutions of other European powers, especially France and Germany, also began to expand abroad. The result was a highly integrated system of international monetary and financial interactions under the Pax Britannica.

Even before World War I however, strains and rivalries were beginning to test the system. Once the war started in 1914, international trade and payments collapsed: of all the world's major financial markets, only New York stayed open for the duration of the conflict. Indeed, by the time World War I ended, the center of international finance had shifted from London to New York, and Wall Street remained the world's principal lender until the Great Depression of the 1930s.

As might be expected, given the reduced economic might of Great Britain, the prewar gold–sterling standard could not be rebuilt. Yet neither was the United States—beset by the isolationist–internationalist conflict at home—willing to simply replace Great Britain at the apex of the world monetary system. What emerged was the so-called gold-exchange standard, where most countries went back to tying their currencies to gold, but no single national currency came to dominate the others. Dollars, sterling, and French francs were all widely used in world trade and payments, yet, given the lack of lasting international monetary cooperation in the period, the arrangement was quite unstable and short-lived. Normal international economic conditions were not restored until 1924, and within a few years the depression brought the system crashing down. With the collapse of the gold-exchange standard and the onset of the depression and World War II, the international monetary and financial systems remained in disarray until after 1945.

As World War II came to an end, the Allied powers, led by the United States, began reconstructing an international monetary system. This Bretton Woods system was based, in the monetary sphere, on an American dollar tied to gold at the rate of thirty-five dollars an ounce; other Western currencies were in turn tied to the dollar. This was a modified version of the pre-1914 gold standard, with the dollar at its center rather than sterling. As in the Pax Britannica, massive flows of capital from the leading nation—Great Britain in the first instance, the United States in the second—were crucial to the proper functioning of the mechanism. Whereas in the British case these capital flows were primarily private loans, from 1945 to 1965 they were essentially government or multilateral loans and foreign direct investment. Only after 1965 did private international finance once again become significant, rapidly reaching historically unprecedented proportions and developing new characteristics.

Even as the new international financial system, generally known as the Euromarket, was gathering steam, the Bretton Woods monetary system was beginning to weaken. It was, as Cohen (Reading 14) points out, more and more difficult to maintain the dollar price of gold at thirty-five dollars an ounce. As pressure built on the dollar, and attempts at reform stagnated, the Nixon administration finally decided that the system was unsustainable. In August 1971, President Richard Nixon "closed the gold window," ending the dollar's free convertibility into gold. The dollar was soon devalued. By 1975, the gold–dollar standard had been replaced by the current floating-rate system. In Reading 15, Barry Eichengreen evaluates the ability of an international political explanation—the so-called theory of hegemonic stability—to explain the evolution of international monetary relations across these historical systems.

Under the current system of floating exchange rates, the value of most currencies is set more or less freely by private traders in world currency markets. Thus, the values of the dollar, the deutsche mark, the franc, and so on, fluctuate on international currency markets. This has led to frequent and rapid changes in the relative prices of major currencies, as well as to frequent complaints about the unplanned nature of the new system. Because of the central role of the United States dollar even in today's floating-rate system, changes in American economic policy can drive the United States dollar up and down dramatically, in ways that have important effects on the economy both of the United States and of the rest of the world. The "unholy trinity" of a fixed exchange rate, capital mobility, and autonomous monetary policy—and the necessary trade-offs engendered by the pursuit of these three goals—is central to understanding the current floating-rate system and the potential for cooperation among the world's leading nations in international monetary affairs. This problem is examined by Benjamin J. Cohen in a second essay (Reading 16).

In the 1970s, as American inflation rates rose, the dollar's value dropped relative to other major currencies. However, in 1979 American monetary policy began to concentrate on fighting inflation. The result was a worldwide rise in interest rates, followed rapidly by a deep recession, a reduction in inflation, and a dramatic rise in the dollar's value. Although inflation was brought down, the strong dollar wreaked havoc with the ability of many American industries to compete internationally. The American trade deficit grew to well above $100 billion, even as the United States government financed large portions of its growing budget deficit by borrowing from foreigners. In the mid-1980s the dollar dropped back down to its lowest levels in nearly forty years, while large American trade and budget deficits continued to be financed by foreigners. Through it all, there was dissatisfaction in many quarters because of the underlying uncertainty about international trade and monetary trends. Today, currencies fluctuate widely, many of the world's major nations are experiencing unprecedented trade surpluses or deficits, and capital flows across borders in enormous quantities.

Monetary uncertainty has led some nations to seek security in a variety of alternative institutions. Some countries and observers support the development of a new international money, of which special drawing rights might be a precursor. Others desire a return to the gold standard and the monetary discipline that system fostered. The principal strategy has been to seek stability through cooperative regional agreements. The most important of these agreements is the European Monetary System, created in 1979. Through the EMS, the different national currencies of the members of the European Union are essentially fixed against each other but move up and down together against the dollar, the yen, and other non-European monies. In tandem with the increasing economic integration of goods and services markets in Europe, the European Union has also proposed and is working toward implementing a monetary union that would involve the adoption of a single currency. The history and politics of European monetary unification are examined by Barry Eichengreen and Jeffry Frieden (Reading 17).

In international finance, the period since 1965 has been extraordinarily eventful. The Euromarket has grown to several trillion dollars, and international banking has become one of the great growth industries in the world economy. The recent explosion of international finance is unprecedented. Net international bond and bank lending was $440 billion in 1989, rising from just $180 billion five years earlier. Capital outflows from the thirteen leading industrialized economies averaged $444 billion in 1989, in contrast to $52 billion in the late 1970s; moreover, today almost two-thirds of such outflows are portfolio investment and only one-third are foreign direct investment, the reverse of only a decade earlier. Indeed, in the late 1970s, total global outflows of portfolio capital averaged $15 billion a year; between 1986 and 1992, they averaged $205.3 billion a year—a more than thirteenfold increase.

To put these annual flows in perspective, capital outflows were equivalent to 7 percent of world merchandise trade in the late 1970s, but rose to 15 percent in 1989; likewise, the outstanding stock of international bank and bond lending was under $200 billion in 1973, equivalent to 5 percent of the aggregate gross national product of the industrialized countries, and $3.6 trillion in 1989, equivalent to 25 percent of aggregate GNP.

In addition, recent changes in regulations and technology have made it possible for money to move across borders almost instantly, giving rise to massive short-term international financial transactions. By 1993, for instance, foreign-exchange trading in the world's financial centers averaged about a trillion dollars a day, equivalent to nearly a billion dollars per minute and fifty times the amount of world trade each day.[1]

Jeffry Frieden's article (Reading 18) discusses the political implications of international capital movements, both for nations and for groups and sectors within nations. The asset positions of nations and groups, he argues, affect their economic interests and, in turn, their political strategies in important ways. John Goodman and Louis Pauly (Reading 19) examine how recent changes in international financial markets have made national capital controls obsolete and produced a remarkable convergence among countries toward more liberal international financial policies. In their view, based on the predominance of international economic factors, increased capital mobility has overwhelmed the kinds of national and group differences discussed by Frieden.

Postwar monetary and financial affairs have given rise to both academic and political polemics. Developing countries especially have argued that the existing systems of international monetary relations and international banking work to their detriment, and have proposed sweeping reforms. Most developed nations believe that current arrangements, imperfect as they may be, are the best available, and that reform schemes are simply unrealistic.

Among scholars, international monetary and financial relations raise important analytic issues. As in other arenas, the very rapid development of globe-straddling international financial markets has led some to believe that the rise of supranational banks has eroded the power of national states. In this view, international monetary relations essentially serve to enrich increasingly global international banks and their allies in such international institutions as the IMF. Other analysts believe that national governments are still the primary determinants of international monetary and financial trends. The specific policies of major states toward their own banks and their own currencies are, in this view, set in line with national interests; banks and currency movements are instruments of national policy and not the other way around. The tension between a monetary and financial system that is in a sense beyond the reach of individual states, and currencies and banks that clearly have home countries, gives rise to a fundamental tension in world politics and in the study of the international political economy.

NOTE

1. These figures are from Jeffry A. Frieden, "Invested Interests: The Politics of National Economic Policies in a World of Global Finance," *International Organization* 45, 4 (1991): 428; and from Bank for International Settlements, *Sixty-Third Annual Report* (Basle: Bank for International Settlements, 1993).

14

A Brief History of International Monetary Relations

BENJAMIN J. COHEN

Benjamin J. Cohen describes the evolution of the international monetary system over the past century. He shows how the system has evolved away from a gold standard toward the use of national currencies not backed by precious metals for international trade and payments. As Cohen indicates, the national goals of independent states have often conflicted with the more general international goal of a stable, workable means of international payments. The two most successful experiences in overcoming the contradiction between national desires and global cooperation have been in the periods before World War I and after World War II, in which Great Britain and the United States, respectively, served as bankers to the world. From an international political perspective, Cohen argues that in these eras one nation managed and enforced international monetary relations in ways that conformed both to the hegemon's national goals and to the maintenance of international monetary stability—which is not to say that the resultant order was benevolent to all concerned, as Cohen points out. In any case, just as the decline of British political and economic power undermined the classical gold standard, so too has the United States' relative decline since 1970 led to a reshuffling of existing international monetary arrangements.

THE CLASSICAL GOLD STANDARD

. . . It is impossible to specify a precise date when the international monetary order began. The origins of international monetary relations, like those of money itself, are shrouded in the obscurity of prehistory. We know that there were well-defined monetary areas in many parts of the ancient world. But it is only with the rise of

Benjamin J. Cohen. "A Brief History of International Monetary Relations." From Benjamin J. Cohen, *Organizing the World's Money.* Copyright © 1977 by Basic Books Inc. Reprinted by permission of Basic Books, a division of HarperCollins Publishers, Inc. and Macmillan Ltd., London.

the Roman Empire that we begin to find documentary evidence of a very explicit international monetary order. The Roman monetary order, which was based initially on the gold coinage of Julius Caesar and later on the gold solidus (bezant, nomisma) for Byzantium, lasted some twelve centuries in all. Though confronted from the seventh century on with competition from a silver bloc centered on the newly emergent Muslim dinar, the Roman system did not break down completely until the sacking of Constantinople in 1203. The next five centuries were characterized by fluctuating exchange rates and a succession of dominant moneys—the "dollars of the Middle Ages," one source has called them[1]—including in later years the Florentine fiorino, the Venetian ducato, the Spanish reale, and the Dutch florin. After the beginning of the Industrial Revolution, it was the British pound sterling that rose to a position of preeminence in world monetary affairs.

As its name implies, the pound sterling was originally based on silver. In fact, however, England began practicing a loose sort of bimetallism—gold coins circulating alongside silver ones—even as early as the fourteenth century. (Gold coinage was first introduced into England in 1344, during the reign of Edward III.) Gresham's Law was coined during the reign of Queen Elizabeth I. Sir Isaac Newton, as Master of the Mint, tried to cope with the problem of bad money driving out good by calculating the value of the gold guinea (named after the region in West Africa where gold was mined) in terms of silver shillings. And in 1817 gold was formally declared legal tender in England alongside silver. From the time of the Napoleonic Wars, the United Kingdom moved rapidly from bimetallism to a single-money system. In 1798 the free coinage of silver was suspended and a £25 limit set on the legal-tender power of silver coins. In 1816 silver's legal-tender powers were further limited to £2. And after 1819 silver could no longer be used to redeem circulating bank notes: paper could be redeemed in gold coin only. From that date onward, the pound was effectively based on gold alone. The British were on a full gold standard.

Other countries, however, resisted the gold standard for several decades more. Most European nations, as well as the United States, remained legally bimetallic for at least another half century; most others, especially in Asia, formally retained silver standards. It was only in the 1870s that the movement toward a full-fledged international gold standard picked up momentum and it is from this decade that the modern history of international monetary relations is customarily dated. In 1871 the new German empire adopted the gold mark as its monetary unit, discontinuing the free coinage and unlimited legal-tender powers of silver. In 1873 a parallel decision followed in the United States (the "Crime of '73"), and by 1878 silver had been demonetized in France and virtually every other European country as well. During this decade, the classical gold standard was born. During succeeding decades, it spread to encompass virtually all of the world's independent countries, as well as all of the various colonial empires of Europe.

The classical gold standard was a comparatively brief episode in world history, ending with the outbreak of World War I in 1914. It was defined by two key features. A country was considered to be "on" the gold standard if (1) its central bank pledged to buy and sell gold (and only gold) freely at a fixed price in terms of the home currency and (2) its private residents could export or import gold freely. Together these two features defined a pure fixed-exchange-rate mechanism of balance-of-payments adjustment. Fixed exchange rates were established by the ratios of the prices at which central banks pledged to buy and sell gold for local currency. Free export and import of gold in turn established the means for reconciling any differences between the demand and supply of a currency at its fixed exchange rate. Deficits, requiring net payments to foreigners, were expected to result in outflows of gold, as residents converted local currency at the central bank in order to meet transactions obligations abroad. Conversely, surpluses were expected to result in gold inflows. Adjustment was supposed to work through the impact of such gold flows on domestic economic conditions in each country.

The mechanism of liquidity creation under the classical gold standard was very nearly a pure commodity standard—and that commodity, of course, was gold. Silver lost its role as an important reserve asset during the decade of demonetization in the 1870s. And national currencies did not even begin to enter into monetary reserves in significant quantities until after 1900. The most widely held national currency before World War I was the pound; its principal rivals were the French franc and the German mark. But even as late as 1914, the ratio of world foreign-exchange reserves to world gold reserves remained very low. The monetary standard even then was still essentially a pure commodity standard.

After World War I, observers tended to look back on the classical gold standard with a sense of nostalgia and regret—a sort of Proustian *Recherche du temps perdu*. As compared with the course of events after 1918, the pre-1914 monetary order appeared, in retrospect, to have been enormously successful in reconciling the tension between economic and political values. During its four decades of existence, world trade and payments grew at record rates, promoting technical efficiency and economic welfare; yet, looking back, it seemed that problems of balance-of-payments adjustment and conflicts of policy between nations had been remarkably rare. The gold standard seemed to have succeeded to a unique degree in accommodating and balancing the efficiency and consistency objectives. For many, it had literally been a "Golden Age" of monetary relations.

The image of a Golden Age, however, was a myth, based on at least two serious misconceptions of how the gold standard had actually operated in practice. One misconception concerned the process of balance-of-payments adjustment, the other involved the role of national monetary policies. The process of balance-of-payments adjustment was said to have depended primarily on changes of domestic price levels. The model was that of the so-called price-specie-flow mechanism: outflows of gold (specie) shrinking the money supply at home and deflating the level of domestic prices, inflows expanding the money supply and inflating domestic prices. National monetary policies, although reinforcing the adjustment process, were said to have been actually concerned exclusively with defense of the convertibility of local currencies into gold. Central banks were said to have responded to gold flows more or less mechanically and passively, with a minimum of discretionary action or judgment. They simply played the "rules of the game," allowing gold flows to have their full impact on domestic money supplies and price levels. Combined, these misconceptions produced a myth of an impersonal, fully automatic, and politically symmetrical international monetary order dependent simply on a combination of domestic price flexibility and natural constraints on the production of gold to ensure optimality of both the adjustment process and reserve supply.

More recent historical research has revealed just how misleading this myth of the Golden Age really was. Regarding the role of monetary policy, for example, Arthur Bloomfield has convincingly demonstrated that central banks before 1914 were rarely quite as mechanical or passive as observers later believed. In fact, central banks exercised a great deal of discretion in reacting to inward or outward flows of gold. The rules of the game could be interpreted in either a negative or a positive sense. In the negative sense, central banks could simply refrain from any actions designed to counteract the influence of gold flows on domestic money supplies; in the positive sense, central banks might have been expected to magnify the domestic monetary influence of gold flows according to their deposit-reserve ratios. Bloomfield has shown that under the classical gold standard, central banks hardly ever adhered to the rules in the positive sense, and sometimes even departed from them in the negative sense. Of course, this was still an era of predominantly laissez-faire attitudes in government economic policy. Yet, even then, central banks were neither entirely unaware of, nor indifferent to, the effects of gold flows on domestic prices, incomes, or public confidence. To counteract such effects when it suited them, monetary authorities developed a variety of techniques for evading the rules of the game—including manipulation of the margins around exchange rates (technically, the "gold points"), direct intervention in the foreign-exchange market, and loans between central banks. Monetary policies in this period were never really either fully passive or simply automatic.

Similarly, regarding the process of balance-of-payments adjustment, Robert Triffin has convincingly demonstrated that domestic price levels rarely played as much of a role before 1914 as observers later believed. In fact, the process of adjustment depended at least as much on changes of domestic income and employment as on price changes. But most of all, the process depended on capital movements. The role of international capital movements in adjusting to payments disequilibria was far more important than any role that the terms of trade may have played. . . .

However, capital movements were not something that all countries could avail themselves of with equal facility. Triffin drew a distinction between countries that were capital exporters and those that were capital importers. Capital-exporting countries usually could avoid the consequences of balance-of-payments deficits—domestic deflation or a possible threat to the gold convertibility of the local currency—simply by slowing down investment abroad. The customary instrument in this regard was the central-bank discount rate (in England, Bank rate); that is, the rate at which the central bank discounted collateral when lending to commercial banks. A rise of the discount rate, cutting back cash reserves of banks, could normally be relied upon to reduce the rate of capital outflow and improve the balance of payments. Borrowing countries, on the other hand, were far less able to control the rate of their capital imports, these being primarily determined by credit conditions in the capital-exporting countries. The Golden Age, therefore, was really limited only to the "core" of advanced nations of Europe and the so-called regions of recent settlement (including North America, Australia, South Africa, and Argentina). Elsewhere, the gold standard was far less successful in preserving payments stability or avoiding policy conflict. . . .

Thus, not only was the gold standard neither impersonal nor fully automatic; it was also not politically symmetrical. In fact, the pre-1914 monetary order was arranged in a distinctly hierarchical fashion, with the countries of the periphery at the bottom, the core countries above, and at the peak—Britain. Great Britain dominated international monetary relations in the nineteenth century as no state has since, with the exception of the United States immediately after World War II. Britain was the supreme industrial power of the day, the biggest exporter of manufactured goods, the largest overseas investor. London was by far the most important world financial center, sterling by far the most widely used of the world's currencies for both current- and capital-account transactions. It is sometimes claimed that the gold standard was in reality a sterling-exchange standard. In one sense this appellation is misleading, insofar as most monetary reserves before 1914 (as mentioned above) were still held in gold, not sterling, and insofar as governments continued to be concerned with maintaining the gold value of their currencies, not the sterling value. Yet in another sense the facts cannot be denied: the classical gold standard *was* a sterling standard—a hegemonic regime—in the sense that Britain not only dominated the international monetary order, establishing and maintaining the prevailing rules of the game, but also gave monetary relations whatever degree of inherent stability they possessed.

This stability was ensured through a trio of roles which at that time only Britain had the economic and financial resources to play: (1) maintaining a relatively open market for the exports of countries in balance-of-payment difficulties; (2) providing contracyclical foreign long-term lending; and (3) acting as lender of last resort in times of exchange crisis. These were not roles that the British deliberately sought or even particularly welcomed. As far as the Bank of England was concerned its monetary policies were dictated solely by the need to protect its narrow reserves and the gold convertibility of the pound. It did not regard itself as responsible for global monetary stabilization or as money manager of the world. Yet this is precisely the responsibility that was thrust upon it in practice—acquired, like the British Empire itself, more or less absentmindedly. The widespread international use of sterling and the close links between the larger financial markets in London and smaller national financial markets elsewhere inevitably endowed Britain with the power to guide the world's monetary policy. Changes of policy by the Bank of England inevitably imposed a certain discipline and coordination on monetary conditions in other countries. . . .

It is important to recall, however, that the stability ensured by British monetary management was confined largely to the core of advanced nations in Europe and the regions of recent settlement—countries that were themselves capital exporters or, when necessary, were capable of availing themselves of the lending facilities of London or other financial centers. The less-developed countries of the periphery were, as emphasized, far less able to control the rate of their foreign capital imports; moreover, they suffered from Britain's related power to avoid the continuing cost of adjustment by manipulating its international terms of trade.... As Fred Hirsch has argued, Britain "managed" the system partly at the expense of its weakest members."[2] Over time, this was bound to become a source of serious policy conflict in the monetary order.

In fact, it may be argued that behind the deceptive facade of the Golden Age, the classical gold standard actually bore within itself the seeds of its own destruction. Not only did the order require the continued acquiescence of periphery countries in order to preserve a semblance of stability in the core; it also depended on the continued hegemony of Great Britain in the world's economic affairs. But as many economic historians have noted, this dominance was already beginning to fade, even as early as the turn of the century. From the decade of the 1870s onward, British industrialists were faced with a mounting wave of competition in world export markets, first from Germany and the United States, and later from France, Russia, and Japan. From the 1890s onward, London was faced with growing competition from newly emergent financial centers like Paris, Berlin, and later New York; the pound found itself rivalled *inter alia* by the franc, the mark, and eventually the dollar. As a result of these developments, the British gradually lost a good part of their power to manage the international monetary order. Thus, when it was brought down by the outbreak of World War I, the classical gold standard had already become a rather fragile thing. It is perhaps too much to argue, as does one economic historian, that "the tree felled by the crisis was already rotten."[3] But signs of decay there most certainly were.

THE INTERWAR PERIOD

When World War I broke out, all of the belligerent nations—and soon most others as well—took action to protect their gold reserves by suspending currency convertibility and embargoing gold exports. The classical gold standard was dead. Private individuals could no longer redeem paper currency in gold, nor could they sell it abroad. But they could still sell one paper currency for another (exchange control not being invented until the 1930s) at whatever price the exchange market would bear. The fixed exchange-rate mechanism of the gold standard, therefore, was succeeded by its absolute opposite: a pure floating exchange-rate regime. In the ensuing years, as currency values varied considerably under the impact of wartime uncertainties, the international monetary order could not even come near to realizing its potential for joint gain.

Accordingly, once the war was over and peace arrangements taken care of, governments quickly turned their attention to the problem of world monetary reform. Lulled by the myth of the Golden Age, they saw their task as a comparatively simple one: to restore the classical gold standard (or a close approximation thereof). The major conundrum seemed to be an evident shortage of gold, owing to the extreme price inflations that had occurred in almost all countries during and immediately after the war. These had sharply reduced the purchasing power of the world's monetary gold stock, which was still valued at its old prewar parities. One plausible solution might have been an equally sharp multilateral devaluation of currencies in terms of gold, in order to restore the commodity value of gold reserves. But that was ruled out by most countries on the grounds that a return to "normal" (and to the Golden Age) must include a return to prewar rates of exchange. Yet at the same time, governments understandably wanted to avoid a scramble for gold that would have pushed up the metal's commodity value through competitive deflations of domestic prices. Some other solution had to be found.

The "solution" finally agreed upon was to *economize* on the use of gold. An international economic conference in 1922 (the Genoa Conference) recommended worldwide adoption of a gold-exchange standard in order to "centralize and coordinate the demand for gold, and so avoid those wide fluctuations in the purchasing power of gold which might otherwise result from the simultaneous and competitive efforts of a number of countries to secure metallic reserves."[4] (Central banks were urged to substitute foreign-exchange balances for gold in their reserves as a "means of economizing the use of gold."[5] Gold holdings were to be systematically concentrated in the major financial centers (e.g., London); outside the centers, countries were to maintain their exchange rates by buying and selling "gold exchange" (i.e., currencies convertible into gold, such as sterling) instead of gold itself. The monetary order was thus to combine a pure fixed exchange-rate mechanism of balance-of-payments adjustment modeled on the classical gold standard, with a new mixed commodity-currency standard to cope with the shortage of gold.

The gold-exchange standard came into formal existence early in 1925, when Britain reestablished the gold convertibility of the pound and eliminated restrictions on gold exports. Within a year nearly forty other nations had joined in the experiment, either de jure or de facto, and most other independent governments joined not much later. But the experiment did not last long. In 1931, following a wave of bank failures on the European continent, the British were forced by a run on their reserves to suspend convertibility once again, and in the chaos that ensued the international monetary order broke up into congeries of competing and hostile currency blocs. The largest of these was the sterling bloc, comprising Britain, its overseas dependencies and dominions (except Canada, which had closer financial ties with the United States), and a variety of independent states with traditionally close trading and banking connections with Britain. This bloc was a shrunken remnant of the world that the British had dominated and in effect managed prior to 1914. Members were identified by two main characteristics: they pegged their currencies to sterling, even after convertibility was suspended; and they continued to hold most of their reserves in the form of sterling balances in London. A second bloc after 1931 was informally grouped around the United States (the dollar area), and a third around France (the "gold bloc"). In addition, there was a large group of miscellaneous countries (including, especially, Germany and the states of Eastern Europe) that abandoned convertibility altogether in favor of starkly autarkic trade and financial policies.

The decade of the 1930s, the decade of the Great Depression, was a period of open economic warfare—a prelude to the military hostilities that were to follow after 1939. Never had the conflictual element in international monetary relations been laid quite so bare. It was truly a free-for-all regime. With public confidence shattered, exchange rates tended to fluctuate widely, and governments consciously engaged in competitive depreciations of their currencies in attempting to cope with their critical payments and unemployment problems. As in the years during and immediately after World War I, the monetary order failed to come even near to realizing its potential for joint gain. In 1936 a semblance of cooperation was restored by the Tripartite Agreement among Britain, France, and the United States for mutual currency stabilization. But this was only the barest minimum that might have been done to restore consistency to international monetary relations. Genuine monetary reconstruction had to wait until after World War II.

Why did the interwar experiment fail? Why did the attempt to return to the Golden Age end so disastrously? Mainly because the Golden Age *was* a myth, a myth based on misconceptions and a fundamental misunderstanding of how much the world economy had really changed. Governments failed to read the signs of decay in the prewar era; more importantly, they failed to realize how anachronistic a restored gold standard would be in the new circumstances of the postwar era. Conditions in the 1920s simply did not lend themselves to the adoption of an impersonal and fully automatic monetary order. In reality, the experiment was doomed from the start.

In the first place, governments were in the process of abandoning their inherited attitudes of laissez-faire in general economic policy. Social and political conditions had changed. A Bolshevik revolution had succeeded in Russia; elsewhere, socialism was almost universally on the rise. Governments could no longer afford to tolerate a certain amount of price or income deflation or inflation simply for the sake of maintaining convertibility of their currencies at a fixed price. Domestic stability now had to take precedence if politicians were to hold onto their jobs. If before World War I central banks rarely adhered to the gold-standard rules of the game in the positive sense, after the war they rarely adhered to them even in the negative sense. Instead, a variety of new instruments were devised to counteract and neutralize the domestic monetary influence of external payments disequilibria, just the opposite of what was needed to make a restored gold standard work. . . .

In the second place, prices and wages were becoming increasingly rigid, at least in a downward direction, under the impact of rising trade unionism and expanding social welfare legislation. Domestic price flexibility was a key requirement for a restored gold standard. Without it (and with exchange rates fixed), a disproportionate share of the adjustment process had to consist of changes of domestic incomes, output and employment. It was precisely in order to avoid such impacts, of course, that governments were becoming increasingly interventionist in economic affairs. But the consequences of such interventionism inevitably included a complete short-circuiting of the external adjustment mechanism that the same governments were laboring so hard to rebuild.

A third problem was the distorted structure of exchange rates established under the new gold-exchange standard. In insisting upon a return to convertibility at their prewar parities, governments were taking insufficient note of the fact that price relationships between national economies had been dramatically altered since 1914. Inconvertibility and floating exchange rates had broken the links between national price movements, and domestic inflation rates had varied enormously. When convertibility was finally reestablished after 1925, many governments found themselves with currencies that were overvalued and undervalued by quite significant amounts. Yet they were prevented from doing much about it by the straitjacket of fixed exchange rates. The pound, for example, restored to convertibility at its old prewar parity of $4.86, was overvalued by at least 10 percent; but since subsequent changes of the parity were ruled out by the gold-standard rules of the game, it was not surprising that the British balance of payments stayed under almost continuous strain until 1931, and British unemployment rates remained uncomfortably high. The French, on the other hand, who were an exception to the general rule in returning to gold (de facto in 1926, de jure in 1928) at just one-fifth of their prewar parity, undervalued the franc by perhaps as much as 25 percent. The result in this case was an almost immediate drainage of funds from London to Paris, adding to Britain's woes and, in the end, contributing importantly to the final collapse of the ill-fated experiment in 1931.

A fourth problem was the war's legacy of international indebtedness, which imposed a severe strain on monetary relations throughout the 1920s. The United States was the net creditor in a complicated network of obligations arising from wartime interallied loans and postwar German reparations; the biggest debtor, of course, was defeated Germany. As it turned out, most countries simply did not have the capacity to generate the net current-account surpluses necessary to effect their obligated transfers on capital account. In large measure, therefore, they had to rely instead on private capital outflows from the United States (much of which went to Germany) in a vast circular flow of funds. The Germans paid their reparations essentially with funds borrowed from America; Germany's creditors then used the same funds or other American loans to pay off their debts in the United States. How precarious all of this was became clear in 1929, when the stock-market crash and ensuing Great Depression abruptly cut off virtually all U.S. investment overseas. It is no accident that within two years reparations and interallied debt payments were abruptly cut off as well.

Finally, there was the problem of divided responsibility in the monetary order. If what ensured the apparent stability of the classical gold standard before 1914 was a single dominant center capable of acting as money manager of the world, what ultimately brought down its successor in 1931 was the emergence of competitive financial centers effectively rendering Britain's traditional hegemonic role impossible. Rivals to London had begun emerging even before World War I. During the 1920s this process continued, as Paris reasserted itself as a financial center and New York suddenly appeared on the scene. Still losing ground industrially and now saddled with an overvalued currency as well, Britain was no longer capable of playing the trio of roles that had provided the prewar monetary order with its semblance of stability. Unfortunately, neither were the French capable of shouldering such heavy responsibilities—they lacked the requisite economic and financial resources—and the Americans, who did have the resources, were as yet unwilling to do so. As a result, the system drifted without a leader. As Charles Kindleberger has written: "The United States was uncertain of its international role. . . . The one country capable of leadership was bemused by domestic concerns and stood aside. . . . The instability [came] from the growing weakness of one driver, and the lack of sufficient interest in the other."[6]

Could the two drivers, together with France, possibly have managed the monetary order cooperatively? Perhaps so. But this would have called for greater mutual trust and forebearance than any of the three seemed capable of at the time. Britain was still trying to lead, albeit from weakness, and the United States had not yet learned how to lead from strength. The French, meanwhile, resented both Anglo-Saxon powers, and all three were competing actively for short-term money flows—and even for gold itself. (After 1928, for example, the Bank of France added to the pressures on the British by suddenly opting to convert its sizable accumulation of sterling balances into gold.) The result of this lack of coordination was a continual problem of large-scale transfers of private funds ("hot money" movements) from one financial center to another—the confidence problem. "This shifting of balances from one market to another [was] inevitable in a gold standard system without a single dominating center."[7] In the end, it was such a shifting of balances out of London in 1931 that finally brought the system down. In fact, it was not until 1936, with the Tripartite Agreement, that the three powers eventually got around to acknowledging formally their mutual responsibility for the monetary order. By that time, however, it was too late.

THE BRETTON WOODS SYSTEM

World War II brought exchange control everywhere and ended much of what remained of the element of cooperation in international monetary relations. But almost immediately, planning began for postwar monetary reconstruction. Discussions centered in the Treasuries of Britain and the United States, and culminated in the creation of the International Monetary Fund at a conference of 44 allied nations at Bretton Woods, New Hampshire, in 1944. The charter of the IMF was intended to be the written constitution of the postwar monetary order—what later became known as the Bretton Woods system. The Bretton Woods system lasted only twenty-seven years, however, and died in August 1971.

The Origins of the Bretton Woods System

The Bretton Woods system originated as a compromise between rival plans for monetary reconstruction developed on the one hand by Harry Dexter White of the U.S. Treasury, and on the other hand by Lord Keynes of Britain. In 1944 the differences between these two plans seemed enormous. Today their differences appear rather less impressive than their similarities. Indeed, what is really striking, a third of a century later, is how much common ground there really was among all the participating governments at Bretton Woods. All agreed that the interwar experience had taught them several valuable lessons; all were determined to avoid repeating what they perceived to be the errors of the past. Their consensus of judgment was reflected directly in the contents of the IMF's Articles of Agreement.

Four points in particular stand out. First, it was generally agreed that the interwar period had demonstrated (to use the words of one authoritative source) "the proved disadvantages of freely fluctuating exchanges."[8] The floating rates of the 1930s were seen as having discouraged trade and investment and encouraged destabilizing speculation and competitive depreciations. Nations were loath to return to the free-for-all regime of the Depression years. But at the same time, they were also unwilling to return to the exchange-rate rigidity of the 1920s. The experience of those years was seen as having demonstrated the equal undesirability of the opposite extreme of permanently fixed rates. These, it was agreed, could "be equally harmful. The general interest may call for an occasional revision of currency values."[9] Accordingly, the negotiators at Bretton Woods were determined to find some compromise between the two extremes—one that would gain the advantages of both fixed and flexible rates without suffering from their disadvantages.

What they came up with has since been labeled the "pegged-rate" or "adjustable-peg" regime. Members were obligated to declare a par value (a "peg") for their currencies and to intervene in the exchange market to limit fluctuations within maximum margins (a "band") one percent above or below parity; but they also retained the right, whenever necessary and in accordance with agreed procedures, to alter their par values to correct a "fundamental disequilibrium" in their balance of payments. What constituted a fundamental disequilibrium? Although key to the whole operation of the Bretton Woods adjustment mechanism, this notion was never spelled out in any detail anywhere in the Articles of Agreement. The omission was to come back to haunt members of the Fund in later years.

Second, all governments generally agreed that if exchange rates were not to be freely fluctuating, countries would need to be assured of an adequate supply of official monetary reserves. An adjustable-peg regime "presupposes a large volume of such reserves for each single country as well as in the aggregate."[10] The experience of the interwar period—the gold shortage of the 1920s as well as the breakdown of fixed rates in the 1930s—was thought to have demonstrated the dangers of inadequate reserve volume. Accordingly, a second order of business at Bretton Woods was to ensure a supplementary source of reserve supply. Negotiators agreed that what they needed was some "procedure under which international liquidity would be supplied in the form of pre-arranged borrowing facilities."[11]

What they came up with, in this instance, was the IMF system of subscriptions and quotas. In essence, the Fund was to be nothing more than a pool of national currencies and gold subscribed by each country.

Members were assigned quotas, according to a rather complicated formula intended roughly to reflect each country's relative importance in the world economy, and were obligated to pay into the Fund a subscription of equal amount. The subscription was to be paid 25 percent in gold or currency convertible into gold (effectively the U.S. dollar, which was the only currency still convertible directly into gold) and 75 percent in the member's own currency. Each member was then entitled, when short of reserves, to "purchase" (i.e., borrow) amounts of foreign exchange from the Fund in return for equivalent amounts of its own currency. Maximum purchases were set equal to the member's 25 percent gold subscription (its "gold tranche"), plus four additional amounts each equal to 25 percent of its quota (its "credit tranches"), up to the point where the Fund's holdings of the member's currency equaled 200 percent of its quota. (If any of the Fund's holdings of the member's initial 75 percent subscription of its own currency was borrowed by other countries, the member's borrowing capacity was correspondingly increased: this was its "super-gold tranche.") The member's "net reserve position" in the Fund equaled its gold tranche (plus super-gold tranche, if any) less any borrowings by the country from the Fund. Net reserve positions were to provide the supplementary liquidity that was generally considered necessary to make the adjustable-peg regime work.

A third point on which all governments at Bretton Woods agreed was that it was necessary to avoid a recurrence of the kind of economic warfare that had characterized the decade of the 1930s. Some "code of action" was needed to "guide international exchange adjustments," some framework of rules to ensure that countries would remove their existing exchange controls and return to a system of multilateral payments based on currency convertibility. At Bretton Woods such a code was written into the obligations of Fund members. Governments were generally forbidden to engage in discriminatory currency practices or exchange-control regulation, although two exceptions were permitted. First, convertibility obligations were extended to current international transactions only. Governments were to refrain from regulating purchases and sales of foreign exchange for the purpose of current-account transactions. But they were not obligated to refrain from regulation of capital-account transactions; indeed, they were formally encouraged to make use of capital controls to maintain equilibrium in the face of "those disequilibrating short-term capital movements which caused so much trouble during the 'thirties."[12] And second, convertibility obligations could be deferred if a member so chose during a postwar "transitional period." Members deferring their convertibility obligations were known as Article XIV countries; members accepting them had so-called Article VIII status. One of the functions assigned to the IMF was to oversee this code of action on currency convertibility.

Finally, governments agreed that there was a need for an institutional forum for international consultation and cooperation on monetary matters. The world could not be allowed to return to the divided responsibility of the interwar years. "International monetary relations especially in the years before the Tripartite Agreement of 1936 suffered greatly from the absence of an established machinery or procedure of consultation."[13] In the postwar era, the Fund itself would provide such a forum. Of all the achievements of Bretton Woods, this was potentially the most significant. Never before had international monetary cooperation been attempted on a permanent institutional basis. Judged against the anarchy of the 1930s, this could be considered a breakthrough of historic proportions. For the first time ever, governments were formally committing themselves to the principle of collective responsibility for management of the international monetary order.

These four points together defined the Bretton Woods system—a monetary order combining an essentially unchanged gold-exchange standard, supplemented only by a centralized pool of gold and national currencies, with an entirely new pegged-rate mechanism of balance-of-payments adjustment. The Fund itself was expected to perform three important functions: regulatory (administering the rules affecting exchange rates and currency convertibility), financial (supplying supplementary liquidity), and consultative (providing a forum for the cooperative management of monetary relations). The negotiators at Bretton Woods did not think it necessary to alter in any fundamental way the mixed commodity-currency standard that had been inherited from the interwar years. Indeed, it does not even seem to have occurred to them that there might be any inherent defect in the structure of a gold-exchange standard. The problem in the 1920s, they felt, had not been the gold-exchange standard itself but the division of responsibility—in short, a problem of management. "The nucleus of the gold exchange system consisted of more than one country; and this was a special source of weakness. With adequate cooperation between the centre countries, it need not have been serious."[14] In the Bretton Woods system the IMF was to provide the necessary machinery for multilateral cooperation. The management problem would thus be solved and consistency in monetary relations ensured.

Implicit in this attitude was a remarkable optimism regarding prospects for monetary stability in the postwar era. Underlying the choice of the pegged-rate adjustment mechanism, for instance, seemed to be a clear expectation that beyond the postwar transitional period (itself expected to be brief) payments imbalances would not be excessive. The adjustment mechanism was manifestly biased in principle against frequent changes of exchange rates, presumably because of the experience of the 1930s; governments had to demonstrate the existence of a fundamental disequilibrium before they could alter their par values. At the same time, no government was prepared to sacrifice domestic stability for the sake of external equilibrium. Yet nations were left with few other instruments, other than capital controls, to deal with disturbances to the balance of payments. This suggests that the negotiators at Bretton Woods felt that the major threat to stability was likely to come from private speculation rather than from more fundamental price or income developments. It also suggests that they were confident that most disequilibria would be of a stochastic rather than nonstochastic nature. Underlying the IMF's financial function seemed to be a clear expectation that its centralized pool of liquidity would be sufficient to cope with most financing problems as they emerged.

As matters turned out, this optimism proved entirely unjustified. Monetary relations immediately after the war were anything but stable, and the transitional period anything but brief. Only the United States, Canada, and a small handful of other countries (mainly in Central America) were able to pledge themselves to the obligations of Article VIII right away. Most others were simply too devastated by war—their export capacities damaged, their import needs enormous, their monetary reserves exhausted—to commit their currencies to convertibility. Payments problems, especially in Europe and Japan, could hardly be described as stochastic; the Fund's initial pool of liquidity was anything but sufficient. After a short burst of activity during its first two years, mainly to the benefit of European nations, the Fund's lending operations shrank to an extremely small scale. (In 1950 the Fund made no new loans at all, and large-scale operations did not begin again until 1956.) The burden instead was shifted to one country, the only country after the war immediately capable of shouldering the responsibility for global monetary stabilization—namely, the United States.

Fortunately, this time, for reasons of its own (see below), the United States was willing. As dominant then as Britain had been in the nineteenth century, America rapidly assumed the same trio of managerial roles—in effect, taking over as money manager of the world. A relatively open market was maintained for the exports of foreign goods. A relatively generous flow of long-term loans and grants was initiated first through the Marshall Plan and other related aid programs, then through the reopened New York capital market. And a relatively liberal lending policy was eventually established for the provision of short-term funds in times of exchange crisis as well. Since monetary reserves were everywhere in such short supply—and since the IMF's pool of liquidity was manifestly inadequate—the United States itself became the residual source of global liquidity growth through its balance-of-payments deficits. At the war's end, America owned almost three-quarters of the world's existing monetary gold; and prospects for new gold production were obviously limited by the physical constraints of nature. The rest of the world, therefore, was more than willing to economize on this scarce gold supply by accumulating dollars instead. The dollar thus was enshrined not only as principal "vehicle currency" for international trade and investment but also as principal reserve asset for central banks. In the early postwar years, America's deficits became the universal solvent to keep the machinery of Bretton Woods running. It may be misleading, as I have indicated, to call the classical gold standard a sterling-exchange (though not, I have suggested, to call it a hegemony); it is not at all misleading to call the postwar monetary standard a dollar-exchange standard. Indeed, the Bretton Woods system became synonymous with a hegemonic monetary order centered on the dollar. Though multilateral in formal design, in actual practice (like the classical gold standard before it) the Bretton Woods system was highly centralized.

In effect, what the United States did was to abjure any payments target of its own in favor of taking responsibility for operation of the monetary order itself. Other countries set independent balance-of-payments targets; America's external financial policy was essentially one of "benign neglect." Consistency in monetary relations was ensured not by multilateral cooperation but by America's willingness to play a passive role in the adjustment process, as the nth country, in effect: "other countries from time to time changed the par value of their currencies against the dollar and gold, but the value of the dollar itself remained fixed in relation to gold and therefore to other currencies collectively."[15] The growth of the world's liquidity supply was largely determined, consequently, by the magnitude of America's deficits—modified only to the extent that these deficits were settled in gold, rather than dollars, reflecting the asset preferences of surplus countries.

Like the British in the nineteenth century, the Americans did not deliberately seek the responsibility of global monetary management. (In the interwar period they had evaded it.) On the other hand, unlike the British, once the Americans found themselves with it, they soon came to welcome it, for reasons that were a mixture of altruism and self-interest. Being money manager for the world fit in neatly with America's newfound leadership role in the Western Alliance. The cold war had begun, and isolationism was a thing of the past. The United States perceived a need to promote the economic recovery of potential allies in Europe and Japan, as well as to maintain a sizable and potent military establishment overseas. All of this cost money: the privilege of liability-financing deficits meant that America was effectively freed from balance-of-payments constraints to spend as freely as it thought necessary to promote objectives believed to be in the national interest. The United States could issue the world's principal vehicle and reserve currency in amounts presumed to be consistent with its own policy priorities—and not necessarily with those of foreign dollar holders. Foreign dollar holders conceded this policy autonomy to America because it so directly contributed to their own economic rehabilitation. America accepted the necessity, for example, of preferential trade and payments arrangements in Europe, despite their inherent and obvious discrimination against U.S. export sales; likewise, America accepted the necessity of granting Japanese exporters access to the U.S. internal market at a time when other markets still remained largely closed to goods labeled "Made in Japan." In effect, as I have argued elsewhere, an implicit bargain was struck.[16] America's allies acquiesced in a hegemonic system that accorded the United States special privileges to act abroad unilaterally to promote U.S. interests. The United States, in turn, condoned its allies' use of the system to promote their own economic prosperity, even if this happened to come largely at the expense of the United States. . . .

The History of the Bretton Woods System

The subsequent history of the Bretton Woods system may be read as the history of this implicit bargain. The breakdown of the system in 1971 may be read as the bargain's final collapse. . . .

The chronology of Bretton Woods can be divided into two periods: the period of the "dollar shortage," lasting roughly until 1958; and the period of the "dollar glut," covering the remaining dozen years or so. The period of the dollar shortage was the heyday of America's dominance of international monetary relations. The term "dollar shortage," universally used at the time, was simply a shorthand expression of the fact that only the United States was capable of shouldering the responsibility for global monetary stabilization; only the United States could help other governments avoid a mutually destructive scramble for gold by promoting an outflow of dollar balances instead. As David Calleo has written: "Circumstances dictated dollar hegemony."[17] Dollar deficits began in 1950, following a round of devaluations of European currencies, at American insistence, in 1949. (Dollar surpluses prior to 1950 were financed largely by grants and long-term loans from the United States.) In ensuing years, deficits in the U.S. balance of payments (as conventionally measured) averaged approximately $1.5 billion a year. But for these deficits, other governments would have been compelled by their reserve shortages to resort to competitive exchange depreciations or domestic deflations; they would certainly not have been able to make as much progress as they did toward dismantling wartime exchange controls and trade restrictions. Persistent dollar deficits thus actually served to avoid monetary instability or policy conflict before 1953. Not since the Golden Age before World War I, in fact, had the monetary order been so successful in reconciling the tension between economic and political values. The period to 1958 has rightly been called one of "beneficial disequilibrium."

After 1958, however, America's persistent deficits began to take on a different coloration. Following a brief surplus in 1957, owing to an increase of oil exports to Europe caused by the closing of the Suez Canal, the U.S. balance of payments plunged to a $3.5 billion deficit in 1958 and to even larger deficits in 1959 and 1960. This was the turning point. Instead of talking about a dollar shortage, observers began to talk about a dollar glut; consistency in monetary relations no longer appeared quite so assured. In 1958, Europe's currencies returned to convertibility. In subsequent years the former eagerness of European governments to obtain dollar reserves was transformed into what seemed an equally fervent desire to avoid excess dollar accumulations. Before 1958, less than 10 percent of America's deficits had been financed by calls on the gold stock in Fort Knox (the rest being liability-financed). During the next decade, almost two-thirds of America's cumulative deficit was transferred in the form of gold. Almost all of this went to governments on the continent of Europe.

It was clear that the structure of Bretton Woods was coming under increasing strain. Defects were becoming evident both in the mechanism of liquidity-creation and in the mechanism of payments adjustment.

Credit for first drawing attention to the defects in the liquidity creation mechanism of Bretton Woods is usually given to Robert Triffin for his influential book *Gold and the Dollar Crisis*.[18] The negotiators at Bretton Woods, Triffin argued, had been too complacent about the gold-exchange standard. The problem was not simply one of management. Rather, it was one of structure—an inherent defect in the very concept of a gold-exchange standard. A gold-exchange standard is built on the illusion of convertibility of its fiduciary element into gold at a fixed price. The Bretton Woods system, though, was relying on deficits in the U.S. balance of payments to avert a world liquidity shortage. Already, America's "overhang" of overseas liabilities to private and official foreigners was growing larger than its gold stock at home. The progressive deterioration of the U.S. net reserve position, therefore, was bound in time to undermine global confidence in the dollar's continued convertibility. In effect, governments were caught on the horns of a dilemma. To forestall speculation against the dollar, U.S. deficits would have to cease. But this would confront governments with the liquidity problem. To forestall the liquidity problem, U.S. deficits would have to continue. But this would confront governments with the confidence problem. Governments could not have their cake and eat it too.

Not that governments were unwilling to try. On the contrary, during the early 1960s a variety of ad hoc measures were initiated in an effort to contain speculative pressures that were mounting against the dollar. These included a network of reciprocal short-term credit facilities ("swaps") between the Federal Reserve and other central banks, as well as enlargement of the potential lending authority of the IMF (through the "General Arrangements to Borrow"). Both were intended to facilitate recycling of funds in the event of speculative currency shifts by private investors. They also included creation of a "gold pool" of the major financial powers to stabilize the price of gold in private markets. Later, in 1968, the gold pool was replaced by a two-tier gold-price system—one price for the private market, determined by supply and demand, and another price for central banks, to remain at the previous fixed level of $35 per ounce. These several measures were moderately successful in helping governments cope with the threat of private speculation against the dollar—the private confidence problem. The official confidence problem, however, remained as acute a danger as ever.

Meanwhile, in the mid-1960s, negotiations were begun whose aim was to establish a substitute source of liquidity growth, in order to reduce reliance on dollar deficits in the future. These negotiations were conducted among ten industrial countries—the so-called Group of Ten (G-10)—comprising Belgium, Canada, France, Germany, Italy, Japan, the Netherlands, Sweden, the United Kingdom, and the United States. What came out of the G-10 negotiations was the agreement to create Special Drawing Rights, an entirely new type of world fiduciary reserve asset. The SDR agreement was confirmed by the full membership of the International Monetary Fund in 1968 and activated in 1969. Between 1970 and 1972 some 9.5 billion SDR units were allocated to members of the Fund. Governments were confident that with SDRs "in place," any future threat of world liquidity shortage could be successfully averted. On the other hand, they were totally unprepared for the opposite threat—a reserve surfeit—which in fact is what eventually emerged.

Any number of authors could be credited for drawing attention to the defects in the payments adjustment mechanism of Bretton Woods. Virtually from the time the Charter was first negotiated, observers began pointing to the ambiguity surrounding the notion of fundamental disequilibrium. How could governments be expected to alter their par values if they could not tell when a fundamental disequilibrium existed? And if they were inhibited from altering their par values, then how would international payments equilibrium be maintained? I have already noted that the adjustment mechanism was biased in principle against frequent changes of exchange rates. In practice during the postwar period it became biased even against infrequent changes of exchange rates. At least among the advanced industrial nations, the world seemed to have returned to the rigidities of the 1920s. Governments went to enormous lengths to avoid the "defeat" of an altered par value. (A particularly sad example of this was the long struggle of the British government to avoid devaluation of the pound—a struggle that ended when sterling was devalued by 14.3 percent in 1967.) The resulting stickiness of the adjustment process not only aggravated fears of a potential world liquidity shortage. It also created irresistible incentives for speculative currency shifts by private individuals and institutions, greatly adding to the confidence problem as well.

Speculative currency shifts were facilitated at the time by the growing integration of money and capital markets in all of the advanced industrial nations. Large-scale capital movements had not originally been envisaged by the negotiators at Bretton Woods; as I have indicated, governments actually were encouraged to *control* capital movements for the purpose of maintaining payments equilibrium. In reality, however, capital movements turned out to be promoted rather than retarded by the design of the Bretton Woods system—in particular, by the integrative power of the par-value regime, and by the return to currency convertibility in Europe in 1958. (Japan did not pledge itself to Article VIII of the IMF Charter until 1964.) After 1958, capital mobility accelerated *pari passu* with the growth of the Eurocurrency market—that well-known market for currencies deposited in banks located outside of the country of issue. From its origin in the mid-1950s, the Eurocurrency market rapidly expanded into a broad, full-fledged international financial market; subject to just a minimum of governmental guidance, supervision, and regulation, it became during the 1960s the principal vehicle for private speculation against official exchange parities. Increasingly, governments found it difficult to "defend" unadjusted par values in the face of the high degree of international capital mobility that had been generated.

The most serious adjustment problem during this period was, of course, the dollar glut—more accurately, the persistent payments imbalance between the United States and the surplus countries of Europe and Japan. On each side, complaints were heard about the policies of the other. America felt that its erstwhile European and Japanese allies could do more to eliminate the international payments disequilibrium by inflating or revaluing their currencies; the Europeans and Japanese argued that it was the responsibility of the United States to take the first steps to reduce its persistent deficit. Each felt discriminated against by the other. The surplus countries felt that America's privilege of liability-financing deficits, growing out of the dollar's reserve-currency role, created an asymmetry in the monetary order favorable to the United States. None of them, after all, had such a degree of policy autonomy. America, on the other hand, felt that the use of the dollar by other governments as their principal intervention medium to support par values—the intervention-currency role of the dollar—created an asymmetry in the monetary order more favorable to Europe and Japan. Many sources argued that the dollar was overvalued. Yet how could its value in terms of foreign currencies be changed unilaterally unless all other countries agreed to intervene appropriately in the exchange market? The United States felt it had no effective control over its own exchange rate (no exchange-rate autonomy) and therefore did not feel it could easily devalue to rid itself of its deficit.

In fact the debate over asymmetries masked a deeper political conflict. The postwar bargain was coming unstuck. In the United States, concern was growing about the competitive threat from the European Common Market and Japan to American commercial interests. The period of postwar recovery was over: Europe and Japan had become reinvigorated giants, not only willing but able to compete aggressively with America in markets at home and abroad. The cost of subordinating U.S. economic interests to the presumed political advantage of now strengthened allies was becoming ever more intolerable. Conversely, concern was growing in Europe and Japan about America's use of its privilege of liability-financing to pursue policies abroad which many considered abhorrent (one example was the U.S. involvement in Vietnam), the "exorbitant privilege," as Charles de Gaulle called it. The Europeans and Japanese had just one major weapon they could use to restrict America's policy autonomy—their right to demand conversion of accumulated dollar balances into gold. Robert Mundell has written that "the sole function of gold convertibility in the Bretton Woods arrangement was to discipline the U.S."[19] But by the mid-1960s this was a discipline that most major financial powers were growing somewhat reluctant to use. America's overhang of liabilities was by now far larger than its gold stock. A concerted conversion campaign could have threatened to topple the whole of the Bretton Woods edifice. Governments—with one major exception—did not consider it in their interest to exacerbate the official confidence problem and provoke a systemic crisis. The one major exception was France, which in 1965, in a move strikingly reminiscent of its behavior toward sterling after 1928, began a rapid conversion of its outstanding dollar balances into gold, explicitly for the purpose of exerting pressure on the United States. France alone, however, was unable to change America's policies significantly.

At bottom, the Bretton Woods system rested on one simple assumption—that economic policy in the United States would be stabilizing. Like Britain in the nineteenth century, America had the power to guide the world's monetary policy. The absence of an effective external discipline on U.S. policy autonomy could not threaten the system so long as this assumption held. And indeed, before 1965, the assumption did seem quite justified. America clearly had the best long-term record of price stability of any industrial country; even for some time after 1958 the United States could not justly be accused of "exporting" inflation, however much some governments were complaining about a dollar glut. After 1965, however, the situation reversed itself, as a direct consequence of the escalation of hostilities in Vietnam. America's economy began to overheat, and inflation began to gain momentum. The Bretton Woods system was tailor-made to promote the transmission of this inflation abroad. With exchange rates pegged, tradable-goods price increases in the largest of all trading nations were immediately radiated outward to the rest of the world economy. And with governments committed to defending their pegged rates by buying the surfeit of dollars in the exchange market, a huge reserve base was created for monetary expansion in these other countries as well.

Now the United States could justifiably be accused of exporting inflation overseas.

The gathering world inflation after 1965 exposed all of the latent defects of Bretton Woods. American policy was no longer stabilizing, yet other governments were reluctant to use the one power of discipline they had. (Indeed, after the creation of the two-tier gold-price system in 1968, the U.S. government made it quite plain that if a serious depletion of its gold stock were threatened, it would be prepared to close the window and refuse further sales.) The adjustment mechanism was incapable of coping with the widening deficit in the U.S. balance of payments (which soared to $9.8 billion in 1970 and an incredible $29.8 billion in 1971), and the confidence problem was worsening as private speculators were encouraged to bet on devaluation of the dollar or revaluations of the currencies of Europe and Japan. Ultimately, it was the United States that brought the drama to its denouement. Concerned about the rapidly deteriorating U.S. trade balance, as well as about rising protectionist sentiment in the Congress, President Richard Nixon was determined to force the Europeans and Japanese to accept an adjustment of international exchange-rate relationships that would correct the overvaluation of the dollar. Feeling that he lacked effective control over the dollar exchange rate under the prevailing rules of the game, the President decided that the rules themselves would have to be changed. Thus, on August 15, 1971, the convertibility of the dollar into gold was suspended, in effect freeing the dollar to find its own level in the exchange market. With that decision, the Bretton Woods system passed into history.

NOTES

1. Carlo M. Cipolla, *Money, Prices, and Civilization in the Mediterranean World: Fifth to Seventeenth Century* (Princeton: Princeton University Press, 1956), chap. 2.

2. Fred Hirsch, *Money International* (London: Penguin, 1967), p. 28.

3. Marcello de Cecco, *Money and Empire: The International Gold Standard, 1890–1914* (Oxford: Basil Blackwell, 1974), p. 128.

4. Currency Resolution of the Genoa Conference, as quoted in League of Nations, *International Currency Experience* (1944), p. 28.

5. Ibid. As another economy measure, central banks were also urged to withdraw gold coins from circulation.

6. Charles P. Kindleberger, *The World in Depression* (Berkeley: UC Press, 1973), pp. 298–301.

7. W. A. Brown, *The International Gold Standard Reinterpreted* (New York: NBER, 1944), 2: 769.

8. League of Nations, *International Currency Experience,* p. 211.

9. Ibid.

10. Ibid., p. 214.

11. Ibid., p. 218.

12. Ibid., p. 220.

13. Ibid., pp. 22–227.

14. Ibid., p. 46.

15. Marina V. N. Whitman, "The Current and Future Role of the Dollar: How Much Symmetry?" *Brookings Papers on Economic Activity,* no. 3 (1974): 542.

16. Benjamin J. Cohen, "The Revolution in Atlantic Economic Relations: A Bargain Comes Unstuck," in Wolfram Hanrieder, ed., *The United States and Western Europe: Political, Economic and Strategic Perspectives* (Cambridge, Mass.: Winthrop, 1974), pp. 113–120.

17. David P. Calleo, "American Foreign Policy and American European Studies: An Imperial Bias?", in Hanrieder, *United States and Western Europe,* p. 62.

18. Robert Triffin, *Gold and the Dollar Crisis* (New Haven: Yale University Press, 1960). The book first appeared in the form of two long journal articles in 1959.

19. Robert A. Mundell, "Optimum Currency Areas," *Economic Notes* 3 (September–December 1975): 36.

15

Hegemonic Stability Theories of the International Monetary System

BARRY EICHENGREEN

Barry Eichengreen evaluates the applicability of hegemonic stability theory (see Krasner, Reading 1, and Lake, Reading 8) to international monetary relations. He examines the argument that the existence of a single dominant power in the international arena is necessary for the establishment and maintenance of stable monetary systems. Eichengreen examines three monetary systems—the classical gold standard, the interwar gold-exchange system, and the Bretton Woods system—to see whether the presence or absence of a hegemon was the primary cause of their development and maintenance. He finds that while hegemons may contribute to the smooth operation of international monetary regimes, international cooperation has been equally important to their design and functioning.

An international monetary system is a set of rules or conventions governing the economic policies of nations. From a narrowly national perspective, it is an unnatural state of affairs. Adherence to a common set of rules or conventions requires a certain harmonization of monetary and fiscal policies, even though the preferences and constraints influencing policy formulation diverge markedly across countries. Governments are expected to forswear policies that redistribute economic welfare from foreigners to domestic residents and to contribute voluntarily to providing the international public good of global monetary stability. In effect, they are expected to solve the defection problem that plagues cartels and—equivalently in this context—the free-rider problem hindering public good provision. Since they are likely to succeed incompletely, the public good of international monetary stability tends to be underproduced. From this perspective, the paradox

Barry Eichengreen. "Hegemonic Stability Theories of the International Monetary System." From *Can Nations Agree? Issues in International Economic Cooperation* (Washington: The Brookings Institution), 1989, pp. 255–98. Reprinted by permission of The Brookings Institution.

of international monetary affairs is not the difficulty of designing a stable international monetary system, but the fact that such systems have actually persisted for decades.

Specialists in international relations have offered the notion that dominance by one country—a hegemonic power—is needed to ensure the smooth functioning of an international regime. The concentration of economic power is seen as a way of internalizing the externalities associated with systemic stability and of ensuring its adequate provision. The application of this "theory of hegemonic stability" to international monetary affairs is straightforward. The maintenance of the Bretton Woods system for a quarter century is ascribed to the singular power of the United States in the postwar world, much as the persistence of the classical gold standard is ascribed to Britain's dominance of international financial affairs in the second half of the nineteenth century. . . . By contrast, the instability of the interwar gold exchange standard is attributed to the absence of a hegemonic power, due to Britain's inability to play the dominant role and America's unwillingness to accept it.

The appeal of this notion lies in its resonance with the public good and cartel analogies for international monetary affairs, through what might be called the carrot and stick variants of hegemonic stability theory. In the carrot variant, the hegemon, like a dominant firm in an oligopolistic market, maintains the cohesion of the cartel by making the equivalent of side payments to members of the fringe. In the stick variant, the hegemon, like a dominant firm, deters defection from the international monetary cartel by using its economic policies to threaten retaliation against renegades. In strong versions of the theory . . . all participants are rendered better off by the intervention of the dominant power. In weak versions . . . either because systemic stability is not a purely public good or because its costs are shunted onto smaller states, the benefits of stability accrue disproportionately or even exclusively to the hegemon.

Three problems bedevil attempts to apply hegemonic stability theory to international monetary affairs. First is the ambiguity surrounding three concepts central to the theory: *hegemony,* the *power* the hegemon is assumed to possess, and the *regime* whose stability is ostensibly enhanced by the exercise of hegemonic power. Rather than adopting general definitions offered previously and devoting this paper to their criticism, I adopt specialized definitions tailored to my concern with the international monetary system. I employ the economist's definition of economic—or market—power: sufficient size in the relevant market to influence prices and quantities. I define a hegemon analogously to a dominant firm: as a country whose market power, understood in this sense, significantly exceeds that of all rivals. Finally, I avoid defining the concept of regime around which much debate has revolved by posing the question narrowly: whether hegemony is conducive to the stability of the international monetary system (where the system is defined as those explicit rules and procedures governing international monetary affairs), rather than whether it is conducive to the stability of the international regime, however defined.

The second problem plaguing attempts to apply hegemonic stability theory to international monetary affairs is ambiguity about the instruments with which the hegemon makes its influence felt. This is the distinction between what are characterized above as the carrot and stick variants of the theory. Does the hegemon alter its monetary, fiscal, or commercial policies to discipline countries that refuse to play by its rules, as "basic force" models of international relations would suggest? Does it link international economic policy to other issue areas and impose military or diplomatic sanctions on uncooperative nations? Or does it stabilize the system through the use of "positive sanctions," financing the public good of international monetary stability by acting as lender of last resort even when the probability of repayment is slim and forsaking beggar-thy-neighbor policies even when used to advantage by other countries?

The third problem is ambiguity about the scope of hegemonic stability theories. In principle, such theories could be applied equally to the design, the operation, or the decline of the international monetary system. Yet in practice, hegemonic stability theories may shed light on the success of efforts to design or reform the international monetary system but not on its day-to-day operation or eventual decline. Other combinations are equally plausible a priori. Only analysis of individual cases can throw light on the theory's range of applicability.

In this paper, I structure an analysis of hegemonic stability theories of the international monetary system around the dual problems of range of applicability and mode of implementation. I consider separately the genesis of international monetary systems, their operation in normal periods and times of crisis, and their disintegration. In each context, I draw evidence from three modern incarnations of the international monetary system: the classical gold standard, the interwar gold exchange standard, and Bretton Woods. These three episodes in the history of the international monetary system are typically thought to offer two examples of hegemonic stability—Britain before 1914, the United States after 1944—and one episode—the interwar years—destabilized by the absence of hegemony. I do not attempt to document Britain's dominance of international markets before 1914 or the dominance of the United States after 1944; I simply ask whether the market power they possessed was causally connected to the stability of the international monetary system.

The historical analysis indicates that the relationship between the market power of the leading economy and the stability of the international monetary system is considerably more complex than suggested by simple variants of hegemonic stability theory. While one cannot simply reject the hypothesis that on more than one occasion the stabilizing capacity of a dominant economic power has contributed to the smooth functioning of the international monetary system, neither can one reconcile much of the evidence, notably on the central role of international negotiation and collaboration even in periods of hegemonic dominance, with simple versions of the theory. Although both the appeal and limitations of hegemonic stability theories are apparent when one takes a static view of the international monetary system, those limitations are most evident when one considers the evolution of an international monetary system over time. An international monetary system whose smooth operation at one point is predicated on the dominance of one powerful country may in fact be dynamically unstable. Historical experience suggests that the hegemon's willingness to act in a stabilizing capacity at a single point tends to undermine its continued capacity to do so over time. . . .

THE GENESIS OF MONETARY SYSTEMS AND THE THEORY OF HEGEMONIC STABILITY

My analysis begins with an examination of the genesis of three different monetary systems: the classical gold standard, the interwar gold exchange standard, and the Bretton Woods system.

The Classical Gold Standard

Of the three episodes considered here, the origins of the classical gold standard are the most difficult to assess, for in the nineteenth century there were no centralized discussions, like those in Genoa in 1922 or Bretton Woods in 1944, concerned with the design of the international monetary system. There was general agreement that currencies should have a metallic basis and that payments imbalances should be settled by international shipments of specie. But there was no consensus about which precious metals should serve as the basis for money supplies or how free international specie movements should be.

Only Britain maintained a full-fledged gold standard for anything approaching the century preceding 1913. Although gold coins had circulated alongside silver since the fourteenth century, Britain had been on a de facto gold standard since 1717, when Sir Isaac Newton, as master of the mint, set too high a silver price of gold and drove full-bodied silver coins from circulation. In 1798 silver coinage was suspended, and after 1819 silver was no longer accepted to redeem paper currency. But for half a century following its official adoption of the gold standard in 1821, Britain essentially remained alone. Other countries that retained bimetallic standards were buffeted by alternating gold and silver discoveries. The United States and France, for example, were officially bimetallic, but their internal circulations were placed on a silver basis by growing Mexican and South American silver production in the early decades of the nineteenth century. The market price of silver was thus depressed relative to the mint price, which encouraged silver to be imported for coinage and gold to be shipped abroad where its price was higher. Then, starting in 1848, gold discoveries in Russia, Australia, and California depressed the market price of gold below the mint price, all but driving silver from circulation and placing bimetallic currencies on a gold basis. Finally, silver discoveries in Nevada and other mining territories starting in the 1870s dramatically inflated the silver price of gold and forced the bimetallic currencies back onto a silver basis.

The last of these disturbances led nearly all bimetallic countries to adopt the gold standard, starting with Germany in 1871. Why, after taking no comparable action in response to previous disturbances, did countries respond to post-1870 fluctuations in the price of silver by abandoning bimetallism and adopting gold? What role, if any, did Britain, the hegemonic financial power, play in their decisions?

One reason for the decision to adopt gold was the desire to prevent the inflation that would result from continued silver convertibility and coinage. Hence the plausible explanation for the contrast between the 1870s and earlier years is the danger of exceptionally rapid inflation due to the magnitude of post-1870 silver discoveries. Between 1814 and 1870, the sterling price of silver, of which so much was written, remained within 2 percentage points of its 1814 value, alternatively driving gold or silver from circulation in bimetallic countries but fluctuating insufficiently to raise the specter of significant price level changes. Then between 1871 and 1881 the London price of silver fell by 15 percent, and by 1891 the cumulative fall had reached 25 percent. Gold convertibility was the only alternative to continued silver coinage that was judged both respectable and viable. The only significant resistance to the adoption of gold convertibility emanated from silver-mining regions and from agricultural areas like the American West, populated by proprietors of encumbered land who might benefit from inflation.

Seen from this perspective, the impetus for adopting the gold standard existed independently of Britain's rapid industrialization, dominance of international finance, and preeminence in trade. Still, the British example surely provided encouragement to follow the path ultimately chosen. The experience of the Latin Monetary Union impressed upon contemporaries the advantages of a common monetary standard in minimizing transactions costs. The scope of that common standard would be greatest for countries that linked their currencies to sterling. The gold standard was also attractive to domestic interests concerned with promoting economic growth. Industrialization required foreign capital, and attracting foreign capital required monetary stability. For Britain, the principal source of foreign capital, monetary stability was measured in terms of sterling and best ensured by joining Britain on gold. Moreover, London's near monopoly of trade credit was of concern to other governments, which hoped that they might reduce their dependence on the London discount market by establishing gold parities and central banks. Aware that Britain monopolized trade in newly mined gold and was the home of the world's largest organized commodity markets, other governments hoped that by emulating Britain's gold standard and financial system they might secure a share of this business.

Britain's prominence in foreign commerce, overseas investment, and trade credit forcefully conditioned the evolution of the gold standard system mainly through central banks' practice of holding key currency balances abroad, especially in London. This practice probably would not have developed so quickly if foreign countries had not grown accustomed to transacting in the London market. It would probably not have become so widespread if there had not been such strong confidence in the stability and liquidity of sterling deposits. And such a large share of foreign deposits would not have gravitated to a single center if Britain had not possessed such a highly articulated set of financial markets.

But neither Britain's dominance of international transactions nor the desire to emulate Bank of England practice prevented countries from tailoring the gold standard to their own needs. Germany and France continued to allow large internal gold circulation, while other nations limited gold coin circulation to low levels. The central banks of France, Belgium, and Switzerland retained the right to redeem their notes in silver, and the French did not hesitate to charge a premium for gold. The Reichsbank could at its option issue fiduciary notes upon the payment of a tax. In no sense did British example or suggestion dictate the form of the monetary system.

The Interwar Gold Exchange Standard

The interwar gold exchange standard offers a radically different picture: on the one hand, there was no single dominant power like nineteenth century Britain or mid-twentieth century America; on the other, there were conscious efforts by rivals to shape the international monetary order to their national advantage.

Contemporary views of the design of the interwar monetary system were aired at a series of international meetings, the most important of which was the Genoa Economic and Financial Conference convened in April 1922. Although the United States declined to send an official delegation to Genoa, proceedings there reflected the differing economic objectives of Britain and the United States. British officials were aware that the war had burdened domestic industry with adjustment problems, had disrupted trade, and had accentuated financial rivalry between London and New York. Their objectives were to prevent worldwide deflation (which was sure to exacerbate the problems of structural adjustment), to promote the expansion of international trade (to which the nation's prosperity was inextricably linked), and to recapture the financial business diverted to New York as a result of the war. To prevent deflation, they advocated that countries economize on the use of gold by adopting the gold exchange standard along lines practiced by members of the British Empire. Presuming London to be a reserve center, British officials hoped that these measures would restore the City to its traditional prominence in international finance. Stable exchange rates would stimulate international trade, particularly if the United States forgave its war debt claims, which would permit reparations to be reduced and encourage creditor countries to extend loans to Central Europe.

The United States, in contrast, was less dependent for its prosperity on the rapid expansion of trade. It was less reliant on income from financial and insurance services and perceived as less urgent the need to encourage the deposit of foreign balances in New York. Influential American officials, notably Benjamin Strong of the Federal Reserve Bank of New York, opposed any extension of the gold exchange standard. Above all, American officials were hesitant to participate in a conference whose success appeared to hinge on unilateral concessions regarding war debts.

In the absence of an American delegation, Britain's proposals formed the basis for the resolutions of the Financial Committee of the Genoa Conference. . . . Participating countries would fix their exchange rates against one another, and any that failed to do so would lose the right to hold the reserve balances of the others. The principal creditor nations were encouraged to take immediate steps to restore convertibility in order to become "gold centers" where the bulk of foreign exchange reserves would be held. Following earlier recommendations by the Cunliffe committee, governments were urged to economize on gold by eliminating gold coin from circulation and concentrating reserves at central banks. Countries with significantly depreciated currencies were urged to stabilize at current exchange rates rather than attempting to restore prewar parities through drastic deflation, which would only delay stabilization.

To implement this convention, the Bank of England was instructed to call an early meeting of central banks, including the Federal Reserve. But efforts to arrange this meeting, which bogged down in the dispute over war debts and reparations, proved unavailing. Still, if the official convention advocated by the Financial Committee failed to materialize, the Genoa resolutions were not without influence. Many of the innovations suggested there were adopted by individual countries on a unilateral basis and comprised the distinguishing features differentiating the prewar and interwar monetary standards.

The first effect of Genoa was to encourage the adoption of statutes permitting central banks to back notes and sight deposits with foreign exchange as well as gold. New regulations broadening the definition of eligible assets and specifying minimum proportions of total reserves to be held in gold were widely implemented in succeeding years. The second effect was to encourage the adoption of gold economy measures, including the withdrawal of gold coin from circulation and provision of bullion for export only by the authorities. The third effect was to provide subtle encouragement to countries experiencing ongoing inflation to stabilize at depreciated rates. Thus Genoa deserves partial credit for transforming the international monetary system from a gold to a gold exchange standard, from a gold coin to a gold bullion standard, and from a fixed-rate system to one in which central banks were vested with some discretion over the choice of parities.

Given its dominance of the proceedings at Genoa, Britain's imprint on the interwar gold exchange standard was as apparent as its influence over the structure of the prewar system. That British policymakers achieved this despite a pronounced decline in Britain's position in the world economy and the opposition of influential American officials suggests that planning and effort were substitutes, to some extent, for economic power.

The Bretton Woods System

Of the three cases considered here, U.S. dominance of the Bretton Woods negotiations is most clearly supportive of hegemonic stability theories about the genesis of the international monetary system. U.S. dominance of the postwar world economy is unmistakable. Yet despite the trappings of hegemony and American dominance of the proceedings at Bretton Woods, a less influential power—Great Britain—was able to secure surprisingly extensive concessions in the design of the international monetary system.

American and British officials offered different plans for postwar monetary reconstruction both because they had different views of the problem of international economic adjustment and because they represented economies with different strengths and weaknesses. British officials were preoccupied by two weaknesses of their economic position. First was the specter of widespread unemployment. Between 1920 and 1938, unemployment in Britain had scarcely dipped below double-digit levels, and British policymakers feared its recurrence. Second was the problem of sterling balances. Britain had concentrated its wartime purchases within the sterling bloc and, because they were allies and sterling was a reserve currency, members of the bloc had accepted settlement in sterling, now held in London. Since these sterling balances were large relative to Britain's hard currency reserves, the mere possibility that they might be presented for conversion threatened plans for the restoration of convertibility.

U.S. officials, in contrast, were confident that the competitive position of American industry was strong and were little concerned about the threat of unemployment. The concentration of gold reserves in the United States, combined with the economy's international creditor position, freed them from worry that speculative capital flows or foreign government policies might undermine the dollar's stability. U.S. concerns centered on the growth of preferential trading systems from which its exports were excluded, notably the sterling bloc.

The British view of international economic adjustment was dominated by concern about inadequate liquidity and asymmetrical adjustment. A central lesson drawn by British policymakers from the experience of the 1920s was the difficulty of operating an international monetary system in which liquidity or reserves were scarce. Given how slowly the global supply of monetary gold responded to fluctuations in its relative price and how sensitive its international distribution had proven to be to the economic policies of individual states, they considered it foolhardy to base the international monetary system on a reserve base composed exclusively of gold. Given the perceived inelasticity of global gold supplies, a gold-based system threatened to impart a deflationary bias to the world economy and to worsen unemployment. This preoccupation with unemployment due to external constraints was reinforced by another lesson drawn from the 1920s: the costs of asymmetries in the operation of the adjustment mechanism. If the experience of the 1920s was repeated, surplus countries, in response to external imbalances, would need only to sterilize reserve inflows, while deficit countries would be forced to initiate monetary contraction to prevent the depletion of reserves. Monetary contraction, according to Keynes, whose views heavily influenced those of the British delegation, facilitated adjustment by causing unemployment. To prevent unemployment, symmetry had to be restored to the adjustment mechanism through the incorporation of sanctions compelling surplus countries to revalue their currencies or stimulate demand.

From the American perspective, the principal lessons of the interwar experience were not the costs of asymmetries and inadequate liquidity, but the instability of floating rates and the disruptive effects of exchange rate and trade protection. U.S. officials were concerned about ensuring order and stability in the foreign exchange market and preventing the development of preferential trading systems cultivated through expedients such as exchange control.

The Keynes and White plans, which formed each side's basis for negotiations, require only a brief summary. Exchange control and the centralized provision of liquidity ("bancor") were two central elements of Keynes's plan for an international clearing union. . . . Exchange control would insulate pegged exchange rates from the sudden liquidation of short-term balances. Symmetry would be ensured by a charge on creditor balances held with the clearing bank.

The White plan acknowledged the validity of the British concern with liquidity, but was intended to prevent both inflation and deflation rather than to exert an expansionary influence. It limited the Stabilization Fund's total resources to $5 billion, compared with $26 billion under the Keynes plan. It was patterned on the principles of American bank lending, under which decisionmaking power rested ultimately with the bank; the Keynes plan resembled the British overdraft system, in which the overdraft was at the borrower's discretion. The fundamental difference, however, was that the White plan limited the total U.S. obligation to its $2 billion contribution, while the Keynes plan limited the value of unrequited U.S. exports that might be financed by bancor to the total drawing rights of other countries ($23 billion).

It is typically argued that the Bretton Woods agreement reflected America's dominant position, presumably on the grounds that the International Monetary Fund charter specified quotas of $8.8 billion (closer to the White plan's $5 billion than to the Keynes plan's $26 billion) and a maximum U.S. obligation of $2.75 billion (much closer to $2 billion under the White plan than to $23 billion under the Keynes plan). Yet, relative to the implications of simple versions of hegemonic stability theory, a surprising number of British priorities were incorporated. One was the priority Britain attached to exchange rate flexibility. The United States initially had wished to invest the IMF with veto power over a country's decision to change its exchange rate. Subsequently it proposed that 80 percent of IMF members be required to approve any change in parity. But the Articles of Agreement permitted devaluation without fund objection when needed to eliminate fundamental disequilibrium. Lacking any definition of this term, there was scope for devaluation by countries other than the United States to reconcile internal and external balance. Only once did the fund treat an exchange rate change as unauthorized. If countries hesitated to devalue, they did so as much for domestic reasons as for reasons related to the structure of the international monetary system.

Another British priority incorporated into the agreement was tolerance of exchange control. Originally, the White plan obliged members to abandon all exchange restrictions within six months of ceasing hostilities or joining the IMF, whichever came first. A subsequent U.S. proposal would have required a country to eliminate all exchange controls within a year of joining the fund. But Britain succeeded in incorporating into the Articles of Agreement a distinction between controls for capital transactions, which were permitted, from controls on current transactions, which were not. In practice, even nondiscriminatory exchange controls on current transactions were sometimes authorized under IMF Article VIII. As a result of this compromise, the United States protected itself from efforts to divert sterling bloc trade toward the British market, while Britain protected itself from destabilization by overseas sterling balances.

In comparison with these concessions, British efforts to restore symmetry to the international adjustment mechanism proved unavailing. With abandonment of the overdraft principle, the British embraced White's "scarce currency" proposal, under which the fund was empowered to ration its supply of a scarce currency and members were authorized to impose limitations on freedom of exchange operations in that currency. Thus a country running payments surpluses sufficiently large to threaten the fund's ability to supply its currency might face restrictions on foreign customers' ability to purchase its exports. But the scarce currency clause had been drafted by the United States not with the principle of symmetry in mind, but in order to deal with problems of immediate postwar adjustment—specifically, the prospective dollar shortage. With the development of the Marshall Plan, the dollar shortage never achieved the severity anticipated by the authors of the scarce currency clause, and the provision was never invoked.

If the "Joint Statement by Experts on the Establishment of an International Monetary Fund," made public in April 1944, bore the imprint of the U.S. delegation to Bretton Woods, to a surprising extent it also embodied important elements of the British negotiating position. It is curious from the perspective of hegemonic stability theory that a war-battered economy—Britain—heavily dependent on the dominant economic power—America—for capital goods, financial capital, and export markets was able to extract significant concessions in the design of the international monetary system. Britain was ably represented in the negotiations. But even more important, the United States also required an international agreement and wished to secure it even while hostilities in Europe prevented enemy nations from taking part in negotiations and minimized the involvement of the allies on whose territory the war was fought. The United States therefore had little opportunity to play off countries against one another or to brand as renegades any that disputed the advisability of its design. As the Western world's second largest economy, Britain symbolized, if it did not actually represent, the other nations of the world and was able to advance their case more effectively than if they had attempted more actively to do so themselves.

What conclusions regarding the applicability of hegemonic stability theory to the genesis of international monetary systems follow from the evidence of these three cases? In the two clearest instances of hegemony—the United Kingdom in the second half of the nineteenth century and the United States following World War II—the leading economic power significantly influenced the form of the international monetary system, by example in the first instance and by negotiation in the second. But the evidence also underscores the fact that the hegemon has been incapable of dictating the form of the monetary system. In the first instance, British example did nothing to prevent significant modifications in the form of the gold standard adopted abroad. In the second, the exceptional dominance of the U.S. economy was unable to eliminate the need to compromise with other countries in the design of the monetary system.

THE OPERATION OF MONETARY SYSTEMS
AND THE THEORY OF HEGEMONIC STABILITY

It is necessary to consider not only the genesis of monetary systems, but also how the theory of hegemonic stability applies to the operation of such systems. I consider adjustment, liquidity, and the lender-of-last-resort function in turn.

Adjustment

Adjustment under the classical gold standard has frequently been characterized in terms compatible with hegemonic stability theory. The gold standard is portrayed as a managed system whose preservation and smooth operation were ensured through its regulation by a hegemonic power, Great Britain, and its agent, the Bank of England. . . .

Before 1914, London was indisputably the world's leading financial center. A large proportion of world trade—60 percent by one estimate—was settled through payment in sterling bills, with London functioning as a clearinghouse for importers and exporters of other nations. British discount houses bought bills from abroad, either directly or through the London agencies of foreign banks. Foreigners maintained balances in London to meet commitments on bills outstanding and to service British portfolio investments overseas. Foreign governments and central banks held deposits in London as interest-earning alternatives to gold reserves. Although the pound was not the only reserve currency of the pre-1914 era, sterling reserves matched the combined value of reserves denominated in other currencies. At the same time, Britain possessed perhaps £350 million of short-term capital overseas. Though it is unclear whether Britain was a net short-term debtor or creditor before the war, it is certain that a large volume of short-term funds was responsive to changes in domestic interest rates.

Such changes in interest rates might be instigated by the Bank of England. By altering the rates at which it discounted for its customers and rediscounted for the discount houses, the bank could affect rates prevailing in the discount market. But the effect of Bank rate was not limited to the bill market. While in part this reflected the exceptional integration characteristic of British financial markets, it was reinforced by institutionalization. In London, banks automatically fixed their deposit rates half a percentage point above Bank rate. Loan rates were similarly indexed to Bank rate but at a higher level. Though there were exceptions to these rules, changes in Bank rate were immediately reflected in a broad range of British interest rates.

An increase in Bank rate, by raising the general level of British interest rates, induced foreign investors to accumulate additional funds in London and to delay the repatriation or transfer of existing balances to other centers. British balances abroad were repatriated to earn the higher rate of return. Drawings of finance bills, which represented half of total bills in 1913, were similarly sensitive to changes in interest rates. Higher interest rates spread to the security market and delayed the flotation of new issues for overseas borrowers. In this way the Bank of England was able to insulate its gold reserve from disturbances in the external accounts. . . .

But why did the Bank of England's exceptional leverage not threaten convertibility abroad? The answer commonly offered is that Britain's unrivaled market power led to a de facto harmonization of national policies. . . . As Keynes wrote in the *Treatise on Money*, "During the latter half of the nineteenth century the influence of London on credit conditions throughout the world was so predominant that the Bank of England could almost have claimed to be the conductor of the international orchestra."

Since fiscal harmonization requires no discussion in an era of balanced budgets, the stability of the classical gold standard can be explained by the desire and ability of central banks to harmonize their monetary policies in the interest of external balance. External balance, or maintaining gold reserves adequate to defend the established gold parity, was the foremost target of monetary policy in the period preceding World War I. In the absence of a coherent theory of unemployment, much less a consensus on its relation to monetary policy, there was relatively little pressure for central banks to accommodate domestic needs. External balance was not the sole target of policy, but when internal and external balance came into conflict, the latter took precedence. Viewed from an international perspective, British leadership played a role in this process of harmonization insofar as the market power and prominence of the Bank of England served as a focal point for policy coordination.

But if the Bank of England could be sure of defeating its European counterparts when they engaged in a tug of war over short-term capital, mere harmonization of central bank policies, in the face of external disturbances, would have been insufficient to prevent convertibility crises on the Continent. The explanation for the absence of such crises would appear to be the greater market power of European countries compared with their non-European counterparts. Some observers have distinguished the market power of capital-exporting countries from the inability of capital importers to influence the direction of financial flows. Others have suggested the existence of a hierarchical structure of financial markets: below the London market were the less active markets of Berlin, Paris, Vienna, Amsterdam, Brussels, Zurich, and New York, followed by the still less active markets of the Scandinavian countries, and finally the nascent markets of Latin America and other parts of the non-European world. When Bank rate was raised in London, thus redistributing reserves to Britain from other regions, compensatory discount rate increases on the Continent drew funds from the non-European world or curtailed capital outflows. Developing countries, due to either the thinness of markets or the absence of relevant institutions, were unable to prevent these events. In times of crisis, therefore, convertibility was threatened primarily outside Europe and North America. . . .

Thus, insofar as hegemony played some role in the efficiency of the adjustment mechanism, it was not the British hegemony of which so much has been written but the collective hegemony of the European center relative to the non-European periphery. Not only does this case challenge the conception of the hegemon, therefore, but because the stability of the classical gold standard was enjoyed exclusively by the countries of the center, it supports only the weak form of hegemonic stability theory—that the benefits of stability accrued exclusively to the powerful.

The relation between hegemonic power and the need for policy harmonization is equally relevant to the case of the interwar gold exchange standard. One interpretation . . . is that in the absence of a hegemon there was no focal point for policy, which interfered with efforts at coordination. But more important than a declining ability to harmonize policies may have been a diminished desire to do so. Although the advent of explicit stabilization policy was not to occur until the 1930s and 1940s, during the 1920s central banks placed increasing weight on internal conditions when formulating monetary policy. The rise of socialism and the example of the Bolshevik revolution in particular provided a counterweight to central bankers' instinctive wish to base policy solely on external conditions. External adjustment was rendered difficult by policymakers' increasing hesitancy to sacrifice other objectives on the altar of external balance. Britain's balance-of-payments problems, for example, cannot be attributed to "the existence of more than one policy" in the world economy without considering also a domestic unemployment problem that placed pressure on the Bank of England to resist restrictive measures that might strengthen the external accounts at the expense of industry and trade.

Under Bretton Woods, the problem of adjustment was exacerbated by the difficulty of using exchange rate changes to restore external balance. Hesitancy to change their exchange rates posed few problems for countries in surplus. However, those in deficit had to choose between aggravating unemployment and tolerating external deficits; the latter was infeasible in the long run and promoted an increase in the volume of short-term capital that moved in response to anticipations of devaluation. Although the IMF charter did not encourage devaluation, the hesitancy of deficit countries to employ this option is easier to ascribe to the governments' tendency to attach their prestige to the stability of established exchange rates than to U.S. hegemony, however defined. Where the singular role of the United States was important was in precluding a dollar devaluation. A possible solution to the problem of U.S. deficits, one that would not have threatened other countries' ability to accumulate reserves, was an increase in the dollar price of gold, that is, a dollar devaluation. It is sometimes argued that the United States was incapable of adjusting through exchange rate changes since other countries would have devalued in response to prevent any change in bilateral rates against the dollar. However, raising the dollar price of gold would have increased the dollar value of monetary gold, reducing the global excess demand for reserves and encouraging other countries to increase domestic demand and cut back on their balance-of-payments surpluses. But while a rise in the price of gold might have alleviated central banks' immediate dependence on dollars, it would have done nothing to prevent the problem from recurring. It would also have promoted skepticism about the U.S. government's commitment to the new gold price, thereby encouraging other countries to increase their demands for gold and advancing the date of future difficulties.

Does this evidence on adjustment support hegemonic theories of international monetary stability? The contrast between the apparently smooth adjustment under the classical gold standard and Bretton Woods and the adjustment difficulties of the interwar years suggests that a dominant power's policies served as a fixed target that was easier to hit than a moving one. . . . [W]hat mattered was not so much the particular stance of monetary policy but that the leading players settled on the same stance. The argument . . . is that a dominant player is best placed to signal the other players the nature of the most probable stance. The effectiveness of the adjustment mechanism under the two regimes reflected not just British and American market power but also the existence of an international consensus on the objectives and formulation of monetary policy that permitted central bank policies to be harmonized. The essential role of Britain before 1914 and the United States after 1944 was not so much to force other countries to alter their policies as to provide a focal point for policy harmonization.

Liquidity

Under the classical gold standard, the principal source of liquidity was newly mined gold. It is hard to see how British dominance of international markets could have much influenced the changes in the world price level and mining technology upon which these supplies depended. As argued above, where Britain's prominence mattered was in facilitating the provision of supplementary liquidity in the form of sterling reserves, which grew at an accelerating rate starting in the 1890s. It is conceivable, therefore, that in the absence of British hegemony a reserve shortage would have developed and the classical gold standard would have exhibited a deflationary bias.

Liquidity was an issue of more concern under the interwar gold exchange standard. Between 1915 and 1925, prices rose worldwide due to the inflation associated with wartime finance and postwar reconstruction; these rising prices combined with economic growth to increase the transactions demand for money. Yet under a system of convertible currencies, world money supply was constrained by the availability of reserves. Statutory restrictions required central banks to back their money supplies with eligible reserves, while recent experience with inflation deterred politicians from liberalizing the statutes. The output of newly mined gold had been depressed since the beginning of World War I, and experts offered pessimistic forecasts of future supplies. Increasing the real value of world gold reserves by forcing a reduction in the world price level would only add to the difficulties of an already troubled world economy. Countries were encouraged, therefore, to stabilize on a gold exchange basis to prevent the development of a gold shortage.

There are difficulties with this explanation of interwar liquidity problems, which emphasizes a shortage of gold. For one, the danger of a gold shortage's constraining the volume of transactions was alleviated by the all but complete withdrawal of gold coin from circulation during the war. As a result, the percentage of short-term liabilities of all central banks backed by gold was little different in 1928 from its level in 1913, while the volume of the liabilities backed by that gold stock was considerably increased. It is hard to see why a gold shortage, after having exhibited only weak effects in previous years, should have had such a dramatic impact starting in 1929. It is even less clear how the absence of a hegemon contributed to the purported gold shortage. The obvious linkages between hegemony and the provision of liquidity work in the wrong direction. The straightforward way of increasing the monetary value of reserves was a round of currency devaluation, which would revalue gold reserves and, by raising the real price of gold, increase the output of the mining industry. As demonstrated in 1931, when the pound's depreciation set off a round of competitive devaluations, sterling remained the linchpin of the international currency system; the only way a round of currency devaluation could have taken place, therefore, was if Britain had stabilized in 1925 at a lower level. But had her dominance of the international economy not eroded over the first quarter of the twentieth century, the political pressure on Britain to return to gold at the prewar parity would have increased rather than being reduced. It seems unlikely, therefore, that a more successful maintenance of British hegemony, ceteris paribus, would have alleviated any gold shortage.

An alternative and more appealing explanation for interwar liquidity problems emphasizes mismanagement of gold reserves rather than their overall insufficiency. It blames France and the United States for absorbing disproportionate shares of global gold supplies and for imposing deflation on the rest of the world. Between 1928 and 1932, French gold reserves rose from $1.25 billion to $3.26 billion of constant gold content, or from 13 to 28 percent of the world total. Meanwhile, the United States, which had released gold between 1924 and 1928, facilitating the reestablishment of convertibility in other countries, reversed its position and imported $1.49 billion of gold between 1928 and 1930. By the end of 1932 the United States and France together possessed nearly 63 percent of the world's central monetary gold. . . .

The maldistribution of reserves can be understood by focusing on the systematic interaction of central banks. This approach builds on the literature that characterizes the interwar gold standard as a competitive struggle for gold between countries that viewed the size of their gold reserve as a measure of national prestige and as insurance against financial instability. France and the United States in particular, but gold standard countries generally, repeatedly raised their discount rates relative to one another in efforts to attract gold from abroad. By leading to the accumulation of excess reserves, these restrictive policies exacerbated the problem of inadequate liquidity, but by offsetting one another they also failed to achieve their objective of attracting gold from abroad. . . .

The origins of this competitive struggle for gold are popularly attributed to the absence of a hegemon. The competing financial centers—London, Paris, and New York—worked at cross-purposes because, in contrast to the preceding period, no one central bank was sufficiently powerful to call the tune. Before the war, the Bank of England had been sufficiently dominant to act as a leader, setting its discount rate with the reaction of other central banks in mind, while other central banks responded in the manner of a competitive fringe. By using this power to defend the gold parity of sterling despite the maintenance of slender reserves, the bank prevented the development of a competitive scramble for gold. But after World War I, with the United States unwilling to accept responsibility for leadership, no one central bank formulated its monetary policy with foreign reactions and global conditions in mind, and the noncooperative struggle for gold was the result. In this interpretation of the interwar liquidity problem, hegemony—or, more precisely, its absence—plays a critical role.

In discussing the provision of liquidity under Bretton Woods, it is critical to distinguish the decade ending in 1958—when the convertibility of European currencies was restored and before U.S. dominance of international trade, foreign lending, and industrial production was unrivaled—from the decade that followed. In the first period, the most important source of incremental liquidity was dollar reserves. Between 1949 and 1958, when global reserves rose by 29 percent, less than one-third of the increment took the form of gold and one-fifteenth was in quotas at the IMF. The role of sterling as a reserve currency was limited almost exclusively to Commonwealth members and former British colonies that had traditionally held reserves in London and traded heavily with Britain. Consequently, the accumulation of dollar balances accounted for roughly half of incremental liquidity in the first decade of Bretton Woods.

In one sense, U.S. dominance of international markets facilitated the provision of liquidity. At the end of World War II, the United States had amassed 60 percent of the world's gold stock; at $35 an ounce, this was worth six times the value of the official dollar claims accumulated by foreign governments by 1949. There was little immediate question, given U.S. dominance of global gold reserves, of the stability of the gold price of the dollar and hence little hesitation to accumulate incremental liquidity in the form of dollar claims. But in another sense, U.S. international economic power in the immediate postwar years impeded the supply of liquidity to the world economy. Wartime destruction of industry in Europe and Japan left U.S. manufactured exports highly competitive in world markets and rendered Europe dependent on U.S. capital goods for industrial reconstruction. The persistent excess demand for U.S. goods tended to push the U.S. balance of payments into surplus, creating the famous "dollar shortage" of the immediate postwar years. While U.S. hegemony left other countries willing to hold dollar claims, it rendered them extremely difficult to obtain.

Various policies were initiated in response to the dollar shortage, including discrimination against dollar area exports, special incentives for European and Japanese exports to the United States, and a round of European currency devaluations starting in September 1949. Ultimately the solution took the form of two sharply contrasting actions by the hegemon: Marshall Plan grants of $11.6 billion between mid-1948 and mid-1952, and Korean War expenditures. Largely as a result of these two factors, U.S. trade surpluses shrank from $10.1 billion in 1947 to $2.6 billion in 1952; more important, U.S. government grants and private capital outflows exceeded the surplus on current account. By 1950 the U.S. balance of payments was in deficit and, after moving back into surplus in 1951–52, deficits returned to stay. Insofar as its singular economic power encouraged the United States to undertake both the Marshall Plan and the Korean War, hegemony played a significant role in both the form and adequacy of the liquidity provided in the first decade of Bretton Woods.

Between 1958 and 1969, global reserves grew more rapidly, by 51 percent, than they had in the first decade of Bretton Woods. Again, gold was a minor share of the increment, about one-twentieth, and IMF quotas were one-eighth. While foreign exchange reserves again provided roughly half, Eurodollars and other foreign currencies grew in importance: their contribution actually exceeded that of official claims on the United States. In part these trends reflected rapid growth in Europe and Japan. More important, they reflected the fact that starting in 1965 the value of foreign government claims on the United States exceeded U.S. gold reserves. Prudence dictated that foreign governments diversify their reserve positions out of dollars.

The role of U.S. hegemony in the provision of liquidity during this second decade has been much debated. The growth of liquidity reflected both supply and demand pressures: both demands by other countries for additional reserves, which translated into balance-of-payments surpluses, and the capacity of the United States to consume more than it produced by running balance-of-payments deficits financed by the willingness of other countries to accumulate dollar reserves. The United States was criticized sharply, mainly by the French, for exporting inflation and for financing purchases of foreign companies and pursuit of the Vietnam War through the balance of payments. Although these complaints cannot be dismissed, it is incorrect to conclude that the dollar's singular position in the Bretton Woods system permitted the United States to run whatever balance-of-payments deficit it wished. Moreover, it is difficult to envisage an alternative scenario in which the U.S. balance of payments was zero but the world was not starved of liquidity. Owing to the sheer size of the American economy, new claims on the United States continued to exceed vastly the contribution of new claims on any other nation. Moreover, U.S. economic, military, and diplomatic influence did much to encourage if not compel other countries to maintain their holdings of dollar claims. Thus U.S. dominance of international markets played a critical role in resolving the liquidity crisis of the 1960s.

The distinguishing feature of Bretton Woods is not that other countries continued to hold dollar reserves in the face of exchange rate uncertainty and economic growth abroad, for neither development has deterred them from holding dollars under the flexible exchange rate regime of the 1970s and 1980s. Rather, it is that they continued to hold dollar reserves in the face of a one-way bet resulting from dollar convertibility at a fixed price when the dollar price of gold seemed poised to rise. In part, the importance of American foreign investments and the size of the U.S. market for European exports caused other countries to hesitate before cashing in their chips. Yet foreign governments also saw dollar convertibility as essential to the defense of the gold-dollar system and viewed the fixed exchange rates of that system as an international public good worthy of defense. Not until 1965 did the French government decide to convert into gold some $300 million of its dollar holdings and subsequently to step up its monthly gold purchases from the United States. But when pressure on U.S. gold reserves mounted following the 1967 devaluation of sterling, other countries, including France, sold gold instead of capitalizing on the one-way bet. They joined the United States in the formation of a gold pool whose purpose was to sell a sufficient quantity of gold to defend the official price. Between sterling's devaluation in 1967 and closure of the gold market on March 15, 1968, the pool sold $3 billion of gold, of which U.S. sales were $2.2 billion. France purchased no gold in 1967 or 1968, presumably due in part to foreign pressure. U.S. leverage undoubtedly contributed to their decisions. But a plausible interpretation of these events is that foreign governments, rather than simply being coerced into support of the dollar by U.S. economic power, were willing to take limited steps to defend the international public good of a fixed exchange rate system defined in terms of the dollar price of gold.

What does this discussion imply for the role of hegemony in the provision of international liquidity? The strongest evidence for the importance of a hegemon is negative evidence from the interwar years, when the absence of a hegemon and the failure of competing financial centers to coordinate their policies effectively contributed greatly to the liquidity shortage. In other periods, when a dominant economic power was present, it is difficult to credit that power with sole responsibility for ensuring the adequate provision of liquidity. Under the gold standard, the principal source of incremental liquidity was newly mined gold; Britain contributed to the provision of liquidity only insofar as its financial stature encouraged other countries to augment their specie holdings with sterling reserves. After World War II, U.S. economic power similarly rendered dollars a desirable form in which to acquire liquid reserves, but the same factors that made dollars desirable also rendered them difficult to obtain.

The Lender of Last Resort

If adjustment were always accomplished smoothly and liquidity were consistently adequate, there would be no need for an international lender of last resort to stabilize the international monetary system. Yet countries' capacity to adjust and the system's ability to provide liquidity may be inadequate to accommodate disturbances to confidence. Like domestic banking systems, an international financial system based on convertibility is vulnerable to problems of confidence that threaten to ignite speculative runs. Like depositors who rush to close their accounts upon receiving the news of a neighboring bank failure, exchange market participants, upon hearing of a convertibility crisis abroad, may rush to liquidate their foreign exchange balances because of incomplete information about the liabilities and intentions of particular governments. This analogy leads Charles Kindleberger, for example, to adopt from the domestic central banking literature the notion that a lender of last resort is needed to discount in times of crisis, provide countercyclical long-term lending, and maintain an open market for distress goods, and to suggest that, in the absence of a supranational institution, only a hegemonic power can carry out this international lender-of-last-resort function on the requisite scale.

Of the episodes considered here, the early Bretton Woods era provides the clearest illustration of the benefits of an international lender of last resort. The large amount of credit provided Europe in the form of grants and long-term loans and the willingness of the United States to accept European and Japanese exports even when these had been promoted by the extension of special incentives illustrate two of the lender-of-last-resort functions identified by Kindleberger: countercyclical lending and provision of an open market for distress goods. Many histories of the Marshall Plan characterize it in terms consistent with the benevolent strand of hegemonic stability theory: the United States was mainly interested in European prosperity and stood to benefit only insofar as that prosperity promoted geopolitical stability. Revisionist histories have more in common with the coercive strand of hegemonic stability theory: they suggest that the United States used Marshall aid to exact concessions from Europe in the form of most-favored-nation status for Germany, IMF exchange rate oversight, and Swiss links with the Organization for European Economic Cooperation. While it is certain that the European countries could not have moved so quickly to relax capital controls and quantitative trade restrictions without these forms of U.S. assistance, it is not clear how far the argument can be generalized. The Marshall Plan coincided with a very special era in the history of the international monetary system, in which convertibility outside the United States had not yet been restored. Hence there was little role for the central function of the lender of last resort: discounting freely when a convertibility crisis threatens. When convertibility was threatened in the 1960s, rescue operations were mounted not by the United States but cooperatively by the Group of Ten.

Kindleberger has argued that the 1929–31 financial crisis might have been avoided by the intervention of an international lender of last resort. The unwillingness of Britain and the United States to engage in countercyclical long-term lending and to provide an open market for distress goods surely exacerbated convertibility crises in the non-European world. Both the curtailment of overseas lending and the imposition of restrictive trade policies contributed greatly to the balance-of-payments difficulties that led to the suspension of convertibility by primary producers as early as 1929. Gold movements from the periphery to London and New York in 1930 heightened the problem and hastened its spread to Central Europe.

But it is not obvious that additional U.S. loans to Britain and other European countries attempting to fend off threats to convertibility would have succeeded in altering significantly the course of the 1931 financial crisis. Heading off the crisis would have required a successful defense of the pound sterling, whose depreciation was followed almost immediately by purposeful devaluation in some two dozen other countries. Britain did succeed in obtaining a substantial amount of short-term credit abroad in support of the pound, raising $650 million in New York and Paris after only minimal delay. Total short-term lending to countries under pressure amounted to approximately $1 billion, or roughly 10 percent of total international short-term indebtedness and 5 percent of world imports (more than the ratio of total IMF quotas to world imports in the mid-1970s). It is noteworthy that these credits were obtained not from a dominant power but from a coalition of creditor countries.

Could additional short-term credits from an international lender of last resort have prevented Britain's suspension of convertibility? If the run on sterling reflected merely a temporary loss of confidence in the stability of fixed parities, then additional loans from an international lender of last resort—like central bank loans to temporarily illiquid banks—might have permitted the crisis to be surmounted. But if the loss of confidence had a basis in economic fundamentals, no amount of short-term lending would have done more than delay the crisis in the absence of measures to eliminate the underlying imbalance. The existence of an international lender of last resort could have affected the timing but not the fact of collapse.

The fundamental disequilibrium that undermined confidence in sterling is typically sought in the government budget. The argument is that by stimulating absorption, Britain's budget deficit, in conjunction with the collapse of foreign demand for British exports, weakened the balance of trade. Although the second Labour government fell in 1931 precisely because of its failure to agree on measures to reduce the size of the budget deficit, historians disagree over whether the budget contributed significantly to the balance-of-payments deficit. The trade balance, after all, was only one component of the balance of payments. The effect on the balance of payments of shocks to the trade balance appears to have been small compared with the Bank of England's capacity to attract short-term capital. If this is correct and the 1931 financial crisis in Britain reflected mainly a temporary loss of confidence in sterling rather than a fundamental disequilibrium, then additional short-term loans from the United States or a group of creditor countries might have succeeded in tiding Britain over the crisis. But the loans required would have been extremely large by the standards of either the pre-1914 period of British hegemony or the post-1944 period of U.S. dominance.

The international lender-of-last-resort argument is more difficult to apply to the classical gold standard. . . . In 1873, as in 1890 and 1907, the hegemonic monetary authority, the Bank of England, would have been the "borrower of last resort" rather than the lender. [This fact] might be reconciled with the theory of hegemonic stability if the lender, Paris, is elevated to the status of a hegemonic financial center—a possibility to which Kindleberger is led by his analysis of late nineteenth century financial crises. But elevating Paris to parity with London would do much to undermine the view of the classical gold standard that attributes its durability to management by a single financial center.

What does this historical analysis of the lender-of-last-resort function imply for the validity of hegemonic theories of international monetary stability? It confirms that there have been instances, notably the aftermath of World War II, when the economic power of the leading country so greatly surpassed that of all rivals that it succeeded in ensuring the system's stability in times of crisis by discounting freely, providing countercyclical lending, and maintaining an open market. It suggests, at the same time, that such instances are rare. For a leading economic power to effectively act as lender of last resort, not only must its market power exceed that of all rivals, but it must do so by a very substantial margin. British economic power in the 1870s and U.S. economic power in the 1960s were inadequate in this regard, and other economic powers—France in the first instance, the Group of Ten in the second—were needed to cooperate in providing lender-of-last-resort facilities.

THE DYNAMICS OF HEGEMONIC DECLINE

Might an international monetary system that depends for its smooth operation on the dominance of a hegemonic power be dynamically unstable? There are two channels through which dynamic instability might operate: the system itself might evolve in directions that attenuate the hegemon's stabilizing capacity; or the system might remain the same, but its operation might influence relative rates of economic growth in such a way as to progressively reduce the economic power and, by implication, the stabilizing capacity of the hegemon.

The hypothesis that the Bretton Woods system was dynamically unstable was mooted by Robert Triffin as early as 1947. Triffin focused on what he saw as inevitable changes in the composition of reserves, arguing that the system's viability hinged on the willingness of foreign governments to accumulate dollars, which depended in turn on confidence in the maintenance of dollar convertibility. Although gold dominated the dollar as a source of international liquidity (in 1958 the value of gold reserves was four times the value of dollar reserves when all countries were considered, two times when the United States was excluded), dollars were the main source of liquidity on the margin. Yet the willingness of foreign governments to accumulate dollars at the required pace and hence the stability of the gold-dollar system were predicated on America's commitment and capacity to maintain the convertibility of dollars into gold at $35 an ounce. The threat to its ability to do so was that, under a system in which reserves could take the form of either dollars or gold (a scarce natural resource whose supply was insufficiently elastic to keep pace with the demand for liquidity), the share of dollars in total reserves could only increase. An ever-growing volume of foreign dollar liabilities was based on a fixed or even shrinking U.S. gold reserve. Thus the very structure of Bretton Woods—specifically, the monetary role for gold—progressively undermined the hegemon's capacity to ensure the system's smooth operation through the provision of adequate liquidity.

Dynamic instability also could have operated through the effect of the international monetary system on the relative rates of growth of the U.S. and foreign economies. If the dollar was systematically overvalued for a significant portion of the Bretton Woods era, this could have reduced the competitiveness of U.S. exports and stimulated foreign penetration of U.S. markets. If the dollar was overvalued due to some combination of European devaluations at the beginning of the 1950s, subsequent devaluations by developing countries, and the inability of the United States to respond to competitive difficulties by altering its exchange rate, how might this have depressed the relative rate of growth of the U.S. economy, leading to hegemonic decline? One can think of two arguments: one that proceeds along Heckscher-Ohlin lines, another that draws on dynamic theories of international trade.

The Heckscher-Ohlin hypothesis builds on the observation that the United States was relatively abundant in human and physical capital. Since, under Heckscher-Ohlin assumptions, U.S. exports were capital intensive, any measure that depressed exports would have reduced its rate of return. Reducing the rate of return would have discouraged investment, depressing the rate of economic growth and accelerating the U.S. economy's relative decline.

The dynamic trade theory hypothesis builds on the existence of learning curves in the production of traded goods. If production costs fall with cumulative output and the benefits of learning are external to the firm but internal to domestic industry, then exchange rate overvaluation, by depressing the competitiveness of exports, will inhibit their production and reduce the benefits of learning. If overvaluation is sufficiently large and persistent, it will shift comparative advantage in production to foreign competitors. The weakness of this hypothesis is that it is predicated on the unsubstantiated assumption that learning effects are more important in the production of traded goods than nontraded goods. Its strength lies in the extent to which it conforms with informal characterizations of recent trends.

Precisely the same arguments have been applied to the downfall of the interwar gold exchange standard. The interwar system, which depended for liquidity on gold, dollars, and sterling, was if anything even more susceptible than its post–World War II analog to destabilization by the operation of Gresham's law. As noted above, the legacy of the Genoa conference encouraged central banks to accumulate foreign exchange. Promoting the use of exchange reserves while attempting to maintain gold convertibility threatened the system's stability for the same reasons as under Bretton Woods. But because foreign exchange reserves were not then concentrated in a single currency to the same extent as after World War II, it was even easier under the interwar system for central banks to liquidate foreign balances in response to any event that undermined confidence in sterling or the dollar. Instead of initiating the relatively costly and complex process of acquiring gold from foreign monetary authorities in the face of at least moral suasion to refrain, central banks needed only to swap one reserve currency for the other on the open market. Gresham's law operated even more powerfully when gold coexisted with two reserve currencies than with one.

This instability manifested itself when the 1931 financial crisis, by undermining faith in sterling convertibility, induced a large-scale shift out of London balances. Once Britain was forced to devalue, faith in the stability of the other major reserve currency was shaken, and speculative pressure shifted to the dollar. The National Bank of Belgium, which had lost 25 percent of the value of its sterling reserve as a result of Britain's devaluation, moved to liquidate its dollar balances. The Eastern European countries, including Poland, Czechoslovakia, and Bulgaria, then liquidated their deposits in New York. Between the end of 1930 and the end of 1931, the share of foreign exchange in the reserve portfolios of twenty-three European countries fell from 35 to 19 percent, signaling the demise of the exchange portion of the gold exchange standard.

The argument that structuring the international monetary system around a reserve asset provided by the leading economic power led eventually to that country's loss of preeminence has been applied even more frequently to Britain after World War I than to the United States after World War II. Because the gold exchange standard created a foreign demand for sterling balances, Britain was able to run larger trade balance deficits than would have been permitted otherwise. In a sense, Britain's reserve currency status was one of the factors that facilitated the restoration of sterling's prewar parity. Despite an enormous literature predicated on the view that the pound was overvalued at $4.86, there remains skepticism that the extent of overvaluation was great or the effect on the macroeconomy was significant. While it is not possible to resolve this debate here, the point relevant to the theory of hegemonic stability is that evidence of reserve currency overvaluation is as substantial in the earlier period, when hegemony was threatened, as in the later period, when it was triumphant.

Of the three monetary systems considered here, the classical gold standard is the most difficult to analyze in terms of the dynamics of hegemonic decline. It might be argued that the pound was overvalued for at least a decade before 1913 and that Britain's failure to devalue resulted in sluggish growth, which accelerated the economy's hegemonic decline. The competitive difficulties of older British industries, notably iron and steel, and the decelerating rate of economic growth in the first decade of the twentieth century are consistent with this view. The deceleration in the rate of British economic growth has been ascribed to both a decline in productivity growth and a fall in the rate of domestic capital formation. This fall in the rate of domestic capital formation, especially after 1900, reflected not a decline in British savings rates but a surge of foreign investment. Thus, if Britain's hegemonic position in the international economy is to have caused its relative decline, this hegemony would have had to be responsible for the country's exceptionally high propensity to export capital. The volume of British capital exports in the decades preceding World War I has been attributed, alternatively, to the spread of industrialization and associated investment opportunities to other countries and continents and to imperfections in the structure of British capital markets that resulted in a bias toward investment overseas. It is impossible to resolve this debate here. But the version of the market imperfections argument that attributes the London capital market's lack of interest in domestic investment to Britain's relatively early and labor-intensive form of industrialization implies that the same factors responsible for Britain's mid-nineteenth century hegemony (the industrial revolution occurred there first) may also have been responsible for the capital market biases that accelerated its hegemonic decline.

Although the classical gold standard experienced a number of serious disruptions, such as the 1907 panic when a financial crisis threatened to undermine its European core, the prewar system survived these disturbances intact. Eventually, however, the same forces that led to the downfall of the interwar gold exchange standard would have undermined the stability of the prewar system. As the rate of economic growth continued to outstrip the rate of growth of gold (the supply of which was limited by the availability of ore), countries would have grown increasingly dependent on foreign exchange reserves as a source of incremental liquidity. As in the 1960s, growing reliance on exchange reserves in the face of relatively inelastic gold supplies would have eventually proven incompatible with the reserve center's ability to maintain gold convertibility.

De Cecco argues that the situation was already beginning to unravel in the first decade of the twentieth century—that the Boer War signaled the end of the long peace of the nineteenth century, thereby undermining the willingness of potential belligerents to hold their reserves as deposits in foreign countries. . . . More important for our purposes, he suggests that the system was destabilized by the growth of U.S. economic power relative to that of Great Britain. Given the experimental nature of U.S. Treasury efforts to accommodate seasonal variations in money demand, the United States relied heavily on gold imports whenever economic conditions required an increase in money supply, notably during harvest and planting seasons. When the demand for money increased, the United States imported gold, mainly from the Bank of England, which was charged with pegging the sterling price of gold on the London market with a gold reserve of only £30 million. As the American economy grew, both its average demand for gold from London and that demand's seasonal fluctuation increased relative to the Bank of England's primary reserve and its capacity to attract supplementary funds from other centers. To rephrase de Cecco's argument in terms of hegemonic stability theory, the growth of the United States relative to that of Britain undermined Britain's capacity to stabilize international financial markets: specifically, its ability to serve simultaneously as the world's only free gold market, providing however much gold was required by other countries, and to maintain the stability of sterling, the reference point for the global system of fixed exchange rates. In a sense, de Cecco sees indications of the interwar stalemate—a Britain incapable of stabilizing the international system and a United States unwilling to do so—emerging in the first decade of the twentieth century. From this perspective, the process of hegemonic decline that culminated in the international monetary difficulties of the interwar years was at most accelerated by World War I. Even before the war, the processes that led to the downfall of established monetary arrangements were already under way.

CONCLUSION

Much of the international relations literature concerned with prospects for international monetary reform can be read as a search for an alternative to hegemony as a basis for international monetary stability. Great play is given to the contrast between earlier periods of hegemonic dominance, notably 1890–1914 and 1945–71, and the nature of the task presently confronting aspiring architects of international monetary institutions in an increasingly multipolar world. In this paper I suggest that hegemonic stability theories are helpful for understanding the relatively smooth operation of the classical gold standard and the early Bretton Woods system, as well as some of the difficulties of the interwar years. At the same time, much of the evidence is difficult to reconcile with the hegemonic stability view. Even when individual countries occupied positions of exceptional prominence in the world economy and that prominence was reflected in the form and functioning of the international monetary system, that system was still fundamentally predicated on international collaboration. Keohane's notion of "hegemonic cooperation"—that cooperation is required for systemic stability even in periods of hegemonic dominance, although the presence of a hegemon may encourage cooperative behavior—seems directly applicable to international monetary relations. The importance of collaboration is equally apparent in the design of the international monetary system, its operation under normal circumstances, and the management of crises. Despite the usefulness of hegemonic stability theory when applied to short periods and well-defined aspects of international monetary relations, the international monetary system has always been "after hegemony" in the sense that more than a dominant economic power was required to ensure the provision and maintenance of international monetary stability. Moreover, it was precisely when important economic power most forcefully conditioned the form of the international system that the potential for instability, in a dynamic sense, was greatest. Above all, historical experience demonstrates the speed and pervasiveness of changes in national economic power; since hegemony is transitory, so must be any international monetary system that takes hegemony as its basis. Given the costs of international monetary reform, it would seem unwise to predicate a new system on such a transient basis.

16

The Triad and the Unholy Trinity:
Problems of International
Monetary Cooperation
BENJAMIN J. COHEN

In this essay, Benjamin J. Cohen explores the attractions and difficulties of cooperation among nations on international monetary
matters, emphasizing how international political realities constrain interactions among independent nation-states. Monetary
policy coordination has some potential benefits, but there are
many uncertainties countries face in engaging in cooperative behavior. The primary dilemma is that governments cannot simultaneously achieve the objectives of exchange-rate stability, capital
mobility, and monetary policy autonomy. As governments are
forced to make trade-offs among these goals, they will abandon
the goal of exchange-rate stability, and thus monetary cooperation, when it is too costly relative to the other policy objectives.
The cyclical and episodic quality of monetary cooperation is
linked to governments' changing incentives to pursue stable exchange rates. Cohen's argument highlights the difficulty of sustaining cooperative arrangements when states' national interests
diverge.

... Among the G-7 [Group of Seven] countries (the United States, Britain, Canada, France, Germany, Italy and Japan), procedures for monetary cooperation have
been gradually intensified since the celebrated Plaza Agreement of September
1985, which formally pledged participants to a coordinated realignment of exchange rates. Ostensibly the aim of these evolving procedures is to jointly manage
currency relations and macroeconomic conditions across Europe, North America
and Japan—the area referred to by many simply as the Triad. Finance ministers
from the G-7 countries now meet regularly to discuss the current and prospective

Benjamin J. Cohen. "The Triad and the Unholy Trinity: Problems of International Monetary Cooperation." From Richard Higgott, Richard Leaver, and John Ravenhill, eds. *Pacific Economic Relations in
the 1990s: Cooperation or Conflict?* Allen & Unwin, 1993, pp. 133–58. Reprinted by permission.

performance of their economies; policy objectives and instruments are evaluated for possible linkages and repercussions; the principle of mutual adjustment in the common interest is repeatedly reaffirmed in official communiqués. . . . Yet for all their promises to curb unilateralist impulses, the governments involved frequently honour the process more in word than deed. In fact, if there has been one constant in the collaborative efforts of the Triad, it has been their lack of constancy. Commitments in practice have tended to ebb and flow cyclically like the tides. In its essence, G-7 monetary cooperation has had a distinctly episodic quality to it.

The main premise of this chapter is that international monetary cooperation, like passionate love, is a good thing but difficult to sustain. The reason, I argue, is systematic and has to do with the intrinsic incompatibility of three key desiderata of governments: exchange-rate stability, capital mobility, and national policy autonomy. Together these three values form a kind of "Unholy Trinity" that operates regularly to erode collective commitments to monetary collaboration. The impact of the Unholy Trinity has been evident in the experience of the G-7. The principal implication . . . is that the conditions necessary for a serious and sustained commitment to monetary cooperation are not easy to satisfy and, without major effort, appear unlikely to be attained any time soon. The irony is that even without such a commitment most . . . governments will find their policy autonomy increasingly eroded in the coming decade—in a manner, moreover, that may seem even less appealing to them than formal cooperation.

The organisation of this chapter is as follows. Following a brief evaluation in Part 1 of the basic case for monetary cooperation, Part 2 reviews the experience of the G-7 countries since 1985 noting, in particular, a distinctly cyclical pattern in the Triad's collective commitment to policy coordination. Reasons for the episodic quality of monetary cooperation with emphasis on the central role of the Unholy Trinity are explored in Part 3, and the question of what might be done about the resulting inconstancy of policy commitments is addressed in Part 4. . . .

1. THE CASE FOR POLICY COOPERATION

Conceptually, international cooperation may take many forms, ranging from simple consultation among governments, or occasional crisis management, to partial or even full collaboration in the formulation and implementation of policy. In this chapter, following the lead of standard scholarship on international political economy, cooperation will be identified with a mutual adjustment of national-policy behaviour in a particular issue-area, achieved through an implicit or explicit process of inter-state bargaining. Related terms such as "coordination" and "joint" or "collective decision-making" will, for our purposes, be treated as essentially synonymous in meaning.

In the issue-area of international monetary relations, the theoretical case for policy cooperation is quite straightforward. It begins with the undeniable fact of intensified interdependence across much of the world economy. In recent decades, states have become increasingly linked through the integration of markets for goods, services and capital. Structurally, the greater openness of economies tends to erode each country's insulation from commercial or financial developments elsewhere. In policy terms it means that any one government's actions will generate a variety of "spillover" effects—foreign repercussions and feedbacks—that can significantly influence its own ability, as well as the ability of others, to achieve preferred macroeconomic or exchange-rate objectives. (Technically the size, and possibly even the sign, of policy multipliers is altered both at home and abroad.) Such "externalities" imply that policies chosen unilaterally, even if seemingly optimal from an individual country's point of view, will almost certainly turn out to be sub-optimal in a global context. The basic rationale for monetary cooperation is that it can *internalise* these externalities by giving each government partial control over the actions of others, thus relieving the shortage of instruments that prevents each one separately from reaching its chosen targets on its own.

At least two sets of goals may be pursued through policy coordination. At one level, cooperation may be treated simply as a vehicle by which countries together move closer to their individual policy targets. (In the formal language of game theory favoured by many analysts, utility or welfare-seeking governments bargain their way from the sub-optimality of a so-called Nash equilibrium to something closer to a Pareto optimum.) Peter Kenen calls this the *policy-optimising* approach to cooperation. At a second level, mutual adjustments can also be made in pursuit of broader collective goals, such as defence of existing international arrangements or institutions against the threat of economic or political shocks. Kenen calls this the *regime-preserving* or *public-goods* approach to cooperation. Both approaches derive from the same facts of structural and policy interdependence. Few scholars question the basic logic of either one.

What is accepted in theory, of course, need not be favoured in practice—however persuasive the logic. . . .

. . . In recent years there has been a virtual avalanche of formal literature citing various qualifications to the basic case for monetary cooperation and casting doubt on its practical benefits. The irony is evident: even as policy coordination since the mid-1980s has ostensibly become fashionable again among governments, it seems to have gone out of style with many analysts. At least five major issues have been raised for discussion by economists working in this area.

First is the question of the *magnitude of the gains* to be expected. Although in theory the move from a Nash equilibrium to Pareto optimality may seem dramatic, in practice much depends on the size of the spillovers involved. If externalities are small, so too will be the potential benefits of cooperation.

Many analysts cite a pioneering study by Oudiz and Sachs designed to measure the effects of monetary and fiscal policy coordination by Germany, Japan and the United States, using data from the mid-1970s. Estimated gains were disappointingly meagre, amounting to no more than half of one per cent of GNP in each country as compared with the best noncooperative outcomes. Although some subsequent studies have detected moderately greater income increases from coordination, most tend to confirm the impression that on balance very large gains should not be expected.

Second is the other side of the ledger: the question of the *magnitude of the costs* to be expected. Theoretical models typically abstract from the costs of coordination. In reality, however, considerable time and effort are needed to evaluate performance, negotiate agreements, and monitor compliance among sovereign governments. Moreover, the greater the number of countries or issues involved, the more complex are the policy adjustments that are likely to be required of each. All this demands expenditure of resources that may loom large when compared with the possibly meagre scale of anticipated benefits. For some analysts, this suggests that the game may simply not be worth the candle. For others, it implies the need for a more explicit framework for cooperation—some formally agreed set of rules—that could substitute for repeated negotiations over individual issues. . . . The advantage of an articulated rule-based regime is that it would presumably be more cost-effective than endless *ad hoc* bargaining. The disadvantage is that it would require a greater surrender of policy autonomy than many governments now seem prepared to tolerate (a point to which I shall return below).

Third is the so-called *time–inconsistency* problem: the risk that agreements, once negotiated, will later be violated by maverick governments tempted to renege on policy commitments that turn out to be inconvenient. The risk, in principle, is a real one. In relations between sovereign states, where enforcement mechanisms are weak or nonexistent, there is always a threat that bargains may be at some point broken. But whether the possibility of unilateral defection constitutes much of a threat in practice is hotly debated among specialists, many of whom stress the role of reputation and credibility as deterrents to cheating by individual governments. In the language of game theory, much depends on the details of how the strategic interactions are structured, for example, the number of players in the game, whether and how often the game is iterated, and how many other related games are being played simultaneously. Much depends as well on the historical and institutional context, and how the preferences of decision-makers are formed—matters about which it is inherently difficult to generalise. In the absence of more general specifications, few definitive judgements seem possible *a priori*.

Fourth is the possible *distortion of incentives* that might be generated by efforts at policy coordination. In an early and influential article, Kenneth Rogoff argued that international cooperation could actually prove to be counterproductive—welfare-decreasing rather than Pareto-improving—if the coordination process were to encourage governments collectively to choose policies that are more politically convenient than economically sound. Formal coordination of monetary policies, for example, could simply lead to higher global inflation if governments were all to agree to expand their money supplies together, thus evading the balance-of-payments constraint that would discipline any country attempting to inflate on its own. More generally, there is always the chance that ruling élites might exploit the process to promote particularist or even personal interests at the expense of broader collective goals. This risk too is widely regarded as realistic in principle and is hotly debated for its possible importance in practice. And here too few definitive judgements seem possible *a priori* in the absence of more general specifications.

Finally, there is the issue of *model uncertainty:* the risks that policy-makers simply are badly informed and do not really understand how their economies operate and interact. Frankel and Rockett in a widely cited study demonstrated that when governments do differ in their analytical views of policy impacts, coordination could well cause welfare losses rather than gains for at least some of the countries involved. For some analysts, this is more than enough reason to prefer a return to uncoordinated pursuit of national self-interest. For others, however, it suggests instead the value of consultation and exchanges of information to avoid misunderstandings about transmission mechanisms and the size and sign of relevant policy multipliers. . . .

Where, then, does all this discussion come out? None of the five issues that have been so thoroughly aired in the literature is unimportant; sceptics have been right to raise and emphasize them. But neither do any of these qualifications appear to deal a decisive blow to the underlying case for cooperation, which retains its essential appeal. For this reason most analysts, myself among them, still remain disposed to view policy cooperation for all its imperfections in much the same light as virtue or motherhood—an inherently good thing. Net gains may be small; motivations may get distorted; outcomes may not always fulfil expectations. Nonetheless, despite all the risks the effort does seem justified. . . .

2. THE EBB AND FLOW OF POLICY COMMITMENTS

A problem remains, however. To be effective, the collective commitment to cooperation must appear credible; and to be credible, that commitment must above all be *sustained.* Individual governments may play the maverick on occasion (the time–inconsistency problem); a little cheating at the margins is after all hardly unexpected, or even unusual, in international relations. But the commitment of the collectivity must be seen to be enduring: there can be no room for doubt about the continuing relevance, the *seriousness,* of the process as such. Otherwise incentives will indeed be distorted for state and non-state actors alike, and outcomes could well turn out to be every bit as counterproductive as many analysts fear. As Peter Kenen has warned, "Sporadic management may be worse than no management at all." Yet, as noted at the outset, that is precisely the pattern that policy coordination has tended to display in practice. The history of international monetary cooperation is one long lesson in the fickleness of policy fashion.

During the early inter-war period, for example, the central banks of the major industrial nations publicly committed themselves to a cooperative attempt to restore something like the pre–World War I gold standard, only to end up in the 1930s energetically battling one another through futile rounds of competitive devaluations and escalating capital controls. And similarly during the Bretton Woods era, early efforts at cooperative institution-building and joint consultations ultimately terminated in mutual recriminations and the demise of the par-value system. In the middle 1970s, endeavours to revive some kind of rule-based exchange-rate regime were overwhelmed by policy disagreements between the

Carter administration in the United States and its counterparts in Europe and Japan, leading to a record depreciation of the US dollar. At the turn of the decade renewed attempts at joint stabilisation were cut short by the go-it-alone policies of the new Reagan administration, leading to the record appreciation of the dollar which, in turn, set the stage for the Plaza Agreement of 1985. The broad picture of monetary relations in the twentieth century is clearly one of considerable ebbs and flows in the collective commitment to policy cooperation.

Moreover, the big picture—much in the manner of Mandelbrot fractals—tends broadly to be replicated in the small. (A fractal is an object or phenomenon that is self-similar across different scales.) Often superimposed on longer waves of enthusiasm or disillusionment with policy cooperation have been briefer "stop–go" cycles of commitment and retreat, such as the short-lived attempts of the London Monetary Conference and later Tripartite Agreement to restore some measure of monetary stability in the 1930s. In the 1960s and early 1970s, even as the Bretton Woods system was heading for breakdown, the major financial powers cooperated at one point to create a new international reserve asset, the Special Drawing Right (SDR), and then at another to temporarily realign and stabilise exchange rates in the Smithsonian Agreement of December 1971. And even before the Plaza Agreement in 1985 there were already regular meetings of finance ministers and central bankers to discuss mutual policy linkages, as well as of lower-level officials in such settings as the Organisation for Economic Cooperation and Development (OECD) and the Bank for International Settlements (BIS). The now-fashionable process of multilateral surveillance was, in fact, first mandated by the leaders of the G-7 countries at the Versailles summit in 1982.

Most significantly, the same cyclical pattern has been evident even . . . since the announcement of the Plaza Agreement. The appetite for mutual accommodation in the Triad continues to wax and wane episodically; inconstancy remains the rule. Formally the G-7 governments are now fully committed to the multilateral-surveillance process. In actual practice, despite regular meetings and repeated reaffirmations of principle, policy behaviour continues to betray a certain degree of recurrent recidivism. . . .

. . . This is not to suggest that the multilateral-surveillance process has been utterly without redeeming social value. On the contrary, one can reasonably argue that for all its episodic quality the effort has on balance been beneficial, both in terms of what has in fact been accomplished and in terms of what has been avoided. Anecdotal evidence seems to suggest that policy-makers have had their consciousness genuinely raised regarding the foreign externalities of their domestic actions; in any event, the regularity of the schedule of ministerial meetings now clearly compels officials to integrate the international dimension much more fully than ever before into their own national decision processes. At the same time potentially severe challenges to regime stability have been successfully averted, including in particular the rising wave of US protectionism in 1985 and the stockmarket crash of 1987.

Collective initiatives have been designed cautiously to avoid the pitfalls of model uncertainty and have not typically been chosen simply for their political convenience. Overall, gains do appear to have outweighed costs.

The gains might have been larger, however. One can also reasonably argue that the positive impact of the process might have been considerably greater than it was had there been less inconstancy of behaviour. That is perhaps the chief lesson to be learned from this brief recitation of recent monetary history. Governmental credibility has undoubtedly been strained by the cyclical ebb and flow of commitments since 1985. With each retreat to unilateralism market scepticism grows, requiring ever more dramatic *démarches* when, once again, joint initiatives seem warranted. *Net* benefits, as a result, tend to be diminished over time. Multilateral surveillance may have redeeming social value, but its stop–go pattern makes it more costly than it might otherwise be. In a real sense we all pay for the fickleness of policy fashion.

3. THE INFLUENCE OF THE UNHOLY TRINITY

Why is international monetary cooperation so episodic? To answer that question it is necessary to go back to first principles. Blame cannot be fobbed off on "karma," accidental exogenous "shocks," or even that vague epithet "politics." Consideration of the underlying political economy of the issue suggests that the dilemma is, in fact, systematic—endogenous to the policy process—and not easily avoided in relations between sovereign national governments.

The central analytical issue, which has been well understood at least since the pioneering theoretical work of economist Robert Mundell is the intrinsic incompatibility of three key desiderata of governments: exchange-rate stability, private-capital mobility, and monetary-policy autonomy. As I wrote in the introduction to this chapter my own label for this is the "Unholy Trinity." The problem of the Unholy Trinity, simply stated, is that in an environment of formally or informally pegged rates and effective integration of financial markets, any attempt to pursue independent monetary objectives is almost certain, sooner or later, to result in significant balance-of-payments disequilibrium, and hence provoke potentially destabilising flows of speculative capital. To preserve exchange-rate stability, governments will then be compelled to limit either the movement of capital (via restrictions or taxes) or their own policy autonomy (via some form of multilateral surveillance or joint decision-making). If they are unwilling or unable to sacrifice either one, then the objective of exchange-rate stability itself may eventually have to be compromised. Over time, except by chance, the three goals cannot be attained simultaneously.

In the real world, of course, governments might be quite willing to limit the movement of capital in such circumstances—if they could. Policy-makers may say they value the efficiency gains of free and integrated financial markets. If polled "off the record" for their private preferences, however, most would probably admit to prizing exchange-rate stability and policy autonomy even more. The problem, from their point of view, is that capital mobility is notoriously difficult to control. Restrictions merely invite more and more sophisticated forms of evasion, as governments from Europe to South Asia to Latin America have learned to their regret. . . .

In practice, therefore, this means that in most instances the Unholy Trinity reduces to a direct trade-off between exchange-rate stability and policy autonomy. Conceptually, choices can be visualised along a continuum representing varying degrees of monetary-policy cooperation. At one extreme lies the polar alternative of a common currency or its equivalent—full monetary integration—where individual governments sacrifice policy autonomy completely for the presumed benefits of a permanent stabilisation of exchange rates. Most importantly, these benefits include the possible improvement in the usefulness of money in each of its principal functions: as a medium of exchange (owing to a reduction of transaction costs as the number of required currency conversions is decreased), store of value (owing to a reduced element of exchange risk as the number of currencies is decreased), and unit of account (owing to an information saving as the number of required price quotations is decreased). Additional gains may also accrue from the possibility of economies of scale in monetary and exchange-rate management as well as a potential saving of international reserves due to an internalisation through credit of what would otherwise be external trade and payments. Any saving of reserves through pooling in effect amounts to a form of seigniorage for each participating country.

At the other extreme lies the polar alternative of absolute monetary independence, where individual governments sacrifice any hope of long-term exchange-rate stability for the presumed benefits of policy autonomy. Most importantly, as Mundell demonstrated as early as 1961, these benefits include the possible improvement in the effectiveness of monetary policy as an instrument to attain national macroeconomic objectives. Today, of course, it is understood that much depends on whether any trade-off can be assumed to exist between inflation and unemployment over a time horizon relevant to policy-makers—technically, whether there is any slope to the Phillips curve in the short-term. In a strict monetarist model of the sort popular in the 1970s, incorporating the classical neutrality assumption ("purely monetary changes have no real effects"), such a trade-off was excluded by definition. The Phillips curve was said to be vertical at the so-called "natural" (or "non-inflation-accelerating") unemployment rate, determined exclusively by microeconomic phenomena on the supply side of the economy. More recently, however, most theorists have tended to take a more pragmatic approach, allowing that for valid institutional and psychological reasons Phillips-curve trade-offs may well persist for significant periods of time—certainly for periods long enough to make the preservation of monetary independence appear worthwhile to policy-makers. From this perspective, any movement along the continuum in the direction of a common currency will be perceived as a real cost by individual governments.

The key question is how this cost compares with the overall benefit of exchange-rate stabilisation. Here we begin to approach the nub of the issue at hand. My hypothesis is that for each participating country both cost and benefit vary systematically with the degree of policy cooperation, and that it is through the interaction of these costs and benefits that we get the episodic quality of the cooperation process we observe in practice.

Assume absolute monetary independence to start with. Most gains from exchange-rate stabilisation, I would argue, can be expected to accrue "up front" and then decline at the margin for successively higher degrees of policy cooperation. That is because the greatest disadvantage of exchange-rate instability is the damage done to the usefulness of money in its various functions. Any move at all by governments to reduce uncertainty about currency values is bound to have a disproportionate impact on market expectations and, hence, transaction costs in foreign exchange; further steps in the same direction may add to the credibility of the collective commitment but will yield only smaller and smaller savings to participants. Most of the cost of stabilisation, on the other hand, can be expected to be "back-loaded" in the perceptions of the relevant policy-makers. That is because governments have an understandable tendency to discount the disadvantages of foreign agreements until they find themselves really constrained in seeking to attain their domestic objectives—at which point disproportionate importance comes to be attached to the compromises of interests involved. Where initial moves towards coordinated decision-making may be treated as virtually costless, further steps in the same direction tend to be seen as increasingly threatening. Thus, the marginal cost of policy cooperation for each country tends to rise systematically even as the marginal benefit may be assumed to fall. . . .

4. CAN COOPERATION BE "LOCKED IN"?

The dilemma posed by the Unholy Trinity thus helps us to understand why international monetary cooperation is so episodic. The question remains: what, if anything, can be done about it?

One answer can be ruled out from the start: the proposition that the observed inconstancy of policy behaviour could be overcome if only governments could be educated to comprehend their own best interests. If my hypothesis is correct, governments are already acting in their own best interests and behaving in a manner consistent with a rational calculus of their own costs and benefits. The issue is not myopia: policy-makers surely are not unaware of the impacts of their behaviour on market expectations . . . and would stick to their commitments if that seemed desirable. Rather, it is a question of how policy incentives change over time as a result of the shifting tide of events. Fundamentally, my reasoning may be understood as a variant of the logic of collective action first elucidated by Mancur Olson more than a quarter of a century ago. A common interest is evident to all, yet individually rational behaviour can, at least part of the time, lead to distinctly suboptimal outcomes. This is true whether the common interest is understood in terms of policy optimisation or regime preservation.

Moreover, my hypothesis has the advantage of being consistent with a wide range of alternative paradigms that have been employed in the standard international political-economy literature. It is certainly compatible with traditional realist or structuralist approaches in which the sovereign state, for reasons of analytical parsimony, is automatically assumed to behave like a rational unitary actor with its own set of well-defined national interests. It is also consistent with more pluralist models of policy-making, in which conceptions of interest are distilled from the interplay of differing combinations of domestic political and institutional forces; and even with models drawn from public-choice theory, in which policy behaviour is assumed to reflect first and foremost the personal interests of policy-makers (the principal-agent problem). For the purposes of my hypothesis, it really does not matter where the policy preferences of governments come from. It only matters that they act systematically on them.

Assuming education is not the answer, the crux of the issue becomes whether any collective commitment to cooperation once made can be "locked in" in some way. If the problem is that governments find it difficult to sustain their enthusiasm for the process, can a solution be found that will effectively prevent them from retreating?

One obvious possibility is the extreme of a common currency, where individual autonomy is—in principle—permanently surrendered by each participating country. In practice, of course, not even full currency unions have proved indissoluble, as we saw in the case of the East African shilling in the 1970s or as evidently we are about to see in the case of the (former) Soviet Union today. But cases like these usually stem from associations that were something less than voluntary to begin with. When undertaken by consenting sovereign states, full monetary unification generally tends to be irreversible—which is precisely the reason why it is seen so seldomly in the real world. During the *laissez-faire* nineteenth century, when monetary autonomy meant less to governments than it does now, two fairly prominent currency unions were successfully established among formally independent nations—the Latin Monetary Union dating from 1865, and the Scandinavian Monetary Union created in 1873—each built on a single, standardised monetary unit (respectively the franc and the krone). Both groupings, however, were effectively terminated with the outbreak of World War I. In the twentieth century, the only comparable arrangement has been the Belgium–Luxembourg Economic Union, established in 1921. (Other contemporary currency unions, such as the CFA franc zone and the East Caribbean dollar area, had their origins in colonial relationships.) The recent difficulties experienced by the European Community (EC) in negotiating the details of a formal Economic and Monetary Union (EMU) illustrate just how tough it is to persuade governments even as closely allied as these to make the irrevocable commitment required by a common currency.

Short of the extreme of a common currency, an effective solution would require participating governments to voluntarily pre-commit to some form of external authority over their individual policy behaviour. The authority might be supplied by an international agency armed with collectively agreed decision-making powers—corresponding to what I have elsewhere called the organising principle of supra-nationality. It might also be supplied by one single dominant country with acknowledged leadership responsibilities (the principle of hegemony). Or it might be supplied by a self-disciplining regime of norms and rules accepted as binding on all participants (the principle of automaticity). Unfortunately, neither experience nor the underlying logic of political sovereignty offers a great deal of hope in the practical potential of any of these alternatives. Supra-nationality and automaticity, for example, have always tended to be heavily qualified in international monetary relations. In the G-7 multilateral-surveillance process, the International Monetary Fund (in the person of its managing director) has been given a role, but limited only to the provision of essential data and objective analytical support, and public articulation of any sort of binding rules (regarding, for example, exchange-rate targets) has been strenuously resisted by most governments. Hegemony, in the meantime, may be tolerated where it is unavoidable, as in the sterling area during the 1930s or the Bretton Woods system immediately after World War II. But as both these historical episodes illustrate, dominance also tends to breed considerable resentment and a determined eagerness by most countries to assert individual autonomy as soon as circumstances permit.

The principal exception in recent years has been the joint currency float (the "snake") of the European Community, first implemented in the 1970s by a cluster of smaller countries effectively aligned with West Germany's Deutschemark, and later extended and formalised under the European Monetary System (EMS) starting in 1979. Under the rules of the EC's joint float, national monetary discretion for most members has been distinctly constrained, despite relatively frequent realignments of mutual exchange rates and, until the end of the 1980s, the persistence of significant capital controls in some countries. German policy, on the other hand, has not only remained largely autonomous but has effectively dominated monetary relations within the group. In effect, therefore, the snake has successfully locked in a collective commitment to cooperation through a combination of automaticity and hegemony. Yet not only has the arrangement proved tolerable to its members, over time it has gradually attracted new participants; and now, despite the difficulties of gaining irrevocable commitments to a common currency, may be about to be extended again in the form of EMU.

The reasons for this success quite obviously are unique and have to do most with the distinctive character of the institutional ties that have developed among EC members. Over time, as Robert Keohane and Stanley Hoffmann have recently noted, the EC has gradually built up a highly complex process of policy-making in which formal and informal arrangements are intricately linked across a wide range of issues. Decisions in one sector are closely affected by what is happening elsewhere and often lead to the sort of inter-sectoral "spillover" effects that were first emphasised in early neo-functional theory. (Note that these effects are quite different from those featured in the theoretical case for policy cooperation, which stresses spillovers in a single sector or issue-area.) More generally, member governments have come to fully accept a style of political behaviour in which individual interests are jointly realised through an incremental, albeit fragmented, pooling of national sovereignty—what Keohane and Hoffmann call a "network" form of organisation, "in which individual units are defined not by themselves but in relation to other units." And this, in turn, has been made possible only because of the existence of a real sense of commitment and attachment—of *community*— among all the countries involved. In this sense, the EC truly is the exception that proves the rule. Among states less intimately connected, resistance to any form of external authority over individual policy behaviour is bound to be correspondingly more stubborn and determined.

Does this mean then that nothing can be done about the episodic quality of monetary cooperation? Not at all. In principle, any number of technical innovations can be imagined to moderate underlying tendencies towards recidivism by cooperating governments. As in the G-7 process, for example, meetings could be put on a regular schedule and based on an agreed analytical framework to help ensure greater continuity of policy behaviour. Much the same impact might also be attained by giving more precision as well as greater publicity to policy guidelines and commitments. And there might also be some benefit to be had from establishing a permanent, independent secretariat to provide an institutional memory and ongoing objective analysis of priorities and issues. The issue, however, is not administrative creativity but political acceptability. Each such innovation makes it just that much more difficult for policy-makers to change their minds when circumstances might seem to warrant it. Is the underlying relationship among the states involved sufficiently close to make them willing to take such a risk? This is not a question that can be answered *a priori;* as the exceptional case of the EC demonstrates, it is certainly not a question of monetary relations alone. Ultimately prospects for sustaining any cooperative effort in this crucial area of public policy will depend on how much basic affinity governments feel in other areas as well—in effect, on the extent to which they feel they share a common destiny across the full spectrum of economic and political issues.

17

The Political Economy of European Monetary Unification: An Analytical Introduction

BARRY EICHENGREEN
AND JEFFRY A. FRIEDEN

European monetary unification—the creation of a single European currency and a European central bank—has been the ostensible goal of the member states of the European Union since the late 1970s. The course of this process has, however, been very uneven. Barry Eichengreen and Jeffry A. Frieden summarize Europe's attempts to develop a common currency, and present potential economic and political factors that may explain the process. They argue that monetary unification is driven primarily by political, rather than economic, considerations, especially those operating at the European regional level.

European monetary unification (EMU)—the creation of a single European currency and a European central bank—is both an economic and a political phenomenon. It is economic in that it will radically transform economic policy and performance in Europe. Transactions costs will be reduced by the creation of a single currency, stimulating cross-border exchange. National monetary autonomy will become a thing of the past, limiting the use by participating countries of the inflation tax and of the exchange rate as an instrument for adjusting to nation-specific shocks.

EMU is also a political phenomenon in that the decision to create a single currency and central bank is not made by a beneficent social planner weighing the costs and benefits to the participating nations. Rather, it is the outcome of a political process of treaty negotiation, parliamentary ratification, and popular referenda. Interest groups support or oppose the initiative depending on how it is likely to affect their welfare, not the welfare of the nation or the Community as a whole.

Barry Eichengreen and Jeffry A. Frieden. "The Political Economy of European Monetary Unification: An Analytical Introduction." From B. Eichengreen and J. Frieden, eds., *The Political Economy of European Monetary Unification,* 1994. Westview Press, 1994. Reprinted by permission.

The pressures they bring to bear are amplified and dissipated by the political institutions through which they are communicated. . . .

A SHORT HISTORY OF EUROPEAN
MONETARY UNIFICATION

Enthusiasts of European integration have long regarded monetary union as a central goal. Economically, fixed exchange rates or a single currency would reduce the cost of doing business within the European Community (EC); concern with exchange-rate volatility is especially strong inasmuch as many European countries are very open to world trade and payments. Politically, movement toward monetary union is seen as a practical and symbolic step toward broader unification of the Community along other dimensions, such as foreign policy and social goals.

Yet movement toward a common EC currency has been hampered by both economic and political factors. Fixed exchange rates and a single currency mean the surrender of national monetary policies to a Community-wide authority. This transfer of responsibility may be desirable in some circumstances for some people. But when major economic dislocations occur, Europe's national governments come under pressure to pursue independent policies tailored to offset national disturbances. Those who shudder at the prospects of common EC foreign, defense, or social policies find monetary union threatening inasmuch as it foreshadows ever greater surrender of sovereign prerogatives in other domains. For these reasons and others, the desirability of European monetary unification has been contested for nearly 30 years, and movement toward the goal has been halting.

Serious discussions within the EC began in the late 1960s, culminating in the 1969 Werner Report. This set forth detailed plans for monetary union but was made obsolete within weeks of its adoption by the beginning of the collapse of the Bretton Woods international monetary regime. Once Bretton Woods crumbled, the most to which the EC's six members could aspire was the maintenance of Bretton Woods–style exchange-rate stability. They resolved in 1972 to hold their currencies within a 2.25 percent band against one another. This arrangement, the "snake," was joined by Great Britain, Ireland, and Denmark in the run-up to their 1973 entry to the Community. But divergent economic conditions, associated with the first oil shock of 1973–74, made the system unworkable. Within three years of its founding only Germany, the Benelux countries, and Denmark remained in the snake. The EC members whose macroeconomic conditions diverged most from those of Germany—the U.K., Ireland, France and Italy—simply left, and the Danes could remain in the union only with continual devaluations.

Renewed discussion of monetary union began in 1977, and in March 1979 a new European Monetary System (EMS) and Exchange-Rate Mechanism (ERM) went into effect. All EC members except the United Kingdom linked to the ERM, which allowed a 2.25 percent band among currencies (6 percent for the lira). Realignments were to be allowed within the EMS, although they were expected to be infrequent. Financing facilities were provided for countries attempting to hold their exchange rates stable in the face of temporary balance-of-payments shocks.

Received wisdom at the time was that the EMS was unlikely to succeed. The inflation rates of EMS countries differed too radically for the maintenance of stable exchange rates. Throughout the 1970s the Community's high-inflation countries had been unable to implement the austerity measures necessary to bring their currencies into line with the deutschemark. Optimism about the EMS required some reason to believe that the system itself would strengthen the willingness or ability of high-inflation countries to implement austerity programs.

Initially, the pessimistic view seemed to be borne out. In the first four years of the EMS's operation, exchange rates were realigned seven times. Monetary policies and inflation rates showed few signs of converging. Then, however, things began to change. Rates of price increase in the high-inflation countries began to decline. From April 1983 to January 1987 there were only four realignments, generally smaller than their predecessors. And from January 1987 to September 1992 there were no major realignments within the ERM. Spain, the United Kingdom, and Portugal joined the mechanism. By the late 1980s, the EC appeared to be well on the way toward becoming a zone of monetary stability.

The success of the EMS was both stimulated by and stimulated progress on European integration more generally. In 1985 and 1986, EC member governments developed and signed the Single European Act (SEA), which called for the removal of all controls on the movement of goods, capital, and people within the Community by January 1, 1993. The prospect of a truly common market propelled forward other aspects of European integration, including monetary unification. In this context, and at the urging of the French and German foreign ministries, in 1988 the European Council empaneled a committee headed by European Commission President Jacques Delors to investigate the prospects for further monetary integration.

In early 1989 the Delors Committee recommended that the EC begin moving toward a single currency, and proposed that EMU be approached in three stages. Stage One involved the elimination of all residual capital controls, accession of all EC members to the ERM, and a hardening of the ERM commitment. In Stage Two, with the EMS credible and encompassing, a common set of macroeconomic policies would be adopted by national authorities, and a European System of Central Banks would coordinate the actions of national central bankers. Stage Three would see the development of an EC-wide central bank, a common currency for all EC members, and Community coordination of fiscal policies.

By 1991, with a detailed plan for EMU in place and all EC members except Greece in the ERM, the single currency seemed only a matter of time. This impression was reinforced when in December 1991, at Maastricht in the Netherlands, EC members agreed to a sweeping treaty on political and economic union.

Soon, however, unanticipated events and political resistance intervened to interrupt the momentum of monetary unification. German reunification was accompanied by large fiscal deficits, which excited Bundesbank fears of inflation and led the German central bank to implement restrictive monetary policies. British and Italian monetary conditions did not converge to those of the rest of the EMS as rapidly as expected, leading the lira and sterling to appreciate in real terms. And stagnant global economic conditions lowered political tolerance for tight money.

The result was pressure on the British and Italian currencies as devaluation expectations grew.

In the midst of the gathering currency crisis, political opposition to Maastricht surfaced. The June 1992 failure of a Danish referendum on the treaty raised the possibility of an indefinite postponement of EMU and thus increased expectations of instability in the ERM. Opinion polls also indicated that a late-September French referendum on Maastricht would be unexpectedly close.

On September 16, 1992 (four days before the French referendum) Britain and Italy withdrew from the ERM and allowed their currencies to depreciate. This, the most serious setback suffered by EMU since the early 1980s, was followed by realignments that drove the currencies of Spain, Portugal, and Ireland downward.

Turmoil in Europe's foreign exchange markets, including additional forced realignments, persisted into 1993. In the summer of 1993, as unemployment grew in many EC members, pressure for interest rate reductions increased. However, the Bundesbank, concerned about German inflation, maintained a tight monetary policy that made it impossible for other EMS members to lower interest rates without risking a devaluation. The dilemma was especially serious in France, where a new conservative government had taken office in March amidst a severe recession and high rates of unemployment. Foreign exchange traders attacked the franc and other currencies in the ERM, forcing the French and other governments to raise already high interest rates, thereby exacerbating unemployment, in order to defend ERM parities that might ultimately prove indefensible.

Tensions in European currency markets were exacerbated by characteristics of the Maastricht Treaty itself. Under the Maastricht criteria, a country qualifies for EMU only if it has maintained its currency within ERM bands for two years. This means that an unsuccessful attempt to defend a currency will lead to unnecessary exchange losses by the monetary authorities. Knowing that they may be able to force a realignment, foreign exchange traders have incentives to speculate against ERM currencies even when there are no fundamental economic reasons for a change in currency values.

In August 1993 this confluence of factors gave rise to irresistible pressure on currency markets. In this context, EMS members agreed to widen currency fluctuation bands to 15 percent (but to keep them at 2.25 percent for the deutschemark and the Dutch guilder). This removed pressure on the EMS, but substantially reduced the fixed-rate component of the system.

Despite these setbacks, plans for EMU remain alive. An assessment of its future prospects requires a systematic analysis of both its economics and its politics.

THE ECONOMICS OF MONETARY UNIFICATION

A standard approach to the economics of monetary unification is to weigh the costs and benefits of replacing multiple currencies with a single currency. In this section, we examine what economic theory and evidence have to.say about the balance of benefits and costs. We show that neither economic theory nor economic evidence provides a clear case for or against monetary unification. The direct economic benefits of monetary unification are likely to be relatively small, and may or may not be dominated by the costs. The absence of a clear economic justification for EMU leads us to conclude that events in Europe are being driven mainly by political factors.

A first economic argument for monetary unification is as an anti-inflationary commitment mechanism. For much of the 1970s and 1980s, European countries suffered high inflation. Pegging to the deutschemark by joining the EMS was a way to import the credible anti-inflationary monetary policies of the Bundesbank and bring down inflation in a relatively painless way. EMU is portrayed as the final step in this process. As a precondition for entering the monetary union, participating countries will be forced to strengthen the independence of their central banks. The Governing Council of the European Central Bank (ECB), on which national central bank governors will sit, will enjoy statutory protection from political pressures. (They will serve long terms in office and be prohibited from campaigning for reappointment, for example.) Hence, by abolishing their national currencies and joining the monetary union, European countries will effectively renounce the option of reverting to inflationary policies. EMU, according to this view, represents an efficient anti-inflationary commitment technology.

A problem with this reasoning is that it is far from clear whether the political independence the ECB possesses in theory will be enjoyed in practice. Europe's traditional high- and low-inflation countries will all have equal representation on the ECB's Governing Council. To be sure, the costs of defecting from EMU, once in, will serve as an effective exit barrier. But while EMU may serve as a technology for credibly committing to a common monetary policy, the inflationary implications of that common policy remain to be seen.

One might think that the reduction in currency-conversion costs due to replacing 12 national monies with one provides a clear economic justification for EMU. This is not so for two reasons: first, the costs of currency conversion are small; and second, the very measures which deliver the reduction in currency-conversion charges may introduce other, even larger, economic costs such as those associated with the loss of policy autonomy. We consider these objections in turn.

The European Commission has estimated that conversion costs absorb no more than 1 percent of GDP for the Community's less-industrialized economies, and that they fall to as little as 0.1 percent of GDP for the large member states for which international transactions are less important. Overall they average only 0.4 percent of EC GDP. This, clearly, is a small return on a monetary unification process riddled with uncertainties and risks.

These calculations may fail to capture the real efficiency gains from a common currency. Such gains may derive from the fact that the creation of a single currency, by eliminating exchange-rate uncertainty, will encourage intra-EC trade and investment. In turn this will lead to a more efficient allocation of resources both within and across member states. Existing evidence suggests, however, that exchange-rate variability and uncertainty have only small effects on trade and investment. Traders can use forward markets, hedges and a variety of financial instruments to lessen the risks attendant on exchange-rate changes; it is not surprising, therefore, that most investigators are unable to find much of a relationship between exchange-rate variability and trade. And exchange-rate variability may actually promote foreign investment insofar as it encourages investors to hold diversified portfolios of assets whose income streams are denominated in different currencies.

A more general form of the argument is that monetary unification is necessary for technical reasons if the EC is to succeed in completing the internal market and reaping its benefits. A truly integrated European market for capital as well as labor and commodities cannot exist in the presence of exchange controls. It is hardly possible to continue restricting the freedom of Frenchmen to open bank accounts in Germany, for example, while at the same time creating an EC-wide capital market free of restrictions on portfolio capital movements and direct foreign investment. The efficiency gains of the single market thus require the removal of capital controls.

The removal of controls, according to this thesis, renders infeasible all monetary arrangements but a single European currency. The EMS, as described above, was a hybrid of pegged and adjustable exchange rates. Extended periods of exchange-rate stability were designed to deliver most of the benefits of fixed rates, while periodic realignments permitted countries to redress serious competitiveness problems. But periods of exchange-rate stability punctuated by occasional realignments were possible only because capital controls protected central bank reserves against speculative attacks motivated by anticipations of realignment. If, for example, France sought to maintain lower interest rates than Germany, huge quantities of financial capital did not flow instantaneously from Paris to Frankfurt, immediately forcing a devaluation. The interest differential had to be large and had to be maintained for an extended period before substantial numbers of French arbitragers found it advantageous to incur the cost of circumventing French capital controls and thereby forcing a realignment. The removal of capital controls, by changing this situation, doomed the EMS as it existed in the 1980s.

It is far from clear, in fact, that monetary unification was the only alternative left by the removal of controls. An obvious alternative is floating exchange rates. But floating retains a bad name in Europe and raises political objections (described below).

Another conceivable alternative stopping short of monetary unification is truly fixed exchange rates among distinct national currencies. A sufficiently credible commitment to intra-EC exchange-rate stability might fix exchange rates even in the absence of capital controls. However attractive in theory, this alternative faces problems in practice. The very existence of distinct national currencies is likely to limit the credibility of policy pronouncements that exchange rates will be irrevocably fixed. In general, it is impossible in a democracy to preclude the possibility that an existing policy instrument like the exchange rate will be utilized. . . . Only under very special circumstances, rarely present in modern industrial democracies, is it possible to assemble the organizational and institutional prerequisites for credibly fixed exchange rates.

In this sense, then, the Single European Act forced the issue. It required the removal of capital controls, which undermined the viability of the EMS and confronted the Community with the choice of reverting to floating or moving forward to monetary unification. Floating was incompatible with Europe's long-standing aversion to exchange-rate variability. Monetary unification was therefore a prerequisite for reaping the benefits of the product- and factor-market integration foreseen by the Single European Act.

Such are the benefits of EMU. But a proper cost–benefit calculus must also consider the other side of the coin.

The theory of optimum currency areas suggests that the costs come from the loss of monetary policy autonomy that follows from the establishment of a single currency. Whether abandoning policy autonomy is costly depends on the shocks to which participating countries are subjected and the effectiveness of monetary policy in facilitating adjustment. If monetary policy is incapable of affecting output and employment, then abandoning monetary independence is costless. But even if monetary policy is effective, abandoning monetary independence will be costless when the same policy response is appropriate for all members of the union. If all suffer deflationary disturbances simultaneously, for example, then a unionwide reflationary monetary policy will suffice. The larger the change in output relative to inflation due to a monetary initiative and the more asymmetric the shocks, the greater the benefits of monetary autonomy and hence the higher the costs of unification.

The evidence on these questions resists easy interpretation. The rigidity of real wages in Europe gives grounds for doubting that monetary policy is as effective as in the United States. Since many of the same industries operate in many European countries, industry-specific shocks will affect these countries in similar ways. On the other hand, econometric studies have found that both aggregate-supply and aggregate-demand shocks are more asymmetrically distributed across European nations than across the regions of existing monetary unions like the United States.

Such asymmetric disturbances do not create a case for policy autonomy if there exist such alternative means of adjustment as labor mobility. Within the U.S., where regional adjustment cannot take place through exchange-rate changes, it occurs mainly through migration. Unemployed auto workers in Michigan load up the U-Haul van and move to the oil fields of Texas when oil prices rise and the auto industry contracts.

By U.S. standards, labor is not very mobile in Europe. Migration between European countries is significantly lower than between U.S. regions. Migration within European countries is lower than in the U.S., as well. Hence region-specific shocks which can no longer be counteracted by exchange-rate changes may give rise to regional concentrations of unemployment more persistent than those characteristic of the United States.

If it is true that shocks to European countries are more asymmetrically distributed than shocks to U.S. regions, while both labor mobility and real wage flexibility are lower in Europe, then the costs of monetary union will be higher than in the

U.S. That the U.S. benefits from monetary union is no guarantee that in Europe the advantages of doing so will exceed the costs.

Uncertainty about the empirical magnitude of every one of these benefits and costs suggests the absence of a clear economic case in favor of EMU. Given the risks and uncertainties that pervade the process, there would have to be a clear margin of benefits over costs for economic considerations, narrowly defined, to provide a justification for such a radical departure in policy. The absence of such a margin implies that the momentum for monetary union must therefore derive from other, primarily political, factors.

THE POLITICS OF MONETARY UNIFICATION

The search for political motivations is hampered by the paucity of theoretical and empirical work on the topic. . . . Nonetheless, as a point of departure we can distinguish three sets of political considerations likely to figure in any such explanation: inter-state bargaining, issue linkage, and domestic distributional factors.

1. Inter-State Bargaining

Even if monetary union does not improve social welfare in all participating countries, it still may be in the interest of some EC governments, which then cajole or coerce others into participation. This approach, generally associated with what some political scientists refer to as "intergovernmentalism," interprets international political outcomes as a result of strategic interaction among national governments.

There are several problems with the approach. Concepts like "power" and "coercion" are difficult to define analytically and measure empirically. Inter-state bargains usually appear to be entered into freely (at least in the proximate sense), and thus presumably involve mutually beneficial exchange. This is not to say that there is no coercion in international relations, only that its invocation for analytical purposes requires careful and systematic attention to both the theoretical bases for the argument and the specific details of the case. Neither is common in application; both are desirable.

Moreover, even where power is defined carefully as one country's possession of bargaining leverage over others, such leverage typically relies on threats and promises, and these threats and promises must possess credibility to be effective. Yet few analyses of intergovernmental bargaining adequately specify what exactly renders credible the threats and promises required for power to be exerted. And . . . there are many circumstances under which pro-EMU countries would be better off keeping more reticent members *out* of a monetary union rather than forcing them to join. Even at the level of theory, then, it is hard to draw explanations of EMU from an intergovernmental bargaining model without further development of the analytical tools used in most such models.

2. Linkage Politics

A framework in which governments trade off objectives along different dimensions seems more appropriate than vague invocations of power politics. A systematic analysis of such trade-offs, however, requires a notion of linkage politics typically lacking in simple analyses of intergovernmentalism.

By linkage is meant the tying together of two otherwise unconnected issue areas, permitting the parties to an agreement to make concessions on one in return for concessions on the other. Thus, one country might "give" monetary union (which it does not inherently favor) in return for "getting" political union (which it does) if the perceived benefits of the latter exceed the costs of the former.

Linkage arguments, though compelling, are not unproblematic. Like inter-state bargaining generally, effective linkage requires credible threats or promises. Otherwise governments will fear that their foreign partners will renege on the commitment and refuse to enter into it in the first place. But even more when issue areas are linked than when bargaining over each issue occurs in isolation, such threats are unlikely to be fully credible. Not only must commitments on each dimension be credible, but the commitment to link dimensions must be credible as well. What, for example, prevents Germany's partners, once they have obtained monetary union, from reneging on their commitment to move ahead with political union subsequently?

Given the importance of credibility, analyses along these lines must devote a great deal of attention to how the parties bind themselves to the linkages they create. Some recent analyses of such commitment mechanisms have become quite sophisticated.

In addition, the domain of linkage politics is likely to be limited. Linkage can only operate when different nations place different values on different issue areas. If all EC members place similar weight (positive or negative) on EMU, there is little room for trading off concessions along different dimensions, and no room for linked bargaining that might improve the likelihood of agreement on EMU. While linkage politics may operate, its analysis requires caution and detail.

3. Domestic Distributional Issues

Just as countries with strong interests in EMU may coerce, cajole or bargain other EC members to participate, specific groups that stand to benefit (or lose) disproportionately may play a similar role domestically. While not benefiting the country as a whole, EMU may still improve the welfare of particular groups within the country, which prevail on the government to pursue their preferred policies. EMU, in this view, is just one example of the distributional politics common in virtually every economic policy arena.

Serious analysis of the distributional implications of EMU is scarce, although there exist some suggestive essays. A few observations are probably uncontroversial. Those for whom currency volatility is most costly stand to gain the most from

EMU. They include major banks and corporations with pan-EC investment or trade interests: for them forgoing national macroeconomic policy is a price worth paying for exchange-rate predictability. Those for whom cross-border and foreign-currency transactions are inconsequential stand to lose the most. For them predictable exchange rates are of little or no value but national autonomy in the formulation of macroeconomic policies may be extremely important.

It is important to recognize that many distributional concerns raised over EMU have to do with the problems of adjusting to a fixed exchange rate. In a high-inflation country, fixing the exchange rate typically leads to a real appreciation, which puts substantial price pressure on producers of import-competing tradables. They can therefore also be expected to have reservations about both fixed exchange rates and monetary union.

Problems with the distributional approach are not so much theoretical as practical. There is almost no empirical work which successfully measures the distributional incidence of different international monetary regimes. Even if such work did exist, it would tell us little about outcomes because interests are mediated through political institutions. Such institutions can magnify the political influence of some groups and diminish that of others so that, for example, similar interests may be expressed differently when parliaments are chosen by proportional representation than when members come from single districts in a first-past-the-post system. In any case, any rounded account of EMU has to pay close attention to domestic political factors, specifically to the role of interest groups with strong views on EMU and how these interest groups operate within national political institutions.

While additional categories of variables can undoubtedly be brought to bear on the political economy of EMU, these three appear central. We need a clear picture of the domestic interests at stake and the institutional setting within which they are situated. We need to understand how the divergent goals of national governments interact at the EC level. And we need to explore the ways in which EMU is linked to other EC policy areas.

THE POLITICAL ECONOMY OF
MONETARY UNIFICATION IN PRACTICE

Though the members of the European Community have pursued the goal of monetary union for more than 25 years, progress has been sporadic. Understanding this trajectory is an obvious prerequisite to predicting whether the EC is likely to achieve this goal.

The domestic distributional effects of international monetary policies have been crucial for European monetary developments. . . . The strongest support for EMU has come from Europe's international banks and corporations, while most of the opposition has come from domestically-oriented economic actors, especially those in high-inflation countries where a fixed exchange rate and subsequent real appreciation has led to a large increase in import competition.

In France and Italy in the early 1980s, for example, the greatest opposition to the policies aimed at sustaining commitment to a fixed exchange rate came from workers in such import-competing industries as steel and automobiles. France's commitment to the EMS during the early years of the Mitterrand government was weakened by the unwillingness of Communists and left Socialists—whose principal constituencies were in declining manufacturing sectors hard hit by imports—to agree to austerity measures needed to bring French inflation in line with that of Germany. A similar dynamic was at play in Italy, where the Communist party and its supporters in the labor movement—again concentrated in such import-competing manufacturing as steel production—were reluctant to agree to real wage reductions needed to keep the lira in line with its ERM partners.

While the differential impact of EMU helps explain political conflict over monetary issues within and among EC members, it can explain changes in support for EMU over time only if the relative importance of different groups shifts or changes occur in the intensity with which the groups favor or oppose different international monetary arrangements. Such shifts may have occurred, especially in the 1980s, due to changing levels of intra-EC capital mobility and trade. As the EC became more financially integrated, the choice between monetary policy autonomy and exchange-rate stability became starker. At the same time, higher levels of intra-EC trade increased the importance of exchange-rate fluctuations for both producers and consumers. And increased cross-border investment among EC members had similar effects, expanding the ranks of those for whom exchange-rate fluctuations caused problems. Inasmuch as the increased openness of EC economies involves more economic agents in cross-border economic activities, and these firms and individuals care about reducing exchange-rate volatility, the drive toward the free movement of goods and capital within the Community strengthens support for EMU.

Many accounts of the political economy of EMU emphasize domestic politics. The crisis the EMS experienced in 1992–93 is a good example. Domestic political factors appeared to impede coordination of EC members' macroeconomic policies. The British government might have raised interest rates to defend sterling, for example, except that the higher rates would have been passed on by mortgage lenders, and many within the ruling Conservative party worried about the objections of property owners. For its part, the Italian government might have enacted drastic fiscal measures to make its commitment to lower inflation more credible, but in the midst of a deep political crisis this was difficult to achieve over the objections of public employees and others who feared that their positions would be threatened. The French government could have raised interest rates to defend the franc, but at the cost of increasing the already-high French unemployment rate. The German authorities might have loosened monetary policy in order to reduce pressure on their EMS partners but for the Bundesbank's traditional concern about inflation, which was reinforced by strong anti-inflationary constituencies in the German body politic such as the country's powerful industrialists.

While there exist many anecdotes about the importance of interest group politics in the debate over EMU, this evidence is hardly systematic. The examples given above indicate that domestic distributional considerations are undoubtedly important, but have not yet been formulated in ways that allow us to arrive at clear conclusions as to their effects.

Inter-state bargaining has of course been central to the EMU process. The coercive strand of inter-state bargaining theories finds support in the fact that EC member states appear to have thrown their weight around in the bargaining process. This is in line with assertions that, for example, the Italian government in the 1980s was not enthusiastic about the EMS but was presented with a fait accompli by the French and Germans. It also accords with the widespread belief that the French government in the 1990s has been eager to use EMU to reduce German influence over European monetary policy while Germany has been somewhat less ardent in its pursuit of EMU.

But there remain problems with too strong a reliance on inter-state analyses relying on coercion. Countries can accede to the ERM or not as they wish, and they can withdraw at will (as they have). Major decisions on the path to EMU restricting countries' freedom of action in significant ways have typically required unanimous votes. While the Maastricht Treaty certainly narrowed the permissible room to maneuver of its signatories, for example, no country was forced to sign. This makes the invocation of power politics questionable.

What most explanations of this type appear to have in mind is not clear-cut coercion, but a bargaining process in which some countries insist to others that refusing to go along with EMU will impose costs on other dimensions of EC policy. This means that the bargaining relationship involves explicit or implicit links between EMU and other issue areas. Linkages are indeed central to what analysts . . . have in mind when they argue that the German government went along with EMU—which it found relatively unattractive on the merits—in return for assurances that the EC would move forward on political matters, especially a common foreign policy. . . . And many analysts have pointed to the connection between the EC's search for exchange-rate stability and its Common Agricultural Policy (CAP), the operation of which is severely complicated by fluctuations in EC currency values.

Evidence of linkage is not easy to find, however. Formal agreements have rarely tied monetary integration to other EC policies. And any analysis that relies on unstated (implicit) links must carefully explain how we know these links exist. For example, while many analysts and policymakers believe that full participation in the single market might be hampered by nonparticipation in the EMS, there is no provision in the Single European Act or any other Community document that even remotely hints at this tie. All of this is not to imply that linkage politics is unimportant, only that its analysis requires care and hard evidence.

All of the factors analyzed here have played a role in the process of European monetary unification. None, however, appears to have earned clear pride of place in our explanatory apparatus. The conclusion we draw is not to abandon systematic economic and political analysis of EMU but to encourage it. It is especially important to insist on explicit analytical arguments and on conscious attempts to disentangle the causes of the processes we observe.

THE FUTURE OF EMU

As we work slowly toward this goal, we can also ponder what 25 years' experience with European monetary unification implies for the future of the process. In the wake of the turbulence that afflicted the European Monetary System following the negotiation of the Maastricht Treaty, a number of scenarios are conceivable.

1. EMU of the 12

All 12 members of the Community (16 if the EFTA countries, other than Iceland and Switzerland, are admitted to the Community) could rededicate themselves to the task of meeting the Maastricht Treaty's convergence criteria and establish an EC-wide monetary union toward the end of the decade.

2. Early Two-Speed EMU

Alternatively, a subset of countries might make substantial progress toward meeting the convergence criteria. If a bare majority of EC countries (including, perhaps, some of the present-day EFTA countries) succeeds in doing so, they could establish a monetary union in short order. The version of the Maastricht Treaty drafted in December 1991 and signed in January 1992 would permit a single currency to be established by a majority of countries after Stage Two began on January 1, 1994, so long as that majority satisfied the convergence criteria, such as two preceding years of exchange-rate stability. Given the exchange-rate instability of 1992–93, in practice it seems unlikely that a majority of countries would satisfy these criteria in the immediate future.

3. Late Two-Speed EMU

The attempt to stabilize exchange rates on a Community-wide basis through the remainder of Stage One and through Stage Two of the transition might fail in the face of market pressures. Only a minority of countries centered on Germany (a "deutschemark bloc" comprising Germany, Benelux and possibly France, Denmark, and—assuming its admission to the Community—Austria) would succeed in maintaining exchange-rate stability and qualifying for EMU in 1999 (the first date, according to the treaty, when EMU can proceed with only a minority of countries).

4. No EMU

Exchange-rate instability could infect even Germany's Northern European neighbors. The Maastricht blueprint would be rendered moot, and would join its predecessors as another failed episode in the effort to achieve monetary unification in Europe.

5. Forced March to Mini-EMU

Realizing the scope for renewed exchange-rate instability, a minority of strong-currency countries centered on Germany and France (encompassing the rest of the deutschemark bloc, possibly including Austria) would establish monetary union well before 1999. Alternatively, France and Germany could attempt to construct a de facto monetary union between themselves. Either option would require that the Maastricht Treaty be revised, replaced or superseded to permit a small subgroup of countries to establish a monetary union prior to 1999.

Neither economic nor political theory is capable of predicting which scenario will obtain. But the combined body of theory, together with the historical record, suggests that some scenarios are more likely than others.

The first scenario (EMU of the 12 by the end of the decade) is unlikely. The asymmetric shock of 1990–91 (German unification) and Europe's 1992–93 recession revealed that many countries' allegiance to the Maastricht process was a "fair-weather" commitment: opposition resurfaced once it became clear that meeting the treaty's preconditions would have economic costs. Recent experience thus suggests that domestic political resistance to belt-tightening measures will prevent some countries from satisfying the convergence criteria, especially if another recession or another asymmetric shock intervenes. German officials, for their part, have rejected suggestions to relax the preconditions for participation in EMU, and have voiced repeated doubts that all 12 member countries will be ready to participate by the end of the decade. . . .

The second scenario (early two-speed EMU) confronts the same problems as does the first scenario, though in somewhat milder form. Moreover, proceeding with a two-speed EMU before 1999 requires, as explained above, that a majority of member countries qualify. Given the exchange-rate instability of 1992–93 and the widening budgetary gaps consequent on Europe's recession, it seems unlikely that a majority of countries would satisfy the convergence criteria at an early date. . . .

This scenario has other obstacles to surmount, as well. In 1992–93, the instability of some European currencies (those of Sweden, Italy and Britain) spilled over to others, even to those of countries apparently meeting all the conditions for having a strong currency (France, for example). This raises the danger that exchange-rate instability within the bloc of countries proceeding at low speed may contagiously infect those attempting to proceed at high speed. The second scenario also raises questions about the viability of other Community programs in a situation where only a subset of member countries form a monetary union. As mentioned above, existing EC programs such as the CAP become difficult to run when intra-European exchange rates are allowed to float. Floating is likely to heighten complaints about competitive pressures associated with the Single European Act if some countries are able to depreciate their currencies in order to steal a competitive advantage in international markets. . . . This scenario also faces the danger that the early participants will resist the subsequent admission of other countries; knowing this, the others will use their leverage in other issue areas to prevent the strong-currency countries from pursuing the second scenario.

The third scenario (late two-speed EMU encompassing only those EC countries—presumably Germany, Benelux and perhaps also France and Denmark—capable of resisting the contagious effects of exchange-rate instability elsewhere) is likely to be viable purely as an exchange-rate arrangement. But this scenario, like the second one, may founder on the incompatibility of floating in parts of the Community with the CAP and the SEA, and on the subsequent admissions problem. . . .

The fourth scenario (no EMU) is conceivable, but it is a fundamental threat to the SEA. It implies either the reimposition of capital controls on a limited basis, and hence modification of the SEA, or a return to generalized floating, which is subversive to the CAP and the SEA.

On purely economic grounds, then, there is reason to attach a higher probability to the fifth scenario (forced march to mini-EMU) than to the others. There is no obvious economic obstacle to establishing monetary union for Germany, France and some of the small Northern European countries. A quick transition would eliminate scope for exchange-rate instability. Excluding countries with more pervasive inflation and budgetary problems would relieve the members of this mini-EMU of their fear that it would exhibit an inflationary bias.

The question about the fifth scenario is whether it is politically viable since it would require thorough renegotiation of existing EMU agreements and the agreement of Germany. Is the bargain that drew the negotiators of the participating countries to accept the Maastricht draft in 1991 still workable today? One view is that the answer is no: Germany, which otherwise had nothing to gain from monetary unification, agreed to EMU in 1991 only as a quid pro quo for the Community's acceptance of German unification. As German unification is now a fait accompli, a new round of negotiations is less likely to meet a successful conclusion. The other view is that Germany will still agree to EMU in return for deeper political union and a renewed foreign policy role. Germany still seeks a renewed foreign policy role within the context of a politically integrated Europe. But the difficulties the Community has experienced in formulating a coherent foreign policy response to the conflict in the former Yugoslavia have dimmed German enthusiasm for this venture. Whether German political leaders and their constituents are really prepared to sacrifice the deutschemark in order to gain a joint foreign policy role, together with France and the other Community countries, is again an open question. . . .

18

Capital Politics: Creditors and the International Political Economy

JEFFRY A. FRIEDEN

This essay analyzes the relationship between international investment interests and foreign economic policy. The first step of the argument, based on an international economic approach, looks at nation-states as the relevant actors, and claims that a country's international investment position tends to affect its policy preferences in ways that are easily understood and anticipated. The international asset positions of a country often have a predictable impact on its policies toward international monetary relations, cross-border investment, and trade. The second step of the argument, founded on a domestic societal approach, looks inside national societies at the international asset positions of various domestic groups. It argues that sectors with varying interests related to their international investment positions contend for influence over national policy. The economic circumstances of each sector lead to sectoral policy preferences with predictable implications for domestic bargaining over foreign economic policy. The general argument is applied briefly to a number of modern creditor countries and sectors, most prominently the United States after World War II.

International monetary and financial relations are at the center of today's international political economy. Currency values, short- and long-term capital movements, debtor-creditor relations, and related issues are crucial to the private sector, to intergovernmental relations, and to private-public sector interaction around the

Jeffry A. Frieden. "Capital Politics: Creditors and the International Political Economy." From *Journal of Public Policy,* 8, 3/4 (July–Dec. 1988). Reprinted with the permission of Cambridge University Press. It is a violation of the law to reproduce this selection by any means whatsoever without the written permission of the copyright holder.

world. A fundamental analytical and practical question for those concerned about the future of the world economy is indeed the extent to which growing international financial ties will lead toward more cooperation among national policy makers, and among nationally-based businesses, or more conflict among them.

The future of international financial relations, and especially the degree of conflict involved in them, is a function of both economic and political considerations. The scholarly literature on the economics of international capital movements grows daily in both quantity and quality. However, this large economic literature is not matched by a comparable body of work on the political factors involved in international money and finance; a *political economy* approach to the topic is only in its infancy. Just as informed academic and general discussion of international trade conflict and cooperation relies on an integration of economic and political considerations, so too must political economy be brought to bear on the study of international finance to improve the level of debate and the effectiveness of policy.

This essay suggests that the starting point for a political economy of international finance should be the relationship between international investment interests and the foreign economic policy preferences they imply. The argument proceeds in two steps, at different levels of analysis. The first step and level of analysis looks at nation-states as the relevant actors, and claims that a country's international investment position tends to affect its international economic preferences in ways that are easily understood and anticipated. Countries' international asset positions often have a predictable impact on their policies toward international monetary relations, cross-border investment, and trade. The second step and level of analysis looks inside national societies at the international asset positions of various domestic groups. It argues that sectors with varying interests related to their international investment positions contend for influence over national policy. The economic circumstances of each sector lead to sectoral policy preferences with predictable implications for domestic bargaining over foreign economic policy.

The general argument is applied briefly to a number of modern creditor countries and sectors, most prominently the United States after World War Two. The United States was a country rich in capital, and its international economic policies reflected the attempt to ensure as high a return as possible to American capital. At a more disaggregated level of analysis, the varied interests of leading sectors of the U.S. economy, with international economic policy preferences that flow from their domestic and international asset positions, provide the basis for an understanding of domestic debates over U.S. foreign economic policy.

The argument and the examples are preliminary and illustrative. The purpose of the essay is only to present the rudiments of a framework for analyzing the domestic and international political economy of international finance, and to show that the framework fits a stylized review of the evidence. As such, the essay reflects the embryonic nature of attempts to develop a political economy of international finance.

INTERNATIONAL FINANCE AND THE
INTERNATIONAL POLITICAL ECONOMY

There are powerful reasons to study the political economy of international capital movements. Economic theory shows that factor movements are substitutes for international trade, and may even perform similar functions more rapidly. If a labor-rich country maximizes its welfare by exporting labor-intensive goods, it does so even more directly by exporting labor and importing capital; the converse holds for a capital-rich country. Trade is only a means to an end, maximizing profits on capital, and exports are only one way of earning profits on foreign activities; it makes as much sense to focus on the end as on the means.

Indeed, international capital markets are today the pivot around which the world economy rotates. The offshore financial markets hold well over a trillion dollars net of inter-bank claims, and hundreds of billions of dollars more are invested abroad in traditional portfolio and direct forms. International capital movements dwarf international trade in sheer size; by rough estimate, more money flows into and out of the United States in a day than goods in a month. In 1984, even according to the inadequate figures available, American overseas investment income was $87.6 billion on overseas private assets of $795 billion. In the same year, merchandise exports were $220 billion; assuming a generous five percent profit margin on overseas sales, this implied that foreign investment earned American businesses eight times as much as did foreign trade. International economic transactions of this size deserve close attention by scholars, especially since the study of the politics of international investment has a long and instructive history.

Another reason to focus systematically on international monetary and financial relations is that there is substantial evidence that these relations themselves help explain developments in other realms of the international political economy. The most obvious example is the effect of real exchange rates on trade: a significant rise in the real exchange rate often leads to protectionist sentiment from traded goods producers whose competitive position is eroded by the currency's appreciation, while a real depreciation tends to dampen protectionist pressure by improving the competitive position of local producers. . . .

Perhaps most obviously, international financial and monetary flows and policy deserve attention from political scientists because they are poorly understood. Trade policy is traditionally a legislative affair, at least in large part, and is thus quite amenable to examination: regional and sectoral interests, trade-offs, and coalitions can be tracked easily. International monetary and financial policies, on the other hand, are almost everywhere centralized in the Treasury and the Central Bank, often in deep secrecy. Yet we know how important foreign economic policy decisions in the monetary and financial arenas can be, from Britain's return to gold in 1925 and America's interwar debts and reparations debates to the 1971 Nixon shocks and the debt crisis of the 1980s.

Many issues in the political economy of international capital movements deserve study. These include the effect of political variables on such economic developments as cross-border capital movements themselves. Our purpose here is more modest: to discuss the origins of government policies directly or indirectly concerning the international movement of capital, especially international monetary policy, the protection of overseas investment, and trade policy.

In analyzing the political economy of international finance, we can draw on two divergent strands within political science. The first, generally associated with what is called the systemic approach to international relations, ignores domestic politics, focuses on the interaction of national states that it assumes to be unitary, and explores how at the level of the international system this inter-state interaction affects the making of foreign economic policy. The second, generally associated with interest-group or class-analytical approaches, focuses explicitly on bargaining among domestic socio-economic and political groups, and investigates how this domestic political interaction affects the making of foreign economic policy.

Systemic studies of international relations contribute two insights to the analysis of the politics of international economics. The first is that the international economic order generally reflects the preferences of the most important states in the system. This bit of common sense is not so trivial as it might seem; its insistence on *states* as the basic ordering principle of the international system highlights the incompleteness of international economic approaches that look only at market forces. The second insight is that, like all atomistic actors, states face difficulties in coordinating their interaction, even when such coordination would be to their mutual benefit. The point here is that inter-state behavior is subject to the same strategic considerations as interaction among firms or individuals. These two insights have been applied, most prominently and with mixed success, to such issues as the construction of an open international trading system by "hegemonic" powers—the United Kingdom in the 19th century and the United States after World War Two.

However, systemic International Relations has not been very successful at going beyond these observations to more systematic analyses of the international political economy. The problem is simple: the two insights mentioned above can only be brought to bear for real analysis if the preferences of the actors (states) can be specified. Scholarship in the systemic tradition regards states as rational units interacting strategically in the international system, but the units have nothing to be rational *for*, no utility function to maximize. Indeed, the strategic interaction of states in the international economic policy arena cannot be understood without a clear picture of the states' prior preferences: a state that wants to be integrated into the international economy will behave very differently in trade negotiations than one that prefers economic autarky. Some have tried to evade the problem by assuming that states maximize their power or prospects for survival and building up from there, but since national power or survival are goals consonant with a myriad of economic policies, the preferences imputed on this basis are *ad hoc*.

One way to avoid this problem is to focus on specific issue-areas in which national economic preferences appear self-evident. There are many studies on the strategic interaction of debtor nations and creditor banks in which, quite plausibly, both debtors and creditors are assumed to be purely economic utility maximizers: debtors trade off the benefits of unilateral reductions in debt service against the costs of creditor retaliation, while creditors do the opposite, all in the context of implicit or explicit bargaining toward an equilibrium outcome. Yet this method has not been generalized to other issue-areas, and it is rarely extended to inter-state interaction in more than one issue-area.

The first cut proposed here to analyze the political economy of international finance is systemic, and focuses on the ways in which nation-states interact in bargaining over global monetary, financial, and trade relations. In line with the systemic focus on unitary state action, we ignore domestic politics, derive the in-terests and preferences of nation-states from their international investment posi-tions, then discuss their behavior as they bargain with other nation-states over in-ternational financial, monetary, and trade issues.

Even the most cursory knowledge of the politics of international financial re-lations is enough to make clear how unrealistic is the fundamental assumption of the systemic approach, that domestic politics do not affect foreign economic policymaking. Different domestic groups have varied, sometimes diametrically opposed, interests in relation to the international economy, and they fight for their interests in the domestic political arena.

The domestic-level alternative to systemic international relations, then, seeks to specify how national economic preferences are derived from bargaining among individuals, firms, and sectors within the nation-state, each of which has prefer-ences derived from its position in society. The analytical bases for this method, which has firm roots in modern political economy, are of course far more devel-oped than systemic interpretations of the international economy. Nevertheless, even at the level of generality of interest to scholars of International Relations the task is extraordinarily complex, since it requires a level of disaggregation suffi-cient to capture the specifics of various individuals, firms and sectors, and then a reaggregation that is able to assign accurate weights to the relevant actors. This is a daunting task in so detailed and variegated a field as international trade, since goods differ so enormously; it is only slightly less daunting in international finan-cial matters.

Our second cut is thus to examine the effect of the different international eco-nomic situations of various groups within national societies on the making of na-tional policies related to international investment. Socio-economic groups with overseas assets are expected to have different interests from those without, and are expected to exert political pressure on policymakers to protect their international interests. These pressures will be brought to bear in issue-areas directly related to international investment, such as international monetary and financial policies, as well as in issue-areas that affect returns on international investment indirectly, such as trade policy.

The remainder of this paper is an attempt to develop and apply these intersect-ing approaches. First we examine how the international investment position of a nation-state as a discrete unit might be expected to affect its interests and actions in bargaining over international monetary policy, cross-border capital movements, and international trade. Then we explore how the international investment posi-tions of various groups *within* each nation-state might be expected to affect the groups' positions in domestic political bargaining over national foreign economic policies on international monetary, investment, and trade issues. For tractability we look only at countries with net external assets, creditors. This restriction in the scope of the analysis is artificial and limiting, since the existence of creditors implies the existence of debtors, and they can be expected to interact in important ways. However, the discussion of creditor interests and actions is complex enough for a preliminary essay.

"NATIONAL" CREDITOR INTERESTS AND THE POLITICAL ECONOMY OF INTERNATIONAL FINANCE

In the process of economic growth and development, countries pass through a series of states in their capital accounts. It is intuitively obvious that, inasmuch as economic development involves capital accumulation, the less developed a country is the more poorly endowed with capital it will be, and the more likely the relative capital scarcity will lead to capital imports. There are of course a number of reasons why the process might take the form, not of capital imports, but of an entirely domestically-driven increase in the country's capital stock and capital-to-labor ratio. Nonetheless, a few not particularly strong assumptions are enough to ensure that almost any model will reflect the empirical observation that relatively poor countries tend to import capital, while relatively rich ones tend to export it.

This secular trend can of course be interrupted by shorter-term fluctuations, for example when a wealthy country borrows heavily abroad (the United States in the Reagan years, Weimar Germany) or when a poor country invests abroad (Argentina and Venezuela in the early 1980s). We ignore the fluctuations and focus on the trend. We also begin our analysis not at the beginning, but at the point at which a country ceases to be a debtor and becomes a creditor.

Creditor countries share certain attributes, but it is useful to distinguish between new lenders and mature creditors. The fundamental distinction between the two is the degree to which overseas assets have been accumulated; a specific indicator might be the relationship between new overseas investments and earnings on existing overseas assets.

When a country begins to export capital, its earnings on overseas assets are substantially less than its new overseas loans and investments. Put another way, a *new lender* pays for most capital exports out of the country's trade surplus. After many years of overseas investment, however, the country's existing stock of foreign assets is large enough that repatriated earnings approach or even surpass new capital exports. Earnings from financial and other services directly related to the country's international financial status (insurance and foreign exchange trading, for example) can be added to this. At the point at which the country is, so to speak, living off its existing overseas assets and international financial sector, it is a *mature creditor* or, in less flattering terms, a rentier state.

A country rich in capital and interested in protecting its overseas investments has a number of interests in international monetary and financial relations. In the global arena, a capital-exporter wants to ensure that capital can move across borders smoothly and without undue interference. This implies a need for formal or informal, bilateral or multilateral, arrangements to facilitate cross-border capital flows. One concern is the adjudication and enforcement of property rights across borders, which can include everything from gunboat diplomacy to investment treaties. Another concern is relatively predictable currency values, whether in the form of the gold standard, the Bretton Woods system, or well-developed forward markets. Creditor countries thus take the lead in maintaining a market for their currency as an international reserve asset, developing international contract law and a mechanism to enforce it, and other such features of financial and monetary stability.

An important aspect of creditor-country status is the financial-center function, by which the country becomes a reliable place for economic agents from other countries to carry out international financial transactions. A financial center's currency must be easily convertible into other currencies and generally trusted, and its financial markets must be strong and reasonably protected from the whims of politicians.

Creditor countries also have important interests in international trade policy. In general, they should be concerned to make their own markets more accessible to their debtors. After all, unless the capital-receiving countries are able, directly or indirectly, to earn the currency of the capital-sending country, creditors will be unable to repatriate their profits. For foreign investing nations, indeed, it is more important that *their own* market be open than that other markets be open; their capital exports can jump trade barriers, but unless foreigners can earn the creditor's currency capital exports can never pay off.

From the standpoint of a major creditor country, such as Great Britain in the nineteenth century and the United States after World War Two, the principal concern is to promote long-term capital movements and short-term exchange stability. World-wide trade liberalization may be of less importance in itself. For a creditor that wishes to enjoy the earnings from its foreign assets, after all, it is *one's own* receptiveness to imports that matters most, for service payments and profit remittances depend on the capital importers' ability to earn or purchase the currency of the lender or investor. Similarly, as the Articles of Agreement of the International Monetary Fund make explicit, short-term currency stability may require trade protection rather than liberalization.

New lenders and mature creditors share a common interest in the security of property outside their borders and international monetary and financial stability, but their positions lead to somewhat different trading considerations. New lenders actively accumulate overseas assets, financing this accumulation out of their trade surplus, while mature creditors consume the returns on already-accumulated assets, so that a trade deficit is a necessary concomitant of receiving the fruits of their previous capital exports. New creditors thus have a stronger interest in securing export markets, and less need to open their own markets, than do mature creditors, while mature creditors have a stronger incentive for inward trade liberalization, and a less powerful one for commercial openness on the part of others.

The brief description of creditor-country interests fits the relevant evidence quite well. Holland in its heyday, Britain before World War One, and the United States since World War Two, are indeed quite adequately described as creditor countries with predictable creditor preferences. In all instances, the countries in question engaged in large outflows of long-term capital, a general commitment to help stabilize the international monetary system, and a reduction in barriers to imports. The central economic aspects of such creditor policies thus gave the rest of the world access to the creditor's capital, medium of exchange, and markets. As other nations joined the ranks of the creditors, especially Germany in the 1960s and Japan in the 1970s, their policies also began to reflect traditional creditor concerns.

Holland's domination of European trade in the seventeenth and early eighteenth centuries eventually permitted the Dutch to invest enormous fortunes abroad. The Dutch became the world's most militant partisans of free trade and investment, invented modern international contract law, and acted as Europe's principal center for international finance and related services for many years. In their quest for lucrative outlets for their capital, Dutch investors looked especially to Europe's most dynamic economy, England. Dutch investors purchased huge quantities of English government securities, as well as shares in developing British private enterprises. By the 1770s well over 40 percent of the English national debt was owed to Dutchmen, and wealthy Amsterdam financiers like the Barings and Ricardos were themselves migrating to London. Throughout, the Dutch maintained their classical creditor commitments.

In the oft-cited British case, massive foreign investments shifted Britain's economic weight from the domestic market toward the foreign sector, and from industry toward finance. By 1914 over one-quarter of Britain's national wealth was invested overseas, and the steady flow of finance out of England made the country the greatest creditor and most important international financial center the world had ever seen. The central role of the United Kingdom in enforcing property rights abroad, stabilizing the international gold standard, and liberalizing its trade relations, is all well-known.

The United States after World War Two similarly pursued policies expected of a country extraordinarily rich in capital. Every effort was made to smooth the flow of capital and goods, and to rebuild an environment in which normal patterns of international investment and trade might resume. The ability of the United States to construct a stable and lasting international investment position depended on the reliability of a number of American commitments. First, U.S. goods markets were generally open to the country's real or potential debtors. Second, the market for U.S. dollars was open and predictable, so that savers and investors at home and abroad would be willing to engage in foreign-currency operations; this also required some form of international monetary cooperation. Third, U.S. capital markets were free enough from major government manipulation to overcome investors' and borrowers' fears of political risk. All over the world, investment was spurred by American capital, demand enhanced by American imports, and international payments made predictable by the gold-backed U.S. dollar.

The pattern of international cooperation among creditor countries on issues of mutual interest can also be examined with the tools discussed here. For example, there would appear to be a strong correlation between creditor status and interest in international monetary cooperation. To take two examples, the important Tripartite Monetary Agreement of 1936 eventually came to include all major creditors (the United States, Great Britain, France, the Netherlands, Switzerland, and Belgium), but never attracted the attention of such debtor countries as Germany and Italy. By the same token, as Japan's overseas investments have expanded, its willingness to take an active role in international monetary matters has grown. Past experience with other creditors would indicate that, although the evolution of Japanese policy has been too slow for the tastes of most American policymakers, it will continue and accelerate as the country accumulates foreign assets.

In another arena, since all creditors share an interest in cross-border property rights, this function has often been carried out in concert. Before World War One, strategic interaction among countries with clear creditor interests in securing foreign investments was of great importance. Multilateral financial control committees to protect the rights of creditors in shaky underdeveloped countries were common. In Serbia, Greece, Tunis, Persia, Egypt, Morocco, and elsewhere committees of private financiers and government officials of the capital-exporting nations were established. In the most limited sense they were charged with ensuring continued debt service, but this task soon involved them in running major portions of the debtors' economies. The best-known example is that of the multinational Ottoman Public Debt Administration, which eventually came to manage a wide variety of the Empire's modern business activities, and to control about one-quarter of Ottoman government revenues.

In the 1920s, during a financial expansion led by the United States and joined by Great Britain, monetary and financial cooperation among creditors was primarily managed by the largest private and central banks of the leading lenders, along with the Economic and Financial Committee of the League of Nations. The Dawes and Young plans to stabilize German finances were emphatically multilateral. The Young Plan indeed gave rise to the Bank for International Settlements (BIS), a formal institution designed to facilitate cooperation among major financial centers.

Since World War Two, multilateral creditor cooperation has evolved along the lines begun in the interwar period. The IMF-World Bank system has raised the multilateral principles inherent in the BIS to much higher levels, and has come to provide and supervise an extraordinary degree of creditor coordination.

The distinction between new lenders and mature creditors is also useful. It helps explain some of the trade-policy differences among creditor countries, such as why pre–World War One Great Britain was so much more willing to keep its markets open than France or Germany. It also helps explain some of the pattern of evolution in the behavior of creditor nations, such as the gradual shift from moderate neomercantilism toward free trade observed as new lenders become mature creditors. Thus, Great Britain in the mid-19th century, the United States in the 1940s, Western Europe since 1960, and Japan in the last decade reflect the transition from aggressive export promotion and moderate to high controls on imports to a reduction in import barriers.

None of this is to imply that there are not problems of competition and coordination among creditor countries. Nor is it to discount the large variations found even where creditor preferences and policies are similar. For example, one creditor's enforcement of property rights in an underdeveloped area makes it possible for other creditors to free-ride on this enforcement; the first creditor might in this circumstance find it attractive to privatize the benefits of enforcement by annexing the underdeveloped area. The approach simply allows the analyst to think more systematically about inter-state relations in such circumstances, in an attempt to understand the conditions in which creditor countries are able to arrive at a cooperative solution (the Ottoman Public Debt Administration) or are driven toward conflict (the late nineteenth-century rush for annexation). Similar exercises could be carried out in the analysis of international monetary cooperation and conflict in the interwar period, or of macroeconomic policy coordination today—all of them attempts to understand how creditor countries with similar preferences can interact in ways that lead to cooperation, conflict, or a combination thereof.

SECTORAL CREDITOR INTERESTS AND THE POLITICAL ECONOMY OF INTERNATIONAL FINANCE

Instead of looking more deeply into the strategic interaction of nation-states with creditor interests, we now turn to a less aggregate level of analysis. It is in fact undeniable that a great deal of the interaction among creditor countries, and between creditor and debtor countries, is driven by domestic rather than international politics. There is, for example, copious evidence that in both the British and American cases much of the impetus for their "hegemonic" international economic policies came from major domestic economic sectors whose interests may not have been identical with those of the nation as a whole. The powerful financial institutions of the City of London are widely regarded as having had a major impact on British international economic policy from the early nineteenth century up to the present; analogous groups, especially American-based international banks and corporations and their employees, have probably played a similar role in the United States.

To speak of *countries* that are rich in capital can indeed be misleading; the capital does not normally belong to "the country" but to economic agents in it. In other words, a capital-rich country is one that has more individuals and firms with a great deal of capital than a capital-poor country. This does not imply that *all* firms and individuals in the country are capital-rich, for the accumulation of capital takes place very unevenly. The most accurate inference would be that, in a capital-rich country, the economic agents well-endowed with capital outweigh those that are poor in capital but, presumably, well-endowed with other factors.

A policy that can be deduced to be in the interests of a creditor country is not necessarily in the interests of everyone in that country. There are of course many examples of conflict among particular groups over national economic policies, in creditors as in all nations. The protection of overseas property rights may benefit overseas investors a great deal, and peasants very little, but the costs may fall primarily on peasants drafted and sent abroad to do the protecting.

Our previous discussion of creditor-country interests is thus quite incomplete. We cannot simply assume that because some local firms and investors have overseas assets, policy will reflect the interests of those with overseas assets. Even where we have reason to believe that overseas asset-holders will dominate foreign economic policy, such as where most firms with strong preferences about policy are overseas investors, there is always the possibility that the political process will be dominated by economic actors with interests different from or opposed to those of creditors. A more detailed analysis of creditor-country preferences requires us to consider the conflicting interests of those *within* creditor countries. In what follows we discuss some characteristic sectoral interests in creditor countries.

We can distinguish two very broad groups of sectoral interests. First are those whose assets are internationally diversified, and who can thus take advantage of both domestic and overseas investment opportunities. This includes most prominently the creditors themselves, those with existing assets abroad. We define this group to include also those involved in the financial-center functions of a creditor country, whose principal function is to service those with foreign investments. This group should also include producers whose domestic output is competitive on world markets but who have not engaged in overseas investment: those that could invest abroad, but at present have no need to. The second group is made up of import-competing sectors and/or those whose assets are not internationally diversified. This encompasses uncompetitive producers, whose domestic output cannot compete with imports and who have not invested abroad, for whatever reason. It also consists of producers of non-traded goods and services, indifferent to international economic conditions. The categorization is schematic but useful; we can demonstrate its utility by discussing how the different sectors respond to several important policy issues in creditor countries.

Government protection of overseas assets is of interest primarily to those who are real or potential holders of such assets. The rest of the economy bears the costs of such protection—insurance, military intervention, membership in consortia—but receives few of the benefits. A similar calculation holds for international financial and monetary cooperation in general; if such cooperation has costs for the country as a whole, those who receive few benefits will oppose it. This can be brought to bear in the analysis of domestic opposition to colonialism, or to multilateral organizations.

Monetary and fiscal policy, which primarily affect international economic policy through the exchange rate, also give rise to different sectoral interests. Overseas investors and competitive producers (and, if they are organized, consumers of imported products) are expected to exert what might alternately be call deflationary, internationalist, or "monetarist" pressures. Their competitive and/or international asset position is such that, other things being equal, they are profitable with a strong exchange rate. Where a strong currency makes their domestic production less competitive, these investors can respond simply by transferring production overseas. Unless information and currency futures markets are perfect, which they rarely are, investors with international portfolios also have an interest in currency stability and predictability, which domestic inflation endangers. They thus fight against fiscally expansionary policies, and for monetary restraint.

On the other hand, uncompetitive, domestically-bound, and non-tradables producers exert pressures that might alternately be called inflationary, weak-currency, nationalist, or "fiscalist." They can only gain from a fiscal stimulus and monetary looseness. A strong currency makes uncompetitive producers even less competitive; depreciation improves their position. By the same token, in most circumstances domestic fiscal stimulation increases demand for domestically produced non-traded goods and services (including goods protected by trade barriers). These groups are thus in the forefront of opposition to monetary stringency and fiscal orthodoxy.

Trade policy is another area of potential conflict. Creditors, along with exporters, have a general interest in inward commercial openness, to avoid retaliation against exports, to allow for profit and interest repatriation and, in the case of multinational firms, for intra-firm trade. For reasons discussed above, creditors in a new lender are less concerned about home-country free trade than creditors in a rentier state. Competitive producers similarly support inward liberalization, for straightforward trade-bargaining reasons. Uncompetitive producers are protectionist; the non-tradable sector is indifferent.

Examples of these sectoral developments recur in the history of creditor states. The Dutch experience is legendary. Even as the country's industries became increasingly unable to compete with foreign manufacturers (especially those protected by British mercantilism), the country's powerful foreign-investment, financial, shipping, and trading interests were able to maintain free trade. . . .

A similar dynamic was at work in Great Britain even at the height of its international creditor status. Industrially-based protectionists, especially supporters of Imperial Preferences, grew steadily stronger after 1880 but were only able to triumph politically, and then only temporarily, in the interwar years. Here, as in Holland, the outcome was not so much national decline as a change in the *domestic* balance of economic and political power as the nation's role in the world was redefined from that of a new lender to a mature creditor. As British investors built up huge international holdings British industry became increasingly uncompetitive, and sectoral conflicts over monetary and exchange-rate policy were particularly striking. To take one famous example, London's City was a primary pressure group for, and a major beneficiary of, Britain's return to gold in 1925 at an overvalued parity. Sterling overvaluation maintained the value of Britain's overseas investments, and helped keep sterling and the City at the center of international finance. Sterling overvaluation also drove Britain's already weak traditional industries into a recession that only ended when it was superseded by the Depression.

A sketch of crucial episodes in domestic conflict over the foreign economic policy of the United States since World War One demonstrates a similar sectoral dynamic. In the 1920s the relatively new creditor sectors that arose during and after the Great War pressed for American membership in the League of Nations and other multilateral organizations, international financial and monetary cooperation, and trade liberalization. Creditors and the financial services sector, led by the New York banks, were allied with America's highly competitive industrial producers, who were already beginning to expand their overseas direct investments. Their opponents were to be found in the uncompetitive heartland industries and non-traded sectors, the bulwark of Taft Republicanism and isolationism. Although creditor and exporting sectors pressed consistently for the United States to revise its traditional protectionism and lack of involvement in international economic negotiations, they were continually defeated in a Congress fundamentally opposed to "internationalism," in economic as in other affairs. It was not until the late 1930s and 1940s that the tides of American politics began to shift toward a less isolationist international economic posture.

In the aftermath of World War Two, with most foreign competition wiped out and economic nationalism discredited, American policy moved in a more traditional creditor direction. Nonetheless, domestic political battles over foreign economic policy continued, on different fronts. "Fiscalist" forces, represented by Henry Morgenthau's Treasury Department, and by the Keynesians more generally, did battle with a powerful strong-currency lobby, based once more in the financial sector. With much of their international and domestic influence eroded by the global and domestic financial disasters of the 1930s, international financial interests were on relatively weak grounds until international trade and payments revived. Thus, while much of American policy accorded with creditor interests, the New York bankers did initially lose the battle to make the International Monetary Fund a tool of financial orthodoxy and to base international monetary relations on a gold-backed dollar.

Over the course of the late 1940s and early 1950s, however, as the U.S. and world economies returned to normalcy, "monetarist" groups reasserted themselves. The Treasury Accord of 1951 reestablished traditional Federal Reserve control over monetary policy. Under orthodox American leadership, the IMF evolved into a paragon of financial rectitude. The crucial question was that of the conditions under which member nations would be allowed to borrow from the Fund, and in successive decisions in 1952, 1955, and 1956, the IMF established rigorous standards upon which borrowing was to depend. By the late 1950s the Fund was often making its loans contingent upon such strict quantitative economic conditions as government spending ceilings and credit supply limits. In addition, international monetary relations as they evolved in the 1950s and 1960s looked far more like the key-currency approach of the New York bankers—with the dollar "as good as gold" and used as an international payments medium—than they did like the wartime plans of American and British Treasury officials.

This framework can also be brought to bear on the political economy of recent

U.S. international economic policy. One set of sectors is internationally integrated and/or competitive; another is uncompetitive and/or internationally insulated. In the American context the position of military contractors is especially important within the latter group, because of the widespread acceptance of relatively high levels of military spending in the United States—which can be regarded for our purposes as a fiscal stimulus to goods producers sheltered from international competition. Whether one sees this military spending as motivated primarily by real security concerns, by an ideologically acceptable military Keynesianism, or by the inordinate power of military contractors, the fact is that a degree of economic nationalism in pursuit of military preparedness has long been politically acceptable in the United States.

When private international capital movements began to accelerate after Europe's 1958 return to convertibility, the tension in the United States between deflationary and inflationary, monetarist and fiscalist, groups was a central problem. The position of the country's creditor sectors was endangered by the erosion of international confidence in the dollar, itself a result of the American government's domestic and international fiscal laxity. Rather than capitulate completely to deflationary pressures—for a more stringent monetary policy, for budgetary restraint, for a compression of domestic consumption—the Kennedy and Johnson administrations attempted to shield the domestic economy from trends in the country's capital account. The outflow of American capital was worsening the country's payments balance, thus exacerbating the deflationary pressures on domestic economic policy, but policymakers attempted to avoid domestic deflation without reducing the overseas activities of American firms. This attempt took a number of forms, leading up to the imposition of capital controls that permitted, perhaps even encouraged, American banks and corporations to engage in offshore funding of their overseas investments. The capital controls, which lasted until 1974, only postponed and may ultimately have magnified the conflict.

The Nixon administration also faced conflicting sectoral pressures as it continued to try to square the circle of American international economic policy. Creditor groups encouraged the government to restrain spending enough to strengthen the dollar, and failing that supported a revision of the Bretton Woods system on a cooperative multilateral basis. Meanwhile, domestically based and uncompetitive sectors were under increasing pressure, and support grew for government policies to stimulate the economy, provide trade protection, and devalue the dollar. Much of this sentiment was expressed in Congress, where protectionist sentiment increased rapidly, and through Treasury Secretary John Connally, who was quite sympathetic to domestic business. In August 1971 Nixon appeared to give in to pressures for a revision of traditional American foreign economic policies, much to the chagrin of internationalists around the world.

Conflict continued through the 1970s and into the 1980s. The early Carter administration stimulated the economy, but the result was a serious loss of confidence in the dollar by international investors. The dollar depreciation aided the competitive position of domestically based producers, but seriously worried those whose international investment interests were threatened by inflation and currency instability. In late 1978, as the dollar dropped vertiginously, Carter moved to defend the currency, with little success until in 1979 Paul Volcker and the Federal Reserve moved resolutely to deflate the economy and strengthen the currency. At the same time, the administration began to exercise some fiscal restraint, but most of the adjustment burden was borne by monetary policy, an arena dominated by the Federal Reserve, which generally reflects the concerns of those who are committed to the international economy and to an anti-inflationary posture.

The conflict between monetarists and fiscalists, deflation and inflation, internationalism and nationalism, accelerated in the Reagan administration. Three varied sets of interests reflected in the Republican Party and the administration can be pointed to. One was based in non-traded sectors, especially trade, real estate, and military contractors from the "Sunbelt" area. These groups were clear influences in favor of fiscal expansion, although the non-traded nature of their activities made them hostile or indifferent to trade protection. A second broad grouping was declining industrial sectors in the Midwest and Northeast—these inflationary *and* protectionist. Of course, traditional internationalist and creditor groups maintained their fundamental opposition to both fiscal stimulation and economic nationalism.

The Reagan administration's policies, and its frequent internal disagreements, reflected the disparate pressures on it. Anti-inflationary internationalist creditor sectors dominated monetary policy, including policies to manage international financial and monetary matters. However, reflationary non-traded or uncompetitive sectors had substantial influence on the fiscal side, and had some trade-policy successes as well. One outcome of the pulling and hauling between fiscal and monetary policies was a massive capital inflow as foreigners funded Federal deficits. By 1986 the United States was a net debtor; although American investors still have enormous overseas interests, the U.S. government has built up huge debts to the international capital markets. The effect of these contradictory American policies has become the central issue in the world economy. The story is still being played out, but there is no doubt that in the future, as in the past decade, the conflict between sectors with contending international financial interests will play a crucial role in American economic policy.

Tension similar to that found in the United States since World War Two has characterized debates over economic policy in most of the rest of the OECD. As international markets have become more and more integrated, the general trend has been for national policy to reflect more and more the interests of internationally diversified investors. Yet policymakers have also tried to meet some demands for protection from international competition by more insular and immobile economic actors. In virtually all countries, groups with important international economic ties have dominated, while groups for whom the rest of the world was a threat rather than an opportunity have fought for protection. Here too, domestic bargaining continues; perhaps the most striking topic of debate is the future of the European Community as 1992 approaches.

PRUDENTIAL DISCLAIMERS AND OBSERVATIONS

The framework presented here does not pretend to be a full-blown theory of the laws of motion of the international political economy. There are many issues that the approach does not address, and many questions it does not answer.

As mentioned at the outset, the initial causes of national-level creditor status are not clearly explained. It is especially important to be able to separate the secular or "natural" evolution of a national economy and sectors within it, from developments that are simply driven by government policy. It would hardly be justified to regard Great Britain in 1914, with a century of international investment experience, as equivalent to a country that became a net creditor solely for perverse policy reasons—as some Third World borrowers with overvalued currencies did after 1980. The same might be said about the United States today: it clearly is not a "natural" net debtor. In this regard a distinction between short- and long-term, and between public- and private-sector, capital movements may be useful.

In much the same way, it is hardly satisfactory simply to assert that some sectors are "natural" overseas investors while others are not. Government action, from tax policy through colonialism, can change the incentives to overseas investment in important ways. Long-term prediction on the basis of the framework presented here requires a stronger prior notion of what kinds of economic agents are more likely to engage in foreign investment.

In other words, the causal arrows implicit in this analysis are not unambiguous. National or sectoral creditor status may itself be the result of prior conditions that are not examined in the model, such as resource endowments, culturally determined savings propensities, or strategic considerations. Nor does the framework presented here provide determinant predictions of the *outcomes* of the sectoral clashes it forecasts. It claims only that the pattern of sectoral conflict, and the policy preferences of the various sectors, will be as set forth above; it says little about the institutional, political, strategic, and other factors that might influence the success of the various sectoral coalitions. These are important points for the extension of this analysis, and for more systematic tests of it.

Despite its preliminary nature, the discussion in this paper demonstrates that only the careful analysis of the roots of national economic preferences can allow International Relations scholars to analyze international monetary and financial interaction in fruitful ways. The implications of the paper are, further, that national economic interests cannot be derived from the system; while a first cut can be extrapolated from national factor endowments, a far more accurate picture requires a sectoral approach. Throughout, we have used the international investment positions of countries and sectors to explain national policies toward both global monetary and financial relations and such related arenas as international trade.

This paper analyzes the implications of national and sectoral international asset positions for national and sectoral economic interests and interaction. By way of example, it argues that creditor countries have certain identifiable international economic interests, and exhibit certain predictable behavior in line with these interests. Illustrations are drawn from a variety of historical and contemporary cases.

National-level phenomena are not sufficient to explain national economic interests, however, for domestic politics impinges strongly on the making of foreign economic policy. For this reason, the article develops a sectoral approach that distinguishes among domestic socio-economic actors with different international portfolios. It identifies the interests, and the expected behavior, of sectors within nations in domestic bargaining over foreign economic policy; illustrations are drawn from historical and contemporary cases. The analytical framework and empirical evidence presented here are meant primarily to suggest ways in which further research and analysis can be pursued in order to understand better the interplay of politics and economics in the international movement of capital.

19

The Obsolescence of Capital
Controls? Economic Management
in an Age of Global Markets
JOHN B. GOODMAN
AND LOUIS W. PAULY

John B. Goodman and Louis W. Pauly explain why countries reduced controls on capital flows from the late 1970s to the early
1990s and why they did so at different times during this period.
Focusing on the international economy as the fundamental cause
of changes in government policy, Goodman and Pauly argue that
transformations in the structure of global production and international financial markets made it both possible and desirable for
firms to successfully evade government controls. This made government attempts to control capital movements more costly and
less effective, and governments eventually abandoned them.
Examining the cases of France, Germany, Japan, and Italy, Goodman and Pauly conclude that the exact timing of the abandonment of controls was a function of whether states were experiencing capital inflows or outflows and, consequently, of the costs of
abandoning the controls.

The movement of capital across national borders has long raised sensitive political
questions. Whatever the benefits, international investment complicates national
economic management. Most research on this subject has focused on the causes
and consequences of foreign direct investment. Less studied, but no less important, are short-term capital flows—those arising from the purchase or sale of financial instruments with maturities of less than one year. In contrast to investments in plant and equipment, short-term flows are highly sensitive to interest rate
differentials and exchange rate expectations. Indeed, the mere announcement of a

John B. Goodman and Louis W. Pauly. "The Obsolescence of Capital Controls? Economic Management in an Age of Global Markets." From *World Politics,* Vol. 46, No. 1 (1993), pp. 50–82. Reprinted
by permission of the authors and The Johns Hopkins University Press.

change in economic policy can trigger massive capital inflows or outflows, undermining the anticipated benefits of the new policy. For this reason, most governments regularly resorted to various types of controls on short-term capital movements in the decades following World War II.

In recent years, however, the world has witnessed a remarkable shift away from the use of capital controls. In country after country, governments have abolished controls and dismantled the bureaucratic machinery used to administer them. And in the rare instances where governments have fallen back on controls, their temporary nature has usually been emphasized. This general trend toward liberalization has stimulated a growing body of research on the political and economic consequences of capital mobility. In this article, our principal aim is to address two prior puzzles: First, why did policies of capital decontrol converge across a rising number of industrial states between the late 1970s and the early 1990s? Second, why did some states move to eliminate controls more rapidly than others? We argue that the movement away from controls on short-term capital flows did not result, as regime or epistemic community theories might predict, from the emergence of a common normative framework or widespread belief in the benefits of unfettered capital mobility. Nor has it simply reflected the overarching power of a liberal state. Instead, we contend that it has been driven by fundamental changes in the structures of international production and financial intermediation, which made it easier and more urgent for private firms—specifically, corporations and financial institutions whose aspirations had become increasingly global—effectively to pursue strategies of evasion and exit. For governments, the utility of controls declined as their perceived cost thereby increased.

Still, not all governments abandoned capital controls at the same pace. In order to examine both the process through which these pressures impinged on policy at the national level and variations in the timing of policy reform, we analyze policy developments in four advanced industrial states that relied extensively on capital controls—Japan, Germany, France, and Italy. The first two moved decisively away from capital controls in 1980 and 1981, the latter two, at the end of the decade. These differences can be traced to the interaction between generic types of external pressure and remaining distinctions in domestic structures. Specifically, governments facing capital inflows liberalized sooner than governments facing capital outflows—a conclusion that is not obvious, since capital inflows can be as threatening to national policy-making autonomy as capital outflows. Our analysis at the national level highlights the mechanisms by which such systemic economic pressures were transmitted to unique domestic political arenas. But it also provides a clue as to the increasingly common constraints governments would now have to overcome if they wanted to move back to policies designed to influence and control short-term capital flows.

In theoretical terms, our argument and evidence address a central question in international political economy regarding the relative importance of, and relationship between, international and domestic variables. In the crucial area of capital flows, the two interact in a clear pattern: global financial structures affect the dynamics of national policy-making by changing and privileging the interests and actions of certain types of firms. Once those interests have been embedded in policy, movement back is not necessarily precluded but is certainly rendered much more difficult.

The rest of this article is divided into four sections. The first section examines the debate over capital controls in the postwar period and shows that the normative conclusion of this debate remained remarkably consistent throughout subsequent decades. The second section analyzes how changes in international financial markets influenced firm behavior and reframed the issue of capital controls for governments. The third section compares the way in which such changes affected government decisions to eliminate controls in Japan and Germany, which confronted problems associated with chronic capital inflows, and in France and Italy, which faced problems associated with capital outflows. Finally, the fourth section explores the conditions under which a retreat from liberal capital policies could occur and speculates on the normative implications of policy convergence witnessed thus far.

CAPITAL CONTROLS IN THE POSTWAR MONETARY ORDER

Following World War II, capital controls were an accepted part of the international monetary system. Despite pressure from the United States to allow investment as well as goods to cross borders without governmental interference, the 1944 Bretton Woods agreement intentionally legitimated the imposition of controls on capital movements that were not directly linked to trade flows. The agreement gave the International Monetary Fund (IMF) a mandate to discourage exchange restrictions and other financial impediments to trade but pointedly did not give it jurisdiction over capital controls. Most industrial countries accepted the logic of restoring currency convertibility but jealously guarded their right to control short-term capital flows. . . .

Facing persistent payments imbalances and problematic exchange rate rigidities in the 1960s, virtually all leading industrial states resorted to some type of control on capital movements. Even the United States adopted controls to prevent "disequilibrating" outflows. Similar controls were put in place by other states with external deficits, while states with external surpluses adopted measures to ward off unwelcome capital inflows. Ironically, these controls gave a boost to incipient "offshore" financial markets in Europe and elsewhere. The subsequent growth of Euro-currency banking, bond, and equity markets reflected a number of factors—including the unwillingness of governments to coordinate their associated regulatory and tax policies and the development of new technologies. . . .

The disintegration in the early 1970s of the Bretton Woods system of pegged exchange rates potentially opened the door for a new normative framework to coordinate efforts to influence international capital flows. An intergovernmental forum on international monetary reform, the Committee of Twenty of the IMF board of governors was established in 1972, and a group of technical experts was appointed by the committee to examine the problem of disequilibrating capital flows. They concluded that controls should not become a permanent feature of a reformed system because of their potentially negative impact on trade and investment flows. But since capital flows could continue to disrupt even a more flexible exchange rate arrangement, they recommended the adoption of a code of conduct monitored by the IMF to govern the future use of controls. In the end, however, their recommendation was not pursued by the committee.

When the IMF Articles of Agreement were finally amended in 1976 to accommodate floating exchange rates, the normative framework guiding international capital movements originally articulated at Bretton Woods remained intact. States retained the right to resort to controls at their own discretion. In sum, at the official level, neither the beliefs concerning capital controls nor the rules governing them changed significantly over the postwar period. The forces behind the wave of policy liberalization that was about to occur were located elsewhere.

GLOBAL FINANCE AND FIRM BEHAVIOR

Between the late 1970s and the early 1990s, the development of truly international financial markets and the globalization of production undercut the rationale for capital controls. To analyze how these changes affected policies designed to limit capital mobility, it is useful to begin by looking at why such policies were deemed necessary in the first place. In the early 1960s strong theoretical support for the use of capital controls was provided by J. Marcus Fleming and Robert Mundell, who demonstrated that a government could achieve at most two of the following three conditions: capital mobility, monetary autonomy, and a fixed exchange rate. Consider what happens when a government decides to tighten monetary policy and maintain a constant exchange rate. Without capital mobility, the rise in interest rates will simply reduce aggregate demand. With capital mobility, such autonomy is lost, as funds attracted from abroad drive interest rates back down to world levels. A decision to loosen monetary policy would have the opposite effect. Of course, few countries have ever sought to insulate themselves completely from capital inflows or outflows. But throughout the postwar period, many did seek to limit the volume of those flows and thus preserve a degree of autonomy.

During the 1960s a growing number of economists argued that a preferable way to preserve national monetary autonomy was to abandon fixed exchange rates. With flexible exchange rates, a decision to tighten monetary policy might still attract capital, but its principal effect would be on the value of the national currency, not domestic interest rates. . . .

In practice, the shift to flexible exchange rates in the 1970s did not provide the desired panacea. The Mundell-Fleming analysis . . . ignored feedback effects between exchange rates and domestic prices. As predicted, a country that sought to stimulate production by lowering interest rates suffered a depreciation of its currency. This depreciation, in turn, raised the price of its imports. If the country could not reduce imports quickly, higher import costs translated into higher prices for domestic production, thereby reducing the anticipated increase in output. Despite the shift to floating rates, many countries therefore still considered capital controls necessary to carve out as much autonomy as possible for their monetary policies.

In the 1970s and 1980s, however, two developments dramatically reduced the usefulness of capital controls. The first was the transformation and rapid growth of international financial markets. Between 1972 and 1985, for example, the size of the international banking market increased at a compound growth rate of 21.4 percent, compared with compound annual growth rates of 10.9 percent for world gross domestic product and 12.7 percent for world trade. Moreover, just as this pool of funds increased in size, technological changes reduced the time it took to transfer funds across borders. Since the early 1970s the daily turnover on the world's exchange markets has risen tremendously. In the midst of the currency crisis in March 1973, $3 billion were converted into European currencies in one day. In the late 1970s, daily turnover around the world was estimated at $100 billion; a decade later, that figure had reached $650 billion.

Just as these changes were occurring, a related development was taking place—an increasing number of businesses were moving toward a global configuration. Multinational enterprises (MNEs) were, of course, not new. What was new was the growth in their number, from just a few hundred in the early 1970s to well over a thousand in 1990. Moreover, for more and more MNEs, the home base was outside the United States. Globalization was also evident in the rapid growth of foreign direct investment. During the latter half of the 1980s, for example, flows of new FDI rose at an annual rate of 29 percent. According to one recent study, more than $3.5 trillion of business assets came under "foreign control" in the 1980s.

These twin changes had dramatic consequences for the use of capital controls. Most importantly, the expansion of financial markets made it progressively easier for private firms whose operations had become increasingly global to adopt strategies of exit and evasion. Evasion had obviously taken place for decades, but the means by which it could be conducted were now multiplied. Multinational structures enabled firms to evade capital controls by changing transfer prices or the timing of payments to or from foreign subsidiaries. The deepening of financial markets meant that firms could use subsidiaries to raise or lend funds on foreign markets. If controls in a country became too onerous, MNEs could also attempt to escape them altogether by transferring activities abroad, that is, by exercising the exit option.

This possibility, in turn, constrained the choices available to governments. Assume that a government maintains a more expansionary monetary policy than the rest of the world in order to stimulate growth and create jobs. Assume further that it recognizes that higher interest rates abroad are likely to attract domestic savings needed to finance domestic investment, and it therefore imposes controls on capital outflows. If MNEs react to these controls by moving certain operations offshore, the domestic savings base essentially shrinks. In this instance, the country finds itself in a worse position than when it started. Clearly, if a government can anticipate this effect, credible threats of exit would deter the imposition of capital controls. To the extent that such threats are indeed credible, they highlight the deepening interrelationship between short-term and long-term investment flows. A government that is truly serious about restricting short-term capital movements would also have to be prepared to restrict offshore direct investments by domestic firms. It would then have to balance the losses (in terms of efficiency) borne by those firms and the national economy against the anticipated benefits of capital controls.

From the perspective of firms, however, neither evasion nor exit is a costless option. Firms surely prefer to avoid capital controls or to have them removed, rather than having to consider either option. Thus, MNEs and financial institutions might be expected to mobilize against controls and promote policies encouraging international capital mobility. Governments concerned with the issue of national competitiveness might be expected to be especially responsive to such entreaties. They might also be expected to press other governments to liberalize.

Government decisions to abandon capital controls during the 1980s reflected fundamental changes in the markets through which capital could flow. In our examination of specific decisions in the cases of Japan, Germany, France, and Italy, we provide examples of how these changes affected decision-making processes. Not surprisingly, indisputable evidence of evasion and exit on the part of firms is difficult to find—the former because firms have little interest in making apparent their use of loopholes; the latter because it involves, in essence, a kind of structural power. It need not be exercised to have effect. What comes out clearly, however, is the perception by national policymakers that capital controls had become less useful and more costly.

Although similar pressures affected all advanced industrial countries, the speed with which specific governments responded depended upon whether they were experiencing capital inflows or outflows. The four countries we examine in the next section provide examples of each. Japan and Germany, typically recording surpluses in their current accounts and experiencing capital inflows, liberalized in 1980–81. France and Italy, typically recording external deficits and experiencing capital outflows, did not abandon capital controls until the end of the decade. This difference in timing should not be exaggerated, but neither should it be overlooked, for it helps to clarify the way in which the pressures discussed above shaped the development of particular national policies.

Countries that sought to control capital inflows faced different incentives from those facing countries that sought to control capital outflows. The reason lies mainly in the asymmetric impact of capital movements on foreign exchange reserves. Current account deficits, capital outflows, weakening exchange rates, and depleting reserves often go together; when they do, governments must either adjust their policies or adopt controls before the loss of reserves is complete. In contrast, governments facing the obverse situation find it easier to abandon controls since their reserve position is not threatened. This asymmetry can be enhanced for deficit countries committed to maintaining a fixed exchange rate, as was the case for France and Italy in the context of the European Monetary System (EMS).

THE FOUR CASES

Germany

Development of Controls   In the early years of the Federal Republic, current account deficits and a dearth of foreign exchange reserves led to a strict prohibition on all exports of capital by residents. The legal basis for these controls was provided in the foreign exchange regulations of the Allied Occupation. By the early 1950s, however, West Germany's current account turned to surplus and the country's war-related external debts were finally settled. Restrictions on foreign direct investment abroad began to be liberalized in 1952, and residents were allowed to purchase foreign securities in 1956. By 1957 export of capital by residents was generally permitted without authorization. The relaxation of controls on outflows was effectively completed following restoration of currency convertibility in 1958, a policy stance legally enshrined in the Foreign Trade and Payments Act of 1961.

Owing largely to structural pressures on the deutsche mark in the Bretton Woods system of pegged exchange rates, however, this liberalization was not matched by similar progress on capital inflows. These pressures first emerged in the mid-1950s, when West Germany's low inflation rate and growing current account surplus increased the attractiveness of the mark relative to other currencies, notably the dollar. Under the Bretton Woods rules, the Bundesbank was required to enter the foreign exchange market and sell marks whenever the intervention point with the dollar was reached. But, of course, such obligatory purchases served to increase liquidity in the banking system and expand the money supply, thus creating inflation. Capital inflows therefore quickly came to be seen as significant threats to the Bundesbank's goal of maintaining price stability. Periodic expectations of revaluation and the resulting increase in speculative capital inflows dramatically underlined the dilemma.

In this situation, Germany essentially had two options as it struggled to maintain control over its domestic money supply. It could either revalue its currency or impose capital controls. Given the strong opposition of export interests to revaluation, transmitted in the subtle interplay between the government (which had responsibility for exchange rate policy) and the Bundesbank, the central bank's inclination tended in the latter direction. In June 1960, for example, the purchase of domestic money market paper by nonresidents was subjected to an authorization requirement. Simultaneously, a ban was imposed on interest payments on bank deposits held by nonresidents. These restrictions remained in place after the mark was revalued in 1961 and were not removed until the second revaluation in October 1969. Controls were reintroduced, however, when pressure once again mounted against the mark in 1971. The following year, the Bundesbank required 40 percent of all loans raised abroad to be placed in non-interest-bearing accounts. It also extended authorization requirements to the purchase of domestic bonds by nonresidents. Capital nevertheless continued to pour into Germany and ultimately necessitated two revaluations. Faced with massive speculative pressures in early 1973, the mark was finally allowed to float.

The transition to floating initially eased many of the pressures on the currency; the Bundesbank therefore began loosening some of its earlier restrictions but not dismantling its control apparatus altogether. Indeed, when confidence in the dollar began to decline in 1977, the Bundesbank again tightened existing capital controls and raised minimum reserve requirements on nonresidents' bank deposits to prevent what it considered an excessive appreciation of the mark. These measures were eased somewhat in 1978, when a shift in U.S. economic policy reduced inflows from abroad.

In the wake of the second oil shock, the German current account moved sharply into an uncharacteristic deficit position. A surplus of DM 17.5 billion in 1978 became a deficit of DM 10.5 billion in 1979. Capital inflows suddenly dried up; indeed, capital began exiting the country. The value of the mark slid, and the Bundesbank was forced to finance the deficit first by borrowing and then by dipping into its reserves, which fell by DM 8 billion in 1980 alone. Faced with the novel need to attract rather than ward off capital, the Bundesbank lifted remaining controls on capital flows in 1981.

Reasons for Liberalization   The sudden lifting of controls in 1981 was certainly triggered by a shift in Germany's external accounts. What is striking, however, is that the Bundesbank did not consider it necessary to reimpose capital controls when the current account returned to surplus in 1982 or when the mark once again began to appreciate after the Plaza Agreement in 1985. The reasons for this policy turnaround are several.

Official views on the deutsche mark clearly underwent a dramatic change in the early 1980s. Throughout the 1960s and 1970s, the Bundesbank had, in effect, sought to prevent the mark from becoming a reserve currency largely to protect its ability to conduct an autonomous monetary policy and to deflect pressures for revaluation. Yet by 1983 the Bundesbank had reluctantly accepted the mark's increasing role in the world economy. Financial openness was seen to promise benefits. . . .

The rapid transformation in the Bundesbank's perspective reflected the changing interests of German banks. By the early 1980s, the large West German banks had become extensively involved in external markets. Their international assets (loans), for example, rose from $6.7 billion in 1973 to $73.3 billion in 1980 and $191 billion in 1985. With such rapidly rising international assets subject to world interest rates, banks became concerned about retaining a similar flexibility on the deposit side. In other words, changes on one side of bank balance sheets required similar changes on the other. Henceforth, the ability of German banks to compete abroad would depend increasingly upon the free movement of capital.

Deregulatory developments in Britain deepened such concerns; so too did policy changes further afield. In 1984, for example, the United States and Japan concluded a bilateral agreement aimed at facilitating the access of American financial firms to the Tokyo markets. West German banks feared that this agreement would forever lock them out of Japan unless their government stopped waiting for multi-lateral liberalization and began to negotiate a similar bilateral deal. The reciprocity provision built into the subsequent German-Japanese discussions of the management of securities issues in one another's markets underlined the new complexities that would have to be addressed if a unilateral movement toward closure were ever again contemplated.

More subtle pressures on official policies also emanated from changing corporate strategies. In the 1970s and 1980s German companies became increasingly multinational and directed larger volumes of their investment overseas. Reflecting this evolution, German foreign direct investment in foreign market rose from DM 3.2 billion in 1970 to DM 7.6 billion in 1980 and DM 14.1 billion in 1985. The growing internationalization of German business strengthened resistance to the reimposition of capital controls.

In the same vein, financial institutions, which had adapted well to the restrictiveness of the German capital market in the early years of the Federal Republic, gradually became willing to threaten the exit option. The decision, for example, by the Deutsche Bank to buy 5 percent of Morgan Grenfell and move its international capital market operations to London provided the West German authorities with a clear signal that something had to be done to prevent international business from gravitating away from Frankfurt to London. The Deutsche Bank, after all, was not just any bank. It dominated the German capital market, led nearly half of all new mark-denominated Eurobond issues, underwrote 90 percent of new West German equity issues, and accounted for nearly one-quarter of all trading in German securities. More generally, since the strength of the major German banks had long been viewed by policymakers as critical to the health of the country's leading industries—for which they served as lenders, shareholders, and advisers—the liberalization of their domestic base quickly became an important goal of policy. The subsequent renewal of integration efforts in the European Community, including adoption of the 1992 program and initial planning for monetary union, accelerated policy efforts to expand "Finanzplatz Deutschland."

By the opening of the 1990s, the desire to see Frankfurt more deeply integrated into global financial markets had overwhelmed residual concerns about the implications of capital decontrol. The perennial issue of enhancing the competitiveness of German industry would be advanced by other means, including the expansion of production facilities outside the Federal Republic. The massive financial challenges posed by unification only reinforced the policy movement away from controls. The inflows that had proved so problematic in earlier decades were now deliberately encouraged.

Japan

Development of Controls   As in Germany, the priority of economic reconstruction in Japan during the immediate years after World War II entailed tight official controls over both inflows and outflows of short-term capital. The policy was put into place during the early days of the occupation and eventually drew its legal justification from the Foreign Exchange and Foreign Trade Control Law of 1949. In principle, all cross-border flows were forbidden unless specifically authorized by administrative decree. Only in the early 1960s did these arrangements begin to loosen, and then only for certain flows closely related to trade transactions. By 1964 this limited liberalization was enough to qualify Japan for Article VIII status in the IMF and for entry into the OECD.

Notwithstanding the first tentative moves toward financial openness, much publicized at the time, an extremely tight regime of controls over most capital movements remained. To be sure, certain inflows of hard currency, mainly U.S. dollars in the form of portfolio investment and foreign currency loans from American banks, were welcomed, but outflows and direct investment inflows were rigorously discouraged. The rationale for this policy stance was obvious. Even twenty years after the war, the country had no foreign currency reserves and was pursuing an ambitious strategy of indigenous industrial development. In effect, the policy amounted to husbanding and rationing scarce national resources. With an export-oriented economic growth strategy in place, the direct beneficiaries of the policy were leading industries selling their products in external markets. Financing was channeled to them mainly through highly regulated banks. Capital controls were key elements in a complex, but bureaucratically organized and directed financial system. In view of its own overarching foreign policy interests, the United States, the only possible challenger to this arrangement, willingly acquiesced.

A string of current account surpluses began to generate increasing volumes of reserves in the early 1970s, and corporate as well as official interest began to shift in the face of impending resource scarcities, domestic environmental problems, and the rise of trade barriers in several foreign markets. Restraints on capital outflows consequently started to loosen, but short-term capital inflows continued to be discouraged through a variety of measures. Strict new limitations, for example, were placed on new foreign currency loans. The goal was to counter the need for an upward revaluation of the yen and thereby to protect the competitiveness of the export sector.

With the international monetary crisis of 1971, the subsequent pressure on the yen, and the first oil shock in 1973, the policy environment turned upside down. For three years, Japan registered deficits in its current account. Controls were quickly eased on short-term inflows and tightened on outflows, particularly those occurring through the overseas networks of Japanese banks. When the situation improved in 1976, and current account surpluses returned, the controls on outflows gradually came off again, but several new controls on short-term inflows were put in place for the familiar purpose of countering upward pressure on the yen. In 1979 a second oil price shock reversed the current account balance, this time for two years. But new controls on outflows were now surprisingly limited. By then, Japanese money markets had become more deeply integrated with international markets, and stabilizing inflows more than matched outflows. Instead of being concerned that the new crisis would hurt the value of their investments in Japan, international investors, including OPEC governments, now focused on the underlying strength of the economy, and funds poured into the country.

Reasons for Liberalization   Having contributed to tensions in its economic relations with the United States and Western Europe in the early 1970s and again in 1976, exchange rate issues were in the background in 1979 when the Ministry of Finance announced its intention to initiate a major liberalization program to cover inward as well as outward capital movements. The relative ease with which the economy was adjusting to the second oil crisis provided a permissive policy context for this shift. In 1980 it was codified in a new Foreign Exchange and Foreign Trade Control Law, which replaced the concept of capital flow interdiction with the concept of automaticity-in-principle.

It is no coincidence that such a regime was put into place at a time when remarkable changes were under way in the international direct investment strategies of Japanese firms. After decades of slight involvement abroad, Japanese FDI went into a period of explosive growth. Comparable to volumes recorded throughout the late 1960s and early 1970s, net long-term capital movements from Japan totaled U.S. $3.1 billion in 1977. In 1978 that number jumped to $12.4 billion, or 1.5 percent of Japan's GNP. By 1986 it had reached $132.1 billion, or 6.7 percent of GNP. In the face of these flows, and the options of evasion and exit that they implied for externally oriented Japanese firms, the control regime originally enshrined in law in 1949 had outlived its usefulness.

Although the new law did not limit the government's formal capacity to intervene in Japanese financial markets, in practice a policy of decontrol was aggressively pursued. The apparatus for controlling capital movements was dismantled, a policy reinforced by parallel moves to free up gradually the operations of both domestic and foreign financial intermediaries. Although external pressures from private markets and foreign governments may have hastened the overt pace of change in each area, it is worth noting that foreign financial interests were far from unanimous in welcoming this shift. Foreign banks long established in Japan, for example, benefited materially from the earlier regime.

It is clear, however, that well-positioned Japanese intermediaries had the most to gain from the deepening of domestic capital markets promised by the twin policies of decontrol and deregulation, while Japanese manufacturing and financial firms overseas benefited to the extent that such policies defended their positions in foreign markets. In the mid-1960s Japan's cross-border banking business was mainly related to trade flows, and the Bank of Tokyo, the officially designated international bank, accounted for most of the fifty Japanese branches abroad. Twenty years later all of the major banks, as well as many smaller intermediaries, maintained physical networks overseas, comprising over two hundred branches and subsidiaries and three hundred representative offices. Japanese securities companies and insurance vendors followed the banks in major international expansions. Japanese intermediaries and some of their foreign rivals formed the institutional infrastructure for Euro-yen markets, whose development received a boost from the so-called yen-dollar negotiations that the United States and Japan concluded in 1984. Thereafter, it would become much more difficult to prevent the yen from evolving into a major international reserve currency.

By the early 1980s Japan was on the way to becoming the world's largest creditor. In practical terms, this meant that Japanese financial institutions began to play an increasingly important role in overseas capital markets—a development that expanded the range of arbitrage (or "exit") opportunities for Japanese investors and borrowers and complicated the problem of economic management for the Japanese government. After Sumitomo Bank purchased a majority interest in the Swiss universal bank Banco del Gottardo, for example, it became exceptionally difficult for the Ministry of Finance to keep the Eurobond market separate from the Japanese domestic market, since major Sumitomo clients could henceforth raise funds more easily in either market.

The private pressure for increased openness thereby generated was matched during much of the 1980s by the effects of rising public sector indebtedness, which further encouraged the deepening of domestic debt markets. Even without the added pressure coming from foreign governmental demands for decontrol, by 1990 high volumes of inward as well as outward capital flows translated into a broadening domestic political base for progressive financial liberalization and capital decontrol. Although countervailing domestic pressures emerged as inward flows pushed up the exchange value of the yen, the authorities now attempted to manage them more generally through the medium of interest rates and more directly through selective policies of compensation.

At the firm level, foreign direct investment was an obvious and increasingly used method for coping with a rising yen. Indeed, such a consideration has been widely cited as an explanation for the rapid pace of growth in Japanese FDI in the 1980s. From a base of U.S. $2.4 billion in 1980, direct investment outflows from Japan increased to $6 billion in 1984, $14.4 billion in 1986, and $34.1 billion in 1988. During the latter years of the 1980s, Japanese FDI grew at an average rate of 35.5 percent per year. For Japanese companies, the progressive internationalization of their production facilities was matched by the increasing global diversification of their financing. In 1975 they raised ¥2.8 billion on domestic capital markets and ¥.5 billion on overseas markets. In 1989 the comparable figures were ¥17.2 billion on domestic markets and ¥11.1 billion overseas.

Despite extreme financial turbulence in the 1990s, including a collapse in stock and real estate prices and an associated pullback of Japanese financial intermediaries from foreign markets, few observers expected a movement back to capital controls. The internationalization of Japanese business and the international integration of Japanese financial markets had proceeded far enough to make such an option much less feasible than it had been even a decade earlier. For leading Japanese firms, in particular, strategies of evasion and exit were now embedded in their very structures. That reality gave them significant new leverage over Japan's capital policies.

France

Development of Controls   Controls on foreign exchange transactions in France, although first introduced in 1915, became firmly established only after the Second World War. Like most other European countries, France initially used capital controls to ensure that its limited foreign exchange be used for domestic reconstruction and development. In later years, controls on capital outflows were kept in place because of persistent current account deficits. In these circumstances, controls were deemed necessary to insulate domestic interest rates from world markets. In 1966 a new law gave the government the right to control all foreign exchange transactions between France and the rest of the world, oversee the liquidation of foreign funds in France and French funds abroad, and prescribe conditions for the repatriation of all income earned abroad.

These new controls on capital movements added to France's already impressive array of administrative measures designed to direct the flow of savings and investment. The Treasury, for example, channeled funds directly from the government budget to industry. It also controlled the country's parapublic banks—such as the Banque Française du Commerce Extérieur and the Crédit National—which had been created to provide favored sectors with access to credit at subsidized rates. And finally, it guided the trajectory of financial flows through its use of controls over domestic interest rates and bank lending (the famous *encadrement du crédit*).

The importance of both capital and credit controls increased with France's decision in 1979 to join the EMS. Although French authorities had never allowed the franc to float freely, the EMS fixed the value of the franc more rigidly. Yet between 1979 and 1984, no government, whether of the Right or the Left, was willing to raise interest rates high enough to maintain the value of the franc in the EMS. Capital controls enabled the government to keep interest rates lower than would otherwise have been required.

The use of capital controls intensified following the 1981 election of François Mitterrand, the first socialist president of the Fifth Republic. Mitterrand inherited a currency that had become substantially overvalued, and his government's commitment to fiscal expansion and income redistribution soon triggered a run on the franc. In the midst of this crisis, Mitterrand and his advisers refused to sacrifice the goal of exchange rate stability. . . . Nor was the government willing to sacrifice monetary autonomy; despite the fact that France's major trading partners were in recession, the government continued with its plans to stimulate the economy. With these options ruled out, the government therefore tightened controls on the foreign exchange positions of French companies, on the overseas accounts of individuals, and on borrowing by nonresidents in France.

These controls provided the government with some breathing space, but the combination of growth at home and recession abroad soon caused France's trade and current accounts to fall deeply into the red. Even with more restrictive capital controls and tighter credit ceilings, however, the socialist government was unable to eliminate pressure against the franc and was therefore forced to devalue on three occasions during its first two years in office. In the aftermath of the third devaluation, the government decided to reverse course and replace its earlier expansion plans with deflationary monetary and fiscal policies. In addition, it adopted draconian capital controls: foreign equities and bonds could only be traded by French citizens among themselves. Importers faced strict limits on their ability to cover their foreign exchange risk, while exporters were forced to repatriate foreign-currency earnings almost immediately. French nationals could only keep a foreign bank account while they resided abroad. French tourists could take only a small amount of foreign exchange outside the country and were deprived of the use of their credit cards.

For the socialists as for their conservative predecessors, heavy reliance on capital controls thus resulted primarily from a desire to keep domestic interest rates lower than those generally prevailing in the rest of the world without abandoning the objective of exchange rate stability. Lower interest rates reduced demand for franc-denominated assets and stimulated domestic demand for imports. Together, these two effects increased net capital outflows and placed pressure on the franc. To avoid a precipitous decline of the franc (even if France left the EMS), tighter capital controls were deemed necessary. As the socialist government discovered, however, such controls had to be continuously tightened if they were to be effective. The controls of 1983 placed the French economy in the tightest corset since World War II.

Reasons for Liberalization   In November 1984 Prime Minister Laurent Fabius announced a dramatic new plan to reform the entire financial system. The government planned not only to eliminate credit ceilings and capital controls, but also to create new money, bond, and futures markets. Such wholesale reform had not been expected. Unlike France's decision to remain in the EMS, pressure from its EC partners was not part of the policy calculation; indeed, the announcement of its financial reform package *preceded* the commission's June 1985 white paper on European financial integration. . . .

What drove this new program of financial liberalization? Evasion strategies on the part of individuals and firms were certainly in the background; the famous stories about suitcases filled with foreign currency being carried into Switzerland come to mind. More subtle and ultimately more decisive pressures emanated, however, from the boardrooms of large French firms and financial intermediaries. In the French case, direct threats of exit were muted by the fact that virtually all of these firms were owned or controlled by the state. In this environment, such an option was transmuted into the rising concerns of government officials regarding the competitiveness of those firms relative to their foreign rivals. Jobs and investment that were promised by growth in the service sector, for example, were seen to be leaving France and migrating to less-restricted markets. In a very real sense, especially in financial services, Paris was increasingly seen to be in direct competition with London and Frankfurt. . . .

By 1984 the situation had become severe, and French policymakers recognized the pressing need to change course. When international capital markets were rapidly developing elsewhere, the competitiveness of both French industry and finance was now seen to be seriously undermined by capital controls. In 1985 the elimination of credit ceilings began, and new money, bond, and futures markets were created. The phaseout of capital controls followed, with major steps taking place in 1986 and 1989; in January 1990 controls disappeared completely with the lifting of the ban on the holding of foreign deposits by French nationals.

The shift in favor of capital mobility eventually tied in directly with plans for European Monetary Union (EMU), and France became a key promoter of the idea. The freedom of capital movements across the member states of the prospective union, indeed, was a prerequisite. But the planning for EMU followed the new commitment to restore and enhance the competitiveness of French industrial firms and financial intermediaries. The Delors Committee report on EMU came in 1988, three years after decontrol became the thrust of financial policy within France. That policy remained consistent despite the election of a conservative government in 1986 and the return of the socialists in 1988. In effect, as international financial integration outside France accelerated, French policymakers came to the conclusion that their preference for national monetary autonomy was unrealistic. The decision to initiate capital decontrol followed and accelerated as the country's external accounts improved.

Italy

Development of Controls   Restrictions on capital movements were initially put in place in Italy during the First World War. They were refined and tightened by Mussolini during the following two decades. Controls were relaxed in the late 1950s, a period of current account surpluses and currency stability. The "hot autumn" of 1969, however, dramatically altered Italy's economic trajectory. Facing increased labor militancy, the government put into place an expansionary fiscal policy to spur growth and ensure social peace. By 1973 this policy resulted in fiscal imbalances and current account deficits. The lira soon came under speculative attack. Rather than reverse its economic policy and risk unrest, the government responded by tightening capital controls.

Italian economic policy after the 1973 oil shock followed a classic stop-and-go cycle that made capital controls even more necessary. The oil shock caught Italy in a difficult position—with both a booming economy and a significant current account deficit. With the backing of the IMF, macroeconomic policy shifted to a decidedly more restrictive course in 1974, and by 1975 the Italian economy had fallen into its deepest recession since the 1950s. A shift to easier monetary and fiscal policy in early 1975, however, brought an exceptionally rapid recovery. Booming imports created downward pressure on the lira, and fears of a communist electoral victory accelerated capital flight. Despite heavy intervention in the foreign exchange markets, which left Italy with only $500 million in reserves, the lira depreciated by 20 percent in the first four months of 1976.

The Italian authorities responded by tightening monetary policy, fiscal policy, and capital controls. The most draconian measures were embedded in Law 159 of 1976, which essentially decreed that every foreign exchange transaction was illegal unless specifically authorized. In particular, the law made it a criminal offense either to send or to hold more than 5 million lire abroad without permission. Moreover, Italians owning residential property abroad were required to sell it and bring the proceeds back to Italy. A year later, these controls were eased somewhat after the communists were finally included in the governing majority, after the trade unions agreed to make wage concessions, and after a standby arrangement was negotiated with the IMF.

Still, government officials viewed capital controls as a means of avoiding hard choices. By the mid-1980s the annual budget deficit had topped 11 percent of GDP and cumulative debt approached 100 percent of GDP. To finance these deficits, the government had long relied on a large domestic savings pool. Household savings in Italy amounted to 20 percent of personal disposable income—the second highest savings rate in the world after Japan. Doing away with capital controls in the face of such deficits meant that domestic savers would be able to purchase foreign assets, forcing the government to offer a higher rate of interest on its own debt. . . .

Italy's decision to join the EMS in 1979 made matters even more difficult. With an economic policy more expansionary than that of its neighbors, exchange markets would not long find credible the country's commitment to maintain a fixed exchange rate. Here, too, capital controls were seen as a way of avoiding hard choices. Controls were eased and then reimposed each time the lira came under attack in exchange markets.

Reasons for Liberalization   The elimination of capital controls in Italy did not begin until 1987 and was not completed until 1992. Given the difficulties faced by Italian policymakers, the source of this policy change is particularly interesting. Of the major EC countries, Italy was the only one whose decision was affected by pressure from its partners, particularly Germany, to comply with the EC directive on capital movements. In July 1986, for example, the European Court of Justice ruled that Italy had to give up insisting that every Italian citizen who held securities abroad had to keep 25 percent of their value in a non-interest-bearing account with the central bank. (In this instance, the Italian government responded by reducing the deposit to 15 percent.)

Still, it would be a mistake to attribute Italy's policy shift primarily to such external pressure, for in Italy—as in Germany, Japan, and France—private pressure for liberalization had become pervasive. Evasion of capital controls, of course, was a national sport, practiced by business executives, government ministers, and even church officials.

More important for the shift in policy, however, was the increasingly assertive position taken by private firms. Financial institutions, for example, had become concerned about the effect of controls on their ability to compete. It was perhaps not surprising that foreign companies opposed capital controls. . . . Yet domestic institutions also believed they were being disadvantaged. . . .

Manufacturing firms, like Olivetti and Fiat, also favored an end to controls. As the power of organized labor diminished in the 1980s, these firms became more profitable and competitive in foreign markets. They were therefore also more directly hampered by restrictions on capital movements and concerned about the prospect of not being able to take full advantage of the expanding EC market. Moreover, throughout the 1980s, many corporate groups—including Fiat, Montedison, and Ferruzi—had entered the financial sector, both individually and in concert with Italian banks. With diversification, these corporations developed new interest in the further development of domestic capital markets, as well as the extension of access to external markets. Capital controls impeded this prospect. So too did the never-ending rise in public borrowing. Accordingly, corporate leaders pushed for the elimination of controls in the hope of forcing greater discipline upon the government. In 1987, in a political environment significantly reshaped by changing corporate structures and preferences, the Italian government began stripping away existing controls on capital movements—a move completed in 1992—and pushed through legislation limiting its own power to reimpose new controls during times of currency crisis.

CONCLUSION

In the early years of the postwar period, governments relied on controls over short-term capital movements for one fundamental purpose—to provide their economies with the maximum feasible degree of policy-making autonomy without sacrificing the benefits of economic interdependence. Controls were a shield that helped deflect the blows of international competition and ameliorate its domestic political effects. In the Bretton Woods system of pegged exchange rates, controls promised to provide both the space needed for the design of distinct national economic policies and the time needed for gradual economic adjustment to a changing external environment. To the surprise of some, they remained essential for many governments even when that system was replaced by managed floating.

Between the late 1970s and the early 1990s, a broad movement away from capital controls was evident across the industrialized world. The rapid growth of liquid international funds and the increasing globalization of production drove this process. Offshore markets eroded national financial barriers, not least by providing ever-widening sources of funding for multinational firms engaged in the process of globalizing their production facilities. In so doing, they enhanced the capability of firms to develop evasion and exit strategies. Governments thus first found that controls had to be tightened continuously to remain useful and then discovered that the resulting or potential economic costs of such tightening soon exceeded the benefits.

To be sure, governments encouraged or at least acquiesced in both the growth of offshore money markets and the international expansion of firms. Yet as our case histories show, governments continued to impose capital controls long after such developments became salient. In this sense, the diminishing utility of capital controls can be considered the unintended consequence of other and earlier policy decisions.

Strategies of evasion and exit on the part of firms, we have argued, threatened to reduce the volume of domestic savings and investment, the promotion of which often constituted the original rationale for controls. Of course, firms could use direct methods for pushing the decontrol agenda, as we saw in the French case where state ownership was a significant factor. But their ultimate influence on policy came from the pressure to evade controls or exit from their national jurisdictions if they were to remain competitive. In the German case, for example, by making moves offshore, the Deutsche Bank effectively made the case that capital controls were inconsistent with the goal of building a strong national financial center.

Other factors have influenced the elimination of capital controls, but our cases suggest that such factors played a secondary role. The principle of international capital mobility, for example, had long been enshrined in the OECD Code on Capital Movements, but until the 1980s virtually every major signatory country had at some point honored that principle in the breach. Similarly, a common European capital market was a key objective of the 1992 program, but the success of this effort was preceded (and made possible) by national programs of capital decontrol in both France and Germany. Fundamental changes at the domestic level also underpinned the apparent success of direct political pressure by other governments. In the Japanese case, for example, American pressure appeared at most to reinforce firm-level pressures associated with the rapid expansion of Japanese financial intermediaries and companies in overseas markets.

Notwithstanding the general movement in the direction of capital liberalization across the advanced industrial world, our cases point to important differences in the timing of actual decisions to decontrol. It was easier for countries facing capital inflows (Japan and Germany) to lift capital controls, than it was for countries facing capital outflows (France and Italy). The difference in timing—roughly a decade—underlines the mechanism by which systemic forces were translated into national decisions. Our cases do not enable us to reach definitive conclusions in this regard, but it seems likely that these differences in timing are correlated with broader variations in domestic political structures. Whether a country is facing chronic capital inflows or outflows may depend upon the structure of the state and the relative strength of domestic interest groups. But the fundamental convergence in the direction of capital mobility noted in all of our cases suggests that systemic forces are now dominant in the financial area and have dramatically reduced the ability of governments to set autonomous economic policies.

Our argument and evidence do not suggest, however, that a movement back toward capital controls or analogous policies to influence the flow of capital is impossible, only that such a movement would be more costly from a national point of view. Indeed, the restoration of controls is not just a theoretical possibility. In the midst of the European currency crisis in September 1992, for example, Spain and Ireland imposed new controls on banks' foreign exchange transactions. Despite the fact that such "temporary" measures did not contravene the letter of a prior agreement to eliminate impediments to capital mobility throughout the European Community, they surely conflicted with its spirit. More generally, continuing instability in global currency markets did subsequently lead the G-7, at the urging of American treasury secretary Nicholas Brady, to commission a new study to explore multilateral approaches to dealing with the consequences of international capital mobility.

If our argument is correct, two theoretical as well as policy implications bear underlining. First, if pressures for capital decontrol are now deeply embedded in firm structure and strategy, any efforts to understand or deal with the political effects of short-term capital mobility would seem to entail dealing with the politics of foreign direct investment. The two issues have long been related, but have also long been viewed as distinguishable for conceptual as well as for policy purposes. The distinction has broken down. The adoption of policies to influence short-term capital flows would now have a clearer impact on long-term investment decisions. Further research on this deepening connection is warranted.

Second, if policy convergence on the issue of capital controls is intimately linked to the development of international financial markets, attempts to understand and manage the effects of short-term capital mobility cannot be divorced from efforts to enhance the cross-national coordination of financial policies. As the negotiators at Bretton Woods recognized in 1944, open and stable markets ultimately depend upon a modicum of shared behavioral norms. Despite deepening interdependence across contemporary financial markets, states retain the right to change their policies on capital movements, either individually or on a regional basis. What remains unclear is their obligation to take into account the consequences of such policies for other states and for the world community. Thus, the time may now be ripe to begin considering new international arrangements to define and demarcate national responsibilities in an age of global markets.

V

TRADE

The international trade regime constructed under American leadership after World War II and embodied in the General Agreement on Tariffs and Trade (GATT) has facilitated the emergence of the most open international economy in modern history. After World War II, political leaders in the United States and many other advanced industrialized countries believed, on the basis of their experience during the Great Depression of the 1930s, that protectionism contributes to depressions, depressions magnify political instability, and instability leads to war. Drawing upon these beliefs, the United States led the postwar fight for a new trade regime based upon the liberal principle of comparative advantage. Tariffs were to be lowered, and each country would specialize in those goods that it produced best, trading for the products of other countries as appropriate. To the extent that this goal was achieved, American decision makers and others believed that all countries would be better off and prosperity would be reinforced.

The American vision for the postwar trade regime was embodied in a plan for an International Trade Organization (ITO) to complement the International Monetary Fund. As originally presented in 1945, the American plan offered rules for all aspects of international trade relations. The Havana Charter, which created the ITO, was finally completed in 1947. A product of many international compromises, the Havana Charter was the subject of considerable domestic opposition within the United States. Republican protectionists opposed the treaty because it went too far in the direction of free trade, while free-trade groups failed to support it because it did not go far enough. President Harry Truman, knowing that it faced almost certain defeat, never submitted the Havana Charter to Congress for ratification. In the absence of American support, the nascent ITO died a quick and quiet death. The GATT was drawn up in 1947 to provide a basis for the trade negotiations then under way in Geneva. Intended merely as a temporary agreement to last only until the Havana Charter was fully implemented, the GATT became the principal basis for the international trade regime with the failure of the ITO.

Despite its supposedly temporary origins, the GATT has emerged as the most important international institution in the trade area. Trade negotiations within the GATT proceed in "rounds," typically initiated by new grants of negotiating authority delegated from the United States Congress to the President. Since 1947, there have been eight rounds of negotiations, each resulting in a new treaty subsequently ratified by member states under their individual constitutional provisions.

The GATT is based on four norms. First, all members agree to extend unconditional most-favored-nation (MFN) status to one another. Under this agreement, no country receives any preferential treatment not accorded to all other MFN countries. Additionally, any benefits acquired by one country are automatically extended to all MFN partners. The only exceptions to this rule are customs unions, such as the European Union.

Second, the GATT is based upon the norm of reciprocity, or the concept that any country that benefits from another's tariff reduction should reciprocate to an equivalent extent. This norm ensures fair and equitable tariff reductions by all countries. In conjunction with the MFN, or nondiscrimination, norm, it also serves to reinforce the downward spiral of tariffs initiated by the actions of any one country.

Third, "safeguards," or loopholes and exceptions to other norms, are recognized as acceptable if they are temporary and imposed for short-term balance-of-payments reasons. Exceptions are also allowed for countries experiencing severe market disruptions from increased imports.

Fourth, in 1965, a development norm was added to the GATT that allowed (1) generalized systems of preferences (or unilateral and unreciprocated tariff reductions by developed countries on imports from their developing counterparts), (2) additional safeguards for development purposes, and (3) export subsidies by developing countries.

The GATT has been extremely successful in obtaining its declared goal of freer trade and lower tariffs. By the end of the Kennedy Round of GATT negotiations in 1967, which was initiated by President John F. Kennedy in 1962, tariffs on dutiable nonagricultural items had declined to approximately 10 percent in the advanced industrialized countries. In the Tokyo Round, concluded in 1979, tariffs in these same countries were reduced to approximately 5 percent. These significant reductions initiated an era of unprecedented growth in international trade that continues today. The two most rapidly growing areas are the overlapping ones of trade between advanced industrialized countries and intrafirm trade (the exchange of goods within, rather than between, corporations).

The GATT remains an active force for liberalization. In the late 1980s and early 1990s, the Uruguay Round focused on the thorny issues of services and agricultural trade—two areas that had been excluded from earlier negotiations. Governments have long regulated many of their domestic service industries, such as insurance, banking, and financial services. Often differing dramatically from country to country, these regulations are among the most politically contentious barriers to trade. Likewise, governments in most developed countries subsidize their agricultural sectors, which leads to reduced imports and creates surpluses that can only be managed through substantial sales abroad. Nearly all analysts agree that national and global welfare could be enhanced by reducing agricultural subsidies and returning to trade based on the principle of comparative advantage; yet, as the prolonged negotiations of the Uruguay Round demonstrated, politicians have found it difficult to resist demands from farmers for continued government intervention. Here, as in other areas, the tension between national wealth and the self-seeking demands of domestic interest groups have created a difficult diplomatic issue—but one that, after years of comparative neglect, finally made it onto the GATT agenda. Concluded in late 1993, the Uruguay Round did make substantial progress toward liberalization on many fronts, including services and agricultural trade; the primary exception, from the American point of view, was entertainment products, such as films, which were excluded from the final agreement at the insistence of the European Union.

While tariffs have been declining and trade increasing, however, new threats to the free-trade regime have emerged. With the success of the GATT, more and more industries have been exposed to increased international competition. Industry demands for some form of protection have multiplied in nearly all countries. Increasingly, governments seek to satisfy these demands for protection through nontariff barriers to trade (NTBs). The most important of these NTBs are voluntary export restraints (VERs), in which exporters agree to restrain or limit their sales in the importer's market. Current estimates suggest that almost one-half of all manufactured goods imported into the United States enter under a VER or other NTB. Nor is the United States unique. Excluding the states of the former Communist bloc, which do not yet meet GATT standards in many other ways as well, nearly half of the world's trade is subject to some form of nonmarket control. While the GATT regime has not been destroyed, it has certainly become weaker and more fragile.

The readings in this section address the causes and implications of the recent trends in trade policy in the United States, but the analytic issues apply to other countries equally well. Cletus Coughlin, Alec Chrystal, and Geoffrey Wood (Reading 20) review the classic economic argument for free trade and survey explanations for protection. Several different theoretical perspectives are then presented. In an international political explanation, Robert Baldwin (Reading 21) relates the rise in protection to the decline of American hegemony. Combining domestic statist and societal explanations, Edward Ray (Reading 22) summarizes recent trends and explains the shift to NTBs as the result of increased group demands for protection filtered through a government that remains committed to free trade. Both are relatively pessimistic about the future of the liberal international trade regime. Helen Milner (Reading 23) and Judith Goldstein (Reading 24), in contrast, are comparatively optimistic about the future, but for very different reasons. Synthesizing domestic societal and international economic explanations, Milner explains the absence of even greater protectionism in the United States and France after the decline of American hegemony by the growth of international interdependence among key industrial sectors. Goldstein, in turn, offers a domestic statist explanation of America's continued commitment to relative free trade that focuses on the importance of ideas that become embedded in government institutions. Finally, Robert Lawrence (Reading 25) surveys recent trends toward regional trade agreements and their implications for the future of the international economy.

20

Protectionist Trade Policies:
A Survey of Theory,
Evidence, and Rationale

CLETUS C. COUGHLIN, K. ALEC CHRYSTAL, and GEOFFREY E. WOOD

In this selection, three economists review traditional arguments in favor of free trade in light of new theories and evidence. Beginning with an exposition of the principle of comparative advantage, Cletus Coughlin, Alec Chrystal, and Geoffrey Wood examine modern forms of protection, the costs of trade protection in the United States and the world, and contemporary arguments for restricting trade. They conclude that free trade remains the optimal policy for all countries. To explain why countries nonetheless adopt protection, they emphasize societal theories focusing on the distributional effects of trade policy and on the incentives for specific groups to seek governmentally imposed trade restrictions.

Protectionist pressures have been mounting worldwide during the 1980s. These pressures are due to various economic problems including the large and persistent balance of trade deficit in the United States, the hard times experienced by several industries, and the slow growth of many foreign countries. Proponents of protectionist trade policies argue that international trade has contributed substantially to these problems and that protectionist trade policies will lead to improved results. Professional economists in the United States, however, generally agree that trade restrictions such as tariffs and quotas substantially reduce a nation's economic well-being.

This article surveys the theory, evidence and rationale concerning protectionist trade policies. The first section illustrates the gains from free trade using the concept of comparative advantage. Recent developments in international trade theory that emphasize other reasons for gains from trade are also reviewed. The theoretical discussion is followed by an examination of recent empirical studies that demonstrate the large costs of protectionist trade policies. Then, the rationale for restricting trade is presented. The concluding section summarizes the paper's main arguments.

THE GAINS FROM FREE TRADE

The most famous demonstration of the gains from trade appeared in 1817 in David Ricardo's *Principles of Political Economy and Taxation*. We use his example involving trade between England and Portugal to demonstrate how both countries can gain from trade. The two countries produce the same two goods, wine and cloth, and the only production costs are labor costs. The figures below list the amount of labor (e.g., worker-days) required in each country to produce one bottle of wine or one bolt of cloth.

	Wine	Cloth
England	3	7
Portugal	1	5

Since both goods are more costly to produce in England than in Portugal, England is absolutely less efficient at producing both goods than its prospective trading partner. Portugal has an absolute advantage in both wine and cloth. At first glance, this appears to rule out mutual gains from trade; however, as we demonstrate below, absolute advantage is irrelevant in discerning whether trade can benefit both countries.

The ratio of the production costs for the two goods is different in the two countries. In England, a bottle of wine will exchange for 3/7 of a bolt of cloth because the labor content of the wine is 3/7 of that for cloth. In Portugal, a bottle of wine will exchange for 1/5 of a bolt of cloth. Thus, wine is relatively cheaper in Portugal than in England and, conversely, cloth is relatively cheaper in England than in Portugal. The example indicates that Portugal has a comparative advantage in wine production and England has a comparative advantage in cloth production.

The different relative prices provide the basis for both countries to gain from international trade. The gains arise from both exchange and specialization.

The gains from *exchange* can be highlighted in the following manner. If a Portuguese wine producer sells five bottles of wine at home, he receives one bolt of cloth. If he trades in England, he receives more than two bolts of cloth. Hence, he can gain by exporting his wine to England. English cloth producers are willing to trade in Portugal; for every 3/7 of a bolt of cloth they sell there, they get just over two bottles of wine. The English gain from exporting cloth to (and importing wine from) Portugal, and the Portuguese gain from exporting wine to (and importing cloth from) England. Each country gains by exporting the good in which it has a comparative advantage and by importing the good in which it has a comparative disadvantage.

Gains from *specialization* can be demonstrated in the following manner. Initially, each country is producing some of both goods. Suppose that, as a result of trade, 21 units of labor are shifted from wine to cloth production in England, while, in Portugal, 10 units of labor are shifted from cloth to wine production. This reallocation of labor does not alter the total amount of labor used in the two countries; however, it causes the production changes listed below.

	Bottles of wine	Bolts of cloth
England	− 7	+ 3
Portugal	+10	− 2
Net	+ 3	+ 1

The shift of 21 units of labor to the English cloth industry raises cloth production by three bolts, while reducing wine production by seven bottles. In Portugal, the shift of 10 units of labor from cloth to wine raises wine production by 10 bottles, while reducing cloth production by two bolts. This reallocation of labor increases the total production of both goods: wine by three bottles and cloth by one bolt. This increased output will be shared by the two countries. Thus, the consumption of both goods and the wealth of both countries are increased by the specialization brought about by trade based on comparative advantage.

TRADE THEORY SINCE RICARDO

Since 1817, numerous analyses have generated insights concerning the gains from trade. They chiefly examine the consequences of relaxing the assumptions used in the preceding example. For example, labor was the only resource used to produce the two goods in the example above; yet, labor is really only one of many resources used to produce goods. The example also assumed that the costs of producing additional units of the goods are constant. For example, in England, three units of labor are used to produce one bottle of wine regardless of the level of wine production. In reality, unit production costs could either increase or decrease as more is produced. A third assumption was that the goods are produced in perfectly competitive markets. In other words, an individual firm has no effect on the price of the good that it produces. Some industries, however, are dominated by a small number of firms, each of which can affect the market price of the good by altering its production decision. . . .

These theoretical developments generally have strengthened the case for an open trading system. They suggest three sources of gains from trade. First, as the market potentially served by firms expands from a national to a world market, there are gains associated with declining per unit production costs. A second source of gains results from the reduction in the monopoly power of domestic firms. Domestic firms, facing more pressure from foreign competitors, are forced to produce the output demanded by consumers at the lowest possible cost. Third is the gain to consumers from increased product variety and lower prices. Generally speaking, the gains from trade result from the increase in competitive pressures as the domestic economy becomes less insulated from the world economy.

FORMS OF PROTECTIONISM

Protection may be implemented in numerous ways. All forms of protection are intended to improve the position of a domestic relative to foreign producer. This can be done by policies that increase the home market price of the foreign product, decrease the costs of domestic producers or restrict the access of foreign producers to the home market in some other way.

Tariffs

Tariffs, which are simply taxes imposed on goods entering a country from abroad, result in higher prices and have been the most common form of protection for domestic producers. Tariffs have been popular with governments because it appears that the tax is being paid by the foreigner who wishes to sell his goods in the home economy and because the tariff revenue can be used to finance government services or reduce other taxes.

In the 20th century, U.S. tariff rates peaked as a result of the Smoot-Hawley Tariff of 1930. For example, in 1932, tariff revenue as a percentage of total imports was 19.6 percent. An identical calculation for 1985 yields a figure of 3.8 percent. The decline was due primarily to two reasons. First, since many of the tariffs under Smoot-Hawley were set as specific dollar amounts, the rising price level in the United States eroded the effective tariff rate. Second, since World War II, numerous tariff reductions have been negotiated under the General Agreement on Tariffs and Trade.

On the other hand, various other forms of protection, frequently termed non-tariff barriers, have become increasingly important. A few of the more frequently used devices are discussed below.

Quotas

A quota seems like a sensible alternative to a tariff when the intention is to restrict foreign producers' access to the domestic market. Importers typically are limited to a maximum number of products that they can sell in the home market over specific periods. A quota, similar to a tariff, causes prices to increase in the home market. This induces domestic producers to increase production and consumers to reduce consumption. One difference between a tariff and a quota is that the tariff generates revenue for the government, while the quota generates a revenue gain to the owner of import licenses. Consequently, foreign producers might capture some of this revenue.

In recent years, a slightly different version of quotas, called either orderly marketing agreements or voluntary export restraints, has been used. In an orderly marketing agreement, the domestic government asks the foreign government to restrict the quantity of exports of a good to the domestic country. The request can be viewed as a demand, like the U.S.-Japan automobile agreement in the 1980s, because the domestic country makes it clear that more restrictive actions are likely unless the foreign government "voluntarily" complies. In effect, the orderly marketing agreement is a mutually agreed upon quota.

Regulatory Barriers

There are many other ways of restricting foreigners' access to domestic markets. . . . The 1983 *Tariff Schedules of the United States Annotated* consists of 792 pages, plus a 78-page appendix. Over 200 tariff rates pertain to watches and clocks. Simply ascertaining the appropriate tariff classification, which requires legal assistance and can be subject to differences of opinion, is a deterrent.

Product standards are another common regulatory barrier. These standards appear in various forms and are used for many purposes. The standards can be used to service the public interest by ensuring that imported food products are processed according to acceptable sanitary standards and that drugs have been screened before their introduction in the United States. In other cases, the standards, sometimes intentionally, protect domestic producers. An example of unintended restrictions may be the imposition of safety or pollution standards that were not previously being met by foreign cars.

Subsidies

An alternative to restricting the terms under which foreigners can compete in the home market is to subsidize domestic producers. Subsidies may be focused upon an industry in general or upon the export activities of the industry. An example of the former . . . is the combination of credit programs, special tax incentives and direct subsidy payments that benefit the U.S. shipbuilding industry. An example of the latter is the financial assistance to increase exports provided by the U.S. Export-Import Bank through direct loans, loan guarantees and insurance, and discount loans. In either case, production will expand.

An important difference between subsidies and tariffs involves the revenue implications for government. The former involves the government in paying out money, whereas tariffs generate income for the government. The effect on domestic production and welfare, however, can be the same under subsidies as under tariffs and quotas. In all cases, the protected industry is being subsidized by the rest of the economy.

Exchange Controls

All of the above relate directly to the flow of goods. A final class of restrictions works by restricting access to the foreign money required to buy foreign goods. For example, a government that wishes to protect its exporting and import competing industries may try to hold its exchange rate artificially low. As a result, foreign goods would appear expensive in the home market while home goods would be cheap overseas. Home producers implicitly are subsidized and home consumers implicitly are taxed. This policy is normally hard to sustain. The central bank, in holding the exchange rate down, has to buy foreign exchange with domestic currency. This newly issued domestic currency increases the domestic money stock and eventually causes inflation. Inflationary policies are not normally regarded as a sensible way of protecting domestic industry.

There is another aspect to exchange controls. The justification is that preventing home residents from investing overseas benefits domestic growth as it leads to greater domestic real investment. In reality, it could do exactly the opposite. Restricting access to foreign assets may raise the variance and lower the return to owners of domestic wealth. In the short run, it also may appreciate the domestic exchange rate and, thereby, make domestic producers less competitive.

COSTS OF TRADE PROTECTIONISM

The specific goal of protectionist trade policies is to expand domestic production in the protected industries, benefiting the owners, workers and suppliers of resources to the protected industry. The government imposing protectionist trade policies may also benefit, for example, in the form of tariff revenue.

The expansion of domestic production in protected industries is not costless; it requires additional resources from other industries. Consequently, output in other domestic industries is reduced. These industries also might be made less competitive because of higher prices for imported inputs. Since protectionist policies frequently increase the price of the protected good, domestic consumers are harmed. They lose in two ways. First, their consumption of the protected good is reduced because of the associated rise in its price. Second, they consume less of other goods, as their output declines and prices rise.

The preceding discussion highlights the domestic winners and losers due to protectionist trade policies. Domestic producers of the protected good and the government (if tariffs are imposed) gain; domestic consumers and other domestic producers lose. Foreign interests are also affected by trade restrictions. The protection of domestic producers will harm some foreign producers; oddly enough, other foreign producers may benefit. For example, if quotas are placed on imports, some foreign producers may receive higher prices for their exports to the protected market.

There have been numerous studies of the costs of protectionism. We begin by examining three recent studies of protectionism in the United States, then proceed to studies examining developed and, finally, developing countries.

Costs of Protectionism in the United States

Recent studies by Tarr and Morkre (1984), Hickok (1985) and Hufbauer et al. (1986) estimated the costs of protectionism in the United States. These studies use different estimation procedures, examine different protectionist policies and cover different time periods. Nonetheless, they provide consistent results.

Tarr and Morkre (1984) estimate annual costs to the U.S. economy of $12.7 billion (1983 dollars) from all tariffs and from quotas on automobiles, textiles, steel and sugar. Their cost estimate is a net measure in which the losses of consumers are offset partially by the gains of domestic producers and the U.S. government.

Estimates by Hickok (1985) indicate that trade restrictions on only three goods—clothing, sugar, and automobiles—caused increased consumer expenditures of $14 billion in 1984. Hickok also shows that low-income families are affected more than high-income families. The import restraints on clothing, sugar and automobiles are calculated to be equivalent to a 23 percent income tax surcharge (that is, an additional tax added to the normal income tax) for families with incomes less than $10,000 in 1984 and a 3 percent income tax surcharge for families with incomes exceeding $60,000.

Hufbauer et al. (1986) examined 31 cases in which trade volumes exceeded $100 million and the United States imposed protectionist trade restrictions. They generated estimates of the welfare consequences for each major group affected. [Their] figures indicate that annual consumer losses exceed $100 million in all but six of the cases. The largest losses, $27 billion per year, come from protecting the textile and apparel industry. There also are large consumer losses associated with protection in carbon steel ($6.8 billion), automobiles ($5.8 billion) and dairy products ($5.5 billion).

The purpose of protectionism is to protect jobs in specific industries. A useful approach to gain some perspective on consumer losses is to express these losses on a per-job-saved basis. In 18 of the 31 cases, the cost per-job-saved is $100,000 or more per year; the consumer losses per-job-saved in benzenoid chemicals, carbon steel (two separate periods), specialty steel, and bolts, nuts and screws exceeded $500,000 per year.

[This study] also reveals that domestic producers were the primary beneficiaries of protectionist policies; however, there are some noteworthy cases where foreign producers realized relatively large gains. For the U.S.-Japanese voluntary export agreement in automobiles, foreign producers gained 38 percent of what domestic consumers lost, while a similar computation for the latest phase of protection for carbon steel was 29 percent.

Finally, [the study] indicates that the efficiency losses are small in comparison to the total losses borne by consumers. These efficiency losses . . . result from the excess domestic production and the reduction in consumption caused by protectionist trade policies. In large cases such as textiles and apparel, petroleum, dairy products and the maritime industries, these losses equal or exceed $1 billion. It is likely that these estimates understate the actual costs because they do not capture the secondary effects that occur as production and consumption changes in one industry affect other industries. In addition, restrictive trade policies generate additional costs because of bureaucratic enforcement costs and efforts by the private sector to influence these policies for their own gain as well as simply comply with administrative regulations.

Costs of Protectionism throughout the World

In 1982, the Organization for Economic Cooperation and Development (OECD) began a project to analyze the costs and benefits of protectionist policies in manufacturing in OECD countries. The OECD (1985) highlighted a number of ways that protectionist policies have generated costs far in excess of benefits. Since protectionist policies increase prices, the report concludes that the attainment of sustained noninflationary growth is hindered by such price-increasing effects. Moreover, economic growth is potentially reduced if the uncertainty created by varying trade policies depresses investment.

. . . [The] OECD study stresses the fact that a reduction in imports via trade restrictions does not cause greater employment. A reduction in the value of imports results in a similar reduction in the value of exports. One rationale for this finding is that a reduction in the purchases of foreign goods reduces foreign incomes and, in turn, causes reduced foreign purchases of domestic goods.

While the reduction in imports increases employment in industries that produce products similar to the previously imported goods, the reduction in exports decreases employment in the export industries. In other words, while some jobs are saved, others are lost; however, this economic reality may not be obvious to businessmen, labor union leaders, politicians and others. . . . [The] jobs saved by protectionist legislation are more readily observed than the jobs lost due to protectionist legislation. In other words, the jobs that are protected in, say, the textile industry by U.S. import restrictions on foreign textiles are more readily apparent (and publicized) than the jobs in agriculture and high technology industries that do not materialize because of the import restrictions. These employment effects will net to approximately zero. . . .

ARGUMENTS FOR RESTRICTING TRADE

If protectionism is so costly, why is protectionism so pervasive? This section reviews the major arguments for restricting trade and provides explanations for the existence of protectionist trade policies.

National Defense

The national defense argument says that import barriers are necessary to ensure the capacity to produce crucial goods in a national emergency. While this argument is especially appealing for weapons during a war, there will likely be demands from other industries that deem themselves essential. For example, the footwear industry will demand protection because military personnel need combat boots.

The national defense argument ignores the possibility of purchases from friendly countries during the emergency. The possibilities of storage and depletion raise additional doubts about the general applicability of the argument. If crucial goods can be stored, for example, the least costly way to prepare for an emergency might be to buy the goods from foreigners at the low world price before an emergency and store them. If the crucial goods are depletable mineral resources, such as oil, then the restriction of oil imports before an emergency will cause a more rapid depletion of domestic reserves. Once again, stockpiling might be a far less costly alternative.

Income Redistribution

Since protectionist trade policies affect the distribution of income, a trade restriction might be defended on the grounds that it favors some disadvantaged group. It is unlikely, however, that trade policy is the best tool for dealing with the perceived evils of income inequality, because of its bluntness and adverse effects on the efficient allocation of resources. Attempting to equalize incomes directly by tax and transfer payments is likely less costly than using trade policy. In addition, as Hickok's (1985) study indicates, trade restrictions on many items increase rather than decrease income inequality.

Optimum Tariff Argument

The optimum tariff argument applies to situations in which a country has the economic power to alter world prices. This power exists because the country (or a group of countries acting in consort like the Organization of Petroleum Exporting Countries) is such a large producer or consumer of a good that a change in its production or consumption patterns influences world prices. For example, by imposing a tariff, the country can make foreign goods cheaper. Since a tariff reduces the demand for foreign goods, if the tariff-imposing country has some market power, the world price for the good will fall. The tariff-imposing country will gain because the price per unit of its imports will have decreased.

There are a number of obstacles that preclude the widespread application of this argument. Few countries possess the necessary market power and, when they do, only a small number of goods is covered. Secondly, in a world of shifting supply and demand, calculating the optimum tariff and adjusting the rate to changing situations is difficult. Finally, the possibility of foreign retaliation to an act of economic warfare is likely. Such retaliation could leave both countries worse off than they would have been in a free trade environment.

Balancing the Balance of Trade

Many countries enact protectionist trade policies in the hope of eliminating a balance of trade deficit or increasing a balance of trade surplus. The desire to increase a balance of trade surplus follows from the mercantilist view that larger trade surpluses are beneficial from a national perspective.

This argument is suspect on a number of grounds. First, there is nothing inherently undesirable about a trade deficit or desirable about a surplus. For example, faster economic growth in the United States than in the rest of the world would tend to cause a trade deficit. In this case, the trade deficit is a sign of a healthy economy. Second, protectionist policies that reduce imports will cause exports to decrease by a comparable amount. Hence, an attempt to increase exports permanently relative to imports will fail. It is doubtful that the trade deficit will be reduced even temporarily because import quantities do not decline quickly in response to the higher import prices and the revenues of foreign producers might rise.

Protection of Jobs—Public Choice

The protection of jobs argument is closely related to the balance of trade argument. Since a reduction in imports via trade restrictions will result in a similar reduction in exports, the overall employment effects, as found in the OECD (1985) study and many others, are negligible. While the *overall* effects are negligible, workers (and resource owners) in specific industries are affected differently.

A domestic industry faced with increased imports from its foreign competition is under pressure to reduce production and lower costs. Productive resources must move from this industry to other domestic industries. Workers must change jobs and, in some cases, relocate to other cities. Since this change is forced upon these workers, these workers bear real costs that they are likely to resist. A similar statement can be made about the owners of capital in the affected industry.

Workers and other resource owners will likely resist these changes by lobbying for trade restrictions. The previously cited studies on the costs of protectionism demonstrated that trade restrictions entail substantial real costs as well. These costs likely exceed the adjustment costs because the adjustment costs are one-time costs, while the costs of protectionism continue as long as trade restrictions are maintained.

An obvious question is why politicians supply the protectionist legislation demanded by workers and other resource owners. A branch of economics called public choice, which focuses on the interplay between individual preferences and political outcomes, provides an answer. The public choice literature views the politician as an individual who offers voters a bundle of governmentally supplied goods in order to vote in elections. Many argue that politicians gain by providing protectionist legislation. Even though the national economic costs exceed the benefits, the politician faces different costs and benefits.

Those harmed by a protectionist trade policy for a domestic industry, especially household consumers, will incur a small individual cost that is difficult to identify. For example, a consumer is unlikely to ponder how much extra a shirt costs because of protectionist legislation for the textiles and apparel industry.

Even though the aggregate effect is large, the harm to each consumer may be small. This small cost, of which an individual may not even be aware, and the costs of organizing consumers deter the formation of a lobby against the legislation.

On the other hand, workers and other resource owners are very concerned about protectionist legislation for their industry. Their benefits tend to be large individually and easy to identify. Their voting and campaign contributions assist politicians who support their positions and penalize those who do not. Thus, politicians are likely to respond to their demands for protectionist legislation.

Infant Industries

The preceding argument is couched in terms of protecting a domestic industry. A slightly different argument, the so-called infant industry case, is couched in terms of *promoting* a domestic industry. Suppose an industry, already established in other countries, is being established in a specific country. The country might not be able to realize its comparative advantage in this industry because of the existing cost and other advantages of foreign firms. Initially, owners of the fledgling firm must be willing to suffer losses until the firm develops its market and lowers its production costs to the level of its foreign rivals. In order to assist this entrant, tariff protection can be used to shield the firm from some foreign competition.

After this temporary period of protection, free trade should be restored; however, the removal of tariff protection frequently is resisted. As the industry develops, its political power to thwart opposing legislation also increases.

Another problem with the infant industry argument is that a tariff is not the best way to intervene. A production subsidy is superior to a tariff if the goal is to expand production. A subsidy will do this directly, while a tariff has the undesirable side effect of reducing consumption.

In many cases, intervention might not be appropriate at all. If the infant industry is a good candidate for being competitive internationally, borrowing from the private capital markets can finance the expansion. Investors are willing to absorb losses *temporarily* if the prospects for future profits are sufficiently good.

Spillover Effects

The justification for protecting an industry, infant or otherwise, frequently entails a suggestion that the industry generates spillover benefits for other industries or individuals for which the industry is not compensated. Despite patent laws, one common suggestion is that certain industries are not fully compensated for their research and development expenditures. This argument is frequently directed toward technologically progressive industries where some firms can capture the results of other firms' research and development simply by dismantling a product to see how it works.

The application of this argument, however, engenders a number of problems. Spillovers of knowledge are difficult to measure. Since spillovers are not market transactions, they do not leave an obvious trail to identify their beneficiaries. The lack of market transactions also complicates an assessment of the value of these spillovers. To determine the appropriate subsidy, one must be able to place a dollar value on the spillovers generated by a given research and development expenditure. Actually, the calculation requires much more than the already difficult task of reconstructing the past. It requires complex estimates of the spillovers' future worth as well. Since resources are moved from other industries to the targeted industry, the government must understand the functioning of the entire economy.

Finally, there are political problems. An aggressive application of this argument might lead to retaliation and a mutually destructive trade war. In addition, as interest groups compete for the governmental assistance, there is no guarantee that the right groups will be assisted or that they will use the assistance efficiently.

Strategic Trade Policy

Recently theoretical developments have identified cases in which so-called strategic trade policy is superior to free trade. As we discussed earlier, decreasing unit production costs and market structures that contain monopoly elements are common in industries involved in international trade. Market imperfections immediately suggest the potential benefits of governmental intervention. In the strategic trade policy argument, governmental policy can alter the terms of competition to favor domestic over foreign firms and shift the excess returns in monopolistic markets from foreign to domestic firms.

Krugman (1987) illustrates an example of the argument. Assume that there is only one firm in the United States, Boeing, and one multinational firm in Europe, Airbus, capable of producing a 150-seat passenger aircraft. Assume also that the aircraft is produced only for export, so that the returns to the firm can be identified with the national interest. This export market is profitable for either firm if it is the only producer; however, it is unprofitable for both firms to produce the plane. Finally, assume the following payoffs are associated with the four combinations of production: (1) if both Boeing and Airbus produce the aircraft, each firm loses $5 million; (2) if neither Boeing nor Airbus produces the aircraft, profits are zero; (3) if Boeing produces the aircraft and Airbus does not, Boeing profits by $100 million and Airbus has zero profits; and (4) if Airbus produces the aircraft and Boeing does not, Airbus profits by $100 million and Boeing has zero profits.

Which firm(s) will produce the aircraft? The example does not yield a unique outcome. A unique outcome can be generated if one firm, say Boeing, has a head start and begins production before Airbus. In this case, Boeing will reap profits of $100 million and will have deterred Airbus from entering the market because Airbus will lose $5 million if it enters after Boeing.

Strategic trade policy, however, suggests that judicious governmental intervention can alter the outcome. If the European governments agree to subsidize Airbus' production with $10 million no matter what Boeing does, then Airbus will produce the plane. Production by Airbus will yield more profits than not producing, no matter what Boeing does. At the same time, Boeing will be deterred from producing because it would lose money. Thus, Airbus will capture the entire market and reap profits of $110 million, $100 million of which can be viewed as a transfer of profits from the United States.

The criticisms of a strategic trade policy are similar to the criticisms against protecting a technologically progressive industry that generates spillover benefits. There are major informational problems in applying a strategic trade policy. The government must estimate the potential payoff of each course of action. Economic knowledge about the behavior of industries that have monopoly elements is limited. Firms may behave competitively or cooperatively and may compete by setting prices or output. The behavior of rival governments also must be anticipated. Foreign retaliation must be viewed as likely where substantial profits are at stake. In addition, many interest groups will compete for the governmental assistance. Though only a small number of sectors can be considered potentially strategic, many industries will make a case for assistance.

Reciprocity and the "Level Playing Field"

. . . U.S. trade policy discussions in recent years have frequently stressed the importance of "fair trade." The concept of fair trade, which is technically referred to as reciprocity, means different things to different people.

Under the General Agreement on Tariffs and Trade, negotiations to reduce trade barriers focus upon matching concessions. This form of reciprocity, known as first-difference reciprocity, attempts to reduce trade barriers by requiring a country to provide a tariff reduction of value comparable to one provided by the other country. In this case, reciprocity is defined in terms of matching changes.

Recent U.S. demands, exemplified by the Gephardt amendment to the current trade legislation, reveal an approach that is called full reciprocity. This approach seeks reciprocity in terms of the level of protection bilaterally and over a specific range of goods. Reciprocity requires equal access and this access can be determined by bilateral trade balances. A trade deficit with a trading partner is claimed to be *prima facie* evidence of unequal access. Examples abound. For example, U.S. construction firms have not had a major contract in Japan since 1965, while Japanese construction firms did $1.8 billion worth of business in the United States in 1985 alone. Recent legislation bars Japanese participation in U.S. public works projects until the Japanese offer reciprocal privileges.

As the name suggests, the fundamental argument for fair trade is one of equity. Domestic producers in a free trade country argue that foreign trade barriers are unfair because they place them at a competitive disadvantage. In an extreme version, it is asserted that this unfair competition will virtually eliminate U.S. manufacturing, leaving only jobs that consist primarily of flipping hamburgers at fast food restaurants or . . . rolling rice cakes at Japanese owned sushi bars. While domestic producers *are* relatively disadvantaged, the wisdom of a protectionist response is doubtful. Again, the costs of protectionism exceed substantially the benefits from a national perspective.

In an attempt to reinforce the argument for fair trade, proponents also argue that retaliatory threats, combined with changes in tariffs and non-tariff barriers, allow for the simultaneous protection of domestic industries against unequal competition and induce more open foreign markets. This more flexible approach is viewed as superior to a "one-sided" free trade policy. The suggestion that a fair trade policy produces a trading environment with fewer trade restrictions allows proponents to assert that such a policy serves to promote both equity and efficiency. In other words, not only will domestic and foreign producers in the same industry be treated equally, but the gains associated with a freer trading environment will be realized.

On the other hand, critics of a fair trade policy argue that such a policy is simply disguised protectionism—it simply achieves the goals of specific interest groups at the expense of the nation at large. In many cases, fair traders focus on a specific practice that can be portrayed as protectionist while ignoring the entire package of policies that are affecting a nation's competitive position. In these cases, the foreign country is more likely either not to respond or retaliate by increasing rather than reducing their trade barriers. In the latter case, the escalation of trade barriers causes losses for both nations, which is exactly opposite to the alleged effects of an activist fair trade policy.

Critics of fair trade proposals are especially bothered by the use of bilateral trade deficits as evidence of unfair trade. In a world of many trading countries, the trade between two countries need not be balanced for the trade of each to be in global balance. Differing demands and productive capabilities across countries will cause a specific country to have trade deficits with some countries and surpluses with other countries. These bilateral imbalances are a normal result of countries trading on the basis of comparative advantage. Thus, the focus on the bilateral trade deficit can produce inappropriate conclusions about fairness and, more importantly, policies attempting to eliminate bilateral trade deficits are likely to be very costly because they eliminate the gains from a multilateral trading system.

CONCLUSION

The proliferation of protectionist trade policies in recent years provides an impetus to reconsider their worth. In the world of traditional trade theory, characterized by perfect competition, a definitive recommendation in favor of free trade can be made. The gains from international trade result from a reallocation of production resources toward goods that can be produced less costly at home than abroad and the exchange of some of these goods for goods that can be produced at less cost abroad than at home.

Recent developments in international trade theory have examined the consequences of international trade in markets where there are market imperfections, such as monopoly and technological spillovers. Do these imperfections justify protectionist trade policies? The answer continues to be no. While protectionist trade policies may offset monopoly power overseas or advantageously use domestic monopoly power, trade restrictions tend to reduce the competition faced by domestic producers, protecting domestic producers at the expense of domestic consumers.

The empirical evidence is clear-cut. The costs of protectionist trade policies far exceed the benefits. The losses suffered by consumers exceed the gains reaped by domestic producers and government. Low-income consumers are relatively more adversely affected than high-income consumers. Not only are there inefficiencies associated with excessive domestic production and restricted consumption, but there are costs associated with the enforcement of the protectionist legislation and attempts to influence trade policy.

The primary reason for these costly protectionist policies relies on a public choice argument. The desire to influence trade policy arises from the fact that trade policy changes benefit some groups, while harming others. Consumers are harmed by protectionist legislation; however, ignorance, small individual costs, and the high costs of organizing consumers prevent the consumers from being an effective force. On the other hand, workers and other resource owners in an industry are more likely to be effective politically because of their relative ease of organizing and their individually large and easy-to-identify benefits. Politicians interested in re-election will most likely respond to the demands for protectionist legislation of such an interest group.

The empirical evidence also suggests that the adverse consumer effects of protectionist trade policies are not short-lived. These policies generate lower economic growth rates than the rates associated with free trade policies. In turn, slow growth contributes to additional protectionist pressures.

Interest group pressures from industries experiencing difficulty and the general appeal of a "level playing field" combine to make the reduction of trade barriers especially difficult at the present time in the United States. Nonetheless, national interests will be served best by such an admittedly difficult political course. In light of the current Uruguay Round negotiations under the General Agreement on Tariffs and Trade, as well as numerous bilateral discussions, this fact is especially timely.

REFERENCES

Hickok, Susan. "The Consumer Cost of U.S. Trade Restraints," Federal Reserve Bank of New York *Quarterly Review* (Summer 1985), pp. 1–12.

Hufbauer, Gary Clyde, Diane T. Berliner, and Kimberly Ann Elliott. *Trade Protection in the United States: 31 Case Studies* (Institute for International Economics, 1986).

Krugman, Paul R. "Is Free Trade Passé?" *Journal of Economic Perspectives* (Fall 1987), pp. 131–44.

Organization for Economic Co-Operation and Development (OECD). *Costs and Benefits of Protection* (1985).

Tarr, David G., and Morris E. Morkre. *Aggregate Costs to the United States of Tariffs and Quotas on Imports: General Tariff Cuts and Removal of Quotas on Automobiles, Steel, Sugar, and Textiles,* Bureau of Economics Staff Report to the Federal Trade Commission (December 1984).

World Bank. *World Development Report 1987* (Oxford University Press, 1987).

21

The New Protectionism: A Response to Shifts in National Economic Power
ROBERT BALDWIN

Robert Baldwin argues that the postwar liberal international order
was a function of United States economic and political hegemony. Because free trade was beneficial to the country as a
whole, the United States led the world toward this goal. In recent
years, however, there have been a number of structural changes
in the world economy, especially the decline in American competitiveness and the role of the dollar, and the growing economic
importance of other countries. Under these altered international
conditions, there have been increased pressures for protectionist
measures both in the United States and abroad. Trade restrictions
will grow and there is the potential for creeping protectionism,
Baldwin concludes, although it is not inevitable that the world
will descend into generalized protection.

INTRODUCTION

The international trading economy is in the anomalous condition of diminishing
tariff protection but increasing use of non-tariff trade-distorting measures. The
former trend is the result of the staged tariff cuts agreed on in the GATT-
sponsored Tokyo Round of multilateral negotiations concluded in 1979. The latter
trend is taking place largely outside the framework of GATT and threatens to undermine the liberal international trading regime established after World War II.

This paper relates the new non-tariff protectionism to significant structural
changes in world industrial production that have brought about a decline in the
dominant economic position of the United States, the concomitant rise to international economic prominence of the European Economic Community and Japan,

Robert Baldwin. "The New Protectionism: A Response to Shifts in National Economic Power." From
Dominick Salvatore, ed., *Protectionism and World Welfare.* Copyright © 1993 by Cambridge University Press. Reprinted with the permission of Cambridge University Press.

and the emergence of a group of newly industrializing countries (NICs). The first two sections describe the rise of the United States to a dominant position in international economic affairs in the immediate postwar period and indicate the types of "hegemonic" actions it took. "Shifts in International Economic Power" explains how changes in trade, finance, and the energy situation have led to modifications in national trade policy behaviour, particularly on the part of the United States. We then speculate about the nature of the international regime that is evolving under the present pattern of economic power among nations. The paper's final section is a summary and conclusion.

THE RISE IN US HEGEMONY

The role of the United States in the evolution of the modern trading system has been central. Although this country became an important trader on the world scene after World War I, it gave little indication at the time of a willingness to assume a major international leadership role. The American share of the exports of the industrial countries rose from 22.1 per cent in 1913 to 27.8 per cent by 1928, but during this period the United States chose political and economic isolation, rejecting membership in the League of Nations and erecting in 1930 the highest set of tariff barriers in its peacetime history. The failure of the London Economic Conference of 1933 due to the inward-looking economic position of the United States marks the low point of US internationalism in the interwar period.

A major policy reorientation toward participation in international affairs began to occur in the United States during the late 1930s and especially in World War II. More political leaders and the electorate generally began to accept the view of key policy officials in the Roosevelt administration that continued isolationism would bring not only renewed economic stagnation and unemployment to the American economy but also the likely prospect of disastrous new worldwide military conflicts. Consequently, active participation in the United Nations was accepted by the American public, as were the proposals to establish international economic agencies to provide for an orderly balance-of-payments adjustment mechanism for individual nations and to promote reconstruction and development. International trade had long been a much more politicized subject, however, and all that was salvaged (and then only by executive action) from the proposal for a comprehensive international trade organization was the GATT.

The economic proposals initiated by the United States were not, it should be emphasized, aimed at giving this country a hegemonic role. They envisioned the United States as one of a small group of nations that would cooperate to provide the leadership necessary to avoid the disastrous nationalistic policies of the 1930s. The envisioned leadership group included the United Kingdom, France, China and, it was hoped, the Soviet Union.

Hegemony was thrust upon the United States by a set of unexpected circumstances. First, the failure of the United Kingdom to return to anything like its prewar position as a world economic power was unforeseen. US officials thought, for example, that the US loan of $3.75 billion to the United Kingdom in 1946 would enable that country to restore sterling convertibility and to return to its earlier prominent international role, but the funds were quickly exhausted and it was necessary to restore exchange control. The 1949 devaluation of the pound was equally disappointing in its failure to revitalize the country. Economic reconstruction in Europe also proved much more costly than envisioned. The resources of the International Bank for Reconstruction and Development proved much too small to handle this task and massive foreign aid by the United States became necessary. Meanwhile the US economy grew vigorously after the war rather than, as many expected, returning to stagnant conditions.

The failure of either China or the USSR to participate in the market-oriented international economy placed an added leadership burden on the United States. But perhaps the most important factor leading to US hegemony was the effort by the Soviet Union to expand its political influence into Western Europe and elsewhere. American officials believed they had little choice from a national viewpoint but to assume an active political, economic and military leadership role to counter this expansionist policy, an action that most non-communist countries welcomed.

HEGEMONIC BEHAVIOUR

The significant expansion of productive facilities in the United States during the war, coupled with the widespread destruction of industrial capacity in Germany and Japan, gave American producers an enormous advantage in meeting the worldwide pent-up demands of the 1940s and 1950s. The US share of industrial-country exports rose from 25.6 per cent in 1938 to 35.2 per cent in 1952. (The combined share of Germany and Japan fell from 24.0 percent to 11.4 per cent between these years.) Even in a traditional net import category like textiles, the United States maintained a net export position until 1958.

Static trade theory suggests that a hegemonic power will take advantage of its monopolistic position by imposing trade restrictions to raise domestic welfare through an improvement in its terms of trade. However, like the United Kingdom when it was a hegemonic nation in the nineteenth century, the United States reacted by promoting trade liberalization rather than trade restrictionism. A restrictionist reaction might have been possible for a highly controlled, planned economy that could redistribute income fairly readily and did not need to rely on the trade sector as a major source of employment generation or growth, but the growth goals of free-market firms, together with the nature of the political decision-making process, rule out such a response in modern industrial democracies.

Industrial organization theory emphasizes that firms in oligopolistically organized industries take a long-run view of profitability and strive to increase their market share. By doing so, they try both to prevent new competitors from entering the market, possibly causing losses to existing firms, and old competitors from increasing their shares to the point where others might suffer progressive and irreversible market losses. US firms organized in this manner seized the postwar competitive opportunities associated with American dominance to expand overseas market shares through both increased exports and direct foreign investment. The desire of US political leaders to strengthen non-communist nations by opening up American markets and providing foreign aid complemented these goals of US business, and business leaders actively supported the government's foreign policy aims. Even most producers in more competitively organized and less high-technology sectors such as agriculture, textiles and miscellaneous manufactures favoured an outward-oriented hegemonic policy at this time, since they too were able to export abroad and were not faced with any significant import competition.

The United States behaved in a hegemonic manner on many occasions in the 1950s and early 1960s. . . . [I]n doing so, it did not coerce other states into accepting policies of little benefit to them. Instead, the United States usually proposed joint policy efforts in areas of mutual economic interest and provided strong incentives for hegemonic cooperation. In the trade field, for example, US officials regularly pressed for trade-liberalizing multilateral negotiations and six such negotiations were initiated between 1947 and 1962. But the United States traded short-term concessions for possible long-run gains, since the concessions by most other countries were not very meaningful in trade terms due to the exchange controls they maintained until the late 1950s. The US goal was to penetrate successfully the markets of Europe and Japan as their controls were eased and finally eliminated.

One instance in which the United States did put considerable pressure on its trading partners to accept the American viewpoint was in the Kennedy Round of multilateral trade negotiations. At the initial ministerial meeting in 1963, US trade officials—with President Kennedy's approval—threatened to call off the negotiations unless the EC accepted the American proposal for a substantial, across-the-board tariff-cutting rule. Members of the Community had regained much of their economic vitality and the United States wanted economic payment for its earlier unreciprocated concessions and its willingness to support a customs-union arrangement that discriminated against the United States.

In the financial area the $3.75 billion loan to the United Kingdom in 1946, the large grants of foreign aid after 1948 under the Marshall Plan, and the provision of funds to establish the European Payments Union in 1948 are examples of hegemonic leadership by the United States. American leaders envisioned the postwar international monetary regime to be one with fixed and convertible exchange rates in which orderly adjustments of balance-of-payments problems would take place. When the IMF proved inadequate to cope with the magnitude of postwar payments problems, the United States provided financial aid until the affected countries were strong enough economically for the IMF to assume its intended role. A US hegemonic role was also exercised in the energy field, as American companies, with the assistance of the US government, gained control over Arab oil during the 1940s and 1950s.

SHIFTS IN INTERNATIONAL ECONOMIC POWER

Trade Competitiveness

The hegemonic actions of the United States, aimed at maintaining the liberal international economic framework established largely through its efforts and at turning back the Soviet Union's expansionism, succeeded very well. By 1960 the export market shares of France, Germany, Italy and Japan had either exceeded or come close to their prewar levels. Among the industrial countries only the United Kingdom failed to regain its prewar position by this time. The restoration of peacetime productive capabilities in these countries meant that the exceptionally high market shares of the United States in the early postwar years declined correspondingly. The 35.2 per cent US export share of 1952 had dropped to 29.9 per cent by 1960, a figure that was, however, still higher than its 1938 share of 25.6 per cent.

For manufactured products alone, the picture is much the same. The US world export share decreased from 29.4 per cent in 1953 to 18.7 per cent in 1959, while the shares of Western Europe and Japan rose from 49.0 per cent to 53.7 per cent and from 2.8 per cent to 4.2 per cent respectively. The export market share of Western Europe remained unchanged in the 1960s, but the Japanese share continued to rise and reached 10.0 per cent in 1971. At the same time the US share of world exports of manufactures fell to 13.4 per cent by 1971.

While aid from the US government played an important part in restoring the trade competitiveness of the European countries and Japan, the governments of these nations themselves were the prime driving force for revitalization. The French government, for example, formulated an industrial modernization plan after the war and two-thirds of all new investment between 1947 and 1950 was financed from public funds. Similarly, the British government under the Labour Party created an Economic Planning Board and exercised close control over the direction of postwar investment, while even the relatively free-market-oriented German government channelled capital into key industries in the 1950s. Government investment aid to the steel, shipbuilding and aircraft industries and the use of preferential governmental policies to promote the computer sector are other examples of the use of trade-oriented industrial policies in Europe during this period.

Japan is perhaps the best-known example of the use of government policies to improve international competitiveness. During the 1950s and 1960s the Japanese government guided the country's industrial expansion by providing tax incentives and investment funds to favoured industries. Funding for research and development in high-technology areas also became an important part of the government's trade policy in the 1970s. Governments of newly industrializing developing countries use industry-specific investment and production subsidies to an even greater extent than any of the developed nations in their import-substitution and export-promotion activities.

Not only had the prewar export position of the United States been restored by the late 1960s, but the period without significant import pressures in major industries with political clout had come to an end. Stiff competition from the Japanese in the cotton textiles industry was evident by the late 1950s, and the United States initiated the formation of a trade-restricting international cotton textile agreement in 1962. A broad group of other industries also began to face significant import competition in the late 1960s. The products affected included footwear, radios and television sets, motor vehicles and trucks, tires and inner tubes, semiconductors, hand tools, earthenware table and kitchen articles, jewelry and some steel items.

Trade-pattern changes in the 1970s and early 1980s were dominated by the price-increasing actions of the Organization of Petroleum Exporting Countries (OPEC). This group's share of world exports rose from 18.2 per cent in 1970 to 27.3 per cent in 1980. By 1984 OPEC's share, however, had fallen to 23.5 per cent as the power of the cartel declined. During this period the US export share fell from 13.7 per cent to 10.9 per cent, while that of the EC dropped from 36.1 per cent to 30.7 per cent. Japan, however, managed to increase its share from 6.1 per cent to 8.4 per cent. The latter figures reflect Japan's continued strong performance in manufacturing; its share of industrial countries' manufacturing exports rose from 9.9 per cent in 1971 to 15.3 per cent in early 1984.

The 1970s and early 1980s were a time of relative stability in the US manufacturing export share, with this figure rising slightly—from 19.6 per cent in 1971 to 20.1 per cent in 1984. In contrast, the EC's manufacturing export share declined from 59.9 per cent in 1971 to 54.6 per cent in 1984. Another major development of this period was the increase in the manufacturing export share of the developing countries from 7.1 per cent in 1971 to 11.0 per cent in 1980.

An important feature of the shifts in trading patterns of industrial countries in the 1970s and 1980s has been that not only have labour-intensive sectors like textiles, apparel and footwear continued to face severe import competition but that large-scale oligopolistically organized industries such as steel, automobiles and shipbuilding have had to contend with such competition. Machine tools and consumer electronic goods have also come under increasing import pressure.

The decline in the dominance of the United States in trade policy matters became apparent in the Tokyo Round of multilateral trade negotiations as well as when the United States proposed a new negotiating round in 1982. As it had in the Kennedy Round, the United States proposed an across-the-board linear tariff-cutting rule at the outset of the Tokyo Round, whereas the EC again proposed a formula that cut high tariff rates by a greater percentage than low duties. This time the United States did not prevail. The other industrial nations treated both the United States and the Community as major trading blocs whose negotiating objectives must be satisfied. The result was a compromise duty-cutting rule that met the US desire for a deep average cut and at the same time produced the significant degree of tariff harmonization sought by the EC. At the 1982 GATT ministerial meeting the United States again called for a new multilateral exercise that included as major agenda items negotiations aimed at reducing export subsidies in agriculture and barriers to trade in services. The Community and the developing countries both rejected the US proposals, and it has become clear that the United States can no longer determine the pace at which such negotiations will be held.

International Financial and Other Economic Changes

As a decline in the dominant trade-competitive position of the United States became increasingly evident in the 1960s, both the United States and many other countries became dissatisfied with the US role in international monetary affairs. Since the supply of gold in the world increases only slowly, the demand for additional international liquidity that accompanied the rapid growth in world trade had to be met by greater holdings of dollars, the other official form of international reserves. As these holdings grew, a number of countries became concerned about the freedom from monetary and fiscal discipline that such an arrangement gave the United States and they resented the seigniorage privileges it granted. The United States also became increasingly dissatisfied with its inability to change the exchange rate of the dollar as a balance-of-payments adjustment means. Another indication of the decline in US hegemony was the creation in 1969 of a new form of international liquidity in the IMF: Special Drawing Rights (SDRs), designed to reduce the dependence of the international economy on the dollar.

The shift to a flexible exchange-rate system in 1971, however, was the clearest manifestation of the decline in US dominance in the monetary field. Although the results of this action have not given countries the expected degree of freedom from US financial influence, the role of the dollar as a reserve and vehicle currency has declined. Another institutional change directed at reducing the monetary influence of the United States was the formation of the European Monetary System in 1979.

The difficulties faced by the industrial nations in the energy field as a consequence of the success of OPEC have already been mentioned, but the importance of this shift in economic power is hard to exaggerate. This development was an especially devastating blow to the international economic prestige of the United States.

TRADE POLICY RESPONSES TO THE REDISTRIBUTION OF NATIONAL ECONOMIC POWER

The non-hegemonic members of the international trading regime (i.e., countries other than the United States) responded to the inevitable industry disruption caused by the shifts in comparative cost patterns in a manner consistent with their earlier reconstruction and development policies. With the greater postwar emphasis on the role of the state in maintaining full employment and providing basic social welfare needs, these governments intervened to prevent increased imports and export market losses from causing what they considered to be undue injury to domestic industries. Assistance to industries such as steel and shipbuilding injured by foreign competition in third markets took the form of subsidies. These included loans at below-market rates, accelerated depreciation allowances and other special tax benefits, purchases of equity capital, wage subsidies and the payment of worker social benefits. Not only had such activities been an integral part of the reconstruction and development efforts of the 1940s and 1950s, but the provisions of the GATT dealing with subsidies other than direct export subsidies also did not rule out such measures.

Because of the difficulties of modifying the tariff-reducing commitments made in earlier multilateral trade negotiations, import-protecting measures generally did not take the form of higher tariffs. By requiring compensating duty cuts in other products or the acceptance of retaliatory increases in foreign tariffs, increases in tariffs could have led to bitter disputes and the unravelling of the results of the previous negotiations. Therefore, to avoid such a possibility, governments negotiated discriminatory quantitative agreements outside the GATT framework with suppliers who were the main source of the market disruption. For example, quantitative import restrictions were introduced by France, Italy, the United Kingdom and West Germany on Japanese automobiles as well as on radios, television sets and communications equipment from Japan, South Korea and Taiwan. Flatware, motorcycles and videotape recorders from Japan and the NICs of Asia were also covered by such import restrictions of various European countries. In the agricultural area, which had been excluded from most of the rules of the GATT, governments did not hesitate to tighten quantitative import restrictions (or restrictions like those under the EC's Common Agricultural Policy that have the same effect) or provide subsidies to handle surpluses produced by high domestic price-support programmes.

In the United States the disrupting effects of the postwar industry shifts in competitiveness throughout the world produced basic policy disputes that continue today. Except for the politically powerful oil and textile industries, until the late 1960s import-injured industries were forced to follow the administrative track provided for import relief under the escape-clause provision of the GATT. Moreover, many of the industry determinations by the ITC were rejected at the presidential level on foreign policy grounds—the need for the hegemonic power to maintain an open trade policy. Industry subsidies provided by foreign governments, though subject to US countervailing duty laws, were largely ignored by the executive branch for the same reason.

The official position of the United States began to change under the strong import pressures of the late 1960s. As their constituents described the competitive problems they were facing, fewer members of Congress accepted the standard argument that a liberal US trade policy was essential to strengthen the free world against communism. The intensity of congressional views on trade issues is indicated by their rejection of President Lyndon Johnson's 1968 request for new trade authority and by the near-approval in 1970 of protectionist legislation. The growing unwillingness of US allies to accept the unquestioned leadership of the United States in international political, military and economic affairs also caused officials in the executive branch to question the traditional American position on trade policies.

The view that gradually gained the support of the major public and private interests concerned with trade matters was that much of the increased competitive pressure on the United States was due to unfair foreign policies such as government subsidization, dumping by private and public firms, preferential government purchasing procedures, and discriminatory foreign administrative rules and practices relating to importation. This argument had appeal for several reasons. No new legislation was required to provide import relief; stricter enforcement of long-existing domestic legislation seemed to be all that was necessary. After a material-injury clause was introduced into the US countervailing duty law in 1979, these laws also were consistent with the provisions of the GATT dealing with unfair trade practices. Consequently, stricter enforcement of US unfair trade laws was unlikely to lead to bitter trade disputes with other countries. By placing the blame for their decline in competitiveness on unfair foreign actions, US managers and workers could avoid the implication that the decline might be due to a lack of efficiency on their part. Finally, government officials could maintain that the United States was still supporting the rules of the liberal international regime that the country had done so much to fashion.

The emphasis on the greater need for fair trade is evident in the 1974 legislation authorizing US participation in the Tokyo Round of multilateral negotiations. In reshaping the proposal of the president, the Congress stressed that the president should seek "to harmonize, reduce, or eliminate" NTBs and tighten GATT rules with respect to fair-trading practices. Officials in the executive branch supported these directives not only on their merits but also because they deflected attention from more patently protectionist policies. . . .

The unfair trade argument has been used in support of most other trade-restricting or trade-promoting actions taken by the United States in recent years. The textile and apparel sectors have been described by government officials as "beleaguered" by disruptive import surges, justifying more restrictive import controls. Similarly, when temporary orderly marketing agreements (OMAs) were negotiated in the 1970s with selected East and Southeast Asian countries, the implication conveyed was that these were responses to unfair export activities of these nations. Even the Japanese voluntary export restraints on automobiles were sometimes justified by American industry and government officials on the grounds that industry's competitive problem was in part due to the unfair targeting practices of the Japanese government. On the export-promoting side, it is routinely claimed that subsidized export credits through the Export-Import Bank and special tax privileges to exporters establishing foreign sales corporations are necessary to counter unfair foreign practices in these areas. In short, fair-trade arguments using such phrases as the need for "a level playing field" or "to make foreign markets as open as US markets" have become the basic justification for the greater use of trade-distorting measures by the United States.

THE FUTURE OF THE INTERNATIONAL TRADING REGIME

The United States fared well economically in its hegemonic role; American exporters and investors established substantial foreign market positions from which they are still benefiting greatly. The open trade policy that US officials were able to maintain for so long also promoted growth and resource-use efficiency and thus extended the period of US economic dominance. But the postwar recovery of Europe and Japan and the emergence of the NICs brought an inevitable relative decline in US economic and political power. The comparative economic position of Western Europe also receded from its postwar recovery level as Japan and the NICs grew more rapidly. The outcome has been an increase in industrial-country protection that takes the form of non-tariff trade-distorting measures.

No country or country group is likely to assume a dominant role in the world economy during the rest of the century. Japan would seem to be the most likely candidate for this leadership role with its highly competitive industrial sector, but it appears to be too small economically to be a hegemonic power. Moreover, like the United States in the 1920s, Japan is still quite isolationist. Government officials and business people are conditioned by the disastrous outcome of the country's expansionist efforts in the 1930s and 1940s and by its past history of inwardness. Furthermore, when a potential hegemonic nation first demonstrates its competitive strengths over a wide range of products, certain traditional sectors (such as agriculture) that are faced with difficult adjustment problems tend to be able to prevent the national commitment to trade openness required of a dominant economic power. This occurred in the early stages of both the British and the American rise to economic dominance and is now keeping Japan from making a commitment to openness commensurate with its competitive abilities. In addition, Japanese consumers have not yet developed the taste for product variety needed to make Japan an important market for foreign-manufactured goods. The EC possesses the size and resources to be the dominant economic power, but the economic diversity among its members and the severe structural adjustment problems faced by almost all of them preclude a hegemonic role for this economic bloc.

The United States remains the country most able to identify its trading interests with the collective interests of all. However, a number of the industries that were the most competitive internationally during the rise of US hegemony have become victims of their success. The high profits these oligopolistically organized industries were able to maintain provided the investment funds needed to take advantage of the expanding market opportunities at home and abroad. But their economic structures were also favourable to the development of powerful labour unions that wished to share these profits through higher wages. The outcome was wage increases in these industries that far exceeded wage increases in manufacturing in general. As other countries developed their productive capabilities, these American industries found themselves penalized by above-average labour costs and an institutional framework that made it very difficult to adjust to the new realities of international competition. Also, management in some of these industries failed to keep up with the most advanced practices. Another important feature of these industries is their ability to obtain protection by exerting political pressure at the congressional and presidential levels, if they fail to gain it through administrative routes involving the import-injury, antidumping and countervailing duty laws.

As a consequence of these developments, protectionism has gradually spread in the United States as such industries as steel and automobiles have come under severe international competitive pressures. European governments are faced with even stronger protectionist pressures for similar reasons and have also moved toward more restrictive import policies. . . .

There seems to be no reason why the recent trend in non-tariff protectionism at the industry-specific level will not continue in the United States and Europe and become more important in Japan. But one should not conclude from this that the present international trading regime will turn into one where protectionism is rampant. There are—and will continue to be—dynamic, export-oriented industries in the older industrial countries that will seek access to foreign markets and see the relation between this goal and open markets in their own country. Moreover, such industries will have considerable political influence, as US high technology and export-oriented service industries have demonstrated. These sectors will continue to provide the United States, Western Europe and Japan with the economic power that makes international openness a desirable trade policy objective, and none of these trading blocs is likely to adopt a policy of general protection.

But will not creeping protection at the industry level eventually bring a *de facto* state of general protection? This is, of course, a real possibility, but this conclusion need not follow because protection usually does not stop the decrease in employment in declining industries. Even politically powerful industries usually have only enough political clout to slow down the absolute fall in employment. Furthermore, while employment tends to increase due to the fall in imports from the countries against which the controls are directed, offsetting forces are also set in motion. These include a decrease in expenditures on the product as its domestic price tends to rise; a shift in expenditures to non-controlled varieties of the product, to either less or more processed forms of the good and to substitute products; a redirection of exports by foreign suppliers to more expensive forms of the item; and, if the import controls are country-specific, an increase in exports by non-controlled suppliers. Also, the larger industry profits associated with the increased protection are likely to be used to introduce labour-saving equipment at a more rapid pace than previously.

The continued decline in employment after increased protection is well documented from histories of protection in particular industries. In the European Community and the United States, even such politically powerful industries as textiles and apparel and steel have been unable to prevent employment from falling despite increased import protection.

There are many factors that determine an industry's effectiveness in protection seeking. Its size in employment terms is one important factor. With declining employment, an industry faces diminution of its political power because of the fall in its voting strength and attendant decrease in its ability to raise funds for lobbying purposes. The decline in the political power of the US agricultural sector as the farm population has declined is an example that supports this hypothesis. It seems likely that highly protected industries such as textiles and apparel will gradually lose their ability to maintain a high degree of import protection. Consequently, in older industrial nations the spread of protection to sectors in which NICs gradually acquire international competitiveness may be offset by a decrease in protection in currently protected sectors. Counter-protectionist pressures also build up as industry-specific protection spreads. The stagnating effect of this policy becomes more obvious, as do the budgetary and economic-efficiency costs. A state of affairs may thus be reached in which protectionism will not increase on balance in the current group of industrial countries, or only at a very slow rate. Meanwhile, export-oriented high-technology and service sectors will encourage continued international cooperation to maintain an open trading regime.

Even if this sanguine scenario takes place, the international trading regime is likely to operate quite differently than it did in the years of US dominance. Industrial countries will seek short-run economic reciprocity in their dealings with each other. In particular, the United States will no longer be willing to trade access to its markets for acquiescence to US political goals and the prospect of long-term penetration of foreign economic markets. The developing countries and nations with special political relationships with particular major trading powers will probably continue to be waived from the full-reciprocity requirement but their trade benefits from this waiver will be closely controlled. Greater emphasis will be placed on bilateral negotiations to reduce non-tariff trade distortions, though the negotiations may still take place at general meetings of GATT members. The articles and codes of the GATT will provide the broad framework for the negotiations, but the variety and discriminatory nature of non-tariff measures make true multilateral negotiations too cumbersome. Bilateral negotiations will also be used to a greater extent in handling trade disputes. The GATT dispute-resolution mechanism will be utilized by smaller countries in their dealings with the larger trading nations and by the larger nations to call attention to actions by one of their members that are outside of generally accepted standards of good behaviour. These means of settling disputes do not differ essentially from the practices followed throughout the history of the GATT.

Greater discrimination in the application of trade restrictions and in the granting of trade benefits is another feature of the emerging international trading regime. The safeguard provisions of the GATT, for example, will probably be modified to permit the selective imposition of quantitative import controls on a temporary basis. It will be justified, at least implicitly, on the grounds that injury-causing import surges from particular suppliers represent a form of unfair competition and thus can be countered with discriminatory restrictions under GATT rules. More state assistance for the development and maintenance of high-technology and basic industries will be another characteristic of the international trading order likely to evolve during the rest of the century. The governments of both industrial and developing nations will continue to insist on domestic subsidies to develop a certain minimum set of high-technology industries and to maintain a number of basic industries on the grounds that these are needed for a country to become or remain a significant economic power.

The international trading regime described above is not one that will gain favour with economists. It will not yield the degree of economic efficiency or economic growth that economists believe is achievable in an open, non-discriminatory trading order. But this is an essay on the probable nature of the future international trading order, not the one economists would most like to see evolve. Free trade is not a politically stable policy in an economic world of continuing significant structural shifts involving severe adjustment problems for some politically important sectors and the demands of infant industries for special treatment. But neither is general import protectionism a politically stable state of affairs in modern industrial democracies with dynamic export sectors. Stable conditions in this type of world economy involve openness in some industries and protection in others, with the industries in each category changing over time. The particular mix of openness and import protection can vary significantly, depending on such factors as the country distribution of economic power and the pace of structural change. The present situation, in which there are three major industrial trading powers and a rapid rate of new technology development and international transfer of old technologies suggests that the currently evolving trading regime will be characterized by more government control and private cartelization than has existed throughout most of the postwar period.

SUMMARY AND CONCLUSION

The new protectionism threatening the international trading regime is related to significant structural changes in world production that have brought about a decline in the dominant economic position of the United States, a concomitant rise of the EC and Japan to international prominence and the emergence of a highly competitive group of newly industrializing countries.

The trading regime expected to develop after World War II involved the major economic powers' sharing responsibility for maintaining open and stable trading conditions. But the unexpected magnitude of the immediate postwar economic and political problems thrust the United States into a hegemonic role. US economic dominance manifested itself in the trade, finance and energy fields and enabled American producers to establish strong export and investment positions abroad. Yet, by facilitating the reconstruction and development of Western Europe and Japan as well as the industrialization of certain developing countries, US hegemonic activities led eventually to a marked decline in the American share of world exports and a significant rise of import competition in both labour-intensive sectors and certain oligopolistically organized industries. These developments significantly diminished the leadership authority of the United States.

Most industrial countries responded to the inevitable market disruptions associated with these shifts in comparative advantage by providing extensive government assistance to injured industries in the form of subsidies and higher import barriers. Such behaviour was consistent with the extensive role the governments of these countries played in promoting reconstruction and development. For the hegemonic power, the United States, the policy adjustment has been more difficult. Government and business leaders have gradually adopted the view that unfair foreign trading practices are the main cause of the country's competitive problems. By focusing on more vigorous enforcement of US statutes and GATT rules on fair trade, they are able to press for important protection and still maintain their support for the type of open trading regime the United States did so much to establish after World War II. Attention has been diverted from the role that high labour costs and inefficient managerial practices in certain industries play in explaining these problems.

No other trading bloc seems able or prepared to become a hegemonic power, but free trade is not a politically stable policy in a dynamic economic world in the absence of such leadership. Without the foreign policy concerns of the dominant power, domestic sectors injured by import competition and the loss of export markets are able to secure protection or other forms of government assistance through the political process in industrial democracies. Nevertheless, these industries are unlikely to be able to stop market forces from preventing the decline in employment in the industries and thus an erosion of their political influence. General protectionism is also not a politically stable policy in a rapidly changing economic environment. Politically important export industries that can compete successfully abroad will press for the opening of foreign markets and they realize the need to open domestic markets to achieve this result.

While it is possible that particular instances of protectionism will continue to spread and bring about an essentially closed international trading order, a more sanguine outcome, involving the support of the three major trading powers (the United States, the EC and Japan) seems possible. This is the emergence of a regime characterized by more trade-distorting government interventions than at the height of American hegemony and by the existence of a significant group of government-assisted industries. But while new industries will be added to this group, assistance will be withdrawn from others as they lose political influence so that, on balance, the list does not increase over time or does so only very slowly. Such a regime will not yield the growth and efficiency benefits of an open-trading system, but at least it will not lead to the disastrous economic and political consequences brought about by the type of trading order that prevailed in the 1930s.

22

Changing Patterns of Protectionism: The Fall in Tariffs and the Rise in Non-Tariff Barriers
EDWARD JOHN RAY

Edward John Ray seeks to explain the pattern of trade protection in the United States, both over time and across industries, and the recent rise of nontariff barriers to trade. Focusing on both domestic statist and societal factors, he argues that trade policy is determined by both the general beliefs and policy positions of the government—in this case, that free trade is the socially optimal policy—and interest-group pressures. At present, he concludes, the government of the United States continues to believe in the general efficacy of free trade, while interest groups have turned increasingly protectionist, resulting in an ambiguous policy of gradually expanding nontariff restrictions on trade.

I. INTRODUCTION

Repeating the current litany of concerns about an apparent rise in protectionist rhetoric in the United States and abroad is not the aim of this Article. Rather, its focus is on describing and explaining changes in the pattern of protectionism that have emerged in the United States and other industrialized nations since World War II through use of a simple analytical framework. With generous reference to the abundant literature on the political economy of trade restrictions, this Article also attempts to explain the shift in protectionism from tariff to non-tariff barriers over the last two decades. It also describes how the changing pattern of protectionism is likely to influence future trade policy in both the United States and abroad.

The model constructed in this Article explains how the efforts of special

Edward John Ray. "Changing Patterns of Protectionism: The Fall in Tariffs and the Rise in Non-Tariff Barriers." From *Northwestern Journal of International Law and Business*, 285 (1988).

interest groups within a nation interact with its domestic political and foreign policy objectives to influence the nation's overall structure of trade regulations. Section II of the Article, therefore, begins by providing a simple analytical framework which can help to explain the evolution of both the pattern and the level of protectionism in the United States and other countries. Section III of the Article reviews the history of United States trade policy and summarizes the current economic and political climate for protectionist legislation in the United States. The Article will then expand its analysis in Section IV by attempting to explain historical events more fully in terms of the framework set out in Section II. Section V describes the reasons behind the growth in non-tariff barriers ("NTBs") over the past several decades.

II. AN ANALYTICAL FRAMEWORK

A. The Micro and Macro Views of Policy Decisionmaking

Historically, there have been two generally accepted explanations of how trade policy is determined. The first—the micro view—is that trade policy is the aggregate outcome of industry battles over protection; government policy simply mirrors the preferences of industrial constituents. The second—the macro view—is that the international policy of a given government may be difficult to trace back to individual industry interests. The central government acts as an independent agent reflecting aggregate or collective interests. In this view, national objectives are the primary determinants of domestic and international policies. National governments interact to determine international trade policies. In this context, protectionist positions are heavily influenced by the means available to nations for adjudicating trade disputes between countries.

Studies stressing the macro perspective have attempted to demonstrate how the mechanisms for adjudicating trade disputes between countries might be changed to move the United States and the rest of the world back toward a more consistent trade liberalization stance. Implicit in many of these papers is the notion that government trade policies are constrained by domestic concerns, such as full employment, price stability, and economic growth, that are not necessarily related to the wants of any particular interest group, but are of great concern to the populace as a whole. In this view, trade policy is an integral part of both national domestic policy and foreign policy.

The micro perspective presumes that special interest groups shape the pattern of protection within a given country. This perspective often leaves the impression that government policy is either a weighted sum of the preferences of special interest groups adopted in a passive fashion or the end product of a sinister calculation by a group of frightened politicians who are committed to nothing but keeping themselves in office.

While there are times when governments appear to behave in a way that is consistent with one or the other of these views, there is little evidence to suggest that either is superior to the other as a general model for predicting government behavior. Within the context of the Stigler-Peltzman-Becker framework, one can argue that in conjunction with the equilibrium distribution of rents established in a regulated market, there is in fact also a political equilibrium that is the product of both self-interest (the micro view) and shared values (the macro approach). This Article argues that contemporary trade policy is best understood in this light. That is, trade policy actually results from the interaction of self-promoting economic interest groups with national economic and political policies. These latter "national" policies represent shared or consensus values which are slow to change and thus are quite durable. This Article describes these values and their effectiveness in checking protectionist demands over the last decade.

B. A Combined Framework

What follows is a simple attempt to define an analytical framework with which one can analyze the post-war pattern of protectionism generally described in Section IV. The debate over trade policy in Congress in the last decade has resulted in the kind of policy drift consistent only with a genuine clash between long-held national principles and the pressures that are generated by special interest groups. The model proposed here is that United States trade policy is the joint product of these two clashing forces. This framework combines elements of both the micro and macro perspectives within it; both national political objectives and economic special interest groups play a significant role in defining trade policy.

The first step in demonstrating the model's efficacy is to show that shared national values actually exist. There is a great deal of evidence supporting this proposition, as seen in the hypothesis that governments in industrialized countries are committed to the shared value of providing a trade restriction safety net for weak industries. Two researchers have demonstrated empirically that declining industries not only were favored by minimal Kennedy Round tariff cuts, but were also given enhanced protection in the form of NTBs. In addition, it has been argued that shifts in United States trade policy, including the adoption of the Generalized System of Preferences ("GSP") and the Caribbean Basin Initiative ("CBI"), resulted from a national foreign policy commitment to aid developing nations trying to compete effectively for exports of manufactured goods. These programs are clearly inconsistent with the long-standing United States policy of adhering to the most favored nation ("MFN") principle. This inconsistency suggests an activist government that is not simply responding to special interests or voters.

Although the aforementioned policies suggest that shared values play an important role in decisionmaking, one must be aware that special interests are also a contributing factor. For example, there is evidence that special interest groups influenced the content of the GSP and effectively undermined its goal of opening up United States markets for key exports from developing countries. One might therefore be led to believe that United States policy is merely the servant of economic special interest groups, and that policies like the GSP and CBI are part of a cruel charade. A brief discussion of the "pure" special interest group model of trade policy decisionmaking is thus in order.

The special interest group model cannot be understood unless one is quite specific about the makeup of the various special interest groups which try to influence trade policy and which groups constitute the winners and losers. One important group is consumers, who always have an interest in freer trade for access to a variety of products at the least possible cost. In addition, highly competitive export-oriented firms and their workers will favor free trade because domestic trade restrictions may lead to retaliation from abroad and reduce foreign market access. In contrast, producers and workers in less competitive or import sensitive sectors of the economy will always favor protection. Trade restrictions can preserve jobs and protect profits that would otherwise be lost to foreign competitors.

Four modest extensions complete a summary of the key elements of all of the special interest models and aid in the construction of a paradigm. First, assume that consumers are a diverse group who cannot form an effective coalition to promote free trade, and the price of producing an effective lobby for protection increases with the size of the interested group. One may conclude that concentrated industries with a handful of dominant firms will be more effective in obtaining protection than industries with many small firms. Second, firms that purchase capital equipment or other intermediate goods abroad will surely favor freer trade for those goods. Third, these importing industries are likely to be more concentrated than consumers, creating a presumption that protection will be biased toward final consumer goods and away from intermediate inputs. Fourth, the government serves simply as the agent for all of these interests while pursuing a trade policy consistent with its own survival or electability.

The pure special interest model clearly presents an incomplete picture of how trade policy is formed, however. Most plainly, it ignores foreign policy. The United States-Israel and United States-Canada free trade agreements, and attempts to provide preferential access to United States markets for manufactured imports from developing countries through the GSP and the CBI, suggest that as a nation we have staked out international political positions which do not easily follow from the pure special interest model. The current battle between the executive branch and Congress over trade policy shows that at a time when special interest groups are quite outspoken in their demands for government trade relief, the government is working hard to maintain the nation's long-standing commitment to continued trade liberalization. This type of conflict cannot be explained by a model in which the government proceeds to make policy decisions based solely on its appraisal of the wishes of special interest groups.

In light of the foregoing, it becomes clear that the federal government, as a distinct, separate entity, is itself a key player in the trade policymaking process. Particular government actions are guided by established national policies subject to feedback from special interest groups. When both national preferences and special interest group preferences favor trade liberalization (as this Article will argue they did in the early post–World War II period), national policy will be unambiguously in favor of freer trade. When national preferences are for freer trade and competition, but special interest preferences are on balance protectionist (as this Article will argue they have been in recent years), United States policy on international trade will reflect the kind of ambiguity we are now observing. The presumption is that national policy can be turned away from the current pro-trade stance if a special interest group bias continues to remain strong for a number of years.

The primary distinction between the model proposed here and the normal special interest group models is that the government is explicitly included as an active player with a long-term agenda of its own. The government is sensitive to special interest group pressures but is not their captive. At the same time government policy is not unrelated to the concerns of special interest groups. If special interest group preferences persist in favoring a particular stand on trade issues, the national agenda may shift to adopt that position. This model highlights the dynamic interaction between individual and collective interests which is so important to an understanding of current United States policy. As this Article proceeds, the value of this model as an analytical tool will become increasingly apparent.

III. THE PATTERN OF PROTECTION IN THE UNITED STATES

The value of providing some historical perspective to any study of trade policy or protectionism is suggested by the now common caution that history does indeed repeat, but never in exactly the same way. Drawing simpleminded historical parallels can thus be as foolhardy as ignoring history altogether. If analyzed properly, however, history can provide useful insights. For example, in the late nineteenth century the United States built a world-class navy in order to assume the role of a major player in international political affairs. Coincidentally, that same period saw the emergence of major manufacturing sectors such as steel and textiles as serious competitors in world markets. That combination of national ambitions and private economic interests played a critical role in shifting United States trade policy away from highly protective tariffs toward freer trade at the turn of the last century.

In the late twentieth century the United States faces changed political and economic fortunes that threaten to end four decades of commitment to trade liberalization. The framework outlined above can explain these changes, if considered in the historical context of the last 100 years. The shift in political support toward protectionist legislation in the United States in the last decade, for example, is not without precedent. Political support for trade liberalization within the United States during the 1950s and 1960s is also not without precedent. A brief review of United States history demonstrates how economic interest groups can and have reinforced or undermined federal government trade policies.

A recent study of trade policy in the United States during the last half of the nineteenth century identified a number of important relationships behind the trade policy of the time. First, contrary to the general thrust of United States trade policy throughout most of the post–World War II period, the United States pursued a policy of high tariffs throughout its period of rapid industrialization between 1870 and 1914. Based on a sample of 97 manufacturing industries (including every industry that proved to be significant in 1914), the average United States tariff rate was 45.8% in 1870, 40.6% in 1910 and 26.3% in 1914 following the substantial tariff cuts associated with the Underwood-Simmons Tariff Act of October 1913.

Second, . . . United States tariff policy appears to have been systematically geared to accommodate rapid industrialization. Specifically, the study found that tariff protection was concentrated on finished manufactured goods rather than intermediate goods. That same general strategy has been used by developing countries in this century to promote import substitution in manufacturing. While the results of contemporary cases are somewhat mixed, the historical evidence suggests that throughout the period from 1870 to 1914, those manufacturing sectors which were highly protected by the tariff structure in 1870 emerged as the most rapidly expanding industries in the United States. Finally, the study noted that tariffs were systematically higher on liquor, tobacco products, and other price inelastic commodities which one would expect to be reliable sources of federal government revenue at a time when tariffs funded well over half of the federal budget.

The point to emphasize is that during its industrialization period the United States was highly protectionist, used tariff policy to promote the growth of its manufacturing sector, and relied heavily on tariffs to fund central government programs. Those policies can be seen in many developing countries today and present a sharp contrast to the trade liberalization stance that the United States has professed for the last fifty years.

Except for the brief interval of time associated with the Smoot-Hawley Tariff of 1930 (resulting in tariffs reaching an all time high average of 59% in 1932), tariffs have declined steadily in the United States from 1914 to 1986 (when the General Agreement on Tariffs and Trade ["GATT"] Tokyo Round tariff cuts were scheduled to be fully implemented). The rapid decline in United States tariffs from 59% in 1932, to a little over 7% after the implementation of the Kennedy Round tariff cuts by the early 1970s, paralleled changes in other industrialized nations and contributed to a genuine sense of progress toward free international trade. The model set forth in Section II should be able to explain how these changes came about.

Another important aspect of the pattern of protectionism in the past several decades is the growth in NTBs. Even before the Kennedy Round concluded, a number of authors noted either that: (1) the multilateral agreements were not providing substantial access to industrial country markets for the manufactured exports of developing countries; or (2) remaining NTBs might affect trade differently than would tariffs. Unfortunately, NTBs have yet to be successfully addressed in any of the GATT negotiating rounds. The negotiators at the Kennedy Round meetings abandoned their efforts to deal with NTBs when it became clear that their work on tariff cuts would warrant their full attention. The negotiators at the Tokyo Round did succeed in hammering out codes of conduct for the use of NTBs, but actual agreements to reduce them in line with tariff cuts remained for later rounds of multilateral negotiations.

The fact that international negotiations have not dealt effectively with NTBs is a crucial element in any explanation of the shifting pattern of protectionism in the last twenty-five years. If trade policy is determined by the impact of economic special interests within a country on the national political agenda through the political process, the outcome at any point will surely be influenced by underlying political and economic circumstances. Which positions ultimately prevail, however, will also depend upon the means available for controlling trade flows. This Article argues that as NTBs have become more effective and more prevalent protectionist devices, they have also increased the likelihood that protectionist interests will be successful in any given set of political and economic circumstances.

IV. EXPLAINING THE HISTORY OF PROTECTIONISM IN THE UNITED STATES

The changing pattern of protectionism in the United States over the course of the last century is not difficult to explain if one keeps the model set forth in Section II in mind. This model suggests that trade policies are ultimately defined by governments which act in accordance with shared social values subject to special interest group pressures. Changes in political and economic conditions and innovations in methods of protection contribute to changes in the protectionist regime within any given country. Applying the model to historical trends provides worthwhile examples of the changing nature of protectionism.

A. Partisan Politics and the Model

After the end of the Civil War, Congress was dominated by eastern economic interests which strongly supported rapid industrialization. This support produced a consensus that the United States should promote industrialization. The rapid industrialization that subsequently occurred undercut arguments that further protection was needed. Consequently, export interests became more important over time and, on balance, special interest groups favored free trade. This shift from protectionism to substantial trade liberalization took nearly twenty years. The Sixteenth Amendment to the United States Constitution, passed in 1913 and authorizing the collection of income taxes, resolved a conflict between the general consensus to liberalize trade and the need to finance rapidly expanding federal programs.

A striking paradox in United States trade policy that the proposed analytical framework must explain are the positions on trade policy which have historically been taken by the two primary political parties. Throughout the late nineteenth century, Democrats opposed the high tariffs adopted by Congress and fought to reduce them. Republicans were equally staunch in their support for high tariffs. By contrast, in the post–World War II era Democrats have systematically championed protectionist legislation over the objections of the Republicans. This apparent reversal of the major parties with respect to trade restrictions is explained by reference to the proposed model.

What has changed since World War II is not the respective parties' constituencies but rather the economic interests of those constituencies. Even before the depression of the 1930s solidified labor support for the Democrats, the basic division between Democrats and Republicans put farmers and industrial workers in the Democrat camp and business in the Republican camp. During the 1950s and early 1960s both Democrats and Republicans supported trade liberalization because United States agricultural and manufactured products dominated competition in world markets. Democrats, however, became divided on the trade issue during the late 1960s and early 1970s. It then became clear that despite continued United States competitiveness in agricultural products and capital equipment, some industries (like textiles, footwear, steel, and automobiles) were beginning to lose sales to foreign competitors. Democrats pushed programs to provide unemployment assistance to steel and auto workers, and they also supported trigger prices and quotas in steel and textiles. Although most of the push for protectionism has come from the Democrats, by the late 1970s Republicans from "rust belt" states (like Michigan, Ohio, Indiana, and Illinois) which were particularly affected by the decline in United States steel and auto sales, also supported relief from import competition. The positions of the two major political parties on trade issues have thus changed in response to the changing preferences of their constituent special interest groups; this shift lends credence to the model proposed above.

B. Historical Data and the Model

An examination of historical data highlights the long-term relationship between tariffs in the United States and key economic variables related to our model for the period 1913 to 1980. This relationship helps illustrate the direct and predictable link between changes in domestic and international economic conditions and United States trade policy over the course of the last century. Specifically, analysis shows that when special interests and national policies coincided to support or oppose trade restrictions, United States trade policies were unambiguous. When the net impact of special interest groups is poised in opposition to declared national policy on trade issues, as seems to be the case today, actual trade policy appears contradictory, ambiguous, or both.

It is clear that tariffs have declined substantially between 1913 and 1980, while per capita income has increased. A more careful look at the data makes it clear that rising incomes in the period from 1913 to 1920 were accompanied by tariff cuts from 17.4% to 6%. As income fluctuated during the 1920s and plummeted during the early 1930s, tariffs rose quickly to almost 12% in 1921 and a high of 24% in 1932. In 1933, average income reached a low point in the United States and, as incomes recovered throughout the post–World War II period, tariff rates generally declined. That inverse relationship between tariffs and incomes is consistent with the assumption that rising incomes are associated with increasing consumer preferences for product variety which consequently leads to pressure for liberalization in international trade.

Data from 1913 to 1980 illustrate the relationship between tariff protection and business cycles, as indicated by the occurrence of recessions in the United States economy in that period. Based on the model discussed in Section II, one would expect special interest groups to be most united against free trade when economic conditions are depressed and most solidly in favor of free trade during relatively prosperous times and the data bear out this expectation. Tariffs increased with the recession of 1921 and 1922 and with the beginning of the depression in 1930. Until 1939, the average tariff rate on imports did not fall below the pre-depression 1929 level of 13.5%. The consequent steady decline in tariffs ended during the recession in 1950, and tariffs rose slightly in 1951. Similarly, tariffs increased slightly during the recessions of 1958 and 1974–75 and following the recession in 1961.

Economic declines, and the job losses and business failures that they inevitably bring, have served to rally support for restrictions on international trade. It is therefore not surprising that pressures to restrict trade were less during the 1950s and 1960s, when recessions were less frequent and severe, than during the 1970s and early 1980s, when the United States experienced its most severe recessions since World War II.

An interesting relationship also exists between tariff protection and the relative commodity export strength of the United States in international trade. This relationship once again highlights the association between special interest group demands for protection from import competition and the ability of United States firms to compete. One expects support for trade liberalization to increase and fall in concert with the success or failure of United States companies in selling more goods and services abroad than foreigners sell in the United States. This expectation, too, is supported by the data. For every year from 1936 to 1970, net merchandise exports from the United States were positive and often quite high relative to the sum of imports and exports. The relative net export figure averaged 37.7% during the 1940s, 10.7% during the 1950s, and 9.8% during the 1960s. During the early post-war period, the United States took the lead in promoting trade liberalization, not only because of its advantage in international competitiveness, but also because this stance helped achieve the foreign policy goals of re-industrializing war-torn Europe and Japan and including developing nations as trading partners in the world economy. In the context of the framework set forth above, it is worth noting that throughout the 1950s and the 1960s these foreign policy goals reinforced the international economic interests of the highly competitive United States business community.

Tariff movements and changes in the relative size of the trade sector in the United States since 1913 also bear out the usefulness of the model. Over this period, the larger the trade sector was (compared to the overall economy), the stronger the special interest group concern, and the more likely it was that domestic economic conditions would be linked to trade policies.

These observations follow directly from the argument in Section II that trade policy is the result of government enforced consensus policies tempered by the influence of special interest groups. This argument is further supported by recent trends in the relative net export figures of the United States. In contrast to prosperous post–World War II years, the United States relative net exports dropped to − 4.2% during the 1970s, and was −16.0% from 1981 through 1986. Moreover, the net merchandise export position for the United States has been negative for each of the last ten years. It is therefore no accident that the United States commitment to liberalization has seemed less certain over this period. In fact, based on the framework set forth in Section II and earlier in this section, one would have expected the recent deterioration in the net merchandise export position of the United States to have generated special interest group efforts to undermine commitment to trade liberalization. This is exactly what happened.

The rapid deterioration in the merchandise export position of the United States since the mid-1970s has created a collision of interests between trade sensitive industries and government. That conflict is evident in the current disagreement between the Congress and the executive branch over trade policy. In addition, it is worth noting that the rapid expansion in the relative size of the trade sector over the past twenty years represents a return to pre–World War II proportions. During that period tariffs averaged well over 10%, and domestic economic problems were closely identified with international economic conditions. This rapid growth of the trade sector—accompanied by a deterioration in the United States trade balance and the two worst recessions since World War II—has fueled the protectionist argument that our domestic economic problems are somehow the fault of our trading partners. Because tariff increases are prohibited by the GATT agreements, protectionism has had to take the form of NTBs since the 1970s.

By the mid-1970s it was clear that while tariffs were declining in the United States and other industrial countries, there remained systematic differences in protection across industries. However, there was no consensus that NTBs were a serious threat to further trade liberalization. Further, there was no particular concern that NTBs might disguise the extent of protectionism and thereby foster a false perception among policy makers that gains in international economic cooperation were actually being achieved. It was not until the emergence of national and international economic crises in the late 1970s that the power of special interest groups in setting trade policies and the effectiveness of NTB protectionism was recognized.

V. THE SHIFT FROM TARIFFS TO NON-TARIFF BARRIERS

A. The Growth in Non-Tariff Barriers

The rise of NTBs as trade restriction devices over the past several decades is a development inextricably linked to governmental preferences as to the form of protection for import sensitive industries. While protection in general was diminishing among industrial countries in the early post–World War II period, the trade restrictions known as NTBs were expanding in several specific areas. For example, in 1956 the United States persuaded Japan to adopt one type of NTB, a voluntary export restraint ("VER"), on exports of cotton textiles to the United States; the United Kingdom concluded a similar agreement with Hong Kong.

There are numerous other examples of NTBs in the post–World War II era. A number of factors help explain this shift in trade policy. The first is that the existence of effective income tax systems in the industrialized countries makes them less dependent on the use of tariffs to finance central government operations than is the case for most developing nations. Second, as explained below, special interest groups that are too large to win tariff protection (because of public resentment) may be able to secure NTBs. These demands for protection, along with the relatively greater number of trade restrictions that are available to industrial country governments, make the industrialized nations likely candidates for the adoption of innovations in NTBs. Finally, there is always some domestic and international political advantage to being able to assist special interests in a less publicizable way. NTBs have the advantage of being more difficult to assess in terms of winners and losers and their general welfare effects. For these reasons, industrial countries that are not required to use tariffs for revenue purposes and prefer the political advantages of NTBs in masking government support for special interest groups are likely to prefer NTBs to tariffs.

The first factor in the industrialized nations' shift to NTBs is the fact that these countries no longer require tariff-related income. Historically, the development of nation-states meant that central governments needed funding. Tariff revenues were one fairly easy way to get that funding. It was not until the early twentieth century that tariffs ceased to provide the majority of federal government revenue in the United States. In many developing countries, tariffs continue to play a major role in financing national government expenditures. It is therefore not surprising that developing countries still rely more heavily on tariffs than do the industrialized nations. Nor is it surprising that, once freed of the need for tariff-generated revenues, the industrialized nations would lead the way in developing NTB innovations for regulating international trade.

A number of historical examples illustrate the link between the need for revenues and the existence of tariffs. First, trade liberalization in England in the 1840s occurred only after the central government instituted an income tax system. A second example is found in the United States. One of the most hotly contested domestic political issues during the 1890s was whether the expanding economic role of the central government should be financed primarily with tariff revenues or through the adoption of an income tax system. The ratification of the Sixteenth Amendment in 1913 was a critical factor in the first dramatic tariff cuts in the United States in over fifty years.

The second advantage of NTBs is that while GATT is equally outspoken in its condemnation of tariff and NTB restrictions on trade, it has been much easier to ascertain the quantitative effects of tariffs than it has been to gauge the effect of NTBs like product standardization requirements, government procurement practices, and others. Therefore, as successive GATT rounds achieved further reductions in tariff rates, NTBs were used either to support already weak industries, or compensate industries that were adversely affected by tariff cuts. That shift is evidenced by multifiber agreements beginning in the early 1960s and in the NTB protection given to the footwear, steel, and auto industries.

A third explanation for the rise in NTBs is that they can be used effectively by special interest groups incapable of getting government support for tariff protection. One study provides empirical support for the notion that, other things being equal, NTBs are found predominantly among less concentrated industries. The importance of this finding derives from this Article's earlier assumption that concentrated industries with a small number of dominant firms have been most successful in gaining government trade protection, and that less concentrated multifirm industries are notably less successful. The study's findings suggest, however, that where NTBs are at issue rather than tariffs, effective coalitions with even large numbers of participants are quite possible, and more likely to be successful.

There is at least one other plausible explanation for the rise in NTBs. Consider an industry composed of fifty firms that are each losing domestic sales to foreign firms and therefore have a collective interest in getting the government to restrict imports with a tariff on foreign goods. One problem which the group faces is a firm's electing not to help in the lobbying effort, thereby benefiting from the reduction in foreign competition along with the other forty-nine which worked for that outcome. The one firm is therefore a free rider because it benefits from the collective effort of the other producers without bearing any of the costs. The more firms there are in an industry, the more likely it is that the free rider problem will prevent an effective coalition from being formed because each of the fifty firms has an incentive to try to get others to do the work and be a free rider.

If, however, the same group of fifty firms could get the government to restrict imports of competitive goods and distribute import licenses among those producers that participated in the coalition to limit imports, the group would have a means by which it could reward participants and exclude free riders. In this case, each participant in the coalition gains not only the benefits of reduced foreign competition but also part of the economic rent which would have gone to the government with a tariff (in this case, excess price) associated with the domestic sale of foreign goods. Firms which try to free ride will still benefit from the increased price of foreign goods but can be prevented from importing and selling foreign goods at the higher domestic price. They will not capture any of the tariff equivalent rents generated by the quota. This reduces the free rider problem substantially and enhances the prospects for a successful coalition.

Another example of an NTB would be "buy American" government purchase plans which provide government contracts to domestic firms that lobbied for the program while excluding free riders from access to those government contracts. Large coalitions which could not get tariff protection might succeed in getting "buy American" status associated with their products. What is disturbing is that the relatively greater effectiveness of NTBs as means of rewarding participants and excluding free riders may increase the overall extent to which protection is granted to domestic industries.

B. Empirical Evidence for the Rise in Non-Tariff Barriers

The GATT Kennedy Round failed to deal with the problem of NTBs and focused instead on tariff reduction. The Tokyo Round developed codes with respect to the *use* of NTBs, but left the issue of how to dismantle them for later GATT rounds. In effect, then, these rounds left countries free to develop NTBs as a response to domestic political economic interests.

A pair of studies found clear evidence of this, demonstrating first that NTBs had been used in the United States and abroad to substitute for lost tariff protection resulting from the Kennedy Round, and second, that NTBs were systematically used to complement tariff protection in industries which were already receiving relatively high tariff protection. These studies indicated that industries which had the highest tariff rates before the Kennedy Round still had the highest tariff rates after the round was implemented. Furthermore, NTBs introduced during the late 1960s and 1970s did not go to industries with low tariff rates after the Kennedy Round; rather, NTB protection was given to those industries which benefited most from tariff protection before and after the Kennedy Round.

Another study provided a more precise test of the substitution and complementary protective effects of NTBs which were implemented in response to the Kennedy Round tariff cuts. The study demonstrated that industries (like steel, textiles, processed foods, and consumer durables) which experienced small if any tariff cuts during the Kennedy Round were precisely the industries which gained NTB protection. In short, NTBs were not used only to substitute for the general loss of tariff protection but also to increase protection for industries least affected by Kennedy Round tariff cuts. One can conclude, therefore, that the Kennedy Round was more effective in changing the *form* of protectionism than in changing the *relative level* of protectionism.

C. Voluntary Export Restraints

There is one NTB innovation particularly worth mentioning in the current context. The VER poses a particular problem for international trade negotiations. Although GATT explicitly condemns the use of quantitative trade restrictions (and allows for retaliatory sanctions by injured parties), it is difficult to imagine a means of policing self-imposed export restrictions negotiated bilaterally. VERs effectively bribe foreign governments and producers with tariff-equivalent revenue if they agree to limit exports. This system avoids open confrontations that ordinary quotas invite, and, as in the case of Japanese restrictions on automobile exports to the United States, can be worth billions of dollars to exporters and to the government of the exporting country. Since VERs produce transfers of wealth to the exporting country, these exporters are unlikely to complain to the GATT Council. This in turn suggests that VERs are likely to become the trade restriction of choice for all but the poorest nations.

Moreover, in contrast to tariffs and multilateral quotas, VERs are extremely well suited to the needs of special interest groups seeking protection. First, they are bilateral agreements worked out by consenting rather than competing nations. They can be structured to provide protection to import sensitive industries and to provide rents to both governments and producers in the exporting countries. This means that producers in both the importing and exporting countries can collude with their governments in restraining competition and capturing monopoly rents at the expense of the consuming public. VERs present no incentive for retaliation and GATT has no effective means for preventing such collusive agreements. Multilateral tariffs and quotas, on the other hand, are likely to generate retaliation; this possibility reduces the likelihood that special interest groups within a country will succeed in having them adopted.

United States trade policy has become clouded by the conflict between protectionist groups and the free trade oriented government. Despite the vacillations, however, the severity of the protectionist threat is easily underestimated. NTBs are an especially dangerous weapon in the protectionist arsenal. The fact that NTBs can reduce the free rider problem and increase the likelihood that special interest groups will be successful in their quest for protection means that NTBs markedly enhance the protectionist threat.

This point is important and bears repetition. Imposing tariffs is a hostile economic action, multilateral in effect and easily observed. Given the common desire of developed nations to liberalize trade after World War II, the GATT member states had no trouble rejecting unilateral impositions of tariffs without just cause. So effective was this commitment that tariffs declined dramatically throughout the period. Special interest groups seeking added tariff protection for their industries generally failed in their efforts because of the obvious international economic and political harm. Multilateral quotas have many of the same characteristics as tariffs and are not a likely vehicle for successful protection. VERs, on the contrary, are not multilateral in effect and are not likely to draw complaints from the participating countries. They are therefore likely to become an increasingly popular protectionist vehicle and deserve close observation. . . .

VII. CONCLUSION

In conclusion, it seems clear that the period of United States dominance in international economic competition is over, and with it the unanimity with which United States politicians pushed for trade liberalization in the early post–World War II period. It is also clear that NTB innovations to restrict trade have had the net effect of strengthening protectionist interests. On balance, however, the continued growth within the United States and the accompanying decline in the unemployment rate to 6% by August 1987 have reduced the pressure to use protectionist measures to provide a safety net for industries and workers. The decline in the dollar has already begun to reduce the commodity trade deficit and moderate the impact of special interest groups. Thus, the United States has not abandoned its commitment to further trade liberalization, although the commitment does remain somewhat shaky.

The world seems poised for a long struggle over international economic cooperation, however. Without greater growth rates in industrial and developing countries, the drive to liberalize world trade will be thwarted by special interest groups. Yet without further—and genuine—liberalization in world trade, the prospects for accelerated real growth rates are not good. It is hoped that this Article has identified some of the factors that determine the nature of the ongoing struggle between free trade and protectionist interests, and shown the importance of NTBs as hindrances to further world economic growth. While this work may not provide the answers, it may provide conceptual tools with which to face the problem.

23

Resisting the Protectionist Temptation: Industry and the Making of Trade Policy in France and the United States during the 1970s

HELEN MILNER

This reading investigates why the advanced industrialized countries generally avoided protectionist policies in response to the economic crises of the 1970s. Helen Milner rejects the arguments that the free-trade regime of the GATT, the structure of the international system, or the character of state institutions explains why free trade prevailed. Instead, she links domestic societal and international market variables to argue that rising interdependence in the international economy reduced the incentives for firms to demand protection. Milner examines the cases of the United States and France and finds, first, that internationalized firms did not support protectionism and, second, that despite quite different state structures these firms were able to influence policy.

In the 1970s, a period of great economic turbulence shook the international economy. Two oil "shocks," the abrupt termination of the Bretton Woods monetary system, severe inflationary pressures, several recessions, and rapidly shifting patterns of international comparative advantage turned this decade away from the previous twenty years of fairly stable growth, employment, and monetary and trade flows. This economic turmoil threatened the stability and openness of the

Helen Milner. "Resisting the Protectionist Temptation: Industry and the Making of Trade Policy in France and the United States during the 1970s." From *International Organization*, Vol. 41:4 (Autumn 1987), pp. 639–665. Copyright © 1987. Reprinted by permission of The MIT Press, Cambridge, Massachusetts and the author.

international trading system. It presented the advanced industrial states with a difficult set of economic problems—ones which, in the past, had often resulted in widespread protectionism.

Advanced industrial democracies adjusted to these conditions in ways that were likely to have a major impact on the international economy. At the time, many observers predicted that these countries would adopt full-scale protectionism, thereby destroying the integrated, liberal world economy erected in the postwar period. In the 1970s, however, the international system remained relatively liberal. Since no aggregate measures of protection, defined broadly, exist, it is difficult to evaluate whether overall protection grew or declined in the 1970s. Certainly some protectionist measures were greatly reduced. For example, tariffs in the advanced industrial democracies reached their lowest level ever when the GATT (General Agreement on Tariffs and Trade) Kennedy Round tariff cuts and the Tokyo Round negotiations began. Progress was made as well with the achievement of new cooperative agreements regulating the use of certain policy instruments such as subsidies and government procurement. In addition, although nontariff barriers still protected U.S. industries, they were less prevalent and restrictive than thirty years before. But as these trade barriers were dismantled, new barriers were erected with the orderly marketing arrangements and voluntary export restraints. These new restrictions reversed some of the decade's liberalization, but others were eventually withdrawn. Despite serious economic difficulties, the advanced industrial states appear overall to have maintained fairly open economies.

In this article, I shall examine why major industrial sectors of these economies stayed open despite the economic and political troubles of the 1970s. A variety of explanations for this have already been proposed. Some have cited the existence of the GATT trade regime as a central factor holding back protectionist forces. Proponents of this view argue that the rules and norms of the GATT system made protection more costly and less legitimate, thus diminishing states' willingness to use it. Others have focused on the structure of the international system. For them, the distribution of power among states, whether still hegemonic or multipolar, prevented recourse to protectionism. Finally, some have maintained that the character of the domestic policymaking system, specifically in the United States, prevented the translation of protectionist pressures into policies. In this view, the lessened role of Congress and the insulation of the process from interest groups held back protectionist pressures.

These studies share two common features. First, many of them examine only one country, the United States. This focus seems too narrow since all the advanced industrial democracies, to some extent, resisted protectionism in the 1970s. Why did these countries not respond to their difficulties by widely protecting their economies? To answer this question, this article examines a global phenomenon that affected all these countries internally. Second, these studies assume that the important domestic social actors in the process are solely forces *for* protection. They fail to consider that some domestic actors may be important sources of anti-protectionist (and pro-liberal) trade pressures. This article shows how certain domestic forces helped maintain a liberal trade system in the 1970s.

Certain aspects of the increased international interdependence of the postwar period altered domestic trade politics by creating new trade preferences among important actors. By exposing industries to new foreign competition, increased interdependence has certainly generated heightened pressures for protection by some industries, but few observed the anti-protectionist interests created by these new international linkages. In particular, rising interdependence has greatly extended international economic ties for firms through exports, imports of production inputs, multinational production, and intra-firm trade. Firms with these types of international linkages are expected to have little interest in protectionism even in times of severe economic distress. Consequently this article focuses on an international-level change that affected the domestic preferences of firms and may have helped to maintain a relatively open economy during the 1970s and early 1980s.

This change in preferences should have occurred in all of the advanced industrial countries that experienced new levels of these international economic linkages. Thus, one test of this thesis compares the process in two countries—in this case, France and the United States. My argument predicts that rising international economic interdependence in the form of exports, multinationality, and global intra-firm trade should have affected firms' preferences similarly in the two countries, regardless of other domestic differences. This similarity would be remarkable given how frequently France and the United States have been characterized as opposites in their domestic political structures. The unlikelihood of finding similarities was the main reason for this particular comparison.

To understand why advanced industrial countries maintained relatively open economies in the 1970s, I shall explore two aspects of the trade policy process. First, I shall examine the formation of firms' trade preferences, and second, the structure of the trade policymaking process. These two aspects are critical to my central argument for several reasons. The proposed thesis suggests that firms' trade preferences should be strongly shaped by their position in the international economy and less by other, more domestic factors. This argument has two implications. First, contrary to some strong assertions about the autonomy of the state, firms' trade preferences should be relatively independent of state influence. This argument contradicts the view of "the democratic state as an autonomous entity capable of shaping societal preferences in accord with its own."[1] Second, it implies that firms with similar positions in the two countries should have similar preferences. It proposes that the way firms determine their preferences should be strongly similar *across* countries. A correlation between similarly placed firms and their trade preferences in France and the United States would help establish these points.

But a further step will show whether these preferences affect outcomes. We must examine how these preferences are involved in the policy process. If policymaking structures in these two countries allow firms' preferences to affect the policy process, then the nature of these preferences and how they are formed will be of central importance in understanding policy outcomes. A comparison of the policy process in the two countries will show if, and how, industry influences these structures.

My argument is not that firms' preferences alone account for outcomes or that the policy processes in these two countries are identical; but rather that firms' preferences are one of the most important influences on trade policy in both countries. Both firms' trade policy preferences and the policymaking process will thus tell us why, given the turmoil of the 1970s, the advanced industrial countries maintained relatively open economies.

The first section of this article develops the argument linking aspects of increased international interdependence with changes in firms' trade policy preferences. I shall discuss how the growing international ties of French and U.S. firms reduced their interests in protection. Industries from the two countries will test this assertion. The second section examines characteristics of the trade policymaking process in the two countries, focusing on how this process allows industry preferences to affect policy. Much of the literature on economic policymaking implies that France and the United States should be differentially sensitive to industry demands. As a "weak state," the United States has been depicted as very susceptible to interest group pressures, while France as a "strong state" has been portrayed as highly resistant to industry pressure with its "state-led" policy system. In this view, the preferences of French industry have little bearing upon policy since the process is seen as insulated from societal influence. Instead, I suggest how the French policy structure also allows firms' preferences into the process, and I argue that it has a much less "strong" state than many claim.

1. INTERNATIONAL INTERDEPENDENCE AND INDUSTRY INTERESTS

The integration of the French and U.S. economies into the global one accelerated greatly during the postwar period. In terms of exports, imports, multinational production, and intra-firm trade, both these economies became more dependent on the international economy, although in different ways. In its trade, France has always been more dependent on the international economy than the United States; however, this dependence increased dramatically in the postwar period. French industrial export dependence rose from 12 percent in 1958 to about 20 percent in 1968 and up to 33 percent by 1981. Import penetration grew from 15 percent in 1958 to around 20 percent by 1968 and to almost 30 percent by 1981. Consequently the economy's openness to trade grew rapidly after 1958, much more than it had in the previous five decades.

American trade dependence was more restricted than France's. But even it grew in the postwar period. U.S. export dependence rose from about 5 percent in the late 1950s to almost 20 percent by the late 1970s. Its import dependence climbed from 5 percent in 1960 to over 20 percent in 1980. While lagging behind France in trade dependence, the United States' multinational ties have been more extensively developed. The internationalization of American firms began before

World War I, resumed in the interwar period, and accelerated greatly after 1945. Thus, by the late 1970s, direct U.S. industrial foreign investment accounted for over 20 percent of its total industrial assets. In addition, the global operations of these firms have become increasingly complex, often creating a web of international trade flows within the firm. In particular, re-export from foreign production sites to the U.S. market by U.S. multinationals has grown immensely. The amount was miniscule in the 1940s, but by 1981, over 15 percent of all U.S. manufactured imports were assembled abroad by U.S. firms. U.S. direct foreign investment and its related intra-firm trade were well developed by the 1980s, even though its trade dependence, while growing, remained less than that of most other advanced industrial countries.

France's multinational production and trade were, in contrast, much less established. French industry was late in developing multinational ties. Most date this development from the mid-1960s, although the greatest growth occurred only after 1974. Indeed, by 1974, foreign French production accounted for only 10 percent of total industrial production. Moreover, France has been slower in creating globally integrated firms. Trade flows within French multinationals were less developed than they were among their U.S. counterparts. In fact, despite home markets of similar size, European multinationals' re-export to the home market amounted to $260 million in 1978, compared to $4.1 billion for U.S. firms. Growth of French trade dependence and multinationality thus occurred in the postwar period. Its levels of interdependence were, however, much greater in trade, particularly trade within the European Community (EC), than in multinational activities, while the opposite held for the U.S., where multinationality was more significant than trade dependence.

The Argument about Industry Preferences

My central claim is that aspects of the increased international interdependence similarly affected the interests of firms in both countries. Firms more extensively involved in the international economy through exports, multinationality, and intra-firm trade should be less likely to seek protectionism even in times of economic distress than firms without such international ties. These internationally oriented firms should find protection costly for several reasons. First, firms that export or have foreign production and trade flows will be concerned about retaliation. Demanding protection at home may prompt greater protection abroad or new restrictions on foreign operations and their trade flows. Second, protection in one market may hurt a firm's exports to third markets as other exporters divert their products to these third markets to compensate for the closure of the market elsewhere. Third, firms enmeshed in a global web of trade and production will view protection as a new cost that may undermine the existing pattern of trade and investment. For these firms, protectionism will be very disruptive and costly. Fourth, for firms dependent on imports, whether from their subsidiaries, subcontractors, or foreign firms, new trade barriers will increase their costs substantially, often eroding their competitiveness. Finally, intra-industry rivalries will create resistance to protectionism. Internationally oriented firms will find that protection puts them at a disadvantage vis-à-vis their domestically oriented rivals. It imposes a cost on the international firms, while providing substantial benefits for the domestically centered firms, thus perhaps enhancing the latter's market position and profitability. The different relative costs and benefits of protection will also prompt internationally oriented firms to oppose it. For these reasons, firms with substantial international ties will find protection of the home market very costly and will probably resist appeals for it.

My argument is that, assuming other solutions to their problems besides protection (such as diversification or exit) are about equally costly to all firms, the internationally oriented firms should be less likely to demand protection, given its higher relative cost to them. Protection will cost more than other options, and protection will benefit these firms less than it will the domestically oriented firms. For these domestically centered firms under import pressure, protection will be less costly and thus preferable. Thus, I claim that serious foreign competition will be more likely to cause domestically oriented firms to seek protection, because protection is so much less costly for them. . . .

Some Results

The investigation of American and French industries reveals a strong correlation between their international ties and their trade policy preferences. For industries that were dominated by firms lacking substantial ties to the international economy, soaring imports tended to produce rising demands for extensive protection. In contrast, protection was not desired for industries whose firms had well-developed multinational operations *and integrated global production and trade flows*—even in times of rapidly rising imports. In fact, they often attempted to further open markets at home and abroad. Between these two extremes lay a range of industries whose firms possess either some multinational ties or some exports. For these intermediate cases, preferences were more complex. They differed greatly from firm to firm. Most commonly, they sought some form of limited or selective protection when they were under strong import competition. For these firms, a compromise tended to develop, which involved protection targeted against their strongest competitors while leaving their other foreign markets undisturbed. Both the French and U.S. cases illustrate this pattern of trade preferences.

The U.S. and French footwear producers typified the industries that lacked substantial international economic ties. All the U.S. producers lacked substantial export or multinational operations. After the mid-1960s when shoe imports surged, the industry, united in its preferences, launched a campaign to get tariff protection. From the early 1970s on, the industry, through its trade association, pursued this goal with increasing intensity; the association filed numerous trade complaints with the ITC, lobbied Congress for relief, developed a coalition of Congress members to promote their cause, and finally launched a public relations campaign to garner public support. In the late 1970s, these activities successfully pushed President Carter to negotiate voluntary export restraints with several East Asian countries. The producers' limited political success since has partially resulted from rising opposition to protection by some U.S. producers who had begun importing or subcontracting offshore. Thus, the industry's waxing and waning protectionist demands were partly a function of the extent of its firms' international ties.

The French footwear industry was much like its U.S. counterpart, except that, before the mid-1970s, the French had been major exporters. Hence, in the early 1970s, the industry resisted attempts to seek protection or government aid despite the import flood unleashed by the Kennedy Round tariff cuts of 1968. By mid-decade, however, as exports shrank dramatically, the smaller producers began searching for ways to get relief. At this point, the industry presented the government with a rescue plan, which contained protectionist elements. Although the plan was approved by the French government, the large exporters in the industry halted it. By the late 1970s, as the industry's international position further deteriorated, the coalition for protection was strengthened, and the industry made new demands. While Italian opposition crushed attempts to use the EC's complaint process to slow imports, the industry eventually negotiated its own voluntary export restraints with a number of East Asian countries. In the two footwear cases, the limited and diminishing international economic ties of the firms removed constraints on demanding protection when imports became a problem.

On the other hand, for a number of large multinationals with extensive international trade flows, protection was not sought largely because it had costly effects on the firms' global operations. The United States producers of automobile tires and of semiconductors are two examples. Due to their failure to develop radial tires, the U.S. producers faced a massive import surge in the early 1970s. These producers, the largest of which were sizable multinationals, reacted differently. The smaller domestic firms and the mid-sized multinationals launched a trade complaint against their strongest competitor, the French firm Michelin, in the early 1970s. Despite the opposition of the global U.S. giant, Goodyear, the U.S. government ruled against Michelin. This suit was later halted at the urging of Michelin and Goodyear. Indeed, further protectionist activity was squashed in large part by Goodyear, the industry leader that controlled the tire producers' association where trade complaints were developed. After this case, the major firms decided that the best way to meet import competition was to adjust internally, choosing various strategies of consolidation, diversification, concentration, and product specialization. The U.S. industry that emerged in the 1980s was smaller but not protectionist. After its one trade complaint in 1973, the industry largely resisted any protectionist urges, despite mounting foreign competition.

During the 1970s, the U.S. semiconductor industry faced serious import competition for the first time. The largest firms in this industry (IBM, Texas Instruments, Motorola) were internationally oriented, with widespread foreign production facilities and intra-firm trade; the smaller firms were more domestically focused. Demands for aid or protection by the industry did not occur in the 1970s. By the late 1970s, however, the smaller firms, united in the Semiconductor Industry Association (SIA), began developing a trade complaint against the Japanese. Because of opposition by the large firms, especially IBM, this complaint was not formalized at the time. Initially, Texas Instruments and IBM refused to join the SIA because they opposed its activities. Later, IBM joined the SIA and helped turn its attention towards negotiations with Japan over further tariff reductions. These negotiations, compelled by the firms, resulted in lowered tariffs; other moves to open the Japanese market followed. In the 1970s, then, the strong, international ties of the leading semiconductor manufacturers helped prevent a turn to protectionism in the face of rapidly rising imports.

In France, the tire and glass industries behaved similarly. The French tire industry, mainly Michelin, faced enormous problems after the mid-1970s. The firm was quite export-dependent and multinational, and planned to become more so. To deal with foreign competition, then, the firm chose to avoid any demands for protection or government aid. Instead, it adjusted through its own economic means, further internationalizing its operations. Protectionism would only upset the firm's global operations, which were considered crucial to its success.

The French glass industry reacted similarly to the intense foreign competition it faced from British, American, and Japanese multinationals in the 1970s. This industry was largely European in its operations and quite export-dependent. Despite an invasion of imports, the French producers never sought protection or government aid. Furthermore, they favored tariff reductions and actively opposed protection for glass in the United States. Like other internationally oriented industries, the glass producers adjusted on their own. The second largest French and European producer, BSN, left the business entirely in the late 1970s, while the largest firm, St. Gobain, adjusted by further "Europeanizing" production and building new glass factories. Once again, neither protection nor government aid was desired, or received, to deal with foreign competition by these internationally oriented firms.

Between these highly domestically oriented and very internationally oriented industries lay a range of intermediate cases. Many of these industries had some exports or some multinational production, but they were still focused mostly on the domestic market. In these cases, demands for selective protection—that is, protection of particular products or against certain countries—usually resulted. Two examples illustrate these intermediate cases: U.S. and French television producers. The U.S. television producers had some foreign operations but were not exporters. In fact, the industry was divided: the two largest producers, RCA and GE, were integrated multinationals; the rest of the industry, including Zenith, Magnavox, and GTE-Sylvania, were primarily domestic producers. In the 1970s, when East Asian imports began pouring into the United States, the domestically oriented producers initiated a series of trade complaints against a few East Asian countries and several specific products. These complaints met with varying success, but RCA, the industry's giant multinational, opposed them all. By the late 1970s and early 1980s, much of this protectionist activity had abated as the American firms began their own adjustment. This adjustment further eroded support for even the limited, selective protection they desired earlier.

Although the French television industry was created behind extensive trade barriers, by the late 1960s, imports began claiming an ever larger share of the domestic market. The French industry, lacking international ties, reacted to this invasion by seeking more protection and government aid. The industry negotiated its own voluntary quotas with the Japanese and designed various industrial policy plans for itself. By the mid-1970s, the industry's strategy had shifted. The dominant and sole French producer, Thomson-Brandt, began foreign operations throughout Europe. Thomson's Europeanization sparked its growing interest in a freer intra-European market. To this end, it worked to eliminate the technical barriers that sealed off the French market. Its interest in containing Japanese color television competition, however, endured. Thus, Thomson's Europeanization created an interest in promoting a European market, while maintaining selective protection against the Japanese.

In all these cases, extensive international economic ties through exports, multinationality, or intra-firm trade prompted firms to resist seeking protection in times of severe import competition. Indeed, in certain cases, these international ties created strong anti-protectionist interests within the industry. This pattern of results appeared in both French and U.S. industries. The two countries' industries discovered the logic of increased interdependence despite their different contexts.

We should note three additional points. First, the cases reveal that firms usually did have a fairly clear conception of their trade policy preferences. In contrast to the findings of R. Bauer, I. Pool, and L. Dexter, the firms and industry associations in this study formed trade policy preferences and pursued them quite actively. Because they faced strong competition and the policies they pursued were sector-specific, their situation differed from the 1950s case examined by Bauer, Pool, and Dexter. Firms may have greater difficulty and less interest in defining their preferences clearly when they are less threatened by imports and faced with a much broader policy issue, such as the delegation of tariff-cutting ability to the president.

A second point deals with collective action problems. It has been argued that there is an asymmetry in the willingness of free trade and protectionist interests to act. Groups interested in free trade will be less likely to act politically since the benefits to them individually will be small and diffuse; for protectionists, however, the benefits of such activity will be sizable and very tangible. The evidence here challenges this claim. It shows that small groups of internationally oriented firms—even one firm—interested in resisting protection or in further liberalizing trade may find the benefits of political activities to be very substantial and worth the costs. Thus, these groups may act to realize their preferences just as much as protectionist groups do. Moreover, the cases reveal that the failures of an industry to develop a strong, common front on trade issues may result less from collective action problems than from divisiveness among the firms over the desired policy. Intra-industry disputes may account in large part for the inability of industries to develop and realize their trade policy positions, as the French and U.S. footwear and semiconductor cases suggest.

Third, firms' preferences were not driven by the state's, but were developed largely by examining their own international positions. In contrast to certain arguments about the autonomy of the state, little evidence shows that even the "strong"

French state played a major role in shaping its firms' preferences. . . . In no case did a firm's preferences appear to be directly shaped by the state. More frequently, firms' preferences shaped the state's activity. Often the firms, and not the state, initiated policy for the sector. For example, the French footwear and television industries both took a central role in developing and initiating the sectoral trade and industrial policies undertaken. Moreover, some French industries had very little need for state help. For instance, the French tire and glass producers adjusted independently without seeking aid or protection.

While perhaps not directly shaping preferences, the state, it has been claimed, may alter the context of economic activity and thereby reshape industry preferences. For the French economy, the creation of the European Common Market and the building of "national champion" firms are linked to this effect. It is likely that the Common Market helped create export and multinational interests, which have since become major supporters of that international market. But it is also true that important support for the Common Market was evident among certain large, internationally oriented French firms before its inception. Institutions and societal interests were interdependent. Societal interests favoring the institution's goals appeared important for its creation. Over time, however, the institution, to remain successful, promoted these interests, thereby establishing further support for itself. This process suggests that the institutional context in which firms operate may, over time, influence firms' calculations of their preferences—but that firms' preferences may also affect the institutions.

Finally, the creation of French "national champions" has provided equivocal support for freer trade. Despite their large size, many national champions have remained domestically oriented, often because of governmental pressures, and they have been unwilling to see their virtual domestic monopolies broken by foreign competition. In contrast, others have developed foreign operations, often at the government's displeasure, and have become anti-protectionist forces. The main point is that while firms take many factors into account when developing their preferences, the extent of their linkage to the international economy plays a critical role.

2. TRADE POLICY STRUCTURES AND INDUSTRY INFLUENCE

This section discusses how firms' preferences affect trade policy outcomes, and whether the structure of policymaking allows business interests to play an important role in shaping policy outcomes. In particular, it examines how these interests are integrated into the policy process, describing the U.S. and French "policy networks" linking state and society in the trade issue-area.

Much of the literature on French economic policymaking implies that answers to this question should differ greatly between the two countries. In these accounts, the French state is viewed as the primary determinant of policy, while societal interests are seen as secondary at best. French policy is "state-led." The French state is depicted as highly centralized, unified, and powerful, relative to its decentralized, divided societal actors; it is a very "strong" state. The preferences of industries in this political structure are seen as much less important than they are in the United States. In contrast, the U.S. state is viewed as a "weak" one—decentralized, divided against itself, and easily permeated by societal interests. These scholars contrast the closed, unified policy process in France with the open, fragmented U.S. policy process.

This contrast appears to be overdrawn. Evidence presented in this study and others reveals that industry preferences are deeply involved in the trade process in both countries. The structure of policymaking allows significant industry influence in both, although the character of this involvement differs in the two countries. Thus, knowledge of the policymaking structure, *as well as the preferences of industries,* is critical in both for understanding policy outcomes.

Four characteristics of the policy process are often used to distinguish policymaking in the United States and France: (1) the degree of unity in the policy process (often the number of state actors involved); (2) the extent of insulation of the policymaking bureaucracy; (3) the number of policy instruments available; and (4) the coherence of policymakers' goals. The less each of these characterizes the policy process, the "weaker" the state is seen to be, and the greater the likelihood that societal influences can significantly affect the process. In terms of these four aspects, the structure of policymaking in France is often viewed as differing greatly from the U.S. structure. The French state is seen as "strong" on each account. Its purported differences from the United States are crucial to my argument because they imply that industry preferences in France, even if formed independently of the state, should have minimal effect on policy outcomes.

Characteristic #1: Unity of State Policymaking Structures

Studies of French policymaking portray it occurring in a highly centralized and unified state, with decision-making controlled by the executive and, within that branch, by the Ministry of Finance and the prime minister. Trade policymaking in France, however, appears much less unified than these accounts suggest. First of all, France de jure has no independent trade policy. As many French policymakers explained, trade policy is made at the EC, not nationally. While overstated, this point is important because most of the traditional trade policymaking apparatus is located in Brussels, not Paris. The negotiation and setting of tariff rates and the use of GATT-sanctioned trade measures—such as antidumping, countervailing duty, and escape clause measures—rest in the hands of the Community. Analogues to the United States' ITC and STR then are found in the European Community's Commission.

Within France, however, mechanisms exist to shape French positions on trade. The Direction for External Economic Relations (DREE), attached before 1975 to the Ministry of Finance and afterward to the Ministry of Foreign Trade, is the central locus for defining French positions within the EC. The DREE is also responsible for French export policies and the control of imports under its old system of import restrictions.

Other ministries also shape trade policy. The Ministry of Industry develops much sectoral policy, including trade complaints and export aid. Industries often bring their complaints and demands first to their division of the Ministry of Industry—as both the footwear and television producers did. The Ministry of Agriculture deals with all agricultural trade policy, while other "tutelles" develop policies for their clients—for example, the Ministry of Health oversees policy affecting the pharmaceutical industry. Finally, the Ministry of Foreign Affairs watches over trade policy developments to ensure that they do not disturb relations with foreign governments.

While the French parliament is not as directly involved with trade legislation as the U.S. Congress is, it plays a significant role in communicating its members' regional interests to the executive. This role was particularly evident in cases where the industry was concentrated regionally. For the footwear, watch and clock, and tire industries, firms' problems and complaints sparked regional representatives' activities, which included not only launching local initiatives, but also pressing the national authorities to help the industries. All these strands of trade activity are supposedly coordinated through an inter-ministerial committee chaired by the prime minister. The actual role of this committee seems quite limited in fact, and policymaking often lacks centralized direction.

The fragmented French trade policy process provides many avenues for industries to voice their preferences. An industry can petition the EC or lodge its complaint with various national authorities. If the EC resists its pressure, it can find allies at home to increase pressure on the EC's Commission, as happened in the television case. If the Ministry of Finance or the DREE resists its appeals, it can turn to its tutelle or regional representatives for help, as occurred in the footwear and pharmaceutical industries. Multiple channels of access exist, then, for industries to express their demands. These channels give industries the ability to play one group off against another, as they often do in the United States. For instance, in the late 1970s the pharmaceutical industry finally succeeded in having the government remove price controls, which served to limit imports, from many of its goods. The industry achieved this aim by allying with the Ministries of Industry and of Health against the Ministry of Finance. Regional authorities and allies in one ministry who can countervail another's authority enable industries to be heard. Overall, trade policymaking in France exhibits a fairly fragmented character, as it does in the United States.

Characteristic #2: Insulation of the Bureaucracy

France's bureaucracy has been portrayed as highly insulated from societal influence, given the bureaucrats' similar backgrounds and strong esprit de corps. Although their similar social backgrounds and educational training may make them a cohesive social group, it does not necessarily set them apart from other sectors of society. . . . This situation has created a community among bureaucrats and business leaders. The two tend to have easy access to one another. Moreover, working groups that are created to define policies for troubled industries bring business leaders and bureaucrats into close contact, as evidence from the television industry shows. Indeed, some have pointed out the "quiet conspiracy" between them in determining postwar economic policy. The French bureaucracy may be a socially coherent group, but its insulation from other groups has been exaggerated given its close relations with business.

Politically, the bureaucracy's independence from societal actors is also limited. The bureaucracy's access to information and development of policy expertise has not been achieved without industry help. In a number of cases, the bureaucracy's understanding of a particular industry's problems and its gathering of statistics depended directly on information from the industry itself. For instance, in the footwear, watch and clock, and television cases, the best information on sales, imports, and exports was provided by the industry associations to the Ministry of Industry. Moreover, in these cases, the industries initially formulated their own industrial policy plans and trade policies. In addition, some of these industries even negotiated their own voluntary export agreements with foreign producers and their governments. The French bureaucracy, then, does not appear independent from industry for its information collection, policy planning, or implementation.

The character of the relations between an industry and the bureaucracy in France may also reduce decision-makers' autonomy. As others have theorized, bureaucrats may sometimes be more willing than politicians to help industries under their auspices. In particular, when bureaucracies have narrowly defined areas of jurisdiction and they compete with one another, keeping one's clients happy is the key to successfully retaining, and perhaps expanding, one's jurisdiction. Such conditions describe the French system, especially the Ministry of Industry. This ministry is organized into sections dealing with specific industries, and it competes with other ministries for jurisdictional control over these industries. In addition, the ministry's sections have very extensive, long-term relations with their industries, which involve much bargaining and consensual decision-making, as the footwear, television, watch and clock, and pharmaceutical cases illustrate. In each case, the industry tended to initiate its own proposals and then negotiate with the bureaucracy to get what it wanted. Studies of the textile, steel, nuclear, and oil industries show these patterns as well. The French bureaucracy thus seems less insulated from industry than others have suggested. Rather, it is engaged in an extensive negotiating relationship with industry, which often produces mutually acceptable outcomes.

Characteristic #3: The Number of Policy Instruments

The French state is often seen as possessing a plethora of policy instruments, partly because of its long history of intervention in the economy. While sizable, its array of trade and industrial policy instruments is not vastly superior to the United States'. In trade, many French policy instruments have been assumed by the EC, namely those involving tariff levels and unfair trade practices. Unlike the United States then, the French cannot impose their own trade law measures. The well-developed U.S. arsenal of legal procedures to redress trade problems is not easily available to the French. Instead, they must petition the EC, a supranational body in which French interests must take their place among many other nations' interests. Additionally, the French cannot legislate trade assistance for particular industries, as the United States Congress does. While these laws would contradict GATT provisions, they are nonetheless possible in the United States and unheard of in France.

On the other hand, the French possess an administrative capability for controlling imports. The French trade laws that were developed in the 1930s made import controls the rule and free trade the exception. While parts of these laws still exist, allowing bureaucrats to monitor and impose quotas on imports, much of their substance has been eliminated by France's decision to participate in the GATT and the EC. Use of these quotas has been foresworn and control of imports has devolved to the EC. Nonetheless, quotas and negotiated import controls have developed in both France and the United States. The proliferation of voluntary export restraints and other non-tariff barriers has affected the two countries very similarly. The use of import controls, then, is not restricted to France. Overall, in terms of traditional trade measures, the French may actually be *less* well-endowed than the Americans because of the EC's important role.

The French, it has been shown, have many non-traditional methods to affect trade. Besides the use of standards, norms, and government procurement, all of which are available in the United States, the French have recourse to industrial policy and export subsidies. Many observers have viewed industrial policy as a substitute for trade policy. The main lines of French industrial policy have involved two measures. First, it has promoted "restructuration" of industries, usually promoting concentration around the leading firms in the industry. Second, the French have given aid for R&D and exports, or simply as a production subsidy. For the cases examined, the two have been intertwined: industries have demanded aid and the government has offered it on condition that the industries restructure. Both policies seek to render the industries more competitive, but only aid has direct protectionist implications.

The amount of aid that industries receive is difficult to estimate since it comes in many forms. For instance, interest rate subsidies are very difficult to calculate. Some estimates of this aid, however, do exist. One estimate places *total* state aid to industry at eight billion francs in 1972 and over twenty billion francs in 1979. This accounted for roughly 3 percent of French industrial production in 1979. But of 15 billion francs in total aid in 1976, only a fifth (3.5 billion) went to promote exports. These export credits equaled 2 percent of France's total exports. In addition to these outright credits, the state's COFACE (Compagnie Française d'Assurances du Commerce Extérieur) provided export insurance to approximately a third of all French exports. Over 60 percent of this state aid, however, was channeled to five industrial sectors—steel, shipbuilding, computers, electronics, and aeronautics. Export aid in France was thus limited, in both its percentage of total aid and its distribution among industries.

Compared with U.S. activity in the same area, the figures show similar *levels* of expenditures in both countries. In 1975, direct state aid to exports totaled $27.3

million in France and $23.7 million in the United States. While the U.S. figure is obviously a much lower percentage of its total exports, the absolute figures show that export subsidies are available to either government. Another figure also reveals that government funding of R&D is very important in the United States as well as in France. Public funding of industrial R&D as a percentage of total funding (public and private) in 1979 was about 29 percent for France and 32 percent for the United States. These comparable figures imply that the United States also has an active industrial policy, one carried out mainly in conjunction with its defense policy.

The French state's control over credit has been the central example of its ample means to control societal actors. Evidence from the cases suggests that this instrument was rarely used as a "stick" towards industry. Instead, financial aid was the "carrot" offered for industry restructuring. Granting aid seemed less the result of the state's autonomous decisions than of negotiations between industry and the state. For example, the watch and clock industry association drew up and presented its own rescue plans to the government and then spent much time negotiating for the aid it had requested and arguing about how to restructure. This bargaining between the two sides was very common, appearing in every case where aid was demanded. In this process the French state did have ample negotiating leverage. In most cases, it was able to prompt restructuring, even if not desired by the industry. But this was a bargained outcome. The state paid for it by giving aid to the industry, even when it did not want to pay.

In the United States, relations appeared far more adversarial, as noted elsewhere. Little could be done to induce industries to change their ways, but threats and denials of help were possible. In the United States, sometimes antitrust policy was used. The threat of antitrust action forced industries to back down from making trade complaints in several cases. For instance, the machine tool industry couldn't file a major trade complaint after all its documents were impounded in an antitrust suit. The outright denial of industry demands was also possible through the ITC's findings or Presidential decision, as happened to the footwear industry several times. Such denials and threats occurred less frequently in France. There, the long standing, close relations between industries and the state fostered the negotiated resolution of industry problems. Overall, it seems inaccurate to portray the French state as significantly better equipped with trade or industrial policy instruments. Both countries have a plethora of their own, specific means for aiding and guiding industries.

Characteristic #4: Coherence of State Policy Goals

Finally, French policymakers have been characterized as possessing a set of goals, distinct from much of their society's, that have directed the postwar French economy. The central goal of French foreign policy has been the pursuit of national autonomy and influence. This goal involved policies to maximize its external dependence. Such goals entailed promoting economic growth, creating and protecting strategic infant industries, and maintaining a rough balance of payments to uphold the franc's value through capital and import controls; all were pursued in the 1950s and 1960s.

Evidence of a coherent policy that followed these goals is very uneven for the 1970s, however. Overall, trade and industrial policymaking in this decade have been characterized as "ad hoc, inconsistent, and short term." No overarching strategy or plan seemed to guide policy. Money was given to ailing industries in the hope that they would recover, while protection was granted to various industries in other cases. Indeed, as the cases here demonstrate, some sectors received protection and aid—for example, footwear, watches and clocks, and television— while other, larger and more significant industries in difficulty went without it— such as pharmaceuticals, tires, and glass—often because they did not want any help. This haphazard "pattern" of protection and aid in France does not support a vision of policymakers unified in the pursuit of common goals, but rather one of a state making ad hoc adjustments partly to meet its industries' demands.

Like American legislators, French policymakers in the 1970s were increasingly caught in the problem of how to preserve their national autonomy in the face of growing international interdependence. External economic shocks multiplied in the decade, and the French found it increasingly difficult to pursue their long standing goals. Their response was not a coherent plan, but a series of ad hoc measures and compromises designed to revive growth and allow for some autonomy without disrupting their new interdependence. In 1981 and 1982, when the Socialists undertook a coherent effort at reflation, France's constrained ability to pursue national goals was starkly revealed. Greatly increased interdependence frustrated French policymakers. However, rather than reduce this interdependence by closing the economy, the French chose to accept it, and instead altered their domestic policies and goals. The management of the economy's new integration into the world economy thus proved an increasing problem for the French after 1968, as it did for many other advanced industrial countries, including the United States.

In sum, the picture of the French state I have drawn is one much less insulated from and remotely imposing over its society than traditional characterizations suggest. This state is in constant negotiation with its industries, and does not dictate policy to them. Trade and industrial policymaking seems less unified and dominated by isolated bureaucrats. Instead, it involves frequent contact between business and the state as well as bureaucrats who depend on industries for help collecting information and implementing policies. Moreover, the policy instruments available in these issue-areas hardly seem so much more numerous than those available in the United States. In addition, French policy in the 1970s does not appear as a coherent, well-planned effort to pursue a set of well-established goals. It was rather a series of ad hoc measures, frequently prompted and designed by industries themselves, to absorb the impact of the decade's external shocks.

The traditional view of the French state as a strong, centralized unit insulated from societal pressures may have been more accurate before the 1970s. But the state's success in transforming its society and increasing its integration into the world economy altered it and its relationship with that society. . . .

My argument thus contends that business in both states may have had the capacity to influence trade policymaking. In neither country did the structure of policymaking keep industry from gaining access to the policy process. But were firms and industries able to influence outcomes? The evidence I have presented can only suggest an answer to this question since it focuses mostly on firms' preferences and activities, not outcomes. The cases do lend credence to the idea that industries' access to the state provided them with influence. In the U.S. cases, firms' preferences seem to have played a role in shaping outcomes. Often intra-industry disputes weakened demands for protection, thereby relieving pressure on policymakers to institute protection. In the tire and semiconductor cases, firms' resistance to protection prevented them from voicing demands for it. In the television and footwear cases, certain firms' opposition to protection seriously weakened the demands made and may have increased policymakers' ability not to respond to these pressures. Conversely, pressure from some industries actually induced policymakers to seek further trade liberalization. For instance, the semiconductor industry was central in encouraging the U.S. government to begin negotiations with the Japanese to reduce trade barriers. These examples suggest that the preferences of these internationally oriented firms were evident in the policy process, thereby contributing to the maintenance of openness in these sectors.

Examples from the French cases also illustrate industry influence. In the footwear and watch and clock industries, the industry associations designed their own industrial policies, which the government adopted without much change. In addition, the footwear and television producers formulated and negotiated their own voluntary export restraints with foreign suppliers. In these cases, the industry shaped policy as much as the state did. Certain industries battled the government, or parts of it, to realize their preferences. The pharmaceutical industry fought for price decontrol, which it largely achieved (thus opening the country's market to imports). The major television manufacturer pushed successfully to have various non-tariff barriers lowered, despite government resistance. All these examples suggest that trade policymaking in France was not immune to industry influence. In these cases, industry preferences helped shape the adopted policy. Conclusions about how general this finding is—both among industries and in different issue-areas—are difficult. But other studies corroborate this argument. Thus, while conclusions about industry influence over outcomes must remain suggestive, one conclusion we can draw is that, in addition to examining state structures, firms' preferences should be taken into account when explaining policy outcomes since they may play an important role in shaping policies.

CONCLUSIONS

This article makes two major points. First, I have argued that aspects of increased international interdependence have wrought changes in the trade policy preferences of industries. Strengthened international economic ties in the form of exports, multinationality, and global intra-firm trade have raised the costs of protection for internationally oriented firms. These firms have thus resisted seeking protection even in times of serious import competition. This finding held for both French and American industries. Differences in the firms' contexts did not override the powerful influence that a firm's international ties exerted on its trade policy preferences. Similar international forces in the two countries shaped firms' calculations of their preferences.

Second, I compared the structure of trade policymaking in France and the United States, examining the way firms' preferences were integrated into these structures. Comparative analysis of trade and industrial policymaking in the United States and France revealed that firms' preferences were a powerful influence. France seemed less immune to industry influence than typical accounts suggest. Its state did not appear "strong" in terms of the unity of its policymaking process, the insulation of its bureaucracy, the relative number of its policy instruments, and the coherence of its goals. Thus, the structure of trade policymaking in France during the 1970s did not prevent industries from having access to and some influence over the process, and the same was true in the United States.

While the structure of trade policymaking seemed more similar between the two countries than is often claimed, the character of this process differed. Industry–state relations in France were characterized by a long-term bargaining process, often producing mutually acceptable outcomes with the industry: the industry received the aid or protection it desired, and the state obtained reorganization of the industry. Trade policymaking in the United States, while as fragmented and ad hoc as in France, involved a more distant relationship between industry and the state. As in France, firms or industries initiated much activity to get protection, but relations in the United States appeared less accommodating. These different policymaking styles undoubtedly reflected the different political resources relevant to industry and the state in the countries. Nevertheless, because of similar "weaknesses" in their policymaking structures, firms' preferences in both states played a central role by helping initiate and shape policy. Thus, not only were the trade policy preferences of firms similarly shaped by certain international forces in France and the United States, but the structure of policymaking in both countries also allowed these preferences to influence outcomes. Consequently, the internationally oriented firms in both countries may have provided important resistance to protectionist pressures in the 1970s and early 1980s.

Finally, we must return to our initial question: why did all the advanced industrial democracies maintain relatively open economies in the 1970s? My argument should apply to all of these countries. It implies that if their industries became more integrated into the international economy, a growing part of their firms should have developed anti-protectionist preferences. Whether these preferences influenced policy would depend in part on the structure of policymaking in each state. For states other than France and the United States, the argument about the influence of these new preferences is more limited. In other states, the policy process may be more insulated from industry influence, or other actors, such as labor, may play a much more important role. Thus, the argument about firm preferences should be more generally applicable, while the one about the policy process more particular to the two countries I have examined. In conclusion, although the cross-national evidence here suggests that my argument may have wider validity, only further research on other countries can determine if anti-protectionist pressure from firms was also important in shaping their resistance to protection in the 1970s and 1980s.

NOTE

1. E. Nordlinger, *On the Autonomy of the Democratic State* (Cambridge, Mass.: Harvard University Press, 1981), 100.

24

Ideas, Institutions, and American Trade Policy
JUDITH GOLDSTEIN

Rejecting international and societal explanations, Judith Goldstein explains United States trade policy, and specifically the maintenance of free trade despite America's hegemonic decline, from a domestic statist perspective. She argues that the structure of state institutions has an important impact on trade policy and shows how different institutional settings—designed to promote the policy ideas of free trade, fair trade, and trade adjustment—influence patterns of protection. This is important, she maintains, because policy ideas become embedded in particular institutions and continually influence the way actors assess problems and formulate strategies. In this way, Goldstein explains why policies persist and continue to shape politics long after the specific purpose for their enactment passes.

Nowhere is America's hegemonic decline more evident than in changing trade patterns. The United States trade balance, a measure of the international demand for American goods, is suffering historic deficits. Lowered demand for American goods has led to the under-utilization of both labor and capital in a growing number of traditionally competitive American industries. Conversely, Americans' taste for foreign goods has never been so great. Japanese cars, European steel, Third World textiles, to name a few, are as well produced as their American counterparts and arrive on the U.S. market at a lower cost.

It is no surprise that as America's trade position suffers, the subject of commercial policy again looms large on the political agenda. The questioning of America's trade policy was common throughout the 19th and early 20th century. In the post–World War II period, however, a consensus arose that America should have an open, liberal trade posture. In the late 1960s, those who questioned that commitment found little support. By the 1980s, however, newspapers and journals

Judith Goldstein. "Ideas, Institutions, and American Trade Policy." From *International Organization*, Vol. 42:1 (Winter 1988), pp. 179–217. Copyright © 1988. Reprinted by permission of The MIT Press, Cambridge, Massachusetts and the author.

were heralding the return of protectionism and sounding the death knell for America's liberal trade policies.

Changes in America's market position also have led academics to predict policy change. Such predictions are no surprise. They derive directly from current analyses of American politics. Among scholars, the explanation for protectionism is often presented as the flip side of a theory of trade liberalization. The lack of the causal structure that explains the choice to pursue openness predicts protection.

Two genres of theory offer predictions for American trade policy. One looks to social pressures as an explanation for policy; the other looks to international structure. Of the two, the former dominates the study of American trade policy. Among American scholars, the seminal analysis of trade policy was conducted by E. E. Schattschneider. His analysis of the 1929–30 Smoot–Hawley Act made tariff policy the prima facie proof of extensive interest group influence over the making of American laws. Although studies of later legislation led to revisions in the original analysis of the tariff-making process, an often implicit belief that interest group activity determines protectionism remains ingrained in analyses of American economic policy.

The alternative approach used by international relations scholars considers trade as a foreign policy issue and looks to international structure as the determinant of state interest. These analysts argue that liberal trade and an absence of protectionism were prefaced by America's ascendancy to hegemony after World War II. With a decline in American power has come a decline in interest and resources with which the U.S. can maintain a liberal trade regime. As in the interest group approach, the loss of American power and market share leads to the prediction of an increase in trade protectionism.

This article argues that neither of these approaches captures the dynamic of protectionism in the U.S. Both approaches envision government as a conduit translating either group pressure or international demands into state policy. Neither approach looks at the institutional arrangements through which domestic demands and international constraints are filtered. In this article, state structure is used to explain policy. The argument made is that state structures are historically determined and reflect the biases of decision-makers present at their creation. Critical in decisions of protection is the evaluation by the state of the legitimacy of claims brought forth by social actors. What the law designates as a legitimate claim for aid has varied systematically over time. This article explains the origins and scope of three types of legitimate claims for state aid.

UNDERSTANDING PROTECTIONISM

The explanation for American protectionism or the systematic exclusion of industries from general American trade policy has three components. First, policy-making is dominated by a belief in the efficacy of free trade. That belief has been encased in post–World War II laws and institutional structures that service continued trade liberalization and ensure minimal legitimacy for social claims for protectionism. Second, U.S. policy has a "fair" trade component. Previous to America's move towards openness in the mid-1930s, policy was protectionist. From the end of the Civil War to 1934, policy reflected the belief that the U.S. could maintain an isolationist policy with respect to imports and still expand trade in foreign markets. The impact of this period is evident in laws and institutions that legitimate social claims for state intervention to favor domestic producers over foreign competitors. Third, there is a welfare component to U.S. policy. Policies exist that are redistributive. The state both compensates uncompetitive sectors and helps industries adjust to foreign competition that results from liberalization. Viewing America's policy on protectionism, an analyst finds state policies based on often contradictory ideas about the correct relationship between state and society. Laissez-faire, intervention against foreign producers, and intervention to redistribute social goods all coexist as legitimate state policies.

How can the coexistence of three apparently contradictory policies be explained? Most simply, these different policies exist because institutions, once created, live substantially beyond the mandate they originally served. Government organizations do change but more slowly than does their environment. In the U.S., a society embalmed in the "rule of law," legal constraints encourage the layering, rather than the replacing, of government institutions.

As in geological surveys, the institutions of American government can be organized by the historical period of their birth. Institutions are created to serve a particular legal mandate. Mandates evolve from a political consensus that was generated to support a particular response to a government or social need. Institutions, then, reflect a set of dominant ideas translated through legal mechanisms into formal government organizations. If ideas become encased in institutions through legal procedures, they will continue to have policy impact over time. Generally, this institutional influence derives from the existence of formal organizations whose rules, norms, expectations, and traditions establish constraints on individuals within these organizations, on elected leaders outside these organizations, and on society in general.

Institutional structures alone are an insufficient explanation for postwar American trade policies. As critical is the belief system of those individuals who enforce laws. In the U.S., liberal beliefs about trade policy have dominated the debate and thinking of those involved with policymaking. In the post-Depression period, liberalism gave decision-makers both a design for economic reconstruction and organizing principles that directed what was then seen as a problematic relationship between government and society. The Great Depression was the necessary prerequisite for the acceptance of liberalism. The Depression not only led to international decline and war but also led to a domestic crisis emanating from the fear that congressional pork-barrel politics had caused or at least contributed in a major way to great economic and political dislocation. Crisis was a requisite, a necessary but not sufficient cause, for liberalism to take on an ideological character. In its early years, liberalism can be explained in that it served the interest of the U.S. and its central decision-makers. However, the existence of unprecedented postwar affluence and power for the U.S., which came to be associated with a particular international economic policy, elevated liberalism into a realm untouchable by interest group politics. Crisis followed by affluence became the necessary and sufficient criteria for the entrenchment of liberal doctrine.

In sum, this article reexamines protectionism in the U.S. In particular, it attempts an explanation for patterns of aid. We begin with the observation that over time, societal actors have become increasingly threatened by foreign producers. In the postwar period, the U.S. has continually lowered barriers to trade at home. The result has been that American producers have encountered increasingly stiff competition at home as well as abroad. Averaged ad valorem tariffs have declined dramatically since the 1930s. . . . Import penetration has increased more quickly than either exports or GNP. In the 30 years following World War II, Americans have almost tripled their consumption of foreign goods. Whereas only 5 percent of personal consumption expenditures were for imports in 1945, that proportion increased to 14 percent by 1984. Both industry and labor have responded to loss in market share by attempting to gain state aid. Petitions for aid increased dramatically in the 1970s in all the categories examined below. Although Congress showed little interest in protectionist legislation in the 1960s, it entertained hundreds of bills pertaining to some aspect of America's trade program in the 1970s and 1980s.

This article focuses on five particular mechanisms available to these complainants. They are differentiated by the historical period in which Congress first created each form of aid. The article maintains that variation in aid is greater across the various forms of protectionism than within each form. Types of aid should be differentiated by the legal criteria used by the government to adjudicate cases. These differences in laws reflect historic shifts in ideas about what constitutes a legitimate claim for state aid. Laws alone, however, cannot explain the pattern of aid in the U.S. Equally important are the beliefs of those who adjudicate the laws. Thus, "ideas" appear twice in the explanation of protectionism. First, they are critical independent variables that explain why different laws arise in different historical periods. Second, the ideas or beliefs of those who administer the laws affect outcomes. However, contemporary beliefs of decision-makers affect the ability of groups to obtain aid only to the extent that there is room for discretion in the administration of these laws.

This article does not seek to give a general theory of American trade policy. Rather, its purpose is to show the value of studying the institutional and cognitive bases for American policy. We argue that neither the disintegration of American power nor the rise of interest group activity fully explains the pattern of protectionism. A more complete explanation resides in the study of state institutions themselves. . . .

THE LIBERAL IDEA

In the postwar period, America's commercial policy has centered on the creation and perpetuation of a liberal trade regime. As envisioned after World War II, that regime called for the opening of national borders to the free flow of goods, services, and capital. Although many aspects of the liberal regime were never accepted by America's trading partners, the U.S. has continually attempted to inculcate the neoclassical economic view of trade into international practice.

Although components of the liberal regime, most particularly the General Agreement on Tariffs and Trade (GATT), have come under criticism, support for liberalism has only minimally eroded among American central decision-makers. Liberalism still holds a social position not unlike a "sacred cow" in the policymaking community. In content, America's liberal ideas stem from two intellectual roots: 19th-century British thought and 18th-century American political philosophy.

The institutionalization of the liberal idea of free trade can be dated to 1934. Although entertained as a policy earlier in the 19th century (for example, see debate on Walker tariff, 1846), it was only after 1934 that American central decision-makers looked to free trade ideas as a basis of policy. The primary event that prefaces this move to liberalism is the Great Depression. The failure of the Smoot–Hawley tariff of 1929–30 to deal with economic decline set up a policymaking crisis. The delegitimization of protectionism forced the political community to search for an alternative theoretical approach to explain past errors and provide guidelines for future behavior.

Economic decline breeds numerous interpretations. The Great Depression was no exception. Two sets of events allowed for the particular shift towards free trade. First, institutional responsibility for tariff-making shifted to the executive. A Democratic Congress relinquished its constitutionally granted mandate under the guidance of a strong Democratic president. Party discipline alone, however, does not explain this change. The president needed to have a cognitive explanation of the interconnections between electoral misfortune, the Great Depression, and the protectionist policies of earlier administrations to gain congressional agreement. These connections were made repeatedly to the president and Congress by "free traders" such as Secretary of State Cordell Hull.

Liberalism began as one policy alternative among many. It became a policy bias only after the U.S. began to prosper under the free trade regime. Although in 1934 Congress undertook a policy of liberalization, there was no immediate opening of America's borders. The lesson of the Depression was far more modest. It was clear that Congress could no longer protect noncompetitive sectors of the American economy. Market forces could not be ignored in the rush to aid constituents. Politically, this meant that powerful private interests wishing protection would have to be ignored. In the 1930s, however, central decision-makers did not agree that free trade was the only policy option for the U.S. Liberalism became ingrained as a policy bias as intellectuals and elected officials attributed the return to abundance and postwar growth to the successive, although incremental, policy of reducing barriers to trade. Success was taken to mean that those who argued that liberalism was the optimal policy for the U.S. were correct. By the early 1970s, liberalism had become more than a policy option, it was a policy bias and a policy constraint.

Liberalization after 1934 was characterized by two processes. First, state mechanisms were developed that supported liberal trade. Not only did Congress allocate tariff-making authority to the executive, but it repeatedly endorsed the right of the U.S. to engage in negotiations to lower tariffs while nurturing bureaucracies whose mandate was to foster liberal trade relations. And second, liberalism was accepted only with safeguards. Understanding that interest groups would continue to demand particularistic import preferences, Congress created a set of safeguards to protect its policies from group interference. The method used was to create alternative mechanisms through which groups could articulate their needs. Instead of going to Congress, interest groups could go to bureaucratic agencies whose legal task was to placate potential congressional clients. As an example of this process, we turn to the escape clause.

Escape Clause

In the postwar years, Congress has instituted a number of measures that protect constituents unable to compete with foreign producers within the U.S. The measure with the longest history of both legislation and adjudication is the "escape clause." As compared with protectionist legislation written before America's move towards liberalism, the escape clause is more difficult to obtain, may be overruled at a number of decision points, and once received, needs repeated renewals to keep protection in force. In short, although potentially a device that could create great barriers to trade, the escape clause was created in a manner making attainment a difficult and arduous process. As such, this legislation has deterred a rise in protectionism and helped maintain liberalism. Cases are decided by the International Trade Commission (ITC), an independent bureaucracy that selects recipients based on a set of objective criteria established by Congress. As opposed to the pre-1934 period, the ITC, not Congress, deals with formal petitions for aid. By distancing congressional representatives, the ITC acts as a buffer, mediating potentially disruptive political pressures.

Since the escape clause was instituted by Executive Order in 1947 and incorporated into statute in 1951, the U.S. has always included safeguard provisions in trade treaties and legislation. The escape clause provision allows an industry that has been seriously injured by imports to be exempted from an American trade agreement that would lower its tariff. The initial intent of the escape clause was to accomplish what the old peril point had failed to do—that is, to keep imports at a level that precluded injury to domestic producers.

The concept of the escape clause was first used as a provision in a 1942 trade agreement with Mexico. The idea reappeared in debate over the 1945 trade act as a compromise by the executive following congressional transference of increased tariff-making authority. In return for legislation, Truman issued Executive Order 9381 (1/25/48), establishing that all future trade agreements were to include escape clause provisions.

To ensure congressional assent, the U.S. backed inclusion of an escape clause provision, similar to domestic law, in the GATT. The provision, Article XIX, was condemned by then President Truman as "an embarrassment to be avoided in the interest of maintaining an image of American leadership and dependability in world and foreign affairs." Once the escape provision was in place, however, the U.S. was the first to invoke it four years later, in a case involving hatter's fur. Under American tutelage, GATT held that the U.S. was "entitled to the benefit of the doubt" in its estimation of criteria of injury. This somewhat loose interpretation of Article XIX led to the prediction that the liberal tenets of GATT would be defeated in an onslaught of cases using a nation's own definition of injury as grounds for protection. However, the use of Article XIX to escape liberalization by the U.S. or any of its trading partners has been limited. In effect, the magnitude of changes in trade patterns over the postwar period has *not* been reflected in the use of Article XIX.

Although the earlier intent of the escape clause procedure was frozen into GATT rules, its American counterpart has evolved over time. In fact, escape clause procedures have been reexamined each time Congress has mandated further liberalization; in substance, however, much of the original program remains. By statute, a request from the president, Congress, Senate Committee on Finance, or House Ways and Means Committee, an ITC motion, or an application from an interested party (industry, union, or association) will induce an escape clause investigation. The investigation, according to the 1951 law, determines whether any industry "product on which a trade agreement concession has been granted is *as a result,* in whole or in part, of the customs treatment reflecting such concession being imported in such increased quantities either *actual or relative,* as to *cause or threaten to cause injury* to the domestic industry producing like or directly competitive products" (emphasis mine). If the ITC rules that imports did threaten an industry, it can recommend an increased import barrier. The finding, however, is by statute only a recommendation to the president. The president could choose to ignore the finding, to accept the finding but choose a different remedy, or to accept the advice of the ITC.

Since 1951, Congress has reviewed this legislation three times. An examination of the textual changes in the law reveals the 1962 criteria to be the most difficult to fulfill. This becomes obvious by looking at the evolution of the phrases emphasized above.

First, the 1951 Act required imports to have "contributed substantially" to injury or threat of injury. In 1962, this criterion was considered too permissive; instead, imports had to be "the main factor" in causing injury in order to justify aid. Under the Trade Act of 1974, the criteria again eased. Increased imports had to be only "a substantial cause" rather than "the major cause" of injury.

Second, the early law required proof that injury resulted from a customs concession. Again, Congress in 1962 voted to stipulate more strictly that causal connection. The 1962 Trade Expansion Act stipulates that injury must have resulted "in major part" from the concession, not just "in whole or in part." When reexamined in 1974, the newer requirement was dropped.

Third, the specification of whether imports have to increase in absolute or in relative terms to constitute grounds for protection has varied. In 1951, either constituted just cause; in 1962, however, the tightening of aid criteria led to legislation which specified that only an absolute increase in imports warranted aid. This interpretation was again overturned in 1974 for the earlier, more flexible interpretation.

The one criterion that has been consistently eased is the specification of what constitutes serious injury. In 1951, the ITC was mandated to consider, among other things, "a downward trend of product, employment, prices, profits, or wages in the domestic industry concerned, or a decline in sales, an increase in imports, either actual or relative to domestic production, a higher or growing inventory, or a decline in the proportion of the domestic market supplied by domestic producers." In 1962 this mandate to the ITC was expanded to include "all economic factors which it considered relevant, including idling of productive facilities, inability to operate at a level of reasonable profit, and unemployment or underemployment." The factors to be considered were further expanded in 1974. Congress declared that the ITC must consider, among other things, the "idling of productive facilities, the ability to reap a profit, unemployment and underemployment and downward trends in production, profits, wages, or employment in the affected industries."

Although these procedural issues have been addressed and changed by Congress, a basic relationship between the executive and the legislature has not been violated. In particular, Congress has never taken from the executive his jurisdiction as final judge on escape clause cases. Although sentiment has been expressed for a renewal of a congressional role in aiding industries injured by imports, the reaction of Congress has been to give more power to the bureaucracy through easing aid requirements, not to take authority from the president. As early as the 1962 hearings, the position expressed on aid was that "relief ought not to be denied for reasons that have nothing whatever to do with the merits of the case. . . . In particular . . . no U.S. industry which has suffered serious injury should be cut off from relief for foreign policy reasons."

Yet the 1962 Act was the most antiprotectionist to come out of committee. During these hearings, Congress expanded executive discretion with the inclusion of adjustment assistance as an additional alternative to using the escape clause without establishing enforceable rules to dictate presidential choice. It was not that curtailment of executive privilege was not discussed. Congress dictated guidelines for the president but did not choose to make them mandatory.

For instance, Congress has expressed preferences for one type of aid to be given over others in positive escape clause cases. In 1974 hearings, a popular opinion espoused in Congress was that in the choice between consumer interests and the interests of those unemployed, "the President should adopt the latter course and protect the industry and the jobs associated with the industry." In terms of preferred remedies, Congress stated that an import duty was to be considered and used first while an Orderly Marketing Agreement (OMA) was to be considered last. This advice has been repeatedly ignored.

In sum, although Congress has argued about the form, amount, and duration of escape clause aid to industries affected by imports, the power to make those decisions has remained with the president. In legislation aimed at affecting the decision-making criteria used by the bureaucracy, Congress has maintained guidelines established in the 1950s, a time when there was little interest and minimal pressure for protectionism. Although a presidential veto of an ITC decision could be overturned by Congress with increased ease over time, the power has never been exercised. Rather, Congress is content with what appear to be symbolic measures to aid industry.

That Congress plays only a symbolic role in aiding industry is counterintuitive, given the structural relationship between Congress and powerful private groups. Congress has been a focal point for societal pressures aimed at gaining relief from imports. Even though negotiating authority was given to the president in 1934, the ability to legislate protective duties remains with Congress. Yet Congress has not responded to industry malaise with legislation—on the occasions when a quota was passed by one of the houses, executive intervention has forestalled implementation. Although the 1980s have been filled with accounts of impending congressional intervention, the large increase in bills entered in the *Congressional Record* has led to relatively few changes in law. The fear of a "slippery slope" to protectionism continues to affect the legislative process.

The role Congress does play is to establish criteria by which the technocrats in the ITC or the other trade-related bureaucracies adjudicate cases. As more pressure is placed on Congress, it responds by expanding the powers of the bureaucracy, not by intervention. Congress retains the right to hold hearings and has done so for key sectors such as the steel and automobile industries. However, once a hearing is completed, it is executive, not congressional, action that dictates whether that industry will receive effective aid. Congressional consent is necessary to appoint commissioners to the ITC. And congressional hearings and pressures from interested private groups affect the constitution of the ITC itself. But, since even a pro-protectionist ruling by the ITC in an escape clause case will be meaningless if the executive does not accept the ITC's advice, the role of Congress is severely constrained.

In sum, two facts emerge from this review of the legal history of the escape clause. First, legislation has changed, but in only marginal ways, over the postwar period. In the periods before 1962 and after 1974, the criteria for escape clause aid were easier to meet than under the 1962 Act. We expect that ITC decisions will reflect these changes in law. Second, although Congress has changed the legal criteria over time, the basic design of the legislation has remained substantially the same. Congress sets standards, the ITC adjudicates cases, but the president makes all final decisions on relief and amount. In short, the law gives much latitude to the president. The power of the executive office to maintain trade policy is the institutional design that has fostered liberalism in the postwar period. . . .

THE DEFENSE OF FAIR TRADE

The escape clause is only one mechanism open to industries needing import protection. The other forms of aid, to which we now turn, are based on differing notions of what constitutes a legitimate claim for protection. These laws, conceived before the Great Depression, reflect a period when the ideas of List and Hamilton dominated those of Smith and Ricardo. It is this period, from the end of the Civil War to Smoot–Hawley, in which ideas of "autarky" led policymakers to see gains from trade only in terms of export expansion. (By 1913, liberal ideas had gained increased acceptance among a subset of policymakers. Only after 1934, however, did legal and institutional changes allow these ideas to be translated into policy.) This period gave rise to what is labeled here as a "fair" trade law.

Indicative of differing views on trade, the legislative debates on tariffs in this earlier period are distinguishable. The question addressed by those debating the tariff in the earlier period was whether a tariff's primary purpose should be to raise revenue or to protect national industry; in the later period the debate turned on the tariff as a foreign policy instrument. In the earlier period, the tariff was subject to congressional logrolling; after 1934, tariff-making authority was given to the executive. Finally, the first set of tariffs was more reflective of the nexus of competing interests of the time. Since no one position on what was an optimal tariff had emerged, the type of tariff passed was a function of the capabilities of particular groups within and outside Congress. After 1934, agreement on one position on tariff policy—that is, liberalism—substantially transformed the interest group process.

What is somewhat unusual in the U.S. move to free trade is that liberalization occurred without the dismantling of pre-liberal norms, values, and institutions. Laws written in America's pre-liberal period reveal a far different set of state interests than would be the case after the Depression. In design these "mercantile" statutes reflect earlier American concerns with economic nationalism, not with later interest in the international gains free trade would afford. These laws changed little, even as the U.S. revamped her basic approach to trade policy. Thus, even in America's most liberal period, a legal mandate existed to exclude imports under these sets of laws.

Three laws are examined in this section. All have their legal roots in the pre-1934 period of American tariff history. All establish a set of criteria for "fair" trade based on a narrow interpretation of legitimate market behavior. Created in a period in which the U.S. wanted to discourage imports, these laws establish criteria for fair trading and state involvement in the production process that could exclude the majority of America's current trading partners. A philosophical difference exists between how cases of "fair" competitive trade that adversely affects an American producer and cases of "unfair" trade that may cause the same result are viewed. Belief in the long-term beneficial aspects of the market has translated into a condemnation by American decision-makers of foreign governments and foreign industries that attempt to interfere with "natural" market mechanisms, especially if the goal of that manipulation is predatory. The relationship between the American state and private industry is the model used to evaluate actions taken by other nations. The law stipulates that no country assist home industries or interfere with consumer market preferences to a greater extent than is done in the U.S.

A number of problems exist in the administration of these "fair" trade laws. First, there is a problem in the discovery and definition of a violation. Rulings in all three types discussed below are subject to difficulties with data collection; administrators must rely on domestic and foreign producers to supply information, which is often incomplete and difficult to assess. In laws in which the intent of the foreign producer to undercut an American producer is critical to the state's ruling, it is even more difficult for American complainants to prove their case. Foreign producers do engage in what Americans view as unfair practices but often without predatory intent. There is a dilemma in how to judge, for example, national pricing policies or subsidized research and development programs. In such cases foreign practices were often not created to gain a market advantage but merely reflect national goals.

Second, administrators must adjudicate cases based on overly ethnocentric standards. States vary greatly in their philosophical and historical relationship to producers. The relationship found in the U.S. is not characteristic of that found in other polities. To use the U.S. case as a benchmark establishes criteria on the extreme end of a continuum. The enforcement of American values of the state-industry relationship not only interferes with a set of foreign policy goals that seek prosperity in noncommunist states but also translates into interference into other states' domestic politics. Such interference alienates allies and in principle deviates from the regime norm of sovereignty.

These issues were not of great importance in the early years of the liberalization program. As competition increased in the American market, however, these laws were rediscovered. Industries filed better claims and increasingly qualified under the narrow interpretation of "fair" trade as embodied in early law. This presented a dilemma for liberal central decision-makers who thought it in the nation's economic interest to keep the American market open. Administrators responded, whenever possible, by obfuscating the law through delays, noncollection of extra duties, and loose interpretations of findings. Such practices are no longer broadly accepted. Unfair trade issues are viewed by Congress, by the population, and by many administrators as more legitimate than their escape clause counterpart. "Cheating" remains antithetical to liberal norms. The problem facing central decision-makers who accept the principle of fair trade, however, is how to maintain openness while adhering to the narrow interpretation of fairness established in American statutes.

Antidumping Legislation

Antidumping legislation appeared in its modern form in 1921, although earlier, in the Revenue Act of 1916, a similar condemnation of unfair trade practices was legislated. The intent of an antidumping law is to counter international price discrimination. Legislation protects home producers from competition arising from imports being sold at values below those at which they are sold in their home market or below their cost of production. If such a practice is found to exist, an additional duty equal to that price differential is assessed on the product.

Until the Trade Act of 1979, the request of a domestic producer to the Customs Bureau of the Treasury Department would trigger a preliminary appraisal of whether just cause existed for an antidumping investigation. If the appraisal was negative, the case was rejected. This preliminary judgment process, which determined the fate of many cases, was often inconsistent and highly discretionary.

Upon a positive preliminary determination, the Treasury Department would launch an investigation. The major component of the investigation determined whether sales were at Less Than Fair Value (LTFV). Compared with the other forms of aid examined in this essay, the criteria for such a determination were quite detailed. Dumping is defined by 300 lines of text in the Antidumping Act with an additional 1,000 lines on administrative regulation in the *Federal Register*. In contrast, the only criterion the Trade Act of 1974 imposed on the president's escape clause decisions was "the national economic interest of the United States," and the criteria by which the 1974 Trade Act charged the ITC with judging injury take up only thirty-five lines.

If a LTFV ruling is made by the Treasury Department, the case goes to the ITC for a determination of whether there has been domestic "injury" as a result of the dumping activity. Until 1979 the ITC had a wide amount of discretion in its determination. No hearing was necessary, even if requested by the petitioners. If the ITC found in the affirmative, a report was issued to the secretary of the treasury, who issued a "finding of dumping." As opposed to escape clause cases, a tie vote in the ITC became an affirmative finding. Until 1979, some redundancy existed between the Treasury Department and the ITC mandate. In particular, the information the ITC studied in making its final determination did not necessarily have to apply only to the injury determination. The ITC could find no injury based on a redetermination that the foreign producer was not, in its judgment, dumping, and overturn the Treasury Department ruling.

The discretionary nature of the injury determination was of central concern to foreign producers in the Tokyo Round of GATT negotiations. The antidumping code agreed to in Geneva incorporated the notion of "material injury," not just any injury, by reason of LTFV imports. In previous hearings on the Kennedy Round of negotiated agreements, Congress had held that the international codes signed in 1967 did not change the 1954 revisions of the antidumping law. In question was whether any degree of injury other than *de minimus* constituted injury. The U.S. agreed that it did, although this conflicted with the view of other signatories of the agreement. To conform with international standards, the Senate instructed the ITC to define "material" as "harm which is not inconsequential, immaterial or unimportant." This move was more symbolic than substantive. The ITC had never determined injury using the "more than *de minimus*" criterion, and had used its discretion to undercut, not increase, dumping rulings.

The changes made in 1979 trade legislation point directly to the weaknesses in the administration of antidumping law. New time limits were set for the assessment of dumping duties. In the past, duties could be delayed for long periods; for example, $400 million worth of duties were delayed seven years in the case of television receivers from Japan. That the Treasury Department did not move quickly to collect these duties reflects the original intent of dumping legislation. In the past, if dumping margins were found to exist, yet were corrected before new merchandise entered the American market, no penalty was levied. It was assumed that foreign producers would change their prices when charged with a dumping finding. The Customs Department never developed the administrative structure necessary to collect back taxes from intransigent producers. Legislation was aimed at stopping future infringements, not punishing past infractions. The incentive thus existed to dump, at least until caught, onto the American market. Since 1979, however, a one-year statutory time limit has been set for collection.

In the period through 1979, when an investigation was in process, an importer was required to make a deposit through a customs bond for the merchandise under question. There were limited direct costs attributed to this bond and thus no incentive to stop a dumping practice until a final judgment or to provide necessary information to the Treasury Department or the ITC. After 1979, deposits of estimated dumping duties on merchandise imposed a far more substantial financial burden on importers. This new practice is consistent with the administrative practices of the European community, with GATT codes, and with the intent of American law; it is not a form of "new protectionism."

Finally, and perhaps most basically, after 1979 LTFV determinations were made by the Department of Commerce, which, as proponents of the bureaucratic transfer suggested, may be more responsive than the Treasury Department to domestic producers. Although the administrative organization has changed, the legal mandate has not. The Treasury Department did use the latitude it was granted under the law to maintain a liberal American market. Commerce may choose not to use its discretionary authority in that way. If adjudicated to the letter of the law, antidumping actions will lead to increased closure of the American market.

Countervailing Duty Legislation

If a nation is directly or indirectly giving a bounty or a grant—that is, a subsidy—to a domestic producer, U.S. law stipulates that an additional duty equal to the net amount of the subsidy should be levied on that product upon its importation into the country. In the U.S., the imposition of a countervailing duty follows a distinct set of procedures; conversely, in most other countries, subsidized exports are not distinguished from sales below cost. The current form of legislation appeared in the Tariff Act of 1930, but similar mandates against such foreign practices appeared in both 1909 and 1913 legislation. . . .

The procedures in countervailing duty cases are straightforward. Upon complaint, the Customs Bureau (Department of Commerce after 1979) initiates an investigation. Until 1979 there was no delineation of how the investigation should be conducted or of the appropriate criteria. Rather, upon completion of the investigation the secretary of the treasury would decide whether to impose the duty, and the appropriate "equalizing" amount. The 1974 and 1979 Trade Acts added an injury requirement in order to make U.S. law consistent with the GATT codes. The 1979 law also specifies, for the first time, procedure and guidelines for the new overseeing agency, the Department of Commerce.

The period between 1930 and 1979 was characterized by great latitude in countervailing duty cases. The size of the duty imposed was not subject to judicial review, and in general the Treasury Department had much freedom to interpret the law. The 1979 reforms came about because of the belief that such freedoms had been at the cost of the petitioner. The laws themselves were repeatedly defended by the Congress. It was the administrative agencies that were seen as undermining the intent of congressional legislation. As with antidumping legislation, the discretionary nature of the legislation had allowed liberal administrators to undercut protectionism. With the move to the Department of Commerce and the mandate from Congress to enforce its legislation, countervailing duty laws could increasingly become an impediment to trade.

Section 337

Section 337 of the Tariff Act of 1930 empowers the ITC to investigate complaints of unfair competition in the importation or sales of items from foreign producers. Section 337 has the potential of applying to a wide variety of predatory import practices. In general, most cases have dealt with patent violations. Under this law, if the ITC found that such practices destroyed or substantially injured an industry "efficiently and economically operated in the U.S.," the product could be excluded from entry into the U.S. Following an ITC exclusion order (a cease-and-desist order after 1974) the president had sixty days (under 1974 law) in which to intervene and override the ITC's decision "where he determines it necessary because of overriding policy reasons." Unlike countervailing duties or cases of dumping, the administration of unfair trade did not change under the 1979 law.

This review leads to three general conclusions about the politics behind unfair trade laws. First, there appears to be significant flexibility in the prosecution of these laws. Such flexibility has undercut the protectionist potential of these statutes. Even with the delineation of the LTFV criteria, the Treasury Department was never fully constrained by Congress to enact a particular type of policy in dumping and countervailing duty cases. In effect, Congress gave to the Treasury Department the right to regulate in this area as it saw fit. And, as the data show, it often decided not to grant protection. In the case of Section 337 violations, Congress gave to the ITC guidelines, but allowed the ITC's decisions to be sidestepped through both legal and extralegal means. Both the courts and the office of the president encouraged settlements.

Second, and related, there appears no clear criterion in the legislative histories by which to assess whether these laws are becoming more or less protectionist. Rather, continuity has existed in the form, basic organization, and use of these laws, even though administrative agencies have changed. This is true even with the 1979 legislation. In the countervailing duty and antidumping cases, the injury determination makes it somewhat more difficult to obtain aid; the change of administrative responsibility to the Department of Commerce may make it easier.

Third, what separates unfair trade laws from escape clause legislation is the autonomy vested in the bureaucracy. In the escape clause cases, the president has the authority to ignore an ITC finding if it is in the national interest. This has been an effective mechanism used by executives to keep the American market open. Most post-Depression legislation has so aggrandized the rights of the president. Of the unfair trade laws studied, only one includes a role for the executive. Neither antidumping nor countervailing duty legislation allows the executive to counteract a protectionist ruling by the bureaucracy. Beginning in the 1970s, this presented a foreign policy problem to central decision-makers. Since the end of World War II, American security interests dictated that the U.S. maintain a strong economic alliance with both Europe and Japan. Analysts who studied postwar trade policy argue that America was willing to allow the EEC and Japan to protect their markets because American security interests took precedence over the establishment of a worldwide liberal trade regime. The onset of negative sanctions in the early 1960s, however, cannot be explained as a sharp reversal in security policy. Rather, the U.S. was able to allow the Japanese and Europeans latitude in the first twenty years after the war because their products posed no threat to American producers. As soon as foreign products began to threaten home producers, the government responded, even though sanctions conflicted with other elements of foreign policy. Although escape clause cases were sidestepped, unfair trade petitions forced central decision-makers to sanction Japan and Europe. These statutes withheld from the executive prerogative he had gained in other foreign policy areas since the 1940s.

In short, unfair trade laws posed little threat to the trade regime in the 1960s. Although infringements of these statutes were prosecuted when found, American producers had little need to resort to them. In the 1970s, however, as competition intensified, producers found that state-society relations in most nations qualified them for state aid under unfair trade statutes. The rise in petitions with potentially positive rulings led liberal administrators to obscure the intent of these laws. The executive, too, in this period attempted circumvention of these statutes. Two examples are noteworthy. First, the 1974 law included a provision allowing a cabinet member, the secretary of the treasury, to waive a countervailing duty if necessary for the nation's interest. Second, negotiation and administration of the extralegal form of aid, trigger prices, gave the executive authority in dumping cases denied him by law. In essence, trigger prices created a powerful alternative to the Treasury Department route for steel petitioners.

With more public attention given to the issues of fair trade, the laws began to be administered more closely to their legislative mandates. Such attention undercut the flexibility members of government had had in interpreting the laws in line with general foreign policy or regime interests. Taken in conjunction with increasing import pressures and growing awareness on the part of producers of their legal rights in these cases, these laws have increasingly posed a problem for government officials who want to maintain openness. Some prosecution of unfair trade laws is helpful to liberalization; the U.S. never understood liberalism to mean that she take the "sucker's payoff." The problem facing central decision-makers, however, is that America's unfair trade laws hold an overly narrow interpretation of the legitimate relationship between producers and the state. . . .

THE IDEA OF TRADE ADJUSTMENT

As with the other two tenets of American commercial policy, the origins of American adjustment policies trace to a cognitive model of the proper relationship between state and society. At issue here is the extent of state involvement in mitigating the social effects of economic fluctuations. After the 1930s, such active state participation gained increased legitimacy. Exigencies due to the business cycle, technological advances, or capital migration, to name but a few, were accepted by state leaders as costs of maintaining the capitalist economy. The role accepted by the government, however, was only that of adjustment; by the 1950s, the position of direct state intervention into the economy, a position that had gained some acceptance in the 1930s, was rejected.

At heart, trade adjustment policies reflect post–New Deal political norms. Adjustment policies are essentially compensatory. The state compensates industries and labor groups adversely affected by trade policy, from an ever-expanding economic "pie." If trade policy had adversely affected constituents, they were entitled to state aid.

Trade Adjustment Assistance (TAA) was first proposed during the Eisenhower administration in a minority opinion to the Randall Commission report. Adjustment was envisioned as a substitute, in the form of federal financial aid, for escape clause aid. With limited support, a weak version of TAA appeared in the 1962 Trade Act, was used in the Automotive Products Trade Act of 1965, and was ultimately expanded in the 1974 bill. Those who understand TAA only as a method to sell trade liberalization fail to appreciate the welfare function the program has played. Though clearly not so conceived in the early 1960s, adjustment assistance evolved as an important component of trade policy as the state was forced to react to the rise in industry petitions for protection.

Under the 1962 Trade Act, workers and firms were eligible for aid. Petitions were filed with the Tariff Commission, which conducted investigations (limited to sixty days) to determine whether the petitioners fulfilled the legislative criteria. The criteria of eligibility were fulfilled (1) if injury was due in major part to a trade concession, (2) if injury resulted in increased quantities of a like or directly competitive product, and (3) if imports were a major factor in causing or threatening to cause serious injury to the applicant firm, domestic industry, or group of workers. Once passed by the Tariff Commission, the president certified the petitions; if the Commission vote was tied, the president was empowered to decide the case. In just about all cases, the president approved aid. Since the criteria used in TAA cases were similar to those dictating escape clause relief, a dilemma existed. In a sense, the Tariff Commission "could not be liberal in approving adjustment assistance petitions without being liberal in approving escape clause petitions. Thus, adjustment assistance—which was supposed to foster freer trade—was included in the Trade Expansion Act in such a way as to make its actual use inconsistent with that objective."

As a response, TAA was revamped under the 1974 law. First, coverage was extended to communities as well as firms and workers. Second, the investigatory responsibilities and determination of injury were given to the Labor Department for worker cases, and to the Department of Commerce for cases involving firms and communities. And third, eligibility criteria changed from the earlier stricter requirements to the following: (1) that a significant number of workers be affected, (2) that there be an absolute decrease in sales and production, and (3) that imports of a like or directly competitive article contributed importantly to a decline in sales or production. "Contributed importantly" was interpreted as a cause that is important but not necessarily more important than any other cause. This last criterion, that imports be of a similar nature to a product made in the U.S., served to disqualify a number of otherwise qualified applicants, especially in cases involving auto production. In the late 1970s, manufacturers of auto parts such as bumpers were being laid off as a result of the sale of foreign cars. Yet, because no foreign bumper was being imported, their case did not meet the necessary criteria.

Once certified, firms and communities received low-cost loans and other development assistance. Workers were paid a weekly adjustment allowance of 65 percent (in the 1962 Act) or 70 percent (in the 1974 Act) of their average weekly wage for up to fifty-two weeks, with a twenty-six-week extension for workers in training or workers over sixty years of age. In no case was aid to exceed 65 percent (70 percent in the 1974 Act) of the average weekly manufacturing wage. Employment services and relocation allowances were offered to facilitate re-employment, but these constituted a small part of the program.

The original 1974 program was extended in 1981 for two years. However, early in the Reagan administration it was announced that the program would be eliminated, and in October 1981, in the Budget Reconciliation Act (Title 25), the benefit program was changed. After 1981, and for the life of the program, aid would be given as an extension to unemployment insurance for the long-term unemployed. The previous concept of an additional payment to those unemployed due to imports (which brought income to 70 percent of previous levels) ceased. Furthermore, after 9 February 1982, cases had to show "substantial cause"—that is, imports had to be the primary cause of industry malaise, the criterion used under the 1962 Trade Act.

In essence, TAA was a program of transfer payments. Liberalism incurs differential costs and benefits. Adjustment assistance was an institutional response to these costs, and has acted both as a welfare policy and as a way to diffuse potential opposition. It was the latter function that propelled its creation, but the former that was its engine for growth. Adjustment assistance or its functional equivalent is a necessary ingredient in a liberal American trade policy. The program ensures support for free trade through redistribution. Liberal trade policy was accepted because it brought wealth; if an unregulated market leads to visible economic upheaval, the cognitive basis of liberalism will be questioned. . . .

CONCLUSION

Two types of conclusions are offered here. The first are more theoretical. The points addressed center on the ability to defend the role of institutions and ideas as important determinants of American politics. The second are substantial. The remarks address the trade data and their implications for the future of general trade policy in the U.S.

This article offers an alternative method for understanding protectionism in the U.S. Neither of the two dominant genres of analysis looks towards the state as the critical variable in explaining policy outcomes. Societally based explanations look to social forces; international explanations look to power structures. Our explanation does not deny the validity of either of these approaches. Rather, we argue they are insufficient in their explanation of American protectionism. This article looks to a dominant role for ideas, as embedded in institutional design and laws, and the beliefs of central decision-makers as an additional explanation for policy.

Protectionism should be viewed in its historical context. Viewed over time, it can be organized by the time period in which protectionist legislation was first written. In particular, laws have varied on what constitutes a legitimate claim against the state for aid, on the institutional structures used to adjudicate forms of aid, and on the discretion granted to administrators. The first type of aid examined we labeled liberal, created after the U.S. moved towards opening up its borders to trade. Philosophically, the period is characterized by limited state intervention; governments serve their societies most efficiently when they do not interfere with market mechanisms. The institutional structure is executive centered, and administrators have considerable discretion in adjudicating cases. The second set of ideas were labeled as "fair" trade. Here the legitimate role of government in trade is to ensure that American producers compete in a fair market. Written in the years preceding World War II, these laws are more Congress centered, are more detailed in the criteria administrators use to adjudicate the case, and on the whole allow less discretion than do other trade laws. The overt use of discretion to counter the intent of these laws by the Treasury Department was the central issue that led Congress to move administrative control to the Department of Commerce.

The third set of beliefs we labeled redistributive. Here, the government is portrayed as having some responsibility for abrogating the ill effects of the market. As with the escape clause, these laws are executive centered. And, as above, the president has the right to overturn decisions. The administration of these laws, however, was given to sympathetic departments with strong ties to affected communities. From the start, this form of aid was envisioned as a method of alleviating the painful aspects of liberalism.

This article shows that each of these three types of protectionism operated according to a different logic and aided a different type of constituent. By examining laws that direct the relationship between the state and society on trade matters, we saw that legislation reflected differing notions about the legitimate role of the state. Viewing laws over time, we saw that each functioned with a different internal logic and a different calculus of politics. Even though the escape clause was potentially a protectionist instrument, the structure of the statute encouraged liberal central decision-makers to undercut the ability of groups to use the law effectively. Conversely, the laws we designated as "fair" trade legislation have consistently forced central decision-makers to protect the American market. Liberal central decision-makers have done *whatever* is possible to undercut these laws. This too is reflected in the data. However, these laws were structured in a period of congressional ascendance. The executive is not granted the rights he gained in post-Depression legislation. To illustrate the third component of policy, we turned to Trade Adjustment Assistance. Adjustment assistance was argued to be a transfer payment to industries hurt by imports.

It is both interesting and important that in the period through the early 1970s these laws did not interfere with America's international commitment to the liberal trading regime. By pushing for fair trade, unfair trade laws served to reinforce the norm that market mechanisms, not government policy, should determine comparative advantage. Later, however, unfair trade laws, with their narrow interpretation of legitimate government policies, posed a problem to the continuation of free trade. Similarly, the TAA program served liberalism during the 1970s. By creating an alternative to a trade barrier, TAA diffused potential industrial pressures on government for a more substantial response. However, TAA became overwhelmed by petitioners in the late 1970s who took financial aid but continued to file more potent suits against the state. Neither of these programs created much interest among central decision-makers in the 1960s; both were seen as problematic to some aspect of American trade policy two decades later.

A general review of the data presented reveals a number of counterintuitive empirical findings. First, it is clear that as the U.S. became increasingly more open, domestic groups put up resistance. Increased resistance, however, is not the explanation for aid receipt. Rather, it is the fit between the strategy employed by groups and state structures that explains state response.

Second, a free trade bias seems to exist among central decision-makers and is part of an explanation for policy. In particular, the Office of the President has been active in protecting America's liberal position. Although the congressional position on trade has varied, the position of the executive has been unambiguous. When confronted by a choice between giving aid or not, the executive gave no aid. When protectionism was mandated by the bureaucracy, the president often chose to give a transfer payment, to give less than recommended, or in the case of countervailing duties, to sanction a tariff waiver. In dumping cases, legislation precludes direct executive action. In response, the president has attempted to control petition activity, using a variety of incentives to convince petitioners to halt the dumping investigation voluntarily.

It is in the category of circumvention of protectionism that we find VERs and OMAs. All were used as mechanisms to give industries less than they would have received either from an ITC, Treasury Department, or Department of Commerce ruling. In terms of fiscal impact, these marketing arrangements constitute a transfer of funds from the American treasury (funds which would have been collected from an equivalent tariff) to foreign governments. They are only rational as a presidential attempt to reconcile systemic interests in maintaining liberalism with a domestic need to respond to industries that fulfill the legal requisites for aid. They are not explicable as a response to group demands for such agreements, as the most efficient mechanism to aid industries, or as a new form of the old protectionism.

Third, of the ideas that have contributed to current trade policy, the notion of redistribution has had the weakest hold on the policymaking community. With budget deficits and a decline in wealth, this policy directive was abandoned. The explanation for the need for adjustment was never as developed as the explanation for free trade or as institutionalized as fair trade practices. Given our review of the functioning of trade policy within the U.S., this lack of an adjustment assistance strategy may ultimately undermine liberalism. The structure of politics in the U.S. places great pressure on government leaders. Some mechanism is necessary to act as a pressure valve. Without this support for groups adversely affected by imports, the pressures on government will lead to a questioning of their cognitive beliefs and make alternative approaches to trade more attractive.

Finally, what is the future of free trade in the U.S.? The U.S.-sponsored trade regime has had a unique character. The U.S. never confronted the political trade-offs associated with free trade doctrine, despite being the major force behind the liberalization of world trade. From free trade's inception, the U.S. never had the institutional capability to maintain all aspects of liberalization. Although accepting the norms of free trade, there was no consensus in Congress to repeal the traditional protections afforded to domestic industry. Thus, the norms and institutions of fair trade coexisted with their liberal counterparts. It is these laws that have the potential of undercutting the regime itself. It is no surprise that of the solutions suggested to America's declining trade balance, it is the call for fair trade and expanded access to export markets, not for the protection of noncompetitive sectors, that has received the greatest attention.

The prosecution of unfair trade laws, however, should not be interpreted as the first step down a "slippery slope" towards high barriers to trade. Liberalism still retains overwhelming support in the U.S. Ideas such as liberalism, however, do have life cycles. The inevitable conflict between free and fair trade in a period of chronic trade imbalance has led to a questioning of the tenets of American trade policy. Currently, however, there is no legitimate theoretical alternative to liberalism. The protectionism of the inter-war period has no support. Welfare-redistributive policies are fiscally not viable. Thus, although there is discontent, a radical change in American policy is unlikely.

25

Emerging Regional Arrangements: Building Blocks or Stumbling Blocks?

ROBERT Z. LAWRENCE

Economist Robert Lawrence examines current trends toward regional trade blocs and concludes that they are likely to contribute to, rather than detract from, future international economic openness. Instead of forming exclusive economic spheres as in the 1930s, he argues, regional arrangements today will, first, create trade by stimulating national growth and, second, encourage further liberalization by creating demands for greater access to the bloc. Lawrence also demonstrates that bloc members remain dependent on trade with nonmembers and suggests that current regional arrangements are motivated not by the desire to exclude others but by the need to secure greater liberalization between the member states. The forces propelling regionalism, he concludes, are fundamentally liberal, not protectionist.

The spectre of global fragmentation is haunting the global trading system and with it international financial markets. The fear is that progress toward global integration over the past four decades will be reversed as the world economy splits up into three regional trading blocs, each centred on a major currency, each closed to outsiders. No one familiar with the history of the 1930s can forget what Charles Kindleberger has called the "disarticulation of the world economy" in which multilateral trade was virtually confined to currency blocs, international capital markets dried up and the international adjustment mechanism failed to operate.[1] But concerns that this scenario could be repeated reflect a fundamental misreading of the evidence. The major regional initiatives currently under way are more likely to represent the building blocks of an integrated world economy than stumbling blocks which prevent its emergence. To be sure, there are risks that these

Robert Z. Lawrence. "Emerging Regional Arrangements: Building Blocks or Stumbling Blocks?" From Richard O'Brien, ed. *Finance and the International Economy: 5, The AMEX Bank Review Prize Essays* (1991) pp. 22–35 by permission of Oxford University Press.

initiatives could go astray. But the forces initiating these developments are the very opposite of protectionism. They represent positive, integrative responses to the pressures exerted by globalization. If accompanied by parallel progress at the GATT, regionalization could be a potent mechanism for freeing world trade and investment and harmonizing national institutional practices.

STUMBLING BLOCKS?

Outsiders have fears about each of the regional initiatives currently under way. In this analysis I will outline some of these concerns and then indicate why they are misplaced.

The European Community's Single Market Initiative (EC92) is viewed with concern because of fears that (i) this initiative will divert more trade than it creates; (ii) as its membership grows, the EC will become increasingly preoccupied with internal concerns and thus neglect its external relations; and (iii) a more centralized European Community would be dominated by the preferences of its more protectionist members and erect new external barriers.

A second concern is that Japan will spearhead a Southeast Asian bloc, principally by moving its manufacturing industry offshore. The favourite analogy is to the migration of geese: Japan is the head goose, with a V-formation of newly industrialized countries (NICs) of Southeast Asia and China following (or expected to follow) closely behind. This formation is motivated by the Japanese desire to exploit cheaper Asian labour to produce for Japan and elsewhere. As Japanese investment rises in other Southeast Asian countries, so goes this argument, Japan will obtain control over these rapidly growing markets, erecting invisible barriers that will make it difficult for other countries to penetrate. And acting through MITI, Japan supposedly will try to manage international specialization in a manner which inhibits the free entry of firms and products from outside the region.

A third concern relates to US initiatives in the Western Hemisphere. One fear is that such an agreement could have substantial trade-diversion effects. A second is that, like the EC, the US would be diverted from global initiatives, which, given the major leadership role it has played in the post-war trading system, would be a major blow to liberalization.

Clearly, any turn inward by the EC or the US could have domino effects. A Fortress Europe would encourage non-European countries shut out of European markets to think about forming their own closed blocs among their neighbours. An Asian bloc run by Japan could topple the global trading system by increasing demands for managed trade.

Moreover, corporate responses to these regional arrangements could enhance global fragmentation. The threat of protection will induce major corporations to adopt multiregional strategies in which each region is served through local production facilities. Once foreign companies are located within a region, they are less vulnerable to trade barriers and thus less inclined to oppose them. Paradoxically, therefore, this form of corporate globalization could weaken, rather than strengthen trade liberalization.

In sum, the apparent movement toward blocs has generated concern among defenders of multilateralism. They fear that, at best, a proliferation of blocs will make future global liberalization more difficult, and at worst, lead to a new round of trade wars.

BUILDING BLOCKS?

But many of these concerns are misplaced. Stronger regional integration need not be associated with higher external barriers. Indeed, as the GATT itself recognizes, such a trend could have positive effects on the rest of the world provided the emerging regional blocs are "open" to trade from outside.

Growth   One key benefit to the rest of the world comes from the impact of regional arrangements in stimulating growth and thus demand for extra-regional exports. These growth effects stem from several sources. One is the income effect of the gains from trade. Secondly, such increased income induces increased investment. For example, Richard Baldwin estimates that the removal of trade and other internal barriers to trade and investment within Europe as part of the Single Market will stimulate sufficient increases in investment to produce "dynamic" growth effects that will be greater than the "static" efficiency gains: up to a 10 per cent increase in total output, as compared to the 4.5 per cent figure (for static gains alone) estimated in the official Cecchini report prepared for the Commission.[2] Another positive source of growth stems from the beneficial macroeconomic effects of these regional initiatives. "Animal spirits" have a major impact on investment. The psychological impact of the 1992 initiative in shifting Europe from "Europessimism" to "Europhoria" should not be underestimated, nor should the impact of increased expected competition. European firms have been convinced that the post-1992 Europe will be different. To prepare themselves they have been investing and merging. Their behaviour is a striking contrast to their sluggish investment in the late 1970s and early 1980s. Regardless therefore of whether the final details of the internal market are actually completed, the changed competitive environment has already brought considerable growth benefits.

Similarly, the restoration of investor confidence is the key to economic recovery in Latin America. The credible integration of these economies with the USA and Canada is a vital mechanism for restoring this confidence. The improved ability to attract foreign investment will permit these countries both to restore growth and to return to their natural positions as nations with trade deficits. This shift will in turn provide increased export opportunities for all their trading partners, not simply those within the region.

Another key reason for benefits to Europe's trading partners stems from the sectoral location of the main benefits of the Single Market. The Single Market will probably make its most important contribution in introducing competition among firms in many of the sectors for goods and particularly for services which were formerly nontradable. While growth in Europe's traded goods sectors could improve or worsen the rest of the world's terms of trade—depending on whether it is biased toward imports or exports—growth in the nontraded goods sector is unambiguously good for the rest of the world, because it results in increased demand for imports.

External Barriers   Open regional blocs can actually promote and facilitate external liberalization, that is, trade with parties outside blocs. On the political front, regions might be more willing to agree to liberalization than individual countries. The postwar experience with the EC is heartening. Increased European integration after the Treaty of Rome was quite compatible with the lowering of Europe's external barriers. Gary Hufbauer, for example, has argued that the Kennedy Round of trade negotiations would not have occurred in the absence of the EC. "France and Italy, in particular, would have strongly resisted making any trade concessions in the 1960s, and Germany would not have made trade concessions in isolation from its continental partners."[3] With the noteworthy exception of agriculture, therefore (an exception for which the EC was not solely to blame), increased regional integration among the original six members of the EC was associated with extensive participation in multilateral tariff reductions. Indeed the formation of the EEC was an important impulse for the Kennedy Round.

The European experience also demonstrates that excluded countries have stronger incentives to liberalize in a system with emerging regional arrangements. Instead of the fragmentation process some fear, an expansionary dynamic is likely. The prospects (indeed, the actuality) that major trading partners could move into arrangements from which they are excluded could well drive countries to join regional liberalization schemes. The EEC's formation, for example, set in motion a cumulative regional liberalization process in which the United Kingdom was initially induced to join EFTA and later the EC itself. For the numerous developing countries which once had close linkages to individual European nations through colonial ties, the EC provided a mechanism for extending these to Europe as a whole through the special arrangements which the Community has with ACP, Mediterranean, and Magreb countries. Similar pressures are now operating under the Single Market in which the EFTA nations, East Europeans and others such as Turkey are clamouring for inclusion.

As was the case with the EC, the North American Free Trade Agreement (FTA) also is not developing as an exclusive process. Indeed, as Mexico has moved into the FTA negotiations with the US it has simultaneously sought to counterbalance this growing dependence on its more powerful partners with new initiatives toward the Pacific and Central and South America. Mexico is seeking, for example, to join the OECD, is negotiating another FTA with Venezuela and Chile, and has signed agreements to achieve freer trade with several Central American countries.

The United States has also not been able to confine its attention to Mexico. President Bush has invited other Western Hemisphere nations to sign FTAs with the US separately or as groups in his "Enterprise for the Americas Initiative." The pressures of being left out of a prosperous regional arrangement are inducing many countries to accept this invitation. But the dynamic effects are not confined to agreements with the United States. This US invitation to Latin America has also stimulated increased interest in regional initiatives throughout Latin America. For example, the five Andean Nations—Bolivia, Colombia, Peru, Ecuador and Venezuela—have signed an accord to lift all barriers to intra-regional trade by 1991, while Brazil, Argentina, Paraguay and Uruguay have agreed to form the Mercosur common market by the end of 1995. It would be extremely difficult for a group of countries to negotiate with the United States with a high dispersion in their external tariffs. Countries seeking to negotiate as a group with the United States are thus stimulated to agree first on common external rates. Since this process is taking place at a time of liberalization, these common tariffs toward all trading partners are likely to be lower than those currently protecting these economies. Again the benefits beyond the region should be evident.

It remains to be seen, however, if the US will be able to confine its free trade area initiatives to the Western Hemisphere (and Israel). Far more likely will be pressures on the US to extend its invitation to willing Asian and other economies. The result will be an open agreement which will then be readily linked in a global arrangement.

The Asian bloc allegedly emerging around Japan is the least likely to develop into a formal protectionist arrangement. This region is particularly dependent on extra-regional trade. . . . To be sure, Japan's influence in the East Asian area is likely to increase, but precisely because other Asian nationals are reluctant to submit to an arrangement with a single dominant economy, progress toward a single regional arrangement centred solely on Japan is likely to be slow. Moreover, the US will be unwilling to concede Asia to Japan and is likely to use its influence to prevent a formal Pacific arrangement from which it is excluded. For a time, the US could well be caught in the hypocritical position of promoting Western Hemisphere integration while resisting an Asian arrangement. Eventually, therefore, it will be forced to extend its invitation to form FTAs to willing Asian nations.

Importance of Extra-Bloc Trade Current trade patterns and trends suggest that extra-bloc trade is vital for each of the current or prospective regional arrangements. While each of the major players may benefit from regional arrangements none can afford to ignore its extra-regional relations. The US, Europe and Japan are all global rather than regional traders. . . .

Over half of the Western Hemisphere's exports and two thirds of Asian exports are outside these regions. Only for Europe are extra-regional exports less than a third of trade. But the share of intra-regional trade in total trade is not the most relevant measure of dependence on extra-regional trade. The importance of extra-regional trade is more usefully measured by the ratio of total extra-regional trade—exports plus imports—to GNP. . . . [M]easured as a share of GDP, extra-regional trade is actually more important to Europe than to North America. Nonetheless, extra-regional trade remains very significant to North America and to the

United States in particular. Since goods are roughly 45 per cent of North American GNP, this implies that about 25 per cent of all American transactions in goods involve an extra-regional buyer or seller. Clearly, efforts to liberalize at the global level through the GATT remain of vital importance.

. . . [There have been no] strong long-run trends towards increased reliance on intra-regional trade. While the share of intra-regional exports in total exports of each region has fluctuated, overall the shares in 1988 for each region were not much different from their levels in 1973.

In sum, the importance of extra-regional trade to nations all over the world means that no region is in a position to sever, or even significantly curtail, its trade ties with the rest of the world by forming closed blocs. While nations have been known to take steps that were against their long term interests, it is clear that each region retains a major interest in the global system. The data thus confirm the importance of extra-regional trade for individual firms in the selling and buying of merchandise.

Motivation The forces driving nations into regional arrangements are dramatically different from those that drove them into preferential trading blocs in the interwar period. The motive for completing the internal market is not to secure the European market for European producers by providing them preferential access, but instead to facilitate the free movement of goods, services, labour and capital throughout the Community. The EC Single Market initiative reflects the recognition that as the European economies became increasingly integrated, it was necessary to move beyond simply removing border barriers to achieve a much deeper degree of integration. To be sure, there is the hope that a larger market will improve European efficiency, but enhanced competition is precisely the mechanism by which the gains from trade are achieved.

Moreover deeper integration within Europe will facilitate trade with the rest of the world. A common set of standards, for example, makes it easier for *all* who wish to sell in Europe—not just insiders. A tough set of rules which inhibits governments from subsidizing domestic firms aids all their competitors, not only those located in the European Community. Once the larger European economies are committed to allow the free flow of resources within Europe, they will no longer be able to ensure each has a national champion in every industry located within its territories. This undermining of the nationalist sentiments which drives much of the protectionism in the larger European countries will benefit outsiders. In addition, some of the mechanisms developed by the EC to deal with national diversity could serve as a model for further integration between the EC and its trading partners.

Similarly, the US-Canada free trade agreement was motivated by concerns beyond those relating simply to tariff barriers to merchandise trade. Canada in particular sought protection from the exercise of US trade laws relating to unfair trade. The United States was concerned about Canadian inhibitions on foreign investment. The agreement was wide-ranging, therefore, and included liberalization in services and a bi-national dispute settlement mechanism which again could serve as a model in other integration arrangements. Moreover, there are plans to extend the agreement in the future to deal with discipline on domestic subsidies. Once Canadian subsidies are disciplined, the benefits will accrue to all its trading partners.

Likewise, Mexico is not seeking an FTA with the United States to avoid liberalization with the rest of the world. On the contrary, since the mid-1980s, Mexico has engaged in an extensive unilateral reduction in external restrictions accompanied by internal liberalization. Moreover, in most sectors, tariff barriers against Mexican products entering the US are relatively low. Instead, much of the appeal of an FTA is that it provides credibility and permanence to Mexico's liberalization measures. A second rationale is that an export-oriented Mexico requires secure access to its major trading partner. The FTA is thus an important complement to an outward-oriented policy which is based on attracting foreign investment.

It is ironic that as developing countries have increasingly shifted toward more liberal trading regimes, the differential treatment accorded them by the GATT has actually become a hindrance rather than a benefit. A major motive behind liberalization has been the attraction of foreign capital. However, pledges to maintain open markets made at the GATT have not been particularly credible, in part because of the weakness of the disciplines imposed on developing countries. By contrast, commitments in regional FTAs with developed countries are likely to be much more credible. The GATT dispute settlement mechanism may be weak, but no one doubts the ability of the lawyers in Washington to enforce agreements.

The key point here is that once Mexico accepts obligations *vis-à-vis* the United States to permit foreign investment, to enforce intellectual property rights, to unwind its elaborate protectionist programs for automobiles and electronics, these changes will provide benefits for all its trading partners—not just the United States. US involvement in particular would dramatically enhance the credibility of intra-Latin American regional liberalization arrangements by making the costs of violating the agreement for any individual Latin American country particularly high.

Again the context and motivation for these efforts in Latin America must be appreciated. Over the past three years, in addition to Mexico, Brazil, Argentina and Colombia have all significantly reduced tariff levels as well as the dispersion of tariff levels, while Chilean liberalization has been in place even longer. It is no surprise that the earlier Latin American regional initiatives were failures, since they were implemented in the context of import-substitution policies. The aim of governments with interventionist philosophies was to achieve scale economies in protected regional markets. But these protectionist motives precluded success. However, the current policies are different. They are being implemented by governments proclaiming market-oriented philosophies seeking domestic liberalization and the attraction of foreign capital to service global rather than domestic markets.

To be sure, if these measures are successful, they will increase competition for other nations seeking to attract foreign capital. Pressures will be felt by other countries to avoid being isolated by securing similar arrangements. But as long as the US and the EC offer such nations conditional access to their regional arrangements, this form of competition should be seen as beneficial and liberalizing.

CONCLUDING COMMENTS

This optimistic viewpoint needs to be qualified. While overt protectionist barriers are unlikely, each of the regional arrangements might well resort to more subtle protectionist measures.

In the case of the United States, these typically involve so-called voluntary restraint arrangements (VRAs) and harassment through the use of anti-dumping actions. However, with a Western Hemisphere FTA, Latin American nations would be less susceptible to such measures and in any case have more recourse through special dispute settlement institutions that will inevitably be part of an FTA agreement.

In the case of Europe, protection could be applied through the strict and less-than-transparent application of anti-dumping rules; increased application of safeguard measures; efforts to nurture European firms (through implicit subsidies, selective government procurement and consortia excluding non-European firms); and the promulgation of standards purportedly addressing environmental and safety concerns that have the effect (if not the purpose) of discriminating against extra-bloc trade.

In the case of Asia, protection might be applied through actions taken by Japanese companies, implicitly sanctioned by the Japanese government. It is a commonplace that foreign companies have found the Japanese market hard to crack, largely because of "hidden barriers" which inhibit them from making sales in Japan.

These concerns highlight the importance of disciplines on these practices at the global level through the GATT. In particular, the Uruguay round contains measures to limit some of these practices. A successful round, which is in the interest of each of the regions, would enhance the prospects that protectionist responses be limited.

Nonetheless, particularly from the standpoint of financial markets, these measures are unlikely to lead to the cataclysmic scenarios resembling the 1930s. Overall, therefore, while progress will undoubtedly not be smooth and linear, the overall direction of the trend toward increased global integration is clear. The key is to appreciate that these deeper degrees of integration cannot necessarily be achieved initially at the global level. Some require much greater and more credible governance than a global institution can provide. Others are acceptable only to particular groups of countries. The correct solution is surely a multitrack approach, with complementary concurrent initiatives proceeding at the global, plurilateral and even bilateral levels. To be sure, there is the danger that this approach will not produce solutions which are completely compatible, but it is surely preferable to restricting progress on integration to the lowest common denominator. If regional arrangements are crafted as open and designed to reinforce rather than resist market forces, they will inevitably become building rather than stumbling blocks in the move towards a more integrated global economy.

NOTES

1. See Charles Kindleberger, *The World in Depression 1929–1939* (University of California Press, 1986), p. 280.
2. Richard Baldwin, "On The Growth Effect Of 1992," *Economic Policy,* 1989, pp. 248–81.
3. See Gary Clyde Hufbauer, "An Overview," in Hufbauer, ed., *Europe 1992: An American Perspective* (Brookings Institution, 1990), p. 5.

VI

ECONOMIES IN DEVELOPMENT AND TRANSITION

The liberal international economy created after 1945 and the increase in international finance and trade discussed in previous sections have helped produce unprecedented levels of national and global growth. Within this broad pattern of economic success, however, there are important variations. While some countries and people enjoy the highest standards of living in human history, many more remain mired in poverty.

Indeed, the gap between the richest and the poorest people on earth not only is large but also is growing wider every year. The richest fifth of the world's population currently enjoys 82.7 percent of global product (aggregate gross national product), while the world's poorest fifth receives only 1.4 percent. And while the ratio between the income of the richest 20 percent and that of the poorest 20 percent of the world's population was 30:1 in 1960, it grew to 32:1 in 1970, 45:1 in 1980, and 59:1 in 1989. This pattern is replicated at the level of individual countries as well. Where all developing countries averaged 9 percent of the GNP per capita of the industrialized countries in 1960, they fell to 5 percent by 1989; the "least" developed countries, those with a GNP per capita of $300 or less, fell from 3 percent to 1 percent and the countries of sub-Saharan Africa fell from 7 percent to 3 percent over the same period. These income trends are repeated in the areas of trade, savings, and investment.[1] While economic growth has increased over the post-1945 period, raising the average standard of living around the globe, the gaps between the world's wealthiest and poorest societies have increased even faster.

For decades, scholars and practitioners have debated the sources of economic growth and the best strategies for producing rapid increases in standards of living. Many analysts argue that development, at least in its initial stages, requires that a country insulate itself from more established economic powers and stimulate key industries at home through trade protection and government subsidies. Indeed, Alexander Hamilton, the first secretary of the treasury of the United States, argued for just such a policy in his famous *Report on Manufactures,* presented to the House of Representatives in 1791. Starting in the 1930s, with the collapse of the international economy in the Great Depression, many so-called developing countries began de facto strategies of import-substituting industrialization (ISI), increasing domestic production to fill the gap created by the decrease in foreign trade. After World War II, especially in Latin America but elsewhere as well, this de facto strategy was institutionalized de jure in high tariffs and explicit governmental policies of industrial promotion. Behind protective walls, countries sought to substitute domestic manufactures for foreign imports, first in light manufactures, such as textiles, apparel, and food processing, and later in intermediate and capital goods production.

Beginning in the 1960s, however, ISI started to come under increasing criticism. The government incentives for manufacturing benefited industry at the expense of agriculture—increasing rural-to-urban migration and often worsening income distribution—and produced tremendous distortions and inefficiencies in the economy. The later stages of ISI, which focused on intermediate and capital goods production and were often more dependent on technology and economies of scale in production, also had the paradoxical effect of increasing national dependence on foreign firms and capital. Yet, despite these criticisms, virtually all countries that have industrialized successfully have adopted ISI for at least a brief period. While many economists argue that success occurs in spite of trade protection and government policies of industrial promotion, historical experience suggests that some degree of import substitution may be a necessary prerequisite for economic development.

In the 1980s, ISI generally gave way to policies of export-led growth. Many developing countries came to recognize the economic inefficiencies introduced by protectionist policies. The debt crisis of the early 1980s and the subsequent decline in new foreign lending increased the importance of exports as a means of earning foreign exchange. Rapid technological changes made "self-reliance" less attractive. There were also important political pressures to abandon ISI. The World Bank and IMF, important sources of capital for developing countries, pressed vigorously for more liberal international economic policies. Proclaiming the "magic of the marketplace," the United States also pushed for more liberal economic policies in the developing world.

Particularly important in reorienting development policy was the success of the newly industrializing countries (NICs) of East Asia: South Korea, Taiwan, Hong Kong, and Singapore. All of these states achieved impressive rates of economic growth and industrialization through strategies of aggressive export promotion. While they all adopted ISI during their initial stages of development, the NICs have generally sought to work with, rather than against, international market forces. With well-educated labor forces and limited raw materials, the NICs have exploited their comparative advantage in light manufactures and, over time, diversified into more capital-intensive production. Today, the NICs are among the most rapidly growing countries in the world, and they have achieved this result with relatively egalitarian income distributions.

The sources of this success remain controversial. Some analysts, especially neoclassical economists, point to the market-oriented policies of the NICs. This view is represented in the article by Lawrence Summers and Vinod Thomas, two former World Bank economists (Reading 26). Others argue that unique domestic political factors were important prerequisites for successful policies of export-led growth—in particular, weak labor movements and leftist parties; strong, developmentally oriented bureaucracies; and, to varying degrees, authoritarian political regimes. These conditions, it is averred, facilitated market-oriented policies that are not feasible politically in other circumstances. Relatedly, critics of export-led growth have suggested that the success enjoyed by the NICs cannot be repeated. The number of countries that can specialize profitably at any given time in labor-intensive manufacturing is limited, and the industrial states have consistently protected their domestic markets when threatened by "too much" competition from the NICs, creating a barrier to further upward movements in the international division of labor. As a result, they argue, the path blazed by the NICs is no longer open to other developing countries. This critical perspective is developed in the essay by Robin Broad, John Cavanagh, and Walden Bello (Reading 27).

Macroeconomic policy in developing countries is central to both perspectives on development. For proponents of export-led growth, successful stabilization policies are a cornerstone of economic advancement; high inflation and rapidly changing fiscal and monetary policies undermine incentives for private investment. For skeptics, such stabilization policies are merely an artifact of underlying political factors; the same conditions that allow export-led growth also facilitate stable macroeconomic policies. The problems and politics of inflation and stabilization are addressed by Stephan Haggard (Reading 28).

With the collapse of Communist rule in Eastern Europe and the former Soviet Union, many "socialist bloc" countries have joined the ranks of the so-called developing world. Abandoning central planning, state ownership of productive assets, and economic insularity, the states of the former bloc now seek to join the liberal international economy as full partners; most have joined the IMF and petitioned to join the GATT. For all, however, the problems of development loom large. While many achieved high rates of industrialization under Communist rule, their economies are not competitive in current international markets; indeed, the system of centralized planning and intrabloc trade that arose under the old regimes can be viewed as an extensive example of ISI, with all the problems that strategy entails. In addition, state ownership of most productive assets and the absence of effective internal markets created further economic distortions. Today, the states of Eastern Europe and the former Soviet Union not only must compete with (and against) other developing countries on international markets, but also must recreate the very foundations of their economies.

There are two distinct views on how the former Communist states can best rebuild their economies and reintegrate themselves into the international economy. The first is similar to that outlined by the proponents of export-led growth and is sometimes referred to as "shock therapy." The economy is a complex system with numerous linkages between issues and policies. According to proponents of shock therapy, piecemeal market reforms cannot succeed. Rather, new foundations must be built across all dimensions simultaneously. Macroeconomic stabilization cannot occur, for instance, without terminating the extensive government subsidies to industry; but which firms are likely to be profitable, and which are not, cannot be known without market-determined prices. Prices cannot be decontrolled, however, without breaking up the huge industrial firms characteristic of Soviet-style planning, and demonopolization cannot proceed without enacting new laws governing private property. Each individual reform is actually part of a large, intricate puzzle, and movement must occur along all fronts together.

Advocates of shock therapy also recognize that, given the uncompetitive economies of many former Communist states, the creation of new economic systems will inevitably produce widespread dislocations and personal suffering. Instead of dragging out the process of reform, and risking an eventual collapse of political support, advocates maintain that the post-Communist regimes ought to draw upon existing reservoirs of goodwill and "rush to the market." Only rapid reform, in this view, is politically viable. The case for shock therapy is summarized in the essay by Jeffrey Sachs (one of the strategy's principal architects) and David Lipton (Reading 29).

Conversely, proponents of a "gradualist" approach argue that for both economic and political reasons effective and competitive markets cannot be created quickly. While agreeing with advocates of shock therapy that the economy is a complex and interdependent system, gradualists draw a different conclusion. Incremental reforms, they argue, can provide entrepreneurs with essential information that is simply unavailable in the more rapid approach; in particular, gradual decontrol of prices can signal to entrepreneurs the direction of change and the general pattern of production and investment that will eventually emerge. Gradualists also argue that shock therapy will produce such large economic dislocations that newly enfranchised citizens will reject the proposed market reforms. They advocate instead a slower process that builds into reform a "social safety net" and other protections against economic disruptions. Such a strategy, they expect, will enjoy greater popular support and reinforce emerging trends toward political democracy. The "perils of the fast track to capitalism," as he calls them, are discussed by Thomas Weisskopf (Reading 30).

The process of political and economic reform now under way in the former Communist states is virtually unprecedented. While similar to Western Europe's transition from mercantilism to liberalism in the eighteenth and, especially, nineteenth centuries (see Kindleberger, Reading 5), the jump from command economy to market economy is greater and states are attempting to traverse this chasm more quickly than ever before. This transition, and the problem of development more generally, raises questions central to the study of the international political economy. How and under what circumstances should countries seek to integrate themselves into the international market? How can the international economy be structured so as to fulfill the needs of separate nation-states? How does the international economy affect politics within states? An examination of the historical and contemporary international political economy can shed important light on these questions and produce essential insights into the future of the "economies in transition." Nonetheless, the final outcome of this process will not be known for many years and depends fundamentally on the weight of decades of past developments. As Karl Marx wrote in 1852: "Men make their own history, but they do not make it just as they please; they do not make it under circumstances chosen by themselves, but under circumstances directly encountered, given and transmitted from the past."

NOTE

1. These figures, for 1989 unless otherwise stated, are from United Nations Development Programme, *Human Development Report 1992* (New York: Oxford University Press, 1992), 35, 141.

26

Recent Lessons of Development
LAWRENCE H. SUMMERS
and VINOD THOMAS

This essay summarizes what the authors, two economists then at the World Bank, consider the main policy conclusions from the development experience of the last thirty years. While shying away from a strict laissez-faire or free-market approach, Lawrence Summers and Vinod Thomas do advocate a limited role for government in development and the adoption of "market-friendly" economic reforms. In particular, they maintain, the state should primarily invest in human and physical infrastructure, create a competitive climate for business, and establish sound macroeconomic policies. The view expressed here contrasts sharply with that of Broad, Cavanagh, and Bello (Reading 27).

Development is the most pressing challenge facing the human race. Despite the enormous opportunities created by the advances in technology, more than 1 billion people, one-fifth of the world's population, live on less than US$1 a day, a standard of living that the United States and Europe attained two centuries ago.

In the past the development effort may have mattered primarily to the citizens of poor countries. But now demographic, political, and technological trends make development an urgent priority for rich countries as well. Ninety-five percent of the growth in the world's labor force will take place in the developing world over the next quarter of a century. With the end of the cold war, economic and environmental issues will occupy the center of the diplomatic stage, and these issues will increasingly involve developing nations. As improvements in transportation and communication shrink the world, the rich and poor countries will inevitably impinge more and more on each other. International television's impact on the less-advanced nations and the sharp increase in refugee flows worldwide are harbingers of things to come.

A remarkable transformation in prevailing views about how governments can best promote economic development has occurred in recent years. Where it was

Lawrence H. Summers and Vinod Thomas. "Recent Lessons of Development." From *The World Bank Research Observer*, 8, 2, (July 1993), pp. 241–54.

once thought that government needed to occupy an economy's commanding heights by allocating credit, rationing foreign exchange, ensuring against dependence, and operating key industries, today it is widely accepted that government's responsibility for directing the production and distribution of goods and services should be much reduced and the private sector's role much enhanced. It is in those tasks for which markets prove inadequate or fail altogether—for example, investing in education, health, or physical infrastructure—that government has a central role.

For some time now, the advice of the Bretton Woods institutions (the World Bank and the International Monetary Fund) has reflected the view that economic progress is impeded by governments that seek to supplant, rather than support, markets. That view has recently been taken on board by policymakers in many parts of the world. Most publicized has been the collapse of communism in what was once the Soviet bloc. China, where one-fourth of the people in the developing world live, calls itself socialist, but the past decade has witnessed spectacular growth of the nonstate sector and very substantial price liberalization. India, where one-fifth of the population of the developing world lives, is now undertaking a program of structural adjustment and liberalization that is mild by Eastern European standards but would have been unthinkable even two years ago. Chile and Mexico have demonstrated to other Latin American nations the benefits that liberalization can bring. And change is coming, albeit slowly, in Africa, as agricultural marketing boards are dismantled and investment licensing schemes are scaled back.

For fifteen years, the World Bank's *World Development Reports* have been distilling the lessons of the record in various aspects of economic development. In a synthesis of what has been learned to date, the 1991 report described the emerging consensus in favor of what was labeled the "market-friendly" strategy, one in which governments sustain rather than supersede markets. . . . This article summarizes what we consider to be the main policy conclusions from the development experience of the past thirty years and then considers a number of unresolved issues and challenges for the future.

THE DEVELOPMENT RECORD

In thinking about development strategy, it is a mistake to lose sight of the enormous progress that has been made and continues to be made in the developing world. Average incomes in developing countries have doubled over the past three decades—faster, that is, than in the United Kingdom during the Industrial Revolution, in the United States during its spurt to industrial maturity in the nineteenth century, or in Japan during its prewar growth spurt. Economic progress in some developing countries has been dramatic: Turkey doubled its average income in twenty years (1957–77), Brazil in eighteen years (1961–79), the Republic of Korea in eleven years (1966–77), and China in ten years (1977–87).

Tremendous social progress has also been achieved in the developing world.

Infant mortality rates have been cut in half, total fertility rates have been lowered by 40 percent, and life expectancy has increased by nearly a decade, equivalent to twice the gain from eliminating both cancer and heart disease in the United States. A child born in Shanghai today has a smaller chance of dying in the first year of life, a longer life expectancy beyond one year, and a greater chance of learning to read than a child born in New York City. Social advance has been most striking in East Asia. It is estimated that the incidence of absolute poverty (that is, the percentage of the population that subsists below the poverty line) in that region has fallen dramatically in the past three decades, from a third of the population in 1970 to a tenth in 1990.

Many people think of the 1980s as a "lost decade" for development. Indeed the economies of Latin America, the Middle East and North Africa, and Sub-Saharan Africa, where average incomes declined in real terms during the decade, did have a difficult time during the 1980s. But growth of income per capita weighted by population was slightly above the historic average during the decade. In other words, the income of the average person worldwide grew more in the 1980s than in the 1970s. This reflects the acceleration of growth in India and China, where more than 2 billion people live: average incomes in China expanded at roughly 8 percent a year in the 1980s, while those in India increased by more than 3 percent a year.

Of course, this relatively favorable record conceals enormous variations in growth rates and poverty reduction across countries. Per capita incomes in some economies have doubled twice over since 1960 and are well on the way to a third doubling. But thirty-six nations with a combined population of nearly 500 million people have seen low or declining average incomes over the past twenty-five years. Poverty remains a formidable problem, and substantial economic progress has yet to touch millions of people. Before turning to the more detailed implications of this record of divergence for national policy, three broad facts of experience are worth emphasizing.

First, peace is a prerequisite to successful development. Most of the economically successful countries have been able to enjoy sociopolitical stability. By contrast, most of the thirty-six countries that have lost ground over the past twenty-five years were involved in a substantial military conflict. In Africa, where development performance has been most disappointing, 7 million lives have been lost in wars in the past thirty years.

Second, nations shape their own destinies. Poor domestic policies, more than an unfavorable external environment, are usually to blame for development failures. By any measure more foreign assistance goes to Africa, where performance has been poor, than to parts of Asia, where it has been better. Net capital inflows over the past quarter of a century to the most successful area of the developing world, East Asia, were less than one percent of the region's gross domestic product (GDP). Moreover, East Asia has not had the benefit of natural resources to export. And countries such as the Republic of Korea and Indonesia, despite debt burdens similar to those of some of the highly indebted countries, have not experienced debt crises because they used the proceeds of borrowing to make investments yielding high returns. The recognition that countries make their own histories has begun to be reflected in models of economic growth, which increasingly factor in aspects of a country's policy environment that affect performance.

Third, the proper blend of state and market in the economy is a decisive factor. A review of the record identifies some important characteristics of successful government intervention. Most of these follow from the general principle of supporting, rather than supplanting, markets and the related idea that, as Keynes put it, "the important thing for government is not to do the things which individuals are doing already and to do them a little better or a little worse; but to do those things which at present are not done at all."

Market development itself requires government action. The socialist economies in transition, from Eastern Europe to East Asia, are finding out that the establishment of the rules of the game by the government is crucial to the success of market reforms. The need for government action goes further, its rationale resting on various notions of market failure.

Investment in human capital and physical infrastructure by the government are usually justified because of externalities or spillover effects in the consumption or production of both of these categories and the inadequate incentives for markets to take them into account. In the case of primary education, for example, there are consumption related spillovers. The benefits to literacy go well beyond the gains to the individuals becoming literate. In the case of physical infrastructure such as roads, there are production related externalities based on the need to make lumpy investments or to integrate the service in large networks. Negative spillovers, too, justify government intervention: environmental pollution and congestion are inadequately accounted for by the market.

The central issue, then, is one of the state and the market, but it is not a question of intervention versus laissez faire—a popular dichotomy but a false one. As discussed below, it is rather a question of the proper division of responsibilities between the two and of efficiency in their respective functions.

LEARNING FROM EXPERIENCE

The relation between government and market can be seen under three broad headings: human and physical infrastructure, competitive climate for enterprise, and macroeconomic management. A fourth area, institutional development, cuts across all three. The areas, of course, are interrelated. A relatively undistorted and competitive domestic economy rewards the buildup of human capital more generously than one that is highly regulated and protected. At the same time, investments in education make the domestic economy more productive by speeding the adoption of new technology. To take another example, a stable macroeconomic framework allows the domestic price system to work effectively because it helps to avoid inflation. But microeconomic efficiency also makes it easier to keep inflation low: with fewer unviable enterprises, there will be less need for subsidies that swell the public sector deficit. And, reforms in all these areas work better if a country's institutional framework, embracing both market and government institutions, is improved.

Human and Physical Infrastructure

Perhaps the most important investments governments need to make are in people. The economic returns from public and private investments in education and health are often extremely high. Improving people's health and education strengthens the demand for smaller families, which, together with better provision of family planning services, helps to tackle the population problem in many parts of the world. Markets in developing countries often cannot be relied upon to provide people—especially the poor—with adequate education (particularly primary education), health care, nutrition, and family planning services. The returns to government development of various forms of physical infrastructure are also usually very high. The incentives for the private sector to develop adequate infrastructure, such as rural roads, are often lacking.

A child born in Africa today is more likely to be malnourished than to go to school at all, and is more likely to die before the age of five than to go to secondary school. And yet because basic health care services are labor-intensive, they can be effectively produced in developing countries. By one recent calculation for Pakistan, providing 1,000 girls with one extra year of schooling would raise their market productivity by between 10 and 15 percent and would avert nearly seven hundred births and close to fifty infant deaths.

Many governments are investing far too little in human development. In Brazil and Pakistan rapid economic growth alone was insufficient to improve social indicators substantially. In Chile and Jamaica, however, these indicators improved even in periods of slow growth. Among low-income countries, Guinea and Sri Lanka have the same per capita income, but average life expectancy is some two-thirds longer in Sri Lanka. Brazil and Uruguay have similar per capita incomes, but infant mortality is two-thirds lower in Uruguay.

Governments must also make necessary tangible investments in infrastructure. However appropriate the incentive framework, firms cannot function if the water runs brown, and nothing happens when a coin is put in the phone. Too often, as in the case of electricity and water supply, failed government efforts to provide or maintain infrastructure lead to very expensive attempts at private sector substitution. For example, in India power plants operate with a capacity utilization of less than 50 percent, yet firms are forced to install their own generators because the risk of interruptions is so great.

Ensuring that governments make the necessary investments in both tangible and intangible infrastructure is partially a matter of making sure they have adequate resources. But in addition to increasing the quantity of human investment, governments must improve its quality. Too often, capital investments go forward without adequate provision for the recurrent expenditures they entail, which results in wasteful underutilization. Too often, water is provided at little or no cost to industry and then is wasted, while clean water is unavailable where it is desperately needed to improve health. Targeting expenditures appropriately is crucial. Expenditures are frequently poorly targeted and involve a great deal of leakage.

The need to shift priorities in spending is wide-ranging. It will pay to reduce heavy subsidies for higher education and to spend much more on primary education, from which the returns are relatively higher. The case for a similar switch in spending on the margin, from expensive curative health care systems to primary systems, is also strong. In too many developing countries half the national health budget goes to a few hospitals that do open heart surgery in or near the nation's capital, whereas immunizations cannot be afforded in rural areas. The question of priorities goes beyond the area of human resources. In many countries there is scope for substantially reducing spending on the military in favor of increased spending on human and physical infrastructure.

Competitive Climate for Enterprise

Growth led by the private sector needs a permissive, rather than a prohibitive, environment. Almost no one disagrees that communism is the longest route from capitalism to capitalism. For all their faults, competitive markets are the most effective way yet found to get goods and services produced and distributed efficiently. External and domestic competition provides the incentives that unleash entrepreneurship and technological progress.

Openness to trade, investment, and ideas encourages domestic producers to cut costs and improve productivity by introducing new technologies and to develop new and better products. A high level of protection for domestic industry, conversely, has held development back by decades in many places. The effect of import protection on firms in Chile and Turkey, for instance, and the effect of greater competition in export markets on firms in Brazil, Japan, and Korea confirm the decisive contribution to efficiency that the external economy can make.

Many developing countries are taking to heart the lessons from worldwide experience in trade liberalization. As a result of the various liberalization episodes of the 1970s and 1980s, the developing world is more open today than at any time in recent history. But the threat of increasing protectionism is ever present, not least from the industrial countries. In fact, as the developing countries liberalized, the industrial countries on average raised trade restrictions in the 1980s: development prospects can be substantially improved if all countries roll back trade barriers.

A permissive domestic environment is one where government seeks to reduce, rather than increase, the cost of doing business. That means doing away with licensing requirements for investment, avoiding debilitating restrictions that limit firms' ability to downsize, and reducing tariffs and quotas on capital goods whose cost is found to affect growth performance significantly. One study found that the price of traded capital goods was 50 percent higher in Africa than in other parts of the developing world. Creating a competitive climate for the private sector also entails avoiding government monopsonies or punitive regulations. The success of the Nigerian government's action in abolishing agricultural marketing boards and moving toward a realistic exchange rate illustrates what deregulation can accomplish. Cocoa output has risen 50 percent since 1986, both rubber and cotton production has more than quadrupled, and soybean production and processing of soybean products have increased even more. A permissive environment is also one where market forces are able to set prices without price controls or large subsidies. The former Soviet Union, where the price of oil at any realistic exchange rate has been less than $1 a barrel for many years, is an extreme example of distortions caused by subsidies, but large subsidies to energy and energy-using products are ubiquitous in developing countries.

Governments have a history of failure in attempting to manage directly the production of private goods and services. Around the world the record of public enterprise management is one of disaster. It may be true in theory that a properly managed public enterprise can often be as productive and efficient as a private one, but the reality is that politics usually intrudes and efficiency is sacrificed. Public enterprise managers are rarely permitted to shed labor in order to produce at minimum cost. And procurement is often treated as a way of enriching contractor and procurement officers rather than producing efficiently.

Nigeria provides an example of what can go wrong when government tries to operate what should be private industry. Between 1973 and 1990 the Nigerian government invested $115 billion in its public sector, or about $1,000 for every citizen. This investment, depending on what exchange rate is used, represented as much as four years' worth of gross national product. Yet there is little growth to show for it. Public sector assets are operating at a capacity utilization rate of less than 40 percent. And a $3 billion steel complex sits empty, awaiting the $1 billion of investment necessary to complete it. Mexico, by contrast, provides an example of what privatization can accomplish. Large-scale privatization has attracted substantial foreign investment and has already considerably improved efficiency. Indeed, several countries have found that the expectation that enterprises will be privatized creates an impetus for increased efficiency.

Macroeconomic Management

Sound macroeconomic policies with sustainable fiscal deficits and realistic exchange rates are a prerequisite to progress. Large government budget deficits absorb domestic saving and foreign funds that could otherwise be channeled to the private sector. Crowding out productive investments by farmers, entrepreneurs, and large businesses, government deficits place the financial system under great strain. Often they induce rapid inflation, which in turn exacerbates the deficit, creating a vicious circle. Deficits also lead to overvalued exchange rates, which stifle exports, damage domestic producers, and create pressures for protectionism. Evidence is accumulating from country experience of widespread ill-effects of large fiscal deficits.

A distinguishing feature of the East Asian experience is that the public sector exercised discipline in its spending; such discipline is essential to ensure that rents from government interventions are kept to a minimum. Fiscal discipline was practiced in different ways. In Taiwan before 1987, a law limited the value of outstanding government bonds to no more than 40 percent of the central government's annual budget. Thailand limits its budget deficit to 20 percent of expenditures. In Indonesia the openness of the capital account has served as a check on irresponsible fiscal behavior that could precipitate currency speculation and crisis. Malaysia, however, ran a large deficit (a high of 19 percent of GDP in 1982) but cut it sharply (5 percent in 1990) when performance was threatened.

To be sure, fiscal and financial instability have sometimes been partly inflicted on governments by external events—or by internal shocks such as civil wars or natural disasters. But governments can choose how to respond to such pressures. In such countries as Côte d'Ivoire, Kenya, Mexico, and Nigeria, the response to a temporary economic upswing was an unsustainable increase in public spending. Countries such as Botswana, Chile, Colombia, Indonesia, Korea, Malaysia, Mauritius, and Thailand managed to keep their macroeconomic policies on course, and their broader economic performance has benefited accordingly.

If a persistent government budget deficit is the surest route to economic failure, an artificially overvalued exchange rate must be the runner-up. Underlying such overvaluation are expansionary fiscal and monetary policies, excessive borrowing, and inadequate trade and exchange rate policies. Overvaluation leads to the rationing of foreign exchange, which is invariably associated with its discretionary allocation and appropriation by government officials and their friends. Overvaluation also creates pressures for layer after layer of controls on imports, capital flows, and even travel. And it destroys emerging export industries, perhaps the most important foundation for growth that any developing country enjoys. The extent of exchange rate misalignment and its deleterious effects on performance are now well documented.

Institutional Development

The better a country's institutional capabilities are, the more effective such actions will be. Similar policy reforms have produced different results across countries, and one of the explanations is the variation in the capacity of institutions to implement the reforms. Institutional development refers to market as well as to government institutions.

In many countries market development requires less government intervention. Market institutions are often stifled by a series of harmful interventions. Governments sometimes intervene in the market to address political instability and other political constraints. But, all too often, the resulting combination of pervasive distortions and predatory states leads to development disasters. Reversing this process is a crucial part of institutional development. It requires political will and a political commitment to market reform and market development.

But it is a myth that "government is the problem, not the solution." When governments do the things they should not do, they are stretched too thin to do the things they must do. Governments need to assist in the efficient development of markets. Only governments can provide the institutional framework for exchanges. This means rules governing property rights, and it means enforcement based on preestablished principles of contracts. The establishment of a well-functioning legal system and judiciary and of secure property rights is an essential complement to economic reforms.

Reform of the public sector is a priority in many countries. In addition to market liberalization and privatization, it includes reforming the civil service, rationalizing public expenditures, and reforming some state-owned enterprises. Related economic reforms include better delivery of public goods, supervision of banks, and legislation to encourage financial development. Adopting these reforms will increase the quality of governance and the capacity of the state to implement development policy and enable society to establish checks and balances.

WHAT ARE THE UNCERTAINTIES?

Across a wide spectrum of opinion there is agreement on the basic principles we have just described. Governments have done too much of the things they cannot do well—regulating markets and producing ordinary goods—and too little of the things they must do well—maintaining macroeconomic stability and making necessary public investments. Governments, in ways that will differ from country to country, need to do less of certain things and to do them better. But the agreement on these points leaves a great deal unresolved. There are questions about implementation and concerns about external constraints of various kinds.

First, the East Asian success stories remain open to differing interpretations. Government, at key stages in each of these countries' development, did seek to affect the allocation of resources across sectors through industrial, trade, and credit allocation policies. *World Development Report 1991* noted some key conditions under which East Asian interventions were far more effective than similar actions in other parts of the world. Government interventions were disciplined by international competition. And they were flexible enough to be changed on the basis of the evidence about their effectiveness.

As the success of Japan, Korea, and Taiwan continues, the position taken by some economists that they succeeded despite government efforts at channeling market forces is increasingly implausible. But there is still room for disagreement, and so for research on two questions: how important in explaining East Asian growth is the contribution of sectoral interventions relative to the contribution of overall macroeconomic stability, outward orientation, and investments in capital and people, and what is unique about these countries that enabled interventionist policies to succeed there when they have been so unsuccessful in the rest of the world? Answering the latter question is essential if the East Asian experience is to provide guidance to other countries.

Second, what is the best sequence and pace of reform? If the role of government that we have just described is agreed to be appropriate, there remains the question of how policies should be reformed. On the sequencing question, experience suggests that it is wrong to think of reform as a series of obstacles, each of which must be surmounted. Policy changes typically occur simultaneously or nearly simultaneously on many fronts. But as a general proposition it appears that macroeconomic stabilization is essential to reform and needs to come early, and that it is usually best to delay financial liberalization until macroeconomic stability has been put in place and the viability of enterprises has been restored. On the question of the pace of reform there is also room for disagreement. Where hyperinflation is rampant or looming, the case for urgent action is clear. But where the threas is not imminent, as in much of Africa, China, or India, the case for "big bang"–style reform is much weaker. Particularly where reform will involve large displacements of workers who will not be quickly reemployed, there are legitimate grounds for favoring gradual transitions. The difficulty, of course, is that gradual transitions are often favored by those whose first choice would be no transition at all.

Third, what is the relationship between political and economic reform? An earlier view that democracy was antithetical to development and that the strong-arm state with a strong leader at the helm was essential has now been discredited. A number of studies . . . have found no systematic relationship between liberties and rates of economic growth and evidence of a positive relationship between liberties and social performance. These findings are reassuring to friends of both economic and political freedom, but doubts remain. Most of the major development success stories—for example, Chile, China, Korea, or Singapore—had governments that were or are authoritarian in many respects. It is possible that democracy can foster growth by making it impossible for hopelessly incompetent and corrupt governments to remain in power, but one also has to wonder whether democracy can be inconsistent with outstanding performance. A related issue involves the sequencing of political and economic reform—the ordering of glasnost and perestroika. It is easier to identify examples of successful economic reform that preceded political reform than that immediately followed it.

Fourth, can adjustment to the "market-friendly" approach work in very low-income countries, especially in Africa? It is hard to answer this question in the absence of a clearly specified alternative strategy. One of the hard lessons of the adjustment efforts of the past decade is that adjustment and reform take time to yield results. Government credibility, once lost, is restored only very slowly. And would-be investors, whether foreign or domestic, can always delay investment, waiting to see how things turn out before deciding whether to invest. Most of the success stories—Japan and Germany after World War II and Chile, Korea, and Mexico more recently—took time, and things often got worse before they got better. The process appears even more protracted in very low-income countries. It is no accident that programs put in place with the cooperation of the Bretton Woods institutions involve a higher ratio of adjustment to austerity than would have been the case a few years ago.

Fifth, will the external global economic conditions make export-led growth possible on a large scale over the next twenty-five years? Export-led strategies have not invariably been the most effective. Looking at the record of the period between the two world wars and of the immediate postwar period, it is not difficult to understand the appeal of import substitution notions. Brazil, with relatively closed markets, was about the fastest-growing country in the world from 1965 to 1980. The liberal advice that most developing countries receive must be based on one of two premises. One is that it will be widely ignored, so the adding-up problem—that is, the problem that increased exports from all will deny benefits to individual countries—will not arise, and those few countries that increase their export capacity will benefit. The other is that many countries will be able to increase exports greatly without depressing their terms of trade, either because industrial markets for domestic products will grow without protectionist policies being imposed, or because trade among developing countries will become more important in the future than it has been in the past. These premises are not self-evident as reform sweeps the developing world, industrial country growth slows, and the Uruguay Round flounders. Although it has been true in the past that the external climate has been a less important barrier to development than misguided domestic policies, this may change as domestic policies improve and protectionism in the industrial world mounts.

Sixth, will natural environmental constraints hold back development or force a new paradigm based on notions of sustainability? Environmental concerns are very important and have been too little reflected for too long in policymaking in both developing and industrial countries. To a large extent environmental problems are a consequence of policies that are misguided on narrow economic grounds—subsidies to energy, failure to give farmers title to their land and adequate credit, public ownership of major industries, inefficient charging for water, and so forth. And where they are not, the difficulty is to do the right cost-benefit analysis and implement the most cost-effective policies for sustainable development. Of particular importance are steps to eradicate the severe forms of environmental degradation, such as poor sanitation and water and air pollution, that threaten human lives and well-being. The agenda for environmental reform is a large one. Accepting the challenge to accelerate development in an environmentally responsible manner will involve substantial shifts in policies and priorities and will require substantial investments. Failing to accept it will be far more costly.

Seventh, and finally, there is the ever present danger that some new problem will surface. The only real constant of experience is the unpredictability of the future.

27

Development: The Market Is Not Enough

ROBIN BROAD, JOHN CAVANAGH, and WALDEN BELLO

This essay challenges the viability of development models based on free-market principles, as advocated by Summers and Thomas (Reading 26). The authors argue that the newly industrializing countries of East Asia are not models of successful development, as evidenced by their recent labor unrest and ecological destruction; that the socialist command economies' failure was not due primarily to their eschewal of market mechanisms; and that policies of "structural adjustment" have not set the stage for sustained development in the 1990s. Instead, the authors advocate development strategies that promote broadly representative government, equitable income distribution, and ecologically sound policies. In their view, such models will better foster environmentally sustainable and equitable growth and enhance political stability and democracy in developing countries.

As the 1990s begin, the development debate has all but disappeared in the West. Monumental changes in Eastern Europe and Latin America are widely interpreted as proof of the superiority of development models that are led by the private sector and oriented toward exports. Free-market capitalism is said to have prevailed because only it promises growth and democracy for the battered economies of Africa, Asia, and Latin America. World Bank President Barber Conable summed up this prevailing view in remarks made in February 1990: "If I were to characterize the past decade, the most remarkable thing was the generation of a global consensus that market forces and economic efficiency were the best way to achieve the kind of growth which is the best antidote to poverty."

Ample evidence exists, however, to suggest caution in the face of triumphalism. Warning signs are surfacing in South Korea and Taiwan, the miracle models

Robin Broad, John Cavanagh, and Walden Bello. "Development: The Market Is Not Enough." Reprinted by permission from *Foreign Policy* 81 (Winter 1990–91). Copyright © 1990 by the Carnegie Endowment for International Peace.

of capitalist development. After decades of systematic exploitation, the South Korean labor force erupted in thousands of strikes during the late 1980s, undermining the very basis of that country's export success. Meanwhile, decades of uncontrolled industrial development have left large parts of Taiwan's landscape with poisoned soil and toxic water.

Additional evidence reveals extensive suffering throughout Africa, parts of Asia, and Latin America, where privatized adjustment has been practiced for more than a decade in a world economy of slower growth. As the United Nations Children's Fund noted in its 1990 annual report, "Over the course of the 1980s, average incomes have fallen by 10 per cent in most of Latin America and by over 20 per cent in sub-Saharan Africa. . . . In many urban areas, real minimum wages have declined by as much as 50 per cent." The World Bank estimates that as many as 950 million of the world's 5.2 billion people are "chronically malnourished"— more than twice as many hungry people as a decade ago.

In Latin America, people are talking about a lost decade, even a lost generation. In Rio de Janeiro, the lack of meaningful futures has given birth to a new sport: train surfing. Brazilian street children stand atop trains beside a 3,300 volt cable that sends trains hurtling at speeds of 120 kilometers per hour. During an 18-month period in 1987–88, train surfing in Rio produced some 200 deaths and 500 gruesome injuries. "It's a form of suicide," said the father of a *surfista* who was killed. "Brazilian youth is suffering so much, they see no reason to live."

This generalized failure of development in the 1980s is producing a very different kind of consensus among people the development establishment rarely contacts and whose voices are seldom heard. A new wave of democratic movements across Africa, Asia, and Latin America is demanding another kind of development. Through citizens' organizations millions of environmentalists, farmers, women, and workers are saying they want to define and control their own futures. They are beginning to lay the groundwork for a new type of development in the 1990s—one that emphasizes ecological sustainability, equity, and participation, in addition to raising material living standards.

The false impression that the free-market model has triumphed in development is rooted in three misconceptions about the past decade:

- that the newly industrializing countries (NICs) of East Asia were exceptions to the "lost decade" and continue to represent models of successful development;
- that socialist command economies in Eastern Europe or the developing world failed principally because they did not use market mechanisms;
- that the export-oriented structural adjustment reforms that were put in place in much of the developing world have laid the groundwork for sustained growth in the 1990s.

The NICs did achieve the fastest growth rates among developing countries over the last three decades. But as the Berlin Wall was dismantled, the costs of high-speed, export-oriented industrialization were beginning to catch up with South

Korea and Taiwan. The foundations of these supposed miracles of capitalist development were cracking.

In South Korea centralized authoritarian development has created a virtual time bomb. From afar, South Korea's spectacular growth may seem to have justified so-called transitional costs like severe labor repression. But many South Korean workers feel differently. Taking advantage of a small democratic opening between 1987 and 1989, more than 7,200 labor disputes broke out, compared with only 1,026 from 1981 through 1986. No major industry was spared; over the 1987–88 period the number of unions increased two and a half times. In perhaps the best known confrontation, 14,000 policemen stormed the Hyundai shipyard in March 1989 to put down a 109-day strike.

The priority of many South Korean workers is not the maintenance of Korea's export competitiveness but rather acquiring what they regard as their overdue share of the fruits from three decades of growth. Indeed, the 45 per cent rise in average Korean wages over the last three years constitutes a central factor behind the erosion of Korea's export competitiveness. As export growth falls, the country is likely to experience its first trade deficit in years in 1990.

While a resentful labor movement threatens South Korea's traditional growth model by demanding greater equity and participation, a powerful environmental movement in Taiwan is challenging the island's fragile social consensus on export-oriented growth. This decentralized multi-class movement comprises consumers, farmers, influential intellectuals, residents of polluted areas, and workers. Although less-publicized than Eastern Europe's environmental devastation, Taiwan's is also severe and results from the same technocratic assumption that "some" environmental damage is the necessary price of economic growth. As it turned out, "some" damage included at least 20 per cent of the country's farmland, now polluted by industrial waste. Dumping of industrial and human waste (only 1 per cent of the latter receives even primary treatment) has been unregulated. Uncontrolled air pollution has also contributed to a quadrupling of asthma cases among Taiwanese children in the last decade.

A growing awareness of these environmental realities has led some Taiwanese to fight back. Citizen actions have halted work on a Dupont chemical plant, shut down an Imperial Chemical Industries petrochemical factory, stopped expansion of the naphtha cracker industry, and prevented construction of a fourth nuclear power plant on the island, thus thwarting the government's plan to build 20 nuclear plants by the end of the century. Large segments of the populations of Korea and Taiwan now reject the path to growth long touted as a model for the Third World. According to one 1985 survey, 59 per cent of Taiwanese favor environmental protection over economic growth.

These points do not mean that South Korea and Taiwan are about to become basket cases. Nor does the argument deny that they experienced periods of economic growth greater than that of most other developing countries. Instead, the evidence demonstrates that both countries can no longer practice a growth strategy based on repression of workers and abuse of the environment. It is now clear that each would have been better off trading some economic growth for more democracy and more ecological sensitivity from the start. Korea and Taiwan hardly serve as exemplary models for development.

While the cracks in the NIC model of development have been largely ignored in the West, the failure of socialism as an agent of development has been overplayed. There is no disputing this model's collapse; one cannot argue with the millions who have taken to the streets across Eastern Europe. Yet an overlay of the NICs experience with that of Eastern Europe suggests a less facile explanation for the failure of socialism than blaming it solely on the suppression of market mechanisms.

During the 1960s in Eastern Europe, the government-led "command" economies achieved growth rates higher than those of the capitalist world, according to a 1984 United Nations Conference on Trade and Development report, while building the infrastructure for further industrial advance. Only the Japanese, who seem less blinded by free-market ideology and more appreciative of the role of a centralized state, have reconciled the two models in a more insightful lesson. . . .

The authoritarian regime in South Korea also achieved spectacular growth rates by practicing command economics. This fact flies in the face of conventional development dogma. Government incentives, subsidies, and coercion fueled the drive for heavy industry in such areas as iron and steel that market forces would have rendered uncompetitive in the early stages. These sectors then built up the infrastructure South Korea needed to become a world-class exporter of such higher value-added goods as cars and VCRs.

South Korea's technocrats enlarged the application of market principles in the early 1980s, whereas the East European economies failed to do so. The South Korean economy's resumption of growth after a brief period of stagnation at the onset of the 1980s and Eastern Europe's slowdown after rapid growth in the 1960s confirm a more complex truth than that purveyed by free-market ideologues: Command economies may propel societies through the first stages of development, but further growth into a more sophisticated economy necessitates a greater role for market mechanisms.

At the same time, there should be no illusions about the adverse consequences of market mechanisms on equity. Both China and Vietnam, for example, have increased agricultural output by freeing market forces. Yet both countries have experienced growing inequalities. While some farmers are getting richer, some consumers are going hungry in the face of rising food prices. Post-1978 economic reforms in China have increased income inequalities in both urban and rural areas.

Other lessons emerge from Eastern Europe and the socialist developing world. While some of these countries did perform redistributive reforms, providing significant health and education services, they, like the NICs, have failed in the realms of ecological sustainability and political participation. Indeed, proponents of the free market fail to address a common demand coming from the citizens of China, Eastern Europe, South Korea, and Taiwan: Free markets are not a panacea; the average citizen must participate in decision making that affects his or her life.

Most developing countries, however, fall neither into the category of the NICs nor into the socialist world. For the development establishment, the lesson drawn from the experience of the NICs and the socialist countries is that developing countries' only hope rests with exporting their way to NIC status through the purgatory of structural adjustment. Dozens of countries across Africa, Asia, and Latin America have been force-fed this harsh prescription.

Supervised by the World Bank and the International Monetary Fund (IMF), these adjustment packages mandate severely cutting government spending to balance budgets, eliminating trade barriers and social subsidies, encouraging exports, tightening money policies, devaluing currencies, and dismantling nationalist barriers to foreign investment.

Part of the West's sense of triumph flows from a feeling that a worldwide consensus has developed about the necessity of these reforms. But many Western development authorities ignore that this "consensus" has been pushed on developing-country governments with a heavy hand. After borrowing sprees in the 1970s most developing countries ran into debt-servicing difficulties in the 1980s. Creditor banks, using the World Bank and IMF as enforcers, conditioned debt rescheduling on acceptance of export-oriented structural adjustment packages. In fact, many least-developed countries (LDCs) faced serious external constraints on export opportunities—from growing protectionism in developed-country markets to increased substitution for raw-material exports.

THE FAILURES OF STRUCTURAL ADJUSTMENT

The strategy urged on the LDCs suffers from other shortcomings as well. Structural adjustment in practice has damaged environments, worsened structural inequities, failed even in the very narrow goal of pulling economies forward, and bypassed popular participation. Now many of the democratic movements expanding across the globe are rejecting the profoundly undemocratic approach of structural adjustment.

Ecological sustainability has been undermined in country after country. In their frenzy to export, countries often resort to the easiest short-term approach: unsustainable exploitation of natural resources. The stories of ecological disasters lurking behind export successes have become common: Timber exporting has denuded mountains, causing soil erosion and drying critical watersheds. Cash crop exports have depended on polluting pesticides and fertilizers. Large fishing boats have destroyed the coral reefs in which fish breed and live. Tailings from mines have polluted rivers and bays.

One example is the production of prawns in the Philippines. Prawns were one of the fastest growing Philippine exports during the 1980s and are heavily promoted throughout Asia by some U.N. and other development agencies. By 1988, Philippine prawn exports had reached $250 million, ranking them fifth among the country's exports. The government's Department of Trade and Industry is seeking to boost that figure to $1 billion by 1993.

Prawn farming requires a careful mixture of fresh and salt water in coastal ponds. Vast quantities of fresh water are pumped into the ponds and mixed with salt water drawn from the sea. But some rice farmers in the Philippines' biggest prawn area fear that as salt water seeps into their nearby lands, their crop yields will fall as they have in Taiwan. Other farmers complain that not enough fresh water remains for their crops. In one town in the heart of prawn country, the water supply has already dropped 30 per cent: Potable water is being rationed. Like many cash crops, prawns do little to increase equity. Invariably, they make the rich richer and the poor poorer, weakening the prospect for mass participation in development. In one typical Philippine province, the substantial initial investment of approximately $50,000 per hectare limited potential prawn-pond owners to the wealthiest 30 or 40 families, including the province's vice governor, the ex-governor, and several mayors. Moreover, as the wealthy renovated old milkfish ponds into high-tech prawn ponds, the supply of milkfish, a staple of the poor, fell and its price rose.

Structural adjustment hurts the poor in other ways, too. As government spending is reduced, social programs are decimated. One May 1989 World Bank working paper concluded that a byproduct of the "sharply deteriorating social indicators" that accompany contractionary adjustment packages is that "people below the poverty line will probably suffer irreparable damage in health, nutrition, and education." Another World Bank working paper, published in September 1989, on Costa Rica, El Salvador, and Haiti suggested that the concentration of land in the hands of a few, along with population growth, was a major cause of environmental degradation. Skewed land distribution, it argued, pushed marginalized peasants onto fragile ecosystems. However, as the report noted, the adjustment programs in these countries failed to address distributional issues, focusing instead on correcting "distorted prices." In this regard, Taiwan and South Korea offer historical precedents: Their economic success rested on an initial redistribution of the land. Although some recent agricultural policies have been biased against the peasantry, extensive land reforms in the 1950s helped create the internal market that sustained the early stages of industrialization.

The failures of structural adjustment in the areas of environment and equity might appear less serious if the adjustment packages were scoring economic successes. They are not. The first World Bank structural adjustment loans were given to Kenya, the Philippines, and Turkey a decade ago; none can be rated a success story today. A new U.N. Economic Commission for Africa study has highlighted the World Bank's own findings that after structural adjustment programs, 15 African countries were worse off in a number of economic categories.

None of these examples is meant to deny that developing countries need substantial reforms, that some governments consistently overspend, or that markets have an important role to play. Rather, the lesson of the 1980s teaches that there are no shortcuts to development. Development strategies will not succeed and endure unless they incorporate ecological sustainability, equity, and participation, as well as effectiveness in raising material living standards.

Countries focusing on any of these principles to the exclusion of others will probably fall short in the long run, if they have not already. The World Bank and the IMF, either by ignoring these first three principles in their structural adjustment reforms or, at best, by treating them as afterthoughts, have adjusted economies to the short-term benefit of narrow elite interests. Their fixation on high gross national product growth rates ensures that the costs in terms of people and resources will mount and overwhelm an economy at a later date, much as they have in South Korea and Taiwan.

PEOPLE POWER

While governmental approaches to development are failing across Africa, Asia, and Latin America, development initiatives are flourishing among citizens' organizations. Indeed, a natural relationship exists between the two levels. The failure of governments in development has given birth to many citizens' initiatives.

Popular organizations are taking on ecological destruction, inequitable control over resources and land, and governments' inability to advance the quality of life. And often the people are struggling in the face of government and military repression. Many citizens' groups are pushing for a central role in development—a concept they do not measure solely in terms of economic growth. At the core of almost all these movements lies an emphasis on participation of members in initiating and implementing plans, and in exercising control over their own lives. Hence, democracy becomes the central theme.

In the Philippines some 5 million people participate in citizens' groups. Alan Durning of the Worldwatch Institute estimated in the Fall 1989 issue of *Foreign Policy* that across the developing world more than 100 million people belong to hundreds of thousands of these organizations. Official development organizations have difficulty taking these groups seriously and to date act as though they have little bearing on national development strategies. Our research suggests the opposite: The programs and experience of these grassroots groups will form the basis for new development strategies of the 1990s.

During the past decade, many of the most vibrant organizations have been born in battles over the destruction of natural resources. The Philippines clearly illustrates this phenomenon as various citizens' groups raise ecological issues as a key measure of sustainable development. By some estimates, the destruction of forests and other natural resources in the Philippines has been among the most rapid in the world. The Philippines loses more than 140,000 hectares of forest a year, leaving only 22 per cent of the country covered with trees—versus the 54 per cent estimated as necessary for a stable ecosystem in that country.

But out of the Philippines' devastation dozens of environmental groups have sprung up, with farming and fishing communities at their core. The largest and most influential is *Haribon* (from the Filipino words "king of birds," a reference to the endangered Philippine eagle). *Haribon* matured in a battle to save Palawan, an island that contains the country's most extensive tropical rain forests. A local citizens' group evolved into a *Haribon* chapter and took on the wealthy logger whose forest concessions control 61 per cent of Palawan's productive forests.

Among other strategies, *Haribon* launched a nationwide campaign to gather a million signatures to save Palawan's forest. In 1989 *Haribon* also joined with other Philippine organizations (more than 500 by April 1990) to launch a "Green Forum" that is defining what equitable and sustainable development would involve at both the project and national levels.

By the end of the 1980s, the thousands of organizations across the developing world were campaigning against timber companies, unsustainable agriculture, industrial pollution, nuclear power plants, and the giant projects that many governments equate with development. In 1989, 60,000 tribal people, landless laborers, and peasants gathered in a small town in India to protest a series of dams in the Narmada Valley to which the World Bank has committed $450 million. On the other side of the world, Brazilian Indians from 40 tribal nations gathered that year to oppose construction of several hydroelectric dams planned for the Xingu River. Soon thereafter, Indians, rubber tappers, nut gatherers, and river people formed the Alliance of the Peoples of the Forest to save the Amazon.

In struggles over the control of resources, many also have ended up challenging powerful entrenched interests and inequitable structures. It is in this context that the president of *Haribon,* Maximo Kalaw, summed up the struggle over Philippine forest resources: "In the past fifteen years we have had only 470 logging concessionaires who own all the resources of the forests. The process created poverty for 17 million people around the forest areas."

In addition to ecology and equity, people's organizations have acted on the inability of governments to meet the most basic human needs and rights outlined in the U.N.'s International Covenant on Economic, Social and Cultural Rights: the rights to "adequate food, clothing and housing." All over the world, informal economic institutions have sprung up to fill the economic void left by cuts in government spending. Development analysts Sheldon Annis and Peter Hakim have filled a book, *Direct to the Poor* (1988), with examples of successful worker-owned businesses, transportation collectives, peasant leagues, micro-enterprise credit associations, and other citizen initiatives across Latin America. Africa specialist Fantu Cheru, in his 1989 book *The Silent Revolution in Africa,* refers to such groups in Africa as participants in a "silent revolution."

Will this decade see coalitions of citizens' organizations drawing on mass participation create governments with sustainable development agendas in Brazil, the Philippines, South Africa, and elsewhere—much as they ushered new governments into Eastern Europe in 1989? Even where citizens' coalitions do not take over the reins of state power, will these new, innovative groups be able to build links to segments of bureaucracies and even militaries that express openness to the sustainable development agenda?

Our research has uncovered positive signs in many countries. But a caveat is important: In order to gauge the success of these initiatives, one must shift away from exclusive interest in aggregate growth figures toward the more meaningful indicators of ecological sustainability, participation, equity, and quality of life for the poorer majority.

Beyond the sheer number of citizen initiatives that advance these indicators, a further measure of success revolves around the ability of local groups to form countrywide associations that address national issues. Over the past half decade in the Philippines, for example, a coalition of dozens of peasant organizations representing 1.5 million members has gathered tens of thousands of signatures for a comprehensive and technically feasible national "People's Agrarian Reform Code." The code could become the centerpiece of a national development strategy in this predominantly agrarian country that suffers from an awful land-tenure situation. The Philippine land distribution problem is also seen in the loophole- and scandal-ridden 1988 land-reform bill passed by President Corazon Aquino's Congress. According to land-reform expert Roy Prosterman, it is "likely to redistribute barely 1 per cent of the Philippines' cultivated land." By contrast, the peasant groups' code would cover all lands, abolish rampant absentee landownership, and offer support services to peasants acquiring land.

As the peasant supporters of the People's Agrarian Reform Code lobby Congress for passage of their code, they are simultaneously taking steps to implement portions of the desperately needed reform on their own. A 1989 report documented 14 representative cases around the country: actions by thousands of poor families to occupy 800 hectares of idle or abandoned lands, the seizure of idle fishponds, boycott of rent payments on land, spread of organic farming techniques, revival of traditional rice varieties, and the reforestation of mangroves in coastal areas. In other African, Asian, and Latin American countries, coalitions of peasants, workers, women, and small entrepreneurs are banding together to craft policy alternatives.

Ultimately, the greatest successes in sustainable development will come when citizens' groups seat their representatives in government. Governments that are more representative can help transform sustainable development initiatives into reality. Such governments can help build up an economic infrastructure and an internal market, create a network of social services, and set rules for a country's integration into the world economy. These three tenets do not represent another universal model to replace those of free marketeers, Marxist-Leninists, or the World Bank; the past four decades are littered with the failures of universal models. However, the outlines of a more positive government role in development can be sketched using the principles of ecological sustainability, equity, participation, and effectiveness.

South Korea and Taiwan offer positive lessons for the ideal governmental role in the economy. The main lesson is not that the government should be taken out of the economy. Instead, the NICs' experiences suggest that success depends on governments standing above vested interests to help create the social and political infrastructure for economic growth. Indeed, though it may sound paradoxical, one needs an effective government to create the market.

The problem in many developing countries is not too much government, but a government that is too tangled in the web of narrow interest groups. The Philippine government, for example, serves as the private preserve of special economic interests. In South Korea, on the other hand, the weakness of the landed and business elite allowed the government to set the direction for development in the 1960s and 1970s. Without an assertive government that often acted against the wishes of international agencies and big business, South Korea would never have gained the foundation of heavy and high-technology industries that enabled it to become a world-class exporter of high value-added commodities.

Placing governments above the control of economic interest groups presents no easy task in countries where a small number of powerful families control much of the land and resources. To increase the chances of success, strong citizens' groups must put their representatives in government, continue to closely monitor government actions, and press for redistributive reforms that weaken the power of special interests.

While independent governments can help push economies through the early stages of development, progress to more mature economies seems to require more market mechanisms to achieve effective production and distribution. For market mechanisms to work, however, there must first be a market. And for the majority of the developing world, creating a market with consumers possessing effective demand requires eliminating the severe inequalities that depress the purchasing power of workers and peasants. The "how to" list necessitates such steps as land reform, progressive taxation, and advancement of workers' rights.

Pragmatism is also essential for the integration of developing countries into the world economy. The choice facing these countries should not be viewed as an ideological one between import substitution and export-oriented growth, neither of which alone has generated sustainable development. Basing development on exports that prove to be ecologically damaging not only ignores sustainability, it fails to ask the more fundamental question of whom development should benefit. But building an export base on top of a strong internal market does make sense. In this scheme, foreign exchange receipts would shift from primary commodities to processed commodities, manufactures, and environmentally sensitive tourism. China, India, South Korea, and Taiwan all based their early industrial development on slowly raising the real incomes of their domestic populations. Each opened up to varying degrees to the world market and to foreign capital only after substantial domestic markets had been developed and nurtured.

Concerted citizen action can bring about more participatory, equitable, and ecologically sustainable development. At least one historical precedent can be cited, albeit on a subnational level: the postwar experience of Kerala, traditionally one of India's poorest states. With a population of 27 million, Kerala has more people than most developing countries. A long history of large movements by people of the lower castes culminated in the election of progressive state governments beginning in 1957. Constant pressure by India's most active agricultural labor unions and other peasant organizations forced these governments to abolish tenancy in what was one of the most sweeping agrarian reforms in South and Southeast Asia and place a high priority on health and literacy. In periods when conservative governments were voted into power in Kerala, the nongovernmental citizens' organizations remained strong enough to win reforms and ensure enforcement of existing laws. Today, despite income levels below the Indian average, Kerala boasts the highest life expectancy and literacy rates among Indian states, as well as the lowest infant mortality and birth rates.

Kerala also highlights an important caveat: New, more accountable governments should not be seen as a panacea. Even popular governments cannot provide the answer to the wide array of development problems. No matter who wields state power, strong independent citizens' groups will continue to be central to sustainable development. Perhaps South Korea and Taiwan would be more successful societies if they had combined their early land reforms and thoughtful state intervention with a prolonged commitment to ecology, equity, and participation.

Democratic participation in the formulation and implementation of development plans forms the central factor in determining their medium- and long-term viability. This, however, is a controversial premise. Indeed, such a pronounced emphasis on democracy flies in the face of political scientist Samuel Huntington's claim in the 1960s that order must precede democracy in the early stages of development. Many still believe authoritarian governments in Eastern Europe, South Korea, and Taiwan served as the catalysts for industrialization that in turn created the conditions for advancing democracy.

Experiences of the last two decades suggest otherwise. Africa, home to dozens of one-party authoritarian states, remains a development disaster. Argentina, Brazil, the Philippines, and other Asian and Latin American countries ruled by authoritarian governments have suffered similar fates. As political scientist Atul Kohli has documented, the economies of the relatively democratic regimes in Costa Rica, India, Malaysia, Sri Lanka, and Venezuela have "grown at moderate but steady rates" since the 1960s and income inequalities have "either remained stable or even narrowed."

Moreover, in South Korea and Taiwan, authoritarian characteristics of the government were not responsible for industrialization and growth. Far-reaching land reforms and each state's ability to rise above factions in civil society deserve credit for sparking growth. The only "positive" growth impact of repression by these governments was to hold down wage levels, thereby making exports more competitive. Yet heavy dependence on exports no longer serves as an option in today's increasingly protectionist global markets. The percentage of imports into the major developed countries that were affected by nontariff barriers to trade rose more than 20 per cent during the 1980s, a trend that is likely to continue. In this hostile global economic climate, respect for workers' rights can lead to the creation of local markets by increasing domestic buying power. Democratic development therefore implies shifting emphasis from foreign to domestic (or, for small countries, to regional) markets. This shift meets more needs of local people and takes into account the difficult world market of the 1980s and 1990s.

The portrait painted at the outset—of a global development crisis masked by triumphant Western development orthodoxy—was a decidedly gloomy one. Why then should citizens' movements pushing for more equitable, sustainable, and participatory development stand a chance in the 1990s? Much of the answer lies in the extraordinary possibilities of the current historical moment.

DEVELOPMENT AFTER THE COLD WAR

For four decades, the Cold War has steered almost all development discussions toward ideological arguments over capitalism versus communism, market versus planning. It has also diverted public attention away from nonideological global concerns (such as environment, health, and economic decay) and toward the Soviet Union as the source of problems. Hence, the dramatic winding down of the Cold War opens great opportunities for development.

At the very minimum, real debate should now become possible, getting beyond sharply drawn ideological categories in order to discuss development in more pragmatic terms. What are the proper roles of government and market? If one values both effectiveness and equity, what kind of checks should be placed on the market? What do the experiences of Japan, South Korea, and Taiwan offer to this discussion?

The 1990s provide other opportunities to cut across Cold War polarities. Paranoid Cold War governments often saw communists lurking behind popular organizations fighting for a better society. But citizens' movements played a central role in the recent transformation of Eastern Europe. A greater openness should emerge from this phenomenon. Not only should governments and development experts treat such nongovernmental organizations with the respect they deserve, but they should realize that these groups have vital roles to play beyond the reach of governments and individuals.

Beyond the Cold War, global economic shifts also offer new possibilities for the sustainable development agenda. While much attention has been focused on the relative decline of the United States, this shift offers potentially positive openings. A decade of unprecedented U.S. military spending, for example, has bequeathed fiscal deficits that preclude significant increases in foreign aid. This situation adds impetus to proposals that the United States give less but better aid. That can be accomplished by slashing military aid that in areas like Latin America has often been used to suppress citizens' movements, and by redirecting development assistance away from unaccountable governments and toward citizens' organizations.

Likewise, persistent trade deficits are pushing the U.S. government to restrict imports that enter the domestic market with the assistance of unfair trade practices. The United States could assist developing-country movements for equity and workers' rights by implementing existing legislation that classifies systematic repression of worker rights as an unfair trading practice. Finally, the failure of the Baker and Brady plans to halt the pileup of debt should reopen the door for substantial debt plans that shift payments toward sustainable development initiatives.

Japan's displacement of the United States as the world's most dynamic large economy and biggest aid-giver provides perhaps more intriguing questions about development efforts in the next decade. Japan stands at a juncture fraught with both danger and opportunity. It can take the easy road and mimic what the United States did: ally with local elites and subordinate development policy to security policy. Or Japan can practice enlightened leadership by divorcing the two policies and opening up the possibility for a qualitative change in North-South ties. Will Japan seize the opportunities? During the Marshall Plan years, the United States bestowed substantial decision-making power on the recipient governments. Can Japan, using that experience as a starting point, broaden the decision-making group to include nongovernmental organizations? In fact, voices within Japan are calling for the Japanese government to redirect its aid flows to include citizens' organizations. . . .

The question also remains whether Japan will follow the U.S. example of using the World Bank and IMF as extensions of its aid, commercial, and trade policies, further eroding the credibility of these institutions in the Third World. Perhaps Japan's ascension will encourage these institutions to delve more objectively into the development lessons of Japan, South Korea, and Taiwan, thus adding realism to their prescriptions.

Finally, both Japan and the United States will have to face the need to respect the emerging citizens' movements as the groups reach out internationally to work with one another. The realization that governments suffer from severe limits in the development field should not be seen as negative. Rather, this understanding opens a variety of possibilities for new forms of government-citizen initiatives. In February 1990, for instance, African nongovernmental organizations, governments, and the U.N. Economic Commission for Africa jointly planned and participated in a conference that adopted a strong declaration affirming popular participation in development. NGOs may also enjoy an enhanced role at the 1992 U.N. Conference on Environment and Development in Brazil as the realization spreads that governments alone can do little to stop forest destruction and other activities that contribute to the emission of greenhouse gases.

In the face of such opportunities, the seeming death of the development debate in the industrial world represents an enormous travesty. Rekindling that debate, however, requires listening to new approaches from the rest of the world. Excessive confidence in free-market approaches melts when one examines the mounting crises in the supposed success stories of South Korea and Taiwan. Exciting alternatives to the dominant development paradigms are emerging in the hundreds of thousands of citizens' groups that flourish amid adversity and repression in Africa, Asia, and Latin America. These voices must be heard in the development establishments of Washington, Tokyo, and Bonn.

28

Inflation and Stabilization

STEPHAN HAGGARD

In this article, Stephan Haggard seeks to explain why some developing countries have been more successful than others in promoting stable macroeconomic policies. Blending domestic societal and state-centered approaches, he argues that both the density and composition of social groups and how they express their interests through state institutions shape policy outcomes. Haggard's analysis of middle-income Latin American and East Asian countries suggests that a combination of interest-group pressure and the nature and design of particular institutions determines the incentives faced by state leaders to pursue stable macroeconomic policies. The developing countries with the highest inflation, he finds, have been those with urban labor movements mobilized into populist parties within relatively polarized party systems.

Why have some middle-income developing countries had histories of high inflation over the past two decades, while others have pursued stable macroeconomic policies? Among countries experiencing inflation, why do some governments move to stabilize with alacrity, while others postpone the adjustment decision, often with disastrous costs? Once the decision to stabilize is taken, why are some countries capable of sustaining stabilization policies while others falter and reverse course?

A wide array of economic factors is important in understanding particular national experiences with inflation, including the severity of exogenous shocks. Nonetheless, inflation often has political roots, and whatever its causes, stabilization poses profound political dilemmas.

This chapter reviews some current thinking about the political economy of fiscal policy and advances some hypotheses about differences in inflation and stabilization efforts among middle-income developing countries. The rent- and revenue-seeking approach of the new political economy is useful for understanding the political incentives to government spending and explains why subsidies

Stephan Haggard. "Inflation and Stabilization." From Gerald M. Meier, ed. *Politics and Policy Making in Developing Countries: Perspectives on the New Political Economy.* The International Center for Economic Growth, ICS Press, 1991, pp. 233–49. Reprinted by permission of ICS Press.

and state-owned enterprises become politically entrenched. This approach, however, does not explain cross-national *differences* in fiscal performance and inflation. Such variation can be accounted for in part by pressures for government spending that result from interest group and partisan conflict. The organization of urban labor and its incorporation into the party system appear to be important factors. The developing countries with histories of high inflation, mostly in Latin America, have been those in which urban "popular sector" and labor groups have been mobilized into populist parties within relatively polarized party systems. Such high-conflict countries also had the greatest difficulties stabilizing in the 1980s, particularly where stabilization episodes overlapped with transitions to democratic rule. It is difficult to disentangle lines of causality because the size of external shocks and initial disequilibria posed greater difficulties for the large Latin American debtors, but the vulnerability to external shocks was itself partly the result of previous policy choices.

The structure of interest groups and the nature of the political regime are, of course, not easily changed. Other political factors affecting fiscal outcomes may offer greater scope for reform, though. The political difficulties of macroeconomic adjustment appear to be less severe where decision making is relatively centralized within the government and insulated from rent-seeking pressures. This suggests the importance of institutional reform for sustaining credible macroeconomic policy.

THE POLITICAL ECONOMY OF INFLATION AND STABILIZATION

Albert Hirschman has pointed out that "the explanation of inflation in terms of social conflict between groups, each aspiring to a greater share of the social product, has become the sociologist's monotonous equivalent of the economist's untiring stress on the undue expansion of the money supply." To construct a political theory of inflation and stabilization demands an explication of the precise mechanisms through which political variables contribute to increases in the price level and difficulties in stabilization.

In studies of the advanced industrial states, cross-national variations in inflation have been traced to differences in wage-setting institutions and relations among business, organized labor, and government. Wage policy has played a role in efforts to control inflation in the developing world, but a growing body of evidence suggests that fiscal policy is a more appropriate focus for an examination of the political economy of inflation in developing countries. Since developing country governments generally have limited scope for domestic borrowing, financing fiscal deficits usually involves recourse to foreign borrowing and the inflation tax. There appear to be few cases of severe and prolonged inflation in the developing world that were not associated with fiscal deficits financed by money creation.

Fiscal policy also helps explain the accumulation of debt and the subsequent vulnerability of debtor countries to external shocks. When net capital inflows ceased abruptly in the early 1980s, debtors were unable to cut expenditures and raise revenues quickly. They thus relied on instruments that constituted implicit taxes on financial intermediation, with adverse consequences for investment.

Not surprisingly, fiscal policy has been central to stabilization efforts. International Monetary Fund stabilization programs invariably target some monetary indicator as the key performance criterion, but the focus on monetary policy reflects the availability of data and the political problems of appearing to interfere in sensitive allocational decisions rather than a belief in the primacy of monetary measures. The actions required to meet monetary targets are usually fiscal: some combination of increased taxes or nontax revenues and cuts in expenditures. The principal political dilemma is that no matter how beneficial these measures may be in the long run for the country as a whole, they entail the imposition of short-term costs and have distributional implications for particular groups.

CONTRIBUTIONS AND LIMITS OF
THE NEW POLITICAL ECONOMY

The new, or neoclassical, political economy relies heavily on interest group models that seek to explain policy, including taxation and expenditure, as the result of political exchanges between welfare-maximizing constituents and support-maximizing politicians. On the demand side of the political market are constituents, conceptualized as individual voters, interest groups, or even bureaucratic groups within the state itself. The political process consists of spending by these constituents to influence the size and direction of fiscal redistribution. Rational constituents will expend resources—on lobbying, political contributions, demonstrations, and so forth—until the marginal cost of their influence efforts equals the expected marginal return from securing their desired policy outcome. Where rival constituencies have conflicting interests, groups expending the most on the influence attempt will prevail.

Politicians constitute the supply side of the market, though the real "suppliers" are those groups from whom income and wealth transfers are ultimately sought. The key insight of the new political economy into fiscal policy is that politicians view expenditures to their constituents not as costs, but as benefits. They will thus seek to increase expenditures to constituents to the point at which the political return is offset by the economic and political costs, including the inflationary consequences of high budget deficits. The lure of deficits is strengthened by fundamental asymmetries between spending and taxing decisions: the means of financing deficits—inflation and borrowing—are less visible than taxation, spread more widely across the population (inflation), or pushed onto future generations (borrowing).

The new political economy underlines the incentives facing politicians to spend and explains puzzles such as the bias against least-cost alternatives and the tendency for projects to assume unnecessary scale. Ultimately, however, this rent-seeking approach cannot predict whether central government accounts will be in surplus, balance, or deficit. Put differently, there is a problem in getting from the microlevel of a particular expenditure or tax to the macrolevel of aggregate fiscal outcomes.

Discussions of subsidies and state-owned enterprises that draw on rent-seeking models illustrate this difficulty. Subsidies give politicians an instrument for building electoral or clientele support. Because they can grow into virtually open-ended government commitments and are seen as entitlements by their recipients, subsidies have been a major factor contributing to fiscal deficits in a number of middle-income countries. Their reduction or elimination has been a central component of most stabilization plans and is one of the most difficult to carry through because of the vulnerability of most governments to urban consumer groups. Yet not all governments have fallen into the subsidy trap, and some have managed to reduce subsidies.

A related example is provided by the growing literature on state-owned enterprises (SOEs). SOEs played a major role in contributing to fiscal deficits and external borrowing in a number of developing countries over the 1970s and 1980s. Some of this expenditure was no doubt for legitimate purposes; viewed politically, however, SOEs represent powerful constituencies within the government because of the resources under their control and their importance in generating employment. In many cases, SOEs are more powerful than the ministries that presumably oversee their activities; state-owned oil enterprises, such as Mexico's PEMEX, are important examples. Governments have also been politically vulnerable to pressures from customers, contractors, and suppliers to maintain purchases of goods and services, limit price increases, raise wages, and retain employees. Again, the puzzle for the new political economy is in explaining variance. In some countries, SOEs have mushroomed and been a major drain on national treasuries, while in others their role has been limited or subject to effective control.

One way of bridging the gap between the micro- and macrolevels of political analysis is through the political business cycle. This literature argues that regardless of the party in power, economic policy will change over the electoral cycle as politicians seek to manipulate the short-run Philipps curve (showing the trade-off between unemployment and inflation) to electoral advantage. The evidence for a political business cycle remains weak for the advanced industrial states. The model assumes short voter memory concerning past performance and myopia concerning future inflation, or, as Brian Barry has put it, "a collection of rogues competing for the favors of a larger collection of dupes."

Many of the political and institutional characteristics that mitigate political business cycles in the advanced industrial states are absent, however, in the developing countries. These include, among other things, informed publics; independent media coverage of economic policy; institutionalized forms of consultation between business, government, and labor; and welfare systems that cushion the costs of unemployment. Given lower levels of income, extensive poverty, and the insecurity of political tenure in a number of polities, it is plausible that politicians' time horizons in the developing world are oriented toward the delivery of short-term benefits for electoral gain.

A second way of joining the micro- and macrolevels is through models emphasizing partisan conflict. In one such model, the economy is divided into two groups, "workers" and "capitalists," each with its own political party. The party in power seeks to redistribute income in favor of its constituency: right-wing governments pursue policies that favor profits; left-wing governments, those that favor wages. In designing fiscal policy, each party will seek to tax its opponents to the maximum feasible extent, while redistributing to its own constituency. Governments in power have a strong incentive to borrow, knowing that the full cost of servicing current obligations will be borne by political successors.

Two hypotheses result from this line of inquiry. First, a high level of political instability, measured by frequent changes of government, is likely to generate higher fiscal deficits, since politicians will have particularly short time horizons. Second, a polarized political system in which the objectives of the competing parties are highly incompatible will generate higher fiscal deficits than those systems in which the objectives of the competing parties overlap and are less zero-sum in nature.

BRINGING INSTITUTIONS BACK IN

Economists who have branched into political economy tend to think of the polity in terms of economic cleavages. Workers have different interests than capitalists; holders of financial assets have different inflation preferences than debtors; urban consumers have different preferences regarding agricultural prices than rural producers. As the partisan-conflict model suggests, economists assume a close "mapping" between economic cleavages and political organization, and see the state and politicians as relatively passive registers of social demands. With this approach, every policy that has a distributional consequence could be explained on the grounds that it favored some group. The more demanding task is to explain why some polities are riddled with revenue seeking, while others have developed mechanisms of fiscal control.

Answering such questions requires greater attention to organizational and institutional factors. First, different types of economic activity may be more or less amenable to political organization and collective action. The agricultural sector may loom large in the economy, but peasants are difficult to organize and rural influence on policy can easily be offset by smaller, but better organized urban forces. It is therefore important to have information not only on economic cleavages, which provides good clues about policy preferences, but also on which social groups are in fact capable of effective organization.

Second, party organization can aggregate interests in different ways. In some polities, the party system reinforces societal and economic cleavages and conflicts, for example, pitting populist or labor parties against conservative and middle-class parties, or urban-based parties against rural-based ones. In other countries, broad, catchall parties cut across class or economic divisions and tend to mute them. These organizational differences can have profound influence on the political appeals parties make, on the demands on public finance, and consequently on the conduct of macroeconomic policy. Macroeconomic stability is more likely in two-party systems with broad, catchall parties than in those that pit class-based parties against one another or in multiparty systems that foster more ideological parties.

It is not enough to know how groups are organized for political action; equally if not more important is the question of how social demands are represented in the decision-making process. The new political economy has focused its attention on the advanced industrial states, and thus assumed the existence of political processes such as general elections. Elections are not relevant for policy making in authoritarian regimes, and may not be relevant for policy making in some arenas even under democratic conditions. For example, monetary policy and the details of budgeting may have more to do with internal bureaucratic politics or the independence of the central bank, than with electoral or party constraints.

The absence of democratic processes in the developing world may help explain the attraction of lobbying and rent-seeking models, which can presumably be applied to both democratic and authoritarian regimes. Democracy may not be ubiquitous, but lobbying is. Yet interest group pressures constrain authoritarian rulers less than they do democratic rulers. It is thus plausible that the political regime can be an important factor in explaining the ability to impose stabilization costs.

These observations suggest the importance of combining interest group and partisan explanations with an analysis of the overall institutional context: the nature of the party system, the budget process, and the type of regime. This analysis can be illustrated, though not definitively tested, by examining some hypotheses about the variation in inflation and stabilization efforts among the middle-income countries.

POLITICS AND INFLATION IN MIDDLE-INCOME COUNTRIES

Although the debt crisis of the 1980s has had global implications, its effects have been felt quite differently in various geographic regions. Among the middle-income countries, Latin America has been the hardest hit. Twelve of the seventeen countries designated by the World Bank as the most heavily indebted are in the Western Hemisphere. The most severe problems with inflation are found in that region as well. By contrast, the middle-income countries of East and Southeast Asia—South Korea, Taiwan, Indonesia, Thailand, Malaysia, and the Philippines—have largely been immune from devastating inflations.

. . . [D]ifferences in inflation are not simply the result of recent events. Before the onset of the debt crisis, Latin America consistently had higher levels of inflation than other developing countries, though there are important contrasts within regions. Brazil, Chile, and Uruguay all have histories of comparatively high inflation. The current hyperinflations in Brazil and Argentina are outside the range of those countries' historical experience, but both have experienced severe inflations before. Other Latin American countries, including Colombia, Venezuela, and

Mexico, have not had chronically high levels of inflation, though all have suffered increasing inflationary pressures in recent times. Peru, historically a low-inflation country compared with the Southern Cone nations (Argentina, Chile, and Uruguay), is now veering toward hyperinflation.

In Asia, Thailand, Taiwan, and Malaysia have had histories of low inflation and all largely escaped the debt crisis of the 1980s. Indonesia had a near hyperinflation in the mid-1960s, but its fiscal and monetary policy have been conservative since. South Korea has had high levels of debt and inflation by Asian standards but adjusted relatively smoothly in the early 1980s. The Philippines, by contrast, had painful problems of adjustment in 1984, though by comparison to the Latin American debtors, that country's difficulties appear relatively mild.

Recognizing that economic circumstances vary across cases as well, what political factors help account for these long-term patterns? The new political economy would suggest that differences in the density and composition of interest group organization should be a starting point. Through most of the postwar period, the Latin American countries can be differentiated from the Asian cases in terms of the size and organization of urban-industrial interest groups, including the so-called popular sector, which has played a crucial role in Latin American politics.

Mexico, Brazil, and particularly the countries of the Southern Cone had longer histories of industrialization, larger urban-industrial populations, and comparatively small agrarian sectors at the outset of the borrowing boom of the 1970s than the East and Southeast Asian countries. These conditions have implied denser and more established networks of unions, white-collar associations, and manufacturers' groups linked to the import-substituting industrialization (ISI) process in Latin America.

This density of urban-industrial groups, in turn, had two implications for economic policy. The first concerns overall economic strategy. There have been important economic barriers to shifting the pattern of incentives toward export-oriented strategies in Latin America, including the problem of setting exchange rates where there is a strong comparative advantage in natural resource export. The number and extent of groups linked to import-substituting industrialization have also been significant factors. Even authoritarian governments with preferences for market-oriented policies, such as Brazil after 1964, faced constraints from groups linked to the ISI process. The well-known balance of payments problems associated with ISI were, in turn, one factor in the expansion of foreign borrowing during the 1970s and the subsequent macroeconomic policy problems.

In South Korea and Taiwan, by contrast, industrialization, and particularly ISI, were of shorter duration, and there were consequently fewer interests opposed to the crucial exchange rate and trade reforms that launched export-led growth. Elite concern with rural incomes may also have had some effect on policy, constituting a political counterweight to ISI forces. This constellation of interest groups may help explain the ability of the Philippines, Thailand, Malaysia, and Indonesia to maintain realistic exchange rates and to shift, though to varying degrees, toward the promotion of manufactured exports.

The second consequence of the density of urban-industrial groups relates more immediately to macroeconomic policy. The political mobilization of urban groups and unions, particularly in a context of high income inequality, is an important factor in explaining the appeal of populist economic ideologies in Latin America. . . . [T]here is a remarkable similarity in populist economic programs across countries. Their main political objective is to reverse the loss in real income to urban groups that results from traditional stabilization policies or simply from the business cycle.

Populist prescriptions include fiscal expansion; a redistribution of income through real wage increases; and a program of structural reform designed to relieve productive bottlenecks and economize on foreign exchange. Populists reject the claim that deficit financing is inflationary, arguing that the mobilization of unused spare capacity, declining costs, and, if necessary, controls, will moderate inflation.

Populist experiments go through a typical cycle, usually triggered by orthodox stabilization efforts:

Phase 1.   Policy makers enjoy a honeymoon as their prescriptions appear to be vindicated. Output grows and real wages and employment improve. Direct controls are used to manage inflation. The easing of the balance of payments constraint and the buildup of reserves under the previous orthodox program provides the populists a crucial cushion for meeting import demand.

Phase 2.   Strong domestic demand starts to generate a foreign exchange constraint, but devaluation is rejected as inflationary and detrimental to maintaining real wage growth. External controls are instituted. The budget deficit widens because of the growth of subsidies on wage goods and on foreign exchange.

Phase 3.   Growing disparity between official and black market exchange rates and general lack of confidence lead to capital flight. The budget deficit deteriorates because of continuing high levels of expenditure and lagging tax collections. Inflation soars.

Phase 4.   Stabilization becomes a political priority, and the principal political debate concerns whether to pursue a more "orthodox" or "heterodox" policy mix.

Why do such cycles appear in one political setting and not in another? Stop-and-go macroeconomic policies themselves are partly to blame, since they carry particular costs for urban workers. One determinant of such populist cycles is the way urban political forces are initially organized—in other words whether historical partisan alignments mute or reinforce sectoral and class cleavages.

In Argentina, Peru, Chile, and Brazil, antioligarchical parties of the center and the left recurrently sought the support of urban workers and small manufacturers by appealing to class and sectoral interests. These appeals produced the kind of political polarization and macroeconomic policy outcomes predicted by the partisan-conflict model outlined above. In Colombia and Venezuela, by contrast, such conflicts were discouraged by the electoral dominance of broadly based patronage parties. In Uruguay, the traditional Colorado and Blanco parties also tended to discourage class and sectoral conflicts that lead to expansionary macroeconomic policies, though by the mid-1960s, the influence of these parties had come under challenge from a coalition of center-left parties with strong bases of support in Montevideo.

Mexico provides an important example of the significance of institutions in determining the ability of new urban-industrial groups to formulate effective demands on the state. Under the leadership of President Lázaro Cárdenas in the 1930s, the ruling Partido Revolucionario Institucional (PRI) encompassed peasant, middle-class, and working-class organizations. Mexico experienced structural changes comparable to those in Brazil and Argentina in the 1950s and 1960s, but under stable macroeconomic policies. This regime of "stabilizing development" was achieved following a painful devaluation in 1954. The government was able to withstand short-term protests to this crucial reform because of the special relationship it enjoyed with state-sanctioned unions. Not until the early 1970s did deepening social problems and the populist political strategy of President Luis Echeverría combine to break the pattern of stable monetary and fiscal policies. Nonetheless, Mexico still managed to pursue more "orthodox" stabilization policies in the 1980s under Presidents Miguel de la Madrid and Carlos Salinas than either of the other two large Latin American countries, Brazil and Argentina. This is due in large part to the PRI's continuing ability to engineer political compromises and exercise discipline over urban workers.

Even when populist forces surfaced in East and Southeast Asian countries, they never succeeded in gaining a political foothold. A larger proportion of the population remained outside the framework of urban interest group politics altogether than in Latin America, and patterns of political organization also differed. Broad, anticolonial movements muted class and sectoral conflicts. Generally, the most serious political challenges came not from the urban areas, but from rural insurgencies. When and where urban working-class politics did emerge, it was either assimilated into corporatist structures or suppressed.

In the Philippines, two diffuse political machines dominated the electoral system before the announcement of martial law by Ferdinand Marcos in 1972. Pork-barrel conflicts were more important than programmatic differences, but elite domination of the political system resulted in extremely low levels of taxation. Beginning in the late 1960s, urban-based leftist organizations grew, but they were crushed following the declaration of martial law. Even when political liberalization provided new opportunities for the left to organize, its influence was counterbalanced by that of the old political machines and the new middle-class democratic political movement, headed finally by Corazon Aquino, which owed little to the left.

In Malaysia, politics was dominated by a single nationalist party and its minor coalition partners, but class and sectoral conflicts were secondary to ethnic rivalries. Indonesia remains a single-party system, with very limited pluralism. Thailand, despite periodic democratic openings, has shown a continuity in economic policy thanks to the central role of the bureaucracy and the continuing influence of the military.

South Korea and Taiwan once again provide sharp contrasts to the Latin American cases. Until the transition toward more pluralist politics in the two countries in the mid-1980s, both South Korea and Taiwan (beginning in 1972 and 1949, respectively) were ruled by strong, anticommunist, authoritarian regimes that limited the possibilities for interest group organization. Taiwan's one-party system effectively organized and controlled the unions and disallowed opposition parties. The South Korean government combined informal penetration of the unions and periodic repression to keep labor and urban-based opposition forces in check. The recurrence of urban-based opposition among students and workers may explain the Korean government's greater tolerance for an expansionist macroeconomic policy, but the opportunity for open political organization and populist appeals was severely limited. Both countries showed a continuity in government unparalleled in any of the Latin American governments except Chile.

This discussion suggests that the middle-income countries of Latin America and East and Southeast Asia can be arrayed on a continuum from very high to low levels of group and party conflict. Argentina, Chile, Brazil, Uruguay, and Peru appear at one extreme, with relatively large popular sectors, and with political movements and party structures that historically tended to reinforce sectoral and class conflicts; these countries have historically also had higher levels of inflation. At the other pole are Indonesia, Taiwan, and Thailand, where the popular sectors were smaller, and both political alliances and party structures less conducive to the emergence of populist movements; these countries have also generally had lower levels of inflation. The other Latin American and Asian countries fall between these two polar types, with varying degrees of urban and working-class mobilization and organization.

THE POLITICS OF STABILIZATION

These stylized patterns of political conflict also help explain variations in the political management of stabilization over time. Stabilization efforts have encountered the greatest difficulties in those countries where intense group conflicts and persistently high levels of inflation have fed on each other over long periods of time. In these circumstances, the capacity to impose stabilization has in the past been linked to the nature of the political regime, suggesting once again the importance of institutional variables in explaining policy outcomes.

There are examples of populist military governments: Bolivia in 1970–1971, the Peruvian experiment in the early 1970s, and the first year of South Korea's military rule in 1961–1962. Typically, however, militaries have seized power in the midst of political-economic crises characteristic of the later stages of the populist cycle outlined above. They have initially pursued policies designed to impose discipline and rationalize the economic system, in part by limiting the demands of leftist, populist, and labor groups. This general pattern was followed, with varying constraints, in Brazil (1964), Argentina (1966, 1976), Indonesia (1965), Chile (1973), Uruguay (1973), and arguably South Korea (1980–1981).

As the initial crisis is brought under control, military regimes begin to face new problems of consolidation or transition. Old political forces resurface, and regimes face pressure to build support and moderate the militancy of the opposition. Brazil provides an example. The government's decision to pursue high-growth policies during the oil shocks coincided closely with the military's decisions concerning the opening of the political system.

The transition to democratic rule in such systems is likely to pose particular problems for stabilization efforts. The transition opens the way for well-organized and long-standing popular sector groups to reenter politics, groups that had been controlled or repressed under military rule. High inflation and erratic growth make the distributional and political costs of fiscal restraint appear particularly formidable, but these costs are compounded by the uncertainties associated with the transition itself. New political leaders are necessarily preoccupied with securing the transition, and thus have relatively short time horizons. Those political forces that have been in opposition, or simply suppressed, are eager to press new demands on the government. As political leaders attempt to accommodate these strongly conflicting demands, it becomes difficult to maintain macroeconomic stability.

It could be argued, however, that the transition process is less important in explaining macroeconomic policy than the nature of the economic problems these governments inherited from their authoritarian predecessors. First, in countries with chronically high inflation, both authoritarian and democratic governments have accommodated conflicts over income shares through indexing. Indexing itself generates inertial inflation and complicates the conduct of monetary and fiscal policy. Second, the severity and speed of external shocks, particularly the withdrawal of external lending, severely narrowed the range of economic policy choice. Economic legacies, rather than political constraints, matter; Argentina simply inherited greater difficulties than the Philippines or South Korea.

Yet in the transitional democracies that faced high inflations, political constraints do appear to be significant in the making of macroeconomic policy. The three experiments with heterodox adjustment strategies—Argentina, Brazil, and Peru—occurred in systems with a high level of popular sector mobilization. Brazil under José Sarney and Peru under Alán García responded to high inflation with heterodox policies in the mid-1980s that included wage-price controls and currency reforms. In contrast to Mexico, however, neither new democratic government placed a high priority on containing wage pressures, reducing subsidies, or controlling spending, and both experiments ran into difficulties. Raúl Alfonsín's middle-class government in Argentina also pursued a heterodox shock policy to manage high inflation, but initially placed greater emphasis on negotiating wage restraint and bringing deficits under control. Nonetheless, fiscal policy remained a source of inflationary pressure, stabilization efforts faltered, and political competition with the Peronists and the anticipation of a change of government ultimately undermined the coherence of macroeconomic policy.

The interesting exception is Uruguay, one of the most economically successful of the new Latin American democracies. The return to constitutionalism in Uruguay restored the dominance of the two, broad-based centrist parties that had dominated political life until the coup in 1973, providing a framework for elite negotiation and accord much like that in more established democratic systems such as Colombia and Venezuela. Negotiations between the Blanco and Colorado parties led to an economic policy agreement in early 1985 that emphasized controlling budget deficits and inflation, promoting exports, and undertaking structural reforms.

The transition to democracy has played a less important role in explaining macroeconomic policy in countries with a lower level of popular sector mobilization and a greater institutional continuity in political and decision-making structures. Not coincidentally, these countries also faced less daunting economic problems, and it can once again be argued that economic circumstance rather than political factors account for the variance. It nonetheless appears plausible that politics had at least an intervening effect on policy choices and outcomes.

In Thailand, the new political order ushered in by parliamentary elections in 1979 might be labeled semidemocratic. In 1980, General Kriangsak was forced to resign over economic mismanagement in the face of rising protest and pressure from within the military. Another general, Prem Tinsulanon, was elected by a large majority in both houses to replace him. Prem moved to incorporate opposition parties into a broad-based coalition, yet to Thailand's "bureaucratic polity," power continued to reside in the army and bureaucracy. There were no fundamental discontinuities in business-government relations and technocrats even gained in influence.

In South Korea, General Chun Doo-hwan's handpicked successor, Roh Tae-woo, was forced to widen the scope of political liberalization and constitutional reforms in the wake of widespread urban protests in 1986 and 1987 that included students, workers, and middle-class elements. Running against a split opposition, Roh captured the presidency with just over one-third of the popular vote. Though the conservative ruling party subsequently lost control of the National Assembly and has been forced to make a number of economic concessions, including those to labor and farmers, the executive and bureaucracy maintain comparatively tight control over fiscal policy.

In the Philippines, Aquino was brought to power by massive middle-class demonstrations against fraudulent elections in February 1986. The "revolution" did not rest on popular sector mobilization; indeed, the left made the tactical error of not supporting Aquino's presidential candidacy. Subsequent development planning focused greater attention on rural problems in an effort to counteract the insurgency, and the government pursued a mild Keynesian stimulus through a public works program. But Aquino also moved quickly to cement ties with those portions of the private sector disadvantaged by Marcos' cronyism and Aquino's economic cabinet was dominated by businessmen-turned-technocrats. The reconvening of Congress in 1987 provided new opportunities for pork-barrel politics, but as in Thailand and Korea, fundamental political and institutional continuities limited political pressures on macroeconomic policy.

More generally, in those countries where underlying class and sectoral cleavages are less intense, or where class and sectoral cleavages have been muted by integrative forms of party organization, the political stakes of stabilization appear lower. This has two further implications. First, the capacity to carry out stabilization programs in these cases is not closely influenced by the type of regime. Democratic governments in Venezuela and Colombia have done as well or better at maintaining fiscal discipline as systems dominated by one party such as Mexico.

Second, where the parties are less polarized and the process of political succession is institutionalized, changes of government should not be expected to produce major shifts in policy. In such cases, unlike in high-conflict societies, newly elected governments do not usually represent previously excluded groups that expect immediate material payoffs. The time horizons of political leaders are therefore likely to be longer.

Democratic governments of this sort may be subject to political business cycles, but they are also in a better position to capitalize on the honeymoon effect by imposing stabilization programs early in their terms. This, too, is related to the time horizons of politicians in more institutionalized systems. With greater expectations that they will be able to reap the political benefits of stable policies, politicians will be less tempted toward unsustainable expansionist policies. . . .

29

Poland's Economic Reform

JEFFREY SACHS
and DAVID LIPTON

In this essay, Jeffrey Sachs and David Lipton—American economists and advisers to the Solidarity government—outline the case
for so-called shock therapy reforms in Poland. As the country engaged in the first and most comprehensive attempt to "leap to the
market," Poland is a critical test of the approach and a source of
important lessons for reforms elsewhere in the former Communist
bloc. Written early in the process of reform, the essay outlines the
failed efforts of the Communist era, the situation inherited by Solidarity when it came to power in 1989, the initial reforms of
1990, and potential dangers and pitfalls that must be avoided in
creating a new market economy. The authors conclude with a
plea for increased Western financial assistance.

The leaders of Eastern Europe's democratic revolution describe their goal as a
"Return to Europe." They seek to overcome the Cold War divisions of Europe as
rapidly as possible by adopting the institutions of parliamentary democracy and a
market economy and by joining the economic and political organizations of Western Europe. The new democratic governments of Poland, Hungary and Czechoslovakia have explicitly rejected the idea of experimenting with a "third way" between capitalism and state socialism, aiming instead to replicate the economic
institutions of Western Europe. The basic economic questions facing East European governments are therefore not mainly about the desired ends of reform, but
rather about the strategy for making the transition from state socialism to a market
economy.

The transition is fraught with danger. The East European economies are not
starting from a stable situation but from a deep and prolonged economic crisis.
Moreover there are no comparable success stories to serve as clear road maps for
reform. Previous reforms conducted under communist rule have backfired. Attempts to decentralize planned economies have tended to worsen financial instability, a pattern now evident in the Soviet Union and one that also occurred in the
1980s in Hungary, Poland and Yugoslavia.

Jeffrey Sachs and David Lipton. "Poland's Economic Reform." From *Foreign Affairs*, 69, 3 (Summer
1990), pp. 47–66.

Of course, the new democratic governments in the region have profound advantages over previous regimes in attempting the necessary reforms. Not only do the new governments command popular trust and support, but they also are not hampered by the ideological baggage and vested interests that weighed down the reform attempts of earlier years. Nonetheless the political situation in Eastern Europe remains fragile. If the reform programs of the new democratic governments fail, the meager living conditions in Eastern Europe will fall further, which could in turn provoke serious social conflict and even a breakdown of the new democratic institutions. But there are also profound possibilities for rapid improvements in living standards, if the East European countries can successfully make the transition from central planning to the market economy.

While there is enormous speculation on the correct strategy for reform, only Poland has so far launched a program of comprehensive reform under noncommunist rule. Poland's pioneering effort, which began on January 1, 1990, is the culmination of a decade in which Poland's Solidarity movement led the region in organized opposition to communist rule, and then in forming a noncommunist government. When Solidarity's Tadeusz Mazowiecki became prime minister in September 1989, his new government was facing a financial crisis among the worst in the world—with inflation of about 40 percent per month and widespread shortages of basic goods. The Polish public was thoroughly demoralized by a long-term crisis of economic and ecological decline that had lasted in acute form since the late 1970s.

Under the leadership of Deputy Prime Minister Leszek Balcerowicz, the government's new economic team fashioned a program of comprehensive and rapid change, aimed at ending hyperinflation and shortages and at creating a market economy as rapidly as possible. The program has been described as an attempt to "leap to a market economy." More precisely, it aims to create during the course of 1990 the legal, economic, financial and administrative conditions needed for a market economy. Nonetheless many key steps, such as tax reform and the privatization of a large portion of state industry, will necessarily take longer. And the actual restructuring of economic activity, involving the rise of small and medium-size firms in the private sector and a shift of production from heavy industry to light industry, services and housing construction, will occur only in the course of the coming decade.

There is much to be learned from Poland's efforts, even at this early stage. Not surprisingly, economic reformers and politicians in the rest of Eastern Europe and in the Soviet Union are studying the Polish experience intently. From our vantage point as economic advisers to Solidarity, we will examine the logic of the Polish economic program, the results to date, the anticipated difficulties in the coming months and years and the lessons for other socialist economies. We will also describe the kinds of assistance from Western governments that would be most effective in supporting Poland's transition to a market economy.

The starting point for Poland's leap to the market economy is the country's Stalinist economic legacy. Most important, more than 90 percent of industry is state owned, with a strong bias toward heavy industry—long held by communist ideology to be the real source of growth in the economy—and a neglect of consumer goods production. Similarly, the service sector is seriously underrepresented. Only 35 percent of the Polish work force is in services, compared with an average of more than 50 percent for most of Western Europe. The emphasis on industrial growth has also been supported by a deliberate distortion of the pricing structure, aimed at keeping the prices for industrial inputs low, especially the price of energy. The "energy intensity of production" (energy use per unit of GNP) is far higher in Eastern Europe than in Western Europe, and this is one of the sources of environmental degradation in the region.

Production, moreover, was organized by state planners to facilitate central control rather than to instill any spirit of competition. Employment tends to be in very large enterprises, to the almost complete exclusion of small and medium-size firms. In all of Poland, there are only 982 enterprises in the state sector with 100 or fewer employees. The average number of employees per state-owned enterprise (excluding cooperatives) is 1,132, and per individual plant is 378. By contrast, there was an average of 66 workers per plant in a 1986 survey of Western economies.

Competition was further reduced by the closing off of domestic markets from imports from the West. In Poland and elsewhere in Eastern Europe, imports have been controlled by strict bureaucratic allocation of foreign exchange and by explicit quotas. In Poland, until the mid-1980s, almost all imports had to be centrally approved, although this system of central control was partially liberalized in the last years of the communist regime. In most cases, importing was carried out through a state trading bureaucracy, which limited the contact of individual state enterprises with the outside world. Individual firms were therefore cut off from the transfer of technology that would usually accompany the import of industrial goods from more technically advanced economies.

Under strict central planning, the flow of physical resources to individual enterprises was set in the central plan. By the early 1980s the deficiencies of this system were so evident that the regime embarked upon a gradual decentralization of production, even as political repression under martial law intensified. Between 1982 and 1989, the regime cut back significantly on the role of central planners, allowing individual firms much greater freedom in the choice of inputs and outputs.

As part of the decentralization and as an attempt to mollify a bitter population, a small measure of worker self-management was introduced into the enterprises during the 1980s. In a sense, this can be thought of as the communist regime's preferred response to the public's growing demands for political representation: no free elections, but a modest degree of worker representation. Workers' councils were given some powers of supervision over plant operations and over management. While this control was illusory in many instances and was easily manipulated by the communist authorities, it was substantial in other cases.

There were two ironic effects of this limited devolution of power to the plant level and to the workers' councils. First, as decentralization progressed, workers gained enough influence to push for higher and higher wages. This contributed to an explosion of wages during 1987–89, which rose far more quickly than official prices, and which in turn contributed to shortages, inflation and a rising budget deficit in the last years of the communist regime. The second effect was to instill in parts of the Solidarity movement a commitment to worker-managed enterprises, which is now complicating the government's desire to convert firms into joint-stock companies organized along Western lines.

The specific patterns of the Polish crisis should also be noted. During the 1970s, the regime of Edward Gierek tried to overcome the inherent shortcomings of the economy and to regain the support of a sullen population by the device of heavy foreign borrowing from the West. By the end of 1979, the economy had taken on $25 billion in foreign debt (since grown to over $40 billion as interest arrears have accumulated). The loans had been singularly poorly used, with almost no increase in export potential to show for the debt. At the end of the 1970s Poland was plunged into a deep foreign-debt crisis when the inflow of money stopped and when payments started to fall due. Living standards collapsed in the period 1979–82, prompting the rise of Solidarity and its brutal repression under martial law. According to the official data, the 1978 levels of per capita income were finally restored in 1988, but in fact it is likely that 1978 living standards have not yet been restored even today.

The regime responded to the deepening crisis by partially eliminating the central planning apparatus and giving more freedom to enterprises. The result was not the birth of a market economy, but rather an intensification of financial instability. There was still no real competition. Production remained highly monopolized, and international trade—which might have allowed for competition from abroad—remained centrally regulated. Some private firms were legalized, but they were hobbled by administrative and tax laws and unable to obtain adequate supplies from the state sector. Also, the state enterprises had the wrong incentives. Workers were able to push for higher wages, either because they actually controlled management or because the managers were given little incentive to resist workers' demands. Managers borrowed funds whenever they could; if an enterprise later got into trouble, the reasoning went, it would surely be bailed out. The regime pumped money into the economy at highly inflationary rates, partly to satisfy the enterprises' voracious appetite for investment funds, partly to bail out money-losing firms, and partly to subsidize consumer goods in a vain hope of calming a bitter population.

In effect the central plan was replaced not by markets but by an unending process of ad hoc negotiations between firms and the government. When an enterprise experienced difficulty, it would go to the finance ministry or the central bank for some combination of cheap credits, tax exemptions, subsidies, and central allocations of a scarce good. Prices, credits, foreign exchange allocations and subsidies were all subject to intensive bargaining between enterprises and the government and among ministries. Rules changed rapidly—to the extent that they existed at all—and the economic environment became increasingly unpredictable.

By this route Poland had fallen into a remarkable combination of explosive inflation and massive shortages by the time Solidarity inherited the government in

September 1989. Huge excess demand in the economy was being stoked by large wage increases, swollen budget deficits and cheap credits from the central bank; since official prices were continually held below market-clearing levels, shortages developed, and goods were available to consumers only after long waits in queues, by the paying of bribes or through the black market.

The inflation at the end of 1989 was further intensified by one of Solidarity's own actions. In the course of the historic roundtable negotiations in early 1989 that legalized Solidarity, and which set up the elections that soon brought Solidarity to power, the trade union movement pressed the government to introduce wage indexation as a defense against inflation. Indexation became a key transmission belt for inflation and quickly pushed monthly inflation to 54 percent in October 1989, thus breaching the 50 percent per month threshold that economists use to define hyperinflation.

Looking back at the 1980s, the failure of the piecemeal approach to reform attempted by Poland's communist regime (along with similar failures in Hungary, Yugoslavia and the Soviet Union under perestroika) seems clear. Ultimately the communist parties of Eastern Europe (and the Soviet Union to date) were unwilling and unable to carry out truly radical reforms to create a competitive, private market economy. Such a transformation was barred by ideology, by party elites intent on preserving power, by the distrust of the public and by the lack of foreign financial support from Western governments, which rightly doubted the commitment of the East European governments to the fundamental and necessary changes.

When the new Solidarity government began to define its strategy, its policymakers knew well the failure of piecemeal change. They recognized that thoroughgoing measures were needed. But at the same time, certain profound barriers stood in the way of comprehensive change. The trick was to find one's way out of the maze of dead ends and false turns left behind by the old system.

Consider, for example, the urgent problem of macroeconomic stabilization. Halting hyperinflation almost always requires an elimination of a large budget deficit and a tightening of monetary conditions by the central bank. Poland's situation presented no exception. At the same time, however, a monetary and fiscal squeeze almost always prompts some bankruptcies, especially of inefficient firms that are suddenly cut off from artificial subsidies and cheap credits. In a socialist economy like Poland's at the end of 1989, the price system is so distorted that there is simply no way to tell which firms should go bankrupt and which should be allowed to stay in operation. Without a realistic set of prices for industrial goods, it is impossible to sustain a tight macroeconomic policy without the risk of excessively high social costs.

This in turn suggests that macroeconomic stabilization measures must be carried out in conjunction with an end of price controls, so that prices can respond to supply and demand and thereby send accurate signals to the economy. But here the next conundrum arises. With the economy as monopolized as it is in Poland

(and the rest of Eastern Europe), policymakers were rightly concerned that price deregulation would result in a new distortion: monopolistic pricing. Nor was the bureaucracy equipped to overcome that problem by administrative controls. The whole history of price setting by the bureaucracy in the 1980s had proven the impossibility of determining a rational set of prices by bureaucratic methods. Only shortages had resulted.

In turn, a demonopolization designed to precede macroeconomic adjustment presented another dead end. Not only was the macroeconomic situation spinning out of control, but demonopolization, like price liberalization, cannot really be carried out by bureaucratic fiat. The kinds of industrial restructuring that are necessary will only be learned in the context of actual market performance. Winners and losers cannot be selected a priori from among Poland's 7,800 industrial enterprises in the state sector. And, as is now evident, the type of production that individual enterprises will undertake in a market environment may be vastly different from that which they have traditionally conducted under a central plan.

A further apparent problem was that real market competition requires a real private sector. While liberalization of private sector activity would allow a new private sector to arise in the course of time, this natural process would be too slow to ensure a proper functioning of the economy in the meantime. Part of the process of building the private sector must therefore also include the privatization of state enterprises, mainly by selling firms to the public. But at what price? A reliable valuation of firms requires a reliable price structure for the inputs and outputs of the enterprises. This in turn requires market competition, which in turn requires an active private sector. How then to cut the Gordian knot?

The new Polish economic team chose several ways out of this dilemma. First and most important, they recognized that international trade would be the most effective means to instill competition in the economy. By allowing foreign firms to import freely into Poland (and Polish firms to export freely to the West), domestic state enterprises would immediately be subjected to intense competition from the world market. At least for goods that can be potentially traded (which includes most industrial and agricultural commodities), a decisive opening of Poland to world markets would immediately create domestic competition as well as a realistic structure of prices that would mimic that of Western Europe.

To implement a regime of free trade quickly requires a series of financial, economic and diplomatic steps. Financially the exchange rate must be made convertible on the trade account, meaning that domestic enterprises can freely buy foreign exchange, without rationing, at a given official price, and that exporters receive the same price in domestic currency for each dollar earned abroad. The government set a unified rate of 9,500 złotys per dollar on January 1, 1990, as the stable convertible rate for all of Poland's international trade with the West—a devaluation from 6,500 złotys at the end of 1989. Next, all sorts of trade barriers, including import quotas and high tariffs, had to be eliminated or at least sharply reduced. Finally, trade treaties with the United States and the European Community were needed to ensure Poland open access to Western markets.

Another way to attack the dilemma was to proceed as rapidly as possible on liberalization in conjunction with macroeconomic stabilization. As an example, farmers were allowed to bring food directly to the market themselves, thereby bypassing the monopolized food-processing industry. In a matter of weeks, farmers' markets sprang up all over Poland, breaking the monopoly power of the state food distribution sector. The free market prices for food are generally lower now than in the official stores, though higher than the official prices that prevailed before the end of food subsidies. Another set of policies aimed to move swiftly to break up monopolies in specific sectors, such as coal, publishing and retail shops, mainly by dividing large, multiplant enterprises into several independent units, and by eliminating industry-wide cartel-like associations.

It was recognized that small-scale privatization—in which a state enterprise sells off a shop, or a piece of machinery—would also help to get thousands of small-scale entrepreneurs in business in a short period of time. On the other hand, large-scale privatization of major enterprises was recognized as something that must follow, rather than precede, the initial stage of stabilization and liberalization.

In the end, therefore, Poland's strategy for a "leap to the market" was based on the following precepts:

— The budget deficit and easy credit policies had to be ended, as the basis for eliminating shortages and halting rampant inflation;
— Prices had to be decontrolled and subsidies eliminated, in order to establish a demand-and-supply-driven system of price determination;
— A regime of free trade with the West had to be established by creating a convertible currency at the outset of the program and by eliminating almost all restrictions on international trade, thus allowing Poland to "import" a realistic price structure;
— Restrictions on the private sector had to be done away with as soon as possible and specific sectors targeted for rapid demonopolization;
— Privatization should proceed as rapidly as possible, recognizing that it would be a long process, involving many or most of the 7,800 industrial enterprises in the state sector.

These measures were to be undertaken rapidly. Even before the Solidarity-led government took office in September 1989, key leaders in Solidarity—such as the current minister of labor, Jacek Kuroń—were pressing hard to use Solidarity's public support to introduce decisive changes in the economy as quickly as possible. Mazowiecki and Balcerowicz shared this point of view. The crisis was clearly getting out of hand, but it was felt that the government would enjoy a vital freedom of action made possible by high public trust and the shared sense of national emergency. The public expected strong measures and the government had the political opportunity to implement them. It was known that many measures would be socially painful, and that the painful steps should not be stretched out in an unending social agony. As former Bolivian Planning Minister Gonzalo Sanchez de

Lozada, who ended his country's hyperinflation in 1986, was fond of explaining: "If you are going to chop off a cat's tail, do it in one strike, not bit by bit."

On the first day of 1990 the official exchange rate was devalued sharply and the złoty was made a stable, convertible currency. As was hoped, the fixed exchange rate has provided an effective "nominal anchor," stabilizing the prices of traded goods in złoty terms. The creation of a convertible currency was accompanied by the liberalization of international trade and the decontrol of domestic prices. Simultaneously most remaining subsidies were cut back sharply or entirely in order to eliminate the budget deficit.

These measures led to a corrective inflation: consumer prices were 78 percent higher on average in January than in December, according to the official price index. But this inflation was a one-time burst, which was quickly dissipated. From the beginning of February until the end of the month, prices rose by less than five percent, and then by about the same rate in March. To ensure that the corrective inflation would not be incorporated into a fruitless wage-price spiral, the government adopted a tax-based wage policy, which meant that wage increases would be held considerably below the increases in prices at the start of the government's program.

From an economic point of view, it was impossible to compensate workers fully for the price increases. In part, the rise in prices resulted from the end of budget subsidies, which in turn was necessary to end the high inflation. Granting higher wages would have simply undone many of the budgetary savings. In addition, the higher prices resulted from the end of price controls under a situation of widespread excess demand for goods. Prices rose as shortages were eliminated.

While households might seem to have been hurt by the lower real wages, the fall in actual living standards is greatly overstated by the official statistics. Households now pay more for goods that they buy, but they also pay less in the form of the hidden "inflation tax," which had been reducing their purchasing power by steadily eroding the value of their currency holdings. Additionally, since the higher prices resulted in part from the elimination of shortages, households are compensated for the price increases by shorter lines, greater availability of goods and an end to the higher-priced black market. Indeed households that had previously been shopping on the black market for particular commodities might not even notice any actual price increases, even though the official statistics report a large jump in prices.

To guarantee that the excessive issuance of money would be firmly stopped, a fundamental adjustment of financial policies was undertaken. Legislation was approved by the parliament prohibiting the National Bank of Poland from extending any long-term credits to the government. At the same time, the budget called for the deficit to be reduced from more than nine percent of gross domestic product in 1989 to around one percent of GDP in 1990. The improvement will come mainly from a sharp reduction of subsidies and the elimination of various tax exemptions. Provision in the budget has been made for new social safety net programs (especially unemployment insurance), other forms of social spending and a fund to assist in the restructuring of industry. At the same time, the national bank has tightened the extension of new credits to the rest of the economy. Interest rates have been set well above the rate of inflation and the lending operations of the major commercial banks have been closely supervised.

The situation was further complicated by Poland's external debt. The debt in convertible currencies stood at $40.3 billion at the end of 1989, of which $27.7 billion was owed to Western governments, $9.2 billion to commercial banks and $2.1 billion to other socialist countries. The annual $3.6-billion interest bill on this debt consumes about 50 percent of the earnings on Poland's merchandise exports to the West.

Western governments provided two forms of financial assistance to Poland as the stabilization program was being launched. First, Poland's foreign exchange reserves were bolstered by balance-of-payments support loans from the International Monetary Fund and the Bank for International Settlements. In addition a special $1-billion stabilization fund was created by the Group of Seven leading industrialized nations, comprising a combination of grants, including $200 million from the United States, and loans from others of the G-7 governments.

Second, virtually all of the principal and interest falling due on Poland's debt to official creditors through March 1991 was rescheduled by Western governments. Poland also unilaterally limited interest payments to its commercial bank creditors, pending completion of negotiations for a deep reduction of its commercial bank debt burden to be arranged under the auspices of the U.S. Treasury's "Brady Plan." The Western governments, the IMF and World Bank have attested to Poland's need for commercial bank debt relief, and to Poland's inability to service its existing debt on a normal market basis.

These two forms of assistance provided a crucial underpinning for the Polish government's efforts to create a convertible currency, which were at the heart of the stabilization effort. The availability of balance-of-payments support made it possible for the financial authorities to contemplate the introduction of a stable, convertible currency, providing much-needed backing for the złoty. Similarly the rescheduling of debt service lessened the claims on export earnings and strengthened the ability of the authorities to make the złoty exchange rate defensible. As other East European countries prepare fundamental reform, these same two forms of financial assistance should be made available to permit the creation of stable, convertible currencies.

The initial goals of Poland's reform program are now within reach. The corrective inflation has passed and the excess demand in the economy—reflected in shortages and high inflation—has been brought under control. Shortages have been eliminated in almost all parts of the economy, both at the household and industrial level. Foreign consumer goods are now widely available.

Household incomes are down by about 30 percent after correcting for inflation, but we believe that this decrease overstates the actual decline in living standards, as we have noted. Public opinion surveys show that households believe that the economic situation and their own economic welfare are somewhat better in March 1990 than they were three months earlier, despite the large recorded decrease in the real wage. Evidently the end of inflation and shortages, and the wider availability of goods, has compensated the population for the higher but now fairly stable prices.

In addition, the combined effect of the austerity measures and the fixed and competitive złoty exchange rate has been a quick turnaround in Poland's external trade situation. The trade balance with the West in the first four months of 1990 totaled a surplus of $1.2 billion, which is more than twice the surplus for the full year 1989. In particular, exports have picked up significantly, reaching nearly $1 billion in March, almost 20 percent higher than a year earlier.

The surplus that has been achieved has several important implications. First, the export increase indicates that the Polish economy can be successfully integrated with Western Europe. Second, the stable exchange rate, which is key to price stability, is better assured because of the rise in foreign exchange reserves. And third, the sacrifices that the Polish public has endured are resulting in a financial cushion that will lessen the risks of further crisis and create a stable environment in which the economic transformation can proceed.

The new "demand barrier," in which enterprises find it difficult to sell their total output, has led enterprises and workers alike to reevaluate their behavior. The managers of Polish firms, now cut loose from the protection of the state, are struggling to produce goods that the public will buy at competitive prices. For the first time, enterprises are faced with the need to market their products actively at home and abroad, and to compete with importers who can also deliver goods to the domestic market. While state enterprises still are likely to be more lax in financial management than are private firms, tight credit conditions and restrained demand are forcing state enterprises to weigh cost considerations as never before.

The state enterprises will need Western management assistance to learn to function properly in a market environment. Polish firms have been more a part of the state bureaucracy than a part of the marketplace. Most enterprises have had few contacts with Western businesses, know little about the potential markets in the rest of the world, and do not produce to Western specifications. Management consultants in the West have the knowledge and experience that could greatly accelerate the insertion of Polish firms into normal market life.

At the same time, the reduction in aggregate demand has caused a cyclical recession in Poland. One effect of the recession is a rise in unemployment. The official data show 266,000 registered unemployed at the end of March [1990], or about 1.5 percent of the 18-million person labor force, in comparison with almost zero at the end of 1989. Note that despite the rise of unemployment in early 1990, the overall unemployment rate remains far below that of almost all market economies, including the United States (where the unemployment rate was 5.4 percent of the labor force in April 1990). It is expected, however, that unemployment will rise further in future months, perhaps to between five and ten percent of the labor force, not out of line with unemployment rates seen in Western Europe. Polish unemployment will probably grow to exceed West European rates at least temporarily, as the restructuring of the labor force takes place in the next year or two.

The rising risk of unemployment has greatly affected the behavior of workers.

Poland's over-full employment has long meant that workers could find new jobs easily, while businesses had difficulty finding workers, combating absenteeism and motivating a strong work effort. Now, with employees worried about potential job losses, sick leave has dropped sharply according to government surveys, wage pressures have abated and strike activity is negligible.

Besides unemployment, the drop in domestic sales is the other indication of recession, and the main source of concern about the state of the economy. Data for January through March show that the percentage of Polish production sold by the state sector was about 30 percent lower than in the same months of 1989. While a recession is undoubtedly in progress, these data overstate the depth of the decline, as they do not include the fastest growing sector of the economy, the private and informal markets (for which little comprehensive data are as yet available).

The first phase of the Polish leap to a market economy is on schedule. Some basic institutional steps remain to be taken in the course of 1990 and 1991, which will be important in setting the proper incentives for the new private sector. These include tax reform, further antimonopoly measures, additional liberalization of private business activity, and changes in profit repatriation rules in order to spur foreign investment.

These changes will be easier than the other, much more profound, structural adjustments still ahead in Poland. The deeper structural adjustments involve both basic institutional change—mainly the privatization of much of state industry—and the reallocation of the work force and capital within the economy. It is really with these deeper changes that the ultimate test of the government and its economic policies will be made.

Privatization is already proving to be one of the most contentious and complex issues facing the country. Britain's prime minister, Margaret Thatcher, who may be regarded as the most fervent privatizer of the 1980s, has presided over some two dozen privatizations in the past decade, most of which were carried out by public offerings of shares of state companies. In Poland, however, there are over 7,000 state enterprises that are candidates for privatization. Poland must therefore find new privatization means that are administratively feasible, economically efficient and politically viable.

The main barrier to privatization, and potentially the ultimate sticking point, is a heated political debate over who really owns the firms. The government is asserting its clear juridical title to the companies. The workers in many enterprises, on the other hand, are asserting a de facto if not de jure claim, and are arguing that shares should be turned over to the workers or held in trust in a form of worker self-management. The government is opposed to this solution on grounds of both equity and efficiency. It is not fair, the government asserts, to give away the majority of shares to current workers when the industrial work force is a mere third of the total work force, and when some workers happen to work in highly profitable enterprises while others work in firms near bankruptcy. The government has instead proposed that a limited (and minority) proportion of shares of an enterprise be sold cheaply to its workers.

The government is also correct, in our view, to oppose worker ownership of firms on efficiency grounds. Not only has the practical experience with worker self-management been dismal in Yugoslavia (the only country where it has been tried on a large scale), but there are compelling theoretical arguments against it. First, workers would be unwise to keep both their financial capital and their labor earning power (human capital) tied up in a single firm. It is better for workers to own (through pension funds, for example) the shares of enterprises other than their own. Second, worker-managed firms tend to be cut off from outside capital markets. As long as workers' councils are the management bodies, and therefore get to decide how much of a company's income stream will be categorized as "wages" versus "profits," the firm will have a difficult time attracting outside investors.

Another barrier to effective and rapid privatization will be the logistical problems. Poland's financial markets are very limited in scope, and the financial purchasing power of households is also very limited. Thus the government will have to come up with ways to sell the firms at very low prices, or will actually have to give shares away through one mechanism or another (e.g., share distributions as a form of employee bonus or retirement benefit). Various innovative schemes for transferring blocks of shares to local governments, state banks or new holding companies are also under intensive study.

In the short term, the government can likely maintain macroeconomic equilibrium even while the industrial sector remains largely in state hands. But privatization must proceed rapidly if the Polish government is to avoid a renewed financial crisis in a few years. Historical experience teaches that public enterprises around the world have been prone to repeated financial crises, through overinvestment and overly generous compensation of employees. Thus, in Latin America (where state ownership often reaches 50 percent of the industrial sector), financial crises in the state enterprises have been commonplace. Even in Western Europe, state firms have been unusually prone to financial embarrassment.

The second, and equally divisive, structural challenge is to close down parts of loss-making heavy industry and to reorient the economy toward light industry, housing construction and services. Declining industrial sectors, such as the coal industry in Britain or the steel sector in the United States, almost always provoke heated political battles in which vested interests in the declining sector lobby the government to slow down the process of decline. The results can be very expensive if protectionism and subsidies are used to keep old and failing industries alive. Poland and other East European economies face special risks in that regard, since it is likely that much of the heavy industrial sector should be cut back in scale and some enterprises should be closed down entirely. A rise in unemployment is inevitable, even in the long run after restructuring is completed, as some workers lose their jobs in declining industries.

This will present not only an economic challenge to the new government, but also a political challenge. It will be vital to have a strong social safety net in place, including unemployment insurance and job retraining and relocation programs. In addition, the government should actively support the formation of new small businesses to absorb the unemployed and to fill in the gaps in services, light industry and housing construction left by the previous system. It can do this with special credit programs directed toward small businesses, and with technical assistance.

Poland has good reason to endure the ongoing recession and persist in its efforts to transform the economy, because the long-run economic prospects are promising. The land is well-endowed with natural and human resources and in close geographic proximity to Western Europe. There is every reason to believe that economic and political integration with Western Europe will enable Poland to raise its living standards decisively, if market forces are allowed to guide the transformation. Although Polish workers currently earn only a small fraction of what their counterparts make in the West, the narrowing of this gap will come naturally through increased trade, transfers of technology and capital inflows aimed at modernizing Polish industry and taking advantage of Poland's low wages.

The long-run promise of Poland will certainly remain unfulfilled, however, if political barriers impede the transformation process. The most immediate risk is that economists and policymakers, misled by faulty data or spurred by populist politics, might attempt to arrest the recession through a renewal of inflationary policies. If Poland were to succumb to the temptation to reactivate the economy artificially at this early stage, the initial gains would be lost, and a resurgence of inflation and a balance-of-payments crisis would not be far off. The second risk is a paralyzing debate over privatization.

The third risk is a descent into protectionism, if coalitions of workers, managers and bureaucrats tied to declining sectors wage a successful lobbying battle to preserve their jobs in the face of adverse market forces. Argentina's fate in the past thirty years—when entrenched special interests frustrated desperately needed structural reforms—represents Poland's potential nightmare in the future. Poland and the rest of Eastern Europe, with their legacy of powerful state enterprises, bureaucratic entrenchment and monopolistic industrial organization, may be especially prone to this tragic denouement, unless political leaders act bravely and decisively to fend off protectionist pressures.

Success in Poland's transition to a market economy will require financial support from Western governments during the period of transition, as well as the determination of the West to welcome Poland as a full partner in the political and economic institutions of the Western nations. If support from the West is timely and on an adequate scale, and if Poland remains steadfast in its reform efforts, the transition period will be brief, and so too will be the period in which financial aid is needed.

The initial phase of Poland's transition to a market economy has already been assisted by the loans and debt relief extended to the Polish government. The $1-billion stabilization fund, the IMF standby loan and the export credits granted by several governments gave the Polish government the financial backing it needed to take the major steps of currency convertibility and price liberalization.

One clear lesson from the case of Poland is that the West should be preparing similar packages of lending and debt-service relief for other East European countries, to be made available, quickly and on an adequate scale, to governments that choose to undertake the key steps of currency convertibility and price decontrol. Holding out the promise of sufficient financial assistance would greatly bolster the new governments of Hungary and Czechoslovakia as they consider the case for making a decisive "leap" to the market.

Poland's state enterprises now face a much harsher economic environment than they did under communism. Without an urgent effort to bring technical assistance to Poland's state firms, much of Poland's state sector will perform poorly, deepening the recession unnecessarily and slowing down the process of privatization (as healthy firms are much easier to privatize than distressed firms). Potentially viable enterprises might slide into bankruptcy before their managements learned how to cope with the competitive forces that have been unleashed. This could put the economic program at political as well as economic risk.

Recognizing the urgency of this problem, Deputy Prime Minister Balcerowicz has called for the creation of a "Minister's Fund," supported by contributions from the West, which would provide individual enterprises with the management assistance that they need in the immediate future. Polish enterprises wishing to acquire Western expertise would be eligible to draw upon the fund, provided that they put up counterpart funds from their own resources. The fund would be administered in a decentralized fashion, with enterprises themselves arranging to receive the services of Western management consultants, marketing experts, accountants, auditors, investment bankers and lawyers.

Poland's most fundamental financial need is for a deep and permanent reduction of its external debt burden. Otherwise, the debt burden will remain as a profound barrier to economic recovery. So far, Western governments have agreed that Poland can participate in the Brady Plan, under which Poland will negotiate a reduction of its debt to commercial banks. The Brady Plan, however, would cover only $10 billion of Poland's $40-billion debt, since the remaining $30 billion is owed to governments rather than to banks. The G-7 governments have not, so far, committed to a policy of debt reduction on Poland's government-to-government debt.

A reduction of debt to commercial banks is certainly needed and should be arranged swiftly, with the assistance of the leading creditor governments and the international financial institutions. The debt could most effectively be reduced through a single, comprehensive "buyback"—agreed to by Poland and the banks—at the price of Poland's debt in the secondary capital markets, between 15 and 20 cents per dollar. With $8 billion of medium- and long-term debt owed to commercial creditors, roughly $1.5 billion would be required to consummate the deal. These funds could easily be raised from the resources allotted for this purpose at the International Monetary Fund and the World Bank, combined with the resources of the $1-billion stabilization fund and loans and grants from friendly governments and the new European Bank for Reconstruction and Development.

In order to arrange for such a simple and straightforward deal, Poland will require the clear backing of the creditor governments, which (as in all debt reduction deals under the Brady Plan) must work with their countries' banks to put such a deal in place. Without official debt relief, Poland will be stuck with an enormous debt overhang, which in turn will frustrate the flow of private funds into Poland that are so vitally needed for the growth of private economic activity.

The case for official debt reduction should be plainly evident to Poland's leading creditor, the Federal Republic of Germany, for no country's history in the twentieth century makes as clear the case for a timely reduction of an unpayable foreign obligation. After World War I, Germany's unpayable reparations bill put forward by the allies helped to create the chaotic economic conditions that eased the rise of Hitler.

After World War II, the allied powers were far wiser. Not only did the United States lend generously to Germany under the Marshall Plan, but it also led a successful effort to cut Germany's debt burden significantly, in order to give that country a fresh start. Now, it is time for a democratic and prosperous Germany to lead a multilateral effort to provide Poland with the same kind of assistance today.

30

Russia in Transition: Perils of the Fast Track to Capitalism
THOMAS E. WEISSKOPF

In this essay, Thomas Weisskopf forcefully challenges the "shock therapy" approach to economic reform in Russia (see Reading 29). He argues that this approach has not successfully redistributed resources within the population and that they remain concentrated in the hands of the economically and politically powerful— principally the members of the old Communist elite. He also maintains that macroeconomic stabilization and current plans for privatization undermine the population's support for economic and political reform. Weisskopf advocates a more gradual program designed, first, to move to a market-based economy without shrinking domestic demand or increasing income inequalities and, second, to produce a thoroughgoing and fair process of privatization.

The social, political, and economic transformation currently under way in Eastern Europe and the successor states of the former Soviet Union has attracted an enormous amount of interest in the West. Rarely are the basic institutions of a society open to the kind of fundamental change now in progress. The fact that the direction of change is from a largely alien and unfamiliar system to one that is less threatening and more similar to Western capitalist market societies has reinforced a sense on the part of many Westerners that the transition should be encouraged to proceed as rapidly as possible.

Indeed, many Western economists have been advocating programs of "shock therapy" and "mass privatization" to accelerate the scuttling of command-administrative economies in favor of free markets and capitalist enterprise. This approach was embraced by Russian President Boris Yeltsin in late 1991, after the failed coup of August 1991 that marked the beginning of the end for the old Soviet Union. During the following year it was implemented by a group of "radical economic reformers" led by First Deputy Prime Minister Yegor Gaidar, and it

Thomas E. Weisskopf. "Russia in Transition: Perils of the Fast Track to Capitalism." From *Challenge*, Nov./Dec. 1992, pp. 28–37.

remains official policy as of October 1992, although it has been encountering increasing public restiveness and political opposition during the course of the year.

In this essay I seek to assess the nature and impact of the fast-track strategy to transform Russia into a capitalist economy, and I explore the possibility of an alternative strategy for reform of the failed command-administrative system. I begin with a sketch of current conditions in Russia; I then turn to key aspects of the policies of shock therapy and privatization carried out by the Yeltsin-Gaidar government; and, finally, I consider economic and political elements of an alternative approach.

STRUGGLE FOR ECONOMIC SURVIVAL

In the wake of the collapse of the old economic system, the dominant concern of every Russian now is individual economic survival. Under the command-administrative form of socialism, people suffered from political oppression, poor pay, limited opportunities and ubiquitous corruption, but they were at least guaranteed a modest standard of living, job security, and price stability. Virtually everyone had low-cost access to such amenities as housing, medical care, education, transportation, cultural activities, and vacation opportunities—though the quality of many of these amenities was often poor.

Within the last year, the breakup of the Soviet Union and the disintegration of economic relations between the former Soviet Union and its East European trade partners, the freeing of prices on most goods and services, and the decentralization of economic decision-making authority has led to an increasingly chaotic social, political, and economic environment. Prices have multiplied ten, twenty, and in some cases even one hundred times during a period in which most people's wages or pensions have increased only five or ten times. Almost everyone is trying desperately to make ends meet.

The well-placed and/or lucky few have met this struggle for survival with great success. Traders and speculators with monopolistic control over commodities whose prices have shot up on the free market, managers or bureaucrats who have succeeded in gaining control of some of the more viable state industrial assets through *de facto* privatization, government officials who dispense permits and licenses worth enormous bribes, and foreign-language speakers who have caught on with joint ventures—these are all members of a small new elite that is doing very well in the new environment. They have joined foreigners in the tiny top tier of the income distribution consisting of people who deal more often in dollars than rubles and who can now find and purchase anything they want on the free market—at prices the vast majority of the population cannot afford.

That vast majority—most urban wage and salary workers, most rural residents, all pensioners—have found their real incomes dropping precipitously with the galloping price inflation. Not only have nominal wages been failing by a large margin to keep up with prices (except in the case of a small number of strategically placed workers who have successfully struck for much higher pay), but a large proportion of wages due have not been paid on time—or at all—because of a shortage of ruble notes. Checking accounts are virtually unheard of, so everyone receives wages in cash. The ability of the printing presses to produce bank notes, however, has been falling well behind the rise in nominal wages; as the presses work overtime to catch up (printing larger-denomination ruble notes), the purchasing power of the overdue wages continues to fall.

The "stagflation" that plagued Western economies in the 1970s consisted of a then unusual combination of high inflation with stagnating or recessionary levels of overall output. But Western-style stagflation would be most welcome now in Russia, where the combination of galloping inflation and plummeting real output requires a new label like "depflation" to reflect the actual conditions of depression. The decrease in output in Russia in 1991 has been estimated at about 11 percent, and production is falling at about twice that rate in 1992. Moreover, many of the goods still being produced are piling up in factory lots and warehouses for lack of buyer purchasing power. As of today, layoffs have still been relatively limited, for enterprise managers are not prepared to face the consequences of massive unemployment; they have been able to prevail upon the Central Bank to keep supplying enough funds on credit to pay their workers—if belatedly. They have not been able to pay most of their suppliers, however, with the result that the level of interenterprise debt (extended reluctantly by sellers trying to maintain markets) has risen to staggering levels. Women have been especially hard hit by the economic crisis; they are most unlikely to have ascended to positions of real power and influence in the old system, and they are the first to be laid off when falling revenues and limited credit leave no alternative but for budgets to be cut and jobs to be trimmed.

Under such circumstances people have been forced to think of nothing but where their next meal is coming from. For many, this means selling off household goods that they have acquired over the years or hoarded in the recent past, or buying some of the few low-priced goods left in state stores and selling them on the street at much higher prices. For others, it means searching for temporary service or trade opportunities during their nonwork time or—increasingly—during the time that they are officially on the job. In the big cities countless sidewalk vendors may be seen at every subway stop and virtually every major street corner, and during the spring and summer of 1992 a common streetside spectacle was row upon row of individuals holding up a commodity or two for sale as passersby searched for the space to proceed. In more recent months, municipal authorities and trade racketeers (the so-called "mafia") have managed to cut down on unregulated street trade; the latter have increasingly been able to monopolize the business, while the former are sharing in the proceeds. In this context, more and more people, frustrated by the difficulty of earning money through honest work or legal trade, are now simply resorting to crime.

The growing number of foreigners (in large cities, especially Moscow) looms as a potential gold mine for desperate local citizens, as a single dollar goes a very long way. A dollar was worth about 100 rubles in early June [1992]—more than most Russians could earn in a day—and it had risen to 200 in September; it reached 400 by late October, and it will surely continue to rise for the foreseeable future. These rates of exchange are way out of line with the true purchasing power of the ruble (even taking into account the rapid rate of internal inflation in Russia); they reflect a growing crisis of confidence in the Russian economy and massive speculation against the ruble. The extraordinary domestic value of the dollar results not only in continuous hawking of souvenirs and other commodities to foreigners, but also in frequent offers of services running from bed-and-breakfast stays, child care, and language lessons to fashion modeling, escort services, and prostitution. Young men accost young foreign women in the hope of developing a relationship that could lead to marriage and emigration. For Russians with foreign language skills, the opportunity to generate any kind of employment with a joint venture is irresistible. For academics and professionals with contacts abroad, the possibility of turning these contacts into funded research, business contracts, or travel abroad is immensely attractive.

Many of the current economic pressures are causing people to abandon useful and productive activities in favor of relatively unproductive activities that appear to be lucrative in the short run. Thus, women students drop out of University classes to "entertain" foreign clients; language teachers quit their teaching jobs and take on secretarial tasks with joint ventures (making phone calls and sending faxes abroad, translating business documents, etc.); and scholars abandon long-term research projects in favor of short-term contract work with local and foreign businesses. In at least one area, however, the economic pressures are generating more productive work. For families with access to land—for example, small plots near ancestral village homes or gardens around summer dachas—the opportunity to supplement store-purchased food with home-grown fruits, vegetables, and/or dairy products has been both attractive and significant. Around every large city, and in many small towns, people are intensively working small patches of land. In this respect, residents of relatively warm areas with good soil in the south are much better off than most of their compatriots who live in the colder and harsher northern regions of Russia.

BORN-AGAIN CONVERSION OF THE NOMENKLATURA

It is remarkable to note that so many of the same Russians who only a few years ago were loudly proclaiming the virtues of communism and central planning are now among the most vociferous advocates of capitalism and the free market. Not only were many current political leaders (for example, Boris Yeltsin himself) once outspoken supporters and prominent beneficiaries of the old system, but many of the people who now most strongly support a rapid move to capitalism—and who are doing very well in the new market environment—are from the upper echelons of the old party apparatus or the upper levels of the old state institutions (the so-called "nomenklatura"). This apparent paradox disappears when one begins to grasp the extent of the opportunism and the corruption that developed in the Soviet

Union over the past few decades: by the 1980s hardly anyone really believed any more in the communist system.

The people who made it to positions of privilege and power in the Soviet Union in recent decades were—for the most part—people who knew or learned how to win within a morally bankrupt and thoroughly corrupt institutional environment. To advance one's interests one had to cultivate important relationships carefully, exchange favors, give and receive bribes, pay lip service to official platitudes, and ingratiate oneself with one's superiors. To be completely principled and honest in this environment came at an enormous personal cost, which only a few unusually strong-willed and dedicated individuals could achieve—often not only to their own but to their family's detriment. For almost everyone else with any ambition, opportunism on some scale was a way of life—and the more privileged one's position, the greater the degree of opportunism that was likely to have been necessary.

Here are just a few examples. Access to the most desirable summer vacation spots and to opportunities to travel abroad typically required membership and good standing in the Communist Party. Access to Western books, newspapers, and films for all but the most privileged required participation in semi-legal or illegal distribution networks, or side payments to government officials. Entry into the more desirable and prestigious departments at Universities could often be assured only with the payment of substantial sums of money to administrators involved in the admissions process. Publication of books and articles, the production of plays and movies, and promotions to high-level jobs called for careful adherence to official ideological positions and policy lines.

After the failure of Mikhail Gorbachev's efforts at economic reform via perestroika, and the collapse of the Soviet Union in 1991, there is now officially an entirely new set of rules of the game in Russia. These rules come under the noble-sounding headings of democracy and the free market. In the context of completely undeveloped democratic and market institutions, however, success in the game requires many of the same assets and talents that were called for under the old system—for example, the cultivating of relationships with key individuals, judicious payments of bribes or exchanges of favors with other people whose goods or services one needs, a willingness to bend rules and engage in semi-legal if not illegal transactions.

Clearly, the new rules of the game do allow vastly greater opportunities for the expression of creative ideas and dissenting opinions. Even though there are now often economic obstacles to freedom of expression, the elimination of ubiquitous political control represents a major social gain. Moreover, the increasingly free-wheeling market environment has opened up a much wider range of economic opportunities for resourceful and skilled individuals (as well as for unscrupulous and criminal ones). Among the beneficiaries of the new environment are enterprising people whose economic activity was in the past either greatly constrained or forced underground by government rules and regulations. Still, it should come as no surprise that some of the biggest beneficiaries of the new system are the very same people who learned so well to parlay their physical, financial, and intellectual assets into positions of privilege and power under the old system. This has led to a very widespread view among ordinary people—with considerable foundation—that "the same people as before are running things now; they are simply whistling a different tune."

SHOCK WITHOUT THERAPY

The economic chaos I have described above is no doubt due in considerable part to the process of economic disintegration that began in the late 1980s and intensified during the period of Gorbachev's perestroika. The sharp drop in trade between the Soviet Union and its former economic partners in Eastern Europe following the "revolutions of 1989," and the weakening of trade ties resulting from the subsequent breakup of the Soviet Union in 1991, cut deeply into both output and input markets in all of the successor states. Moreover, disintegrating central supply and distribution networks could not easily or rapidly be replaced by market forces in a context of severely undeveloped market institutions. Under such circumstances it is hardly surprising that the overall economic situation in the former Soviet Union has been deteriorating for the last several years. The situation appears to have worsened significantly in Russia, however, since the introduction of "shock therapy" at the beginning of this year.

In January 1992, shortly after assuming full power as president of the newly defined Russian nation, Boris Yeltsin initiated the program of shock therapy in an effort to revitalize the disintegrating economy bequeathed by the Soviet Communist regime. Modelled after the program introduced two years earlier by the first post-communist government in Poland, the Russian shock therapy treatment involved sudden and dramatic price liberalization and macroeconomic stabilization—with privatization of state assets due to follow. Prices of most goods and services were decontrolled in an effort to allow the market to equate supply and demand, and government subsidies to consumers, enterprises, and institutions were sharply reduced in an effort to bring a runaway government budget deficit under control. The Central Bank was instructed to reduce sharply the rate of growth of the money supply and, in particular, to cut back on the extension of credit to state enterprises. Plans were formulated for the privatization of state enterprises and public property.

In its embrace of a shock therapy approach to Russia's enormous economic problems, Yeltsin's economic policy team, under the leadership of Yegor Gaidar, was committing itself firmly to the economic strategy long advocated by the International Monetary Fund (IMF) to restructure state-dominated developing economies. Their commitment to this strategy reflected both the dominant economic outlook of the radical intellectuals most closely associated with the political struggle against the old Communist regime, and a strong desire to enlist IMF support in their effort to attract foreign aid and foreign capital to the new Russia. They hoped that the freeing of prices would bring scarce goods back into shops, that the curbing of budget deficits and the slowing of monetary growth would bring stability to a careening economy, and that the privatization process would encourage new entrepreneurship and the restructuring of old ailing enterprises—and that all of this would attract foreign aid and foreign investment to contribute to the process of economic revival.

. . . [T]he deepening economic and social crisis in Russia has already led many previous enthusiasts of rapid transition to a capitalist market economy to begin to question the shock therapy approach. The critics by no means include only hard-line defenders of the old order, unrepentant managers of state enterprises, and left-wing advocates of democratic socialism. Among them are such prominent capitalist reformers as Grigory Yavlinksy—one of the main authors of the "500-day plan" for transition to a market economy, which was proposed in the last year of Gorbachev's rule, widely applauded by mainstream Western economists, but ultimately rejected. The Yeltsin-Gaidar-IMF shock therapy approach—designed to spur a more rapid transition to capitalism—can be faulted along the following lines.

First, this strategy emphasized, above all, price liberalization and macroeconomic stabilization—before any effective program for the restructuring, demonopolizing, and privatization of state enterprises had been developed. It is of course much simpler to free prices, to cut back government spending, and to restrain monetary growth than it is to formulate and implement a serious program of restructuring and privatization. Such a program involves not only complex economic issues but also thorny political problems, requiring as it does a host of new legislation that must be approved by the executive and legislative branches of government. Although the executive is largely under the control of Yeltsin and his allies, the legislative branch—the Supreme Soviet (or Russian parliament) elected in the Gorbachev period—reflects a wide range of political and social forces in contemporary Russia and contains only a minority of deputies closely aligned with the radical economic reform movement.

The consequences of pushing rapidly ahead on the liberalization and stabilization fronts, without meaningful progress in restructuring and privatization, have become very clear this year. This approach has enabled well-placed individuals—traders and speculators who can dominate the emerging and largely unregulated markets, government officials whose authority is needed to approve various transactions, and enterprise managers with de facto control of important state assets—to enrich themselves handsomely at the expense of the general public. A process reminiscent of early capitalist "primitive accumulation" has enabled a new class of successful merchants and businessmen (some of them genuinely resourceful entrepreneurs, but many more appropriately dubbed "mafiosi" because of the illegal or semi-legal nature of their activities), as well as part of the nomenklatura, to accumulate enormous wealth. These people live lavishly in the new market environment, where anything can be bought at a high enough price, but also stand to be the ones in the best position to acquire full legal ownership of state assets once the privatization process finally gets going. Yeltsin has spoken out about his desire to assure a big class of small owners rather than a small class of big owners in the

new capitalist Russia, but current developments are leading in precisely the opposite direction. Indeed, there has already been a good deal of "wild privatization"—
effective takeovers of productive assets by highly placed insiders and mafiosi.

Second, the shock therapy program has been introduced without any concern
about its consequences for income redistribution. The freeing of prices resulting
from the policy of liberalization, and the cutbacks of government spending resulting from the effort at stabilization, have led to a tremendous polarization between
the small class of the well-to-do and the vast majority of the population who have
been depending on the state for much of their income and benefits. Although the
suffering of ordinary Russians has not (yet) led to the widespread outbreak of riots
and revolts anticipated by some observers, it has led to increasing embitterment
and resentment among ordinary people. This is evident in declining popular support in Russia for Yeltsin and his team of radical reformers and in a growing back-
lash against Yeltsin and Gaidar on the part of politicians representing many different parts of the political spectrum. Although this opposition is often described in
the Western press as coming mainly from "hard-line conservatives" associated
with the old communist rulers, in fact it comes from many other sources as well—
rank-and-file workers, factory managers, pensioners, intellectuals, and even quite
a few of the democrats associated with the political liberalization and market-
oriented economic reform of the Gorbachev years.

Third, the combination of polarizing liberalization and punitive stabilization
(coming on the heels of the disruption of trade ties) has aggravated the fall in
overall demand for the output of domestic industries. This has deepened the ongoing depression and led to further cuts in production levels, mounting stocks of
unsold goods, higher and higher levels of interfirm indebtedness, and a growing
loss of jobs. There is still no evidence of any government program to bolster aggregate demand, nor to retrain workers, nor to generate new job opportunities in
the context of the decline of the old industrial enterprises. It is simply hoped that
the free market and the coming program of privatization will take care of such
problems.

148 MILLION CAPITALISTS?

The Yeltsin-Gaidar government turned its attention seriously to privatization after
the shock therapy program got under way in early 1992. It sought to accelerate the
process of privatizing small enterprises, many of which were under the control of
local authorities. These enterprises were to be sold primarily at auctions or via
competitive tenders to the highest or most qualified bidder. In the longer run the
program envisaged a form of mass privatization of medium-sized and large enterprises in which most of these enterprises were to be converted into open joint-
stock companies, whose shares would then be made available for sale and trade on
a market in company shares.

The process of privatization of small enterprises in Russia has thus far proved
to be seriously deficient. First of all, the liberalization of prices and subsequent

rapid inflation have greatly reduced the real purchasing power of what limited savings the general population had managed to accumulate in past years. This has rendered the vast majority of people quite unable to acquire any stake in small enterprises. Moreover, being excessively concerned with reducing budgetary expenses, the government has not undertaken any significant programs to support potential and actual new property owners and entrepreneurs. In spite of the proclaimed objective of getting the government off people's backs, the privatization process has actually been dependent to a large extent on government bureaucrats at many levels. There has therefore been an unprecedented growth of abuse and corruption among public officials, leading to all kinds of limitations and delays in "legal" privatization and to a great deal of "spontaneous" (quasi- or extra-legal) privatization in which bureaucrats themselves have been major beneficiaries. Finally, the critical task of privatizing land and housing remains unresolved in most parts of the country.

While plans for privatization of medium-sized and large state enterprises remained somewhat unclear in early 1992, the Yeltsin-Gaidar government—with strong support from Western economic advisors—was clearly seeking to promote a system of external ownership of firms based on an active Anglo-American-style stock market. Before the privatization process could begin, however, detailed legislation would have to be enacted by the Russian parliament. Many of the parliament members (elected while Gorbachev was still in power) were much more sympathetic to an alternative approach that would favor acquisition of enterprises by their own managers and workers, through the receipt of some ownership shares at a discount and the opportunity to buy back other shares with the help of bank credit. The stage was thus set for a drawn-out economic and political battle between supporters and opponents of the Yeltsin-Gaidar approach, which culminated finally in June [1992] with the passing of a comprehensive new law on privatization. This law established for medium-sized and large state enterprises a "voucher" system of mass privatization, similar in many ways to the voucher model introduced earlier in Czechoslovakia. Under this scheme the enterprises would be transformed into joint-stock companies with shares traded on a stock market, and every Russian citizen—adults and children alike—would receive a voucher that entitled the holder to buy shares in the new stock market.

The June law offered medium-sized and large state enterprises two principal privatization options. The first option grants to enterprise workers 25 percent of the enterprise shares free of charge, but—unlike all the other shares—these carry no voting rights; workers are also enabled to purchase another 10 percent, and managers 5 percent, of the shares at a concessionary price; the remaining 60 percent of the shares are to be made available to external purchasers, including citizens (using their own savings and/or their vouchers) and investment funds that are encouraged to come into existence. The second option allows managers and workers together to buy up to 51 percent of the (voting) shares of an enterprise, but they must do so with substantially smaller price concessions and without access to credit from the Central Bank. This would make it difficult for most workers and managers to come up with the necessary funds. Selection of the second option requires a favorable vote by two-thirds of the workers (or their representatives), failing which the first option will be adopted. This second option was included at the insistence of supporters of insider ownership in the Russian parliament, but the fact that it requires a two-thirds majority to go into effect, and the fact that it will be difficult for workers and managers in most enterprises to come up with the funds to purchase 51 percent of the shares in the absence of significant price concessions, testify to the ability of the Yeltsin-Gaidar administration to get its way in shaping the privatization policy.

A series of decrees issued during the summer of 1992 by President Yeltsin and by the Russian State Property Committee (in charge of privatization) further specified how this privatization law was to be implemented. A target date of October 1 was set for enterprise workers to decide on their privatization options. On the same date the Russian government began issuing vouchers to each citizen, with a face value of 10,000 rubles (worth about $40 at the time, but now considerably less because of the continuing fall of the ruble against the dollar). The voucher distribution was to be completed by the end of the year 1992, after which people could put their vouchers to use—by purchasing enterprise shares, by investing in newly created investment funds, or simply by selling the voucher at whatever it could fetch in the open market. The initiation of the voucher distribution scheme led the *New York Times,* in a lead editorial under the heading "Suddenly, 148 Million Capitalists," to declare that now "every Russian will become a capitalist."

The buoyant triumphalism of the *Times*'s editorial writer obscured a whole series of unpleasant realities (many of which were amply documented in a series of reports from Moscow by the *Times*'s own reporters). First of all, there is widespread public ignorance about the privatization process in general and about the value of enterprise shares in particular. Most people have no idea what to do with their vouchers and will probably end up selling them to the few people who have some useful inside information. Far from creating a whole country of capitalists, or even a big class of small owners, the scheme seems likely to serve as a convenient way for those who have already acquired vast financial resources to launder frequently ill-gotten gains. Many Russians appear to agree with former USSR President Gorbachev, who declared the voucher plan "a sham . . . that will only alienate people."

While the concentration of share ownership that is most likely to result from the voucher plan contradicts the democratic and egalitarian rhetoric surrounding its inauguration, it may not be unwelcome to many of the radical reformers. Their primary goal is to establish new external ownership of state enterprises in order to force managers to restructure their enterprises or go out of business altogether (no matter what the cost of either course in terms of unemployment and social upheaval). From this point of view, it is desirable that share ownership be concentrated in controlling blocks held by one or a few wealthy investors, rather than widely dispersed among many small shareholders.

The radical reformers appear to be supremely confident that individual external large shareholders can determine far better than current enterprise managers or workers what is best for the enterprise. There is much evidence, however, that even in developed market economies, such an Anglo-American system of external ownership, linked to an active stock market with the ever-present threat of a hostile takeover, is inferior to a system with more emphasis on stable insider management, long-term employment relations and worker involvement, and monitoring by external bank creditors. This is precisely the kind of alternative found in economies like those of Japan and Germany, which have been among the most successful of the advanced capitalist countries. In the contemporary Russian economy—characterized by completely undeveloped capital markets and regulatory processes, and a very low degree of potential and actual labor mobility—it is hard to imagine how a mechanism of industrial restructuring that depends on a high degree of capital and labor mobility can possibly succeed at an economic level, let alone in social and political terms.

By making it very difficult for enterprise workers to own their own enterprises and participate in their management, the radical reformers are displaying a particularly pointed distrust of workers. Their preferred privatization option is explicitly designed to prevent workers from having any opportunity to influence management. Providing workers with nonvoting shares not only contradicts practice in the West (where employee stock-ownership plans are growing in popularity and workers' shares do confer voting rights), but also flies in the face of a great deal of evidence that worker motivation and productivity can be significantly enhanced by various forms of participation in enterprise decision-making.

If a large proportion of Russian state enterprises are economically unviable in their current mode of operation, as most observers believe, it would appear sensible to provide incentives and opportunities for their own workers and managers to render them more viable—rather than to allow external owners to break up or liquidate the enterprises, selling off their assets and dispatching their workers to the labor market. From a social and political point of view, it is even more obvious that any strategy which treats workers as dispensable commodities is going to be fiercely resisted and will give rise to enormous social costs that will ultimately have to be paid.

A MORE HOPEFUL ALTERNATIVE

However much one may justifiably complain about the effects of shock therapy and voucher-style privatization, there is simply no workable path of economic reform and revitalization in the post-communist economies other than one which leads toward price liberalization, macroeconomic stabilization, and privatization. Comprehensive government price controls distort incentives and are in any case unenforceable; rather than try to defeat the market, one has to learn to work with it. Out-of-control government budget deficits and unrestrained monetary growth simply feed inflation and uncertainty, creating an economic environment in which speculation is far more rewarding than productive economic activity; this must not be allowed to continue. Centralized state control of enterprises perpetuates bureaucratic mismanagement and corruption; some form of privatization (understood in its broadest sense as a decentralization of enterprise ownership and control to autonomous agents with responsibility and reward for enterprise performance) is surely essential for economic revitalization—and indeed unavoidable with the collapse of central economic authority in Russia. But the issue now is: what is the best form of liberalization, stabilization, and privatization, and how quickly can these essential economic reform tasks be undertaken?

Critical to the success of the economic reform process is that it be conducted in a way that maintains the impetus for reforms while they are taking place. One of the most damaging aspects of the shock therapy approach—in Poland, in Russia, and wherever else it has been tried—is precisely the way in which it has undermined popular support for economic reform. A viable and successful reform program must be one that has both the economic and political staying power to be continued over a period of many years, through thick and thin. No one can deny that there will be significant costs to bear during at least the first few years of the transition from an administrative-command to a market economy. This means that it is vitally important to limit those costs and to assure that the distribution of gains and losses during the transition is sufficiently fair and equitable to maintain popular support in a democratic environment.

A progressive alternative economic strategy, one that would promote viable and durable economic reform and reinforce, rather than undermine, political democracy, would require all of the following elements:

(a) *A gradual process of liberalization and stabilization,* designed to move to a market-based economic system while preventing the collapse of demand for domestic products and limiting the growth of inequalities in real purchasing power. Prices must be decontrolled, but the immense structure of explicit and implicit government subsidies and taxes that characterized the administrative-command system can and should be gradually dismantled and reoriented to a market environment, so as to avoid huge economic disruptions and social tensions. The government deficit must be reduced, but not in one fell swoop and not by cutting essential social and economic expenditures; instead, the deficit should be gradually brought under control through a combination of tax increases and cuts in military and other nonessential spending.

Advocates of the drastic shock therapy approach usually argue that it is necessary to impose the pain of liberalization and stabilization suddenly and harshly in order to get it over with before public opposition thwarts it. But there is no way to compress the process into a short time period, following which confidence-building improvements would quickly begin to materialize. Instead, the sudden-and-harsh approach leads to dramatic declines in real incomes and production levels, quickly undermining public support for the economic reform process. It is true that "one cannot leap over a chasm in two jumps"; but it is surely better to take the time to build a bridge across it rather than to take one leap into the abyss.

(b) *A substantial role for the public sector,* in undertaking investment in physical infrastructure and human resource development as well as in guiding the process of economic development. Government must play a leading role in the development of desperately needed new infrastructural facilities, in the renovation of the educational system, in the promotion of job training and retraining centers, and so on—for even in developed market economies the market-oriented private sector simply does not find it profitable to undertake such essential activities. Although many aspects of the needed government activities must be funded and guided at the national level, much of the responsibility for the execution of these activities can and should be decentralized to lower levels of government.

One of the most pernicious effects of the prevailing right-wing Hayekian ideology is its denigration and rejection of a significant state role in promoting and guiding economic development, a role that has in the past proven indispensable to the economic development of all but a few entrepôt city-states. Although this anti-state position may be understandable in the light of the overweening bureaucracy and rampant corruption that characterized government in the communist era, it reflects an underlying contempt for the potential of democratic political institutions. In both the public and the private sector there are economically essential activities to be undertaken and significant potential sources of failure; neither sector can or should be expected to bear the whole burden of economic revitalization, and both require political as well as economic mechanisms of regulation to minimize behavior that serves particular, at the expense of general, interests.

(c) *A thoroughgoing and fair process of privatization,* which would transfer effective control of enterprises to people with the abilities and the incentives to make them efficient and productive and which would at the same time assure a reasonably equitable distribution of claims to the nation's wealth. First of all, a systematic effort to break up monopolies and oligopolies is essential to foster overall efficiency through product market competition. The extent of such competition is at least as critical a determinant of enterprise efficiency as the structure of enterprise ownership. Those responsible for managing individual enterprises must have a strong stake in the performance of the enterprise and detailed knowledge of the potential as well as the problems of the enterprise and its personnel. To rely primarily on new external owners to restructure enterprises is to lay the blame for past problems on enterprise managers and workers who in fact had little authority to do anything in a top-down, bureaucratically controlled economic system. Involving workers in a meaningful way in both asset ownership and enterprise control can be very helpful both in stimulating labor productivity and in internalizing some of the social benefits and costs of enterprise activity. The benefits of successful enterprise performance can spread beyond insiders to the general public through a combination of lower output prices, taxes paid for government services, and capital returns to citizens.

For the whole privatization process to be fair and to maintain popular support, huge asset acquisition by the nomenklatura, by mafiosi, or by any other wealthy individuals must be prevented, and all citizens must be assured of continuing benefits from the returns to capital assets. A voucher system designed to spread claims to the nation's accumulated capital stock equitably throughout the population may not be a bad idea—provided that mechanisms are introduced to assure that these claims do not become highly concentrated among a wealthy minority and that they do not preclude a significant role for workers in enterprise management. It is perfectly possible to design a system that combines insider responsibility for enterprise management with outsider participation in enterprise asset ownership, in such a way as to meet the dual objectives of productive efficiency and distributional equity.

What is needed for economic revitalization, most basically, is a genuine social partnership that enlists all elements of the population in a common economic endeavor—rather than pitting groups against groups and individuals against individuals in myriad struggles for economic survival and dominance. Many fundamental economic problems in market economies, whether newly developing or already advanced, require for their solution a substantial degree of coordination and cooperation, with key functions having to be performed by politically constituted public agencies. The trust on which such cooperation must be built—and the effectiveness of the democratic institutions through which public action is determined—can only be assured by fairness and a reasonable degree of equity in the distribution of property, income, and social services. An economic system based on such principles, whether it is closer to a social-democratic form of capitalism or a market-oriented form of socialism, remains the best prescription for both advanced and developing economies. Moreover, it would seem particularly appropriate for post-communist economies emerging from a system that, for all of its failures, did assure a basic modicum of economic security to virtually all its citizens.

THE POLITICS OF AN ALTERNATIVE STRATEGY

For their willingness to pursue a fast-track strategy to create a market capitalist economy, the Yeltsin-Gaidar team has received high marks and strong verbal support (but as yet precious little capital inflow) from the IMF and from Western governments. But in imposing this drastic program on the Russian people, the team may well be undermining the impetus for much-needed economic reform; indeed, they may even be endangering the long-run prospects for democracy in Russia, as more and more people long for an escape from economic chaos and a return to some semblance of order and stability. In a telling joke now circulating in Russia, the question is raised: "What has one year of capitalism achieved that seventy-five years of communism could not?" The answer: "To make communism look good."

As much as an alternative strategy of economic reform is needed, there remain formidable political problems in assembling a viable progressive political force that could lead the campaign for such an alternative. These problems include the following:

(a) Many professionals and intellectuals still don't trust anything that appears to smack of socialism, such as a significant role for the state. Their fear that this would allow old elites to maintain their power and their ways is not altogether unreasonable, but it reflects both an unwarranted distrust of democratic institutions and an unwillingness to recognize the extent to which the former elites have profited and will continue to profit from the current state of affairs.

(b) Many workers cling to a defensive position that would protect them against the rigors of a market system, rather than welcoming greater involvement in the operation of enterprises within a new market environment. Defending one's old job and benefits against the kind of economic free-for-all promoted by the most radical free-marketeer reformers is surely justifiable; but the long-run interest of workers lies in active participation in the building of a new system with greater competition as well as adequate social protection.

What can be done? Progressives should try to form alliances among the growing number of people within the radical reform camp who are beginning to realize that shock therapy doesn't work—if only because of the social and political tensions to which it gives rise—and workers and labor leaders who can be persuaded that defensive approaches are shortsighted and that their real interests lie in a gradual, equitable, worker-involved process of liberalization, stabilization, and privatization.

Even a successful alliance of this sort will face formidable political opposition—not so much from the free-marketeer camp (which is visibly weakening day by day), but by conservative and nationalist forces (which are growing in strength). It is vitally important to draw the line clearly between democratic progressive reformists and authoritarian conservative nationalists, and not to allow the former to be identified with the latter by free-marketeers.

It is of course much more difficult to devise a successful economic reform program based on gradualism, a substantial state role, and equitable privatization than it is to impose shock therapy and hope for rich external investors to come to the rescue. But the success of economic reform and political democracy in Russia depends critically on the ability of progressive forces to accomplish this enormously challenging task.

VII

CURRENT PROBLEMS IN INTERNATIONAL POLITICAL ECONOMY

The second half of the 1990s will be important years in the international political economy. Among the complex economic and political issues of the decade, three stand out. The first is the environment. As we become increasingly aware of the effects of environmental degradation, pressures build for greater governmental regulation to control pollution and manage scarce natural resources. But these pressures have increased at different rates in different countries, creating difficult problems of international policy coordination. Alison Butler (Reading 31) surveys the economics of environmental degradation, examines how efforts to protect the environment affect trade, and explores how countries with different preferences and policies on the environment can best manage their relations and influence environmental quality without damaging trade relations.

Second, United States–Japanese economic relations will be central to the future of the international economy. The United States and Japan are among each other's most important economic partners. Trade and investment in the Pacific Rim area are growing far more rapidly than in the Atlantic region. America's economic future rests in important ways on its trade and investment relations with Japan. Nonetheless, economic friction between the two countries has been growing since at least the 1970s. With the end of the Cold War and the declining salience of security relations between the United States and Japan, many fear that economic tensions will escalate further. There is a vibrant debate under way among academics and policymakers over the source of this friction and the best way to manage relations between these two economic "superpowers."

Many argue that economic disputes, manifested in and exacerbated by America's continuing trade deficits with Japan, result from both the failure of American business to adapt to and compete effectively in the Japanese market and the government's mismanagement of the American economy. Relatedly, analysts agree that in those areas where Japan has not fully complied with its international economic obligations, it should be pressed to conform with multilaterally negotiated rules. Others argue, however, that the liberal rules of the GATT and related monetary and financial regimes are inappropriate for managing relations with Japan and other East Asian newly industrializing countries. Rather, these countries are pursuing a mercantilist economic strategy based on state-led industrial development. The United States must not only seek to increase its market access in Japan, these "revisionists" argue, it must also become more concerned with the health of its own domestic economy—abandoning its traditional arm's-length relationship between government and business, if necessary. Clyde Prestowitz (Reading 32) presents a revisionist analysis of current United States–Japanese economic relations and an argument for a more activist domestic economic policy.

The third issue of major importance is the future of the liberal international regimes created by the United States after World War II. The end of the Cold War has removed the unifying effect of a common enemy and reduced America's willingness to subordinate economic disputes to the need for security cooperation. Likewise, the continuing decline of the United States relative to the other advanced industrial states increases the potential for serious economic disputes as issues of international economic burden-sharing rise to center stage. Benjamin J. Cohen (Reading 33) examines the prospects for international economic cooperation and argues that a more variegated economic order—one that varies substantially across economic partners—is likely to replace the multilateral system that grew up after 1945.

31

Environmental Protection and Free Trade: Are They Mutually Exclusive?

ALISON BUTLER

In this essay, Alison Butler surveys the complex relationship between environmental protection and trade. Beginning with an economic analysis of pollution and environmental protection, Butler identifies the primary effects of environmental regulation on international trade. Environmental regulation typically reduces the supply of a controlled good in a regulated country; therefore producers in other states increase production of that good and export it to the regulated country. Whether such a shift in production and trade improves welfare, Butler argues, depends on national preferences for environmental quality. She then examines transboundary pollution issues and current international regulations on the environment and trade.

> *Having to compete in the United States in a totally free market atmosphere with companies and countries who have yet to develop such environmental standards is inherently unfair. It puts us into a game where the unevenness of the rules almost assures that we cannot win or even hold our own.*
> —James E. Hermesdorf, *Testimony to Senate Finance Committee on Trade and the Environment,* October 25, 1991

Comments like the one cited above are being heard with increasing frequency. In fact, protecting the environment has always had implications for international trade. In 1906, for example, the United States barred the importation of insects

Alison Butler. "Environmental Protection and Free Trade: Are They Mutually Exclusive?" Federal Reserve Bank of St. Louis. May/June 1992.

that could harm crops or forests. Similarly, the Alaska Fisheries Act of 1926 established federal regulation of nets and other fishing gear and made it illegal to import salmon from waters outside U.S. jurisdiction that violated these regulations. More recently, a U.S. law restricting the method of harvesting tuna to protect dolphins has been the subject of a trade dispute between the United States and Mexico.

In recent years, as global warming and other environmental concerns have multiplied, environmental issues have played an increasing role in trade negotiations, further complicating what are generally difficult negotiations. Negotiating environmental regulations multilaterally is especially problematic because of differences in preferences and income levels across countries. What's more, scientific evidence is not always conclusive on the effects of certain types of environmental degradation. Finally, environmental considerations can be used to disguise protectionist policies.

This paper examines the different ways environmental policy can have international ramifications and their implications for international trade and international trade agreements. A general introduction to environmental economics is given, followed by an analysis of the relationship between environmental policy and international trade. The paper concludes with a discussion of the status of environmental considerations in multilateral trade agreements.

AN ECONOMIC RATIONALE FOR ENVIRONMENTAL POLICY

The environment is used primarily in three ways: as a consumption good, a supplier of resources and a receptacle of wastes. These three uses may conflict with one another. For example, using a river as a receptacle of wastes can conflict with its use as a supplier of resources and as a consumption good. When either the production or consumption of a good causes a cost that is not reflected in a market price, market failures that are termed "externalities" may exist. Such market failures frequently involve the environment.

A. C. Pigou, in *The Economics of Welfare* (originally published in 1920), presented one of the classic examples of an externality. In the early 1900s, many towns in Great Britain were heavily polluted by smoke coming from factory chimneys. Laundered clothes hung outside to dry were dirtied by the smoke. A study done in the heavily polluted city of Manchester in 1918 compared the cost of household washing in that city with that of the relatively cleaner city of Harrogate. According to the Manchester Air Pollution Advisory Board:

> The total loss for the whole city, taking the extra cost of fuel and washing materials alone, disregarding the extra labour involved, and assuming no greater loss for middle-class than for working-class households (a considerable understatement), works out at over £290,000 a year for a population of three quarters of a million.

Thus, a by-product of production—smoke—unintentionally had a negative effect on another economic activity—clothes-washing.

Why Do Externalities Occur?

Externalities exist when the *social cost* of an activity differs from the *private cost* because of the absence of property rights. In the preceding example, because no one "owns" the air, the factory does not take into account the extra washing costs it imposes on the citizens of the town. As a result, more pollution than is socially optimal will occur because the private cost of the smoke emissions to the firm (zero) is lower than the social cost (£290,000 a year). In general, if nothing is done about negative externalities, environmental damage will result as ecologically harmful products are overproduced and the environment is overused.

To eliminate externalities, the divergence between the social and private costs must be eliminated, either by assigning private property rights (that is, ownership rights) or by direct government regulation. The approach taken often depends on whether property rights can be assigned. The advantage of assigning property rights to an externality is that it creates a market for that product and allows the price mechanism to reflect the value of the externality.

Example of Assigning Property Rights

Suppose a chemical factory locates upstream from a small town and emits waste into the river as part of its production process. Suppose further that the town uses the river as its primary source of water. As a result of these emissions, the town must process the water before use. Clearly there is an externality associated with the firm's use of the water—it is no longer usable to the town without cost. If property rights to the river could be assigned to either the town or the firm, then the two parties could bargain for the most efficient level of pollutants in the water.

If property rights are assigned to the firm, the town pays the firm to reduce its pollution. The town's willingness to pay for reduced levels of pollution depends on the benefits it receives from cleaner water. Generally speaking, as the water becomes more pure, the additional (marginal) benefits to the town likely decrease. On the other hand, the firm's willingness to reduce pollution depends on the costs it incurs to reduce pollution by, for example, changing to a more costly production or waste-disposal method. Generally speaking, as the firm pollutes less, the additional (marginal) costs to the firm increase. The amount of pollution agreed upon will be such that the added benefits to the town of a further reduction in pollution are less than the added costs to the firm of the further reduction.

If property rights are assigned to the town, on the other hand, the firm pays the town [for the right] to pollute. The firm's willingness to pay for the right to pollute depends on the benefits it receives from polluting. These benefits are directly related to the costs it incurs from using a more costly production or waste-disposal method. Similarly, the town's willingness to sell pollution rights depends on the costs it incurs from additional pollution. The amount of pollution agreed upon is where the additional benefits to the firm of increasing pollution are less than the additional costs to the town of additional pollution.

The Coase theorem proves that the equilibrium level of pollution is the same in the preceding cases. Furthermore, such an outcome is efficient. Thus, when property rights are clearly defined and there is an explicitly designated polluter and victim, the efficient outcome is independent of how the property rights are assigned.

Limitations of the Coase Theorem

The key result of the Coase theorem, that the allocation of property rights does not affect the efficient amount of pollution, has limited application. If there are multiple polluters and/or many parties affected by the pollution, the outcome *can* depend on how property rights are assigned. Similarly, if there are significant transactions costs, such as measurement and enforcement costs, the Coase theorem may not hold.

Assume, for example, that two towns are affected by the factory's emissions, one further downstream than the other. Suppose that the town further away from the chemical plant has lower costs associated with cleaning the water. In this case, the amount of compensation the towns would be willing to pay to reduce emissions by any given amount would differ. Thus, the allocation of property rights among the firm and the two towns would affect the outcome of their bargaining.

Suppose, instead, that more than one firm is polluting. Determining how much pollution is coming from each firm, along with ensuring that each firm lives up to any agreement, may be difficult and costly. If monitoring costs are high, the Coase theorem may not hold and the allocation of property rights again affects the choice of optimal emissions.

The lack of general applicability of the Coase theorem is not an indictment of using market-oriented incentives (which usually requires assigning property rights). Most economists believe that market-oriented solutions will lead to the most efficient use of resources because, rather than having the government attempt to estimate preferences, it allows the market mechanism to reveal them.

Government Regulation

Property rights are not always assigned because many uses of the environment are considered public goods. A pure public good is one that has two qualities: First, it is impossible or extremely costly to exclude people from the benefits or costs of the good (non-excludability). For example, even if a person does not contribute to cleaning the air, she still cannot be excluded from breathing the cleaner air. Second, the consumption of the good by one person does not diminish the amount of that good available to someone else (non-rivalry). For example, the fact that one person is breathing clean air does not reduce the amount of clean air others breathe. In this case, property rights cannot be assigned because rationing is impossible.

While few uses of the environment are pure public goods like air, many have enough features of non-excludability and non-rivalry to make assigning property rights virtually impossible. The functions of the environment that are public goods, such as breathable air and clean water, are summarized by the term *environmental quality*.

Regulating environmental quality is difficult because the government first needs to determine the public's demand for environmental quality before deciding the efficient level of pollution. The *free-rider* problem that occurs with public goods makes this determination especially difficult. When people cannot be excluded from use, they have an incentive to understate their willingness to pay for environmental quality because they can gamble that others will be willing to pay. Similarly, if they are asked their preferences and know they will not have to pay, people have an incentive to overstate their desire for a given public good. The degree to which free-riding is a problem depends on the size of the non-rival group affected. The larger the group, the greater the free-rider problem.

For the purposes of this paper, we will assume that to determine the "true" value of public goods, the government measures the costs of pollution reduction and the benefits of pollution abatement accurately. Using a cost-benefit approach, the optimal outcome is where the marginal cost of pollution reduction equals the marginal benefit of pollution abatement.

It is important to recognize that the socially optimal level of pollution is generally not zero. Achieving zero pollution would require an extremely low level of production or an extremely high cost of pollution control. In determining the optimal amount of pollution, both the costs to individuals and industry need to be taken into account.

Example of Government Regulation
of the Environment: An Emissions Tax

Recall the previous example of a firm emitting pollutants into a river. Suppose the government decides to regulate the industry because there are too many polluting firms on the river to define property rights adequately. After determining the socially optimal level of pollution, the government imposes a per-unit tax on emissions to reduce pollution to the optimal level.

What happens to production? Figure 1 shows the supply and demand curves for the industry's output. The effect of the tax is to shift the supply curve the distance AB (the additional per-unit cost of output given the new tax). The price rises from P_1 to P_2, and the quantity of output falls from Q_1 to Q_2, which is the output level associated with the efficient emission level. Emissions are reduced and environmental quality improves.

Figure 1
The Effect of an Emissions Tax on Industry Price and Output

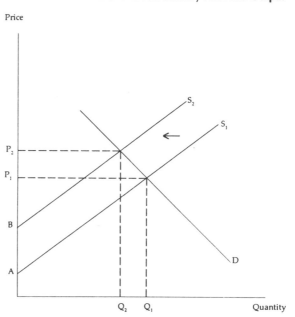

THE TRADE-RELATED ASPECTS OF ENVIRONMENTAL QUALITY

Pollution can have international effects in two ways. First, it might be localized within national boundaries but, through the impact of environmental policy, affect a country's international trade. On the other hand, pollution may be transported across borders without the consent of the countries affected (so-called transfrontier pollution). These two types of environmental damage have different effects on international trade and, therefore, are discussed separately.

Why Do Countries Trade?

Countries trade because of differences in comparative advantage. The idea of comparative advantage suggests that, given demand, countries should export products that they can produce relatively cheaply and import products for which they have a relative cost disadvantage. Traditional international trade models ignore externalities such as non-priced uses of the environment.

By not explicitly including the environment as a factor of production, the costs associated with using the environment are ignored. More recent economic models have extended the definition of factors to include *assimilative capacity,* that is, the capacity of the environment to reduce pollutants by natural processes. The degree to which the environment will be affected by its use or by the production of ecologically harmful products depends on its assimilative capacity. The higher the assimilative capacity, the less the environmental damage caused by the emission of a given amount of pollutants. Assimilative capacity can differ across regions and countries and thus is an important factor in determining the effects of environmental use on trade.

Traditional trade models also ignore the non-priced use of the environment as a consumption good. This underestimates the value consumers may place on the environment and therefore the cost of using the environment for other functions. These two factors can be significant in determining a country's comparative advantage.

Why Would Countries Choose Different Levels of Environmental Quality?

Assimilative capacity is one of the principal factors affecting a country's choice of environmental quality. In general, assimilative capacity is lower in industrialized countries because of the effects of past pollution. Less-industrialized countries often have greater assimilative capacities and thus can tolerate a higher level of emissions without increasing pollution levels. Population density and geography also affect a country's assimilative capacity. For example, the introduction of a polluting industry in a sparsely populated area, all else equal, will likely not affect the assimilative capacity of that area as much as it would in a densely populated area.

Other factors can also affect a country's willingness to accept environmental degradation. For example, poor countries may put a higher priority on the benefits of production (such as higher employment and income) relative to the benefits of environmental quality than wealthy countries. As income levels increase, however, demand for environmental quality also rises. Thus, countries with similar assimilative capacities might choose different levels of environmental quality. As the example below demonstrates, environmental policies that result from differences in countries' preferences and income levels can have significant trade effects.

Environmental Policy When Pollution Is within National Boundaries

How does environmental policy affect trade? Recall that, in the emissions tax example, the higher production costs that resulted from the tax caused the price of the industry's output to increase and the quantity produced to fall. Assume there is a chemical industry in another country producing the same product with the same level of emissions. For simplicity, assume that, prior to the implementation of environmental controls, each industry produced just enough to meet its home demand, and the price was the same in both countries. As a result, trade did not occur. Suppose, because of different preferences, income levels or assimilative capacity, it is optimal to impose environmental controls in one country but not in the other. What happens to price, output and environmental quality in the two countries?

The answer depends in part on whether the two countries can trade. If trade does not occur, the effect is the same as in the previous example. As figure 1 shows, in the country where pollution controls were imposed, the price will rise to P_2 and the quantity of output will fall to Q_2, while in the other country nothing changes. Figure 2 shows the effect of an emissions tax on price and output in the two countries when trade occurs. The reduction in supply of the chemical in the taxed country (Tax) will reduce the world supply of that product, causing the world supply curve to shift upward to the left. At the new world equilibrium D, the

Figure 2
The Effect of an Emissions Tax on Industry Price and Output in a Two-Country World

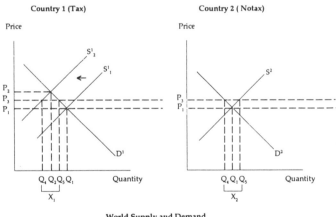

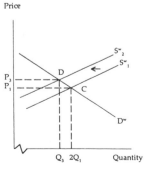

price P_3, is lower than the autarkic (no trade) equilibrium price in Tax (P_2), but higher than the autarkic equilibrium price in the other country, Notax (P_1). At P_3, consumers in Notax demand Q_4, but firms are willing to supply Q_5. The distance X_2 is exactly equal to the distance X_1, which measures the difference between what firms in Tax are willing to supply at P_3 (Q_4) and what consumers demand at that price (Q_5). As a result, Notax exports the quantity X_2 of the chemical to Tax.

What is the effect on other economic variables? Consumption of the chemical falls in Notax, even though output rises. In general, because of the increased production in Notax, there will be an increase in pollution emissions in that country. How much the pollution *level* actually increases in Notax (if at all) depends on the assimilative capacity and the method of production used in that country. Whether the people in Notax are better off at the potentially higher level of pollution that resulted from increased production depends on that country's willingness to accept higher pollution for higher income.

Pollution declines in Tax. If the assimilative capacity is higher in Notax, world pollution will likely be lower after environmental controls are implemented. The effect on world employment is ambiguous and depends on certain country-specific variables. The terms of trade will deteriorate for the country with the emissions tax.

If the new level of emissions in each country is optimal given preferences and income, both countries are better off by trade. The taxed country is able to consume more at a lower price than in the autarkic case, while the value of total output rises in Notax. If measures of national income or wealth accurately reflected environmental damage, they would increase in both countries.

Does Environmental Protection Distort Trade?

One concern is that environmental regulation unfairly discriminates against domestic firms when they compete with firms in a country that has lower environmental standards. In the example discussed above, an externality existed in Tax but, by assumption, not in Notax. As a result, introducing environmental controls eliminated a distortion that previously existed. This changed the flow of trade, but caused all the costs of using the environment, both as inputs in production and as consumption items, to be reflected in market prices. Thus, assuming that environmental quality was not socially optimal before protections were enacted, pollution-intensive sectors in Tax were actually receiving an implicit subsidy from those who had been incurring the external costs of pollution.

The difficulties in trying to determine the optimal amount of environmental quality within a country, as discussed above, are substantial. The optimal level of environmental quality in one country is unlikely to be optimal in another, particularly if the two countries have significantly different income levels. Attempting to impose one country's environmental standards on another by using import restrictions does not allow countries to capitalize fully on their comparative advantage. As discussed later, it is also illegal under current international trading rules.

Environmental Policy When Pollution Crosses National Boundaries

The previous section discussed the international effects of environmental policy when environmental damage is contained within national borders. Many other uses of the environment cause environmental damage across borders, such as acid rain, which results from sulphur dioxide emissions or worldwide, such as ozone depletion, which results primarily from chlorofluorocarbons (CFCs). Transfrontier pollution may occur in essentially four ways:

1. A firm's production takes place in one country, but pollutes *only* in another.
2. Both countries have firms whose production processes pollute, but each country's pollution is experienced *only* in the other country.
3. Pollution occurs as a result of production in one country but the effects are felt in *both* countries.
4. Both countries pollute, and the pollution generated by each is felt in *both* countries.

If pollution is of form 1 or 2, in the absence of an international agreement, the polluting country has no incentive to curtail its polluting activities by implementing an environmental policy. If, instead, pollution is of form 3 or 4, pollution may be regulated domestically. Without taking into account the pollution in the other country, however, these controls will not likely be optimal internationally. In the absence of a globally optimal international agreement, domestic policymakers have less incentive to take into account the costs imposed on a foreign country than if the costs were borne domestically. Thus, from a global perspective there will be excessive use of the environment.

International Policy in the Presence of Transfrontier Pollution

Suppose, as in case 1, the river being polluted by the chemical firm runs directly into another country and all the towns affected are in the foreign country. How is an appropriate policy determined? Previously, we assumed that a country weighed the costs and benefits of pollution, given its preferences for environmental quality, its income level and its assimilative capacity. Unfortunately, in the case of transfrontier pollution, this is no longer sufficient. In this case, domestic policymakers will be less concerned with the costs imposed on a foreign country than those borne domestically. In addition, the desired level of pollution could differ significantly between the two countries because of their preferences and income levels. Other issues contribute to the difficulties in negotiating an international agreement on pollution control. For example, should the polluter pay to reduce emissions or should the residents of the country affected by the pollution pay to induce the firm to reduce emissions?

In the early 1970s, countries belonging to the Organization for Economic Cooperation and Development (OECD), the multilateral organization of the industrialized countries, adopted the Polluter Pays Principle (PPP) to deal with purely domestic pollution. This principle requires that the polluter bear the cost of pollution-reducing measures. This approach, however, provides no guidance about how to determine environmental damage or what to make the polluter responsible to pay for. For example, should a polluter be responsible for damage that has already occurred, or should it be required only to pay to reduce current emission levels? In addition, PPP offers no instruction regarding transfers between governments to resolve problems of transfrontier pollution.

As a result of an OECD conference on transfrontier pollution, it was suggested that the OECD adopt the so-called "mutual compensation principle." This proposal requires the polluting country to provide an estimate of the costs of pollution abatement for various levels of pollution, while the polluted country similarly provides an estimate of the costs of treating the damages. An independent agency determines the optimal level of pollution with these two cost functions. Given the level of pollution set by the agency and the cost functions provided by the two countries, the polluting (polluted) country pays a pollution (treatment) tax based on the cost of the cleanup (control) estimated by the other country and is also required to pay for the cost of pollution abatement (cleanup) in their own country. The advantage of this approach is that it induces countries to reveal their "true" value of the environment. Unfortunately, because of the problems inherent in determining the optimal level of pollution as well as negotiating and implementing such a proposal, the mutual compensation principle has never been used.

There are other impediments to reaching international agreements on environmental use. For certain types of environmental degradation, there is debate about how much damage is actually being done to the environment. An obvious example of this is global warming. Many environmentalists and governments are concerned that excessive emissions of carbon dioxide, nitrogen oxide and methane gas from energy use are irreversibly warming the planet. Many others, including the U.S. government, however, feel that the evidence is insufficient at this point and are unwilling to significantly alter their environmental policy. Scientific evidence on global warming is inconclusive. An August 31, 1991, survey on energy and the environment in *The Economist* pointed out one of the difficulties with transfrontier environmental damage such as global warming: the appropriate policy may need to be implemented before conclusive proof of the damage appears, because of the cumulative effects of some types of environmental damage over time.

Nevertheless, some international agreements have been reached . . . and, if the significant increase in articles, studies and conferences on transfrontier pollution is any indication, there will be additional pressures to find new ways to deal with the increasing problem of transfrontier pollution.

NORTH-SOUTH ISSUES

One of the main reasons environmental policy affects trade is because countries are at different levels of industrialization and thus have different income levels, which can cause their optimal levels of pollution to differ. Because the interests between high- and low-income countries may differ, it is important to look more closely at these so-called North-South issues.

Currently the industrialized countries, in general, are greater polluters than less industrialized countries and thus tend to put a relatively greater demand on world-wide assimilative capacity. One concern heard in developing countries is that industrial economies, rather than reducing their own demand for assimilative services, could impose their environmental standards on developing countries without any assistance in paying for them, thereby reducing the opportunity for less-industrialized countries to grow. . . .

Other types of environmental issues have a particular North-South nature. For example, many of the world's nature preserves are in developing countries in Africa. Currently, trade in elephant hides and ivory, along with other endangered species, is prohibited under the Convention on International Trade in Endangered Species (CITES). At a recent conference on CITES in Kyoto, Japan, several African countries argued that their elephant herds are large enough to be culled without endangering the species. In addition, they argued, revenue generated by the sale of ivory and other elephant products is needed to fund future preservation.

Here, the interest of the industrialized countries, who do not have a native elephant population, is to protect an endangered species. The African countries, however, face a trade-off between the benefits of protecting the species and the loss of revenue associated with the prohibition of trade in elephant products. As a result, less-industrialized countries are putting increased pressure on industrialized countries to help pay for the services they are providing (such as species diversity).

In March 1992, the General Agreement on Tariffs and Trade (GATT), the main body regulating international trade, released a report entitled "Trade and the Environment" that takes a non-traditional approach to North-South problems. One hotly debated issue concerns the protection of the rainforests, most of which are located in Latin America. Industrialized countries have moved to bar wood imports from Brazil and Thailand, for example, as a way to reduce deforestation in those countries. GATT argues that, rather than barring imports of wood products (much of which is GATT-illegal), the industrialized countries should compensate rainforest countries for providing "carbon absorption services."

Although this approach is novel, its advantage is that poorer countries are assisted with financing environmental protection, so that it does not come at the expense of economic development. This approach also reduces the free-rider problem that enables much of the world to benefit from the carbon absorption services provided by rainforests and the diversity of species provided by countries that are not the primary users of the environment. In addition, the approach directly protects the rainforests, rather than barring certain types of wood products in the hopes that doing so will cause the exporting countries to protect them.

Other approaches taken to improve environmental standards in lower-income, less-industrialized countries include debt-for-nature swaps. Here, foreign debt is purchased by environmental groups and sold back to the issuing governments in exchange for investment in local environmental projects, including the purchase of land that is then turned into environmental preserves.

CURRENT INTERNATIONAL REGULATIONS

At present, international agreements do not allow a country to discriminate against products based on their production techniques. Under GATT, barring imports because the production methods used do not meet the standards of the importing country is illegal. This rule has come under fire recently, particularly in light of the controversial tuna-dolphin dispute between the United States and Mexico.

The justification for prohibiting trade restrictions based on the production method is to prevent countries from using such restrictions to protect domestic industries. Unfortunately, GATT was not designed to address some of the more complicated issues of environmental protection, particularly regarding production methods that could have transborder or global effects. . . .

GATT's recently released report on the environment attempts to address some of these issues. Some have suggested, in addition, that GATT focus the next round of talks on environmental issues (assuming the current "Uruguay Round" of talks is successfully completed). The United Nations–sponsored "Earth Summit" in Rio de Janeiro [held in spring 1992, was] is also an attempt to increase international cooperation on protecting the environment, particularly in regard to North-South issues.

CONCLUSION

This article examines the role of environmental policy on international trade. Environmental policy is justified because of the nature of externalities associated with using the environment. When the divergence between the social and private costs of using the environment is ignored, polluting activities receive an implicit subsidy. Environmental regulations may change international trade, but enhance social welfare by removing this subsidy. The optimal amount of environmental protection, however, can differ significantly across countries because of differences in preferences, income and assimilative capacities.

One important concern is that countries will use environmental policies as an excuse to establish protectionist policies. As environmental protection and environmental use take on a more transnational nature and the assimilative capacity is reduced worldwide, new agreements will have to be designed to both protect scarce resources and protect countries from being discriminated against because of how they choose to use their environmental endowments domestically. As the recent GATT report suggested, however, it is possible to protect the environment without distorting trade flows. Thus, free trade and environmental policy are not mutually exclusive but can work together to encourage both economic growth and environmental quality worldwide.

32

Beyond Laissez Faire

CLYDE V. PRESTOWITZ, JR.

This reading disputes the traditional laissez-faire approach to economic policy making in the United States. The author argues that this approach leaves America disadvantaged in international economic competition with the newly industrializing countries of East Asia and, especially, Japan. Breaking with the central tenets of neoclassical economics, Clyde Prestowitz insists that maintaining a strong industrial base in the United States is important to the country's economic future. The United States must abandon laissez-faire rationalizations for inaction and develop a proactive policy that targets high-growth and high-wage industries. The country must also reform the rules of international trade and monetary relations, he concludes, in order to facilitate and reinforce this proactive strategy.

Markets, open to trade, and minds, open to ideas, will become the sole battlefields.

—Victor Hugo

We did the opposite of what the American economists said. We broke all the rules.
—Naohiro Amaya, MITI vice minister

Europe's choice is between survival and decline.
—Jacques Delors, president of the
Commission of the European Communities

As the end of the Cold War opens the door on the new era once envisioned by Victor Hugo, Americans are coming to realize what the Japanese and Europeans have long understood: that economics will be the key to world affairs. That real-

Clyde V. Prestowitz, Jr. "Beyond Laissez Faire." Reprinted with permission from *Foreign Policy* 87 (Summer 1992), pp. 67–87. Copyright © 1992 by the Carnegie Endowment for International Peace.

ization—along with growing suspicions that fundamental American premises about the nature of economic competition are wrong—has brought to a boil a great debate over U.S. economic policy that has simmered during the past decade as trade friction increased and American industry lost out in one technology after another.

At the heart of that debate is the question of whether what a country makes—the structure of its economy—matters. The conventional wisdom, captured in a quip that Bush administration economic advisers deny having made, is that it does not matter: "Potato chips, computer chips, what's the difference? They're all chips. A hundred dollars of one or a hundred dollars of the other is still a hundred dollars."

For most of the past 45 years, U.S. policy has been based on such logic. Partly because they believed it and partly to avoid the kind of economic conflict that helped cause World War II, postwar U.S. leaders fostered a doctrine of laissez faire that separated economic interests from others. The exception was, of course, policy toward the communist world, in which the United States implemented an economic strategy as part of its general policy of containment. Toward all others, though, U.S. economic doctrine was best expressed by Herbert Stein, chairman of the Council of Economic Advisers during the Nixon and Ford administrations:

> The world economic order was to be universalist and private. We were floaters and free traders. In a strict sense, there would be no economic relations between countries. There would be economic relations between individuals who happened to live in different countries but who operated in a world market that didn't distinguish between friend and foe.

That view, based on the classical Ricardian concept of comparative advantage, holds that countries do best when they concentrate on producing those goods naturally favored by their resources, climate, or location, and then trade for other goods. Thus, the United States does well to trade wheat from its temperate Midwest for coffee from tropical Brazil. National policy should not, goes the argument, encourage the production of any particular items such as airplanes or supercomputers. Indeed, such policies are seen as counterproductive. Trade is always envisioned as a positive sum game; one country cannot gain at the expense of another. If the United States fails to commercialize an important technology or loses a large industry, there is no cause for alarm as long as the work is being done by a noncommunist state.

That kind of thinking was evident at a high-level 1985 White House meeting about foreign firms that were illegally dumping semiconductors on the U.S. market and damaging American producers. As a high-ranking Reagan administration official put it: "Why do we want a semiconductor industry? We don't want an industrial policy in this country. We don't want to pick winners and losers. If our guys can't hack it, let them go."

In effect, the economic orthodoxy defined U.S. welfare as being identical to that of the entire world economy. The terms "globalization," "mutual interdependence," and "borderless world" became popular, rationalizing a lack of concern for the structure and nature of interdependence. Because the international economy was thought to be freely floating, the key to prosperity was not U.S. policy so much as the strengthening of international rules, procedures, and institutions. The International Monetary Fund (IMF), the World Bank, and the General Agreement on Tariffs and Trade (GATT) became the trinity for spreading and maintaining the orthodox gospel, a task initially facilitated by their apparent success. Indeed, the birth of those institutions was followed by unprecedented worldwide economic growth, and the first rounds of GATT tariff-cutting negotiations coincided with an impressive increase in world trade, reinforcing the conviction that the main task before U.S. leaders was the expansion of international rules and institutions without regard for their impact on the U.S. economy.

As economist Robert Kuttner and foreign policy analyst Alan Tonelson have noted, that laissez-faire doctrine was the perfect philosophy to rationalize American hegemony. Political leaders felt no qualms about granting economic concessions in exchange for votes in the United Nations or military basing rights. And since it did not matter what was produced in the United States, damage to major U.S. industries resulting from U.S. allies' trade and industrial policies was not a cause for great concern. The laissez-faire consensus was also domestically convenient, defining out of existence any need to think about the structure of the American economy—or how various policies, domestic or foreign, were fundamentally changing it.

Having long denied the approach of the new era, the orthodox have recently begun to respond to it with concern and calls for more of the same. They see great potential danger in any weakening of the old regime or of the U.S. world role that has underpinned it. In the words of a leading economist, there is real danger of "a nationalist upsurge triggering new trade controls, restrictions on foreign investment and a generalized withdrawal from international economic cooperation" in the United States. Abroad, there is risk of "a breakdown of economic cooperation" that could "produce new global divisions that would be profoundly destabilizing." To avoid these threats, the orthodox call for maintaining U.S. hegemony, and they argue that this can only be done by shoring up the old system. They propose a new monetary conference to replace the old Bretton Woods system with a new construct of reference ranges, as well as close monetary and exchange rate policy coordination, with the IMF providing forecasts. Not only do they see successful completion of the Uruguay Round of GATT as essential, but they also call for the exhausted negotiators to go on to strengthen GATT's power to police the international trading system, create a GATT for investment, and eliminate all tariffs and quantitative trade barriers by the end of the century. The orthodox goal is global trade and investment essentially free of government intervention by the end of the century. This consolidation of the "free floaters" system is to be presided over by a smoothly cooperating troika of the European Community, Japan, and the United States. But as Yogi Berra would say: "It's déjà vu all over again." It will not work.

POTATO CHIPS VS. COMPUTER CHIPS

The orthodox doctrine is elegant in its design and even noble in its thrust. It can be quantified and modeled, and its vision of international consensus and cooperation is idealistic. Unfortunately, it is based on false premises, the first and foremost of which is that what we make does not matter. It does matter—profoundly.

First, some industries experience very rapid growth, increases in productivity, and reductions in cost, and have a major impact on many other sectors. Such industries contribute more to economic welfare than others. The semiconductor business has grown exponentially over the past 20 years, sparked development of large new industries such as personal computers, increased productivity in many industries (such as aircraft design by supercomputer), and brought millions of workers to a higher than average level of skills and wages. While most of us love potato chips, they have not had the same dynamic impact on our economy. This is not to say that the United States should stop making potato chips, but if it substituted potato chips for computer chips, its long-term ability to create wealth would be diminished.

Moreover, domination by national producers of an imperfectly competitive industry may result in extra profits and wages for the domestic economy. Long disputed by orthodox economists, the validity of the concept of economically strategic industries has been confirmed by the recent work of James Brander, Paul Krugman, and Barbara Spencer. They point out that dominating a technology or an industry in which there are only a few players, such as aircraft, enables producers to obtain supernormal profits. Since the location of such industries is not dependent on the weather or special natural resources, it can be influenced by policy so that a clever country could raise its living standards by capturing a preponderance of these industries. For example, American domination of the aircraft industry is a great plus for the U.S. economy and is largely the result of U.S. policy decisions dating back to creation of the National Advisory Commission on Aeronautics in 1915.

Second, some industries bring greater training and wages to workers. Unique or highly differentiated complex production of goods such as 747 aircraft or microprocessors requires training and skills that bending hula hoops does not. Because they do not compete primarily on price as commodities do, such products typically yield higher than normal wages. By the same token, high growth often means rapid productivity gains, and industries with high productivity usually pay high wages. This cycle is self-reinforcing because such industries invest more in research and development and training to assure the high skills that yield higher wages.

Third, it will be easier for the United States to expand into new high-growth, high-wage industries if it has not entirely abandoned important older industries. Many industries are closely linked. A major reason why no VCRs are made in America is that most U.S. producers were forced out of the TV industry. The loss of world market share by the U.S. semiconductor industry over the past 12 years has been matched by a similar loss of position by the U.S. semiconductor equipment industry. The U.S. auto industry is the largest customer of the U.S. semiconductor industry. The decline of the U.S. auto industry has hurt the U.S. semiconductor industry because foreign-based auto producers often do not buy semiconductors from U.S. manufacturers.

Finally, there is the obvious question of defense production and its increasing dependence on commercial technology. We are now in the age of spin-on rather than of spin-off. In the past, military technology was often commercialized for civilian use (e.g. 707 aircraft). Today the opposite is the case (e.g. flat-panel displays).

Not only does it matter what Americans make, but the Europeans and Asians alike pursue policies designed to foster a favorable mix of industries. It is foolish to pretend they do not. All of them, particularly the East Asians, have a producer rather than a consumer mentality; all take a relaxed attitude toward antitrust principles (indeed, the Japanese and Koreans foster huge *keiretsu* and *chaebol* arrangements); and all see trade issues in strategic terms.

If America's economic partners do not view interdependence with indifference, neither should America. Of course, interdependence will inevitably increase. The trends of technology and the scale of production needed for global markets guarantee it. But in a world in which what is made matters, the precise terms of interdependence are very important. Boeing needs foreign airlines as customers, and together they are interdependent. For the United States, though, the fact that Boeing is the producer and exporter rather than the reverse is advantageous. Even among allies, national interests do not always intersect. A healthy desire to maintain enough freedom of action to defend one's interests argues for care in the matter of globalization.

The truth is that there are different forms of capitalism, each deeply rooted and in competition with the others. Indeed, a 1991 book by a top Japanese Ministry of Finance official, Eisuke Sakakibara, titled *The Japan That Has Surpassed Capitalism,* argues that Japan is a noncapitalist market economy, far superior to the garden-variety capitalist type. The competition between these systems need not be hostile, but neither should it be ignored.

Just as the orthodox underestimate the important differences between the U.S. economy and those of its trading partners, so too do they overestimate the role of GATT (and other institutions) in the postwar international economic boom. There is no doubt that GATT made positive contributions. But it is unrealistic to ignore the impact of the Marshall Plan, the role of a long overvalued dollar, the impact of the Common Market, and the influence of a technological revolution that has vastly improved communication and transportation networks. Certainly, GATT tariff cutting has stimulated trade, but in many areas outside of GATT—such as services and agriculture—trade has actually grown faster than trade in general. Indeed, renewed growth may originally have made postwar trade liberalization possible (by creating a more benign environment)—not the other way around.

The true force behind the success of the international economic regime was the power of the United States and its ability and willingness to open its markets unilaterally while providing liquidity and technology to others. As American power has waned, the system has run into increasing difficulty. Calls for renewed coordination and cooperation will not repair it. Although America's partners are often cooperative in times of crisis, their fundamental differences with conventional U.S. economic wisdom make attempts to revitalize the old system futile and even dangerous. The philosophical consensus required to make the old structures work is missing, and U.S. efforts amount to trying to persuade others to be like the United States. If the United States could not do that when it had overwhelming power, how can it possibly persuade others while it is in a state of relative decline? It cannot, of course, and its attempt to do so will only anger its partners and neglect the factors behind the continuing erosion of its economic power.

The United States is facing an era of unprecedented economic competition without the benefit of its past superiority in industry, technology, and finance. It is not possible to speak of an international economic policy without addressing the domestic basis of such a policy. In the past, others deferred to U.S. military and economic power. Today, Americans cannot expect to have influence or even minimal cooperation so long as they continue to pile up debt, fail to develop and maintain key technologies, and lose positions in major industries. Some reports from Japan, for example, tell of a growing contempt for the United States. Countries do not long listen to those they do not respect. It will not suffice to recast U.S. international economic policy; the United States must develop a wholly new economic strategy in which international competitiveness is a natural extension of the revitalization of the domestic economy.

The heart of the new strategy must be a recognition that what America makes matters and an explicit, high-priority commitment to American leadership in important industries and technologies. The United States must abandon its laissez-faire rationalizations for inaction and develop a proactive and comprehensive program. . . .

It must be understood at the outset that the tired debate over "picking winners and losers" is beside the point. The United States has a large government that determines the shape of its economy through the tax, regulatory, and spending decisions it makes every day: The savings and loans bailout, the Pentagon's research and development spending, NASA's space shuttle, the breakup of AT&T, the investment decisions of the Defense Advanced Research Projects Agency (DARPA), and the U.S. Trade Representative's recent emphasis on agriculture and services rather than on manufacturing—all affect the structure of the U.S. economy. As a complex country with a diversified economy and an unavoidably large government, the United States cannot shun policy choices that influence its economic structure.

It is often argued that given the U.S. political system, any conscious effort to affect the structure of the U.S. economy would inevitably become hopelessly politicized and result in large subsidies for politically powerful sectors. In fact, the opposite is true. At the moment, in lieu of any overall guiding criteria, the choices are inevitably the victim of politics or happenstance. The space station and super-collider, for instance, will be of very questionable benefit to the U.S. economy for many years, if ever. Yet with no way to evaluate them in regard to other possible choices, they have proceeded because they happen to enjoy political support. We see the same dynamics at play with U.S. trade policy. Why has rice been such an important part of our agenda with Japan? Certainly not because analysis shows major economic gains from opening Japan's rice market.

Thus, a comprehensive policy would be based on the development of productivity and growth criteria to guide choices affecting the structure of the economy so that politicians will be forced to cease the present practice of rewarding favored groups. For instance, should DARPA focus its limited resources on strictly military technology or on dual-use technology? Should NASA be pouring money into the space station or into refurbishing the wind tunnels that underpin commercial aircraft research? It is often said that the government cannot pick winners, but we should not forget that some of the strongest U.S. industries—such as agriculture, aircraft, telecommunications, supercomputing, and networking—were the result of cooperative ventures between industry and government. None of these involved large subsidies; all involved a careful evaluation of global technology and market trends as well as the development of public policies that allowed U.S. industry to capitalize on those trends.

Several groups, including the U.S. Commerce Department, the Japanese Ministry of International Trade and Industry (MITI), the European Commission, and the private-sector U.S. Council on Competitiveness, have compiled lists of key industries and technologies for the twenty-first century. All the lists are essentially the same: Biotechnology, advanced materials such as industrial ceramics and engineered plastics, broad-band communication, and microelectronics clearly will be important in the future. It is desirable that those technologies and industries be realized here. A high-wage, high-growth economy will be far more likely with healthy performers in those sectors than it will be without them.

Americans must also understand that an optimal economic structure involves not only high technology, but the supporting and customer industries that inspire further innovation as well. For example, the auto industry is not only one of the largest customers of the semiconductor industry, but it demands chips of the highest quality and performance. Thus, to assure a healthy computer chip industry, thought must be given to how to maintain a competitive auto industry, particularly in view of the fact that many large foreign auto producers use virtually no U.S. semiconductors.

To ensure that the United States has a leading presence in the new industries— and the necessary strength in the industries that support them—it is imperative that Americans create a governmental mechanism to guide public policy choices in the direction of high growth, high value added, high productivity, and high technology. Congress could charge the General Accounting Office with developing criteria to evaluate the structural impact of legislation, and the Joint Economic Committee could act as the overall coordinator and evaluator of economic bills. In the executive branch, the present economic policy council could develop criteria to guide policy development while evaluating all new proposals with regard to their overall competitive and structural effect. Of course, other organizational structures are possible. The key is not bureaucratic forms. It is recognizing that what we make matters. Such a philosophy and such a mechanism would be the basis both for revitalizing the domestic economy and for developing an effective international economic policy to confront the new era of geo-economics. . . .

In looking at the economic challenges before the United States, there is broad agreement among economists on several key points. Most agree that the world economy is moving inexorably toward greater integration; few see any salvation in isolation and protection. In the future, most see some kind of world trade organization, the continued removal of barriers to trade and investment, the development of a more predictable exchange rate system, and greater funding of development for Eastern Europe and the underdeveloped world. But the key for U.S. policy over the next several years is not so much the goal as how to get there.

The classic U.S. approach has been to maintain dollar dominance despite monetary instability, while proceeding with a trade policy based on the principle of laissez faire. Deviations from this line, such as suggestions to pursue a conscious industrial policy, have been condemned as unfair, and enormous efforts have been exerted in talks like the Structural Impediments Initiative with Japan that seek to bring foreign economic structures into accordance with American ones. The result has been little concrete success and growing resentment of U.S. demands at the bilateral level, and stubborn deadlock of GATT's Uruguay Round at the multilateral level.

Thus, the most important development on the international economic scene is not the Uruguay Round but EC '92. The Europeans have understood that to have truly free trade and deeply integrated national economies, a high degree of homogenization is necessary; otherwise, adjustment costs resulting from structural disparities will undermine the effort. Thus the harmonization of regulatory, labor, social, and technical standards, judicial and corporate governance, and monetary and other regimes has gone hand in hand with freer trade. Even in the context of moving toward integration, no European country is prepared to accept damage to its major industries as a result of structural asymmetries or the industrial policies of its trading partners. The Europeans have recognized that the only way to truly free trade is to integrate.

This should be the model to guide future U.S. policy globally. The United States must move toward ever greater liberalization and world economic integration. Americans must always be prepared to negotiate and ready to take the initiative. But negotiations must be based on the principle that the United States will not allow important segments of its economy to be damaged as a result of structural asymmetries with other countries, foreign industrial policies, or international monetary instability.

The United States must reorient its trade strategy. If what a country makes matters, then what it trades also matters. Trade frictions among the EC, Japan, and the United States have been generated more by the composition of trade deficits than by their size. It is often said that the major problem between Japan and the United States is the large bilateral trade deficit, yet the United States also has a large trade deficit with Saudi Arabia but very few trade frictions. Theoretically, Americans could ship enough logs, scrap metal, and waste paper to Japan to balance the value of all the VCRs, semiconductors, and autos that they import, but such a balance would probably not resolve the trade frictions. The real problem is that major U.S. industries are being displaced by Japanese competitors.

The Uruguay Round and the GATT are foundering because their two core principles—national treatment and unconditional most favored nation (MFN) status—ignore the importance of the composition of trade, thus avoiding the most difficult and important issues. Under the national treatment standard, countries reciprocate in applying the same laws and regulations to the goods and firms of other countries as they do to their own. Under unconditional MFN, countries that extend special favors to one of their trading partners must extend the same favors to all.

That system is based on the premise that its members pursue similar objectives in a similar way. But what if one country has an open and transparent legal and political system as well as an immigrant tradition of welcoming newcomers, while another country has a history of exclusivity and a tradition of granting preferences to insiders? What if one enforces strict antitrust laws and eschews industrial policy, while another allows or even encourages quasicartels and embraces industry targeting? Over time, the industries that the latter country targets will predominate.

That is precisely what is happening. When Amaya said Japan broke all the rules, he meant that it ignored the comparative advantage concepts of the GATT and actively targeted industries such as steel, machine tools, and semiconductors. When Delors spoke of survival or decline he meant that being present in key industries is a matter of life or death: That is why Europe has resisted U.S. efforts to persuade it to reduce Airbus subsidies. That these views and policies are at odds with conventional U.S. concepts does not necessarily make them unfair. Nevertheless, they may put important U.S. industries at a disadvantage.

Beyond industrial targeting is the issue of structural asymmetries, which also give economic advantages to some countries under the GATT system. Take the auto industry, for example. To sell autos, a manufacturer must have dealers. In the United States, the same dealer may sell Ford and Nissan or Chevrolet and Toyota. In Japan that is rarely the case, meaning that to sell in Japan a U.S. company must set up an entirely new dealership network, a time-consuming and costly proposition. Because markets with such closed dealer systems are more difficult to penetrate than the U.S. market, the American auto industry is at a long-term disadvantage. Even if its quality and productivity are perfect, it will be less able to sell in the world's major markets than its Japanese competitors. In view of the importance of economies of scale, this is a major disadvantage.

Finally, there is the free-rider problem. The MFN system allows countries to pocket the concessions made by others without reciprocating: As long as a country's trade barriers are nondiscriminatory, its barriers may be as high as it likes. South Korea, for example, has relatively high tariffs. They are considered fair, however, because they are high for everyone, even though South Korea enjoys the benefit of low U.S. tariffs.

Because the current international institutions do not address the problems of industrial targeting, structural asymmetries, and free riding, they effectively discriminate against the most open societies, which—ironically—have been the most fervent supporters of these institutions. Eventually, however, ardor cools in the face of rejection. The tragedy of the Uruguay Round is that it has left unresolved most of the really difficult trade issues of the past decade—structural issues in industries like steel, semiconductors, and aircraft—and that it is providing no way to address them in the future. . . .

While working toward an integrated world economy, we must deal with a world of industrial policies and structural asymmetries. With respect to goods like sugar, which can be produced in several countries but for which some have a clear natural cost advantage, the United States should strive to open its own—and international—markets. Developing countries typically need open markets for their primary exports in order to build their economies. The United States should provide them with this opportunity, but with three conditions. First, the costs of adjustment must not fall entirely on low-wage workers: Those affected should be assisted in finding new positions. Second, U.S. markets should only be opened to those that meet minimal levels of social and environmental performance. The United States should not open its markets to the products of slave labor or give free run to products from nonmarket economies. Finally, market opening must be reciprocal. If Americans open their market to countries that sell low-cost apparel, then those countries must be prepared to open their markets to American low-cost fabrics and fibers, rather than using apparel sales in the United States to subsidize development of their own fabric and textile industries behind high trade barriers.

The most important exports are those industrial and advanced technology goods that a number of countries are more or less equally capable of producing. Those industries are the primary object of industrial and structural policies, and a strong U.S. position in many of those areas is important. Here U.S. policy must offset or eliminate artificial, policy-based disadvantages to its industry. That should not be done in a moralistic way. It is not unfair for other countries to have a different view of industrial or antitrust policy than the United States. If the Europeans want to subsidize Airbus, and if the Japanese want to target supercomputers, that is their business. Lambasting them as unfair will only poison relations. The United States should, however, be prepared to offset the negative effects of their policies on its own industry. Americans should always be willing to negotiate, but they must be prepared to act unilaterally with countervailing subsidies or other measures, not out of moral outrage, but for self-preservation. Surely Delors and Amaya would understand.

The same holds for structural asymmetries. That the Japanese, for example, have a different market structure is not wrong; Americans should not blame them or insist that they become more like Americans. At the same time, the way the Japanese (and others) do business does sometimes put important U.S. industries at an unacceptable disadvantage. The long-term solution to this problem is, of course, structural convergence. Since it will not come quickly, however, Americans must reconcile themselves to a certain amount of trade management with Japan.

That does not mean negotiating strict bilateral, sector-by-sector market shares. A model for trade management might be the deregulation of telecommunications. In America, because of the past history of the industry and its consequent structure, it was clear that one could not simply remove regulations and tell AT&T's challengers that they could compete: AT&T would have crushed any newcomer. Certain restrictions were therefore put on AT&T in order to give a degree of affirmative action and a significant market share to MCI, Sprint, and others. By managing competition in telecommunications for a time, the government hoped to change the market's structure and make it more competitive. If the United States recognizes that simple commitments to "free trade" or "open markets" do not always bring healthy—or even fair—results domestically, it should also be able to have a more sophisticated approach internationally. To break old structures and overcome the effects of industrial policies it may be necessary to negotiate affirmative action for imports and foreign investment. . . .

Beyond the need to reorient its trade strategy, the United States should help build a more stable international monetary system that shares the burdens equally among the major economies. The current instability arising from a weakened U.S. position causes conflict and protectionism while undermining long-term investment planning.

Even after the 1971–73 collapse of the Bretton Woods system—under which the dollar was used to back up fixed exchange rates—the United States has continued to bear the brunt of the costs of maintaining the world's monetary system. Without a strong replacement for Bretton Woods (the current non-system of loose G-7 coordination hardly qualifies), the dollar has remained the major reserve currency.

Being the printer of the world's money does have it attractions. Americans can borrow in their own currency and thereby escape the disciplines normally applied to debtors. They can pay debts by simply printing more dollars. They can partially export the consequences (like inflation) of poor domestic economic policy, and they have financial leverage that others do not.

But there are costs as well. Capital tends to flow abroad more readily because there are fewer transaction costs and risks. Underinvestment at home may be the result. Other countries tend to undervalue their currencies with regard to the dollar, thereby giving them an advantage in trade. Also, dollar dominance tends to encourage bad economic habits by releasing the United States from normal financial discipline; such habits, in turn, slowly undermine the whole U.S. economy. Those costs, along with the burden of providing liquidity to an expanding world economy from a relatively declining economic base, led the United States to sink Bretton Woods. Unfortunately, the floating exchange rate system that replaced it from 1973 to 1985 was marked by speculative overshooting that again made the costs unbearable for the United States and resulted in the Plaza and Louvre Accords of 1985 and 1987. In the context of substantial philosophical differences among the major industrialized countries, however, the weak coordinating institutions of the current G-7 process have not been particularly successful. The United

States continues to bear the costs of overdependence on the dollar, and the international system continues to bear the costs of inadequate coordination and the resulting monetary instability.

In the long run, the only solution will be some kind of world central bank. Our objective might be a modified version of John Maynard Keynes's original vision of the IMF: With the creation of a world currency, all countries could borrow up to specified limits without bank review, and all would be subject to a mechanism that would force countries with chronic trade surpluses as well as those with deficits toward balance. Obviously, such an ambitious plan would have to include an intermediate stage marked by the shared hegemony of the dollar, yen, and European currency unit (ECU), as well as an expanded role for the IMF.

To get things moving in that direction, the United States should begin unilaterally to reduce the dollar's international role. U.S. leaders should not block expanded IMF funding and should press for greater use of the IMF's special drawing rights in international dealings. America should encourage European monetary union and the establishment of the ECU as the single European currency. At the same time, the United States should press for greater use of the yen, deutsche mark, and eventually the ECU in international transactions. The Japanese trading companies, for example, might be persuaded to bill in yen instead of dollars, and the Organization of Petroleum Exporting Countries might consider at least partial settlement in currencies other than the dollar.

Finally, as the world's monetary system has outrun the ability of the United States to underpin it, so have the demands for development capital outrun the ability of the United States to meet them. To meet the enormous need for development capital—in the former USSR, in Eastern Europe, and throughout the Third World—capital-rich countries such as Germany and Japan must pick up the burden. From the U.S. viewpoint it is desirable that they do so through international institutions rather than by expanding the reach of their global enterprises, which could put U.S. industry at a further disadvantage. Keynes's concept of an IMF surcharge on chronic surplus countries should also be revisited. Not only would it create greater pressure toward trade balance, but it could also be an important source of development capital. The United States should do its best to increase its own contributions to the IMF and the development bank system. Rather than blocking others from raising their contributions because of concerns over voting weights, America should press them to do so. All of this must, of course, be coupled with meaningful debt relief, which would entail a reduction of interest rates on accumulated Third World debts, proportional sharing of the losses among all creditors, and the introduction of new funds from international lending institutions to ensure the flow of new resources to poor countries.

In the end, the United States cannot hope to confront the new era of geo-economics successfully if as a matter of highest priority it does not revitalize its domestic economy. It must concentrate on building broad leadership in industry and technology through a comprehensive economic strategy. U.S. international economic policy must be an extension and integral part of that strategy; that policy should focus on stimulating world economic integration on the basis of a de-emphasis of the dollar, a favorable trade composition, broad reciprocity and affirmative action in key trading relations, and a commonsense foreign investment policy. But to do so, Americans will have to abandon much of the conventional wisdom of economics that has misguided U.S. policy for years.

33

Toward a Mosaic Economy: Economic Relations in the Post–Cold War Era
BENJAMIN J. COHEN

In this essay, Benjamin J. Cohen discusses the future of the international economic order. Pointing to forces that both reinforce
and undermine the existing system, he concludes that there is no
predictable pattern for future international economic relationships. The end of the Cold War and the decline of the United
States have reduced the interest of all countries in cooperative
arrangements. At the same time, the persistence of international
economic regimes, domestic groups with vested interests in the
current system, and prevailing social values reinforces cooperation. In opposition to Prestowitz (Reading 32), Cohen argues that
the United States should work to strengthen the existing order
with multilateral policies whenever possible but be prepared to
accept regional solutions when necessary.

At the outset of the final decade of the twentieth century, the world economy has
entered a critical period of transition. Change, as usual, is driven primarily by
developments in the advanced industrial nations—the countries that for decades
have dominated every aspect of international economic relations. Recent developments in the industrial world have been momentous: the emergence of Japan as a
financial and commercial superpower, the revived pace of regional integration in
Europe, the continued erosion of America's industrial competitiveness, not to
mention the end of the cold war. Taken together, these developments suggest that
fundamental changes may now be anticipated in the design and management of
the global economic system.

Despite emerging strains, it will be possible to preserve the essential elements
of the open, multilateral order erected after World War II. Tensions and friction
will undoubtedly be amplified across a broad range of issues, but resistance to

Benjamin J. Cohen. "Toward a Mosaic Economy: Economic Relations in the Post–Cold War Era."
From *The Fletcher Forum of World Affairs,* 15, 2 (Summer 1991), pp. 39–54. Reprinted by permission.

disruptive forces will also be strong, owing to certain enduring characteristics of the postwar system. If we are in transition to anything, it is toward a much more variegated and mutable order than we have grown accustomed to in the past, one which can best be described as a mosaic of international economic relationships.

CATALYSTS FOR A CHANGING ECONOMIC ORDER

In the aftermath of World War II, the industrial nations succeeded in creating a remarkably open and prosperous international economic order. Rising volumes of foreign trade and investment played a key role in promoting the continued growth of domestic economies. National markets, in turn, became increasingly integrated on a scale not previously seen in this century. Until now at least, the governments of industrial nations have succeeded in maintaining and even extending the liberal postwar order despite ever-lurking forces of parochial nationalism and particularist interest. Policy conflict has not been absent, for tensions and friction are endemic to any system of economic relations among sovereign states. The important point, however, is that for over four decades conflict has been kept manageable, as national policymakers have cooperated to avert any serious threat of disintegration or breakdown in the global economy such as occurred in the 1930s. The caliber of economic management may not be to everyone's taste, but it has contrived, by and large, to preserve the acknowledged benefits of commercial and financial interdependence.

As the decade of the 1990s begins, those benefits seem increasingly at risk as a result of two recent and dramatic developments in global affairs. The apparent ending of the cold war can be expected to alter significantly the calculations that citizens and governments of the industrial world are likely to make in dealing with their common economic problems. Additionally, the accelerating redistribution of economic power among western nations—in particular, America's relative eclipse in the shadows of a resurgent Europe and an increasingly assertive Japan—may affect both the ability and the willingness of the United States to bear its traditionally large share of the costs of economic leadership. Together these two developments threaten to shrink dramatically the supply of cooperative behavior in international economic relations even as the need for it increases in order to cope with a mounting array of troublesome issues.

The end of the cold war is a critical challenge because it removes one of the most important adhesives that, for forty-five years, held the western world together: the specter of a security threat from the Soviet Union. Europe, North America, and Japan may have been competitors in the marketplace, divided by their divergent commercial and financial interests, but they never permitted themselves to forget that they shared a common security interest as well. Because all industrial nations attached considerable value to the "public good" of collective security, economic rivalries, no matter how potentially explosive, were never allowed seriously to endanger the underlying foundations of the Western Alliance. All ultimately preferred to shelter themselves under their joint "security blanket."

With the waning of the Soviet threat, the perceived value of the postwar alliance system is bound to erode. Some common security interests will remain, as Saddam Hussein's invasion of Kuwait in the summer of 1990 clearly demonstrated. But nothing frightens like the danger of nuclear annihilation. Absent that threat, the value of the western security blanket will almost surely be considerably discounted, and this in turn will likely intensify the narrow egoism of key actors in each of the industrial nations, inside as well as outside of government. *Ceteris paribus,* greater weight will be attached to self-interest at the local or national level or, as in the European Community (EC), at the regional level. Correspondingly, nations will devote less attention to collective interests, and will increasingly be tempted to "free ride" in international economic relations. Resistance to concessions under present cooperative arrangements can certainly be expected to grow, and possibly there will even be unilateral defections from commitments previously made, risking greatly amplified tensions and friction across a broad range of issues in global economic relations.

The accelerating redistribution of economic power among the industrial nations represents a critical challenge because of its effect on the West's ability to contain the adverse consequences of increased free riding by individual governments. For many years nations relied, first and foremost, on the resolve and capacity of the United States to preserve the liberal postwar order against the corrosive effects of mutually uncooperative behavior. One does not have to be a fanatical devotee of the familiar "theory of hegemonic stability" to acknowledge the extent to which the benefits of economic interdependence long depended on America's willingness to shoulder a disproportionate share of the burdens of leadership. This required timely concessions or sacrifices when necessary to resolve conflict and promote the welfare of its allies. In return for acknowledgement of America's dominant role in the western security system, Washington self-consciously accepted a special responsibility for management of economic affairs. In addition to providing relatively open markets for goods and capital and an abundant supply of the world's major international currency, America's most crucial contribution was strong and effective leadership in multilateral negotiations and in the major international organizations. An implicit bargain was struck in which Washington's allies acquiesced in a system that accorded the United States special privileges to act abroad unilaterally to promote US interests. The United States, in turn, condoned its allies' use of the system to promote their own economic prosperity, even if this happened to come in good part at the expense of the United States.

However, with the continued erosion of America's postwar economic predominance, best symbolized by its rapid transformation in the 1980s from the world's largest creditor nation to its largest net debtor, the crucial assumption that the United States will not push its own private agenda to the point of fatally disrupting broader economic ties is beginning to look exceedingly complacent, if not downright unrealistic. The United States possesses neither the resolve nor the capacity it once had. The economic ascendancy of Europe and Japan has sapped not only America's ability but, more importantly, its willingness to make painful sacrifices for the common interest. Increasingly, the burdens of economic leadership are being abandoned or rejected as too costly. Concessions on trade or monetary is-sues are now less freely offered, and foreign discriminatory practices less readily tolerated. Demands and threats are both more numerous and more frequently es-calated and tend to be increasingly assertive, even aggressive, in tone. The infa-mous "Super 301" procedure of the 1980 Omnibus Trade Act, with its threat of possible retaliatory measures against nations labeled unfair traders, is indicative of this tougher attitude. US Trade Representative Carla Hills has called Super 301 her "crowbar" to pry open the markets of Japan and other targeted countries.

Washington now looks to other industrial nations to shoulder more of the costs of economic stewardship. The United States has urged Japan, for example, to pro-vide the bulk of the funds needed to underwrite the Brady Plan for Third World debt that was first announced in March 1989. Later in 1989 the United States pres-sured the EC to take principal responsibility for organizing the West's financial contribution to the reconstruction of the newly liberalizing economies of Eastern Europe. And in 1990 America pressed both the Japanese and the Europeans to make major trade concessions in an unsuccessful attempt to ensure a satisfactory conclusion to the Uruguay Round of the General Agreement on Tariffs and Trade (GATT) negotiations. In effect, the United States has grown weary of being the main bulwark against free riding by others, becoming increasingly intemperate in its own pursuit of economic self-interest. This compounds the already heightened risk of amplified tensions and friction in economic relations resulting from the ending of the cold war. The key question for the industrial nations today is whether the liberal postwar order can still be preserved in the face of these critical challenges to mutually cooperative behavior.

THE PROSPECTS FOR CONTINUED ECONOMIC COOPERATION

In some quarters, it has become fashionable to take a rather pessimistic view on this question. Fears generated by the obvious erosion of America's economic pre-dominance have of course already been in vogue for some time. Some scholars, labeled "declinists" by Samuel Huntington, are persuaded of the irreversibility of present trends in favor of Europe and Japan. Not all analysts agree that the relative eclipse of the United States is permanent. Indeed, some authors have recently ar-gued that America's apparent decline, as measured by various indicators of com-parative economic performance, either has been greatly exaggerated or else can be more or less easily corrected. Yet even most of these so-called "revivalists" con-cede that the balance of power among western economies has in fact grown more diffuse and that this spreading of influence is almost certain to make collective management of commercial and financial affairs more difficult. . . .

The end of the cold war seems to exacerbate this trend. Though still a compar-atively recent development, the sudden waning of the Soviet threat at the end of the 1980s has already provoked an anguished chorus of concern, not to say alarm, from informed specialists stressing the dangers of removing the security blanket from western economic relations. Shafiqul Islam of the Council on Foreign Relations has written that "[t]he decline of the West's old common enemy of communism . . . is sowing the seeds of a capitalist cold war." And Fred Bergsten of the Institute for International Economics has asserted that "the end of the Cold War could sharply heighten the prospect of a trade war." For such commentators, it is almost as if the clock has now simply been turned back to the interwar period, or even to the nineteenth century, when economic rivalries were similarly unconstrained by a common security threat. The denouements of those earlier eras—first the Great War, then the Great Depression—certainly give little ground for optimism about the prospects for relations among the industrial nations in the future.

But is such pessimism justified? Is the liberal postwar order today really threatened with disintegration or breakdown? Or are such fears perhaps more than a little exaggerated? Certainly it is not implausible to argue that the postwar order, based as it was on the bipolar cold war, constituted a rather exceptional interlude in the broad sweep of global history. As political theorist Joanne Gowa has formally demonstrated, bipolar international systems are far more conducive to openness and stability in alliance economic relations than are their multipolar counterparts, since stronger incentives for intra-alliance cooperation exist in a bipolar world. Hence it is not unlikely, as she suggests, that "the opening of postwar western markets" can indeed be attributed "to the transition from a multipolar to a bipolar international security system that occurred simultaneously."[1] The success of the postwar order can plausibly be said to have been the product of a very special set of historical circumstances.

Even so, the end of bipolarism hardly justifies alarmist pessimism about what is to come next. Not all the gains of the remarkable postwar interlude must inevitably be lost as we move once again toward multipolarism in international affairs. And the reason, quite simply, is that not all other relevant circumstances are being reversed at the same time, in tandem with the recent dramatic developments in superpower relations. The clock has not simply been turned back to an earlier, less cooperative era. In reality many other fundamental changes have also occurred in the world economy over the last forty-five years that will not disappear even with the end of both the cold war and US economic predominance. A good number of these changes act as countervailing forces to help lock in many of the benefits of commercial and financial interdependence that have been achieved since 1945. The success of the postwar order may not be so fragile after all.

At the systemic level, for instance, a variety of international regime structures have been set in place to help promote collective economic management. These are often formally institutionalized in multilateral organizations like the International Monetary Fund (IMF) and the GATT or in regularized procedures such as the annual economic summits of the so-called Group of Seven. The existence of international regimes by no means guarantees that all state behavior will be mutually cooperative, but it certainly does increase the probability that the tensions and friction so endemic in international economic relations will generally be successfully contained. International regimes facilitate cooperation by reducing uncertainty and transaction costs. They also help to suppress parochial nationalism by underscoring the importance of reputation and, if necessary, by providing collective enforcement mechanisms. Most importantly, as Robert Keohane has pointed out, they are easy to maintain once established. Hence international regimes tend to resist erosion, often for very long periods of time, even after the circumstances responsible for their creation, such as America's postwar predominance, have passed. In Keohane's words: "The decline of hegemony does not necessarily sound cooperation's death knell."[2] On the contrary, the persistence of existing regime structures for trade, money, and the like suggests that the benefits of economic interdependence probably are in fact rather more robust than they might seem at first glance.

Similarly, at the state level, a variety of influential domestic and transnational constituencies have been created by the integration of national economies that now have an important stake in the maintenance of open markets for international commerce and finance. Particularist interests have always played a role in determining the foreign economic policies of sovereign governments, but where traditionally the balance of political forces at home might have tended to encourage protectionist restrictions and increased free riding abroad, today the reverse is often true. Equally powerful pressures on the "anti-protection" side of policy debates have emerged, often spurred by firms and industries now dependent on exports, imports, or multinational production and investments for a substantial portion of their earnings. As Helen Milner has argued: "Increased economic integration of advanced industrial states into the world economy [has] altered the domestic politics of trade."[3] The result is an augmented line of defense within every western nation against any assault on the cohesion and viability of the system as a whole. These internal defenses are likely to persist and remain effective as countervailing forces even after the circumstances responsible for their creation have passed.

Finally, at the cognitive level, a variety of attitudinal changes have been bred by the achievements of the liberal postwar order that can also be expected to oppose any shrinkage in the supply of cooperative behavior in economic relations. Nearly half a century of successful experience with growing commercial and financial interdependence has clearly altered the dominant "economic culture" in all the advanced industrial nations. Social values and perceptions have quite obviously shifted in favor of greater appreciation of the benefits of mutual restraint and open markets in international affairs. No longer is free riding accorded the same legitimacy as it was in the nineteenth century or interwar period. Today the burden of proof is on those who would disrupt foreign economic ties rather than those who would preserve them. There seems little reason why these changes as well should not persist and remain influential even in the new circumstances of the 1990s.

Precisely *how* influential any countervailing forces are likely to be is difficult to say. In principle, international regimes, domestic politics, and social values all matter greatly to policymakers. In practice, however, their effectiveness in determining state behavior clearly varies from one issue to another and even, for any single issue, from one time to another. Thus prospects for relations among the industrial nations in this period of transition are also likely to vary both across issues and across time, depending on the relative strength of disintegrative and countervailing forces in each individual instance.

In short, the basic message is that no uniform or predictable pattern of change in the liberal postwar order should be expected in the post–cold war era. Global economic relations have of course always been messily ambiguous and differentiated to some extent. But now they are likely to become even more variegated and multilayered than ever—growing closer in some instances, widening in others, and occasionally even reversing direction under the pressure of events. Increasingly the system will take on the characteristics of a colorful and complex mosaic, creating a world not easily reduced to simple aggregative analysis or broad facile generalization.

ISSUES OF AGREEMENT AND CONTENTION

The message of cooperation and conflict is clear in the pattern of relations between the United States and each of its major economic allies. The threat of amplified tensions and friction among the industrial nations in coming years is obviously very real. So too, however, is the promise of forceful resistance to disintegration or breakdown of the close economic ties that have been carefully cultivated since the end of World War II.

Competing American and Japanese Interests

By the end of the 1980s the atmosphere between the United States and Japan had grown highly acrimonious. Clearly the most contentious issue was the persistent imbalance in their mutual balance of trade. During the 1980s Japan's bilateral surplus with the United States soared above $50 billion a year, generating a rising tide of resentment and complaints from American business and labor. Americans criticized the Japanese for their habitual strategy of massive penetration of the US market in relatively narrow product lines which often caused severe injury to America's domestic producers.

In the early 1980s most US actions to counter the imbalance in trade stressed negotiation of so-called "voluntary" restraint agreements on Japanese shipments of such products as automobiles, textiles, finished steel, and machine tools. More recently, however, the major focus has been to promote increased American market penetration in Japan. In effect, Washington has cast itself in the role of *demandeur*, repeatedly assaulting the Japanese over allegedly unfair trade practices and, in the name of reciprocity, pressuring Tokyo for a variety of unilateral policy concessions. One commentator has labelled this America's "blame-thy-neighbor policy." The objective, ostensibly, is to ensure equal opportunity for US firms and products in the Japanese market—the proverbial "level playing field."

Japanese reactions to all these pressures, not surprisingly, have tended to become increasingly testy over time. Gradually abandoning their customary diplomatic deference, Japanese officials and businessmen have begun to lash back, citing their own grievances against the United States, such as discriminatory government procurement programs, restrictions on the sale of Alaskan oil, and arbitrary interpretations of existing anti-dumping and countervailing duty regulations. America, they correctly point out, employs a wide array of tariffs and nontariff barriers of its own to tilt the playing field in its favor. Many Japanese feel that their country is as much sinned against as sinner and, as an emerging economic superpower, should stand up more firmly to Washington's persistent demands.

A Resurgent Europe

In the 1990s the US-Europe relationship is likely to be dominated by three key interrelated developments: the reunification of Germany, the revived pace of integration in the EC, and the reform and reconstruction of Eastern Europe. All three developments entail dramatic changes in the ordering of commercial and financial relations on the European continent. The risk inherent in each of them is that they could tend to turn Europe inward, tempting its governments to promote their own regional interests at the expense of outsiders like the United States.

Germany's reunification certainly alters the balance of economic power among the industrial nations. Germany's net creditor position in the world economy is exceeded only by Japan's and the Deutsche mark is more widely used internationally than any money other than the US dollar. Even before political reunification was formally complete, the Germans were already beginning to assert themselves more forcefully in various international economic forums. As the new era advances, there seems little reason to suppose that the Germans might shrink from further exploitation of their new-found commercial and financial leverage.

Moreover, the Germans are not alone. They are also part of the broader European Community, whose remarkable revival since the mid-1980s has served to further accelerate the redistribution of economic power. The launching of the EC's "1992" program triggered ambitious initiatives at the start of the 1990s for monetary unification and perhaps even some form of political union. The deeper the process goes, the greater ultimately will be the EC's impact on commercial and financial affairs. One observer has likened the single-market project to "an economic earthquake in the making." If a reunified Germany alone poses new challenges for the world economy, what of a reinvigorated and truly integrated Community? Together, the Twelve have a population of some 325 million and can boast of levels of production and trade that are already larger even than America's. Increasingly, Europe will become essential to foreign business as a market for goods or capital and as a magnet for investment; its influence in international economic negotiations and organizations is bound to rise as it continues to centralize major elements of policymaking in Community institutions. Outsiders are already treating the EC less like a disparate collection of separate states and more like a coherent entity that is a force in itself. Conversely, almost from the moment the single-market project was launched, fears were expressed about the possibility of an insular "Fortress Europe" in the making.

Then there are the former Communist nations of Eastern Europe, also in effect new actors on the world economic stage. Following the momentous events of 1989, all of the Soviet Union's erstwhile Warsaw Pact allies, as well as Yugoslavia, have embarked on programs of extensive liberalization and regeneration of their economies. All have declared their intention to rejoin Europe by moving as close as possible to the European Community (East Germany, of course, being a special case by reuniting with West Germany). None of the Eastern European states has a particularly large economy: taken together, their output amounts to less than one-tenth that of the EC. But given their needs and the prospective costs of their reconstruction, their reform efforts will surely add to the flux of intra-European relations in the 1990s, particularly if over the course of the decade they are joined even by parts of the Soviet Union itself. Given such profound changes, there is a risk that the Europeans will attach a higher priority to their own agenda of regional problems than to issues of concern elsewhere. Furthermore, there could be a temptation to ease the transition or resolve local conflicts of interest by deliberately discriminating against outside commercial and financial rivals.

Maintaining the Balance

Despite increasing possibilities for conflict among the advanced industrial nations, it hardly follows that in the 1990s governments will necessarily choose the path of overt enmity or trade warfare. One must not forget that there are also many countervailing forces working in the opposite direction to limit acrimony and keep interdependent relationships intact. All sides are tied together by an extensive network of overlapping bilateral and multilateral regime structures as well as a broad heritage of shared values. At the market level, these economies have become highly dependent on their mutual prosperity, and powerful business constituencies have emerged with a vested interest in promoting and preserving even closer economic ties. All have long become accustomed to the occasional storms in their not-always-sunny relationships that somehow manage to pass without lasting damage. For all these reasons, it appears more probable that these countries will simply end up continuing down the familiar path already travelled for more than four decades—a passage marked by intermittent tensions and conflict, sometimes quite serious, but with few irreversible detours or dead ends.

THE VITAL YEARS AHEAD

Clearly, with the fading of the cold war and growing diffusion of economic power among the industrial nations, amplified tensions and friction must be anticipated. Yet across the Pacific and the Atlantic powerful countervailing forces are also at work to limit any damage to the liberal postwar order. Prospects seem good that essentially cooperative relationships can be preserved, but not without much effort and certainly with a lot of contention over individual issues. In principle, four broad options may be identified in this period of transition: multilateralism, minilateralism, regionalism, and unilateralism.

A strategy of multilateralism would involve a renewed commitment to the liberal trade and payments regimes established after World War II, stressing the broadest possible participation of all nations and a reinvigorated role for the GATT, IMF, and other key international economic organizations. Principal emphasis would be on collective management of common problems to suppress economic conflict and promote policy cooperation. The rationale for such an approach is the same as it has been ever since the start of the postwar era: a non-fragmented global economy is the best possible guarantor of enduring prosperity and world order.

Like multilateralism, minilateralism would also involve a renewed commitment to liberal trade and payments arrangements and collective management of common problems. Initially limited to an "inner club" of industrial nations, the participants in a minilateralist scheme would be willing to go beyond the lowest common denominator that can be accomplished in broader global forums. Principal emphasis here would be on a presumed trade-off between inclusiveness and achievement. The argument is that much more progress is possible over a wider range of issues when cooperation is restricted to a like-minded and relatively homogeneous group of countries.

Taking the logic of minilateralism one step further, regionalism would involve mutual commitments limited to even smaller groups of partners, on the model of the European Community or the US-Canada Free Trade Agreement (FTA). Here too emphasis is on the presumed trade-off between inclusiveness and achievement but with a more explicitly defensive rationale: to safeguard national interests against the risk of discrimination by inward-looking blocs elsewhere. The main targets of such an approach would be an emergent "Fortress Europe" or a possibly insular "yen bloc" in the Pacific.

Finally, unilateralism would eschew collective approaches altogether in favor of a more narrowly defined policy of national self-interest in commercial and financial affairs. The emphasis here would be on intensifying the kind of assertive and even aggressive tone that has already become evident recently in a growing range of economic initiatives by the United States and others. The rationale would essentially be one of despair: in a world of amplifying tensions and friction, *sauve qui peut.*

Of these four options, unilateralism clearly represents the highest-risk strategy insofar as it heightens the danger of non-cooperation or even retaliation by others. The more countries reject concessions in economic negotiations, or make unilateral demands on other governments, the more they are likely to provoke precisely the same egoistic behavior elsewhere, thus jeopardizing many of the benefits of interdependence for all. In the past that risk seemed rather less acute. Owing to the West's common security imperative and America's economic predominance, unilateralist impulses, particularly from the United States, generally encountered only limited resistance or complaint. This was certainly evident in the trade field, where US blame-thy-neighbor policies have time and again resulted in policy reforms, reluctant but resigned, from Japan or the EC. It has also been evident in the macroeconomic area, where no amount of reproach from other western nations in the Group of Seven or other forums has sufficed to alter America's domestically oriented fiscal or monetary priorities. But this is no longer the postwar era. In the new "post-postwar era" of the 1990s such tolerance for American free riding is likely to prove notably less reliable. Washington will not always be able to count on the patience and forebearance of its economic rivals.

Non-cooperation or retaliation obviously would be most likely if US unilateralism were to take the form of old-fashioned protectionism, as advocated *inter alia* by the American labor movement today. Even ostensibly more liberal policies, such as Washington's repeated market-opening initiatives promoting reciprocity and level playing fields, may generate conflict rather than compliance. Neither the Japanese nor the Europeans are persuaded that America faces as much unfair discrimination in international trade as it insists. Both Japan and the EC now seem more prepared than ever to respond in kind to any retaliatory measures undertaken by the United States. Although strong countervailing forces may be at work to rein in acrimony across the Pacific and Atlantic, a strategy deliberately designed to test the limits of those forces hardly seems the most promising way to keep America's balancing acts from tumbling. . . .

Much more attractive would be multilateralism, a renewed commitment to the basic principles of the increasingly threatened postwar order. Still accorded greatest respectability by the dominant economic culture, multilateralism continues to be widely championed in US policy debates. America, urges economist Jagdish Bhagwati, must "save the multilateral trading system which has served the United States and the world economy so well in the post–World War II period." Worthy as the goal may be, however, such entreaties essentially beg the question. Can the liberal postwar order as a general system be saved in the altered circumstances of the post-postwar era? In practice, a much more differentiated outcome must be anticipated in the mosaic economy of the 1990s. On many issues, from agriculture to high technology, disintegrative forces will almost certainly dominate international economic relations. It is obviously desirable that Washington should continue to promote collective management of common problems, based on the broadest possible participation and backed by the key international organizations: the greater the supply of cooperative behavior, the better. But a policy that nailed its flag solely to the mast of multilateralism would be sadly unrealistic and could even prove irrelevant.

More realistic, and certainly more relevant, would be increased emphasis on the minilateralist and regionalist options, albeit as supplements to and not substitutes for the goal of a broad liberal order. On many issues there is indeed a trade-off between inclusiveness and achievement. In order to promote further openness in commercial or financial relations or simply to prevent backsliding toward regressive behavior, it may indeed be necessary to confine initiatives to smaller groups of nations prepared to join together in common commitments. But such progress should never be sought at the expense of the wider structure of interdependence. The slogan should be: multilateralism where possible, minilateralism or regionalism where necessary, and unilateralism only as the very last resort. Policy should be designed in modular form in order to conform to the complexity of a mosaic economy.

To some extent policy in the industrial nations has always been effectively modular, operating on several tracks at once. Certainly this is true of the United States. Even while promoting broad multilateralism in such settings as the IMF and GATT, Washington has by no means neglected the other strategic options available. Minilateralism has been evident in the wide variety of informal groupings that Washington has occasionally helped bring together to deal with specific problems. These have included the Paris Club (representing official creditors of developing countries), the Cooke Committee of the Bank for International Settlements (comprising banking supervisors and regulators), and the new Group of Twenty-Four organized to help underwrite the economic reconstruction of Eastern Europe. Regionalism was obviously apparent in the US-Canada FTA, and unilateralism has certainly been evident in the Super 301 crowbar and other recent US trade initiatives.

To be successful, however, modular policies must be implemented with a clear sense of strategic design as well as with the tactical subtlety and finesse needed to fit existing resource means to ends. Most governments are not well organized to formulate and implement coherent economic strategies and will be challenged by the need to adapt more systemically to the altered economic and political circumstances of the 1990s. If policies are to operate on several tracks at once, they must all be programmed to arrive at the same destination.

Toward that objective, two conditions are critical. First, nations must clearly communicate the hierarchy of their preferences in economic relations. There must be no mistaking that the highest priority remains an open world economy on the broadest possible basis. Perhaps the best way to assure this purpose would be to insist that any arrangements worked out on a more limited basis be strictly nonexclusionary in structure. They should be open-ended, allowing for participation by nations prepared to make the same commitments. One possible model is provided by several "codes of conduct," each dealing with a separate substantive issue, drafted during the Tokyo Round of GATT negotiations in the late 1970s. While each code is legally binding for all governments that become formal signatories, adherence itself is purely voluntary. An alternative model might be provided by Gary Hufbauer's far broader and more ambitious proposal for a comprehensive free trade and investment area for all twenty-four members of the OECD—an OECD Free Trade and Investment Area (FTIA). This proposal would be attractive, Hufbauer argues, in part because it "would have soft boundaries, not hard edges," and hence "could eventually succeed in realizing the goals of free and open trade that have so long inspired and frustrated the GATT."[4]

The second condition is that the United States must clearly communicate its readiness to share its traditional leadership role more fully with the other industrial nations. This means not only looking to others to bear more of the costs of stewardship, as Washington has already begun to do, but also acknowledging, in deed and not just in word, that the distribution of economic power is becoming more diffuse. The United States must learn that it can no longer frame policies solely in terms of domestically oriented priorities; nor can it still achieve its goals abroad simply by asserting demands more aggressively. Above all, the United States must be prepared to give more direct recognition to the role of the Japanese and Europeans as fully equal comanagers of the global economic system.

Sharing leadership does not mean going so far as to establish an explicit triumvirate of blocs led by the Big Three—the United States, Japan, and Germany—as some have advocated for the future and others have suggested exists even now. That would be carrying a desirable objective to an undesirable extreme. A formalized Big Three system would emphasize the mutual exclusiveness of emerging economic alignments rather than the reciprocal interests that exist among all western nations, and could even crystallize into mutual antagonisms and conflict. Far more preferable would be a more informal reallocation of responsibilities through the many international regime structures that are already in place, institutionalized where appropriate by a more equitable distribution of voting rights and positions of influence in the major economic organizations. In effect, the emerging mosaic of the world economy should lead to a mosaic of authority as well. Again, the principle should be multilateralism where possible, minilateralism or regionalism where necessary, and unilateralism only as a last resort. The industrial nations are on their way to a more complex set of relations than has ever existed. The best strategy would be to aid rather than resist the transition.

NOTES

1. Joanne Gowa, "Bipolarity, Multipolarity, and Free Trade," *American Political Science Review* 83, 4 (December 1989): 1253.

2. Robert O. Keohane, *After Hegemony: Cooperation and Discord in the World Political Economy* (Princeton: Princeton University Press, 1984), 9.

3. Helen V. Milner, *Resisting Protection: Global Industries and the Politics of International Trade* (Princeton: Princeton University Press, 1988), 290.

4. Gary Clyde Hufbauer, "Beyond Gatt," *Foreign Policy* 77 (Winter 1989–90): 72, 76.

INDEX

ABOUT THE AUTHORS

Jeffry A. Frieden (Ph.D, Columbia University) is Professor of political science at the University of California—Los Angeles. He has also held many Visiting Researcher, Professor, and Consultant appointments within the United States, Latin America, England, and Russia, and is widely published in books and journals in the areas of international relations, political economy, economic development, Latin American politics, and Western European politics. His book publications include *Debt, Development, and Democracy: Modern Political Economy and Latin America, 1965–1985* (Princeton: Princeton University Press, 1991) and *Banking on the World: The Politics of American International Finance* (New York: Harper & Row, 1987), which has been issued in both Japanese and British editions.

David A. Lake (Ph.D, Cornell University) is Professor of political science at the University of California—San Diego. Currently, he is the Research Director for International Relations at the university's Institute on Global Conflict and Cooperation. He is also the principal investigator for a major research project, funded by the Pew Charitable Trusts, on the spread and management of ethnic conflict. Professor Lake edited *The International Political Economy of Trade* (Cheltenham, England: Edgar Elgar Publishing, 1993), and is author of *Power, Protection, and Free Trade: International Sources of U.S. Commercial Strategy, 1887–1939* (Ithaca, NY: Cornell University Press, 1988).